WORKS of
ST. BONAVENTURE

St. Bonaventure's Commentary ON THE
GOSPEL OF LUKE
Chapters 9-16

WORKS of
ST. BONAVENTURE

St. Bonaventure's Commentary
ON THE
GOSPEL of LUKE
Chapters 9-16

With an Introduction, Translation and Notes
By Robert J. Karris, O.F.M., Th.D.

Franciscan Institute Publications
The Franciscan Institute
Saint Bonaventure University
Saint Bonaventure, NY 14778
2003

Library of Congress Card Catalogue Number: 2003101961

ISBN: 1-57659-183-2

Printed in the United States of America
        Bookmasters
        Mansfield, Ohio

TABLE OF CONTENTS

INTRODUCTION

In this Introduction I consider four topics. While the first three topics are relatively short, the fourth topic, Bonaventure's anti-Judaism, merits an extensive treatment.

BONAVENTURE'S VERBAL PLAYFULNESS

As I work my way through Bonaventure's commentary on Luke's Gospel, I continue to be amazed at his verbal playfulness, especially in his introductions to new sections. At first I thought that his use of rhyme and alliteration was idiosyncratic. In researching Bonaventure's sermons for what they have to contribute to an analysis of Bonaventure's anti-Judaism, I have come across a possible source for Bonaventure's agility with words – word lists for preachers. I give an example. Bonaventure introduces his commentary on Luke 10:20b–24 in this wise: "And indeed Christ does this by proposing a four-fold cause or reason for joy. For he shows that there will be joy for the disciples concerning God's infallible prescience, irreprehensible providence, incomprehensible potency, desirable presence" (*de Dei praescientia infallibili, de providentia irreprehensibili, de potentia incomprehensibili, de praesentia desiderabili*). A reason for Bonaventure's use of these rhymes may be found in Géraud du Pescher's *Ars faciendi sermones*: "For the words of Sacred Scripture must be presented in an attractive way that will spur curiosity, so that listeners may be enticed by these means and may be more attentive to grasp and more ready to assimilate the information given them" (*Verba enim sacre Scripture debent esse ornata et proposita curiose, ut per hec alliciantur auditores et sint magis solliciti ad intelligendum et informationem eorum avidius audiendam*).[1]

Chapter 7 of the Géraud du Pescher's *Ars faciendi sermones* contains twelve sub-chapters of word lists (186–197). The second sub-chapter deals with Latin words ending in -*is* and -*bilis*. As the reader goes down the alphabetical list of words ending in -*bilis*, she finds: "Infallible: the promise of God, friendship with God, purity, the divine embrace, the reward of God, divine love, supernal glory, happiness" (*Infallibilis: Dei promixio, Dei amicitia, puritas, divinus amplexus, stipendium Dei, divinus amor, gloria superna, felicitas*) (p. 190).[2] It is to be recalled that Bonaventure used *infallibilis* as he set up his commentary on Luke 10:20b–24.

---

[1] I quote from p. 186 of the critical edition by Ferd. M. Delorme, "L' 'Ars faciendi sermones' de Gérard du Pescher," *Antonianum* 19 (1944): 169–198.

[2] For more on the significance and function of these word lists, see D. L. D'Avray, "The Wordlists in the 'Ars faciendi sermones' of Geraldus de Piscario," *Franciscan Studies* 38 (1978): 184–193 and D'Avray's *The Preaching of the Friars: Sermons diffused from Paris before 1300* (Oxford: Clarendon Press, 1985), 248–254.

I am not saying that Bonaventure utilized such a word list from an author who flourished in the first half of the fourteenth century. Rather I am suggesting, along with D'Avray,[3] that such word lists were common in his day as a means of enticing the preacher's audience to listen to his message and of alleviating the tedium of long sermons or lectures. Perhaps, there was some mnemonic purpose also. I would also suggest that Bonaventure creatively used this tradition of rhyming introductions, for I cannot find any example of Bonaventure's slavish use via mix-and-match of Géraud du Pescher's word lists.

BONAVENTURE'S DEPENDENCE UPON HUGH OF ST. CHER

In my article, "A Comparison of the *Glossa Ordinaria*, Hugh of St. Cher, and St. Bonaventure on Luke 8:26–39,"[4] I tracked Bonaventure's borrowing of Scripture quotations from his older contemporary, Hugh of St. Cher (d. 1263). In preparing this annotated translation of Bonaventure's commentary on Luke 9–16, I began to note that the Quaracchi editors often said: "Cardinal Hugh makes the same comment."[5] Having learned from Bonaventure to follow the wisdom of one's elders, I followed the lead of the Quaracchi editors and began to compare in a rather systematic way Bonaventure's exegesis with that of Hugh of St. Cher. As a result of my

---

[3] *Preaching of the Friars*, p. 254: "This *ars* is, of course, an extreme case, and furthermore the author belongs to the first half of the fourteenth century, but it seems symptomatic of a tendency that is well under way in the period which more immediately concerns us."
[4] *Franciscan Studies* 58 (2000): 121–236.
[5] See, for example, QuarEd on p. 299, n. 9 say this about Bonaventure's commentary on Luke 11:31: "Card. Hugh (on Matthew 12:42 and on Luke 11:31) proposes the same seven preeminent characteristics."

comparative study, this volume is rich in its notations of Bonaventure's dependence upon Hugh of St. Cher, not only for Scripture quotations, but also for quotations from ecclesiastical and other authorities. I refer readers, who are interested in even more detail than I can provide in the confines of this commentary, to my article, "Bonaventure's Commentary on Luke: Four Case Studies of his Creative Borrowing from Hugh of St. Cher,"[6] where I treat Luke 11:29–32, 11:41, 13:20–21, and 16:16. It is my firm opinion, substantiated by the four test cases studied in this article, that Bonaventure is a child of his culture and borrows from his predecessors and that his borrowing is not what we today call plagiarism. Rather it is his creative adaptation of tradition to his purposes.[7]

CONTEMPORARY RELEVANCE OF BONAVENTURE'S INTERPRETATION OF THE PARABLES

In a future monograph I plan to explore in full detail the contemporary relevance of Bonaventure's interpretation

---

[6] *Franciscan Studies* 59 (2001): 133–236.

[7] Zachary Hayes, "Bonaventure of Bagnoregio: A Paradigm for Franciscan Theologians?" in *The Franciscan Intellectual Tradition: Washington Theological Union Symposium Papers 2001*, ed. Elise Saggau; (St. Bonaventure, New York: Franciscan Institute Publications, 2002), 43–56, esp. pp. 46–47 has called attention to Bonaventure's view of himself as "a poor and needy compiler." See what Bonaventure says about his work in the introduction to Book II of his Sentence Commentary in Opera Omnia 2:1: "For I do not intend to champion new opinions, but to repeat commonly held and approved ones. Let no one think that I want to be the fabricator of new doctrine. For I know and confess that I am a poor and needy compiler." Of course, Bonaventure is not merely mouthing what his master and father, Alexander of Hales, taught him. But the point is clear that Bonaventure is deeply beholden to tradition.

of Jesus' parables in Luke's Gospel.[8] Of the many parables that occur in Luke 9–16 I single out that of the Good Samaritan and provide brief comments on the contemporary relevance of Bonaventure's exposition as a down payment of the promised monograph.

It seems to me that vast majority of New Testament scholars maintain that most of the parable interpretation before the advent of Adolf Jülicher's two volumes on the parables was allegorical and thus to be devalued. Surely there are nuances in the viewpoints of individual scholars, for no one wants to make a sweeping generalization that all pre-Jülicher parable interpretation was allegorical. Nonetheless, I would venture to say that most New Testament scholars bypass medieval parable interpretation as irrelevantly allegorical. Perhaps, the judgment of Klyne R. Snodgrass may be taken as representative: "Allegorizing, in fact, was the primary method for the interpretation of Jesus' parables from at least the time of Irenaeus to the end of the nineteenth century. . . . Some Church Fathers and Reformers, of course, protested such allegorizing. . . . Still, allegorizing is no legitimate means of interpretation. It obfuscates the message of Jesus and replaces it with the teaching of the church."[9]

---

[8] For some indication of the contemporaneity of Bonaventure's commentary on Luke, see *Bonaventure's Commentary on the Gospel of Luke, Chapters 1–8*, Introduction, Translation and Notes by Robert J. Karris, Works of St. Bonaventure VIII/I (St. Bonaventure, New York: Franciscan Institute Publications, 2001), xxii–xxxvii and Robert J. Karris, "Bonaventure and Talbert on Luke 8:26–39: Christology, Discipleship, and Evangelization," *Perspectives in Religious Studies* 28 (#1, Spring 2001): 57–66.

[9] "From Allegorizing to Allegorizing: A History of the Interpretation of the Parables of Jesus" in *The Challenge of Jesus' Parables*, ed. Richard N. Longenecker (Grand Rapids: Eerdmans, 2000), 3–29 (5). On page 4 Snodgrass summarizes Augustine's interpretation of the

In this regard I would refer interested readers to
Bonaventure's postill on the literal sense of Luke
10:30–37 (#52–61). In his literal exegesis of the parable
of the Good Samaritan Bonaventure uses Bede, Ambrose, and the Glossa Ordinaria once each. But as is his
dominant mode for interpreting scripture, he interprets
these eight verses via other scripture passages. An indication of the breadth of his knowledge of scripture is the
fact that he takes quotations from sixteen different Old
Testament books and eight different New Testament
writings. The most scripture quotations stem from
Psalms (8), Isaiah (5), and Sirach (5). I give a small example of Bonaventure's literal exposition from what he
has to say about Luke 10:34 (#58): ". . . And because this
injured man was in need not only of medication, but also
of a means of transport and hospitality and food, the
text adds: *And setting him on his own beast*, as a means
of transport, *brought him to an inn*, for hospitality, *and
took care of him*, by giving him food. And thus he
fulfilled what Isaiah 58:7 says: 'Break your bread with
the hungry and bring the needy and homeless into your
home.'" In my opinion Bonaventure's interpretation of
the literal sense of Luke 10:30–37 is very much in
accord with contemporary exegesis as represented in the
master work of Arland J. Hultgren.[10] Most amazing in
this context is the fact that Bonaventure does not al-
legorize, for he first presents "the spiritual sense" in
#62–64 as a distinct type of interpretation.

---

parable of the Good Samaritan as the best known example of theological and ecclesiastical allegorizing.
[10] *The Parables of Jesus: A Commentary* (Grand Rapids: Eerdmans,
2000), 93–101.

BONAVENTURE'S ANTI-JUDAISM

THE CONTEXTS OF ANTI-JUDAISM IN ST. BONAVENTURE'S
WRITINGS

The bibliography on anti-Judaism in the Middle Ages is
immense.[11] Skilled guides for our concerns are Jeremy
Cohen,[12] Gilbert Dahan,[13] and Robert E. Lerner.[14] I first
set Bonaventure's writings in various contexts and then
deal with specific texts in his nine folio volumes.

---

[11] Gavin Langmuir, "Anti-Judaism as the Necessary Preparation for
Anti-Semitism," *Viator* 2 (1971): 383–389 provides this definition of
"anti-Judaism" on p. 383: "Anti-Judaism I take to be a total or partial opposition to Judaism – and to Jews as adherents of it – by men
who accept a competing system of beliefs and practices and consider
certain genuine Judaic beliefs and practices as inferior. Anti-
Judaism, therefore, can be pagan, Christian, communist, or what
you will, but its specific character will depend upon the character of
the specific competing system."
[12] "Mendicants, the Medieval Church, and the Jews: Dominican and
Franciscan Attitudes towards the Jews in the Thirteenth and Fourteenth Centuries" (Ithaca: Cornell University, 1978, PhD. Disserta-
tion); *The Friars and the Jews: The Evolution of Medieval Anti-
Judaism* (Ithaca: Cornell University Press, 1982); *Living Letters of
the Law: Ideas of the Jew in Medieval Christianity* (Berkeley: University of California Press, 1999).
[13] "Saint Bonaventure et les Juifs," *Archivum Franciscanum His-
toricum* 77 (1984): 369–405; *Les intellectuals chrétiens et les juifs au
moyen âge* (Paris: Cerf, 1990); and *The Christian Polemic against the
Jews in the Middle Ages* (Notre Dame, IN: University of Notre Dame
Press, 1998).
[14] *The Feast of Saint Abraham: Medieval Millenarians and the Jews*
(Philadelphia: University of Pennsylvania Press, 2001).

Bonaventure's Theological Context[15]

At the risk of simplification in an area that is very complicated[16] I state that the two primary theological influences on Bonaventure's views of the Jews were St. Paul, especially his Letter to the Romans, and St. Augustine. As I read through the bibliography on medieval anti-Judaism, I was amazed to see how seriously patristic and medieval writers took Romans 11:25–26: "A partial blindness has befallen Israel until the full number of the Gentiles enter. And thus all Israel will be saved." For it is only within the last thirty years that we New Testament scholars have done justice to Romans 9–11 and not considered it a mere "appendix." In today's scholarly literature on Paul and Romans a common view is that Romans 9–11 is the main point of Romans, as Paul vigorously argues for God's fidelity to promises made to Israel, even though Israel has largely failed to come to faith in Jesus, the Messiah and Lord.[17]

---

[15] It is impossible in the course of this presentation to go into all types of Christian anti-Jewish polemics. See Amos Funkenstein, "Basic Types of Christian anti-Jewish Polemics in the Later Middle Ages," *Viator* 2 (1971): 373–382. Funkenstein considers four types: The various forms of "Dialogues with the Jews"; rationalism and/or philosophy applied to religious topics; attacks on post-biblical Jewish literature; argumentation that Jewish post-biblical literature contains references to Christ. See further Dahan, *The Christian Polemic against the Jews in the Middle Ages.*

[16] See Cohen, *Living Letters of the Law,* p. 391: "The selected images of Jews and Judaism in Christian theology from late antiquity to the High Middle Ages that we have considered underscore the complexity and extent of that role, one that defies any simple summary or generalization."

[17] I give some significant titles from a vast bibliography: Krister Stendahl, *Paul Among Jews and Gentiles and Other Essays* (Philadelphia: Fortress, 1976); N. T. Wright, *The Climax of the Covenant: Christ and the Law in Pauline Theology* (Minneapolis: Fortress, 1992); *Pauline Theology,* Volume III: *Romans,* ed. David M. Hay and E. Elizabeth Johnson (Minneapolis: Fortress, 1995). James D. G.

Augustine's contribution to the medieval view of Jews
was at least threefold and very influential. First, in the
first part of his commentary on Psalm 58 Augustine un-
derscores God's mercy and maintains that the very existence of the Jews is a witness to God's mercy. He writes:
"It was on Cain, and, significantly, after he had slain his
brother, that God put a mark, to prevent anyone killing
him. This is the sign that the Jews bear today. They
preserve tenaciously the remnants of their law; they
practice circumcision, observe the Sabbath, slaughter
the paschal lamb, and eat unleavened bread. The Jews
abide; they have not been killed, for they are necessary
to Gentile believers. Why? So that God may give us
proof of his mercy by his dealings with our enemies."[18]

Second, the scriptures of the Jews bear independent
witness to the Gentiles of the truth of Christianity, for
neither Christians nor Jews invented the testimonies
contained in these scriptures. Augustine comments on
Psalm 58:1–2 in Book 18.46 of his *The City of God*: "Although they were conquered and oppressed by the Romans, God did not 'slay' them, that is, he did not destroy
them as Jews. For, in that case, they would have been
forgotten and would have been useless as witnesses to
what I am speaking of. Consequently, the first part of
the prophecy, 'Slay them not lest they forget thy law,' is
of small import without the rest, 'Scatter them.' For, if
the Jews had remained bottled up in their own land
with the evidence of their Scriptures and if they were
not to be found everywhere, as the Church is, the

Dunn, *The Theology of Paul the Apostle* (Grand Rapids: Eerdmans, 1998).
[18] See *Expositions of the Psalms 51–72*, translation and notes by Maria Boulding, Works of Saint Augustine Part III – Books, Volume 17 (Hyde Park, New York: New City Press, 2001), 166. Cf. CCSL xxxix, p. 744.

Church would not then have them as ubiquitous witnesses of the ancient prophecies concerning Christ."[19]

Finally, Augustine conveys the truth of Paul's promise of the conversion of Israel at the end of days. In his commentary on Malachi 4:5–6[20] in Book 20.29 of his *The City of God* Augustine alludes to Romans 11:25–26 as he writes: "It is most widely maintained in the speech and hearts of the faithful that through the exposition of the Law by Elijah, that great and marvelous prophet, to the Jews in the last days before the judgment, the Jews will believe in the true Messiah, that is, our Christ."[21]

In summary, the Augustinian legacy to the Middle Ages about the Jews focused on their witness value, which was predicated on fidelity to Jewish scriptures and praxis, and the hope of their conversion at the end of days.

Bonaventure's Ecclesiastical Context

Sicut Judeis

Papal protection of the Jews, especially those living in Rome, dates back to Pope Gregory I (d. 604) and found articulation in the Bull *Sicut Judeis* of Pope Calixtus II (d. 1124). This Bull was reissued, modified by many subsequent Popes, and found its way into the Church's

---

[19] See *Saint Augustine: The City of God Books XVII–XXII*, translated by Gerald G. Walsh and Daniel J. Honan, FC 24 (New York: Fathers of the Church, Inc., 1954), 165. Cf. CCSL xlviii, pp. 643–645, esp. pp. 644–645.

[20] Septuagint numbering is employed.

[21] This is my translation of CCSL xlviii, p. 752: Per hunc Heliam magnum mirabilemque prophetam exposita sibi lege ultimo tempore ante iudicium Iudaeos in Christum verum, id est in Christum nostrum, esse credituros, celeberrimum est in sermonibus cordibusque fidelium.

Canon Law. As Solomon Grayzel states: "Moreover, it appears to have been repeated more frequently than any other papal utterance concerning the Jews: being used by six popes during the twelfth century (including Innocent III), by ten popes during the thirteenth, by four popes during the fourteenth (including an antipope), and by three during the fifteenth century."[22] It seems worthwhile to quote *Sicut Judeis*, for few have ever seen or read it in its entirety:

"Even as the Jews ought not have the freedom to dare to do in their synagogues more than the law permits them, so ought they not suffer curtailment of those [privileges] which have been conceded them.

"This is why, although they prefer to persist in their obstinacy rather than acknowledge the words of the prophets and the eternal secrets of their own scriptures, thus arriving at an understanding of Christianity and salvation, nevertheless, in view of the fact that they have begged for our protection and our aid and in accordance with the clemency which Christian piety imposes, we, following in the footsteps of our predecessors of happy memory. . . . Grant their petition and offer them the shield of our protection.

---

[22] See "The Papal Bull *Sicut Judeis*," in *Studies and Essays in Honor of Abraham A. Neuman,* ed. Meir Ben-Horin; Bernard D. Weinryb; Solomon Zeitlin (Leiden: Brill, 1962), 243–280 (here pp. 243–44). See also Edward A. Synan, *The Popes and the Jews in the Middle Ages* (New York: Macmillan, 1965); Solomon Grayzel, *The Church and the Jews in the XIIIth Century: A Study of their Relations During the Years 1198–1254: Based on the Papal Letters and the Conciliar Decrees,* revised edition (New York: Hermon Press, 1966); Shlomo Simonsohn, *The Apostolic See and the Jews, Documents: 492–1404,* Studies and Texts 94 (Toronto: Pontifical Institute of Mediaeval Studies, 1988).

"We decree that no Christian shall use violence to force them into baptism while they are unwilling and refuse, but that [only] if anyone of them seeks refuge among the Christians of his own free will and by reason of faith, his willingness having become quite clear, shall he be made a Christian without subjecting himself to any opprobrium. For surely none can be believed to possess the true Christian faith if he is known to have come to Christian baptism unwillingly and even against his wishes.

"Moreover, without the judgment of the authority of the land, no Christian shall presume to wound their persons, or kill them, or rob them of their money, or change the good customs which they have thus far enjoyed in the place of their habitation. Furthermore, while they celebrate their festivals, no one shall disturb them in any way by means of sticks and stones, nor exact forced service from any of them other than such as they have been accustomed to perform from ancient times. Opposing the wickedness and avarice of evil men in such matters, we decree that no one shall dare to desecrate or reduce a Jewish cemetery, or, with the object of extorting money, exhume bodies there interred.

"Should anyone, being acquainted with the contents of this decree, nevertheless dare to act in defiance of it – which God forbid – he shall suffer loss of honor and office or be restrained by the penalty of excommunication, unless he make proper amends for his presumption. We desire, however, to place under the protection of this decree only those [Jews] who do not presume to plot against the Christian faith. Given. . . ."[23]

---

[23] Modified translation from Grayzel, "The Papal Bull *Sicut Judeis*," p. 245.

If one asks about the effectiveness of the frequently re-issued *Sicut Judeis*, one must remember that the medieval papacy was far less powerful than its contemporary counterpart and that *Sicut Judeis* really had no penal bite. As Grayzel soberly comments: "The penal clause, contained in this Bull as in practically all others, was rarely, if ever, enforced. No one, as far as one can tell, was actually removed from office or made to suffer excommunication for converting Jews by force or even for the tortures and murders to which they were subjected throughout the bleak years of the Middle Ages."[24] And implicitly harkening back to Augustine's notion of Jewish witness and God's plan of salvation for Jews, Grayzel concludes his article: "Probably the greatest protection offered by the Church was its constant reminder of human decencies and its reference to the Jewish people as an integral part of the Divine Plan."[25]

IV LATERAN COUNCIL

Decrees 67–70 of IV Lateran Council (1215), which concerned the Jews, reveal another dimension of Bonaventure's ecclesiastical context.[26] Decree 67 forbade Jews, under any pretext, from extorting heavy and immoderate usury from a Christian. Decree 68 stated that Jews and Saracens "of either sex, and in all Christian lands, and at all times, shall easily be distinguishable from the rest of the populations by the quality of their clothes." This decree also forbade Jews from going about in public during the Sacred Triduum and on Easter Sunday.[27] Decree 69 continued the ban on Jews holding public office

[24] "The Papal Bull *Sicut Judeis*," p. 279.
[25] "The Papal Bull *Sicut Judeis*," p. 280.
[26] See Grayzel, *The Church and the Jews in the XIIIth Century*, pp. 307–311.
[27] Grayzel, *The Church and the Jews in the XIIIth Century*, p. 309.

and thereby having power over Christians, and Decree 70 concerned those who, despite voluntary baptism, still retained elements of their former faith.

THE BURNING OF THE HEBREW TALMUD AT PARIS IN 1242

Nicholas Donin, a convert from Judaism, persuaded Pope Gregory IX that the Jewish Talmud contained deviations from biblical norms and blasphemies. The only secular ruler to follow the Pope's demand[28] that the Talmud be investigated was King Louis IX of France. Jeremy Cohen describes what happened after Louis IX had the Talmud put on trial: "The clerical court found the Talmud guilty as charged and condemned it to the stake. . . . Twenty or twenty-four wagonloads of manuscripts – probably ten to twelve thousand volumes – were burned in Paris in the Place de Grève over the course of one and one-half days in 1242."[29] At least two things are significant about this tragic event. First, it raised the question about the Augustinian theory of the value of the witness of the Jews. Were the Jews giving witness solely to the Bible or also against Christianity in their halackic and haggadic commentaries on the Bible found in their Talmud? Second, Bonaventure was a student in Paris in 1242. To what extent, if any, were his views of the Jews influenced by the burning of the Talmud?[30]

---

[28] For the texts, see Grayzel, *The Church and the Jews in the Thirteenth Century*, pp. 240–243.
[29] *The Friars and the Jews*, p. 63. See also Robert Chazan, *Daggers of Faith: Thirteenth Century Christian Missionizing and Jewish Response* (Berkeley: University of California Press, 1989), pp. 31–32.
[30] See Thomas H. Bestul, *Texts of the Passion: Latin Devotional Literature and Medieval Society* (Philadelphia: University of Pennsylvania Press, 1996), 92–93. On p. 93 Bestul claims too much: "I am by no means about to suggest that the spectacular events surrounding the trial and the burning of the Talmud provided the occasion for

I pause to give an answer to this second question by taking a quick look at what Bonaventure's teacher, Alexander of Hales (d. 1245), taught about the Jews.[31] It is very instructive to see how Alexander of Hales argues the question, "Whether the Jews are to be tolerated?"[32] He gives a positive response, arguing by means of the Decretals of Pope Gregory IX and the Augustinian legacy of Jewish witness and Jewish salvation at the end of time. Alexander is very much aware of the burning of the Talmud at Paris in 1242. In the second point of his argument he raises an objection to the toleration of the Jews: "Moreover, in their book, which is called *Talmud*, many things were contained that blasphemed Christ and the Blessed Virgin. Therefore, since they observe the teaching of this book as a law, they are to be dispersed together with books of this kind." To this objection he responses: "Concerning the second point it must be said that their books, in which blasphemies of this sort are contained, are to be burned. But they, if they pertinaciously persist in blasphemy of this kind, having been convicted before a judge, are to be fittingly punished. But it is a different matter if they blaspheme secretly."

Bonaventure's passion treatises, in any narrow sense, but only to position them within a Parisian 'textual environment' that was also rich in symbolic action, to see them in association with what Paul Strohm has termed, in speaking of late fourteenth-century England, 'a broad array of roughly contemporary statements and gestures.'"

[31] While admitting Bonaventure's creativity, I also recognize how traditional he was and underscore what he says at the beginning of his commentary on Book II of the Sentences about his dependence upon his Master, Alexander of Hales. See Opera Omnia 2:1.

[32] See his *Summa Theologica III: Secunda Pars Secundi Libri* (Quaracchi: College of St. Bonaventure, 1930) #740 (pp. 729–730). This question occurs under the title of "Concerning Jews and pagans," which in turn is a subheading of "Concerning those sins by which divine omnipotence is dishonored," which for its part falls under the larger section "About the species of actual sin."

Alexander of Hales argues from the bases tradition provided him: Pope Gregory IX's version of *Sicut Judeis* and the Augustinian legacy. He also manifests the fairness of a judge: First show me the public evidence and a recalcitrant blasphemer, then I'll mete out a fit punishment.[33] It would seem that Bonaventure, Alexander of Hales' student, would follow in his master's footsteps.

COMPULSORY JEWISH ATTENDANCE AT CHRISTIAN SERMONS

Beginning around 1245 a new wave of Christian missionary activity among the Jews commenced. In a 1245 letter to the Archbishop of Tarragona Pope Innocent IV incorporates an earlier royal edict of King James I of Aragon: "'Likewise, we desire and we hereby decree, that whenever the Archbishop, bishops, or Dominican or Franciscan Friars, visit a town or a place where Saracens or Jews dwell, and whenever they want to preach the word of God to the said Jews or Saracens, these shall gather at their call, and shall patiently listen to their preaching. And our officers, if they want to attain our favor, shall, heedless of excuse, compel them to do so.'"[34] In Robert Chazan's view: "A militant Church sought, and often received, the support of the secular overlords of the Muslims and Jews in forcing them to hear Christianity's message delivered by trained, learned, and elo-

---

[33] For a positive assessment of Alexander of Hales from a Jewish perspective, see J. Guttmann, "Alexandre de Hales et le Judaisme," *Revue des etudes juives* 19 (1889): 224–234. On p. 225, n. 1 Guttmann indicates that he used the 1482 edition of Alexander of Hales' *Summa*. This edition contains slight variations from the 1930 edition.

[34] See Grayzel, *The Church and the Jews in the Thirteenth Century*, p. 257.

quent preachers."[35] There is no evidence that Bonaventure trained preachers for this new mission.

LEARNED JEWISH RABBIS REQUIRED TO DEBATE WITH CHRISTIAN PREACHERS

The most celebrated example of such disputations is that between Paul Christian and Rabbi Nahmanides. Paul Christian (d. 1274) was converted from Judaism by the Dominican Raymond of Penyafort (d. 1275) and joined the Dominican Friars. In the summer of 1263 King James I of Aragon summoned Rabbi Moses ben Nahman (Nahmanides) of Gerona to debate with Paul Christian before the royal court in Barcelona. According to the Latin source for this debate Paul Christian intended to prove the truth of four propositions: 1) "that the messiah, which means Christ, whom the Jews have been awaiting, has undoubtedly [already] come; 2) that the same messiah, as had been prophesied, should at once be divine and human; 3) that he in fact suffered and died for the salvation of the human race; 4) that the legal or ceremonial [provisions of the Old Testament] terminated and were supposed to terminate after the arrival of said messiah."[36] What is amazing is that Paul Christian's proofs are taken from the Old Testament and from the self-same Talmud which had earlier been found to contain blasphemies and errors.[37] There was no doubt in the mind of King James I who had won the debate. The king proceeded to order the Jews to attend sermons of the Dominican friars, that blasphemous passages be deleted from Jewish books, that a censorship commission be established to accomplish the aforemen-

---

[35] *Daggers of Faith*, p. 48.
[36] See Cohen, *The Friars and the Jews*, p. 111.
[37] See Cohen, *The Friars and the Jews*, p. 112.

tioned expurgation, and that Paul Christian be empowered to engage in missionary activity among the Jews.[38]

Such disputations along with sermonizing in synagogues established a new pattern of Christian missionary activity among the Jews. The Jew was no longer "the intellectual Jew"[39] or "the hermeneutical Jew,"[40] but the real Jew. One can ask whether Bonaventure ever moved beyond treating the Jew as an abstraction, "the intellectual Jew," and ever got caught up with the new evangelization of the Jews, "the real Jew." I think that Gilbert Dahan is correct to answer in the negative.[41] Bonaventure seems to have been a dyed in the wool Augustinian traditionalist. That is not to say, however, that Bonaventure transcended the milieu of anti-Judaism in which he was reared. But I'm ahead of myself and will return to my presentation of the contexts of Bonaventure's anti-Judaism.

THE REPRESENTATION OF THE JEWS IN PREACHING

The Jews are portrayed negatively most frequently in sermons that deal with themes of Christ's passion.[42] They are also the subjects of "exempla," which were very

---

[38] See Cohen, *The Friars and the Jews*, p. 110. The literature on the 1263 Barcelona disputation is considerable. See Robert Chazan, *Daggers of Faith*, pp. 49–85, 189–195; Robert Chazan, *Barcelona and Beyond: The Disputation of 1263 and Its Aftermath* (Berkeley: University of California Press, 1992; Jeremy Cohen, *Living Letters of the Law*, pp. 334–342.

[39] See Dahan, *Les intellectuels chrétiens et les juifs*, p. 585.

[40] See Cohen, *Living Letters of the Law*, pp. 2–3 and n. 3.

[41] See Dahan, *Les intellectuals chrétiens et les juifs*, pp. 539, 583–585.

[42] See also treatises on Christ's passion, e.g., *Sermo de Vita et Passione Domini*, which is attributed to St. Anselm and also bears the title, *Stimulus Amoris*, and is found in PL 184:953D–966A. For a full discussion, see Thomas H. Bestul, *Texts of the Passion*, especially pp. 92–98 where Bestul discusses Bonaventure's "passion texts."

popular in medieval sermons. One example story, dating from about 1250, can be titled "A Jew Falls into a Stinking Pit." Although it ostensibly deals with the necessity of repenting when one is young, it is really an attack on Jewish literal interpretation of scripture, which prevents Jews from seeing the true spiritual and messianic meaning of scripture. The preacher says: "There are some who are advised to turn from sin, but they say that they are still too young. They say that when they are older, they will stop sinning. It will happen to them as it did to a Jew that I read of. There was once a Jew who on their Sabbath fell into a foul, stinking pit. Along came a man who saw him in this pit and wanted to help him out. But the Jew said no, because it was his Sabbath day: 'Therefore, you shall not labor for me, and I will not labor for you.' And so this passerby let the Jew remain there. Within a little while the stench of this pit was so great that the Jew died there. Truly, I'm very afraid that these men will not turn from their sin until such time as they die of its stench."[43]

Sara Lipton makes the persuasive case that *exempla* against the Jews were the basis for their largely negative portrayal in the *Bible moralisée*, two representations of which she studied and dated to Paris in 1225.[44] Lipton writes: "The fact that numerous visual signs in the *Bible moralisée* seem to be inspired by exempla confirms the suspicion that the imagery of the manuscripts was created by, and conforms to the approaches of, those early thirteenth-century clerics who were engaged in formu-

---

[43] Translation adapted from Joan Young Gregg, *Devils, Women, and Jews: Reflections of the Other in Medieval Sermon Stories* (Albany, New York: State University of New York Press, 1997), 215, 233.
[44] Sara Lipton, *Images of Intolerance: The Representation of the Jews in the Bible moralisée* (Berkeley: University of California Press, 1999).

lating and disseminating effective popular preaching techniques."[45]

But there is also a very positive image of the conversion of the Jews in the *Bible moralisée*. Here the roots are not in St. Paul or St. Augustine, but in Venerable Bede's allegorization of Tobit. Lipton presents two examples. In her figure 4 she provides a roundel of Tobit 11:10–11 along with its commentary roundel which shows that the elder Tobit's joyous welcome of his son and daughter-in-law is compared to the ultimate conversion of the Jews at the end of the world.[46] Lipton writes of figure 85: "The text interpreting the elder Tobias' cure from blindness (Tob 11:13–16) confidently predicts the collective conversion of the Jews: 'The gall of the fish [applied to Tobias' eyes] signifies the malice of the devil, which first the Judaic people will have perceived working within the Antichrist; then when the Lord will have taken it [or: him] away from their midst at the end of the world, all will be illuminated by the faith of Christ.'"[47] Lipton has directed me to Bede's commentary on Tobit and to the sculptures of Tobit at Chartres.[48]

I translate Bede's allegorical commentary on Tobit 11:11–14, which stands behind Lipton's figures 4 and 85: "*And embracing him, he kissed him along with his wife, and was weeping for joy.* Judea, at the end of time, embraces Christ with joy and weeps for joy because it believes, and it weeps for sorrow because it has come to the Lord so late. *Then Tobit, taking the fish's gall, anoints his father's eyes.* And the Lord reveals to believ-

---

[45] "The Root of All Evil: Jews, Money and Metaphor in the *Bible moralisée*," *Medieval Encounters* 1 (1991): 301–322 (320).
[46] *Images of Intolerance*, p. 19.
[47] *Images of Intolerance*, p. 116.
[48] *Images of Intolerance*, p. 205, n. 20.

ers more clearly how great was the wickedness of the ancient dragon, which once ago tried to devour him in the passion, but instead killed his members through this, that is, he lost those he had formerly held in his grasp. *From the eyes of Tobias a white skin began to come off like the skin of an egg*, after his eyes had been anointed with the fish's gall. And he received his sight. And the people of the Jews, after they realize that the most wretched malice of the most wicked enemy has been dispersed, will receive the light."[49]
Bede's very positive view of the Jews harkens back to St. Paul and to St. Augustine, but he alone is the one who sees this interpretation in Tobit 11. Bede's interpretation of Tobit is found in the sculpture work at Chartres Cathedral, whose building is almost co-extensive with the life of Bonaventure – 1200–1260. As Adolf Katzenellenbogen comments: "The cycle of Tobit and Tobias occupies the whole outer archivolt (of the north transept) and acts as frame for the four other cycles. It has to be read clockwise from the left to the right. If interpreted in accordance with the commentary of Venerable Bede, the cycle . . . gives an all-inclusive illustration of the final salvation of the Jews by Christ and the Church."[50] If we recall that the artwork in me-

---

[49] *Bedae Venerabilis Opera*, Pars II, 2B Opera Exegetica, ed. D. Hurst; J. E. Hudson, CCSL cxixb (Turnhout: Brepols, 1983), 16. Joachim of Fiore concludes his *Adversus Judeos* with his eschatological interpretation of Tobit 11:11–14. See *Adversus Iudeos di Gioacchino da Fiore*, ed. Arsenio Frugoni, Fonti per la storia d'Italia 95 (Rome: Instituto Storico Italiano, 1957), 95–101. Joachim is the end-time prophet, preaching repentance to the Jews. In the terms of Joachim's allegorical interpretation Joachim is the dog that runs ahead to announce the joyful news of the return of the son and his wife and the return of Tobias' sight. See Robert E. Lerner, *The Feast of Saint Abraham*, pp. 5–7, 126.
[50] *The Sculptural Programs of Chartres Cathedral: Christ, Mary, Ecclesia* (New York: Norton, 1964), 72. On p. 73 Katzenellenbogen

dieval cathedrals not only inspired admiration, but also taught the faithful, we can see what a positive view of the Jews the cycle of Tobit and Tobias projected.

THE LARGELY NEGATIVE VIEW OF THE JEWS IN ARTWORK

My last point about the teaching value of medieval art-work in its various forms, especially at Chartres Cathe-dral, leads naturally to this point. I refer to the work of Heinz Schreckenberg.[51] Although much that Schrecken-berg presents comes from a later period, there is suffi-cient material from miniatures in psalters or evan-gelaries, panel paintings, and sculptures to indicate the largely negative way such art depicted the Jews, espe-cially under the categories of Ecclesia and Synagoga. But in his section on "Reconciliation of the adversaries" Schreckenberg presents some art pieces that give a posi-tive view of the Jews.[52] I give the one example of a miniature contained in a manuscript of Honorius Autun's exposition of the Shunamite woman in The Song of Songs 6:13. This miniature dates from the sec-ond half of the twelfth century and depicts the Shuna-mite woman along with five Jews in a carriage whose wheels are the four gospels. Above the carriage, which is heading towards salvation, is the word *Jews*.[53] In his interpretation of The Song of Songs 6:12 Honorius Autun states: "For the Jews who have converted at the end of the world will display such great behavior that the Church will be amazed and use their example. For

---

observes: "No antagonism is apparent, and the cycle ends with the salvation of Israel."

[51] *The Jews in Christian Art: An Illustrated History* (New York: Con-tinuum, 1996).

[52] *The Jews in Christian Art*, pp. 66–74.

[53] *The Jews in Christian Art*, p. 72, n. 11.

they will be converted by Elijah and Enoch at the evening of the world. . . ."[54]

THE POLITICAL CONTEXT OF THE JEWS

The First Crusade marks the beginnings of Jewish expulsion from Europe. In 1096 bands of armed crusaders and uncontrollable mobs attacked Jewish settlements in western and central Germany: Speyer, Worms, Mainz, Cologne, Metz, Trier, and Regensburg and Prague to the east. There were forced conversions, slaughter of those who would not convert, and self-immolation of entire families who would rather kill themselves than experience violence, forced conversion, or death at the hands of their attackers. Eleven hundred Jews fell.[55] As far as Jewish expulsion from Europe is concerned, Gavin I. Langmuir observes: "Once Europe had fully accepted medieval Christianity, the expulsion of Jews began in earnest: from England and southern Italy in 1290, from France first in 1306 and finally in 1394, from many parts of Germany by 1350, and from Spain in 1492 and Portugal in 1497. While these expulsions were the work of secular authorities, impelled primarily by self-interested motives, no pope spoke out against them, and

---

[54] PL 172:455C. My translation. See also John C. Gorman's edition of *William of Newburgh's Explanatio Sacri Epithalmii in Matrem Sponsi: A Commentary on the Canticle of Canticles (12th C)* (Spicilegium Friburgense 6) (Fribourg: University Press, 1960), 300–301 for William of Newburgh's similar commentary on The Song of Songs 6:13. William of Newburgh died ca. 1200.

[55] For basic details and multiple interpretations of the event see Jeremy Cohen, "A 1096 Complex? Constructing the First Crusade in Jewish Historical Memory, Medieval and Modern" in *Jews and Christians in Twelfth Century Europe,* ed. Michael A. Signer and John Van Engen (Notre Dame, IN: University of Notre Dame Press, 2001), 9–26.

by 1500 much of Europe was *judenrein*."[56] Even though
he considers his comparison a "superficial" one, there is
much truth in the remark of Ivan G. Marcus: "A superficial comparison might suggest that just as the Christian
Middle Ages were getting 'made,' to use Southern's idiom, the Jewish Middle Ages were getting 'unmade.'"[57]

Scholars debate the causes for the increase of anti-
Judaism to the point of Jewish expulsion from most of
Europe. For our purposes I cite two scholars. In his 1982
book Jeremy Cohen laid heavy blame on "the friars,"
who moved away from the Augustinian view of the Jews
and confronted real Jews for having deserted biblical
religion.[58] In his 1999 monograph Cohen recapitulated
his earlier thesis: "Some fifteen years ago I advanced
the thesis that Dominican and Franciscan friars of the
thirteenth and early fourteenth centuries developed a
new anti-Jewish ideology in Latin Christendom. I ar-
gued that this outlook condemned medieval Jews for
having deserted the biblical religion which, in Augustinian terms, justified a Jewish presence in Christian
society; that, seeking to diminish such a presence, the
mendicant orders thereby contributed to the decline and
virtual disappearance of European Jewry during the
later Middle Ages; and that the new, 'mendicant' anti-
Judaism derived from the 'evolving self-consciousness' of
medieval Christian civilization – from the critical place

---

[56] *Toward a Definition of Antisemitism* (Berkeley: University of California Press, 1990), 303.
[57] "The Dynamics of Jewish Renaissance and Renewal in the Twelfth
Century" in *Jews and Christians in Twelfth Century Europe*, 27–45
(28–29).
[58] *The Friars and the Jews*. Among the notable weaknesses of this
book are Cohen's unwarranted generalizations about the key role
"the friars" had in medieval anti-Judaism. It is difficult, for example,
to see how Cohen's generalizations would apply to all 30,000 Franciscan friars who existed in 1250.

of the thirteenth century in its development and, ultimately, from factors having little to do with the Jews
themselves."[59] In his 1999 book Cohen strengthens his
arguments, but is less sweeping in his conclusions. On
p. 396 he writes: "In all, the movement away from Augustinian doctrine was typically gradual, often incomplete, and notably erratic. Officially, the medieval
Catholic Church never advocated the expulsion of all
Jews from Christendom or repudiated the doctrine of
Jewish witness; where it had effectively ceased to be operative, as in the polemic of Raymond Martin, at least
an acknowledgment of Paul's eschatological vision for
the Jews remained. Still, late medieval Christendom
frequently ignored the mandates implied in 'Slay them
not, lest at any time they forget your law.' The expulsion, harassment, and persecution of its Jews by prince,
cleric, and layperson alike all bespoke opposing con-
structions of the Jew and his Judaism – to the effect
that they had no proper place in Christendom – regard-
less of whether such ideas directly caused any particular
act of hostility."[60]

From the evidence Cohen has presented it is clear that
Dominican and Franciscan friars were involved in con-
frontations with "real Jews." One bemoans any contribution the friars, Dominican or Franciscan, might have
made to medieval anti-Judaism. Shortly I will present
Bonaventure's contribution and set it in the context of
his total output and let my readers pronounce judgment
upon it.

---

[59] *Living Letters of the Law*, p. 313.
[60] *Living Letters of the Law*, p. 396. E. Randolph Daniel, *The Franciscan Concept of Mission in the High Middle Ages* (St. Bonaventure,
New York: The Franciscan Institute, 1992), does not occur in Cohen's
bibliography.

R. I. Moore locates the change in attitude and behavior towards the Jews in the fears of the Christian persecuting society, namely, Christian fear of the Jews' ancient culture and religion, educational prowess, positions as advisers to princes and even as advisers at the papal court. Moore writes: ". . . Since Jews were in fact better educated, more cultivated and more skilful than their Christian counterparts legend must reduce them below the level of common humanity, filthy in their persons and debased in their passions, menacing Christian society from below, requiring the help of the powers of darkness to work evil far beyond their own contemptible capacities."[61] Moore, whose hypothesis has been highly influential, is more concerned with clerical grasping for power than with the thought of theologians, be these friars or not.

CONCLUSION ON BONAVENTURE'S CONTEXTS

In brief compass I have presented the theological, ecclesiastical, cultural, and political contexts of Bonaventure's anti-Judaism. As a way of summary, I present what David Berger says about the attitude of St. Bernard of Clairvaux (d. 1153) towards the Jews,[62] for I think that Bonaventure is much like Bernard, whose published Opera Omnia runs to eight folio volumes and can provide evidence of diverse viewpoints. Bernard's contact with Jews was minimal, and he formed his attitude towards them almost totally on the basis of theological considerations. In his attacks upon the Cistercian monk Radulph, who was encouraging the mobs to

---

[61] *The Formation of a Persecuting Society: Power and Deviance in Western Europe, 950–1250* (Oxford: Blackwell, 1987), 152.

[62] David Berger, "The Attitude of St. Bernard of Clairvaux Toward the Jew," *Proceedings of the American Academy for Jewish Research* 40 (1972): 89–108.

massacre Jews as he preached the Second Crusade in 1143, Bernard was a strong proponent of the Augustinian views about the Jews, especially Paul's teaching about the ultimate conversion of the Jews in Romans 11:25–26. This is not to say that Bernard was not a conveyer of anti-Jewish prejudices. As Berger concludes: ". . . he was an unusually strong opponent of the destruction of Jews, yet an equally strong spokesman for anti-Jewish stereotypes and prejudices. Bernard himself, because of his very strong belief in the Biblical promises which he cites and his devotion to canon law, was able to overcome his prejudices and protect Jews from physical violence, but this achievement was no simple matter."[63]

ANTI-JUDAISM IN BONAVENTURE'S WRITINGS[64]

I treat the relatively few references to the Jews in Bonaventure's oeuvre under the following three generalizations. Bonaventure is a proponent of the Pauline teaching that the Jews will be saved at the end of time. Second, there is anti-Jewish invective in Bonaventure's writings, especially when he deals with Christ's passion. Third, Bonaventure does not address real Jews, but Jews in the abstract, the intellectual Jew.

THE JEWISH PEOPLE ARE ASLEEP UNTIL THE END OF TIME

In his "Sermo 20 de Diversis" (Feria Sexta in Parasceve) #6 Bonaventure interprets 1 Samuel 19:9–10 and Saul's attempt to kill David by throwing a spear at him: "Saul,

---

[63] "The Attitude of St. Bernard of Clairvaux Toward the Jews," pp. 106–107.
[64] See Dahan, "Saint Bonaventure et les Juifs" for a very fine overview.

who was the first king chosen by God, but who afterwards was rejected, signifies the Jewish people who first were accepted by the Lord and afterwards prepared the cross for its Savior. . . . David, strong in hand, signifies Christ. Saul, the reprobate king, signifies the Jewish people who were rejected by the Lord, wanted to crucify the Lord, but the Lord was unharmed, *the spear was thrust into the wall*, into his flesh because his divinity did not suffer anything evil. And it is said there that when Saul had fallen asleep, the spear was removed from him. This spear is Christ's cross that had been among the Jews, but Emperor Constantine transferred it to the Christians. Saul, who is sleeping, signifies the Jewish people who are still sleeping."[65]

It seems to me that for Bonaventure the contemporary Jewish people is asleep until the last day. Relative to Bonaventure's interpretation of the future of the Jews on the last day, we have his last published sermons or "Collations on the Six Days of Creation." Collation 15:25 reads: "The fact that the Jews will be converted is certain because of Isaiah and the Apostle who teaches authoritatively: Though the number of the children of Israel are as the sands of the sea, the remnant will be saved. And again: A partial blindness only has befallen Israel, until the full number of the Gentiles should enter."[66] In Collation 16.4 Bonaventure interprets the two

---

[65] This is my translation of *Saint Bonaventure, Sermons de Diversis* Volume I, ed. Jacques Guy Bougerol (Paris: Les Editions Franciscaines, 1993), 304. See also Bonaventure's *Lignum Vitae* #30 in Opera Omnia 8:79 for a like interpretation of 1 Samuel 19. In 1993 Bourgerol also published his second volume of Bonaventure's *Sermones de Diversis*. The passage I quoted above from Sermon 20.6 is the only passage of anti-Judaism contained in these sixty-two occasional sermons which take up some 765 pages.

[66] Opera Omnia 5:401–402. Translation modified from José de Vinck, *The Works of Bonaventure V: Collations on the Six Days* (Paterson:

sons of Judah by Rahab, namely, Zerah and Perez, in Genesis 38:27–30 to refer to the calling of the Gentiles and the calling of the Jews that will be at the end: "The Jews believed at first, but they immediately drew back their hand at the time of the primitive church. But after all of the Gentiles have come in, then Zara will be born and the Jewish people will be converted."[67]

There are also seven passages in Bonaventure's Commentary on Luke's Gospel where his hermeneutic of Romans 11:25–26 is at play. In his commentary on Luke 3:2a (#5) Bonaventure clearly refers to the first part of Romans 11:25: "Likewise, it is shown that Judea is divided while Rome is united, because the plenitude of the Gentiles had to enter and the multitude of the Jews be scattered because of the sin of unbelief."[68]

In his commentary on Luke 4:31–44 (#85), which deals with the healing of a man and the healing of a woman, Bonaventure provides an allegorical interpretation that the man is a Gentile and Simon's mother-in-law is the Jewish synagogue: "And therefore, the cure of a man comes first, because as it is said in Romans 11:25–26: 'When the full number of Gentiles will have entered, then all Israel will be saved.'"[69]

In his postill on Luke 7:1–10 (#17) Bonaventure uses Romans 11:25–26 to provide an allegorical reading of this miracle story: "*The sequence of the cure* shows that the greatness of Gentile faith is preferred to Israelite

---

St. Anthony Guild Press, 1970), 25–26. Bonaventure's references are to Romans 9:27 and 11:25, which continues with: "and thus all Israel will be saved."

[67] Opera Omnia 5:404. Translation modified from de Vinck, 5.233.

[68] *Commentary on the Gospel of Luke*, p. 229 and n. 11.

[69] *Commentary on the Gospel of Luke*, p. 362 and n. 133.

faith. Romans 11:25–26 has: 'A partial blindness has befallen Israel until the full number of the Gentiles enter. And thus all Israel should be saved.'"[70]

In his exposition of Luke 8:10 (#16) Bonaventure utilizes Romans 11:25 to explain the blindness of the Jews to the meaning of Jesus' parables: "And this happened because of a divine judgment, according to what Romans 11:25 has: "Brothers and sisters, I would not have you ignorant . . . that a partial blindness has befallen Israel until the full number of the Gentiles should enter." [71]

In his exegesis of Luke 13:30 (#38) Bonaventure interprets "the Jews" who were first and "the Gentiles" who were last by means of Romans 11:25–26: "A special example of this appears in the two people, namely, the Jews, who are blinded, and the gentiles who are elected. Romans 11:26–26 reads: 'For I don't want you to be ignorant, brothers, of this mystery . . . that a partial blindness has befallen Israel until the full number of the Gentiles should enter. And thus all Israel will be saved.'"[72]

Bonaventure interprets Luke 13:35: "And I say to you: You will not see me until the time comes when you will say: Blessed is he who comes in the name of the Lord" in this wise (#76): "So the Lord wants to say that this Jewish people will not see Christ for their salvation unless it converts to faith and praises him. This is the final expectation in the last days after the full number of the Gentiles. So Romans 11:25–26 has: 'A partial blindness

---

[70] *Commentary on the Gospel of Luke*, p. 582.
[71] *Commentary on the Gospel of Luke*, p. 669.
[72] This is my translation.

has befallen Israel until the full number of the Gentiles should enter. And thus all Israel will be saved.' And Romans 9:27 says: 'Isaiah cries out concerning Israel: Though the number of the children of Israel are as the sand of the sea, the remnant will be saved.' And in this the depth of the divine dispensation is manifestly apparent, which causes the Apostle to exclaim in Romans 11:33: 'Oh, the depth of the riches of the wisdom and of the knowledge of God. How incomprehensible are his judgments and inscrutable his ways.'"[73]

In his postill on Luke 19:40 (#62) Bonaventure interprets "the mystery" of the stones crying out to refer to the praise of the Gentiles: "Thus the Glossa comments: 'If blindness has befallen Israel, so that it ceases to praise God, the people of the Gentiles, their stone hearts having been softened, will believe in and proclaim their Creator.' According to what Romans 11:25–26 says: 'A partial blindness has befallen Israel until the full number of the Gentiles should enter. And thus all Israel will be saved.'"[74]

It seems to me that Bonaventure's assimilation of the thought and hope of Sts. Paul and Augustine about the future conversion of the Jews was strong. Put in other words, Bonaventure is not addressing "real Jews," for they are sleeping.

BONAVENTURE'S TREATMENT OF CHRIST'S PASSION

I look at this subject from what Bonaventure says in some of his shorter, devotional works, in some of his

---

[73] This is my translation.
[74] This is my translation.

fifty Sunday sermons, and in his commentary on chapters 22–23 of Luke's Gospel.

BONAVENTURE'S PERFECTION OF LIFE ADDRESSED TO SISTERS

In the middle of his *De Perfectione Vitae ad Sorores*, a short work of twenty pages in his Opera Omnia,[75] Bonaventure offers his sixth meditation, which is a three and a half page reflection on Christ's most ignominious, most cruel, most general, and most lengthy passion under the heading of "On Remembering Christ's Passion." In contemplating Christ's most ignominious passion, Bonaventure observes in 6:4: "O good Jesus, O benign Savior, for not once, but multiple times you were put to shame! The more places in which a person is put to shame, the greater and more public becomes his ignominy. And behold, Lord Jesus, you are bound in the garden, slapped in the house of Annas, spat upon in the courtyard of Caiphas, derided in the palace of Herod, carried your cross on the road, crucified on Golgotha. Woe is me! Woe is me! Behold, the liberator of captives is captured. The glory of angels is mocked. The life of human beings is killed. O miserable Jews, you have well fulfilled what you have spoken beforehand: For you said: Let us condemn him to a most wretched death."[76]

---

[75] Opera Omnia 8:107–127.

[76] This is my translation of Opera Omnia 8:121. At the end of his observation Bonaventure quotes the mockers of the just person from Wisdom 2:20. Thomas H. Bestul, *Texts of the Passion,* p. 93, highlights this single passage as one that "contains a typical outburst against the Jews as the murderers of Christ." Bestul fails to translate the "me" in the double *Heu me! Heu me!* ("Woe is me! Woe is me!) and thereby misconstrues the nature of Bonaventure's affective meditation. See how Bonaventure moves his sixth meditation to a practical conclusion of repentance for his readers in 6.10: "Woe also to those whose hearts not even such bloodshed, not even the payment of such a price, can soften with pity, inspire with kindness, inflame with zeal for good. Assuredly, these enemies of the cross of Christ are hurling at the Son of God – now enthroned at the right hand of the Father –

BONAVENTURE'S MYSTICAL VINE OR TREATISE ON THE LORD'S PASSION

I call attention to two passages in Bonaventure's *Vitis Mystica seu Tractatus de Passione Domini*, which runs for thirty pages in his Opera Omnia.[77] In Chapter IV Bonaventure treats the seven bonds by which the vine is tied. Bond six is the crown of thorns by which his mother, the Synagogue, that is, the Jewish people, offer coronation to Jesus Christ, our peace.[78] As Bonaventure continues his reflection on this sixth bond, he considers the blood shed thrice by the faithful soul's Spouse: "Behold, O bride, your spouse, blood red in his perspiration, flagellation, crucifixion. Lift up the eyes of your mind and see whether this is the tunic of your Spouse or not. Behold, a most evil wild beast, a rabid dog, the Jewish people[79] devours him. A most evil wild beast condemns your son, your brother, your Spouse."[80]

---

worse blasphemies than did the Jews of old while he hung on the cross." I have modified de Vinck's translation, 1.245–246. See Opera Omnia 8:123.

[77] Opera Omnia 8:159–189.

[78] Opera Omnia 8:166.

[79] I have translated *plebs* by "people." Bestul, *Texts of the Passion*, pp. 93–94 makes much of this single passage and even goes so far as to give a quasi-Marxist interpretation of *plebs* as "the mob," who are opposed by the dominant class. His conclusion is redolent of special pleading: "By the thirteenth century *plebs* was *undoubtedly* a disparaging term, describing the un-noble and the subjected, a resonance that *must be* heard in Bonaventure's usage" (p. 94; emphases mine).

[80] This is my translation of Opera Omnia 8:167. Bonaventure will also employ this typological reference to the Joseph story of Genesis 37:32–33 in his *Lignum Vitae*. See below and Opera Omnia 8:80. See also Bonaventure's use of the Joseph story in his interpretation of Luke 20:14. On the Glossa Ordinaria's anti-Judaistic treatment of Genesis 37, see Michael A. Signer, "The *Glossa ordinaria* and the Transmission of Medieval Anti-Judaism" in *A Distinct Voice: Medieval Studies in Honor of Leonard E. Boyle, O.P.*, ed. Jacqueline Brown

Chapter XX continues Bonaventure's reflection on the rose of Christ's passion as he discusses Christ's third shedding of his blood, which occurred when "impious Jews" plucked his cheeks and drew blood. Bonaventure concludes his meditation: "I see the sacrilegious hands of this most impious nation, which is not content with striking, slapping, and covering with spittle the adorable face of Jesus all-good, but now is also enkindled to pluck his cheeks and draw from that most sweet face the blood which reddens our rose. I see in this Lamb without blemish a patience worthy of admiration and imitation, as he turns in all meekness his most pure cheeks to the harrowing of most impure nails, so that, if ever shame should cover our own face for his sake, we may suffer patiently."[81]

Bonaventure's *Tree of Life*

There are four anti-Judaistic passages in Bonaventure's *Lignum Vitae*, which is eighteen pages long in his Opera Omnia.[82] In this work Bonaventure discusses four fruits of The Tree of Life found in the mystery of Christ's passion. He opens his meditation on "Jesus, handed over to Pilate" with these words: "O horrible impiety of the Jews, which could not be satiated by such insults but went further and, raging with the madness of wild

---

and William P. Stoneman (Notre Dame, IN: University of Notre Dame Press, 1997), 591–605.

[81] Opera Omnia 8:184–185. Translation of de Vinck 1:196 modified. Note the exhortation to imitation that concludes this meditation. See Bestul, *Texts of the Passion*, p. 95 for an argument that Bonaventure's attempt to inspire resulted "in a subtext with a strong, but much different meaning, a subtext that *surely* led to the arousal in the reader of emotions quite other than love of Christ" (emphasis mine). It seems that Bestul commits a methodological error as he universalizes from his own private experience.

[82] Opera Omnia 8:68–86.

beasts, exposed the life of the Just One to an impious
judge as if to be devoured by a mad dog!"[83]

In his meditation on "Jesus, joined with thieves"
Bonaventure twice considers Jesus' prayer that his Father forgive his enemies: ". . . the most mild Lamb
prayed out of the sweetness of his kindness to his Father for those who were crucifying him and deriding him
. . . 'who in all his torments did not once open his mouth
to say even the slightest word of complaint or excuse or
threat or abuse against those accursed dogs. Rather he
poured upon his enemies words of a new blessing not
heard since the beginning of the world.'"[84]

In his multi-layered meditation on "Jesus, pierced with
a lance" Bonaventure comments: "Behold how the spear
thrown by the perfidy of Saul, that is, of the reprobate
Jewish people, through the divine mercy fastened in the
wall without making a wound (1 Samuel 19:10) and
made a cleft in the rock and a hollow place in the cliff as
an abode for doves (The Song of Songs 2:14)."[85]

Finally, there is the long meditation on "Jesus, bathed
in gore" where Bonaventure uses the Joseph story from
Genesis 37:31–33 in a typological manner: "Recognize,

---

[83] Opera Omnia 8:77 (#23). Translation is from Ewert Cousins, *Bona-venture: The Soul's Journey into God, The Tree of Life, The Life of St. Francis* (Mahwah, NJ: Paulist, 1978), 145. Bonaventure introduces his reflection on "Jesus, condemned to death" with: "Pilate was not ignorant of the fact that the Jewish people were aroused against Je-sus not out of zeal for justice but out of envy" (Opera Omnia 8:77 [#24]; Cousins, p. 146).

[84] Opera Omnia 8:78 (#27); Cousins, p. 150. Bonaventure is depend-ent on Anselm here; see PL 158:155D–156A.

[85] Opera Omnia 8:79 (#30); Cousins, p. 155. See above on Sermo 20.6 of Bonaventure's *Sermones de Diversis* for a similar interpretation of 1 Samuel 19:9–10.

therefore, O most merciful Father, the tunic of your beloved son Joseph, whom the envy of his brothers in the
flesh has devoured like a wild beast and has trampled
upon his garment in rage, befouling its beauty with the
remains of blood, for it has left in it five lamentable
gashes. For this is indeed, O Lord, the garment which
your innocent Son willingly gave over into the hands of
the Egyptian prostitute, that is, to the Synagogue,
choosing to be stripped of the mantle of his flesh and to
descend into the prison of death rather than to seek
temporal glory by acquiescing to the shouts of the adulterous people."[86]

BONAVENTURE'S SUNDAY SERMONS

In his fifty Sunday Sermons I have found five passages
that relate to Christ's passion and contain anti-Jewish
sentiments.[87] Bonaventure's Sermon 6, "Dominica infra

---

[86] Opera Omnia 8:80 (#31); Cousins, p. 156. See above on Bonaventure's *Vitis Mystica* in Opera Omnia 8:186 where Bonaventure also
uses Genesis 37:31–33 in his interpretation of the cross. Consult
Bonaventure's source, Anselm, in PL 158:756D–757A. Bonaventure
changes Anselm's "voice," namely, that of Potiphar's adulterous wife,
to "people." See Bestul, *Texts of the Passion*, pp. 95–96 for his interpretation of Bonaventure's treatment of the Jews in his *Lignum Vitae*.

[87] Bonaventure preached many more sermons than these fifty, which
were edited by Bonaventure and his secretary, Friar Marcus de
Montefeltro, sometime during the years 1267–1268. These fifty sermons are thus representative of and an "official" redaction of
Bonaventure's sermons. See *Sancti Bonaventurae Sermones Dominicales,* ed. [J.] G. Bougerol, Bibliotheca Franciscana Scholastica Medii
Aevi 27 (Grottaferrata: Collegio S. Bonaventurae, 1977), 127. I do
not consider *Sermones Dominicales*, p. 183 (Sermon 7 #10 on Luke
2:48 for "Dominica infra Octavam Epiphaniae"), which deals with
the Virgin Mother's third sorrow concerning the blindness and malice of the Jews, to whom she extends the compassion she has for sinners. Nor do I take into account *Sermones Domincales*, p. 377 (Sermon 35 #9 on Luke 16:2 for "Dominica Octava post Pentecosten)

Octavam Nativitatis," has as its text Luke 2:34, "This child is destined for the ruination and resurrection of many in Israel and for a sign that will be contradicted."[88] It is a long meditation on Christ the good physician and the salvific medicine that he brings. I translate paragraph 6 as a representative passage of Bonaventure's anti-Judaism:[89]

"Third, Christ as salvation on account of his voluntary acceptance of the death inflicted upon him *was destined for the ruination* of the impious. For on the cross Christ, like a bunch of grapes crushed in the winepress, gave forth through the wounds of his flourishing body a fragrant liquid for the healing of all diseases and most sufficient for salvation. But the impious Jews take so much offence at this medicinal liquid that they incur the ruination of death and multiply ruination upon ruination by spurning the medicament that is most salubrious and the antidote by which the human race was saved. They are like toads,[90] which are so repulsed by the good

where Bonaventure discusses the carnal Jews in the desert, who abandoned their reasoning power on account of their gluttony and murmured against God. In *Sermones Dominicales*, pp. 448–449 (Sermon 46 # 5 on Matthew 22:7 for "Dominica Decima Nona post Pentecosten) Bonaventure has almost the identical treatment of the carnal Jews in the desert.

[88] *Sermones Dominicales*, pp. 169–178.

[89] See also paragraphs 5, 16–18 in *Sermones Dominicales*, pp. 172–173, 176–178. There is none of this anti-Judaism in Bonaventure's commentary on Luke 2:34. See *Commentary on the Gospel of Luke*, pp. 194–196.

[90] I have been unable to discover an exact reference for Bonaventure's view of the toad fleeing the vineyard. See, however, Louis Charbonneau-Lassay, *The Bestiary of Christ: With Woodcuts by the Author*, translated & abridged by D. M. Dooling (New York: Parabola Books, 1991), who on p. 170 says this about the medieval view of the toad: "Although the frog does not necessarily inspire disgust, the toad on the contrary is everywhere the object of general revulsion, as much because of its pitiable gait as it drags itself along as on account

and fragrant aroma that issues from the vineyard that they turn around and flee. Of this it is said in Proverbs 29:16: 'When the impious are multiplied, crimes will be increased. But the just will behold their ruination.' Truly when the impious Pharisees were multiplied, crimes were increased, when 'the high priests and the Pharisees took counsel how they might seize Jesus by stealth and put him to death.'[91] But the just, that is, the apostles, saw their ruination when the children and heirs of the kingdom were cast outside through divine reprobation and the Gentiles reclined in the bosom of Abraham through merciful adoption."[92]

Bonaventure's Sermon 14, "Dominica in Quinquagesima," has as its text Luke 18:32–33: "For he will be delivered to the Gentiles, and will be mocked and scourged and spit upon. And after they have scourged him, they will put him to death."[93] In paragraph 13, after his description of how in their cruel malice the Jewish people fulfilled Luke 18:32–33, Bonaventure comments: "And what is worse: they put him to death solely out of jealousy, according to what was prefigured in the murder of Abel, about whom it is said in 1 John 3:12: 'Cain, who was of the evil one . . . why did he kill his brother? Because his own works were wicked, but his brother's just.' Perverse Cain, who killed his just brother solely out of jealousy, signifies, by reason of his malignity, the Jewish people, who killed Christ, born from the Jewish people and nation, because they were envious of his good deeds. And this is what Christ said to them: 'I have per-

---

of its warty skin, which exudes at times a disgusting, poisonous slime."
[91] This quotation is a conflation of John 11:47 and Matthew 26:4.
[92] The allusions are to Matthew 8:11–12. See *Sermones Dominicales*, p. 173.
[93] See *Sermones Dominicales*, pp. 227–234.

formed many good works among you. For which work do
you want to kill me?"[94] For this is Christ who has fulfilled all mysteries whatsoever of the Old Testament."[95]

In Sermon 29, "Dominica Secunda post Pentecosten,"
Bonaventure preaches on Luke 14:16: "A certain man
made a great supper and invited many." In paragraph 5
we read: "Third, Christ is said to be that man in a most
fitting way on account of the power of his wondrous
strength in working many miracles. So John 11:47 states:
'The Pharisees said: What are we to do since this man is
performing many signs?' For he has raised the dead,
cleansed lepers, given sight to the blind, extended mercy
to the lame and feeble, liberated those oppressed by demons, and cured every disease. And despite these good
works which he has performed among you, most wicked
Jews, you seek to kill him. 'O insanity and greatest perversity! You are angry with the one who brings healing,
but are not angry with the one who wounds."[96]

In Sermon 32, "Dominica Quinta post Pentecosten,"
Bonaventure takes as his text Matthew 5:22: "Everyone
who is angry with his brother will be liable to judgment." In paragraph 12 Bonaventure presents what
seems like a stereotypical remark about the Jews: "Certainly, if angry people would attend to this judgment
(Jude 14–15), they would never crucify their brother by

---

[94] This is not an exact quotation from John 10:32.
[95] This is my translation of *Sermones Dominicales*, pp. 232–233.
[96] *Sermones Dominicales*, p. 336. Bonaventure alludes here in a general way to Bernard of Clairvaux' Sermon 42, n. 3 on The Song of
Songs. Bonaventure also "quotes" this same passage in Sermon 6.5
in *Sermones Dominicales*, p. 172. See SBOp 2:34: "O astonishing
perversity! The person is angry with his physician when he should
be angry with the archer who shot him."

xlvi   ST. BONAVENTURE'S COMMENTARY ON THE GOSPEL OF LUKE

means of the poison of slander, as the Jews are said to have crucified the Lord through poisonous speech."[97]

In Sermon 46, "Dominica Decima Nona post Pentecosten," Bonaventure gives a homily on Matthew 22:7: "But when the king heard of it, he was angry, and, having sent his armies, destroyed those murderers." In paragraph 4 Bonaventure interprets "the armies" of the parable as the Romans under Titus and Vespasian and "the murderers" as the Jews who persecute the saints, that is, the apostles who were sent to them.[98]

In conclusion to my presentation of the passages of anti-Judaism in Bonaventure's Sunday Sermons I offer the generalization similar to the one I made earlier about Bonaventure's Occasional Sermons: Considering that Bonaventure's Sunday Sermons cover 350 pages,[99] five passages or two pages, while hardly excusable, is not overwhelming.

BONAVENTURE'S COMMENTARY ON CHRIST'S PASSION IN LUKE 22–23

There are eight passages. In his commentary on Luke 22:4 (#5) Bonaventure writes: "The thirst of avarice motivated Judas, and the thirst for cruelty motivated the high priests. And therefore, they together entered into an evil and perverse pact."[100]

Luke 23:10 reads: "But the chief priests and the scribes were standing by, constantly accusing him." In his

---

[97] *Sermones Dominicales*, p. 360.
[98] See *Sermones Dominicales*, p. 448.
[99] *Sermones Dominicales*, pp. 131–480.
[100] Opera Omnia 7:541. Translations are mine.

comment (#12) Bonaventure observes: "Now this constancy was not a virtue, but it was pertinacity, because it did not spring from a love of justice, but from the malice of envy. For it is this that arms the heart to impugn one's neighbor, as Augustine says: 'Through every sin the virus of the ancient enemy floods the human heart, but the passion of envy swamps all human emotions. It is this that armed Cain against his brother Abel, and the sons of Jacob against Joseph, the Babylonians against Daniel, and the Jews against Christ.'"[101]

In his commentary on Luke 23:11–12 (#15) Bonaventure quotes part of the Glossa Ordinaria: "And so these two (Herod and Pilate) designate the persecution of the two peoples against Christ. So the Glossa: Like Herod and Pilate, so the Jews and Gentiles, although dissimilar in nationality, religion, and perspective, nevertheless are united in persecuting Christians and destroying faith in Christ."[102]

In remarking on the Jewish preference for Barabbas in Luke 23:19 (#23), Bonaventure notes: "And this was the greatest wickedness: to grant life to a destroyer of life and to seize life away from the fount of all life."[103]

---

[101] Opera Omnia 7:568–569.
[102] Opera Omnia 7:569. The Glossa Ordinaria, however, in column 987 continues: "In the type of Herod and Pilate who became friends because of Jesus a figure of the Jews and Gentiles stands forth, so that through the passion of Christ a future concord of both will be made, so that first the Gentiles receive the kingdom of God, and transmit the devotion of their faith to the Jew, so that they, too, may be clothed with the body of Christ through the glory of his majesty, which they previously had despised." It is obvious that behind the Glossa Ordinaria's commentary stands Romans 11:25–26.
[103] Opera Omnia 7:570.

About the Jewish demand that Jesus be crucified in Luke 23:21 (#25) Bonaventure comments: "The wicked demanded this out of cruelty and anger."[104]

In his commentary on Luke 23:34 (#41) Bonaventure writes of Jesus' prayer to the Father for forgiveness of his enemies: "Wherefore, it is also manifest in this that he was a pious and merciful high priest, offering himself and interceding for the salvation of the people. And on account of this Luke alone, who has a special interest in Christ's priesthood, describes and narrates this prayer. Thus Bede comments: 'Since Luke was disposed to depict Christ's priesthood, it is fitting that the Lord in his gospel intercedes for his persecutors by reason of his priesthood.'"[105]

In his postill on Luke 23:44–45 (#55) Bonaventure observes: "Now one must pay attention that in that darkening of the sun is understood the blindness of the Jews, and in the rending of the veil the revelation of the scriptures which was made to the Gentiles. So it is said in John 9:39: I have come for judgment on this world, so that those who do not see may see and those who see may become blind. Or, it could refer to the end of time about which Psalm 103:20 says: You have appointed

---

[104] Opera Omnia 7:571

[105] Opera Omnia 7:577. In Opera Omnia 7:577 QuarEd rightly state in n. 2 that Bede's text is the basis for the Glossa Ordinaria. In CCSL cxx, p. 403 Bede goes on to say: "It is sobering to note that he does not pray for those who, incited by the spurs of envy and pride, preferred to crucify him whom they knew to be the Son of God rather than to believe in him. . . ." The Glossa Ordinaria in column 991 comments: "Not for those does he pray, who knew he was the Son of God, but deny and crucify him out of envy and pride."

darkness, and it became night. During it all the beasts of the forest will go about."[106]

Bonaventure in his commentary on Luke 23:47–48 (#57–58) follows Bede and the Glossa Ordinaria: "So in this centurion appeared the quickness among the Gentiles to believe, and on the contrary the hardness among the Jews leading to disbelief" (#57). And #58: "Now 'this crowd' refers to the people of the Jews, who even though they saw the truth, as the centurion had, only beat their breasts, but did not break out with a vocal confession."[107]

BONAVENTURE DOES NOT ADDRESS REAL JEWS, BUT JEWS IN THE ABSTRACT

In his commentary on the meaning of "the elder brother" of Luke 15:24 Hugh of St. Cher distinguishes between four meanings of "the Jews." Since Hugh of St. Cher's distinctions have important bearing on Bonaventure's consideration of the Jews, I quote him at length: "Notice, however, that in the development of the parable about the Jewish people, they are mentioned in different times and different persons, according to the *Rule of Ticonius*.[108] For at one time the text speaks of the Jewish people according to the state of certain ones among the

---

[106] Opera Omnia 7:581. The Glossa Ordinaria in columns 993–994 does not mention the blindness of the Jews, but states: ". . . but Luke is concerned to join the miracle of the sun with the miracle of the veil. Now the veil is torn, so that the ark of the covenant and all the sacraments of the law which had obtained may appear and go over to the Gentiles."

[107] Opera Omnia 7:582.

[108] Ticonius [d. ca. 423] is famous for his seven rules of interpretation [of the Bible]. See Augustine's *Doctrina Christiana* III, 30–37 for these rules, none of which seems to apply to the case at hand. Nonetheless, Hugh's point is very well taken.

modern Jews who search deeply into the prophets and attain some degree of spiritual understanding. At other times it speaks with respect to the state of those who preceded the coming of Christ and did not worship idols. And at other times it speaks with respect to the state of those who were there at the time of Christ; namely, the Scribes and Pharisees. At other times it speaks with respect to those living in the last times who will convert at the preaching of Elijah and Henoch."[109]

From what I have been able to observe, Bonaventure focuses attention on the Jewish people from three aspects: those who preceded the coming of Christ and often serve as types of the New Testament; the scribes and Pharisees who were present at the time of Christ and were mainly his opponents; those living at the last times. Like Hugh of St. Cher, Bonaventure does not address contemporary or "modern" Jews. Or in terms of our current scholarly argot Bonaventure deals with "the intellectual Jew"[110] or "the hermeneutical Jew."[111]

In our preceding discussions we have seen that Bonaventure deals with the Jews living during the last times through his dependence upon St. Augustine, who in turn was dependent on what St. Paul said in Romans 11:25–26. In our considerations of what Bonaventure

---

[109] *A Commentary on The Parable of the Prodigal Son by Hugh of St. Cher, OP (†1263)*, translated, with introduction and notes by Hugh Bernard Feiss (Toronto: Peregrina, 1996), 63. In his interpretation of Luke 15:28, "His father, therefore, came out and began to entreat with his elder son," Hugh of St. Cher comments: "that is, the last Jews, whom the Lord will call at the end through his preachers. Not the modern Jews, because no one preaches to them and they are not now called to faith." See *A Commentary on The Parable of the Prodigal Son*, p. 71.

[110] Dahan, *Les intellectuals chrétiens et les juifs*, p. 585.

[111] Cohen, *Living Letters of the Law*, pp. 2–3 and n. 3.

said about Christ and the Jews in his accounts of the Passion we have glimpsed his typological use of the Old Testament. For example, both Joseph and David are types of Christ.

The onus of this final section is to view additional passages in Bonaventure's works that deal with his treatment of the Jews who lived during the time of Christ. The first group of passages comes from Bonaventure's Sentence Commentary and might as readily be discussed under the rubric of Bonaventure's presentation of Christ's passion. The second group of passages stem from Bonaventure's Commentary on the Gospel of Luke.

OBSERVATIONS ABOUT THE JEWS IN BONAVENTURE'S COMMENTARY ON THE SENTENCES

The greatest single bulk of Bonaventure's corpus consists of the 3,868 pages that comprise his four folio volumes of commentary on the Sentences of Peter Lombard. In these four volumes there are four small passages, actually *dubia* or doubts that need clarification. These, in one theological way or another, deal with the role of the Jews during Christ's passion. I summarize and sometimes translate these passages.

In Book I of his Sentence Commentary distinction 48 dubium II Bonaventure considers the cause of the Passion. I summarize: In the genus of action the Jews did not cause the passion, whose cause was Christ's good intention, which directed his voluntary passion towards a noble end. The action of the Jews was evil and displeasing to God, but Christ's passion was good and pleasing to God.[112]

---

[112] See Opera Omnia 1:860–861.

In Book I of his Sentence Commentary distinction 48 dubium III Bonaventure takes up the evil of Christ's passion. I offer this summary: It is a good action that Christ suffered by the Jews, that is, Christ endured the penalty that the Jews inflicted upon him. However, the infliction of the passion upon Christ is evil.[113]

In Book II of his Sentence Commentary distinction 40 dubium III Bonaventure deals with the question "that the Jews, in crucifying Christ thought that they were showing obedience to God." And he answers: "I respond that this does not refer to all Jews, but only to the simple who were deceived by their leaders. For the Jewish leaders, that is, the high priests and scribes, were moved out of envy and malice, because they well knew his sanctity and innocence, even though his divinity escaped them. But the simple and common people were moved out of ignorance, for hearing from their leaders that he had blasphemed, they thought that by killing Christ, a blasphemer, they were thus showing obedience to God. This ignorance, however, does not excuse, because the works that Christ performed could offer an indication of his sanctity not only to the great, but also to the little."[114]

Book III of his Sentence Commentary distinction 20 dubium III concerns the teaching that "Christ was handed over by the Father and that he handed himself over" and asks whether God was somehow responsible for Christ's death. Bonaventure resolves: "And thus it is obvious that death on the part of the one undergoing it was pleasing and acceptable to God, but on the part of

---

[113] See Opera Omnia 1:861.
[114] Opera Omnia 2:934.

those inflicting it was merely permissible."[115] Bonaventure goes on to say that his consideration of the rule of God's providence, as treated in Books I and II of his commentary on the Sentences, answers the question of why God permitted another to be killed when God could have prevented it.

WHAT BONAVENTURE'S COMMENTARY ON LUKE'S GOSPEL SAYS ABOUT THE JEWS WHO LIVED DURING CHRIST'S TIME[116]

As I worked through Bonaventure's 601-page commentary on Luke's Gospel, I was shocked by the virulence of some of his anti-Judaistic comments and pleasantly surprised that his anti-Judaism was as limited as it was. I present the passages of Bonaventure's anti-Judaism that I have detected.

It is common for Bonaventure to engage in anti-Judaism when he comments on polemical passages. Take, for example, his commentary on Luke 7:31 (#57): *"Now the Lord said: To what then will I liken, etc. After our Savior had extolled the privilege of virtue in John, he now argues against the perfidy of disbelief among the people. His argument against their disbelief is fourfold. For he points out their infidelity, hardness, detraction, and blasphemy."*[117]

---

[115] Opera Omnia 3:433.

[116] I presuppose that the remarks Bonaventure makes about the Jews in his Commentary on Luke are similar to those he makes about the Jews in his Commentary on John. See Opera Omnia 6:237–530.

[117] *Commentary on the Gospel of Luke*, p. 620. For similar comments about the "perfidy" of the Jews, see Bonaventure's exposition of Luke 14:2 (#4) and Luke 14:4 (#7) which occur in a polemical context.

Two of Bonaventure's most virulent anti-Judaistic passages occur in the commentary published in this volume. In his interpretation of Luke 11:32 (#68) Bonaventure quotes Chrysostom and does so by following the text of Chrysostom he found in Hugh of St. Cher's commentary on this verse: "Therefore, the hardness of the unbelieving Jews is greatly condemned. So Chrysostom says: 'Within three days the Ninevites became God's people, although they had not had prophets. Within the three days of the crucifixion the Jews became the people of the devil. The former escaped imminent vengeance; the latter have suffered the most atrocious vengeance.'"[118]

In his commentary on Luke 11:51 (#98) Bonaventure again quotes Chrysostom: "This is the generation, from which punishment will be required. But in this punishment it will be especially required of the Jewish nation, for perfidy was consummated in them. So Chrysostom says: 'Just as God promised to good people through many generations that Christ would come, but bestowed him as a gift to the last holy ones, so too what God threatened to evil people through individual generations God has now rendered to the final generation. For never was such grace given to men and women as that which came in Christ or has such destruction come upon impious people as upon the Jews.'"[119]

During the course of his interpretation of the parable of Luke 19:11–27 Bonaventure expounds Luke 19:14, "But

---

[118] See the commentary below on Luke 11:32 where the details of Bonaventure's borrowing from Hugh of St. Cher are also given. For greater detail see Robert J. Karris, "Bonaventure's Commentary on Luke: Four Case Studies of his Creative Borrowing from Hugh of St. Cher," *Franciscan Studies* 59 (2001): 133–236.

[119] See the commentary below on Luke 11:51 for more detail.

his citizens hated him," under the category of "the obduracy of human perfidy in the rebellion of the Jewish
people." He agrees with the Glossa Ordinaria that "the
citizens" refer to the Jews.[120]

As he gives his postill on the parable of Luke 20:9–19,
Bonaventure comes to Luke 20:14: "Let us kill him that
the inheritance may become ours." His interpretation is:
"They said this in a perverse scheme, not in order to acquire a new inheritance since Christ was extremely
poor, but to preserve the old one. . . . So this evil pro-
posal stems from avarice as well as from envy. . . . A
figure of this occurred earlier in the story of Joseph.
Genesis 37:18–20 states: 'His brothers thought of killing
him and said to one another: Behold, the dreamer is
coming. Come, let us kill him and cast him into some old
cistern. We will say that a most evil wild beast devoured
him.'"[121]

Luke 21:4 reads: "For all these from their abundance
have put gifts into the Temple treasury, but this poor
widow from her want has put in all that she had to live
on." Bonaventure interprets the rich to be "the Jews,"
whose abundance is their presumption in their own
righteousness. The poor widow is the church gathered
from the Gentiles.[122]
If I add the aforementioned six instances of anti-
Judaism to the eight I detected in Bonaventure's com-

---

[120] Opera Omnia 7:479 (#21).
[121] Opera Omnia 7:506–507. On p. 507, n. 3 QuarEd mention that in
the Roman Breviary for the Friday of the Second Week of Lent the
Joseph story is read in conjunction with Matthew 21:33, which is a
Synoptic parallel to Luke 20:14. See my earlier discussions of Bonaventure's use of the Joseph story in his *Mystical Vine* and *Tree of
Life*.
[122] Opera Omnia 7:522–523 (#8).

mentary on Luke 22–23, I come to fourteen embarrassing occurrences. While I deplore these references, I note that they come to some four pages in a commentary of six hundred and one pages.

CONCLUSION

During the course of this long section on Bonaventure's anti-Judaism I have set Bonaventure within his larger context and have provided anti-Judaistic passages from the nine volumes of his massive output. To me it seems manifest that Bonaventure is a traditionalist in the mold of St. Paul and St. Augustine when it comes to the Jews. But no matter how learned and saintly he was, he could not successfully slough off his medieval skin of anti-Judaism. As one pours through his voluminous writings, his anti-Judaism will surface, especially when he is considering Christ's Passion and dealing with the failure of the Jews of Jesus' time to acknowledge Christ, who worked so many miracles, as Son of God.

I give the last word to Robert E. Lerner, who concludes his study of Bonaventure and others who went against the medieval grain by being more favorably disposed to the Jews: "To avoid clumsiness I have occasionally fallen back on the term philo-Judaism, but the more accurate phraseology for the stance of my subjects would be 'relatively more benign attitude towards the Jews than the late medieval Christian norm.'"[123]

---

[123] *The Feast of Saint Abraham*, p. 120. Lerner treats the views toward the Jews of Joachim of Fiore (d. 1202), Gerardino of Borgo San Donnino (d. ca. 1276), St. Bonaventure (d. 1274), Peter Olivi (d. 1298), John of Rupescissa (d. 1365), John of Bassigny (fl. 1360), Frederick of Brunswick (d. ca. 1392), Francesc Eiximenis (d. 1409), and Nicholas of Buldesdorf (d. 1446). For Peter Olivi's positive view of the Jews in his Commentary on the Apocalypse, see Warren Lewis,

"Freude, Freude! Die Wiederentdeckung der Freude im 13 Jahrhundert: Olivis 'Lectura super Apocalipsim' als Blick auf die Endzeit" in *Ende und Vollendung: Eschatologische Perspektiven im Mittelalter*, ed. Jan A. Aertsen and Martin Pickavé, Miscellanea Mediaevalia 29 (Berlin/New York: Walter de Gruyter, 2002), 657–683, esp. pp. 675–676.

OUTLINE OF ST. BONAVENTURE'S COMMENTARY ON LUKE, CHAPTERS 9-16

Before giving a detailed outline of this volume of commentary, I remind my readers that Bonaventure has a fourfold division of Luke's entire Gospel:

I.   Luke 1-3: The Mystery of the Incarnation;
II. Luke 4-21: Christ's Magisterial Preaching;
III. Luke 22-23: The Medicine of the Passion;
IV. Luke 24: The Triumph of the Resurrection.

So Bonaventure's commentary on Luke 9-16 occurs in Part II of his overall outline and has the following sections:

LUKE 9

LUKE 10

LUKE 11

ABBREVIATIONS AND SHORT TITLES

ACW	Ancient Christian Writers
Bonaventure on Luke, chapters 1-8	*St. Bonaventure's Commentary on the Gospel of Luke Chapters 1-8*. With an Introduction, Translation and Notes by Robert J. Karris. Works of St. Bonaventure VIII/I. St. Bonaventure, New York: Franciscan Institute Publications, 2001.
CC	Corpus Christianorum
CSEL	Corpus Scriptorum Ecclesiasticorum Latinorum
CCSL	Corpus Christianorum. Series Latina
CCSL xiv	*Sancti Ambrosii Mediolanensis Opera Pars IV Expositio Evangelii secvndum Lvcam, Fragmenta in Esaiam*. Cura et stvdio M. Adriaen; Corpvs Christianorvm Series Latina. Turnhout: Brepols, 1957.
CCSL lxxii	*S. Hieronymi Presbyteri Opera Pars I Opera Exegetica 1: Hebraicae Qvaestiones in Libro Geneseos, Liber Interpretationis Hebraicorvm Nominvm, Commentarioli in Psalmos, Commentarivs in Ecclesiasten*. P. Antin; Turnhout: Brepols, 1959.
CCSL cxx	*Bedae Venerabilis Opera Pars II Opera Exegetica 3: In Lvcae Evangelivm Expositio, In Marci Evangelivm Expositio*. Cura et stvdio D. Hurst. Corpvs Christianorvm Series Latina CXX. Turnhout: Brepols, 1955.
Douay Version	*The Holy Bible Translated from the Latin Vulgate...The Douay Version of The Old Testament; The Confraternity Edition of The New Testament*. New York: P. J. Kenedy & Sons, 1950.
FC	The Fathers of the Church.

Fitzmyer	*The Gospel According to Luke (I-IX), (XXXIV).* Introduction, Translation, and Notes by Joseph A. Fitzmyer. Anchor Bible 28/A. Garden City, New York: Doubleday, 1981/1985.
GGHG	Gregory the Great's Homilies on the Gospels.
Glossa Ordinaria	*Sacrorum Bibliorum cum Glossa Ordinaria... Tomus Quintus.* Lugduni: 1590.
Hayes, *The Hidden Center*	Zachary Hayes, *The Hidden Center: Spirituality and Speculative Christology in Saint Bonaventure.* Franciscan Pathways. St. Bonaventure, New York: The Franciscan Institute, 2000.
Hugh of St. Cher	*Hugonis de Sancto Charo... Tomus Sextus in Evangelia secundum Matthaeum, Lucam, Marcum & Joannem.* Venice: Nicolas Pezzana, 1732.
Hurst	*Gregory the Great: Forty Gospel Homilies.* Translated from the Latin by Dom David Hurst. Cistercian Studies Series 123. Kalamazoo, Michigan: Cistercian Publications, 1990.
LCL	Loeb Classical Library
NAB	New American Bible
NJBC	*New Jerome Biblical Commentary.* Edited by Raymond E. Brown, Joseph A. Fitzmyer, Roland E. Murphy. Englewood Cliffs, NJ: Prentice Hall, 1990.
NPNF1/2	Nicene and Post-Nicene Fathers, First or Second Series. Ed. Philip Schaff. Peabody, Massachusetts: Hendrickson, 1994-95. Reprint of 1888/93 editions.
NRSV	New Revised Standard Version
Opera Omnia	*S. Bonaventurae Opera Omnia.* Studio et Cura PP. Collegii a S. Bonaventura (Ad Claras Aquas). Quaracchi: Collegium S. Bonaventurae, 1882-1902. There are nine volumes of text and one volume of indices. The volume number is

first given and then the page number, e.g., 5:24.

PL   Patrologiae Cursus Completus. Series Latina. Ed. J. P. Migne.

QuarEd   The editors who produced the text and the notes of Bonaventure's Opera Omnia 7, which contains the text of Bonaventure's Commentary on Luke (*Commentarius in Evangelium S. Lucae*).

SBOp   *Sancti Bernardi Opera I-VIII*. Ed. J. Leclercq and H. M. Rochais with the assistance of C. H. Talbot for Volumes I-II. Rome: Editiones Cisterciensis, 1957-77.

SBSermons *St. Bernard's Sermons for the Seasons & Principal Festivals of the Year*. Volumes 1-3. Translated from the Original Latin by a Priest of Mount Melleray. Westminster, Maryland: Carroll Press, 1950.

Vulgate   *Biblia Sacra Iuxta Vulgatam Versionem*. Adiuvantibus B. Fischer, I. Gribomont (†), H. F. D. Sparks, W. Thiele recensuit et brevi apparatu critico instruxit Robertus Weber (†) editionem quartam emendatam cum sociis B. Fischer, H. I. Frede, H. F. D.Sparks, W. Thiele praeparavit Roger Gryson. Stuttgart: Deutsche Bibelgesellschaft, 1969. 4th ed. 1994.

A WORD ABOUT THIS TRANSLATION

I know of only two contemporary translations of Bonaventure's Commentary on the Gospel of St. Luke. In 1985 Thomas Reist translated Bonaventure's Commentary on Luke 18:34-19:42 into English.[124] In 1999 the Italian Conference of OFM Provincial Ministers in conjunction with Città Nuova Press published in its series on the Works of St. Bonaventure an Italian translation of Bonaventure's Commentary on Luke 1-4.[125]

This is the second of three volumes. My primary goals in translation have been readability and fidelity. I have not twisted the English language in attempts to match Bonaventure's playfulness with rhyme and alliteration, especially in his introductory sentences to a new section. Rather I have frequently fashioned footnotes at such places to call attention to these displays of Bonaventure's art.

In translations from the Vulgate I have not slavishly followed the Douay Version, but have adapted my translations to contemporary English usage and to the demands of Bonaventure's exegesis.

---

[124] *Saint Bonaventure as a Biblical Commentator: A Translation and Analysis of his Commentary on Luke XVIII, 34 - XIX, 42* (Lanham: University Press of America, n.d. [1985]).

[125] *Commento al Vangelo di San Luca/1 (1-4)*, Introduzione, revisione e note a cura di Barbara Faes de Mottoni, traduzione di Paola Müller (cc. I-III) e Silvana Martignoni (c. IV), Sancti Bonaventurae Opera IX/1 (Rome: Città Nuova), 1999).

A WORD ABOUT THE INDICES

The indices are theological goldmines. The scripture index indicates Bonaventure's profound appreciation of God's wisdom. His use of Ambrose, Augustine, Bede, Bernard of Clairvaux, Gregory the Great, and Jerome manifest his dependence on tradition. He even quotes the principles of Seneca, Cicero, and Aristotle.

ACKNOWLEDGMENTS

I thank Fr. Anthony Carrozzo, OFM, the inspiration behind this annotated translation; Sr. Margaret Carney, OSF, director of the Franciscan Institute for her unfailing encouragement; Frs. Michael Cusato, OFM and Michael Blastic, OFM Conv., who have generously loaned me treasured books; Fr. Thomas Nairn, OFM, who has uncovered rare books for me in Chicago libraries; Dr. Timothy Johnson, who offered helpful guidance on Bonaventure's anti-Judaism; Mrs. Theresa Schafer, who has used her marvelous skills to gather interlibrary loans for me from near and far; Ms. Noel H. Riggs, who has patiently and generously printed many and many copies of this work in progress; Jean François Godet-Calogeras, who has enthusiastically overseen the editing process. In the biblical last place of prominence I owe a debt of gratitude to Fr. Zachary Hayes, OFM, general editor of Bonaventure Texts and Translations Series, for expertly reading through my work.

The Franciscan Institute gratefully acknowledges generous funding from the Academy of American Franciscan History, the OFM Province of St. John the Baptist in Cincinnati, the OFM Province of the Sacred Heart in

Saint Louis, and the OFM General Definitorium in Rome.

THIS VOLUME IS GRATEFULLY DEDICATED TO THE OFM PROVINCES OF ST. JOHN THE BAPTIST AND SACRED HEART.

LUKE 9

1. *Then having summoned the Twelve, Jesus,*[1] etc. In the
previous three main sections of this part of the Gospel
the Evangelist dealt with the teaching of Jesus Christ.
Through this teaching the disciples themselves had
been inspired in what they should believe, encouraged
in the things they should imitate, and instructed in
what they should understand. Now follows the fourth
section which concerns *the sending forth of those who
understand and how they should preach*. Now the order
of this section is sufficiently clear in itself. For some
preachers are of higher status, but others are of lower
status. So this section has two parts. The first deals

---

[1] On p. 216 n. 8 QuarEd rightly mention that the Vulgate does not
have *Iesus* ("Jesus"). See Bonaventure's Commentary on Luke 4:1 for
his outline of Luke's Gospel.

with *the mission of the Apostles.* The second with *the mission of the seventy disciples,* where Luke 10:1 below reads: *Now the Lord appointed seventy others,* etc.

Luke 9:1–62
THE MISSION OF THE APOSTLES

The present chapter itself forms the first part and has three sections, according to the three things that the Evangelist considers necessary for Apostles and prelates[2] who have been sent forth to preach. The first is *the form to be used in preaching.* The second concerns *the way to be used in making progress,* which the Evangelist explains in verse 18: *And it came to pass as he was praying in private.* Third is *the norm to be used in presiding,* which is described in verse 46: *Now a discussion arose among them which of them was the greatest.*

Luke 9:1–17
THE FORM TO BE USED IN PREACHING

Now he explains the form to be used in preaching in a twofold way. First, a divine precept stands behind it. Second, it has a divine example where Luke 9:10 reads: And the Apostles on their return announced[3] to him.

---

[2] The main point behind Apostle and prelate is "having been sent by one in authority."

[3] On p. 216, n. 11 QuarEd correctly indicate that the Vulgate has *narraverunt* ("told") whereas Bonaventure reads *nuntiaverunt* ("announced").

Luke 9:1–9
THE FORMATION OF PREACHERS THROUGH DIVINE PRECEPT

Now relative to the formation of preachers through divine precept the Evangelist introduces three points, namely, the authority committed to them, the integrity enjoined upon them, and the benefit attached to their work. Authority is given first place as the leader. Integrity is present on the way, as 9:3 says: And he said to them: Take nothing for your journey. In third place he adds benefit as the consequence of the mission where 9:6 reads: And going forth, they went about . . . preaching the gospel and working cures everywhere. – Now words, no matter how genuine their preacher may be, are ineffectual unless divine testimony backs them up. And such are the divine miracles. So in this first part there is first an explication of the granting of power to perform miracles and then the commissioning with the authority needed to preach the mysteries. For the first paves the way for the second.

2. (Verse 1). So with regard to *the granting of power to perform miracles* the text says: *Then Jesus, having summoned the twelve apostles,* that is, as the primary prelates, chosen from all others, according to what is said in Luke 6:13 above: "Jesus summoned his disciples. And from these he chose twelve, whom he also named *Apostles.*" Therefore, these had been *summoned,* that is, called together into unity to commend unity, for which the Holy Spirit is given, according to what is said in Acts 2:1: "And when the days of Pentecost were drawing to a close, all the disciples[4] were together in one place." Thus Numbers 11:16–17 has: "The Lord said to Moses: Gather unto me seventy men . . . at the door of the tab-

---

[4] The Vulgate does not read *discipuli* ("the disciples").

ernacle of the covenant. . . . And I will take of your spirit and give it to them." – That is the way it is now. So the text adds: *He gave them power and authority*, so that they would have *power* over spiritual matters and *authority* over corporal matters. And to give a further explanation of this the text continues: *over all the demons*, referring to their *power*; *and to cure diseases*, referring to their *authority*. And by this means their mission would have a double type of witness, in accord with the two types of creature, namely, spiritual and corporal. And this is what is expressly mentioned in Mark 3:15: "He gave them power to cure sicknesses and cast out demons." So there is true fulfillment of what the Psalmist says: "The Lord will give the word to those who preach good tidings with great power" (67:12).

3. (Verse 2). Now concerning commissioning with the authority needed to preach the mysteries the text says: And he sent them forth to preach the kingdom of God. For in their mission rests their authority, without which no one must preach. Therefore, Romans 10:15 has: "How are they to preach, unless they be sent?" So too Isaiah did not dare to preach unless he were sent. Isaiah 6:8 reads: "Behold, here am I. Send me." Jeremiah 23:21 shows the opposite about the false prophets: "I did not send prophets, yet they ran." But such were not the Apostles, who were called in such a way that their authority might be commended. For the word, Apostle, means having been sent. And they had been sent to preach, according to what 1 Corinthians 1:17 says: "The Lord did not send me to baptize, but to preach." – They had been sent to preach, not some small matter, but a great one, namely, the kingdom of God. By this can be understood the teaching of the truth, according to what Matthew 21:43 has: "The kingdom of God will be taken away from you, and will be given to a people yielding its

fruits." It can also be said to be the grace of the Holy Spirit, in accord with what Romans 14:17 reads: "The kingdom of God does not consist in food and drink, but in justice and peace and joy in the Holy Spirit." Luke 17:21 below says: "The kingdom of God is within you." Further, it can also be said to be eternal glory, according to what John 3:5 has: "Unless a person is born again of water and the Spirit, he cannot enter the kingdom of God." Through all these ways the Apostles are sent forth to preach the kingdom of God, namely, through true doctrine, divine grace, and eternal glory. – And since he had granted them the power to cure to enhance the authority of their preaching, the text adds: And to cure diseases. That is, he sent them with this power to confirm the truth they preached, according to what Mark 16:20 says: "They went forth and preached everywhere, while the Lord worked with them and confirmed the preaching by the signs that followed." So a sign and goal of the spiritual mission of preaching is the healing of the diseases of vices in the listeners.

4. Now there are three types of evidence that the preacher is sent forth by the Lord to preach the Gospel. First is *the authority* of the one sending, be this of the bishop or especially of that bishop who takes the place of Peter, who for his part takes the place of Jesus Christ. So the person sent by him is sent by Christ. Second is *the zeal for souls* in the person who is sent, when that individual's primary goal is the honor of God and the salvation of souls. Third, the preaching brings forth *good fruit and conversion* in the listeners. – By means of the first sign they are heralds of the Father, by the second heralds of the Son, and through the third heralds of

the Holy Spirit.[5] Concerning such preachers it is said in John 15:16: "I have appointed you that you should go and bear fruit, and that your fruit should remain." And the person who is thus sent can say what Isaiah 61:1 has: "The Spirit of the Lord is upon me, because the Lord has anointed me," etc.[6]

5. (Verse 3). *And he said to them: Take nothing for your journey.* After explaining the authority by which the Apostles were commissioned, the Evangelist gives *a description of the integrity of life enjoined upon them.* Now there are three components to this life style, namely, *a paucity of things needed to sustain life, bare essentials in clothing,* and *humble manner of life.*[7]

First, with regard to *a paucity of things needed to sustain life*, it is said: *And he said to them: Take nothing for your journey,* that is, in the form of temporal sustenance, so that you may preach by example what 1 Timothy 6:7 says: "For we brought nothing into the world, and certainly we can take nothing out." And in order for his meaning to be more clear, he gives specific instructions when he says: *Neither staff,* namely, for support, *nor wallet,* for storing things, *nor bread,* for eating, *nor money,* for buying things. This verse prohibits all sustenance, so that it may be shown that the preacher must rely with deep hope on God alone, according to what 1

---

[5] Bonaventure does not give any more detail on this somewhat cryptic interpretation.

[6] In its entirety Isaiah 61:1 says: "The Spirit of the Lord is upon me, because the Lord has anointed me. He has sent me to preach to the meek, to heal the contrite of heart, and to preach release to the captives, and deliverance to those who are in prison."

[7] It is virtually impossible to do justice to Bonaventure's verbal playfulness: *In paupertate victus, tenuitate vestitus, et humilitate convictus.* Obviously, the boundaries between these three categories are quite fluid.

Peter 5:7 reads: "Cast all your care upon him, because he cares for you." So also Blessed Francis, when he used to send the brothers out to preach, used to say to them the words of the Psalm: "Cast your care upon the Lord," etc. (54:23).[8] However, in this matter the Lord does not forbid, as Augustine says, careful providence, but over-wrought anxiety,[9] according to what Matthew 6:34 says: "Do not be anxious about tomorrow. . . . For . . . sufficient for the day is its own trouble."

6. And so (we move) to the correct understanding of this precept which one Evangelist negates, namely, Luke, and another Evangelist affirms, namely, Mark, who in 6:8 says: "And Jesus instructed them to take nothing for their journey, but a staff only." About this matter Augustine in his *The Harmony of the Gospels* says: "Both precepts are from the Lord: to take nothing but a staff, and not to take a staff. *Not to take a staff* means not to be anxious. *To take nothing but a staff* refers to the power granted to preachers to receive what they need."[10] Wherefore, Luke 10:7 below reads: "Eating and

---

[8] See 1 Celano 29: "Accepting the command of holy obedience *with much joy and gladness,* they humbly prostrated themselves on the ground before Saint Francis. Embracing them, he spoke sweetly and devotedly to each one: *'Cast your care upon the Lord, and he will sustain you.'* He used to say this phrase whenever he transferred brothers by obedience." Translation from *Francis of Assisi: Early Documents,* Volume I: *The Saint,* edited by Regis J. Armstrong, J. A. Wayne Hellmann, William J. Short (New York: New City Press, 1999), 207. Cf. St. Bonaventure's *Life of St. Francis,* chapter 3.

[9] On p. 218, n. 5 QuarEd refer to Book II, chapter 30, n. 73ff. of Augustine's *The Harmony of the Gospels.* As far as I can ascertain, Bonaventure is providing the gist of what Augustine says in n. 73–78.

[10] On p. 218, n. 6 QuarEd refer to Book II, chapter 30, n. 73ff of Augustine's *The Harmony of the Gospels.* Their reference is so general, because as they astutely continue in their note 6: Augustine's opinion is found in the Glossa Ordinaria's interpretation of Luke 9:3. That is, Bonaventure did not check Augustine's opinion directly or

drinking what they have."[11] – Now *the literal* observance of this precept pertains to the perfect preachers, who perfectly imitate Christ. In their person Peter says in Matthew 19:27: "Behold, we have left all and have followed you."[12] But *its spiritual* observance applies to all preachers, so that the preacher of truth may contemn earthly things. Otherwise, if they proclaim the word of God out of cupidity for lucre, they are not disciples of Christ, but of Balaam the soothsayer, according to what 2 Peter 2:14–15 says: "They have their hearts exercised in cupidity. Children of a curse, they have forsaken the right way," that is, the way of poverty. From this way "they have gone astray. They have followed the way of Balaam . . . who loved the wages of wrongdoing." – Therefore, the preacher of truth must avoid above all else the vice of cupidity. Otherwise, he will not be a preacher, but a flatterer. For which reason 1 Thessalonians 2:5 reads: "At no time have we used words of flattery, as you know, nor any pretext for avarice. God is our witness." For he knew that by this he would provoke God's wrath, as it is said in Micah 3:11–12: "Her princes have rendered judgments for the sake of bribes, and her priests have taught for hire, and her prophets have di-

---

independently. The pertinent passage in Augustine is n. 74. See NPNF1, Volume 6, p. 158: "For the sentence might also have been briefly expressed in this way: 'Take with you none of the necessaries of life, neither a staff, save a staff only.' So that the phrase 'neither a staff' may be taken to be equivalent to 'not even the smallest things;' while the addition, 'save a staff only,' may be understood to mean that, in virtue of the power which they received from the Lord, and which was signified by the name 'staff' [or, 'rod'], even those things which were not carried with them would not be wanting to them."

[11] Bonaventure's point might have been strengthened if he continued with what Luke 10:7 says: "For the laborer deserves his wages."

[12] Luke 18:28 is the same, but Bonaventure has quoted the parallel passage from Matthew in his commentary on Luke.

vined for money. . . . For this reason Zion will be plowed as a field," etc.

7. Second, with regard to *the bare essentials in clothing*, the text adds: *Neither have two tunics*, so that the teaching of the Master may thus agree with the teaching of the Precursor in accordance with what Luke 3:11 has: "Let him who has two tunics share with him who has none." And also this is according to what 1 Timothy 6:8 says: "Having food and sufficient clothing, let us be content with these." Now by forbidding not one garment, but two, he provides for necessity and avoids anxiety in changing and superfluity in possessing. So Bede says: "*One* garment is whatever is necessary for a person according to different places and times. *Two* refers to what is beyond necessity."[13] And this is apparent with regard to the Lord himself, who besides his seamless garment had other garments, which were divided, as it is said in John 19:23. – But according to *the spiritual* understanding the duplicity of simulation and hypocrisy is forbidden, lest they retain one garment in hiding and use one for public appearance and lest they be counted among those of whom it is said in Matthew 7:15: ". . . who come to you in sheep's clothing, but inwardly are ravenous wolves."[14] Similarly Blessed Francis avoided such duplicity, for when he was ill, he refused to have a piece of fur put on his chest inside his habit if a

---

[13] On p. 218, n. 12 QuarEd indicate that these words come from the Glossa Ordinaria on Luke 9:3. Bede's interpretation ultimately stems from Book I of Jerome's Commentary on Matthew 10:10 (PL 26:65A) and is generalized in the Glossa Ordinaria. See CCSL cxx, p. 195 for Bede's actual words.

[14] On p. 219, n. 1 QuarEd note that the Glossa Ordinaria on Luke 9:3 reads: "Allegorically, by means of the two garments he forbids duplicity."

piece of fur would not also be placed on the outside of his habit.[15]

8. (Verse 4). Third, relative to *humble manner of life*, the text says: *And whatever house you enter, stay there*, that is, being content with the hospitality that obtains there. *And do not leave the place*, in order to seek something better, because, as it is said in Sirach 29:31, "It is a miserable life to go as a guest from house to house." For going from house to house as a guest manifests an impatient spirit that changes at a slight provocation and cannot rest, according to what Jeremiah 14:10 reads: "This people loved to move their feet, and have not rested, and have not pleased the Lord." – And the preacher must painstakingly avoid such conduct, for, according to what Proverbs 19:11 says, "The learning of a man is known through his patience." And so Ambrose comments: "It is out of place for the preacher to run from house to house and change the laws of immovable hospitality."[16] But pride is the mother of this inconstancy and impatience. And pride cannot live in peace with anyone, according to what Proverbs 13:10 says: "Among the proud there are always contentions."

---

[15] See 2 Celano 130. *Francis of Assisi: Early Documents,* Volume II: *The Founder,* edited by Regis J. Armstrong, J. A. Wayne Hellmann, William J. Short (New York: New City Press, 2000), 332 reads: "The blessed Francis answered him (his guardian): 'If you want me to put up with this (piece of fox fur) under my tunic, have another piece of the same size sewn on the outside, telling people that a piece of fur is hidden underneath.'"

[16] See CCSL xiv, p. 197 for Ambrose's comment: . . . *alienum a praedicatore regni caelestis adstruens cursitare per domos et inuiolabilis hospitii iura mutare* (". . . adding that it is out of place for the preacher of the heavenly kingdom to run from house to house and change the laws of inviolable hospitality").

9. (Verse 5). And since it is characteristic of genuine humility to associate with all and also not to be a burden to anyone, the text adds this concerning the perfection of humility: *And whoever does not receive you,* namely, by despising your teaching like those who did not even receive the Lord. John 1:11 reads: "He came unto his own, and his own received him not." – And because this is a great offence in which one must not participate, the text continues: *Go forth from that town,* that is, by turning away from their iniquity according to what Numbers 16:26 has: "Depart from the tents of these wicked men and touch nothing of theirs, lest you be involved in their sins." Isaiah 52:11 says: "Go out from their midst; touch nothing unclean." And Jeremiah 48:28 reads: "Leave the cities and dwell in the rock." – And do this, lest you be tainted with foreign pollutants. For this reason the text adds: *And shake off the dust from your feet for a witness upon them,*[17] that is, to show your innocence. Barnabas and Paul did this. Of them it is said in Acts 13:51 that "having shaken the dust from their feet . . . they went to Iconium."[18] Now *to shake the dust from one's feet* is to permit nothing of vain human glory to adhere to one's affections. For vain glory is fittingly designated by *dust,* which is blown away by the wind, according to what the Psalmist says: "It will be

---

[17] On p. 219, n. 8 QuarEd rightly indicate that Bonaventure's quotation has two variations from the Vulgate. The Vulgate has *etiam* ("even") instead of *et* ("and") and *supra* ("against") instead of *super* ("upon").

[18] The Vulgate of Acts 13:51 reads: *At illi excusso pulvere pedum in eos venerunt Iconium.* Bonaventure adds *suorum* ("their") after *pedum* ("feet") and omits *in eos* ("against them"). The Confraternity translates: "But they shook off the dust of their feet in protest against them and went to Iconium."

like the dust which the wind drives from the face of the earth" (1:4).[19]

10. (Verse 6). *And going forth, they went about,* etc. After treating the authority committed to them and the integrity of life enjoined upon them, the Evangelist now adds in a third point *the benefit attached to their work.* Now there is a fourfold benefit which follows from the preaching of the Apostles. That is, they move people *to listen.* They move the listeners *to confer among themselves.* They move those conferring among themselves *to stand in admiration.* They move those standing in admiration *to want to see* what they admire.[20]

So first with regard to *moving people to hear,* it is said: *And going forth, they went about from village to village, preaching the gospel and working cures everywhere,* so that what the Psalm says was already beginning to be fulfilled: "Their sound has gone forth into all the earth" (18:5). For although not all would accept their teaching, nonetheless because of the miracles they wanted to listen to their teaching. Wherefore, it is said in Acts 8:6: "The crowds gave heed to what was said by Philip, with one accord listening to him and seeing the signs that he worked." And so these Apostles not only preached, but also cured everywhere, so that all might be moved to listen to them because of their zeal, their words, and their signs. In this an explanation is not only provided of the benefit to the listeners, but also of the fidelity of

---

[19] The actual subject of Psalm 1:4 is "the wicked," who are blown away like dust. On p. 219, n. 9 QuarEd quote Jerome, Hilary, and Ambrose on the meaning of "shaking the dust from their feet."
[20] By this fourfold description Bonaventure interprets Herod's questions and actions in Luke 9:7–9. As he moves through his interpretation, Bonaventure begins to substitute *finis* ("goal/end/purpose") for *utilitas* ("benefit/use").

the preachers. For since *they went about,* they were free from idleness. Since they went about *from village to village,* they were free from pride.[21] Since *they preached the gospel,* they were free from frivolity. Since *they cured everywhere,* they were free from partiality. And therefore, they had the goal in mind to speak with such ability to move and persuade their listeners. And this is the first and general goal.

11. (Verse 7.) The second goal or special benefit is *moving the listeners to confer with one another.* With regard to this it is said: *Now Herod the tetrarch heard of all that was being done by him,* with the result that the reputation of Christ's name was being conveyed by the Apostles not only to the people, but also to kings, as it is said of Paul in Acts 9:15: "He is a chosen vessel to me, to carry my name among nations and kings and the children of Israel." So the listeners could already say what the Gibeonites said in Joshua 9:9: "We have heard the reputation of the power of your God, of all that he has done."[22] And from hearing these things he was moved to inquire and was in doubt because of the variety of opinions.

12. (Verse 7–8). So the text continues: *And he was perplexed, because it was said by some that John has risen from the dead.* And Herod was a staunch adherent of this opinion. Therefore, Matthew 14:1–2 says: "Herod

---

[21] Bonaventure seems to presuppose the preaching of missions of his own day. To get assigned to preach in a big city could easily lead to pride. Getting assigned to preach in tiny, insignificant places could be a great deterrent to pride.

[22] Bonaventure has rewoven Joshua 9:9 to suit his purposes. The Vulgate reads: *Audivimus enim famam potentiae eius, cuncta quae fecit in Aegypto* ("For we have heard of the reputation of his power, of all that he did in Egypt").

heard about the reputation of Jesus and said to his servants: This is John the Baptist. He has risen from the
dead, and that is why miraculous powers are operating
through him."[23] Now he was of this opinion because of
the eminent sanctity of his life. For, as it is said in Mark
6:20, "Herod feared John, knowing that he was a just
and holy man." But to this opinion he didn't adhere
firmly. Thus the text says that *he was perplexed,* that is,
he vacillated, according to what James 1:6 says: "The
person who vacillates is like a wave of the sea, driven
and carried about by the wind." – And this happened
because of other opinions. So the text adds: *And* it was
said *by some that Elijah has appeared.* And this opinion
seemed probable because of his *eminent power.* Thus
Sirach 48:4 says: "Elijah was magnified in his wonderful
works." And this opinion seemed to be more credible,
for, as it is said in John 10:41, "John indeed worked no
sign." So Christ who did work miracles seemed more
clearly to be Elijah. – However, not everyone agreed
with this assessment. So the text adds: *And by others
that one of the prophets of old has risen again.* And they
were of this opinion because of *their knowledge of the
truth,* for, according to what Amos 3:7 says, "The Lord[24]
will not act on any word without revealing his secret to
his servants the prophets." And thus it is obvious that
there was a threefold opinion because of the triple excellence they heard about Christ, namely, of sanctity, of
power, and of knowledge of the truth. And therefore,
they were conferring with one another, and some believed this, and others believed that.

---

[23] On p. 220, n. 3 QuarEd refer to Book II, chapter 45, n. 93 of
Augustine's *Harmony of the Gospels* and to Book III of Bede's commentary on Luke 9:7–8, but give no details.
[24] The Vulgate has *Dominus Deus* ("Lord God").

13. (Verse 9). Now the third goal was to bring *those conferring together to admiration*. With regard to this point the text continues: *And Herod said: John I beheaded.* That is, he was mortal and subject to suffering. Herod beheaded him because John spoke the truth and Herod was evil, according to what is said in Matthew 14:4: "John said to Herod: It is not lawful for you to have the wife of your brother."[25] And it happened afterwards that he beheaded him for this reason. And so however much John was preached as someone great, Herod judged John, whose death he had ordered, to be weak. – And through comparing Christ to John, Herod admired Christ's power. So the text adds: *But who is this about whom I hear such things?*[26] That is, such great wonders. Thus, he could say: "Who is great like our God? You are the God who does wonders" (Psalm 76:14–15). That is, the likes of which had not been heard of beforehand, according to what John 9:32 says: "Not from the beginning of the world has it been heard that anyone opened the eyes of a man born blind."

14. The fourth goal is *the moving of those standing in admiration to want to see what they admire*. For this reason the text says: *And he endeavored to see him.* For we want to see what we admire. But he would not attain his goal now, according to what is said in Luke 10:24: "Amen, I say to you that many kings and prophets have desired to see what you see and have not seen it." Now

---

[25] Bonaventure has actually combined Matthew 14:3–4 into one quotation: "For Herod had taken John and bound him and put him into prison because of Herodias, his brother's wife. For John had said to him, 'It is not lawful for you to have her.'"

[26] There are three slight verbal discrepancies between what the Vulgate and Bonaventure have. The Vulgate reads: *Quis autem est iste de quo audio ego talia?* Bonaventure has: *Quis est autem hic de quo audio talia?*

he did not attain this goal, because he did not seek it in a wise manner. Thus, Proverbs 14:6 reads: "A scorner seeks wisdom and finds it not." Therefore, one must very solicitously consider how God should be sought, so that God can be seen and found by those seeking him.

Luke 9:10–17
FORMATION BY DIVINE DEED AND EXAMPLE

15. *And the Apostles on their return reported to him.* After describing the formation of the Apostles given by word or command, the Evangelist presents here their formation *by a deed* or example. Now this section has two parts. For in the first Christ forms them by a *familial* example, but in the second through an example that is *figurative* where Luke 9:12 says: *Now the day began to decline.* The first deals with *the spiritual instruction* of the crowds whereas the second concerns their *corporal nourishment*, which supplies the form and figure of spiritual nourishment.

Now the Lord's *instruction* of the crowds, which provides a model for preachers in teaching the faithful, presents a fourfold explanation of the things required in preaching. The first is *fidelity in fellowship.* The second is *the availability of the place.* Third is *the docility of the people.* Fourth is *the affability of the Teacher.* And the results are that nothing is lacking for the word of God on the part of those assisting, those opposing, those listening, and those teaching and that the word of God will have its due effect.

16. (Verse 10). So first, with regard to *fidelity in fellowship* the text says: *And the Apostles on their return reported to him all that they had done.* In this their fidel-

ity is manifest, for they *quickly returned* to fellowship with the divine. Wherefore, they were not like the raven, about which Genesis 8:7 has: "Which went forth and did not return." Rather they were like the dove, about which Genesis 8:9 reads: "She, not finding where her foot might rest, returned to Noah[27] in the ark," like a faithful friend. So too the Apostles, endowed with dove-like simplicity, have quickly returned to Christ like faithful messengers. – Their fidelity is also evident in that they *hid nothing from God*, but *reported to him all that they had done*. Not in order that they might teach the Lord, to whom nothing is hidden, but in order to show that they did not want to hide anything from him, even if they could. Isaiah 29:15 gives a contrary example: "Woe to you that are deep of heart, to hide your counsel from the Lord," etc. Another interpretation is this. *They reported*, so that might not seek glory for themselves from the good they had accomplished, but might refer all to God, in accordance with what 1 Corinthians 10:31 has: "Do everything for the glory of God" and against those who say in Deuteronomy 32:27: "Our mighty hand, and not the Lord, has done all these things."

17. Second, relative to *the availability of the place*, the text adds: *And taking them with him*, as his faithful companions in fellowship, *he withdrew apart to a desert place, which belongs to Bethsaida*, that is, to a quiet and restful location. So Mark 6:31 reads: "Come apart into a desert place and rest a while." And this place is fitting for instruction according to what Hosea 2:14 says: "I will lead[28] her into the wilderness, and I will speak to her

---

[27] The Vulgate reads *ad eum* ("to him").
[28] The Vulgate has *ducam* ("I will lead") while Bonaventure has *adducam* ("I will lead").

heart." Now this desert place was near the Sea of Gene-
sareth, which is evident from the words, *which belongs
to Bethsaida*. For Bethsaida is "the town of Andrew and
Peter," as it is said in John 1:44. And note that the text
does not say *Bethsaida*, as if to say that the place was
near the town or in the town. Rather the text has *which
belongs to Bethsaida*, because it was a remote place, but
pertained to the town of Bethsaida. So it is said in Mark
6:45 that after the multiplication of loaves he commanded them "to cross the sea ahead of him to Bethsaida." Thus, there is no contradiction between Luke
and Mark, but one gives an explanation of things about
which the other remains silent.[29]

18. (Verse 11). Third, concerning *the docility of the people* the text continues: *But the crowds on learning it followed him,* namely, so that they might receive his instruction which they desired, according to what Hosea
6:3 says: "We shall know, and we shall follow on, so that
we may know the Lord." Whence Bede in the Glossa
writes: "*They followed* him, not on animals nor in conveyances, but by the labor of their own feet, so that they
give evidence of the fire of their spirit."[30] Wherefore, it is
said in Mark 6:33 that many "from all the towns hurried
on foot to the place." And John 6:1–2 gives the reason
for this: "After this Jesus went away to the other side of

---

[29] On p. 221, notes 8–9 QuarEd cite the opinions of Bede, Jerome, the
Glossa Ordinaria, and the Glossa Interlinearis on this discrepancy.
Bonaventure's view rests on solid tradition.
[30] On p. 221, n. 10 QuarEd quote the Glossa: "*They followed,* not on
animals, not in conveyances," etc. In CCSL cxx, p. 198 Bede writes:
". . . not on animals or in various conveyances, but as other evangelists by the labor of their own feet."

the sea of Tiberias.[31] And a great crowd followed, because they witnessed the signs he was performing," etc.

19. Fourth, concerning *the affability of the Teacher*, the text has: *And he welcomed them.* Thus, the graciousness of Christ is shown *through the sign of welcoming.* The Apostle exhorts us to such graciousness in Romans 15:7: "Welcome one another, as Christ has welcomed you to the honor of God." Not only through such a sign, but also *in word.* Therefore, the text continues: *And he spoke to them of the kingdom of God,* in speech that was kind and friendly, so that what the Psalmist says may be truly fulfilled: "I will declare your name to my brothers" (21:23). And although he was speaking to them in an affable manner, his speech was not idle nor earthbound, because it was about the kingdom of God and not about worldly matters.[32] So 1 Peter 4:11 reads: "If anyone speaks, let it be as with words of God." And John 3:31 has: "The one who is from the earth . . . speaks of the earth." And John 6:69 says: "You have the words of eternal life." – Not only did the Lord show his affability in *sign* and *word,* but also in *deed.* So the text reads: *And those in need of cure he healed.* In this he shows the perfection of love, about which 1 John 3:18 says: "Let us not love in word neither with the tongue, but in deed and in truth." For "he . . . who sees his brother in need and closes his heart to him, how does the love of God abide in him?" (1 John 3:17). Christ had such love. So Acts 10:38 has: "He went about doing good and healing all who were in the power of the devil," and thus did more than speaking well. – So in this passage the

---

[31] The Vulgate reads *trans mare Galilaeae quod est Tiberiadis* ("the other side of the sea of Galilee, which is that of Tiberias.)"

[32] On p. 221, n. 13 QuarEd refer to the Glossa Interlinearis on Luke 9:11: "*And he spoke to them,* he teaches the ignorant, *of the kingdom of God,* not about secular matters."

preacher or prelate is taught that he should manifest himself as gracious to the sheep, namely, in sign, word, and deed. And what was said thrice to Peter in John 21:17 is a sign of this: "Feed my sheep."

20. *Now the day began to decline*, etc. After the formation of the disciples through a familial example the Evangelist notes their formation through a *deed with figurative meaning*, that is, the feeding of the crowds. In his description the Evangelist mentions two things. First is *the occasion* provided by the need of the multitude. The second is *the largess* shown by the mercy of the Savior where 9:14 has: *And he said to his disciples: Make them recline*, etc.

Now there are four aspects to the occasion set up by the need of the multitude, namely, the lateness of the hour, the barrenness of the place, the scarcity of food, and the great number of people. And thus this occasion is established by circumstances of time and place, the amount of food, and the number of people.

21. (Verse 12). First, then, concerning *the lateness of the hour*, it is said: *Now the day began to decline*. And so it was the hour for having something to eat, as it is said in Luke 24:29 below: "For it is getting towards evening, and the day is far spent." And through this the wonderful dedication of the crowds shines forth, for they had forgotten about corporal food as they listened to divine speech. Something similar is read in Acts 20:7 which states that "Paul . . . prolonged his address until midnight."

Second, with regard to *the barrenness of the place*, the text continues: *And the Twelve came up to him and said: Send the crowds away*. And they were persuaded to offer this advice because of the barrenness of the place. – So they also advise: *so that they may go into the villages and farms roundabout and find lodging and food,* namely, lest they perish of hunger. And this is the wise counsel which the children of Israel followed. Genesis 42:3 says: "The sons of Jacob went down to Egypt to buy food,"[33] like the Apostles did in John 4:8: "For his disciples had gone away into the town to buy food." – And they were also offering this advice on account of the utter destitution of the place. Therefore, the text adds: *For we are in a desert place here,* where food is lacking according to what Exodus 16:3 has: "Why have you brought us into this desert, that you might kill all the multitude with famine?"[34] And because it is difficult to find food in the desert, they give voice to the Psalmist's words: "Can God furnish a table in the desert?" (77:19). This is what the non-believers were saying, heaping scorn on God's power. But the Apostles were offering counsel about the human necessity for food, for they did not want to tempt the Lord.

22. (Verse 13). Third, relative to *the scarcity of food,* the text has: *But he said to them: You yourselves give them some food. You yourselves,* as their prelates, according to what 1 Peter 5:1–2 has: "Elders . . . tend the flock which is among you." Now he said this to ascertain from their response how scarce the amount of food was. – For this reason the text continues: *And they said: We have no more than five loaves and two fish.* From this it is obvious that the Apostles don't have enough food for the

---

[33] Genesis 42:3 reads: "So the brothers of Joseph went down to Egypt to buy corn."

[34] On p. 222, n. 8 the QuarEd note slight differences between the Vulgate and Bonaventure's text. Bonaventure's Latin is: *Cur induxisti nos in desertum, ut occideres.* . . . The Vulgate has: *Cur eduxistis nos in desertum istud, ut occideretis.* . . .

crowd, nor even enough to assuage their own hunger.
And in order to underscore how inadequate their supplies were, John mentions the type of bread.[35] For Andrew says in John 6:9: "There is a young boy here who
has five barley loaves and two fish. But what are these
among so many?" In this they were like that widow
whose flour Elijah multiplied. 1 Kings 17:12 reads: "As
the Lord God lives, I have no bread, but only a handful
of flour." And in 2 Kings 4:43 the servant said to Elisha:
"How much is this that I should set it before a hundred
men?" In a similar way the Apostles answered here. Or
Andrew responded for them all, as it is said in John
6:9.[36] Or he spoke first, and the others afterwards. In
any case, there is no contradiction. In whatever way
these words were spoken, they demonstrate the powerlessness of the disciples to feed the crowd. – But lest
they be thought to have said this not out of powerlessness, but out of laziness, they offer their services to buy
bread. The text has: *Unless we are to go and buy food for
all this crowd*. And their response can be taken to mean
that *they are offering this service* as Mark 6:37 has: "Let
us go and buy two hundred denarii worth of bread and
give them to eat."[37] Or it can be construed as a response
that *manifests their powerlessness* to feed the crowd, not
only because of the amount of bread on hand, but also
because of the cost. Whence it is said in John 6:7: "Two
hundred denarii worth of bread is not enough for them,
that each one may receive a little." And some of the dis-

---

[35] Throughout his discussion Bonaventure seems to be dependent
upon Bede. In Book III of his commentary on Luke 9:13 Bede states
that barley loaves are food especially for animals and rustic servants
and designate the Law. See CCSL cxx, p. 199.

[36] On p. 222, n. 11 QuarEd refer to Bonaventure's Commentary on
John 6, n. 12. See Opera Omnia 6:319.

[37] This is normally taken to be a question: "Are we to go and buy two
hundred denarii worth of bread and give them to eat?"

ciples were expressing the matter in one way, and others in another. And John puts it one way, and Mark in another. But Luke in the passage under discussion includes them both, which is evident from the very way he has treated the subject.[38]

23. (Verse 14). Fourth, concerning *the great numbers of people*, the text has: *There were about five thousand men present.* And for such a large crowd one loaf of bread would have to make do for one thousand men. Now the text calls them *men* and gives their number. From this it is evident how great a crowd of others there was and whose numbers are not given. So it is said in Matthew 14:21 that there were "five thousand, without counting children and women." Now he states the number because *five* was a fitting number for *the Law*, which trained carnal and sensate men and women. And on account of *the perfection of one thousand* it was fitting to denote the reception of instruction in evangelical perfection.[39]

24. (Verses 14–15). *Then he said to his disciples*, etc. After describing the occasion provided by the need of the

---

[38] On p. 223, n. 1 QuarEd refer to Book II, chapter 46, n. 96 of Augustine's *Harmony of the Gospels.* A comparison of Augustine's solution to these evangelical variants with Bonaventure's solution would reveal how insightful Bonaventure really is.

[39] On p. 223, n. 3 QuarEd point to Book III of Bede's commentary on Luke 9. On Luke 9:14 CCSL cxx, pp. 199–200 reads: "Because there are five senses in the exterior person, the five thousand men who followed the Lord designate those who, while still abiding in secular positions, knew how to use well the exterior things they possessed. Those who are properly nourished by the five loaves are those who still have need of instruction in legal precepts. Now those who have thoroughly renounced the world are the four thousand, fed with seven loaves. They are sublime on account of evangelical nourishment and have been trained by spiritual grace." Bonaventure's commentary seems to be a significant abbreviation of Bede's. Cf. Bonaventure's Commentary on John 6, n. 19 in Opera Omnia 6:321.

multitude for food, the Evangelist now mentions *the liberality that flows from the bountifulness of the Savior.* And the liberality of the Savior is shown in a fourfold manner: *the arrangement of those eating together; the abundance of food; the urbanity of those serving; the satiety of those eating.* And thus perfect liberality is shown by the order of those reclining, the abundance of food, the promptness of those serving, and great number of those eating.[40]

First, relative to *the arrangement of those reclining,* it is said: *Then he said to his disciples: Make them recline in groups of fifty. And they did so.* For it is fitting for the glorious and beneficent Lord to attend to order in dispensing his gifts, according to what is said in 1 Kings 10:4–5: "When the queen of Sheba saw all the wisdom of Solomon and the meat of his table and the dwellings of his servants and the order of his ministers...she was breathless." Now there was a definite order with a set number of people. So it is said in Mark 6:40 that "they reclined in groups of hundreds and of fifties." For fifty times one hundred is five thousand. Indeed, the number fifty is used here, for five fittingly corresponds to the Law and also to the five loaves used in the feeding.[41] From this Christ displays his wonderful wisdom through which he foreknew the number of the men and instructed the disciples about the seating arrangements. There is no doubt that he was the one of whom Wisdom 11:21

---

[40] Again Bonaventure shows his literary flair, as the letter "m" concludes eight out of nine words: "ordinem discumbentium, multitudinem victualium, promptitudinem ministrantium et plenitudinem manducantium." And is it coincidence that "m" occurs an additional five times in the nine words used?

[41] On p. 223, n. 5 QuarEd refer to the Glossa Ordinaria which borrowed from Bede who in turn borrowed from Gregory the Great for an interpretation of fifty in accordance with the laws of jubilee rest.

spoke: "You have ordered all things in measure, number, and weight."

25. (Verse 16). Second, with regard to *the abundance of food* it is said: *And he took the five loaves and the two fish, and looking up to heaven, blessed them.*[42] In this blessing the multiplication of the loaves occurred, according to what Genesis 1:28 says: "God blessed them and said: "Increase and multiply, and fill the earth." And in Genesis 30:27 Laban said to Jacob: "I have learned by experience that God has blessed me on account of you." Therefore, as he blessed, *he looked up to heaven*, in order to show that such a multiplication did not come about because of earthly power or power inherent in the elements, but because of heavenly power, reserved to first causes, of which it is said in the Psalm: "Whatsoever the Lord pleased, he has done, in heaven, on earth, in the sea, and in all the deeps" (134:6). – And note that it is said: *He looked up and blessed. He looked up*, indeed, out of human humility, and *he blessed* out of divine power. The Psalm has: "I have lifted up my eyes to the mountains" (120:1).

26. Third, concerning *the urbanity of those serving*, the text adds: *And he broke the loaves and distributed them to his disciples to set*[43] *before the crowds.* For the noble ministers of Christ themselves were stewards and prompt to serve, according to what 1 Corinthians 4:1 reads: "Let a person so account us as ministers of Christ and stewards of the mysteries of God." For it is fitting for a noble Lord to have noble ministers in accordance

---

[42] On p. 223, n. 7 QuarEd rightly note that the Vulgate has *illis* ("them") whereas Bonaventure has *illos* ("them").

[43] On p. 223, n. 10 QuarEd correctly indicate that the Vulgate has *ponerent* ("set") whereas Bonaventure has *apponerent* ("set").

with what Esther 1:8 says: "As the king had appointed, who set over every table one of his nobles, that everyone might take what he wanted." Now in the curia of Jesus Christ those who are more noble are ministers and servants, as it is said in Luke 22:26–27: "Let him who is greatest among you become as the youngest, and him who is the chief as the servant. . . . But I am in your midst as he who serves."

27. (Verse 17). Fourth, about *the satiety of those eating* the text continues: *And all ate and were satisfied*, so that what the Psalm said was thus verified: "The poor will eat and will be filled, and those who seek the Lord will praise him" (21:27). And also what Psalm 77:29 has: "They ate and were filled exceedingly." *They were filled*, I say, with the fullness of *justice*, about which Proverbs 13:25 has: "The just man eats and fills his soul." Matthew 5:6 says: "For blessed are those who hunger and thirst for justice, for they will be satisfied." Not with the fullness of *avarice*, of which Qoheleth 5:11 has: "The satiety of the rich will not allow him to sleep, because he is filled with things for which he will always hunger." – And because divine abundance is far greater than our indigence, the text has: *And what was left over to them was gathered into twelve baskets of fragments*. The magnitude of God's superabundance is shown through what is in the baskets and in the number of baskets. For twelve is a *superabundant even number*, according to the teaching of arithmetic.[44] And thus there is fulfillment of

---

[44] See Bonaventure's commentary on Luke 6:13 (#29) above on the Twelve Apostles. In translating Bonaventure's interpretation of the Twelve in Luke 6:13, I followed a translation of Augustine's number theory and translated *duodecimus est primus numerus abundans* with "twelve is an abundant prime number." In this instance I have followed the translation of Michael Masi, *Boethian Number Theory: A translation of the* De Institutione Arithmetica *(with Introduction*

that whose figure occurred beforehand in 2 Kings 4:43–44. Elijah said of the few loaves: "The Lord says this: They will eat, and something will be left over. So he set it before them. And they ate, and there was something left over according to the word of the Lord." But in the instance of Elijah there was not such an abundance of food left over as is the case here. And this occurred because of the greater and more abundant *perfection* found in the Gospel in accordance with Matthew 5:20: "Unless your justice exceeds that of the Scribes and Pharisees, you will not enter into the kingdom of heaven." Another interpretation is that the greater abundance is due to its *deeper meaning*. For those twelve baskets signify the twelve Apostles. *Baskets* are everyday containers, and these are filled with the fragments of the five barley loaves, that is, the teaching of the five books of Moses, about which 1 Corinthians 14:19 says: "In church I had rather speak five words with my understanding," etc.[45]

---

and Notes), Studies in Classical Antiquity 6 (Amsterdam: Rodopi, 1983), 96. In Book I chapter 19 Boethius describes "another division of even numbers according to perfect, imperfect, and superabundant." Twelve is a superabundant (or superfluous) number. Twelve and 24, "when compared to the sum of their parts factored out of the total body are found to be larger than that sum. Half of 12 is 6, a third part is 4, a fourth part is 3, and a sixth part is 2, and a twelfth part is 1. The total sum [6+4+3+2+1] amounts to 16. This surpasses the total of the entire body. . . . In this matter, it is obvious that the sum of the parts is greater than and exceeds the size of the original number." It is not surprising to me that Bonaventure follows different theories of the meanings of numbers in Luke 6:13 and 9:17.
[45] On p. 224, n. 5 QuarEd refer to the commentaries of Bede and Augustine. See Book III of Bede's commentary on Luke 9:17. I translate CCSL cxx, pp. 200–201: "For by the baskets are signified the twelve Apostles and all the choirs of teachers who followed them. Indeed, on the outside these were held in contempt by people, but inwardly they have gathered together from the fragments of the salutary food of bread to nourish the hearts of the humble. For baskets are accustomed to perform servile tasks, but he filled the bas-

28. From this a lesson is provided for preachers that they should not search out new things from their hearts, for the Lord did not create new loaves to feed the crowd. But as the Lord multiplied five barley loaves by means of a divine blessing, so too must every abundance of true teaching be taken from *the foundation of Sacred Scripture*, multiplied by *prayer*, through which one looks to heaven, and *devotion*, through which it is blessed, and *meditation*, through which it is broken, and *preaching*, through which it is distributed and explained.[46] – For catholic teaching is first to be taken from Sacred Scripture through *reading*,[47] whose words are *bread*. Matthew 4:4 reads: "It is written: Not by bread alone do human beings live, but by every word that comes forth from the mouth of God." – But to reading one must join *prayer*. Matthew 7:7 says: "Seek, and you will find. Ask, and you will receive.[48] Knock, and it will be opened to

---

kets with the fragments of the loaves, he who has chosen the weak in this world to confound the strong." And in Tract 24, n. 5 of his Commentary on John Augustine writes: "The five loaves are understood to be the five books of Moses, rightly not made from wheat, but from barley, for they pertain to the Old Testament."

[46] It seems that Bonaventure is dependent here on Book III of Bede's commentary on Luke 9:16, but adapts it to his own purposes. I translate from CCSL cxx, p. 200: "The Savior did not create new food for the hungry crowds, but having accepted what the disciples had, he blessed it. For he came in the flesh, not to preach anything other than what had been predicted and to demonstrate that the words of prophecy were pregnant with the mysteries of grace. He looked into heaven to direct the mind to find keenness there and to teach that the light of knowledge is to be sought there. He broke and distributed the loaves to the disciples to place before the crowds, for he laid open the hidden meanings of the law and prophecy to those who will preach through the world."

[47] Bonaventure is alluding here to "lectio divina" or meditative reading of Sacred Scripture.

[48] Bonaventure has reversed the order of the first two imperatives of Matthew 7:7 (and Luke 11:9). The Vulgate reads *dabitur vobis* ("it

you." *We ask* by reading. *We seek* by praying. *We knock* by working with our hands. – But to prayer must be added *devotion* and *thanksgiving*. Whence Colossians 4:2 has: "Be assiduous in prayer, being wakeful therein with thanksgiving." So Matthew 26 reads: "Having lifted up his eyes to heaven, he blessed and gave thanks."[49] – To devotion must be joined *meditation* and *explanation of the truth*, which is nothing other than *the breaking* of the bread. Isaiah 58:7 reads: "Break your bread with the hungry, and bring the needy and homeless into your house." – And *it is distributed* when it is ministered to people according to their capacity to hear it. The Psalmist says: "Distribute and count Zion's houses, so that you may tell of it in another generation" (47:14).[50] And from this the listeners are filled. Sirach 15:3 reads: "She will feed him with the bread of life and understanding and will give him the water of salvific wisdom to drink." – And so it is clear that the Lord formed preachers not only through his own example of fellowship, but also through a mystical and figurative example. For the Lord performed this miracle more to form minds than to feed bodies. And the reason is that as Wisdom 11:27 has, he is an extraordinary lover of souls.[51]

---

will be given you") in Matthew 7:7 (and Luke 11:9) whereas Bonaventure has *accipietis* ("you will receive").

[49] On p. 224, n. 8 QuarEd correctly maintain that the thought comes from Matthew 26:26–27, but that the wording comes from the Canon of the Mass found in the Roman Missal. Nowhere in the New Testament accounts of the institution of the Lord's Supper is there mention of Jesus' lifting his eyes to heaven.

[50] I have supplied some of the context of the Psalmist's praise of Zion's strength to clarify Bonaventure's quotation.

[51] Wisdom 11:27 reads: "But you spare all, because they are yours, O Lord, who love souls."

Luke 9:18–45
THE WAY TO BE USED IN MAKING PROGRESS

29. *And it came to pass as he was alone*, etc. After the Evangelist has expressed the form to be used in preaching, he now turns in this part to *the way to be used in making progress*. For this consideration two things come together, namely, *the difficulty of the way*, which brings about merit, and *the joy of the heavenly homeland*, which forms the reward. Therefore, after explaining *the difficulty of the way*, the Evangelist devotes a second section to *the joy of glory* in 9:28: *Now it came to pass after these words*, etc.

Luke 9:18–27
THE DIFFICULTY OF THE WAY

Now *the way* to the heavenly homeland consists specially in two things, namely, in *perfect knowledge* of Christ through faith and *perfect imitation* of him through the cross. So the first section teaches how Christ *is to be known through faith* whereas the second how *he is to be imitated through the cross* where verse 23 has: *And he said to all: If anyone wishes,* etc.

Luke 9:18–22
CHRIST IS TO BE KNOWN THROUGH FAITH

With regard to the first point it is to be noted that *the perfect knowledge of faith* consists of four things: *the approval of divine honor, rejection of human error, confession of Christ as mediator, consideration of the mystery of redemption.* For four things come together for perfect faith: approbation of religion, detestation of superstition, public confession, and secret contemplation.[52]

30. (Verse 18). So first and with regard to *approbation of divine honor* it is said: *And it came to pass as he was praying in private*, so that he might show fitting worship and reverence to God the Father and indicate how this is to be manifested. And this reverent worship is specially shown through prayer, according to what John 4:23 has: "The hour is coming . . . when the true worshippers will worship the Father in spirit and truth." So the Psalm says: "Call upon me in the day of tribulation, and I will deliver you. And you will give me honor" (49:15). – Now since this reverence must lack *all ostentation*, it is said that "*he was praying in private*," according to what Matthew 6:6 reads: "But when you pray, go into your room," etc. This prayer must also be without *any restlessness*. Therefore, he is also praying *alone*, according to what Lamentations 3:28 has: "He will sit solitary and be quiet, because he has taken it upon himself," namely, lest he be disturbed by any loud noise. And therefore, it is said in Matthew 14:23 that "after he had dismissed the crowd, he went up the mountain by himself to pray."[53] – And since the disciples were not disturbers of Christ's reverent prayer through disrup-

---

[52] Bonaventure's playfulness with words and depth of understanding are manifest.

[53] On p. 225, n. 5 QuarEd cite the Glossa Ordinaria which simplifies the insights of Bede on Luke 9:18: "But he alone prays to the Father. For the Saints can be joined to the Lord in faith and love...but he alone penetrates the secret and incomprehensible matters of the Father's design. And he alone prays, knowing what he should pray for...He alone makes petitions, because human hearts do not grasp God's counsel. . . ." And the editors also quote from Euthymius Zigabenus on Matthew 14:23: "For the mountain is a fitting place for prayer. Furthermore, night and solitude promote silence, freedom from distraction, and resoluteness in prayer."

tion, but gave their approbation through true faith, the text continues: *His disciples were also with him.* So when the text says *alone* or *in private*, it does not exclude the companionship of the disciples, but rather the tumult of the crowds. For he admitted *the disciples* into his company like sons. So he even spoke of them in the words used by the Apostle in Hebrews 2:13: "Behold, I and my young men whom God has given me." But he excluded *the crowds* as one would servants. A figure of this is found in what Abraham did in Genesis 22:5 when "he said to his young men:[54] Wait here in the valley with the ass. But the boy and I will go with speed as far as yonder, and after we have worshipped, we will return to you." – Another interpretation is that this does not mean that both were together at the same time, but that first he prayed alone, and was then afterwards immediately joined by his disciples. Nonetheless, they were joined together, because, even if the Apostles were absent from the physical surroundings, they, however, were present with him through affection of spirit and approbation of faith, according to what Paul says in Colossians 2:5: "Though I am absent in body, yet in spirit I am with you, rejoicing at the sight of your orderly array," etc.

31. Second, concerning *the rejection of human error*, the text adds: *And he asked them, saying: Who do the crowds say that I am?* Now he did not ask them to learn the truth, which he knew, according to what John 2:25 has: "He had no need that anyone should bear witness to him concerning human beings, for he himself knew what was in them." But his purpose in asking was to

---

[54] The Douay and Confraternity translations of *pueri* in Genesis 22:4 and Hebrews 2:13 respectively are not the same. I have followed the Douay in both instances and used "young men."

demonstrate that the erroneous opinion of earthly creatures was inimical to genuine faith. For many times the
multitude contradicts the wise, and crowds generate the
judgment of a mob. For which reason Exodus 23:2 says:
"You shall not follow the mob to do evil. Neither shall
you yield in judgment to the opinion of the multitude
with the result that you stray from the truth."[55] And
therefore, it is no wonder that sensual human beings
did not think rightly about Christ as God, for as 1 Corinthians 2:14 has: "The sensual human being does not
perceive the things of God."[56]

32. (Verse 19). For which reason the text adds three
opinions based on three outstanding qualities. Concerning the first it says: *And they answered and said:
John the Baptist.* And they said this, because they saw
in him *the spirit of sanctification* that was in John, according to what Luke 1:15 above has: "He will be great
before the Lord . . . and will be filled with the Holy
Spirit," etc.[57] – But not all agreed with this opinion.

---

[55] On p. 225, n. 10 QuarEd refer to Book V of Rabanus Maurus'
Commentary on Matthew 16:15 (which, they say, is taken from
"Bede, II. Homil. 16. in Natale B. Apost. Petri et Pauli, and III. in
Matth. 16, 15"): "But it was not in ignorance that he asked his disciples and others their opinion of him, but . . . so that he might give a
fitting reward for the confession of the right faith made by the disciples."

[56] The Vulgate reads *ea quae sunt Spiritus Dei* ("the things that are
of the Spirit of God"). On p. 225, n. 2 QuarEd quote the Glossa Ordinaria (from Bede) on Luke 9:18: "As the Lord is about to inquire
about the faith of his disciples, he first asks about the opinion of the
crowd, lest the faith of the Apostles seem to be founded on the viewpoint of the crowd and not on recognition of the truth. Rightly are
these people called *the crowds*, who present divergent opinions about
the Lord, whose wording and sense are unsure and vague. From
such opinions he distinguishes his own when he asks: *But you, who
do you say that I am?*" See CCSL cxx, p. 201.

[57] Contrast what Ambrose says in Book VI, n. 96 on Luke 9:19. I
translate from CCSL xiv, p. 208: "Now why do the people think that

Thus the text continues: *But others: Elijah*, namely, on account of his *burning zeal*, according to what Sirach 48:1 reads: "Elijah the prophet rose up like a fire, and his word burnt like a torch." And this opinion seemed probable, for Elijah the prophet was outstanding not only in his way of life, but also in his power. And also because his return had been promised according to what Malachi 4:5 says: "Behold, I will send you Elijah the prophet, before the coming of the great and dreadful day of the Lord." – Nor did all agree with this viewpoint. Wherefore, the text continues: *Others: that one of the ancient prophets has risen again.* And they maintained this opinion because of *the sense of discernment* they saw in him. Luke 7:16 above has: "A great prophet has arisen among us." And John 6:14 reads: "This indeed is the prophet who is to come into the world." But since they thought he was simply a man, they said *one of the ancient prophets*. In this they were mistaken, for he was not one of the ancient prophets. Rather he was unique, and the one for whom all the ancient prophets have prepared. Of him Deuteronomy 18:15 says: "The Lord will raise up a prophet from your nation. You shall listen to him as you did to me."[58] – Thus, from such a variety of opinions it is evident that the crowds were far from the truth and the singleness of the faith. For which reason it is said in Ephesians 4:14: "So that we may not be like

---

he is John unless perhaps because while he was in his mother's womb he sensed the presence of the Lord? But this one is not John. He worshipped him from the womb. This one was worshipped. He baptized with water. Christ (baptized) in the Spirit. He persuaded people to repent. This one forgave sins."

[58] Has Bonaventure tailored this quotation to abet his christological purposes? The Vulgate reads *Prophetam de gente tua et de fratribus tuis sicut me suscitabit tibi Dominus Deus tuus. Ipsum audies* ("The Lord your God will raise up for you a prophet from your own nation and from your brothers like unto me. You will listen to him").

children, tossed to and fro and carried about by every wind of doctrine . . . according to the wiles of error."

33. (Verse 20). Third, about *the confession of Christ as Mediator*, this is added: *And he said to them: But who do you say that I am? You*, namely, *as chosen from among the others*, according to what John 6:71 says: "I have chosen you, the twelve." And John 15:16 reads: "You have not chosen me, but I have chosen you." Or *You, my friends*, according to what John 15:15 has: "But I have called you friends." Or *You, my special disciples*, according to what Luke 8:10 above says: "To you it is given to know the mystery of the kingdom of God." But *you*, who believe in me, *Who do you say that I am?* That is, do you confess that "with the heart a person believes unto justice, and with the mouth confession of faith is made unto salvation," as Romans 10:10 has? – So the text continues: *Simon Peter answered and said: You are the Christ of God.* One answers for all, so that the unity of the Church in faith, confession, and governance might be commended. Thus, Peter, as the single prelate of the universal Church, answers for all. For this reason Paul said in 1 Corinthians 1:10: "I beseech you . . . that you all say the same thing and that there be no schisms among you." – Rightfully, therefore, is the name of *Peter* confirmed for this confession of the one for all, and universal governance over the Church is granted, according to what is said in Matthew 16:18: "And I say to you." So it is obvious that Peter answers first not out of impulse, but prompted by the Holy Spirit. And this is what is said in the Glossa: "One for all and before all, because he is the senior and the leader of the Apostles."[59]

---

[59] On p. 226, n. 9 QuarEd provide this listing of opinions: "'Glossa Interlinearis: *Simon Peter answered and said*, one for all.' Cardinal Hugo attributed this opinion to Bede, who, however, quotes the fol-

34. Now by confessing him to be *the Christ of God*, he is simultaneously confessing that he is true God and man. Thus, Ambrose in the Glossa says: "He has joined together everything that expresses both his *nature* and *name*. For in the name of *Christ* there is the expression of both divinity and incarnation and faith in his suffering."[60] For *Christ* expresses *one person in two natures* and *the kingly and priestly dignity* and *the fullness of grace* which are prerogatives from his *anointing*, of which the Psalmist says: "God, your God, has anointed you with the oil of gladness" (44:8). So in the name of *Christ* is understood *the anointed, the one anointing, and the means of anointing*. And for this the Father, Word and Spirit work simultaneously, according to what Isaiah 61:1 says: "The Spirit of the Lord is upon me, because the Lord has anointed me."[61] – Also here is under-

---

lowing words from Ambrose (Book VI., n. 93 on Luke): 'Although the other Apostles know, Peter, however, answers before the rest.' The Glossa Interlinearis on Matthew 16:16 has: '*He answered*, etc., the Apostles also know, but Peter answers for all.' The Glossa Interlinearis says the same thing on Mark 8:29. Cf. Chrysostom, Homily 54 (alias 55) on Matthew, n. 1: 'Therefore, why is Peter the mouth of the Apostles? Always zealous, leader of the apostolic chorus, he himself answers, after all have been asked.'"

[60] Wherever the Glossa Ordinaria derived this statement, it did not get it totally from Ambrose. CCSL xiv, p. 207 gives Ambrose's opinion in Book VI, n. 93 as this: *Conplexus est itaque omnia, qui et naturam et nomen expressit, in quo summa uirtutum est* ("Therefore, he has joined together everything that expresses both his nature and name, in which is the sum of powers").

[61] On p. 226, n. 11 QuarEd quote Book I chapter 3, n. 44 of Ambrose's *De Spiritu Sancto*: "If you say Christ, you also designate God as Father, by whom the Son was anointed, and him as the Son who was anointed, and the Holy Spirit with whom he was anointed. For it is written (Acts 10:38): *This Jesus of Nazareth, whom God anointed with the Holy Spirit*, etc." The editors go on to quote from the Third Book of Bonaventure's Commentary on the Sentences, Quaestio 3, dubium 2. See Opera Omnia 3:394: ". . . *Son of God* names the person in *one* nature. But *Christ* and *Jesus* name the person in *two* natures. Now *Christ* names the person in *human* nature related to the

stood *the nature* of the anointed, *the grace* by which he is anointed, and *the dignity* or office to which he is anointed. Daniel 9:24 reads: "The Saint of Saints will be anointed, so that vision and prophecy may be fulfilled."[62] – Now understood here is *kingly, prophetic, and sacerdotal dignity*, according to his triple excellence, namely, of power and of truth and of holiness. As a figure of this in the Old Testament these three persons were customarily anointed. – And in this it is obvious how the three previously expressed opinions are false, although they have enough persuasive power to obscure the issue. Wherefore, it is evident that Christ in this word has confounded these errors and laid the foundation of complete faith, according to what 1 Corinthians 3:11 states: "No one can lay another foundation." From this it is clear that he was called *Peter*, and to him was granted that the true faith would never be missing from his Church. Luke 22:32 below has: "I have prayed for you, Peter, that your faith may not fail," etc.

35. (Verses 21–22). Fourth, with respect to *recognition of the mystery of redemption*, the text says: *But he strictly charged them,*[63] *and commanded them not to tell this to anyone.* And he did this because the mystery of redemption, which by God's just judgment was to be hidden from the rulers of the world, had not been accomplished. Thus 1 Corinthians 2:7–8 reads: "We speak the wisdom

---

divine nature, because he is said to be *anointed*. Now *Jesus* names the person in the divine nature related to the human nature, because *Jesus* is said to be Savior. And therefore, in the name of *Jesus* Christ every knee must bend, as in the name *Son of God*."

[62] It seems to me that Bonaventure has altered this text for his purposes. The Vulgate has: *Et impleatur visio et prophetes et unguatur sanctus sanctorum* ("And so that vision and prophecy may be fulfilled and the Saint of the Saints may be anointed").

[63] On p. 227, n. 4 QuarEd rightly mention that the Vulgate has *illos* ("them") whereas Bonaventure reads *eos* ("them").

of God in a mystery, which has been hidden, . . . which none of the rulers of this world knew. For if they had known it, they would never have crucified the Lord of glory." – But although it was not to be made known to all, it was, however, to be predicted to the disciples. For which reason the text continues: *Saying: The Son of Man must suffer many things*. Now the reason for this prediction is designated in John 14:29: "Now I have told you before it comes to pass, that when it has come to pass, you may believe." For the disciples themselves had not yet grasped this, according to what is said in Luke 18:31 below: "But Jesus, taking to himself the Twelve, said to them: Behold, we are going up to Jerusalem" and afterwards Luke 18:34 adds: "And they understood none of these things, but they accepted this after the consummation."[64] Wherefore, it is said in Luke 24:44–45: "These are the words which I spoke to you while I was yet with you, that all things must be fulfilled that are written . . . concerning me. Then he opened their minds that they might understand the Scriptures."

36. But he said: *Must*, that is, it is *necessary*, not absolutely, but seen from the presupposition of divine disposition and promise, according to what Acts 3:18 says: "But God fulfilled what he had announced beforehand by the mouth of all the prophets that his Christ should suffer." Another interpretation of *must* is that *it is opportune* and expedient, in accordance with what Caiphas predicted. John 11:50 reads: "It is expedient that one person die for the people instead of the whole

---

[64] Indeed, the first part of this sentence comes from Luke 18:34, but the second part does not. It is not a variant reading in the Vulgate, and despite word searches I have been unable to locate the words: *sed hoc acceperunt post consummationem* ("but they accepted this after the consummation"). Did Bonaventure take these words from the liturgy?

nation perishing." I say: *He must suffer many things* to redeem many souls, to forgive many sins, to pardon many condemned people. Isaiah 53:5–6 has: "He was wounded for our iniquities. He was bruised for our sins....All we like sheep have gone astray. Everyone has turned aside into his own way. And the Lord has laid upon him the iniquities of us all." – Now he suffered *many* and *great* things. He suffered at the hands of *many and great people.* For which reason the text continues: *And be rejected by the elders and chief priests and Scribes. The elders* were outstanding because of their age, *the chief priests* because of their authority, but *the Scribes* by reason of their teaching, so that in this way Isaiah 1:2 might be fulfilled: "I have brought up children and exalted them, but they have despised me." – And since the suffering of Christ had been determined to result in death, the text adds: *And be put to death,* that is, he must be put to death, according to what Daniel 9:26 has: "Christ will be slain."[65] But lest it be thought that he was *unwilling,* Isaiah 53:12 says: "He has delivered his soul unto death." – But since this passion and suffering had brought about life from the dead, the text adds: *and on the third day rise,* according to what Hosea 6:3 reads: "He will give us life after two days, and on the third day he will raise us up." The Savior said that a figure of this occurred beforehand in the person of Jonah. Matthew 12:40 has: "Just as Jonah was," etc. – From these considerations, therefore, it is obvious that Christ founded his Church on perfect understanding of the faith, namely, through this faith divine honor is approved, human error is refuted, the me-

---

[65] I have translated Bonaventure's quotation from Daniel 9:26 via Bonaventure's context. Literally, *Christus* means "anointed," and as such could mean "an anointed" or "the anointed."

diator is pronounced, and the restorer[66] is acknowledged.

Luke 9:23–27
CHRIST IS TO BE IMITATED BY MEANS OF THE CROSS

37. (Verse 23). *And he said to all*, etc. Having shown how Christ is to be known by faith, here a second point is made, namely, how *he is to be imitated by means of the cross*, for "faith is dead without works."[67] Because it is difficult to carry the cross, he invites people to this by means of a fourfold consideration, namely, by consideration of *his own example, the danger to oneself, future judgment*, and *the divine kingdom*. The result is that if warnings do not motivate a person, examples may move them or at least dangers, or future judgments, or at least promises.[68]

So he first invites all by means of a *consideration of his own example*, when he says: *And he said to all: If anyone wishes to come after me*, that is, to imitate me. To this I do not compel anyone, but offer an invitation. Therefore, he says: *If anyone wishes*. Sirach 15:16–17 reads: "If you want to keep the commandments . . . they will preserve you. God has set water and fire before you. Stretch forth your hand to the one you want." Whence Chrysostom says: "If one were giving out gold or handing over a treasure, that person would not be inviting with violence. Rather people would run. How much more to

---

[66] One would expect *redemptor* ("redeemer") here, but Bonaventure uses *reparator*.

[67] James 2:26.

[68] On p. 228, n. 1 QuarEd indicate that the Vatican manuscript reads: "or certainly future judgments, or finally promises." In brief, Bonaventure's fourfold listing here is hardly smooth.

those things which are in heaven! For if the nature of things persuades, run for them. If you do not run, you are not worthy to receive what is offered."[69] So he says: *If anyone wishes* to follow my example. – *Let him deny himself*, through *every kind of humility*, bringing sense, affection and thought "into captivity to the obedience of Christ."[70] He notes this when he says: *himself*. And this is the counsel of Sirach 7:19: "Humble your spirit very much." And this, indeed, is necessary for the person who wants to follow the humble Christ. So Gregory in the Glossa says: "Unless a person forsakes himself, he does not come near him who is above him."[71] – But this is not enough. So the text continues: *And take up his cross daily*, through *continuous austerity*, so that he could say with Paul in Galatians 2:19: "With Christ I have been crucified."[72] And 2 Corinthians 4:10 has: "Always bearing about in our body the dying of Jesus Christ."[73] And therefore, it is said in Galatians 5:24: "And those who belong to Christ have crucified their flesh with its vices and passions."

---

[69] On p. 228, n. 3 QuarEd refer to Chyrsostom's Homily 55 (alias 56) on Matthew, n. 1. The editors note that instead of Bonaventure's *sed currerent homines* ("Rather people would run"), the original text has *si vero ad haec sine violentia itur* ("If indeed one can travel to these things without violence").

[70] On p. 228, n. 4 QuarEd mention Bonaventure's quotation of 2 Corinthians 10:5 here.

[71] On p. 228, n. 5 QuarEd specify the Glossa as Ordinaria and Homily 32, n. 2 of GGHG. Bonaventure's text is virtually the same as Gregory's (the Glossa Ordinaria's). See PL 76:1234A: *Quia nisi quis a semetipso deficiat, ad eum qui super ipsum est non appropinquat.* Bonaventure writes: *Nisi quis a se ipso deficiat, ad eum qui supra se est, non appropinquat.*

[72] Is Bonaventure drawn to this passage in Galatians 2 because Gregory uses Galatians 2:20 in his commentary on Luke 9:23–27 from which the Glossa and Bonaventure just quoted? See PL 76:1234A.

[73] The Vulgate simply has *Iesu* ("Jesus").

38. Note that he says: *Daily*, because daily the penitence of the cross must be new and fresh, so that he may always say: "I said: Now I have begun" (Psalm 76:11) like Blessed Francis, who, when he was dying, said that now he was beginning to do good: "Brothers, let us begin and make progress, for up unto now we have made little progress."[74] For the cross of Christ has a renewing nature. Thus 2 Corinthians 4:16 says: "Even though our outer man is decaying, yet our inner man is being renewed day by day." – But for perfect imitation of Christ it is not sufficient to have humility and austerity. For *poverty* is also necessary. So the text adds: *And follow me*, namely, through *the highest poverty*, by which he did not want to carry anything whatsoever on the way, so that he might rightly and expeditiously arrive at the homeland. Wherefore, Peter said in Matthew 19:27: "Behold, we have left everything and have followed you." About this Bernard comments: "Peter, you have spoken well and are no fool. . . . For burdened down with things, you could not follow him who was running ahead."[75] And this is exceedingly honorable, although it seems base, because, as Sirach 23:38 says, "It is a great glory to follow the Lord."

Now from this saying is derived the three counsels and vows of religious, that is, *obedience* with abnegation, *chastity* with the cross, and *poverty* with subjection. But

---

[74] On p. 228, n. 7 QuarEd refer to chapter 14 of Bonaventure's *The Major Legend of Saint Francis*. See *Francis of Assisi: Early Documents: The Founder*, p. 640: "Let us begin, brothers, to serve the Lord our God, for up to now we have done little."

[75] On p. 228, n. 8 QuarEd point their readers to Chapter II "On Leaving All Things" of *Declamationes de Colloquio Simonis cum Jesu, Ex S. Bernardi sermonibus collectae* of Geoffrey the Abbot. See PL 184:438B. See Bonaventure's interpretation of Luke 14:33 (#66) below where he quotes this same abbreviated passage from "Bernard."

as it is said in Matthew 19:11, "Not all can accept this teaching, but those to whom it is given by my Father."[76] So that no one may excuse himself, as if he didn't have the grace, he says: *If anyone wishes*, etc., as if to say that the grace of God is there for us, if the will is not wanting. Hebrews 12:15 says: "Take heed, lest anyone be wanting in the grace of God."

39. (Verse 24). Secondly, he invites a consideration of *danger to oneself*, when he says: *For he who would save his life will lose it*,[77] that is, the person who wants to save life in the present will lose life in the future, that is, for momentary life he loses eternal life. Whence John 12:25 says: "The person who loves his life loses it." For the person who loves too much loves iniquitously. And "the person who loves iniquity hates his soul," as it is said in Psalm 10:6. For the person who loves his life more than God loses God, and by losing God has as a consequence the loss of himself. And therefore, Paul said in Acts 20:24: "I do not count my life more precious than myself." – And since this seems to be a difficult teaching, he offers a proof from the contrary: *But the person who loves his life for my sake*, namely, in this life, *will save it*, namely, in the future life,[78] according to what 2 Maccabees 7:9 has: "Indeed, you destroy us in

---

[76] On p. 228, n. 10 QuarEd correctly mention the blend of Matthew 19:11 and John 6:66 in Bonaventure's quotation. Matthew 19:11 reads: "Not all can accept this teaching, but those to whom it has been given." John 6:66 has: "No one can come to me unless he is enabled to do so by my Father."

[77] On p. 228, n. 12 QuarEd correctly state that the Vulgate reads *illam* ("it") while Bonaventure reads *eam* ("it").

[78] On p. 228, n. 13 QuarEd point to the Glossa Interlinearis on Luke 9:24 as a possible source for Bonaventure's thought and wording. The pertinent words are: "*For*, arguing from the contrary, *the person who loses his life*, his present life, *for my sake*. etc." While Bonaventure has *a contrario sensu*, the Glossa Interlinearis has *e contrario*.

this present life, but the King of the world will raise us up, who die for his laws, in the resurrection of eternal life." And wherefore, Paul said in Acts 21:13: "I am ready not only to be bound, but even to die in Jerusalem for the name of the Lord Jesus." So therefore, *to love one's life* for Christ is *to save it. To want to save one's life* is *to expose it to loss*, in accordance with what Romans 8:13 states: "If you live according to the flesh, you will die." And that is the greatest danger.

40. (Verse 25). And so to make his point even more clear, he adds: *For what profit is it to a person, if he gains the whole world*, and this temporally, *but ruin or lose himself?*, and this eternally, as if he were saying: Nothing, since the person who loses himself loses everything. Therefore, there is no advantage, but only disadvantage. So James 5:1 reads: "Come now, you rich, weep and howl over your miseries which will come upon you." And the reason for this is, as Augustine says in his Sermon on the Innocents, "No one possesses unjust lucre without just punishment; lucre in one's safe, condemnation on one's conscience. He made off with a garment and lost trust. He acquired money and lost justice," and as a consequence his soul.[79] Therefore, Isidore writes: "If you had the wisdom of Solomon, the handsomeness of Absalom, the strength of Samson, the longevity of Enoch, and wealth and power of Octavian, what good is it to you, if at the end your flesh is given

---

[79] Through their note 4 on p. 229 QuarEd have led me to Augustine's Sermon 220 on the Feast of the Holy Innocents in PL 39:2152. Bonaventure has past tenses for Augustine's present tenses. In his commentary on Luke 16:10 (#18) below Bonaventure again quotes Augustine's Sermon 220.

to the worms and your soul together with Dives is endlessly tormented by the demons?"[80]

41. (Verse 26). Third, he invites all to carry the cross by means of a consideration of *future judgment*, when he says: *For whoever is ashamed of me,* that is, of imitating me, *and my words,* namely, of confessing them, by contemning the cross of Christ as ignominious and even his teaching from wicked ashamedness, of which it is said in Sirach 4:24–25: "For the sake of your soul do not be ashamed to say the truth. For there is a shame that produces sin, and there is a shame that produces glory and grace."[81] From this we are given to understand that we must not be ashamed of the truth of Christ. Take the example of the Apostle who said in Romans 1:16: "I am not ashamed of the Gospel, for it is the power of God," etc. But we must be ashamed of the vileness of sin, according to what Romans 6:21 has: "What fruit had you then from those things of which you are now ashamed?" But many are not ashamed of the deformity of sin, of whom Jeremiah 8:12 says: "They are ashamed, because they have committed abomination. Yea rather, they are not afflicted with shame, and they have not known how to be ashamed." And again Jeremiah 3:3 has: "A harlot's forehead was made for you," etc.[82] Such a person is ashamed of Christ's humility. – And concerning this he

---

[80] On p. 229, n. 5 QuarEd indicate that Cardinal Hugo and Gorranus also attribute this saying to Isidore. Then they ask: "But where is it?" They further note that Hugo writes *si divitias Anchi* and that Gorranus has *si divitias Croesi.* They also refer to Christianus Druthmarus on Matthew 16:26 in PL 106:1400. See Hugh of St. Cher, p. 186n for a quotation of Isidore that is very close to that found in Bonaventure.

[81] While the word "shame/ashamed" connects these lines together, the Latin words are different, namely, *erubescentia* and *confusio.*

[82] Jeremiah 3:3 concludes: "and you would not be ashamed" (*noluisti erubescere*).

adds: *Of him will the Son of Man be ashamed*, that is, he will make him ashamed or he will reject him by his just judgment as one who is to be shamed. About this it is said in 1 Samuel 2:30: "Whoever will glorify me, I will glorify him. But they that despise me shall be despised." And this on the day of judgment. – And wherefore, the text continues: *When he comes in his glory and that of the Father and of the holy angels.* This text touches upon the judiciary power with regard to *the principle of causality* in the Father, *the privilege of excellence* in himself, and *the service of obedience* in the multitude of the angels. So Matthew 24:30 reads: "Then will appear the sign of the Son of Man in heaven, and then will all tribes of the earth mourn, and they will see the Son of Man," etc. And Isaiah 3:14 has: "The Lord will come in judgment with the elders[83] of his people." In this judgment the proud will be ashamed, and the humble will be exalted, according to what the Psalm says: "I will break all the horns of the sinners, and the horns of the just will be exalted" (74:11).

42. (Verse 27). Fourth, there is an invitation to consider *the divine kingdom*, which Christ shows to his imitators, when he says: *But I say to you truly: There are some standing here*, through the lifting up of their minds, according to what the Psalmist says: "Our feet were standing in your courts, O Jerusalem" (121:2). – The kingdom must be shown to such people, so that their desire may be completed. So the text continues: *who will not taste death*, through the separation of soul and body, *until they see the kingdom of God*, through revelation, not by open vision. For it was said to Moses in Exodus 33:20: "A human being will not see me and live." But Christ's saying concerns some special revelation, by

---

[83] The Vulgate reads *senibus* ("ancients").

which it was said to Moses: "I will show you all good" (Exodus 33:19). Through this it is given to understand that those standing in the words of Christ will not taste death, but will pass over to life, according to what John 8:51 says: "If anyone keep my word, he will not taste death forever."[84] – Therefore, through these words Christ promises such a great reward to those who imitate him by bearing the cross, warns of such a severe judgment, paints so great a danger, shows so great an example, that it is an extraordinarily obstinate person who is not motivated to imitate him. For this reason it is said in Hebrews 12:1: "Having such a cloud of witnesses over us, . . . let us run," etc. And Hebrews 13:13–14 says: "Let us go forth to him outside the camp, bearing his reproach. For we have no permanent city here, but we see the city that is to come."

Luke 9:28–45
THE JOY OF GLORY

43. *Now it came to pass about eight days after these words.* To the exhortation to an austere way of life the Evangelist joins a *demonstration of the joy of glory.* Now he proceeds in this order. For first he describes *the revelation of the promised glory.* Second comes a *consideration of the glory revealed* in verse 32 which reads: *Now*

---

[84] Bonaventure has modified John 8:51 to suit his interpretive purposes by changing *videre* ("to see") to *gustare* ("to taste"). John 8:51 reads: "If anyone keep my word, he will not see death forever." On p. 229, n. 14 QuarEd point to the Glossa Ordinaria (taken from Ambrose VII, n. 2) on Luke 9:27: "The person who stands with Christ does not taste death, for the person who has merited companionship with Christ will not have the slightest sense of eternal death. Nor for this person will the order of living be interrupted in death." See CCSL xiv, p.215.

Peter and his companions. A third point is *the confirma-*
tion of the revelation shown in verse 37 which has: *Now*
it came to pass on the following day. And he made this
confirmation through a wondrous cure of a demoniac.

Luke 9:28–31
REVELATION OF PROMISED GLORY[85]

The Evangelist describes *the revelation of future glory* in
a twofold manner. First, with regard to its antecedents.
And secondly, with regard to those things that accompany it, as verse 29 indicates: *And it happened as he*
prayed, etc. – Now it should be realized that relative to
the Transfiguration of Christ there were three antecedents or occasions, scilicet, *the necessity of the time*
frame, the select nature of his companions, and *the emi-*
nence of the place. Now these are the three things that
God observes in communicating divine revelations.

44. (Verse 28). So first, with respect to *the necessity of*
the time frame it says: *Now it came to pass about eight*
days after these words. Since the Lord had promised
that he would show himself in glory to his disciples,
and "the Lord does not delay in his promises" as is said
in 2 Peter 3:9, only a short space of time, that is, a
week, should intervene between the promise and its ful-

---

[85] For more detail on Bonaventure's view of contemplation and
Christ's Transfiguration, see Timothy J. Johnson, *Iste Pauper Cla-*
mavit: Saint Bonaventure's Mendicant Theology of Prayer, European
University Studies, Series XXIII Theology, Vol. 390 (Frankfurt am
Main: Peter Lang, 1990), 181–236; Timothy J. Johnson, *The Soul in*
Ascent: Bonaventure on Poverty, Prayer, and Union With God, Stud-
ies in Franciscanism (Quincy, IL: Franciscan Press, 2000), 133–176;
Hayes, *The Hidden Center,* pp. 29–32.

fillment.[86] A figure of this occurred beforehand in the
marriage of Rachel. In Genesis 29:27 Laban said to Jacob in her regard: "Make up a week of days of this
match, and I will give you her also." – And note this,
when he says: *It came to pass about eight days*, that he
did it on the eighth day in the sequence of a week which
did not have eight full days because part of the first day
and part of the last day were missing. And in Matthew
17:1 and Mark 9:1 the first and last days were not
counted, but only the full days. For there it is said: "It
came to pass after six days." And in this there is no contradiction, but one expression explains the other.[87] Now
the Holy Spirit wanted to use both expressions to convey
the mystery. Since God created the world in six days
and rested after the sixth day, work is to be done on six
days and the remaining time is to be used for rest and
contemplation.[88] Therefore, to convey this Matthew
says: "After six days." But since the perfect and consummate rest and contemplation do not take place before the eighth day, namely, the resurrection, it says
here: Eight days. And this is what is said in the Glossa
by Bede and Ambrose concerning Luke 9:28: *After these
words*, etc.[89]

---

[86] On p. 230, n. 5 QuarEd refer to Homily 32, n. 6 of GGHG: "For he
had to promise something to his unlearned disciples even in this present life, so that they might be more robustly established for the future." See PL 76:1257A.

[87] On p. 230, n. 7 QuarEd write that Bonaventure's interpretation
follows those of Book III of Jerome's Commentary on Matthew 17:1,
Book II chapter 56, n. 113 of Augustine's *Harmony of the Gospels*,
and Damascene's Homily on the Transfiguration of the Lord, n. 6.

[88] See Genesis 2:2; Exodus 20:10–11; Deuteronomy 5:13–14; Hebrews 4:4

[89] On p. 230, n. 9 QuarEd do not quote Ambrose or Bede, but give
these references: Ambrose, VII n.7 on Luke and III Bede on Luke
9:28. Further investigation of CCSL xiv, p. 217 and CCSL cxx, pp.
204–205 respectively would reveal to what extent Bonaventure is
actually quoting Ambrose and/or Bede.

45. Second, concerning *the select nature of his compan-ions* it is said: *And he took Peter, John, and James.* He took these three as his more close and intimate disci-ples, just as he took them with him when he raised the girl from the dead in Luke 8:51 above. He took *three* to commend the mystery of the Trinity and to lay a foun-dation for firm testimony. So in the Glossa it is said: "So that the entire world might believe on the basis of three suitable witnesses."[90] Now he specially selected *these three* because of *the eminence* that he ascertained in them. For *Peter* was to be the future primate in the Church to be governed, as Matthew 16:18–19 says: "You are Peter . . . I will give you the keys of the kingdom of heaven." And *James* was the first to be killed among the Apostles for the Church to be increased. It is said in Acts 12:2 about Herod that "he killed James, the brother of John, with the sword." *John* is outstanding in regard to the mother to be cared for. John 19:26 says: "When Jesus saw his mother and the disciple standing there," etc.[91] – Another interpretation is that he took these three for the sake of *teaching through figures.* Through these is designated the threefold state in the Church of those to be saved, namely, *the prelates* in Peter, *the ac-tive believers* in James, *the contemplative believers* in

---

[90] On p. 230, n. 10 QuarEd refer to the Glossa Interlinearis which has in mind Deuteronomy 19:15: "In the mouth of two or three wit-nesses every word will stand." Bonaventure's reference to the Trinity may stem from Ambrose VII, n. 9. See CCSL xiv, pp. 217–218: "Whence three are selected . . . for no one can see the glory of the resurrection, except those who have preserved intact, with the genuine sincerity of faith, the mystery of the Trinity."
[91] On p. 230, n. 11 QuarEd point to the interpretation of Ambrose VII, n. 9. See CCSL xiv, p. 218: "Peter ascends the mountain. He received the keys of the kingdom of heaven. John, to whom his mother was committed. James, who was the first to ascend the sac-erdotal throne."

John like Noah, Daniel, and Job.[92] Another interpretation is that *the married* are designated by Peter, *the continent* in James, and *the virgins* in John, according to the triple continence to which thirty, sixty, and a hundredfold growth is due.[93] For we read of Peter's wife, of the virginity of John, and neither is expressly stated about James.

46. Thirdly, with respect to *the eminence of the place* the text has: *And he went up the mountain to pray.* For a *mountain* is an elevated place that stretches out between heaven and earth and therefore is suitable for contemplation and prayer. Such was this mountain. Wherefore, it is said in Matthew 17:1 that "he led them up a high mountain by themselves," namely, so that they might be separated from the crowd and from earthly matters. And such places are fitting for divine revelation. So it is said of Moses in Exodus 3:1–2 that "after he had driven the flock to the inner parts of the desert, he came to the mountain of God, Horeb," where the Lord appeared to him in the burning bush. It was similar with regard to obtaining the Law. Exodus 24:12 reads: "The Lord said to Moses: Come up to me into the mountain and be there. And I will give you tables of stone." In a similar way relative to the determination of the promised land, according to what Deuteronomy 34:1

---

[92] See Bonaventure's commentary on Luke 7:16 (#31) above: "*Noah* refers to the *prelates. Daniel* refers to those who are gifted with the understanding of visions, namely, the *contemplatives. Job* refers to those in the *active life.*"

[93] See Bonaventure's commentary on Luke 8:8 (#11) above and the note there: Book II of Jerome's commentary on Matthew 13:23 has: the hundredfold refers to virgins, the sixtyfold refers to widows who remain unmarried, the thirtyfold to those in a chaste marriage. On p. 230, n. 13 QuarEd provide a long note, at whose end they cite the Glossa Ordinaria on Luke 9:28: "By Peter the engaged or married, by James the penitents or active, by John virgins or contemplatives."

says: "Moses went up from the plains of Moab unto
Mount Nebo, to the top of Pisgah over against Jericho.
And the Lord showed him all the land of Gilead as far
as Dan." – Therefore, from this one gathers that a
mountain is an apt place for God to appear, to teach,
and to be contemplated. So Bede in the Glossa says:
"He goes up the mountain to pray, so that he may give a
sign that those who are waiting for the resurrection
must elevate their minds on high and be persistent in
continuous prayer."[94] And he does this on a mountain
because of its prominence, according to what Deuteronomy 33:2 says: "The Lord came from Sinai, and from
Seir he rose up to us. He appeared from Mount Paran,
and with him thousands of saints. In his right hand was
a law of fire." And Deuteronomy 33:3 continues: "And
those who come near to his feet will accept his teaching." And thus there are three things that dispose one to
the divine transfiguration even according to the *literal*
understanding.

47. Now *spiritually* in these three there is profound formation for those desiring to attain to seeing the transfiguration of the Lord through the vision of contemplation. For *in the number of days* we are given to understand *the steps* of contemplation that follow upon one
another just as one day comes after another. And according to Matthew 17:1 *six days* are enumerated to indicate *the six steps* of contemplation. Richard gives expression to these in his book *On the Ark* or *On Contem-*

---

[94] On p. 231, n. 3 QuarEd refer to the Glossa Ordinaria apud
Lyranum on Luke 9:28 (apud Strab. on Mark 9:1). See what Bede
says in CCSL cxx, p. 205: "For he goes up the mountain to pray and
so be transfigured, in order to show those who are waiting for the
fruit of the resurrection and who desire to see the king in his splendor that they must dwell on high in their minds and recline there
through continuous prayer."

plation. He says in Book I, Chapter 6: "There are six kinds of contemplation in themselves, and within each there are many divisions. The first is *in imagination* and according to *imagination only*. The second is *in imagination* and according to *reason*. The third is *in reason* and according to *imagination*. The fourth is *in reason* and according to *reason*. The fifth is *above reason*, but not *beyond* reason. The sixth is *above reason* and seems to be *beyond* reason. And therefore, there are two in imagination, two in reason, and two in understanding."[95] – The first two concern *corporeal* matters, the second two deal with *spiritual* matters, the third two are taken up with *eternal* and *incomprehensible* matters.[96] – Now these six kinds of contemplation are understood both by the *six days* and by the *six steps*, by which one climbed up to the throne of Solomon, according to what 1 Kings 10:18–19 has: "Solomon made for himself a great throne of ivory and overlaid it with the finest gold. It had six steps." And the number of perfection gives fitting expression to this, for six is the prime number of the perfect.

48. But according to Luke the days are computed to be *eight*. For Luke treats this apparition from the perspec-

---

[95] This translation of Richard of St. Victor's *The Mystical Ark (Benjamin Major)* I.6 is based on that of Grover A. Zinn. See *Richard of St. Victor, The Twelve Patriarchs, The Mystical Ark, Book Three of the Trinity*, translation and introduction by Grover A. Zinn, The Classics of Western Spirituality (New York: Paulist, 1979), 161. Zinn, p. 151, translates the opening words of Book I, Chapter 1: "If the One with the key of knowledge allows, I wish through a gift of His inspiration to unlock somewhat the mystical ark of Moses, by presenting the results of our nightly work."

[96] On p. 231, n. 6 QuarEd rightly state that Bonaventure is adapting the teaching of Book I, Chapter 7 of Richard of St. Victor. They also refer to Bonaventure's *Breviloquium*, Part V, chapter 6 and his *Itinerarium mentis in Deum*, Chapter 1, n. 5 and Chapter 7, n. 1. See *Opera Omnia* 5:258–260, 5:297, 5:312 respectively.

tive of *glory* after the resurrection. This is evident because in 9:32 he touches on *sleep* and *awakening*. Therefore, he indicates an *eighth step*. The first seven concern
the way whilst the eighth is reserved for the homeland.
Of these seven Augustine says towards the end of his
book, *De Quantitate Animae*: "To serve the purpose of
instruction, let us, following the ascending order, call
the first step *vitalization*, the second *sensation*, the third
art, the fourth *virtue*, the fifth *tranquillity*, the sixth
initiation, the seventh *contemplation*."[97] Afterwards,
nothing remains except *the beatific vision*. And so there
are approximately eight days. And as Augustine continues: "The first step is *concerning* the body, the second
through the body, the third *about* the body, the fourth
toward itself, the fifth *in itself*, the sixth *toward God*,
the seventh *in God*."[98] And these steps not only concern
the steps of contemplation, but also are the means by
which one arrives at contemplation.

Now a certain Brother Giles, although unsophisticated
in speech, but not in knowledge and of whom it was
proven that he was most often rapt in contemplation,
distinguished the steps in this wise: There are seven
steps of contemplation. The first is *fire*, the second is
anointing, the third is *ecstasy*, the fourth is *contemplation*, the fifth is *enjoyment*, the sixth is *rest*, the seventh

---

[97] The translation of Chapter 35, n. 79 of *The Greatness of the Soul* is
based on: *St. Augustine: The Greatness of the Soul: The Teacher*,
translated and annotated by Joseph M. Colleran, ACW 9 (Westminster, MD: Newman, 1950), 109. On p. 231, n. 9 QuarEd rightly indicate that Bonaventure adapts the quotation from Augustine by
changing *primus actus* ("first act") to *primus gradus* ("first step").
See *Sancti Avreli Avgvstini Opera Sect. I Pars IV*. CSEL lxxxix, p.
228.
[98] This translation of Augustine's *The Greatness of the Soul* is also
based on that of Colleran in the ACW 9, p. 109. Again, Bonaventure
has changed Augustine's *actus* to *gradus*. See the previous note.

is *glory*. And after these nothing remains except *eternal happiness*.[99] – Thus, through these seven days one arrives at the eighth day of glory. And this is what the Holy Spirit wanted to designate by setting out the days in this manner.

49. Now by *the three persons* Christ took with him *the three virtues* necessary for contemplation are to be understood, namely, *faith, hope, charity. Faith* by Peter, whose name means *understanding. Hope* by James, whose name means *wrestler. Charity* by John, whose name means *in whom is grace*.[100] Without these wings no one can ascend to the mountain. – Another interpretation of the three persons is this. We are to understand them as *the three dispositions* necessary for the contemplative soul, that is, *industry, discipline*, and *grace*. The first is found in Peter, the second in James, the third in John. For the contemplative soul must be illuminated by *understanding*, conquered by *desire*, and inflamed by *affection*, so that we can be carried aloft with the Lord. If one of these is lacking, the business of contemplation

---

[99] On p. 231, n. 11 QuarEd point to Luke Wadding's *Annales Minorum* II for the year 1262, n. 23 as the source for Brother Giles' teaching. After the editing of Bonaventure's Opera Omnia, the Quaracchi Friars published *Dicta Beati Aegidii Assisiensis Sec. Codices MSS. Emendata et Denuo Edita,* Bibliotheca Franciscana Ascetica Medii Aevi 3 (Quaracchi: Collegium St. Bonaventurae, 1905). Chapter XIII, "De contemplatione," reads: *Et dixit sanctus frater Aegidius: 'In contemplatione sunt septem gradus: Ignis, unctio, ecstasis, contemplatio, gustus, requies, gloria* (p. 48). On p. 48, n. 2 the editors refer to Bonaventure's Commentary on Luke 9:28 (#48), to Bonaventure's *Serm.* 1 in Sabb. s. p II, and to *Chron. XXIV general.,* p. 107. I have translated *gustus* by "enjoyment" in an attempt to see a progression in the Brother Giles' seven steps.

[100] See Bonaventure's commentary on Luke 6:14 (#36) and the notes there for these interpretations of the Apostles' names. On p. 232, n. 1 QuarEd refer to the Glossa Ordinaria on Luke 9:28: "[The three Apostles] signify those who have faith, hope, and charity."

ceases.[101] – Another interpretation takes these three persons to be *the three ways of ascending* to the height of contemplation. For one way is that of ascending by the road of *splendor*. And Blessed Augustine teaches this way of ascending, and it is designated by Peter.[102] Another way of ascending is by means of the road of *sorrow and lamentation*, and this is designated by James and is the way common to those engaged in prayer. The third way is that of *love*. Dionysius teaches this way, which is designated by John.[103] And this is the outstanding way of them all, in which grace is most effective. But in the first way industry or knowledge is very important. And

---

[101] On p. 232, n. 2 QuarEd refer to Bonaventure's *Itinerarium mentis in Deum*, Chapter 7, n. 5. The reference should be to Chapter 7, n. 6. See *Itinerarium mentis in Deum*, with an introduction, translation and commentary by Philotheus Boehner, Works of Saint Bonaventure II (St. Bonaventure, New York: The Franciscan Institute, 1956/1998), 101: "If you wish to know how these things may come about, ask grace, not learning; desire, not the understanding; the groaning of prayer, not diligence in reading; the Bridegroom, not the teacher; God, not man; darkness, not clarity; not light, but the fire that wholly inflames and carries one into God through transporting unctions and consuming affections."

[102] On p. 232, n. 3 QuarEd refer to n. 48 of Augustine's *The Greatness of the Soul*. Unfortunately, n. 48 has nothing to do with the splendor of the soul. As a matter of fact, the very extensive "Index verborum" of CSEL lxxxix gives no reference to "splendor" in Augustine's *The Greatness of the Soul*. Bonaventure seems to be referring to chapter 33, n. 70–76 of Augustine's *The Greatness of the Soul*. Colleran (ACW 9, p. 104) translates n. 76: "Now at last we are in the very vision and contemplation of truth, which is the seventh and last level of the soul; and here we no longer have a level but in reality a home at which one arrives via those levels. What shall I say are the delights, what the enjoyment, of the supreme and true Goodness, what the everlasting peace it breathes upon us?"

[103] On p. 232, n. 4 QuarEd provide this information about Dionysius: "De Div. Nom. c. 3 § 1, c. 4 § 1. seqq., c. 7. § 1. et de Mystica Theolog. c. 7. § 1. seqq. Cfr. de his Qq. disp. de Scientia Christi, q. 7. in corp. et in fine."

the second way consists of a mixture, as it were, of grace and natural and acquired industriousness.

50. Now *the place*, to which he ascended, can be fittingly understood as the eminence or height of the *contemplative life*. For a mountain is the place *for teaching*. Thus it is said in Matthew 5:1 that "Jesus went up the mountain. And when he was seated," etc. And from this it is given us to understand that the contemplative life abounds in *understanding*. And therefore, in the person of contemplatives Isaiah says in 2:3: "Come, and let us go up to the mountain of the Lord and to the house of the God of Jacob, and he will teach us," etc. So it is also said of Moses in Exodus 24:18 that "he went up into the mountain, and was there for forty days and forty nights," and then received the Law. – A mountain is also a place for *sacrifice*, according to what Genesis 22:2 has: "Take your only begotten son Isaac, whom you love . . . and offer him for a holocaust upon one of the mountains that I will show you." And Exodus 3:12 reads: "When you will have brought the people out of Egypt, you will offer sacrifice to God upon this mountain." From this one gathers that the contemplative life abounds in *devoted dedication*. So the contemplative soul speaks in The Song of Songs 4:6: "I will go to the mountain of myrrh and to the hill of frankincense," etc. – The mountain is also the place for *fire* on account of the rays of the sun. So Sirach 43:4 says: "The sun burns the mountains three times as much and breathes out fiery rays." And this because of its great reflections according to what 1 Maccabees 6:39 reads: "The sun shone upon the shields of gold and of brass, and the mountains glittered therewith . . . like lamps of fire." From this it is understood that the contemplative life abounds in *love*. As a sign of this it is said in Exodus 19:18: "All Mount Sinai was smoking, because the Lord had come down

upon it in fire." – A mountain is also a place of *refuge*. So Genesis 19:17 says: "Save yourself on the mountain." And it is said in Matthew 24:16 about imminent persecution: "Then let those who are in Judea flee to the mountains." From this it is understood that the contemplative life abounds in *having defenses*. So in the person of the contemplative man it is said in the Psalm: "I have lifted up my eyes to the mountains, from whence help will come to me" (120:1) – A mountain is also a place of *silence*. Whence it is said in 1 Kings 19:8–9 that "Elijah came to the mountain of God,[104] Horeb . . . and abode in a cave." And of Christ it is said in Matthew 14:23 that "he went up the mountain by himself to pray." From which it is understood that the contemplative soul abounds in *tranquility*. Wherefore, it is said of contemplatives in the Psalm: "Let the mountains receive peace for the people, and the hills justice" (71:3). – A mountain is also a place for *pasturing*, according to what Job 39:8 has: "He looked round about the mountains of his pasture and every green thing." Ezekiel 34:14 reads: "I will feed them in the most fruitful pastures. Their pastures will be on the high mountains of Israel." From which it is understood that the contemplative soul abounds in *sweetness*. Wherefore, Joel 3:18 says this about contemplation: "On that day the mountains will drop down sweetness, and the hills will flow with milk and honey."[105] – And finally, the mountain is a place of *eminence or peak*, according to what Isaiah 2:2 has: "The mountain of the house of the Lord will be prepared on the top of mountains." And of Elijah it is said in 1 Kings 18:42–44 that "he went up to the top of the mountain"

---

[104] Bonaventure has adapted Genesis 19:8 to his purposes. It reads: "And he (Elijah) arose, and ate, and drank, and walked (*ambulavit*; Bonaventure has *pervenit*) in the strength of that food forty days and forty nights, unto the mountain of God, Horeb."

[105] The Vulgate does not have *et mel* ("and honey").

and a little while later that he saw a little cloud rising up from the sea. From this we understand that the contemplative life exceedingly abounds in *the ability to rise up*. As a sign of this the Lord ascended into heaven from the Mount of Olives. And of the holy soul it is said through the figure of Anna in Tobit 11:5 that "she sat on the top of a mountain," for in the person of such people it is said in Philippians 3:20: "Our way of life is in heaven." – From these considerations we can see the excellence of the contemplative life, and how desirable it should be. For it is full of *discernment, devoted dedication, love, security, tranquility, sweetness,* and *the ability to rise up.*[106]

51. (Verse 29). *And it happened that as he was praying*, etc. After treating the antecedents to Christ's Transfiguration, the Evangelist now mentions the things that *accompany* it. And these were threefold, scilicet, *the brightness of Christ's countenance, the radiance of his clothing, his honorable companions*, so that Christ may appear to possess glory within himself, around and alongside him, and thus be in no way lacking in glory.

So first, with regard to *the brightness of his countenance*, it is said: *Now it came to pass that as he prayed, the appearance of his countenance was changed.* Indeed, it was changed through the unsurpassable refulgence of brightness. So it is said in Matthew 17:2 that "He was transfigured before them, and his face shone as the sun." It is no wonder, for in this way he shows the glory of the resurrection, of which Matthew 13:43 says: "Then the just will shine forth like the sun in the kingdom of their Father." And so in the manifestation of this glori-

---

[106] In this section I have translated Bonaventure's *sursum-agilitas* and *agilitas* as "the ability to rise up."

ous brightness he showed his disciples the kingdom of God, for *brightness and glory* are the principal gifts of the resurrected, according to what 1 Corinthians 15:40–42 reads: "There is one glory for the earthly, another for the heavenly, another brightness for the sun, another brightness for the moon, and another of the stars. For star differs from star in brightness. So also with the resurrection of the dead."[107] – Now Christ assumed this gift of *brightness and glory*, from its aspect of *subtlety,* when he was born, although his mother's womb was closed. From its aspect of *agility* when he walked on the water. From its aspect of *impassibility* when he handed over his body to his disciples in the Sacrament.[108] And so also here he assumed *brightness and glory* for the moment, but did not lose his own shape. Rather he had his own shape, and the quality took place like an *affected quality* with the brightness and glory like *something to be taken on.* For just as a person with a pale face blushes for a time on account of shame and then after a while resumes his pale face, so too has the earthly body been affected by supernal and wonderful power and for a time has become refulgent and heavenly.[109] Either there was another gift of bright-

---

[107] I have preserved the difference Paul makes between *gloria* ("glory") and *claritas* ("brightness") and have brought these two meanings into my translation of Bonaventure's use of *claritas* ("brightness and glory").

[108] On p. 233, n. 4 QuarEd say that Bonaventure's opinion here stems from Hugh of St. Victor and Innocent III and refer to Bonaventure's Opera Omnia 6:324, n. 5 for more detail.

[109] On p. 233, n. 5 QuarEd helpfully point to Aristotle as the source for Bonaventure's thought here. I refer to Aristotle's *Categoriae,* chapter 9 which deals with "qualities." I quote from *The Works of Aristotle,* Volume I (London: Oxford University Press, 1928), 9b, lines 28–34: "Those conditions, however, which arise from causes which may easily be rendered ineffective or speedily removed, are called, not qualities, but affections: for we are not said to be such and such in virtue of them. The man who blushes through shame is not

ness and glory in him or not. But there was another brightness and glory, and it was conformable to that supernal brightness and glory, which by divine power did not destroy the eyes of the disciples.[110] Rather it comforted them, so that they could say what Qoheleth 11:7 has: "The light is sweet, and it is delightful for the eyes to see the sun."

52. Now second, with respect to *the brightness of his clothing* the text continues: *And his clothing radiant white*, that is, became so. For the white was so great, that it shone exceedingly bright, as it is said in Mark 9:2: "His clothing became shining, exceedingly white as snow, as no fuller on earth can whiten." This is no wonder, for this designated the brightness which will appear in the saints, according to what Revelation 3:5 reads: "The person who conquers will be arrayed thus in white garments." Revelation 7:13 has: "These who are clothed in white robes, who are they? And whence have they come?," etc.

53. (Verses 30–31). Third, with regard to *his honorable companions* the text adds: *And behold, two men were talking with him.*[111] For it was not fitting for the Lord of glory to be seen alone, but to have honorable companions. Therefore, the text continues: *And these were Moses and Elijah, appearing in majesty.* Now these two

---

said to be a constitutional blusher, nor is the man who becomes pale through fear said to be constitutionally pale. He is said rather to have been affected. Thus such conditions are called affections, not qualities."

[110] Bonaventure seems to bring 1 Corinthians 15:40–42 back into his discussion, but his usual clarity suffers as a result. On p. 233 n. 6 QuarEd refer to the Glossa Ordinaria (from Bede) on Luke 9:29. See CCSL cxx, p. 205.

[111] On p. 233, n. 9 QuarEd correctly indicate that the Vulgate reads *cum illo* ("with him") while Bonaventure has *cum eo* ("with him").

were persons to be held in honor. I say: *Moses* because of *the giving of the Law*, according to what Numbers 12:7–8 states: "But it is not so with my servant Moses, who is the most faithful in my entire house. For I speak to him face to face and plainly and without riddles and figures. He sees the Lord." And *Elijah* because of the outstanding character of his prophecy together with his miracle working. Wherefore, Sirach 48:4–5 says, speaking to Elijah: "Who can glory like you? Who raised up a dead man from below, from the lot of death, by the word of God?" So in order to show their outstanding nature the Lord appeared to both in a special manner in a figure on Mount Horeb. Indeed, he appeared first to Moses, as it is said in Exodus 3:1–6, then afterwards to Elijah, as it is said in 1 Kings 19:8–13, namely, on that same Mount Horeb. – Thus, because of their extraordinary honor and dignity he appeared in their company. Of course, another interpretation is that he appeared with them because one of them was dead, the other alive; one from heaven, the other from the netherworld, so that there may be a witness of every kind and show that he it is who will make the living and the dead glorious.[112] So it is said in the Glossa: "Therefore, the living and the dead appear, so that they may signify Christ about to die and again about to be victorious, and so

---

[112] On pp. 233–234, n. 13 QuarEd quote three authorities. In Book III of his commentary on Matthew 17:3 Jerome observes: "So that he may deepen the faith of the Apostles, he gives as a sign from heaven, Elijah descending thence whither he had ascended, and Moses rising up from the netherworld. . . . " Chrysostom's Homily 56 (alias 57) on Matthew, n. 2 reads: "So that they might learn that he has power both over life and death and can equally command heavenly and terrestrial beings. For which reason he brings forth him, who had been dead, and the one who had not yet died. . . . " The Glossa Ordinaria (from Bede) on Luke 9:30 comments: "Through *Moses* the infernal, through *Elijah* the heavenly, through *the Apostles* the earthly are signified as coming to judgment." See CCSL cxx, p. 205.

that we may live to God and be dead to the world."[113] –
Another interpretation is that these two appear, so that
it may be shown that the Law and the Prophets were in
harmony with the Lord Jesus Christ. Therefore, the
Glossa of Bede comments: "Moses, the lawgiver, and
Elijah, the most distinguished of the Prophets, appear
with the Word in order to demonstrate that he was the
one spoken of in the Law and the Prophets and whom
the Law and the Prophets promised,"[114] so that what
Matthew 21:9 says may be verified: "Those who went
before and those who followed cried out: Hosanna to the
son of David."

54. (Verse 31). And since the Law and the Prophets not
only attested to the glory of Christ, but also to his *passion*, which is the way to glory, the text adds: *And they
were speaking of his exodus,*[115] *which he was about to
fulfill in Jerusalem.* Rightly is his passion called an *excess*, for in it was an excess of *humility*, according to
what Philippians 2:7–8 says: "He emptied himself, taking the form of a servant. . . . He humbled himself," etc.
There was also an excess of *poverty*, according to what
Lamentations 3:19 states: "Remember my poverty and
transgression, wormwood and gall." There was an excess of *sorrow*, according to what Lamentations 1:12
has: "O all you who pass by the way," etc.[116] There was
also an excess of *love*, according to what Ephesians 2:4
states: "God, who is rich in mercy, by reason of his very

---

[113] On p. 234, n. 1 QuarEd state that this is the Glossa Ordinaria.
[114] On p. 234, n. 3 QuarEd state that this is the Glossa Ordinaria.
See CCSL cxx, pp. 205–206.
[115] In what follows Bonaventure will play on the dual meaning of
excessus ("exodus" and "excess").
[116] The first part of Lamentations 1:12 reads: "O all you that pass by
the way, attend and see whether there be any sorrow like to my sorrow. . . . "

great love . . . when we were dead by reason of our sins," etc. And Romans 8:32 reads: "Who did not spare his own Son, but delivered him for us all, how has he not granted us all things with him?"[117] – He fulfilled this excess/exodus in Jerusalem, where he was crucified, where the consummation of our redemption took place, according to what Hebrews 2:10 says: "It was fitting for him, for whom are all things and through whom are all things, who had brought many sons into glory, to perfect through sufferings the author of their salvation." Wherefore, he himself also predicted this to his disciples in Luke 18:31: "Behold, we are going up to Jerusalem, and all things will be consummated," etc.[118]

55. Now according to the *spiritual* understanding during prayer and contemplation *the human face is made to shine*, because while the face of our mind is turned to God, it is being illuminated, made better, and perfected. There was a figure of this in Exodus 34:29 where it is said: "when Moses came down from the mountain, . . . his face appeared radiant from conversation with the Lord."[119] So 2 Corinthians 3:18 also has: "But we all, with faces unveiled, reflecting as in a mirror the glory of the Lord, are being transformed into his very image from glory to glory, as through the Spirit of the Lord." – Not only this, but also *their clothing shines brightly*, be-

---

[117] Bonaventure's quotation does not have *etiam* ("even") which occurs twice and has *donavit* ("granted") instead of *donabit* ("will grant").

[118] In the last three sentences Bonaventure has been playing on the Latin *consummatio/consummare* ("to perfect, to consummate, to accomplish").

[119] A translation of all of Exodus 34:29 is: "And when Moses came down from the mount Sinai, he held the two tables of the testimony, and knew not that his face appeared radiant from conversation with the Lord." The Vulgate uses *cornuta* (literally "horned") which I have translated as "radiant."

cause their way of life has become blameless, according
to what Philippians 2:15 says: "that you may be guile-
less, without blemish . . ."[120] in the midst of a depraved
and perverse people, among whom you shine like stars
in the world." One should not wonder at this, for such
people are conformed to the Lord Jesus Christ, in accordance with what Romans 13:12–14 reads: "Let us put on
the armor of light. Let us walk becomingly as in the
day. . . . Not in revelry and drunkenness . . . but let us
put on the Lord Jesus Christ." – Not only this, but also
they converse with Moses and Elijah, for in prayer understanding is given to men and women of the Scriptures and of the mysteries proposed therein, according
to what Daniel 2:17–19 says: "And Daniel went into the
house . . . and indicated to his companions that they
should seek mercy . . . from the God of heaven concerning this secret. . . . Then was the mystery revealed to
Daniel . . . at night." And Wisdom 7:7 has: "I desired,
and understanding was given to me. I called upon God,
and the spirit of wisdom came upon me." Therefore,
Moses and Elijah are speaking with the transfigured
Lord to give certitude to the vision, for, as Richard says:
"In no way must one give adherence to any revelation
that cannot conform to the New and Old Testament."[121]

---

[120] For some reason Bonaventure leaves out of his quotation of Philippians 2:15 the expression *sine reprehensione* ("without blame")
which would correspond to the point he has just made, to wit, "their
way of life has become blameless" (*irreprehensibilis*). He also leaves
out *filii Dei* ("children of God").

[121] Bonaventure's quotation is based on chapter 81 of Richard of St.
Victor's *The Twelve Patriarchs* (*Benjamin Minor*). See PL
196:57B–58A, esp. 196:57C: *Suspecta est mihi omnis veritas quam
non confirmat Scripturarum auctoritas nec Christum in sua clarifi-
catione recipio, si non assistant ei Moyses et Elias* ("Every truth is
suspect to me which the authority of Scripture does not confirm. Nor
do I accept Christ in his glorification if Moses and Elijah are not assisting him"). See also Grover A. Zinn, *Richard of St Victor*, pp.
138–39, for a translation of chapter 81 of *The Twelve Patriarchs*.

Luke 9:32–36
Consideration of the Glory Revealed

56. *Now Peter and his companions*, etc. After the manifestation of the glory promised the Evangelist now adds contemplation of what had been manifested. Moreover, he gives this sufficient narrative development, for he treats it in four stages. First, with regard to its *beginning*. Second, relative to its *progress* where verse 33 says: *And it came to pass as they were parting from him*. Third, concerning its *consummation* where verse 34 reads: *And as he was saying these things*. Fourth, about its *cessation* where verse 35 has: *And there came a voice out of the cloud*, etc.

Now it is to be noted that in *the contemplation* of divine revelations two things occur, as it were, *in the beginning*, namely, a *heaviness* on the part of nature and *assistance* on the part of grace. The first creates drowsiness, the second kindles a fire.

57. (Verse 32). So first, regarding *the heaviness* of sleeping nature it is said: *Now Peter and his companions were heavy with sleep*. And thus all were faint. That is no wonder, for they were surrounded by weakness. So Wisdom 9:15 says: "The corruptible body is a load upon the soul, and the earthly dwelling weighs down the mind that reflects on many things." – Further, since the nature of the external senses impedes us from keeping a steady eye on the eternal light, it is necessary at the beginning of contemplation that men and women, as people drifting off to rest, remove themselves from their senses, as if through sleep which does not occur without the senses becoming drowsy. So the contemplative soul says in The Song of Songs 5:2: "I sleep, and my heart keeps vigil." And Job 33:15–16 reads: "When deep sleep

falls upon men and women,[122] and they are sleeping in their beds, then he opens their ears and through teaching instructs them in what they are to learn." And of this it is said in Genesis 2:21: "The Lord cast a deep sleep upon Adam."

58. Secondly, concerning *the assistance* on the part of grace that kindles a fire, the text continues: *And awakening, they saw his majesty and the two men who were standing with him.* This *keeping awake* occurs through the desire and love of the Holy Spirit, according to what Isaiah 26:9 says: "Lord, my soul has desired you in the night, but with my spirit within me I will keep awake and watch for you in the early morning." Now this is very necessary in *prayer.* So the Lord says to Peter and his companions in Matthew 26:41: "Keep awake and pray, that you may not enter into temptation. The spirit indeed is willing," etc. Mark 13:33 has: "Take heed, keep awake, and pray." And Mark 13:37 reads: "What I say to one,[123] I say to all: Keep awake." – Now to this watchfulness he principally challenges us with *the promised reward*, according to what Luke 12:37 below has: "Blessed are those servants whom the master on his return will find watching. Amen I say to you," etc. He also challenges through *the danger envisioned*, according to what 1 Peter 5:8 says: "Be sober. Be watchful, for your adversary the devil," etc. And Matthew 24:43 reads: "Amen, I say to you: If the householder had known at what hour the thief was coming, he would certainly have watched," etc.[124]

---

[122] The Vulgate reads *virorum* ("of men").

[123] The Vulgate has *Quod autem vobis dico* ("But what I say to you").

[124] On p. 235 n. 5 QuarEd suggest that Bonaventure may have transferred the beginning of Matthew 24:34 ("Amen I say to you") to the beginning of Matthew 24:43 which reads "But of this be assured that."

59. *Watchfulness* is exceedingly necessary for *contemplation*, for the grace proffered is very quickly withdrawn. So The Song of Songs 5:6 says: "I opened the bolt of my door to my beloved, but he had turned aside and was gone." – Through this *watchfulness* is seen *the divine majesty in creatures*, in accordance with what Wisdom 13:5 reads: "From the greatness of the beauty and of the creature," etc.[125] Wherefore, Isaiah 6:1–3 has: "I saw the Lord sitting upon a high throne . . . and full," etc.[126] *The divine humility in the Scriptures* is seen. For which reason it says: *And two men*, that is the Law and the Prophets, concerning which vision Luke 24:45 below says: "He opened their minds that they might understand the Scriptures." And again in Luke 24:27 it says: "Beginning with Moses and all the Prophets, he interpreted to them in all the Scriptures," etc. – For the sake of these two ways of contemplating a twofold book was made: the Scriptures and creatures, which are designated by the ascent and descent on *Jacob's ladder* in Genesis 28:12, by *the going in and the going out through the gate* in John 10:9, and by *the eagle and its young* in Job 39:27, 30: "Will the eagle soar up at your command?" "Its young will lick up blood."[127]

---

[125] Wisdom 13:5 in full reads: "From the greatness of the beauty and of the creature, the creator of them may be seen, so as to be known thereby."

[126] As with Wisdom 13:5, Bonaventure gives such an abbreviated quotation that his reason for using it is almost lost. Isaiah 6:1–3 reads: "I saw the Lord, sitting upon a high and elevated throne. And his train filled the temple. Upon it stood the seraphim. The one had six wings, and the other had six wings. With two they covered his face, and with two they covered his feet, and with two they flew. And they cried out one to another, and said: Holy, holy, holy, the Lord God of hosts, all the earth is full of his glory."

[127] Bonaventure's last example is truncated. Job 39:27–30 describes the eagle's soaring to places where there is no access and how the mother eagle brings the food of bloody prey to her young.

60. (Verse 33). *And it came to pass, as they were parting from him.* After the initiation of contemplation the text adds *the progress of contemplation*. In this two things are primarily required, namely, exceeding *joy at the gift bestowed* and exceeding *desire that it continue*, in accordance with what Sirach 24:27–29 reads: "My spirit is sweet beyond honey. . . . They that eat me will still hunger, and they that drink me will still thirst." For through these two the soul in the act of contemplation is depicted, as one eating food to satiety and at the same time longing for more.

First, then, with regard to joy at the gift bestowed, it says: And it came to pass as they were parting from him, that is, their desire was to depart. Peter said to Jesus: Master, it is good for us to be here. In this Peter shows in what a wonderful manner he has accepted the glory of contemplation for himself, as if he were saying what the prophet says in the Psalm: "But it is good for me to adhere to God" (72:28). For as it is said in Lamentations 3:25: "The Lord is good to those who hope in him, to the soul that seeks him." And the reason Peter said: It is good for us to be here, is that it is good to wait for Christ, according to what Lamentations 3:26 says: "It is good to wait with silence for the salvation of God." – But it is a greater good to taste Christ. I Peter 2:3 says: "If, indeed, you have tasted that the Lord is sweet." So Wisdom 12:1 also has: "How good and sweet is your Spirit, O Lord, in all," that is, in the right of heart, according to what the Psalmist says: "How good is God to Israel, to those who are right of heart" (72:1). Wherefore, in the person of Christ and of the contemplative soul Elkanah says to Hannah, his wife: "Hannah, why are you weeping? . . . Why are you tormenting your heart? Am I not better to you than ten children?" – But the greatest good is to rejoice with Christ, according to what Philippians 1:23 reads: "To depart and be with Christ is much better." And Matthew 25:23 has: "Well done, good and faithful servant. Since you have been faithful over a few things, I will set you over many. Enter into the joy of your Lord." – The first is good, for it is merit. The second is a greater good, for it is provision for a journey or viaticum. The third, however, is the greatest good, for it is reward. Peter wanted to include all these ways in what he said, especially the way of joy: It is good for us to be here.

61. Second, with regard to *the desire that the gift continue*, the text adds: *And let us set up three tents*, so that our joy may continue, as the children of Israel did figuratively according to what Leviticus 23:42–43 says: "Every one that is of the race of Israel will dwell in tents, so that your posterity may know that I made the children of Israel to dwell in tents." – Since, however, he did not want these three to dwell in a uniform manner or have one tent for all three, he sought to make an individual tent for each one. So the text continues: *One for you*, as the leader. *One for Moses*, as the legislator. *And one for Elijah*, as the excellent preacher. In this way the tents of their mansions[128] are distinguished by reason of their differences in dignity. For it will be so in the kingdom of heaven, according to what John 14:2 reads: "In my Father's house there are many mansions." – Now Peter said this out of *the surpassing desire* that contemplatives customarily possess. And therefore, it is added: *Not knowing what he said*, namely, on account of the overpowering nature of the desire, according to the Psalm: "For my heart has been inflamed, and my innards have been overturned. And I am reduced to

---

[128] Bonaventure smuggles in "mansions" here to prepare for his subsequent quotation from John 14:2.

nothing, and I knew nothing" (72:21–22). And on account of *the profundity of the mystery*, in accordance with what The Song of Songs 6:10–11 says: "I went down into the garden of nuts, to see the fruits of the valleys and to look. . . . I did not know. My soul troubled me on account of the chariots of Aminadab."[129] And because of this twofold reason Peter did not know what he was saying. So the Glossa reads: "Even though Peter through his weakness does not know what to say, he, nevertheless, gives an indication of the zeal which is innate to him when he was delighted to see them and even sought to make them stay. He was in error, for he wanted the kingdom to be given to him and his fellow Apostles on this earth and in this mortal flesh. But this kingdom was promised to those in heaven who have been stripped of their mortal flesh."[130]

62. Now it is to be noted that Peter was wrong in the first place because *he wanted to remain in a state* from which one has to move. For it is said in Hebrews 13:14: "Here we have no lasting city." But Peter wanted to remain here. In this some are indeed reprehensible. They want to ascend to the height of contemplation, want to rest there, and refuse to descend to the labor of action.[131] And these are designated by *the sons of Ruben*, of whom it is said in Numbers 32:5 that they did not want to re-

---

[129] The Song of Songs 6:10 reads in its entirety: "I went down into the garden of nuts to see the fruits of the valleys, and to look if the vineyard had flourished, and the pomegranates budded." It is not clear what The Song of Songs 6:11 means. Bonaventure obviously quoted it, for it had the words "I did not know."

[130] On p. 236, n. 9 QuarEd indicate that Bonaventure quotes the Glossa Ordinaria (from Bede) apud Lyranum on Luke 9:33. For Bede, see CCSL cxx, p. 206. Their note also indicates a number of variant readings. I have tried to produce a smooth translation of a difficult text.

[131] This seems to be a circumlocution for "the active life."

main on the other side of the Jordan. In Numbers 32:6 Moses said to them: "What? Shall your brothers go to fight, and will you sit here?" As if to say: No. Therefore, "Jacob saw a ladder in his sleep," in Genesis 28:12, and "angels," not resting, but "ascending and descending on it." – Second, he was wrong in this that *he believed that the shadow had given way to reality*, although the Apostle said in 1 Corinthians 13:12: "We see now in a mirror in an obscure way." Further, he believed that the tent of glory was *material*, when, however, it is *spiritual*, according to what the Psalm says: "I will enter into[132] the place of the admirable tent and tabernacle" (41:5). This is "the tabernacle which the Lord has erected, and not human beings," as it is said in Hebrews 8:2. And contemplatives must be especially beware, lest they be deceived by figures said to have come to fulfillment. – Third, he was in error because *he wanted to separate what was united*, and wanted to divide into three what was one. For there is one tent and tabernacle in the glory of the Saints according to what John 17:24 reads: "Father, I will that where I am, they also . . . may be with me." And Revelation 21:3 says: "Behold, the tabernacle of God with men and women, and he will dwell with them." And John 10:16 has: "There will be one fold and one shepherd." Now Peter's mistake did not stem from a judgment or assent on his part. Rather he was out of his mind, a state about which 2 Corinthians 5:13 says: "If we were out of our mind, it was for God," etc. And the Psalm says: "There is Benjamin a youth, who is out of his mind" (67:28).[133]

---

[132] On p. 236, n. 12 QuarEd rightly indicate that the Vulgate reads *transibo* ("I will go over") whereas Bonventure has *ingrediar* ("I will enter").

[133] I have not used the customary translation "to be in ecstasy," in order to preserve Bonaventure's play on the word *excessus* throughout this section. A rewarding study would be an investigation of the in-

63. (Verse 34). *As he was speaking thus*, etc. After dis-
cussing the beginning of and progress into contemplation, the Evangelist sets down here *the state* or consummation *of contemplation*. Now contemplation is consummated in a twofold way. The first of these is *the
manifestation of frightful majesty*. The second is *the
revelation of credible truth*.

So the first deals with *the manifestation of frightful
majesty* where the text says: *But as he was speaking
thus, there came a cloud*. This cloud was manifesting the
divine majesty. So the frightful God appeared to the
children of Israel in a cloud, as it is said in Exodus
40:31–33: "After all things were perfected, the cloud
covered the tabernacle of the testimony, and the glory of
the Lord filled it. Neither could Moses go into the tabernacle of the covenant, since the cloud was covering all
things and the majesty of the Lord was shining
brightly." Similarly, it is said in 1 Kings 8:10–11: "It
came to pass when the priests had come out . . . , a cloud
filled the house of the Lord. And the priests could not
minister because of the cloud. For the glory of the Lord
had filled the house of the Lord." Whence a cloud was a
sign of supernal glory and majesty.[134] – And therefore,
the text continues: *And overshadowed them, and they
were afraid*. For they felt the divine power in the cloud,
about which Luke 1:35 above says: "The power of the
Most High will overshadow you." And therefore, *they
were afraid* because of the presence of the highest

---

fluence that Richard of St. Victor's *The Twelve Patriarchs* (*Benjamin
Minor*) and *The Mystical Ark* (*Benjamin Major*) had on Bonaventure's interpretation of Christ's Transfiguration.

[134] On p. 237, n. 4 QuarEd quote part of Chrysostom's Homily 56
(alias 57), n. 3, where Chrysostom cites other biblical parallels to
"cloud" as the place where God always appears: Psalm 96:2; 103:3;
Isaiah 19:1; Acts 1:9; Daniel 7:13.

power, like Job, who said in Job 31:23: "I have always feared God as waves swelling over me." And Jeremiah 10:7 reads: "Who will not fear you, O king of the nations," etc.[135]

64. Now according to *the mystical* sense *the cloud* can be understood to be the flesh of Christ.[136] First, because it tempers the light of divinity for our eyes, so that we can see. Exodus 19:9 has: "Now I will come to you in the darkness of a cloud, that the people may hear me speaking with you." – Second, because it is the vehicle of divine light upon a dark earth, according to what Isaiah 19:1 has: "The Lord will ascend upon a slight cloud and will enter into Egypt."[137] – Third, because it had its origin in bitter human nature which is worthy of punishment, with the Virgin Mary as mediatrix. This was prefigured

---

[135] On p. 237, n. 5 QuarEd provide a lengthy, but ultimately unconvincing parallel from Book III of Jerome's Commentary on Matthew 17:6. Jerome gives three reasons why the Apostles were afraid.

[136] On p. 237, n. 6 QuarEd refer their readers to the opinions of Augustine and Bernard of Clairvaux with the indication: "Confer Volume 6, page 358, n. 6." I have ferreted out the texts the editors refer to. In Sermon 20.7 on The Song of Songs Bernard writes: "The shade of Christ, I suggest, is his flesh which overshadowed Mary and tempered for her the bright splendor of the Spirit." See *On the Song of Songs I*, translated by Kilian Walsh, The Works of Bernard of Clairvaux, Volume 2, Cistercian Fathers Series 4 (Kalamazoo: Cistercian Publications, 1976), 153. In his Tractate 34., n. 4 on the Gospel of John Augustine writes: "Do not despise the cloud of the flesh; he is covered with a cloud not that he may be darkened, but that [his brightness] may be rendered endurable." See *St. Augustine, Tractates on the Gospel of John 28–54*, translated by John W. Rettig, FC 88 (Washington, D.C.: Catholic University of America Press, 1993), 64. Further, see Bonaventure on John 8:12 in his Opera Omnia 6:338 (#18).

[137] On p. 237, n. 7 QuarEd indicate that Jerome comments on Isaiah 19:1 in this vein: "*The Lord ascended upon a slight cloud*, the body of Holy Virgin Mary...or certainly, his body which was conceived by the Holy Spirit. And he entered into the Egypt of this world, etc."

in 1 Kings 18:44: "Behold, a little cloud like a human foot arose out of the sea."[138] – Fourth, because it pours forth the water of salvific grace which it has drawn from its source, when it is moved by the wind of prayer. Thus, Sirach 43:24 says: "A remedy for all is the speedy coming of a cloud."[139] – From this contemplatives learn that they not only lift their eyes to the radiant light of the deity, but also to the dark cloud of humanity. This is prefigured in John 1:51 where the Lord said to Nathanael: "You will see angels," that is, contemplatives, "ascending and descending upon the Son of Man," because in his humanity is hidden divine majesty.

65. (Verse 35). Now second, with regard to *the revelation of credible truth*, the text has: *But as they entered the cloud*,[140] that is, which instilled reverence in them, according to what is said in Exodus 24:18: "Moses, entering into the midst of the cloud, ascended the mountain," where he heard divine revelations. – So the text now

---

[138] On p. 237, n. 8 QuarEd offer a very helpful parallel to Bonaventure's third point. They quote "Ioan. 44. episc. Ierosol., in libro de Institutione monachorum, c. 32. 9 Bibliothec. Patrum etc. per Marg. de la Bigne, Paris, 1610. tom. VIII, pag. 778." I translate the text the editors provide: "For through this, namely, that Elijah's servant saw a little cloud arise from the sea, God revealed to Elijah that a certain infant girl (scilicet Blessed Mary), signified by that little cloud and small like that cloud because of her humility, would be born of sinful human, nature, designated by the sea. This infant girl would be pure of all filth of sin already from her beginning, just as that little cloud came from the bitter sea without any bitterness. For although that little cloud was originally of the same, nature as the sea, it has different qualities and properties. Indeed, the sea was heavy and bitter, but the little cloud was light and sweet. So . . . etc."

[139] On p. 237, n. 9 QuarEd state: "Cfr. Serm. 40 in Appendice serm. August. (alias 201. de Tempore), n. 5, et Isid., Qq. in III. Reg. c. 8, n. 4."

[140] On p. 237, n. 11 QuarEd rightly state that the Vulgate does, not have *autem* ("but") and concludes Luke 9:34 with "as they entered the cloud" and commences Luke 9:35 with "And there came a voice. . . . "

states: *There came a voice out of the cloud, saying: This
is my beloved Son.* He shows who he is *through distinctions*, so that he may manifest that he alone is *Son by
nature.* Whence the Psalm says: "From the womb before
the day star I begot you" (109:3). And the distinctions
are found here in this that he says *this*, and that he says
my, and that he says *beloved.* In this he declares that
the property of sonship in Christ is *personal* and *connatural* and *co-equal.* It is shown to be *personal* through
the pronoun which indicates a particular person. So he
himself said in John 8:25: "I am the beginning, who is
speaking to you."[141] – It is shown to be *connatural*
through this that he says *my*, according to what the
Psalmist has: "The Lord said to me: You are my son.
This day I have begotten you" (2:7). For he has no other
father except God. Relative to this distinction it is said
in John 20:17: "I ascend to my Father and your Father."
– It is further shown to be *co-equal* in this that he adds
beloved, that is, first and best. Therefore, The Song of
Songs 5:10 reads: "My beloved . . . is chosen out of thousands." And John 5:20 says: "The Father loves the Son
and shows[142] everything to him."

66. And since this truth was credible and was the basis
of the credibility of everything said of Christ, the text
continues: *Hear him*, not only with your bodily ears, but
also with your heart as the Prophet says in the Psalm:

---

[141] Bonaventure also quotes John 8:25 in his commentary on Luke
7:14 (#25), 8:15 (#22), 11:31 (#66), and Luke 22:44 (#51). See my detailed, note on Luke 11:31 (#66) below where I emphasize that
Bonaventure has linked John 8:25 via its use of *principium* ("beginning") to John 1:1 ("In the beginning was the Word") and 1:3 and
generated a profound christological affirmation, which is entirely
lost in the Confraternity version: "Why do I speak to you at all?" See,
nAB of the Greek of John 8:25: "What I told you from the beginning."

[142] The Vulgate has *demonstrat* ("shows") while Bonaventure reads
ostendit ("shows").

"I will hear what the Lord may speak in me" (84:9). *Hear*, I say, with all *reverence*, according to the counsel of Sirach 32:9: "Hear in silence, and for your reverence good grace will come to you." *Hear him*, with all *obedience*, according to what Sirach 24:30 says: "Those who hear me will not be confounded, and they who work by me will not sin."[143] *Hear him*, with all *diligence*. Therefore, Luke 19:48 below has: "All the people hung on his words, listening to him," etc. – Now this voice strengthened the hearts of the disciples, so that their teaching itself might become authentic because of it, according to what 2 Peter 1:16–18 says: "For we were not following unlearned tales,[144] when we made known to you the power and coming of our Lord Jesus Christ, but we had been eyewitnesses of his grandeur. For he received from God the Father . . . when we were with him on the holy mountain."

67. (Verse 36). *And after the voice had ceased*, etc. Here in the last place and after the consummation of contemplation, the Evangelist mentions *its cessation*, concerning which he introduces two points. The first deals with *the return to the apostles' customary vision*. The second treats *the concealment of what had been shown in the vision*.

First, with regard to *the return to the apostles' customary vision*, it is said: *And when the voice ceased, Jesus was found alone*, namely, without Moses and Elijah and as he was before they had joined him. And this is what

---

[143] On p. 238, n. 5 QuarEd correctly indicate that the Vulgate has *audit* ("who hears me") while Bonaventure has *audiunt* ("who hear me").
[144] On p. 238, n. 6 QuarEd rightly mention that the Vulgate reads *doctas fabulas* ("learned tales") and propose an explanation for Bonaventure's reading and that of the Vulgate.

the spouse desired in The Song of Songs 8:1: "Who will give you to me for my brother, sucking the breasts of my mother, that I may find you alone[145] outside and kiss you and that now no one may despise me?" And here therefore, he is found *alone* with them, so that they may understand the transitory nature of the Law and prophecy and the permanence of evangelical truth, according to what is said in Matthew 24:35: "Heaven and earth will pass away, but my words will not pass away." Whence in the Glossa Bede says: "He is perceived *alone*, for, the shadow of the law and prophets having departed, the true light, the grace of the Gospel shining brightly, is revealed."[146] – Another interpretation is to show that he himself is the only one to be adored and for whom a tent or tabernacle is to be built, in accordance with Deuteronomy 6:13: "You shall fear the Lord your God and shall serve him only."[147] – Another interpretation is to show that he himself is the only one who can save. Therefore, Acts 4:12 reads: "There is no other name under heaven given to men and women by which we must be saved." And Hebrews 7:24–25 says: "But Jesus, because he continues forever, has an everlasting priesthood. Therefore, he is able to save at all times . . . he lives always to make intercession for us."[148]

68. Second, concerning *the concealment of what had been shown in the vision*, the text says: *And they kept*

---

[145] It seems that Bonaventure has adapted the quotation to his purposes, for the Vulgate does, not have *solum* ("alone").

[146] On p. 238, n. 9 QuarEd say that this is the Glossa Ordinaria apud Lyranum. They quote Book III of Jerome's Commentary on Matthew 17:8.

[147] On p. 238, n. 10 QuarEd refer to the Glossa cited in the previous, note and write: "You see, not Elijah,, not Moses, but him only, for whom one must construct a tabernacle in one's heart, etc."

[148] The Vulgate has *pro eis* ("for them") instead of Bonaventure's *pro, nobis* ("for us").

silence. For they realized what was written in Tobit 12:7: "It is good to conceal the secret of a king." For the time for speaking had not yet come. Rather it was the time for concealment, according to what Qoheleth 3:7 says: "There is a time for keeping silent, and a time for speaking." And Sirach 20:6–7 reads: "There is a person who keeps silence and who knows the right time. The wise person will keep silent till he sees the time to be an opportune time,[149] but a babbler and a fool will have no regard for time." – And such were the Apostles. For which reason this is added: *And told no one at that time any of those things they had seen.* Not because they wanted to conceal them out of covetousness, but because they were silent out of divine obedience. For the Lord had commanded this of them, according to what Matthew 17:9 has: "You shall not tell the vision to anyone, until the Son of Man has risen from the dead."

69. A triple reason can be given for this prohibition. The first concerns instruction for *contemplatives*, whose responsibility is to conceal divine secrets, according to what Isaiah 24:16 says: "My secret is kept to myself, my secret is kept to myself." Wherefore, Mary concealed her virginal childbirth for thirty years, Elizabeth her conception for five months, as it is said in Luke 1:24 above: "She secluded herself for five months." Paul kept his rapture secret for fourteen years, according to 2 Corinthians 12:2: "I know a man . . . who fourteen years ago," etc. – The second reason deals with the instruction for *preachers* that they not propose the word of truth unless they have discerned the capacity of their listeners to believe and accept the word, according to what Sirach 32:6 reads: "Where there is no hearing, do not pour out

---

[149] Bonaventure and Cardinal Hugh of St. Cher follow the expansive "the time to be an opportune time" of the Vulgate.

words." So in the Glossa it says: "The Lord commands that they keep silent until the Son of Man rise from the dead, lest it be incredible because of its magnitude and lest after such a great glory his subsequent crucifixion create a scandal."[150] And Jerome says: "So it is incumbent on teachers to consider the people in their audience, lest they begin to laugh before they listen."[151] – The third reason is for the instruction of *everyone*, lest anyone want to be praised or lest anyone might dare to praise in this life, according to what Sirach 11:30 has: "Praise not anyone before death, for a man is known by his children." So Ambrose states: "Praise after a person has died. Preach after his death."[152]

---

[150] On p. 239, n. 2 QuarEd identify this Glossa as Ordinaria apud Lyranum on Luke 9:36 (Strab. on Matthew 17:9 and Mark 9:8). They also state that this opinion is found in Book III of Jerome's Commentary on Matthew 17:9 where Jerome adds *apud rudes animos* ("among unsophisticated souls") after *tantam gloriam* ("such a great glory").

[151] On p. 239, n. 3 QuarEd state: "Even Cardinal Hugh (on Luke 9:36) attributes this opinion to Jerome (but where?) and indicates that it ends in this way: 'lest it is laughed at before it is heard.'" See Hugh of St. Cher, p. 188e. They then quote Isidore's III Sent. c. 43 in which he deals with discretion in teaching: "Now the primary strength of prudence is to discern the type of person one has to teach."

[152] On p. 239, n. 4 QuarEd indicate that this opinion, attributed to Ambrose, stems from Homily 78 or 2 of St. Maximus on St. Eusebius, Bishop of Vercelli. They also advise readers to check the second, nocturn for the Common of a Bishop Confessor in the Roman Breviary. Lectio VI of the Second, nocturn for this Common, taken from Homily 59 (or 2) of St. Maximus the Bishop about St. Eusebius of Vercelli, contains these words: *Lauda post vitam, magnifica post consummationem* ("Praise him after his life is over. Exalt him after he has died"). It seems that Bonaventure has introduced the strange verb *praedicare* ("to preach") to fit his earlier and second lesson that was for "preachers."

Luke 9:37–45
CONFIRMATION OF THE GLORY MANIFESTED

70. *Now it came to pass on the following day,* etc. After the manifestation of the glory promised and the contemplation of the glory manifested the Evangelist introduces here *confirmation of the glory considered* through the marvelous cure of a demoniac, who was mute and epileptic.[153] Relative to this healing the Evangelist makes three points in order to provide a perfect explication. First is *the occasion.* Second is *the efficient power* where verse 41 has: *And Jesus answered and said to them,*[154] etc. The third is *the consequent benefit,* and this where verse 44 reads: *And all were astounded,* etc.

The occasion consists of three items: the presence of the crowd that was gathering; the insistence of the man crying out; the violence of the demon possessing.[155]

71. (Verse 37). So the first item mentioned is *the presence of the crowd that was gathering,* where it says: *Now it came to pass on the following day, when they came down from the mountain,* namely, returning to the plain, *that a large crowd met them.* For they believed and were hoping to see signs, according to what John 6:2 reads: "And a great crowd followed Jesus, seeing the signs[156] that he worked on those who were sick." – And

---

[153] See #43 above where Bonaventure first presented this division of Luke's materials.

[154] On p. 239, n. 6 QuarEd rightly mention that the Vulgate has *dixit* ("he said") whereas Bonaventure reads *ait illis* ("he said to them").

[155] In this instance it is possible to capture in English some of Bonaventure's Latin playfulness: *praesentia multitudinis occurrentis, instantia hominis obsecrantis, violentia daemonis obsidentis.*

[156] The Vulgate reads: *Et sequebatur eum multitudo magna quia videbant signa* ("And a great crowd followed him, because they saw the signs"). Bonaventure has *videntes signa* ("seeing the signs").

note that a crowd did not accompany him going up the mountain, since they did not grasp sublime matters. So Exodus 19:23 says: "The people cannot ascend the mountain." But the crowd met him descending from the mountain, for it willingly embraced the humble matters of Christ.[157] Whence Matthew 8:1 has: "When Jesus had descended from the mountain, great crowds followed him."

72. Now from this it can be *spiritually* understood that the leisure of contemplation is for the few and is designated by *the ascent up the mountain*. But for many the exercise of action is designated by *his descent from the mountain* and meeting the crowd. And this was designated in Noah's ark, which, although it was 300 cubits in length, was completed with a single cubit at its height, as is evident from Genesis 6:15–16.[158] And therefore, the top of the mountain is fitting for *the contemplatives* and the level plain for *the workers*, in accordance with the Psalmist: "The mountains ascend, and the plains descend" (103:8). And this is what Bede said in the Glossa: "On the mountain he prays, teaches, manifests his majesty, reveals the voice of the Father to the

---

[157] To this, new Testament scholar it seems that Bonaventure's thought here echoes that of Paul in Romans 12:16: *Id ipsum invicem sentientes,, non alta sapientes, sed humilibus consentientes* ("Be of one mind towards one another. Do, not set your mind on high things, but condescend to the lowly"). On p. 239, n. 8 QuarEd refer to Ambrose Book V, n. 46. See CCSL xiv, p. 151 on Luke 6:17: "For how might the crowd see Christ except in the lowly? It did, not follow him to the heights. It did, not ascend to the sublime, etc." They also refer to Bede on Luke 9:37. See CCSL cxx, p. 208.

[158] Genesis 6:15–16 reads: "And thus shall you make it. The length of the ark shall be three hundred cubits, the breadth of it fifty cubits, and the height of it thirty cubits. You shall make a window in the ark, and with a single cubit shall you complete the top of it." On p. 239, n. 9 QuarEd refer to Opera Omnia 5:258, n. 2 for more detail on Bonaventure's interpretation of Genesis 6.

Apostles. But descending from the mountain, he is received by the crowd, struck by the weeping of the afflicted, reproves the sins of infidelity, and expels evil spirits."[159] In this place he touches upon the four acts of *contemplation*, which he designates by *the ascent* to the mountain, namely, *prayer, lectio divina, meditation on the divine,* and *revelation of secrets.* The four actions of *the active life* are shown in the *descent* from the mountain. For the prelate must condescend in four ways in the performance of actions for his subjects, that is, by *visiting them, having compassion on them, reproving their vices,* and *alleviating their needs.*[160] – But according to *the literal sense* the crowd meets Christ descending because they wanted to see the expulsion of the demon, which could not be accomplished by the disciples, as verse 40 adds a little later on: "I asked your disciples to cast it out, but they could not." So from such a great presence and desire of the people the stage is set for the performance of the miracle.

73. (Verse 38). In second place he introduces *the insistence of the man petitioning,* when he says: *And behold, a man from the crowd cried out.* In this he shows his affection in making supplication, in accordance with the Psalm: "When I cried to the Lord, he heard my voice" (30:23).[161] So 1 Maccabees 5:33 has: "They cried out to

---

[159] On p. 239, n. 10 QuarEd state that this is the Glossa Ordinaria. See CCSL cxx, p. 208 for Bede's more discursive contrasts, e.g., *Sursum discipulis mysteria regni reserat; deorsum turbis peccata infidelitatis exprobrat* ("Above he reserves the mysteries of the kingdom for the disciples; below he reproves the crowds for the sins of infidelity").

[160] On p. 239, n. 11 QuarEd write: "Cfr. Isido., III. Sent. c. 46, n. 1. seqq."

[161] On p. 240, n. 1 QuarEd are right to question whether this loose quotation is based on Psalm 30:23 or Psalm 21:25.

heaven[162] with trumpets and cried out in prayer." And of
Samuel it is said in 1 Samuel 15:11 that "grieved, he
cried unto the Lord all night." – And that this was *the
cry of prayer* is evident from what follows: *saying: Master, I entreat you. Look at my son, for he is my only one.*
In this prayer he confesses *the preeminence of Christ,*
offers *reverence*, petitions for *clemency*, and manifests
his *neediness*. And thus his prayer is exceedingly perfect. When he says: *Master, he confesses his preeminence*
according to what is said to the disciples in John 13:13:
"You call me *Master* and *Lord*, and you say well." Therefore, he calls him *Master* rather than the disciples because he has judged that he has greater power and
knowledge than the disciples who were unable to cure
his son and did not know how to cure his son. And therefore, the Lord said to the disciples in Matthew 23:10:
"Neither be called masters, for one is your master, the
Christ."[163] – Furthermore, in the words *I entreat you, he
manifests his reverence.* For it is characteristic of the
petitioner to humble himself and offer reverence, in accordance with what it said in 1 Timothy 5:1: "Do not rebuke an elderly man, but entreat him as you would a
father." And a person must do this especially in prayer.
For it is said in Sirach 35:21: "The prayer of the person
who humbles himself will penetrate the clouds." – By
saying the words, *Look at my son, he seeks mercy*, in accordance with what Sirach 36:1 reads: "Have mercy
upon us, O God of all, and look upon us, and show us the
light of your mercies." In this regard it is said in the
Psalm: "He looked upon the prayer of the humble and
did not scorn their petition" (101:18). – By adding the

---

[162] The Vulgate does, not have *in caelum* ("to heaven") which is found
in a parallel place in 1 Maccabees 4:40.
[163] On p. 240, n. 3 QuarEd rightly mention that the Vulgate reads,
n*ec* ("Neither") whereas Bonaventure has, n*e* ("Neither").

words, *Because he is my only one, he acknowledges his neediness*, as if he were saying with the Psalmist: "Look upon me and have mercy on me, for I am alone and needy" (24:16). For the only son *is tenderly loved*, according to what 2 Samuel 1:26 says: "As a mother loves her only son, so did I love you." And *he is perishing with sorrow*. So in Genesis 42:38 Jacob said of Benjamin: "He alone is left. If any mischief befall him in the land . . . you will bring down my gray hairs with sorrow to hell."

74. (Verse 39). Third, he mentions *the violence of the demon possessing*: *And behold, a spirit seizes him, and he suddenly cries out.* From this it is apparent that the demon is afflicting him with a sudden affliction. So it is said in Matthew 17:14 about this same person: "Have pity on my son, for he is an epileptic and suffers severely. For often he falls into the water and often into the fire."[164] So such an illness was *sudden*, as is the sickness of epileptics. Now such a person was Saul, about whom it is said in 1 Samuel 16:23 that "whenever the evil spirit from the Lord seized Saul, David took up his harp." In this it is designated that the true David, Christ, was coming to tame the demonic violence. – And not only was this sickness sudden, but it was also *harmful*. So the text continues: *And it throws him down and convulses him so that he foams.* This is a sign of grave pain and affliction. Whence he could already say: "Our bones are scattered by the side of hell" (Psalm 101:18), because he was being scattered about by an infernal spirit. – This illness was not only painful, but also *persistent*. For which reason the text has: *and bruising him sorely, it scarcely leaves him.* Thus, he could say what Job 19:12 has: "Robbers have come together and have

---

[164] The Vulgate has the sequence "fire . . . water."

made a way for themselves through me and have besieged my tabernacle all around."

75. (Verse 40). And the difficulty of the cure makes it obvious that his suffering was of long duration. Whence the text adds: *And I asked your disciples to cast it out, but they could not.* Now the reason for this was that they could not cast it out through earthly power, according to what Job 41:24 says: "There is no power upon earth," etc.[165] And moreover, the power of divine efficacy was absent because of human incredulity. Therefore, Matthew 17:18–19 reads: "The disciples said to the Lord: Why could we not cast it out? And he answered and said: Because of your incredulity." But contrariwise Mark 9:22 has: "If you can believe, all things are possible to the person who believes."

76. According to *the spiritual* sense, in this demoniac who is so sorely afflicted is understood the person who is possessed by *spiritual sin*, who is seized by *pride*, which as the principal sin brings about the devil's extending his grip over a human being according to what Job 41:25 says: "He is king over all the children of pride." – Secondly, *he cries out* because of *vainglory*. Isaiah 5:7 has: "I looked that he should do . . . justice and behold, a cry." Such were the Pharisees, according to what Matthew 23:5–6 says: "They widen their phylacteries, enlarge their tassels, love the first places at suppers," etc. – Third, *he throws down* because of *envy*, according to what Job 30:22 reads: "You have lifted me up, and setting me as it were upon the wind" through arrogance, "you have mightily thrown me down" through envy, for, as Job 5:2 says, "envy slays the little one." – Fourth, *he*

---

[165] The full text is: "There is no power upon earth that can be compared with him who was made to fear, no one."

convulses because of *anger*, which disturbs every thought, according to what Job 17:11 has: "My thoughts are convulsed, tormenting my heart." And in the Psalm: "Convulsed and unrepentant . . . they bruised me with their teeth" (34:16). Fifth, *it bruises* because of *sadness of heart*. And this precipitates impatience, through which conscience is also bruised. Wherefore, Sirach 38:19 reads: "Sadness of heart bows down the neck," etc. – And from this it happens that *it scarcely leaves* because of *faithlessness*. Wisdom 12:10 says: "They were a wicked nation, and their malice natural, and the thought of their heart could never be changed."[166]

77. (Verse 41). *And Jesus answered and said to them,*[167] etc. After setting forth the occasion the Evangelist explains in second place Christ's *efficacious power*, which is described here as *just, loving*, and *great*.

First, it is described as *just* in exposing their incredulity of heart when he says: *O unbelieving and perverse generation!* With *infidelity* in thought and *perversity* in affection, according to what Deuteronomy 32:20 says: "For it is a perverse generation and unfaithful children." Infidelity made them *fools*, and perversity *hard*, according to what Qoheleth 1:15 has: "The perverse are corrected

---

[166] On p. 241 QuarEd give, no sources for Bonaventure's spiritual interpretation, which seems strained and whose scriptural sources seem somewhat inadequate. Bonaventure may have had a model in what Hugh of St. Cher calls "the seven effects of the devil in sinners." See Hugh of St. Cher, p. 188v, c. Hugh quotes Job 30:22 to support his attack on "pride" whereas Bonaventure quotes it to attack "envy." Hugh quotes Job 17:11 against "avarice" while Bonaventure quotes it against "anger." As far as I can tell, Bonaventure and Hugh have, no other scripture quotations in common.

[167] The Vulgate has *Respondens autem Iesus dixit* ("And Jesus answered and said") for Bonaventure's *Respondens autem Iesus ait illis* ("And Jesus answered and said to them").

with difficulty, and the number of fools is infinite."
Therefore, they are not only to be admonished, but also
strongly reproved. – Therefore, the text adds: *How long
shall I be with you*, that is, performing good things for
you, *and put up with you?*, namely, putting up with your
evil. He does not say this out of impatience, since he
himself is the one of whom it is said in Matthew 5:45:
"who makes his sun rise on the good and the evil." And
in Luke 6:35 above: "He is kind towards the ungrateful
and evil." But he says this, so that through a sharp reproof he may expel their hardness of heart, according to
what Titus 1:13 reads: "Reprove them sharply, so that
they may be sound in faith."

78. Second, Christ's efficacious power is described as
loving in his summoning of the possessed child, where it
says: *Bring your son here*, that is, into the presence of
the Savior, so that what Isaiah 49:22 says may already
be seen as fulfilled: "They will bring their sons in their
arms, and they will carry their daughters upon their
shoulders."[168] *Bring*, I say, through your faith, him who
cannot come through his own faith, like those men carried the paralytic. Of them it is said in Matthew 9:2:
"Jesus, seeing their faith, said: Your sins are forgiven
you."[169] So in Mark 9:22 the Lord said to this man: "If
you can believe, all things are possible for the person
who believes." For it is faith, acting as a mediator, by
which one is led to Christ, for faith itself is the way of
arriving at the light. So the Apostle says in the Letter to
the Hebrews 11:6: "The person who comes to God must

---

[168] On p. 241, n. 9 QuarEd correctly mention that the Vulgate has
filios tuos ("your sons") and *filias tuas* ("your daughters").
[169] Luke 5:20 makes the same point: "And seeing their faith, he said:
Man, your sins are forgiven you."

believe . . . for without faith it is impossible to please God."[170]

79. (Verse 42). And because "there is no harmony between Christ and Belial nor between light and darkness,"[171] the text adds: *And as he was coming near, the demon threw him into convulsions.* In this it is shown that he came to the light unwillingly, as someone who does evil according to John 3:20: "The person who does evil hates the light."[172] At the same time this action shows that the devil fights the strongest to prevent anyone possessed by him from being converted to Christ, according to what Bede says in the Glossa: "So the boy approaching the Lord is thrown down, for those who have converted to the Lord are very often more severely beaten up by the demon, so that they may revert to their vices."[173] We have an example of this in Exodus 4:4 in the person of the Pharaoh who pursued the people as they left Egypt.

80. (Verse 43). Third, Christ's efficacious power is described as *great* with the expulsion of an unclean spirit, as it continues: *And Jesus rebuked the unclean spirit,* as he restrains him with a mere word, according to what

---

[170] Bonaventure has inverted the first two sentences of Hebrews 11:6: "And without faith it is impossible to please God. For the person who comes to God must believe. . . . "

[171] Bonaventure quotes from 2 Corinthians 6:15 and 14 in reverse order. Was he dependent on some ecclesiastical usage of this scripture passage?

[172] The Vulgate of John 3:20 begins with *Omnis enim* ("For everyone").

[173] On p. 241, n. 13 QuarEd say that this is the Glossa Ordinaria and offer this quotation: "While the boy is approaching the Lord, he is thrown down . . . are severely beaten up, so that either they may be led back to their vices or that the devil may avenge himself for his expulsion."

Luke 4:41 above says: "He rebuked them and did not permit them to speak." Thus, the angel of the Lord in Zechariah 3:2 said: "May the Lord rebuke you, Satan." – And since the demon was cast out by means of this rebuke, the text adds: *and healed the boy.* So that rebuke was salutary. On this account Job 5:17–18 says: "Do not refuse the rebuke of the Lord, for he wounds and will cure. He strikes, and his hands will heal." – And since the faith of the father had deserved this, the text adds: *and restored him to his own*[174] *father*, to relieve his sorrow, so that he could say to his only son what Jacob did in Genesis 46:30: "Now will I die with joy, for I have seen your face and leave you alive."

81. Now from what has happened, the prelate is given *spiritual* instruction on how he must return to the King of the heavens the subject who is possessed by the devil through sin, namely, by *rebuking* and *healing. By rebuking* out of justice, and *healing* out of clemency. Further, the rigor of justice must be exercised relative to the sin, but the gentleness of clemency must be operative relative to human nature. So Augustine says: "Let correction take place with love for the person and hatred for vices."[175] And Gregory states: "We must have strictness

---

[174] On p. 242, n. 1 QuarEd accurately indicate that the Vulgate has *eius* ("his") for Bonaventure's *suo* ("his own").

[175] On p. 242, n. 2 QuarEd quote Hugh of St. Cher. See Hugh of St. Cher, p. 188v, q: "Augustine says: Each should correct and judge and accuse the other out of love for the person and hatred for vices." They continue by referring to what Augustine himself wrote. I quote the Latin text of the *Regula Sancti Avgvstini* IV.11 from George Lawless, *Augustine of Hippo and his Monastic Rule* (Oxford: Clarendon Press, 1987), 92: *Et hoc quod dixi de oculo, non figendo etiam in ceteris inueniendis, prohibendis, indicandis, conuincendis uindicandisque peccatis, diligenter et fideliter obseruetur, cum dilectione hominum et odio uitiorum.* I modify Lawless' translation (p. 93): "Diligently and faithfully, then, attend to my words about suggestive glances at women. Such advice holds also for detection, prevention, disclosure,

in dealing with vices and compassion in dealing with human nature." "For true justice breathes compassion, and false justice indignation."[176] Thus it is also said in Luke 10:34 below about the Samaritan who was taking care of the wounded man that he poured wine and oil on his wounds, the wine that stings and the oil that smoothes, according to the two approaches that have just been discussed.

82. (Verse 44). *And all were astounded*, etc. After setting forth the occasion for the exercise of Christ's efficacious power, the Evangelist now treats *the consequent benefit*. And this benefit is twofold. First, it is *universal*, and second, it is *particular*. The first consists of *instilling in all a reverence for divine majesty*. The second *is care that the disciples understand the truth*.

So first, concerning *instilling in all a reverence for divine majesty*, it is said: *And all were astounded at the majesty of God*, for it was a great power that perfectly cured so great an illness in so short a time with a mere word. So they were chanting with the Psalmist: "Great is our Lord, and great is his power" (146:5). And also what Jeremiah 10:6–7 says: "You are great, O Lord, and great

---

proof, and punishment of other offences, with love for the person and hatred for vices." The editors conclude by quoting the Glossa Ordinaria (from Bede) on Luke 9:43: "The boy does, not suffer the blow, but the devil is the object of the blow of the rebuke. For the person who wants to cure a sinner must argue against and cast out the vice, but must renew the person through love until he may return him healed to the spiritual fathers of the church." See CCSL cxx, p. 209.

[176] On p. 242, n. 3 QuarEd indicate that the first quotation is from Homily 33, n. 3 and the second from Homily 34, n. 2 of GGHG. See PL 76:1241A and PL 76:1246D respectively. The quotations are verbatim with the exception of one word in PL 76:1246D. Bonaventure has *indignationem* ("indignation") while Gregory's text reads *dedignationem* ("indignation").

is your name. . . . And in all the kingdoms of the earth[177] there is none like you." And Exodus 15:11 reads: "Who is like you, O Lord, among the strong?. . . . Inspiring terror and worthy of praise and working wonders."

83. Second, relative to *care that the disciples understand the truth,* the text continues: *But while all were marveling at all the things that he was doing, and also saying and stating, he said to his disciples: Store up these words in your hearts.* It was as if he were saying to them: While others are recalling and admiring the greatness of the miracles, you should think about the humility of future opprobrious events and "of the precious blood, by which the world is to be redeemed. Fix the event in your mind, while all others stand in awe only at the deeds of divine sublimity."[178] So *store up,* that is, put this in your memory, according to what The Song of Songs 8:6 says: "Put me as a seal upon your heart." Therefore, to the miraculous display he joins a prediction of future punishment, lest his passion might come suddenly and entirely surprise his disciples. So Sirach 11:27 reads: "In the day of good things be not unmindful of evils." And lest anyone be exalted at a time of prosperity, according to what Proverbs 27:1 says: "Boast not of tomorrow, for you know not what the day to come may bring forth." And therefore, Sirach 11:4 has: "Be not exalted in the day of your honor." – These words, which he wants them to commit to memory, con-

---

[177] The Vulgate reads *eorum* ("their") where Bonaventure reads *terrarum* ("of the earth"). In his commentary on Luke 8:35 (#62) above Bonaventure also quotes Jeremiah 10:7, but there he reads *eorum*.
[178] On p. 242, n. 6 QuarEd give the Glossa Ordinaria (from Bede) as the source for this quotation, whose beginning is: "*Store up,* you who are members of my band of disciples, to whom I have opened more fully my mysteries, of the precious. . . . " See CCSL cxx, p. 209.

cern his passion.[179] So the text adds: *The Son of Man*[180] *is about to be handed over into the hands of men and women. He is to be handed over,* I say, out of *the clemency* of God the Father. Romans 8:32 says: "He who has not spared his own Son, but has handed him over for us all," etc. He is handed over out of *obedience,* on his own. Isaiah 53:12 has: "For this that he has handed over his soul to death." He is handed over out of *the malice* of Judas the traitor. Matthew 26:23 reads: "He who dips his hand into the dish with me, he will hand me over." And these words encompass the entire passion.

84. (Verse 45). And because this was a hidden mystery, the text continues: *But they did not understand this saying, and it was hidden from them, that they might not perceive it.* For they were still *rustic* and *sensual.*[181] They did not understand the past and therefore, not the future. Thus, Qoheleth 8:7 says: "The person who is ignorant of things past cannot know of things to come, no matter who the messenger." – Furthermore, because they were still not *perfectly instructed,* the text adds: *And they were afraid to ask him about the saying.* For they had not yet heard from him what John 15:15 has: "No longer do I call you servants, for the servant does not know what his master is doing," etc. – Now there is a triple reason for this ignorance. For it partly stemmed from the love of charity, partly from faith in his divinity,

---

[179] On p. 242, n. 7 QuarEd quote the Glossa Ordinaria (from Bede) on Luke 9:44: "Amidst the marvels of divine power he very often unfolds the debasements of human suffering, lest their sudden coming terrify, whilst their prior consideration may enable them to be borne more readily." See CCSL cxx, p. 209 for Bede's text which the Glossa Ordinaria has quoted faithfully, but, not verbatim.

[180] On p. 242, n. 8 QuarEd correctly indicate that the Vulgate reads *enim* ("For").

[181] This is my rendering of Bonaventure's *rudes erant et animales.*

and partly from his customary way of speaking in parables. And the Glossa from Bede touches on this: "This ignorance," etc.[182] Now although the Lord knew that they would not understand, he nevertheless predicted this to them. This prediction prepared them for what happened afterwards, when after his resurrection he spoke with them and rebuked them: "O foolish ones and slow of heart to believe" (Luke 24:25) and "opened their minds" (Luke 24:45). John 14:29 gives as the reason for this: "I have told you this before it comes to pass, so that, when it has come to pass, you may believe." He also said this, so that, as was stated above,[183] he might teach us that in every one of our exaltations we should remember our death and mortality. Thus Sirach 7:40 reads: "Remember your last end, and you will never sin."

Luke 9:46–62
THE NORM OF PRESIDING

85. *Now a thought entered into them*, etc. This is the third section of this part which is taken up with *the mission of the Apostles*. After an explication of the form of preaching and of the way of making progress, the Evangelist presents *the norm of presiding*. For the Apostles

---

[182] On p. 243, n. 2 QuarEd come to the readers' rescue by quoting in full the Glossa Ordinaria that Bonaventure summarizes so tersely: "*But they did, not understand*. This ignorance is born, not so much out of dullness of mind but from love, for they were still carnal and ignorant of the mystery of the cross. They could, not believe that the one they acknowledged as God was going to die. But as they were accustomed to hear him speak in figures, so, now when he was speaking about his being handed over, they thought he was signifying something figuratively." This is almost verbatim from Bede. See CCSL cxx, p. 209.
[183] See #83 above.

were in their persons *preachers, men of perfection,* and *prelates.* Now since three things are necessary for *prelates* in governing the people, namely, *humility in soul, moderation in zeal,* and *perspicacity in judgment,* this section has three components. In the first of these there is instruction about *humility of soul.* In the second *equanimity in zeal,* where verse 51 states: *Now it came to pass when the days had come,* etc. In the third *sharpness in judgment,* where verse 57 has: *And it came to pass as they went on their journey,* etc.

Luke 9:46–50
HUMILITY OF SOUL

The first component has two parts. For the first gives instruction about *humility towards one's family* whilst the second towards *outsiders,* where verse 49 reads: *But John answered,* etc.

In his instruction about showing *humility towards family members,* the Evangelist introduces three points. The first is *an occasion for praising humility* on account of its opposite. The second provides a tangible example of *laudatory teaching.* The third is *the conclusion of perfect praise* by means of a definitive judgment.

86. (Verse 46). Now first, *an occasion for praising humility* is introduced by rejecting its contrary. The text continues: *Now the thought entered into them which of them was the greatest.* – And note that Luke says: *the thought entered into them.* In Mark 9:33 they are said *to have disputed.* In Matthew 18:1 they are said *to have asked* the Lord. There is no contradiction here, for the entire matter could have happened in this way, so that first *the thought* entered their minds, then *a dispute* ensued,

and finally *a question* was deferred to the Master. And what one of the Evangelists does not mention, another does. – Now this *thought* was the road to pride and had entered into them from the ancient corruption, of which Genesis 8:21 speaks: "The perception and thought of the human heart are prone to evil from youth," and especially to pride. For, as it is said in Tobit 4:14, "Never permit pride to reign in your mind or in your words. For from it all perdition took its beginning." Therefore, to the man who is thinking proud thoughts it is said in Job 15:12: "Why does your heart elevate you, and why do you stare with your eyes as if you were thinking great things?" Such were the Apostles then and contrary to the counsel of Sirach 6:2: "Do not extol yourself in your thoughts like a bull, lest your strength be thrown to the ground." Now this proud thought gained entrance into their minds from this fact that he had led three disciples with him up the mountain. And moreover, he had said to Peter only: "To you will I give the keys of the kingdom of heaven," as is said in Matthew 16:19. Therefore, some wanted to put John on a par with Peter. Others wanted Peter to be eminent. And this is what is said in the Glossa: "For they had seen Peter," etc.[184]

---

[184] On p. 243, n. 12 QuarEd quote the Glossa Ordinaria (from Bede) on Luke 9:46: *"Now the thought entered*. Because they had seen Peter and James and John led off by themselves to the mountain and seen that some secret had been handed over to them. But also they reckoned that the keys of the kingdom of heaven had been promised to Peter earlier [Matthew 16:18ff.] and that the church was to be built upon him. Another interpretation is that these three were prelates over the rest or that Peter was over all the Apostles. Another interpretation is because they had seen that Peter was put on a par with the Lord himself in the payment of the tribute [Matthew 17:26; Book III of Jerome's Commentary on Matthew 18:1 offers this explanation], they reasoned that he was to be preferred to the rest. But it should be known that this question came up both before and after the payment of the tribute." Again the Glossa Ordinaria on Luke 9:46 is heavily indebted to Bede. See CCSL cxx, pp. 209–210.

87. (Verse 47). Second, *laudatory teaching* is given by means of a sensible example as the text continues: *But Jesus, knowing the reasonings of their*[185] *heart,* as true God, according to what 1 Samuel 16:7 says: "Human beings see what is manifest.[186] God looks into the heart." And Sirach 23:28 has: "The eyes of the Lord are far brighter than the sun, beholding round about all the ways of men and women and the bottom of the deep, and looking into human hearts." – And because he saw that their reasonings were heading towards sickness, he, like a wise physician, set forth the remedy as he said: *Taking a little child, he set him at his side,* as one like him and kin. So in Matthew 19:14 he said: "Let the little children come to me,[187] and do not hinder them from coming to me, for of such is the kingdom of heaven." And Hosea 11:1 reads: "Because Israel was a boy, I loved him." And on account of this the Wise Man said in Wisdom 9:4–5: "Cast me not off from among your children, for I am your servant and the son of your handmaid." Therefore, he set the little child *at his side,* in order to show that the person who wants to be a friend of God must become a little child.[188]

---

[185] On p. 243, n. 13 QuarEd correctly indicate that the Vulgate reads *illorum* ("their") while Bonaventure has *eorum* ("their").

[186] On p. 243, n. 13 QuarEd rightly mention that the Vulgate reads *parent* ("are evident") whereas Bonaventure has *patent* ("are manifest").

[187] The Vulgate does not have the words *venire ad me* ("come to me").

[188] On p. 244, n. 1 QuarEd quote the Glossa Interlinearis (from Bede) on Luke 9:47: *"But Jesus, seeing,* and understanding the causes of their errors, wants to cure their desire for glory through their striving after humility." See CCSL cxx, p. 210. On p. 244, n. 2 QuarEd cite the parallel passage from Matthew 18:3 and then present the various attempts of authors to identify and, name "the little boy," e.g., the later St. Ignatius of Antioch.

88. (Verse 48). And he notes this when he adds: *And he said to them: Whoever receives this little child for my sake, receives me.* By this he shows how great an affection he has towards the little ones and the lowly that what happens to them he considers to have happened to him. So in Matthew 25:40 he will say at the judgment: "What you did to one of my least ones you did to me." For such he especially receives according to the Psalm: "The Lord is high and has regard for the lowly" (137:6) and according to Isaiah 66:2: "For whom shall I have regard, but for the poor and contrite in spirit," etc. – Furthermore, from this one gathers the great excellence that exists in the little child, when in that person Christ is received not only according to human lowliness, but also according to divine authority. To teach this the text continues: *And whoever receives me, receives him who sent me.* From this one garners that the person who honors and receives a little child of Christ receives and honors God. Therefore, the honor and glory of little ones is great.[189] – Through this example Christ is persuading them not to strive to be someone great, but to endeavor to be little ones. And to this behavior the Apostle summons in Philippians 2:3–7: "In humility regard others as superior to yourself. . . . For have this mind in you which was also in Christ Jesus, who, although he was in the form of God . . . emptied himself, taking the form of a slave." Moreover, the Apostle acted similarly, according to what 1 Corinthians 9:19 says: "Although I was free as to all, I have made myself a slave of all." And 1 Thessalonians 2:7 has: "We were little children in your midst, as if a nurse cherishing her own children."

---

[189] On p. 244, n. 4 QuarEd quote the Glossa Ordinaria (from Ambrose) on Luke 9:48: "Who receives the imitator of Christ receives Christ, and who receives the image of God receives God." See CCSL xiv, p. 222.

89. Third, *the conclusion of perfect praise* through a definitive judgment in the words: *For the one who is the least among you*, on account of reputation and lowliness, *is the greatest*, according to divine acceptance and truth. For the least is the greatest, and this because that one is ordained to great rewards, according to what is said in Luke 18:14 below: "The one who humbles himself will be exalted." If this is true by itself as God's statement, namely, that the one who humbles himself in a great manner is great, then the one who humbles himself in the greatest manner is the greatest. – And the reason for this is that the more humble we are, the more free we are from the tumor of pride. And the more free we are from the tumor of pride, the more full we are of love. And the ones who are more full of love, are the greatest.[190] For of love it is written in 1 Corinthians 13:13: "Now the greatest of these is love." And therefore, Sirach 3:20 states: "The greater you are, humble yourself in all things. And you will find grace before God." And Sirach 10:27 has: "The great man and the judge and the mighty are in honor, but there is none greater than the one who fears God." – Another interpretation is that *the lesser* is greater, for to the extent that someone is the more humble, to that extent he is more similar to Christ. And because of this is closer to him. Now Christ is the greatest, but to the extent that anyone becomes closer to the greatest, to that extent he becomes greater.

---

[190] On p. 244, n. 7 QuarEd quote Augustine's Tractate 1, n. 6 on 1 John: "Pride extinguishes love. Therefore, humility strengthens love." They also refer to Augustine's *De Trinitate*, Book VIII c. 8., n. 12 where I have found a wonderful "parallel." See *Sancti Aurelii Avgvstini De Trinitate Libri XV (Libri I–XII)*. CCSL 1 (Turnhout: Brepols, 1968), 287: *Quanto igitur saniores sumus a tumore superbiae tanto sumus dilectione pleniores. Et quo, nisi deo plenus est qui plenus est dilectione?* ("Therefore, the more we are cured of the tumor of pride, the more we are full of love. And of what, if, not of God, is the person full who is full of love?").

Therefore, to the extent that one is the lesser, to that extent he is greater. And this is what he himself teaches in Luke 22 below: "But I am in your midst as he who serves" (verse 27). And therefore, he says: "Let him who is the greatest among you become as the least, and him who is the chief as the servant" (verse 26). And Mark 9:34 has: "If anyone wishes to be first, he will be last of all and the servant of all," because it is said in Matthew 20:16: "Even so the first will be last, and the last first."[191] And Paul, considering this, said in 1 Corinthians 15:9: "I am the least of the Apostles, and am not worthy to be called an Apostle." And Ephesians 3:8 has: "To me, the least of all the saints, there was given this grace." – Therefore, among spiritual men there must not be this contention about the first place, but about the last, because it is the more honorable, as it is said in Luke 14:10 below: "When you are invited to a wedding, recline in the last place," etc. [192]

90. (Verse 49). *But John answered*, etc. After giving instruction about being humble towards one's family, he now offers teaching about humility towards *outsiders*. Three things are introduced about this teaching. For the first is introduced from the perspective of *the exercise of power by a man outside the group of disciples*. The second from the perspective of *the prohibition of the disciples' rashness*. The third from the perspective of *the Master's teaching about humility*.

So he first introduces *the exercise of power on the part of an outsider* when he says: *But John answered and said:*

---

[191] The Vulgate reads *Sic erunt, novissimi primi et primi, novissimi* ("Even so the last will be first, and the first last").
[192] Bonaventure seems to have conflated Luke 14:8 and 14:10 For example, *ad, nuptias* ("to a wedding") comes from Luke 14:8.

Master, we saw a man casting out demons in your name.
For since the Lord had taught humility, John wanted to
know whether he extended that teaching to outsiders.
So he responds and introduces this foreigner who was
performing miracles. Now those who are outside of
Christ's circle can perform miracles, according to what
Matthew 7:22 has: "Many will say to me: Lord, . . . we
cast out demons in your name. And in your name we
worked many miracles." Then he will say to them in
Matthew 7:23: "Depart from me, you workers of iniquity." Now this happens when a person has faith in the
name of Christ without the love of charity, according to
what 1 Corinthians 13:2 says: "If I have faith so as to
remove mountains and do not have charity, I am nothing." And this is because charity is what makes a person
a friend of Christ. But the power of the name of Christ is
manifest and its great efficacy is invoked by outsiders in
accordance with what Philippians 2:10 says: "At the
name of Jesus every knee should bend of those in
heaven, on earth and under the earth." So Luke 10:17
below has: "Lord, in your name even the demons are
subject to us."

91. Second, he introduces *the prohibition against rashness on the part of the disciple* as he says: *And we forbade him,* namely, I with the others. This did not happen without a hint of presumption, for Proverbs 3:27
says: "Do not prevent the person who is able to do good.
If you are able, do good yourself." – Further since what
is done out of vanity and pride is frequently covered
over with the zeal of justice,[193] the text continues: *Be-*

---

[193] On p. 245, n. 7 QuarEd refer to Homily 34, n. 2 of GGHG. See PL
76:1247A: *Sed aliud est quod agitur typho superbiae, aliud quod zelo
disciplinae* ("But it is one thing to be moved by vanity and pride,
another by zeal for discipline"). They also refer to Homily 9, n. 13 of
Book I of Gregory's Homilies on Ezekiel: "Thus it happens that pride

cause he is not following you[194] *with us.* And therefore, he
is not worthy to be like us in working miracles. He is not
similar to us in the fulfillment of the counsels. But in
this pride lay hidden, as if he were saying what Isaiah
65:5 has: "Who say: Depart from me. Do not come near
me, for you are unclean." And jealousy appeared here
like that concerning Eldad and Medad in Numbers 11
who prophesied in the camps during Moses' absence.
Joshua, son of Nun, said to Moses: "My lord Moses, forbid them. But he said: Why are you jealous for my
sake?" (11:28–29). So John, who was the outstanding
lover of the Lord and was zealous for his honor, wanted
to exclude everyone who did not love the Lord from
preaching in the name of Christ. So Bede in the Glossa
says: "John, lover of the Lord and beloved by the Lord,
thought that the person who did not enjoy their obedience should be excluded from their ministry."[195] Nevertheless he was wrong, for Philippians 1:18 says:
"Whether in pretense or in truth Christ will be proclaimed.[196] But in this I rejoice and will rejoice."

92. (Verse 50). Third, with regard to *teaching about humility on the part of the Master* the text adds: *And Jesus
said to him: Do not forbid him,* but rather humbly bear

---

cloaks itself with authority and human fear with humility, so that
the one is, not able to consider what it owes to God and the other
what it owes to one's, neighbor."

[194] On p. 245, n. 7 QuarEd correctly indicate that the Vulgate does,
not read *te* ("you"), which Blessed Albert and St. Thomas, along with
Bonaventure, have.

[195] On p. 245, n. 9 QuarEd state that this is the Glossa Ordinaria. It
is very close to what Bede has in CCSL cxx, p. 210. I have translated
"Bede's" play on *beneficium* and *obsequium* in an ecclesiastical sense,
to wit, "benefice/ministry" and "obedience."

[196] The Vulgate reads *annuntiatur* ("is proclaimed"). In commenting
on Luke 8:38 (#68) above, Bonaventure quotes both Numbers 11:29
and Philippians 1:18. In that quotation of Philippians 1:18 he writes:
"Whether in truth or in pretense Christ will be proclaimed."

with him, although he is imperfect, for Romans 15:1 says: "We, the strong, ought to bear the infirmities of the weak and not to please ourselves." And especially when the weak person is not an opponent of the truth.[197] – For this reason the text continues: *The person*[198] *who is not against you is for you.* And therefore, that person is helpful to us and bearable, since he is not fighting against us, but is helping us. So Sirach 11:9 reads: "You should not fight[199] in a matter that is of no consequence to you."

93. But this seems contrary to what Matthew 12:30 has: "The person who is not with me is against me, and the person who does not gather with me scatters." But this person was not with the Lord nor did he follow him. Therefore, he was *against him* and his disciples. Now how was he *for them?* – From this we are given to understand that there are three types of preachers. Some are *genuine pastors.* And these seek only the honor of God and the salvation of their subjects, according to what John 10:11 states: "The good shepherd lays down his life for his sheep." And these are *to be accepted and honored.* And these are the imitators of Christ like Timothy of the Apostle as Philippians 2:21–22 has: "They all seek their own interests, not those of Jesus Christ. But know his worth, for as a child serves a fa-

---

[197] On p. 245, n. 10 QuarEd quote from the Glossa Ordinaria: "*Do, not forbid him, for the person.* John is, not reproached, for he did this out of love. Rather he is taught that he might learn the difference between the strong and the weak, for the Lord, even though he rewards the strong, does, not exclude the weak." The Glossa Ordinaria follows Ambrose quite closely. See CCSL xiv, p. 223.

[198] On p. 245, n. 11 QuarEd rightly mention that the Vulgate reads *Qui enim* ("For the person").

[199] On p. 245, n. 11 QuarEd are correct to, note that the Vulgate reads, *ne certeris* ("Do, not fight") while Bonaventure reads, *ne certaveris* ("You should, not fight").

ther he has served with me in the Gospel." – But some are *hirelings*, who preach out of convenience, but preach what is true and good. Of them it is said in John 10:13: "But the hireling flees because he is a hireling." And these are *to be tolerated*. – Some are *wolves*, like the heretics, who disagree with Christ in the teaching of the truth. Of them it is said in John 10:12: "The wolf snatches and scatters the sheep." And Acts 20:29 reads: "Fierce wolves will enter among you and will not spare the flock." And these are *to be shut up*. Now of *such people* is Matthew 12:30 to be understood. The Lukan passage under consideration concerns the second group only. So it is said in Mark 9:38: "There is no one who shall work a miracle in my name, and forthwith be able to speak ill of me." Therefore, Acts 19:13–16 says this about the sons of Sceva that "they attempted...to invoke the name of the Lord Jesus. . . . The evil spirit said to them: Jesus I acknowledge and Paul I know, but who are you? . . . And he overpowered them both, so that they fled from the house naked and bruised."[200]

Luke 9:51–56
EQUANIMITY IN ZEAL

94. *Now it came to pass, when the days had been fulfilled,* etc. After he had formed the Apostles, the prelates of the Church, in humility of soul, he now gives them a second lesson, namely, in *equanimity in zeal*.[201] And this part is twofold. The first section treats *the occasion for tempering their zeal*. The second section contains *the correc-*

---

[200] The second part of Acts 19:16 reads thus in the Vulgate: *Et dominatus amborum invaluit contra eos, ita ut, nudi et vulnerati effugerent de domo illa* ("And overpowered them both with such violence that they fled from that house, naked and bruised").

[201] See #85 above where Bonaventure introduced this analysis.

tion of their intemperate zeal, through which they are given instruction about equanimity in zeal. And the second section commences in verse 54: *But when his disciples.*

Now *the occasion for tempering their zeal* arises from three things, namely, *the neediness of the Lord* for hospitality, *the authority of the disciples* to require said hospitality, *the inhumanity of the Samaritans* in denying said hospitality.

95. (Verse 51). First is the mention of *the Lord's neediness*, for the time of his pilgrimage had arrived. The text notes this as it says: *Now it came to pass when the days of his being taken up were being fulfilled.* That is, when the time was drawing near for his passion, through which he had to be taken up into heaven after the resurrection. Therefore, the Psalm of Resurrection has the title "Of the Morning Assumption."[202] John 13:1 reads: "Jesus, knowing that the hour had come," etc. – Since the time of his passion had come, it was fitting to travel to the place where he would suffer. And therefore, the text adds: *He steadfastly set his face to go to Jerusalem to suffer.* For it is said in Luke 13:33 below: "It cannot be

---

[202] On p. 246, n. 8 QuarEd refer to Psalm 21:1 whose title in the Vulgate is: *In finem pro assumptione matutina Psalmus David* ("Unto the end, For the Morning Assumption. A Psalm of David"). The editors refer to a commentary on this Psalm found among the works of Venerable Bede. This commentary, notes that some texts have "Morning Reception" and others have "Morning Assumption." The commentary's solution is: "Now the resurrection itself is said to be morning *reception* or *assumption*. For when the Lord was assumed into eternal life, receiving the mortal flesh he had put off. . . . Indeed, this reception is called *morning*, for it happened historically *on the morning of the first day of the week* (Mark 16:2)."

that a prophet perish outside Jerusalem."[203] Therefore, he wanted to travel there as a place of shame and disgrace. For this reason he states significantly that *he steadfastly set his face*, namely, through constancy and divine patience, according to what Ezekiel 3:8–9 says: "Behold I have made your face stronger than their faces and your forehead harder than their foreheads, and I have made your face like steel and flint." So set was his face that not only did he not flee, but also he was not afraid to travel to a shameful death, even though he needed to pass through the land of foreigners, according to what is said in Luke 17:11 below: "While Jesus was traveling to Jerusalem, he passed between Samaria and Galilee." And thus it was necessary for him to beg for hospitality from strangers, according to what Jeremiah 14:8 has: "Why will you be as a stranger in the land and as a wayfarer turning in to lodge?"

96. (Verse 52). Secondly, *the authority of the disciples*, through which they ask for hospitality, is mentioned: *And he sent messengers before his face.* For it is fitting that the great Lord have messengers announcing his coming, according to what is said in Malachi 3:1: "Behold, I am sending my angel," that is, messenger, "who will prepare the way before your[204] face." So we also read of Jacob in Genesis 32:3 that "he sent messengers before him." – And since good messengers faithfully and swiftly

---

[203] On p. 246, n. 9 QuarEd quote the Glossa Interlinearis (from Bede): "... *to Jerusalem*: With a resolute and undaunted mind he sought the place where he had decreed to suffer." See CCSL cxx, p. 211.

[204] On p. 246, n. 12 QuarEd are right to mention that the Vulgate reads *meam* ("my"). But in his commentary on Luke 7:27 (#51) above Bonaventure also deals with Malachi 3:1 and reads *ante faciem tuam* ("before your face"). Matthew 11:10 and Mark 1:2 read: *ante faciem tuam* ("before your face").

execute the command of their Lord, the text adds: *And they went and entered a Samaritan town that they might make ready*[205] *for him.* The Samaritans were those inhabitants who had been settled in the cities of Samaria in place of the children of Israel who had been transported to Assyria. As it is said in 2 Kings 17:24, "The king of the Assyrians brought men from among the citizens of the Assyrians[206] and placed them in the cities of Samaria instead of the children of Israel. They possessed Samaria and dwelt in its cities." And of these people 2 Kings 17 later adds in verse 41 that "they feared the Lord, but nevertheless also served their own idols."[207] Into their cities the disciples entered, not on their own volition, since it is said in John 4:9 that "Jews do not deal with Samaritans," but compelled either by the necessity that knows no law[208] or by the special command of the Lord. For concerning the mission of the Apostles it is said in Matthew 10:5: "Do not go in the direction of the Gentiles nor enter the towns of the Samaritans." But that was said about preaching and not about the requirements of seeking hospitality. For John 4:8 says this about a Samaritan town that "the disciples had gone into the town to buy food." And they were doing

---

[205] On p. 247, n. 1 QuarEd correctly indicate that the Vulgate reads *pararent* ("that they may make ready"). It is understood that they are arranging hospitality for their Lord.

[206] The first part of 2 Kings 17:24 is Bonaventure's abbreviation of the Vulgate's: "And the king of the Assyrians brought people from Babylon, and from Cuthah, and from Avva, and from Hamath, and from Sepharvaim. . . . "

[207] It seems that Bonaventure's point would have been strengthened if he had quoted all of 2 Kings 17:41: "So these, nations feared the Lord, but, nevertheless served also their idols; their children also and grandchildren, as their fathers did, so do they unto this day."

[208] On p. 247, n. 2 QuarEd say that the principle, "necessity knows, no law" (*necessitas, non habet legem*), was used by Pope Felix IV (d. 530) and refer to "Gratian, C. *Sicut, non alii* [c. 11] de Consecrat. d.1."

this at the command of the Lord who was demonstrating that no person is to be contemned, but each one is to be loved as a neighbor, as it is said in Luke 10:36 of the Samaritan in the parable that "he was the neighbor to the person who fell among the robbers."

97. (Verse 53). Third, *the inhumanity of the Samaritans*, who deny hospitality, is introduced: *And they did not receive him*, even though he was their Lord, so that what John 1:11 says might be fulfilled: "He came unto his own, and his own received him not." Their inhumanity was similar to that shown to the Levite by the people of Gibeah. It is said in Judges 19:15 that "they sat in the street of the city, and no one would receive them and offer hospitality." The Jews did not allow the Samaritans to their worship of God, and therefore, they were against those traveling to Jerusalem. – And therefore, the text continues: *Because his face was set towards Jerusalem*, that is, because they clearly recognized that he was going to Jerusalem to worship God according to Jewish ritual. Wherefore, the Samaritan woman said to him in John 4:19–20: "Sir, our fathers worshipped on this mountain, but you say that at Jerusalem is the place where one ought to worship." And the Jews and the Samaritans are opposed to one another about the place of prayer, as even now happens *spiritually* when spiritual men and worshippers of God are derided and despised and rejected by those who love the world. So Proverbs 14:2 has: "The person who walks in the right way and fears the Lord is despised by him who journeys along the path of infamy." And Sirach 13:21 says: "As the wolf has fellowship with the lamb, so too the sinner with the just person." Thus, Wisdom 2:12–15: "The wicked said: Let us lie in wait for the just, because . . . he is contrary to what we are doing. . . . He is burdensome to us, even to behold. For his life is not like

that of others, and his ways are very different." For those who lead dissimilar lives do not easily interact with one another. And therefore, the Samaritans, hating Jerusalem, did not want to act with humanity to a person traveling to Jerusalem.

98. (Verse 54). *But when his disciples saw*, etc. Having set up the occasion for the disciples' inordinate zeal, the Evangelist now mentions *the correction of this inordinate zeal*. About this he makes three points, namely, *reprehensible indignation, comprehensible correction, memorable instruction*.[209] The first occurs in the soul of the disciples. The second in the word of the Lord. The third in a deed of the Lord.

So first with regard to *the reprehensible indignation* in the soul of the disciples it is said: *But when his disciples James and John saw this*, that is, that the cruelty of this town was such that they could say with the Psalmist: "I have seen iniquity and opposition in the town" (54:10). And again the Psalmist says: "I was zealous against the wicked, seeing the prosperity of sinners" (72:3). So they are moved with indignation, for they saw the Lord being despised on earth, whose majesty they had seen on the mountain with Moses and Elijah. – For this reason the text continues: *Lord, are you willing that we bid that fire come down from heaven and consume them?*[210] This shows the furor of the indignation by which they are moved that they want them to perish from the earth. But it was these two who were especially vocal about this, because they were the zealous preservers of the

---

[209] I rejoice in this rare opportunity to imitate in English Bonaventure's playfulness in Latin: *indignatio reprehensibilis, increpatio rationabilis, informatio rememorabilis*.
[210] On p. 247, n. 9 QuarEd correctly indicate that the Vulgate reads *illos* ("them") whereas Bonaventure has *eos* ("them").

Lord's honor. So it could be said of them what Romans 10:2 has: "I bear them witness that they have zeal for God, but not according to knowledge." They are like the two sons of Jacob, who driven by zeal against the injury done to them, destroyed the city of the Sichemites, as it is said in Genesis 34:24–29.[211] – Another interpretation is that they said this because they had been with the Lord on the mountain where they had acknowledged his majesty and had seen that Elijah was his companion. And therefore, they wanted to exact a punishment similar to the one exacted by Elijah according to what is said in 2 Kings 1:10: "Elijah said: If I be a man of God, let fire come down from heaven and consume you and your fifty men." And it happened thus.

99. (Verse 55). Second, with regard to *the reasonable rebuke* contained in the Lord's word the text says: *But he turned and rebuked them, saying: You do not know of what manner of spirit you are.*[212] He said this because they believed that they were moved by the spirit of rectitude. In reality they were being moved by acrimonious zeal, which they should not have as it says in James 3:14: "But if you have acrimonious zeal and contentions in your heart, do not glory and be liars against the truth." And therefore, it is said in 1 John 4:1: "Do not trust every spirit, but test the spirits to discern whether they are from God." For the Spirit of Christ is a spirit of meekness according to what Isaiah 61:1 has: "The Spirit of the Lord is upon me, because he has anointed me and sent me to preach to the meek." And it says in Isaiah 42:1-3: "Behold, my servant, I will uphold him....I have

---

[211] Simeon and Levi are also zealous to avenge the rape of their sister Dinah.

[212] Contemporary critical texts of the Vulgate do, not contain the words:, n*escitis, cuius spiritus estis* ("You do, not know of what manner of spirit you are").

bestowed my spirit upon him. . . . The bruised reed he will not break, and the smoking flax he will not extinguish."[213] And these disciples should have this spirit as good disciples and imitators of the Master.

100. (Verse 56). And wherefore, the text states: *For the Son of Man did not come to destroy people's lives, but to save them.*[214] For his coming was not made out of justice, but out of mercy, according to what John 3:17 says: "God did not send his Son into the world to condemn the world, but that the world might be saved through him." So with this goal in mind he received the name that he might be called *Jesus*, according to what Matthew 1:21 has: "You will call his name Jesus, for he will save his people from their sins." And Matthew 20:28 reads: "The Son of Man did not come to be served, but to serve and to give his life as a ransom for the many." And therefore, whoever has the spirit of Christ must not seek vengeance, but exhibit patience, according to what Ambrose says in the Glossa: "Perfect virtue,[215] I say, does not seek after punishment. Where there is the fullness of charity, there is not any anger."[216] Therefore, it is said in Romans 12:19: "Do not avenge yourselves, beloved, but give place to the wrath."[217]

---

[213] Did Bonaventure use Isaiah 42:1 here because in Matthew 12:20 it is applied to the ministry of Jesus?

[214] Contemporary critical texts of the Vulgate do, not contain this sentence. In them Luke 9:56 reads simply: *Et abierunt in aliud castellum* ("And they went to another village").

[215] I cannot help but think that Ambrose is playing on the dual meaning of *virtus*, that is, "virtue" and "power." Perfect power is, not vindictive.

[216] On p. 248, n. 6 QuarEd state that this is the Glossa Ordinaria. In CCSL xiv, p. 224 Ambrose concludes his thought with:, *nec excludenda infirmitas, sed iuuanda* ("weakness is, not to be excluded, but helped").

[217] Bonaventure fails to give the motivating clause of Romans 12:19: ". . . for it is written, Vengeance is mine. I will repay, says the Lord."

101. Third, relative to *the memorable instruction* contained in the Lord's action it is said: *And they went to another village.* In this he gave a lesson to his disciples that they should flee from men and women rather than fight with them, according to the lesson he gave his disciples in Matthew 10:23: "When they persecute you in one town, flee to another." Further, we have an example of this in the case of Abraham and Lot in Genesis 13:8–9: "Abraham said: Let there be, I beseech you, no quarrel between me and you. . . . For we are brothers. . . . If you will go to the left, I will take the right."[218] In this he taught perfect meekness, which befits Christ's servants according to what 2 Timothy 2:24 says: "But the servant of God must not quarrel, but must be meek." Wherefore, James 1:19–20 has: "Let everyone be slow to anger. For a man's anger does not bring about the justice of God." For if the Lord of majesty did not want to become angered at such great inhumanity, how much less should we become indignant over it? And this meekness must be found especially among those set up over the Church. Wherefore, the Apostle exhorts in 2 Timothy 4:2: "Reprove, entreat, rebuke with all patience and instruction." For in the Psalm it is said: "Meekness has come upon us, and we will be corrected" (89:10). And Seneca writes: "The soul of a generous person is more easily led than dragged."[219] So he said that the king of the bees has no sting.[220]

In other words, "the wrath" is a circumlocution for God's just activity.

[218] Bonaventure has changed "Abram" to "Abraham" in verse 8.

[219] In his commentary on Luke 5:3 (#5) above Bonaventure uses the identical quotation from Seneca. The general reference is Book I, chapter 24 of Seneca's *De Clementia*. Bonaventure's "quotation" is, nowhere found in Seneca in the exact same words. See *Seneca: Moral Essays I,* translated by John W. Basore, LCL (New York: Putnam's Sons, 1928), 423: "Man's spirit is by, nature refractory, it struggles against opposition and difficulty, and is more ready to follow than to

Luke 9:57–62
PERSPICACITY IN JUDGMENT

102. *And it came to pass as they went on their journey,*
etc. After instruction has been given to the Apostles
about the norms of humility of soul and equanimity in
zeal for leaders, he now gives them a third instruction
relative to *perspicacity in judgment* and uses Jesus
Christ as an example.[221] Now this sagacity in judgment
is manifested in this section in a threefold manner. First
by repelling duplicity, second by *advocating simplicity*
where verse 59 has: *And he said to another*, etc. Third
by *reproving instability* where verse 61 reads: *And another said: I will follow you, Lord*, etc.

Concerning *the repulsion of duplicitous people* two points
are made: First is *the pretense of simplicity*. Second is
the detection of duplicity.

---

be led (*sequitur facilius quam ducitur*); and as well-bred and high-
spirited horses are better managed by a loose rein, so a voluntary up-
rightness follows upon mercy under its own impulse...." Does
Bonaventure the exegete put the opinion of the, non-Christian Latin
philosopher Seneca on the same level as that of the Apostle and the
Psalmist?
[220] See Seneca's *De Clementia* Book I, chapter 19, n. 3: *Rex ipse
(apum) sine aculeo est* ("But the king (of the bees) himself has, no
sting"). I quote all of, n.3 in Basore's LCL translation, p. 411: "His
(the king's) greatest mark of distinction, however, lies in this; bees
are most easily provoked, and, for the size of their bodies, excellent
fighters, and where they wound they leave their stings; but the king
himself has, no sting., nature did, not wish him to be cruel or to seek
a revenge that would be so costly, and so she removed his weapon,
and left his anger unarmed." Interested readers can consult what
QuarEd have on p. 248, n. 10 about the opinions of Aristotle and
Pliny and how the king bee really should be the queen bee, etc.
[221] See #85 above for this triple division of the text.

103. (Verse 57). Therefore, with regard to *the pretense of simplicity* the text has: *And it came to pass as they went on their journey*, that is, the disciples were walking with the Lord on the way of perfection, as it is said of Noah in Genesis 6:9: "Noah, a just and perfect man, . . . walked with God." And similarly the Lord said to Abraham in Genesis 17:1: "Walk before me, and be perfect." Of this way Isaiah 30:21: "You will hear the word of your teacher: This is the good way. Walk in it."[222] – And because it often happens that evil people want to be joined to the good along this way by simulation, the text adds: *A certain man said to Jesus:*[223] *I will follow you wherever you go.* In this he showed that he has the will to follow Jesus perfectly, but nevertheless had something else in his heart. He is like Simon Magus of whom it is said in Acts 8:12–13 that "after the men and women were baptized, then Simon himself . . . was also baptized." But as the story in Acts 8 continues, it is clear that Simon's heart was evil and duplicitous. Therefore, Jerome says: "This man wanted to follow Jesus and like Simon Magus wanted to have the power to perform miracles, so that he might get wealthy from them."[224] But against this is what Sirach 1:36–37 says: "Do not approach the Lord with a double heart. Be not a hypocrite in the sight of men and women." Such are those who promise great things and do little. Against them Sirach 4:34 states:

---

[222] Bonaventure seems to have adapted Isaiah 30:21 to suit his interpretive purposes: "And your ears will hear the word of one admonishing you behind your back: This is the way. Walk in it."

[223] On p. 249, n. 2 QuarEd correctly mention that the Vulgate has *ad illum* ("to him").

[224] On p. 249, n. 4 QuarEd refer to Book I of Jerome's Commentary on Matthew 8:19ff. And then quote what the Glossa Interlinearis says about that passage: "*He said to him*: With the desire that Simon Magus had of buying (the power to work miracles), so that he might enrich himself by working miracles."

"Be not hasty with your tongue, and slack and remiss in your deeds."

104. (Verse 58). Second, concerning the detection of duplicity the text says: *And Jesus said to him: The foxes have dens,* that is, in which to hide, *and the birds of the air have nests,* in which to spend the night, *but the Son of Man has nowhere to lay his head.* In this he shows wondrous poverty, as if he were saying that the person who loves earthly things will not have him as a companion. Therefore, Luke 14:33 below says: "Whoever has not renounced all that he possesses cannot be my disciple," that is, a perfect imitator. So Chrysostom has: "The Lord responds to his mentality, as if saying: Why do you follow me for the sake of money when you see that money is as alien to me as it is to the birds?"[225] – At the same time he also points out the exterior deceit which is understood in the word fox, according to what is said of Herod in Luke 13:32 below: "Go, and tell that fox." And for this reason foxes are understood to be heretics,[226] for they are crooked and deceitful and carry fire in their

---

[225] On p. 249, n. 7 QuarEd say that this quotation comes from Chrysostom's Homily 27 (alias 28) on Matthew, n. 2. See Hugh of St. Cher, p. 191a for almost the identical quotation.

[226] On p. 249, n. 8 QuarEd quote the Glossa Ordinaria (from Ambrose) on Luke 9:58: "Foxes are tricky animals, intent on treachery, given to destruction and deceit, even living in dens among human dwellings themselves. Thus the heretics, lacking the home of faith, draw others into their tricks and seduce them from the faith." See CCSL xiv, pp. 225–226. John A. Darr, *On Building Character: The Reader and the Rhetoric of Characterization in Luke-Acts,* Literary Currents in Biblical Interpretation (Louisville: Westminster/John Knox, 1992), says this on p. 141 in his chapter on "Herod the Fox": "Foxes were alternatively perceived as wise, tricky, cunning, wily, deceitful, inferior, base, of little or, no concern or consequence, cowardly, greedy, rapacious and destructive. Such traits made the fox a favorite subject of figurative applications to human beings."

tails, as it is said of the foxes of Samson in Judges 15:4–5.[227]

105. Note that he detects *interior simulation* in him through the word *bird*, which seeks high places. Such is the proud person, as it is said in Obadiah 1:4: "Even though you be exalted like an eagle and though you built your nest upon the stars, I will cast you down from there, says the Lord."[228] – And on account of these two things the Lord shows that this person's companionship is to be rejected, for 1 Corinthians 1:28–29 says: "God has chosen the base things of the world and the despised, and the things that are not, to bring to naught the things that are, lest any flesh should pride itself before him." – And therefore, as an example of such imitation of the Lord is the mendicant, according to what 2 Corinthians 8:9 has: "He became poor for our sakes, so that by his poverty we might become rich." Wherefore, the imitators of Christ have been made rich by Christ's poverty. For exceedingly rich is the person who only has as much as the King of heaven and earth. Now a person of this type is the one who has nothing in property, but possesses everything in charity, like those in 2 Corinthians 6:10: "as having nothing, but possessing all things." Blessed are those who turn earthly dens into

---

[227] Judges 15:4–5 reads: "And he (Samson) went and caught three hundred foxes and coupled them tail to tail and fastened torches between the tails. And setting them on fire, he let the foxes go that they might run about hither and thither. And they presently went into the standing corn of the Philistines. Which being set on fire, both the corn that was already gathered together, and that which was yet standing, was all burnt, so much so that the flame consumed also the vineyards and the olive groves."

[228] On p. 149, n. 9 QuarEd quote Bede on Luke 9:58. See CCSL cxx, p. 213: "He is understood to be moved by the Lord's miracles and to have wanted to follow him out of vainglory and pride, which the birds signify."

heavenly palaces. "For blessed are the poor in spirit," etc. (Matthew 5:3). – At the same time as you note this, consider that poverty is not acceptable unless it is *simple* against the *deceitfulness of the fox*, and *humble* against *the exaltation of the bird*. So Isaiah 66:2 reads: "But on whom will I have regard except the one who is poor and of a contrite spirit and who trembles at my words?" Here he joins poverty to simplicity and humility. Whence Augustine says: "What profit is there in giving up riches if the pitiful person has become more proud in contemning riches than in possessing them?"[229] For the proud pauper is hateful to God and humankind, according to what Sirach 25:3–4: "Three sorts my soul hated. . . . A poor man who is proud," etc.[230]

106. (Verse 59). *And he said to another.* After repelling duplicity, the Evangelist now treats *the advocating of simplicity* and introduces two elements about it. First is *the call of a blameless person*. Second is *the instruction of an ignorant person*.

Now relative to the first point, *the call of a blameless person*, it is said: *And he said to another: Follow me*, as *a son follows his father*. Jeremiah 3:19 says: "You shall call me father and shall not cease to walk after me." Or like *a disciple a teacher*, as the Lord said to the youth seeking his counsel in Matthew 19:21: "If you want to be

---

[229] This quotation is based on *Regula Sancti Augustini* I.7. See Lawless, *Augustine of Hippo*, pp. 82–83: *Quid prodest dispergere dando pauperibus et pauperem fieri, cum anima misera superbior efficitur diuitias contemnendo, quam fuerat possidendo?* ("What benefit is there in giving generously to the poor and becoming poor oneself, if the pitiful soul is more inclined to pride by rejecting riches than by possessing them?). See Bonaventure's commentary on Luke 9:43 (#81) above where he also quoted Augustine's Rule.

[230] The other two are "a rich man who is a liar, and an old man who is a fool and doting."

perfect, go, sell all[231] that you have and give it to the poor . . . and come and follow me." And he called this one specifically as he did Peter in John 21:22: "You, follow me." – And with significance it calls this person *another*, for he had another disposition than the first. Moreover, he was *single-minded* and *humble*. And to depict this the text adds: *But he said: Lord, permit me first to go and bury my father.* In this his *purity of mind* is obvious, for he did not hide the affection of his heart nor did he oppose the Lord's counsel. Therefore, Isidore has: "He did not despise the call to be a disciple, but once he had fulfilled the filial piety due the burial of his father, he wanted to follow more freely."[232] His *humility* was evident, for he wanted to show obedience to his dead father, according to what Sirach 3:8–9 says: "The person who fears the Lord honors his parents and will serve them as the masters who brought him into the world . . . in deed and word and all patience." *Obedience to the divine commandment* also moved him to do this. Exodus 20:12 says: "Honor your father." He was also moved by *clemency of soul*, for to bury the dead was an act of mercy. For such acts Tobit was commended in Tobit 1:21: "When the king . . . slew many of the children of Israel, Tobit buried their bodies." A *praiseworthy custom* also moved him, according to what Sirach 38:16 reads:

---

[231] Bonaventure has smuggled in *omnia* ("all") from the parallel passage in Luke 18:22.

[232] On p. 250, n. 2 QuarEd provide this information: "Also Cardinal Hugh of St. Cher and Gorranus attribute to Isidore this interpretation which is also found in the Glossa Interlinearis on Matthew 8:24 and the Glossa Ordinaria (apud Lyranum) on Luke 9:59. These aforementioned Glossae have taken this interpretation from Bede's commentaries on those two passages." In CCSL cxx, p. 213 Bede writes:, n*on discipulatum respuit sed expleta primum paterni funeris pietate liberior hunc assequi desiderat. . . .* ("He did, not reject discipleship, but having first completed the filial duty due the burial of his father, he desired to follow him more freely. . . .).

"Shed tears over the dead, and begin to lament as if you had suffered some great harm. And with discretion cover his body and neglect not his burial." So it is apparent that he did not say this out of carnal desire, but from a certain piety and humility, as Elisha said to Elijah in 1 Kings 19:20: "Let me, I beseech you, kiss my father and my mother, and then I will follow you."

107. (Verse 60). Second, with regard to *the instruction of the ignorant* the text continues: *But Jesus said to him:*[233] *Let the dead bury their dead.* The first point he teaches is *not to associate with sinners.* For *the dead* here refer to sinners and unbelievers. So Ephesians 2:1–2 says: "You, when you were dead in your offenses and sins, in which you once walked." A holy man must forsake consorting with such people, according to what Sirach 13:22 has: "What fellowship does a holy person have with a dog?" That is, with sinners and unbelievers. So no matter how intimately one is joined, nonetheless the connection must be severed, especially when it hinders the good. Therefore, Deuteronomy 33:9–10 reads: "Who has said to his father and to his mother: I do not know you. And to his brothers: I know you not. . . . These have kept . . . your judgments, O Jacob, and your law, O Israel."[234]

108. He is also teaching him that *minor goods are to be put in second place for the sake of greater goods.* So Ambrose teaches: "Minor goods are to be set aside for the benefit of greater goods. For it is greater to raise up the

---

[233] On p. 250, n. 6 QuarEd correctly mention that the Vulgate reads *ei* ("to him") while Bonaventure has *illi* ("to him").

[234] On p. 250, n. 7 QuarEd call attention to Ambrose's opinion. See CCSL xiv, p. 228: "The son is, not called away from a duty due his father, but the faithful person is separated from consort with the perfidious."

souls of the dead by preaching than to hide the body of
the dead in the ground."[235] – And therefore, the text
adds: *But you, go and preach the kingdom of God*, as if
he were saying: Put aside the minor good for a greater
good, according to what is said in 1 Timothy 4:7–8:
"Train yourself in godliness. For bodily training is of little benefit," etc. From this it is obvious that according to
the teaching of the Apostle and the Lord works of spiritual piety are entirely to be preferred to corporal works.
For although it is a great work of piety to bury the dead
and this especially for a father, Christ, nevertheless,
wants it to be set aside for the office of preaching. On
account of this the Apostles said in Acts 6:2: "It is not
right that we should forsake the word of God and wait
on tables." For just as the soul is superior to the body, so
too it is better to feed the soul by preaching than to
minister food to the body. Or especially, because there
are more who are fit to provide a burial than to teach
doctrine. So the Apostles said in Acts 6:3–4: "Select men
of good reputation . . . that we may put them in charge
of this work. But we will devote ourselves to prayer and
to the ministry of the word." For it is said in Luke 10:42
below: "Mary has chosen the best part." And thus, Daniel
12:3 has: "Those who instruct many to justice as stars,"

---

[235] On p. 250, n. 8 QuarEd write: "This opinion (VII, n. 34) is shown
according to the Glossa Ordinaria (from Bede) apud Lyranum on
Luke 9:59)." Indeed, the opinion that Bonaventure attributes to Ambrose is, not found in Ambrose. See CCSL, xiv, p. 226. Rather it is
found in Bede. See CCSL, cxx, p. 213: *Postponendum, namque erat
obsequium huius ministerii officio praedicationis quia illo carne mortuos in terram conderet isto autem anima mortuos ad uitam resusci-
taret* ("For obedience to this ministry is to be given second place to
the office of preaching, for the one plants into the earth persons dead
in the flesh whereas the other resurrects to life those dead in the
spirit"). And Bede derives his interpretation from Gregory the
Great's *Moralia*. See PL 76:125A.

etc.[236] – And note that he says: *Proclaim the kingdom of God*, that is, to those who are willing to repent, according to what Christ said in Matthew 4:17: "Repent, for the kingdom of heaven is at hand." Therefore, just as it is a great sin when a rich person does not give alms to a needy person, so it is a greater sin when a learned person does not communicate doctrine. So Proverbs 11:26 says: "The person who hides corn, will be cursed among the people." Therefore, he says: *Proclaim*, and do not hide.

109. (Verse 61). *And another said: I will follow you*, etc. After repelling duplicity and advocating simplicity, he treats *reproving instability* as his next topic.[237] There are two points. First is *vacillation of will*. Second is *the reproof of instability*.

Therefore, with regard to the first point, *vacillation of will*, he says: *And another said: I will follow you.*[238] Behold, with the resolve to attach oneself to God as to a teacher. For he heeded that dominical saying in John 8:12: "The person who follows me does not walk in the darkness." And Sirach 23:38 has: "It is great glory to follow the Lord." – But in this resolve he was not strong. For this reason the text adds: *But let me first go and tell those at home.*[239] From this it is manifest that he is still

---

[236] Daniel 12:3 in its entirety reads: "but they who are learned will shine as the brightness of the firmament; and those who instruct many to justice as stars for all eternity."

[237] See #103 above for this division.

[238] On p. 251, n. 3 QuarEd correctly indicate that the Vulgate reads *te, Domine* ("you, Lord").

[239] The Vulgate reads: *Sed primum permitte mihi renuntiare his qui domi sunt* ("But let me first say farewell to those who are at home"). The main difference between the text of the Vulgate and Bonaventure's text revolves around two verbs. The Vulgate has *renuntiare* while Bonaventure has, *nuntiare* ("tell/announce"). On p. 250,

attached to his family, against what is said in the Psalm: "Forget your people and your father's house" (44:11). And this person was not like Paul, who said in Galatians 1:15–16: "When it pleased him . . . who had called me by his grace . . . I did not immediately consult with flesh and blood." Carnal friends are opposed to spiritual counsel, and therefore are to be dismissed like enemies. Wherefore, it is said in Matthew 10:34–36: "I have not come to send peace, but the sword. I have come to set a man at variance with his father. . . . And a man's enemies will be those of his own household." And thus it is said in the person of the good religious in Jeremiah 12:7: "I have forsaken my house. I have left my inheritance." This man was not such, for his eye was fixed on his family. Similar to this man are the religious who are inquisitive about what is going on among their relatives. Against this Bede says in the Glossa: "If a disciple who is about to follow the Lord is convinced that he must say goodbye to his household, what will become of those who often and to no one's benefit visit the homes they have abandoned?"[240] Such do not heed what was said to Abraham in Genesis 12:1: "Go forth out of your country and from your kindred and from your father's house and come into the land that I will show you."

110. (Verse 62). Second, concerning *the reproof of insta-bility* it says: *Jesus said to him: No one, having put his hand to the plow*, etc. that is, to the practice of divine perfection and preaching, which is fittingly designated by *the plow* because of its use for cultivation and pro-

---

QuarEd provide a lengthy note 4 on the variant readings of Luke 9:61 and on the meaning of *renuntiare*. They give evidence for the meaning "to say farewell." The dominant dictionary meaning, however, is "to announce" and "to renounce."

[240] On p. 251, n. 6 QuarEd state that the quotation is from the Glossa Ordinaria.

duce, in accordance with what Hosea 10:11 has: "Judah will plough, and Jacob will break the furrows for himself." – *No one*, I say, and such exist, *and looking*[241] *back*, that is, to the world, *is fit for the kingdom of God*, that is, to possess the kingdom of God. For, according to what 2 Timothy 2:4 says, "No one serving as God's soldier entangles himself in worldly affairs, so that he may please him whose approval he has secured." – A figure of this occurred beforehand with the wife of Lot, who, "looking behind her, was turned into a statue of salt" (Genesis 19:26). For such a person is rendered useless and sterile. And therefore, it is said in Luke 17:31–32: "Let the person who is in the field not turn back. Remember Lot's wife."

111. Such a person is not fit for the kingdom, but rather *derision*. Whence 2 Peter 2:21–22 reads: "It were better not to have known the way of truth[242] than having known it, to turn back from the holy commandment delivered to them. For what that true proverb says has happened to them: A dog returns to its vomit," etc. Which can fittingly be understood of recidivists and apostates. And therefore, contrary advice is given by Sirach 5:12: "Be steadfast in the way of the Lord." Such was the Apostle, as it is said in Philippians 3:13–14: "Forgetting what is

---

[241] On p. 251, n. 9 QuarEd correctly state that the Vulgate reads *respiciens* ("looking") whereas Bonaventure (Bede, Cardinal Hugh, et al.) has *aspiciens* ("looking").

[242] The Vulgate has *viam justitiae* ("the way of justice"). The proverb quoted is from Proverbs 26:11. Both 2 Peter 2:21–22 and Proverbs 26:11 were widely applied in medieval times to those who abandoned religious life. See, e.g., St. Francis of Assisi, Admonition 3:10 and my commentary thereon in *The Admonitions of St. Francis: Sources and Meanings,* Text Series 21 (St. Bonaventure, New York: The Franciscan Institute, 1999), pp. 69, 159–160.

behind, I strain forward to what is ahead.[243] I press on towards the goal, the prize of a heavenly calling. . . ." And therefore, he gave the admonishment in Ephesians 3:17–18: "Rooted and grounded in love, you may be able to comprehend," etc. For he knew what had been said by the Lord in Matthew 10:22: "The person who perseveres to the end will be saved." To this perseverance Scripture especially challenges us. Wherefore, throughout the Law and the Prophets[244] the children of Israel were forbidden to return to Egypt, that is, men and women should not convert from divine service to the world. Thus and on account of this sin almost all the children of Israel were killed by the Lord in the desert.

---

[243] Bonaventure's quotation varies somewhat from the Vulgate which reads: *Quae quidem retro sunt obliviscens ad ea vero quae sunt in priora extendens me* ("But forgetting what things are behind me, I strain forward to what things are on ahead").

[244] On p. 252, n. 3 QuarEd give these biblical references: Numbers 14:2ff.; 1 Corinthians 10:10; Hebrews 3:17 as well as Isaiah 30:1ff.; 31:1ff.; Jeremiah 2:5ff.; Ezekiel 20:5ff.

LUKE 10

Luke 10:1-11:13
THE MISSION OF THE DISCIPLES

1. *After this*[1] *the Lord appointed*, etc. Having dealt with the mission of the Apostles, the Evangelist considers here *the mission of the disciples* as *minor prelates*. Now this section has three parts. The first concerns *the form of preaching*. The second, whose object is *the form of living*, commences in verse 25: *And behold, a certain lawyer*, etc. The third part focuses on *the form of praying* and begins in 11:1: *And it came to pass as he was praying in a certain place*, etc.

---

[1] On p. 252, n. 4 QuarEd correctly indicate that the Vulgate has *autem* ("now"), and Bonaventure does not.

Luke 10:1–24
The Form of Preaching

This part has three components, the first of which deals with *the mission of the disciples who are accompanying Christ*. In the second notice is made of *the formation of those going forth* where verse 4 reads: *Carry neither purse*, etc. *The consolation of those returning* is the subject of the third component where verse 17 has: *Now the seventy-two returned with joy*, etc. Now the disciples *are sent* with the authority of divine command, *are formed* by the truth of divine teaching, *are consoled* by the familiarity of being associated with the divine.

Now the Lord *sends* the disciples to preach in this order. First by *appointing* them according to a fitting number. Second by *sending ahead* those appointed into every city and place. Third by *speeding on their way* those sent ahead for the salvation of the elect. Fourth by *strengthening* those sped on their way against the fury of persecutors.

Luke 10:1–3
The Appointment of the Disciples Who Are Accompanying Christ

2. (Verse 1). First, then, with regard to *the appointment of the disciples* according to a fitting number the text says: *After this the Lord appointed seventy-two others*, etc. Now *he appointed*, that is, he carefully chose, in accordance with what John 15:16 has: "I have chosen you and have appointed you that you should go," etc. Wherefore the Glossa reads: "As the form is that of bishops in the case of the Apostles, so the form is that of presbyters

of the second order in the case of the seventy-two."[2]
These must be *appointed* by God, that is, to be brought
to this honor, according to what Hebrews 5:4 says: "And
no one takes the honor to himself, but the one who is
called by God, as Aaron was." In witness of this appointment they must be signed with the seal of their order and the sacerdotal character, the seal of the tonsure
and the assumption of a most holy way of life and discipline,[3] so that it may be manifest that they pertain to
the number of those about whom Ephesians 4:30 says:
"You have been sealed by the Holy Spirit for the day of
redemption."[4] – Now he appointed them *seventy in number*,[5] according to what they had been signified in the
Old Testament in Exodus 15:27 by *seventy palms*. Exodus 15:27 says that "in Elim there were twelve fountains of water" with regard to the Apostles "and seventy
palms" with regard to the disciples.[6] And in Numbers

---

[2] On p. 252, n. 7 QuarEd state that this is the Glossa Ordinaria,
whose words are taken from Bede. See CCSL cxx, pp. 213–214 for
Bede's complete comment which has "those seventy-two are a figure
of the presbyters, that is, of the second order of priests." The first
order of priests is occupied by the bishops.

[3] In this section Bonaventure is interpreting the seventy-two as
priests who were singled out in medieval theology by the tonsure and
a regimented way of life externally and by the sacerdotal character
on their souls internally.

[4] The Vulgate actually reads: *Et nolite contristare Spiritum Sanctum
Dei, in quo signati estis in die redemptionis* ("And do not sadden the
Holy Spirit of God, in whom you have been sealed for the day of re-
demption").

[5] Even though he does not say so explicitly, Bonaventure seems
aware of the textual variation (in Greek) between the reading "seventy-two" and "seventy." He interprets both numbers.

[6] On p. 252, n. 10 QuarEd give a helpful, but vague referent for this
strange interpretation: "Cf. Jerome, Epistle 78 (alias 127) VI. Man-
sio." In PL 22:703–704 I found Jerome's Letter 78 "Seu Liber Exe-
geticus ad Fabiolam." In this passage Jerome is interpreting Numbers 33:9, which is almost identical with Exodus 15:27. PL 22:704
reads: "We have the hospitality of the sixth mansion. For the most

11:25–26 these were signified by *the seventy men*, to whom the Lord gave the Holy Spirit of prophecy: "The Lord spoke to Moses, taking away from the spirit that was in Moses and giving to the seventy men . . . who prophesied and did not cease thereafter. Now in the camp two of the men had remained . . . upon whom the spirit rested. For they also had been enrolled." In this these had been expressly prefigured. – Now the *literal* reason why these were seventy-two in number is this: that just as the Apostles were twelve to preach to the twelve tribes, so these were seventy-two according to what is said in the Glossa: "Seventy-two are sent who would preach the Gospel to the same number of languages in the world."[7] According to *the mystical sense* there are seventy-two because this number contains in itself a sevenfold and twofold measure. Through it is signified the sevenfold gift of the Spirit bestowed for their ministry of implementing the Decalogue and the two precepts of charity.[8] – Another interpretation is that

---

pure fountains never flowed forth in any other place except where the doctrine of the teachers sprang forth. There is no doubt that this refers to the Twelve Apostles, from whose fountains waters gush forth to satisfy the dryness of the entire world. Alongside these waters seventy palms flourished, whom we understand to be those instructors of a second order. The Evangelist Luke testifies that there were Twelve Apostles and seventy disciples of minor grade, whom the Lord also sent ahead of him two by two (Luke 6 and 10)."

[7] On p. 253, n. 1 QuarEd state that this is the Glossa Ordinaria, refer to various authors, and have pointed me to Book I, chapter 9 of pseudo-Augustine's *Libri Tres De Mirabilibus Sacrae Scripturae*. See PL 35:2161: "Now many authors agree that the number of those languages were seventy-two, because they say that the total number of the fathers congregated at the building of that tower in the land of Sennaar, which is now Babylon, was such. So the Lord is also said in the Gospel to have chosen seventy-two disciples, in addition to the first Apostles, through whom he might afterwards preach the same gospel to all peoples."

[8] On p. 253, n. 2 QuarEd give insight into Bonaventure's terse opinion here by quoting St. Albert's commentary on Luke 10:1: "So sev-

seventy-two is chosen because the hours of three days add up to seventy-two, because they had to preach faith in the Trinity, as it is said in the Glossa, according to the three-day circuit of Christ the Sun, namely, the incarnation, passion, resurrection.[9]

3. Secondly, with regard to *the sending ahead of those appointed* the text adds: *And he sent them forth two by two before him.* *He sent,* I say, by divine authority, because, as it is said in John 20:21, "as the Father has sent me, I also send you." Now *two by two* he sent them. *Literally,* so that they might mutually guard and help each other, according to what Qoheleth 4:9 reads: "It is better that two should be together than one, for they have the advantage of their companionship." *The spiritual interpretation,* as Bede says, is this: "From the fact that he sends them two by two he indicates that no one should assume the office of preaching who does not have charity towards another person."[10] As a designation of

---

enty was the number of years before their liberation from captivity (cf. 2 Chronicles 36:21–23; Jeremiah 25:11–12; Jeremiah 29:10). To the number of seventy, two is added on account of the two commandments of love, so that the seven gifts of the Holy Spirit may lead them to fulfill the ten commandments of the Decalogue and that all these may be informed by the two commandments of love."

[9] On p. 253, n. 3 QuarEd state that the Glossa Ordinaria on Luke 10:1 reads: "Since Christ calls himself *the day* and his Apostles *the hours* of this day (John 11:9), he gives a sign through this number of preachers that they are going to proclaim faith in the Blessed Trinity to the world, just as the sun regularly makes three circuits of radiating its light over the course of seventy-two hours." See CCSL cxx, p. 214 for the basis of the Glossa Ordinaria's comment.

[10] See CCSL cxx, p. 214: . . . *quia qui caritatem erga alterum non habet praedicationis officium suscipere nullatenus debet* (". . . that the person who does not have charity towards another person should in no way assume the office of preaching"). And Bede has taken this quotation from Homily 17, n. 1 of GGHG. See PL 76:1139B: "The person who does not have charity towards another person should in no way assume the office of preaching." Gregory's Homily 17 is on

926 ST. BONAVENTURE'S COMMENTARY ON THE GOSPEL OF LUKE

this reality The Song of Songs 4:2 reads: "Your teeth," that is, the preachers whose responsibility it is to chew[11] the food for the little ones, "are as flocks of sheep that are shorn and have come up from the washing, all with twins. And there is none barren among them."[12] As a *figure* of this reality, as the Glossa says, the animals entered Noah's ark two by two, as is mentioned in Genesis 6:19–21.[13] – And since this mission was nothing except a certain preparation for Christ, the text adds: *into every city and place where he himself was about to come.* Wherefore, they went forth like heralds according to what Isaiah 40:3 says: "Prepare the way of the Lord. Make straight . . . his paths."[14] So the Glossa says: "Where the words of preaching sound forth and run ahead, the Lord finds a dwelling place in people's minds."[15]

Luke 10:1–9. On p. 253, n. 5 QuarEd quote Augustine, *Quaestiones Evangeliorum* II, question 14: "Now that he sends them two by two is a sacrament of charity, either because there are two precepts of charity or because every act of charity needs at least two people." See CCSL xlivb, pp. 58–59.

[11] Bonaventure uses the verb *masticare*, which has a double meaning in medieval ecclesiastical Latin: "to chew" or "to meditate."

[12] On p. 253, n. 5 QuarEd state that Gregory the Great in his commentary on The Song of Songs also applies 4:2 to preachers. I have been unable to verify their observation. St. Bernard of Clairvaux never got as far as 4:2 in his extensive commentary on The Song of Songs.

[13] On p. 253, n. 6 QuarEd mention that this is the Glossa Ordinaria which stems from Ambrose. See CCSL xiv, p 229: "What is the reason why he sent them two by two? For the animals were sent into the ark two by two."

[14] Bonaventure has abbreviated Isaiah 40:3: "The voice of one crying in the desert: Prepare the way of the Lord. Make straight in the wilderness the paths of our God."

[15] On p. 253, n. 7 QuarEd indicate that this is the Glossa Interlinearis and state that it is based on Gregory the Great and Bede. For Gregory's comments, which Bede adapts, see PL 76:1139B: "For the Lord follows his preachers because the preaching goes first and then the Lord comes to the dwelling place of our mind. When the words of

4. (Verse 2). Thirdly, concerning *speeding on those who have been sent ahead* for the salvation of the elect the text continues: *And he said to them: The harvest indeed is great*, that is, the crowd is prepared for conversion. Whence in John 4:35, when the Samaritans had believed, the Lord said: "See the fields which are already white for the harvest." This harvest was sown *during the law of nature*, then grew *during the law of figure*, but was gathered *during the time of grace*. So it is said in John 4:38: "I have sent you to reap what you have not sown.[16] Others have labored, and you have entered into their labors." Now the gathering of this harvest is twofold. It is *universal* at the end of time, about which it is said to the angel in Revelation 14:15: "Put forth your sickle and reap, for the hour to reap has come, because the harvest of the earth is ripe."[17] There is another gathering or harvest, and that is *the particular* one in the preaching of the Gospel. – But since good harvesters are indeed few, the text adds: *but the laborers are few*. It is significant that he says *laborers*, for it is necessary that if the sickle of preaching is to gather the harvest, *the hand of work* should hold it, according to what Gregory says in his Commentary on Ezekiel: "In order to ensure the truth to be preached, a high moral standard of living is necessary."[18] Those who practice what they preach are *laborers* and are to be rewarded by the Lord, according to what Matthew 20:8 says: "Call the laborers and give

---

exhortation sound forth and run ahead, truth is also taken into the mind through them."

[16] The Vulgate reads *non laborastis* ("you have not labored").

[17] On p. 253, n. 9 QuarEd rightly indicate that the Vulgate has *aruit* ("has dried up") where Bonaventure has *maturavit* ("is ripe").

[18] On p. 253, n. 10 QuarEd refer to Book I, Homily 11, n. 7: "Therefore, in order to ensure the truth to be preached, a high moral standard of living is held to be necessary."

them their reward."[19] But few are *industrious* laborers, but many are *malicious*, according to what 2 Corinthians 11:13 reads: "They are false apostles, deceitful laborers, transforming themselves into Apostles of Christ." Then many are *slothful*. Thus the Lord in Matthew 20:6 said to the laborers: "Why do you stand here all the day idle?" There are many similar to those, about whom Matthew 23:3 has: "They talk and do nothing. For they bind together heavy and immovable burdens...but not with one finger of their own do they choose to move them." – And since the harvest is lost if there are no good laborers, the text continues: *Pray therefore the Lord of the harvest to send forth laborers into his harvest*, namely, good preachers, who carry not only in their mouth, but also in their hand the sword of the divine word by which the grain is harvested. Thus the Psalm has this about good preachers: "The high praises of God will be in their mouth, and two-edged swords in their hands" (149:6). So preaching is a sword, which, unless it is held in the hand, does not strike fear in the adversary. This was well prefigured in Nehemiah 4:17 concerning the rebuilding of Jerusalem where it is said that "each one labored with one of his hands, and the other hand held the sword."[20] Such laborers are given from heaven, according to what was signified in Genesis 2:15: "God placed the man in the paradise of pleasure, so that he might labor and guard it." And therefore, God is to be asked for these, so that he might hire them with a promise and send those hired with a command, according to what Matthew 20:1–2 has: "who went out early in

---

[19] I have translated this verse to convey Bonaventure's sense. Customarily it is translated: "Call the laborers and pay them their wages."

[20] Bonaventure has made some slight adjustments to the Vulgate, especially by adding *unusquisque* ("each one") at the beginning.

the morning to hire laborers for his vineyard. And having agreed with the laborers," etc.

5. (Verse 3). Now the fourth point deals with *the strengthening of those sped on their way* against the fury of persecutors. The text reads: *Go. Behold, I send you forth as lambs in the midst of wolves.* *Go*, that is, *hasten expeditiously* like those animals in Ezekiel 1:14: "The animals ran and returned like flashes of lightning." And Proverbs 6:3 has: "Run forth, make haste, stir up your friend." Another interpretation is this: *Go*, that is, *expose yourselves to dangers* for the salvation of the sheep according to what John 10:11–12 has: "The good shepherd lays down his life for his sheep. But the hireling sees the wolf coming and leaves the sheep and flees." As if the Lord is saying: Go forth into a situation of *lamentation*, so that later you may receive joy according to the Psalm: "Going, they went and wept, casting their seeds. But coming back, they will come with exaltation," etc. (125:6–7). Another interpretation is: Go forth to *battle*, so that you may gain victory, according to what Joshua 1:14 says: "Go forth[21] armed among your brothers, all of you who are strong of hand and fight for them."

6. And since the most awesome armaments are meekness and patience, he says: *as lambs amidst wolves*, that is, as dedicated, humble and meek in the midst of the impious, proud and ferocious, so that you may win them over by your meekness just as Christ did according to what Isaiah 53:7 has: "As a lamb before his shearer, he was dumb and did not open his mouth."[22] So with lamb-

---

[21] The Vulgate has *transite* ("pass over") while Bonaventure reads *ite* ("go forth").
[22] Bonaventure has changed the Vulgate's future tenses into past tenses.

like meekness the Apostles tamed wolf-like ferocity, and Isaiah 11:6–7 was fulfilled: "The wolf will lie down[23] together with the lamb . . . and the lion will eat straw like an ox." And Isaiah 65:25 reads: "The wolf and the lamb will feed together." Thus Christ by his meekness converted the wolf Paul into a lamb, and what Genesis 49:27 said has been fulfilled in him: "Benjamin, a ravenous wolf, in the morning he will eat the prey, and in the evening divide the spoils."[24] For earlier he was the wolf who persecuted Christ, and later he was the lamb that suffered persecutions for Christ. The prelates of the church must be like this, according to what 1 Peter 5:1–3 says: "Elders, . . . tend the flock that is among you . . . not by lording it over your charges, but by becoming a genuine pattern for the flock." As if to say: Do not be like wolves among the lambs, but rather lambs among the lambs and wolves, so that you may strengthen the good and tolerate the bad. So Chrysostom says: "The grace of God is stronger than nature. While we might be sheep, we are victorious, even though the wolves are many. Also if we were once wolves, we are won over, and the assistance of the supreme shepherd in our regard does not stop."[25]

---

[23] The Vulgate has *habitabit* ("will dwell") whereas Bonaventure reads *morabuntur* ("will lie down").

[24] On p. 254, n. 8 QuarEd have led me to the three readings of the second nocturn of the Feast of the Conversion of St. Paul (January 25). St. Augustine's "Sermon 14 on the Saints" supplies the text for these readings. In brief, Augustine interprets Genesis 49:27 thus: Jacob foretold that Paul, from the tribe of Benjamin, is the wolf whom Christ turned into a lamb, for in the morning or early part of his life he was ferocious against Christians, but in the evening or later part of his life he was the lamb in their midst.

[25] On p. 254, n. 10 QuarEd state that this comes from Homily 33 (alias 34) on Matthew, n. 1. See Hugh of St. Cher, p. 192h for basically the same quotation.

Luke 10:4–16
THE FORMATION OF THOSE GOING FORTH ON MISSION

7. *Do not carry*, etc. After the description of the mission of the disciples two by two the text continues with *the formation of those going forth on mission*. Now this section consists of two points. The first deals with *the common formation* of all. The second concerns *the special formation* of certain individuals where verse 8 reads: *And into whatever city you enter.*

Luke 10:4–7
THE COMMON FORMATION FOR ALL GOING ON MISSION

Through his *general formation* he invites us to consider four topics, namely, *to embrace want, to shun talkativeness, to be courteous and peaceful,* and *to be steadfastly mature.*[26]

8. (Verse 4). First, then, with regard to *embracing want* the text has: *Do not carry a sack*, namely, for depositing money. For it is commonly accepted that *a sack* is used as a purse for money, according to what Proverbs 7:20 says: "He took with him a sack of money." *Nor a wallet,* that is, for holding bread, according to what Matthew 6:31 has: "Do not be anxious for tomorrow,[27] saying: What will be eat," etc. *Nor shoes,* that is for covering one's feet. For in Mark 6:9 it is said: "But to be shod

---

[26] I have translated the last two characteristics via context through paraphrase. Bonaventure wrote: *ad exhibendam humanitatem et ostendendam maturitatem.*

[27] The Vulgate does not have *in crastinum* ("for tomorrow"). Nor does the parallel passage in Luke 12:22.

only[28] with sandals." For *sandals* protect one's feet from injury, but do not cover them, like the sandals of the brothers.[29] Now the Lord wanted to enjoin these things on his disciples, so that they not only *would be* poor, but indeed *would appear* to be so, and that they might invite others to poverty more by their example than by their words. As Seneca says: "But poverty is a hateful good."[30] And therefore, while poverty appears to be shameful and vile, the Lord has united the greatest *dowry* to it, so that through it one can enter into the heavenly nuptials as Matthew 5:3 says: "Blessed are the poor in spirit, for theirs is the kingdom of the heavens."[31]

9. Secondly, relative to *shunning talkativeness* the text continues: *And greet no one on the way.* About this passage the Glossa says: "Lest by confabulation with someone along the way they might be deflected from fulfilling their office."[32] For he was sending them forth in haste,

---

[28] The Vulgate does not have *tantum* ("only"). Bonaventure's addition of "only" in Mark 6:9 leads to his next point.

[29] By "brothers" Bonaventure refers to his Franciscan confreres.

[30] On p. 255, n. 3 QuarEd give evidence of having ransacked the Epistles of Seneca for this quote. According to them in Epistle 17 Seneca shows that poverty, although it may be feared, is a good. In Epistle 80 Seneca teaches that there is nothing evil in poverty, but much that is commendable. Epistle 123, n. 13–16 contain a more exact parallel: "There are two classes of objects which either attract us or repel us. We are attracted by such things as riches . . . we are repelled by toil, death, pain, disgrace, or lives of great frugality. We ought therefore to train ourselves so that we may avoid a fear of the one or a desire for the other. . . . 'Poverty is an evil to no one unless he kick against the goads (*Paupertas nulli malum est nisi repugnanti*)'" (LCL). The LCL does not indicate the source of Seneca's quotation. QuarEd continue with a long quotation from Aristotle.

[31] I don't know how Bonaventure got from poverty to "dowry" and "nuptials."

[32] On p. 255, n. 4 QuarEd state that this is the Glossa Ordinaria which is based almost word for word on Ambrose. See CCSL xiv, p. 235.

as Elisha sent his servant in 2 Kings 4:29: "If any man meet you, do not salute him. And if anyone salutes you, do not respond." Now the Lord enjoined this not to avoid extending a sign of affability, since he himself was most gracious and most courteous, but rather to shun garrulous chatter. Concerning which Proverbs 10:19 has: "In multiplication of words sin will not be absent." And therefore, Sirach 19:5 reads: "The person who hates babbling extinguishes evil." Now this was a common practice among travelers, and frequently was the occasion for contentions. So it is said in Mark 9:33 about the disciples: "For on the way they had discussed[33] which one of them was the greatest." For this reason it is said in Genesis 45:24 that "Joseph said to his departing brothers: Do not be angry on the journey."

10. Now according to *the spiritual sense* he prohibits them for seeking a greeting *on the journey*, but does not prohibit a greeting[34] *in the heavenly homeland which is the goal of the journey*. This is noted when the text reads: *on the journey*. For salvation is to be sought for all, as it is said in 1 Timothy 2:4 that "God desires that all people be saved." And God does this because God is *salutation* and savior. But that *salvation* must be sought of which the Psalmist says: "But the salvation of the just is from the Lord" (36:39). The Apostles always sought this salutary greeting, and concerning it Sirach 22:31 reads: "You will not be ashamed to salute a friend." And Romans 16:16 says: "Greet another with a holy kiss." And the Psalm has: "You yourself are my king and my God who command the salutation of Jacob" (43:5) – Another

---

[33] The Vulgate has *inter se* ("among themselves").
[34] Throughout this first part of the spiritual sense Bonaventure will be playing on the dual meaning of *salus* ("greeting/salutation" and "salvation"). At times it almost seems that Bonaventure intends both meanings in the same sentence.

possible explanation is this: *Salute no one on the way*, that is, as if you were saying to people that they are already saved. They still can be damned, for they are still on the way. For Matthew 10:22 says: "The person who has persevered to the end will be saved." Therefore, *salvation* comes at the end of the journey, not at its mid point nor at its beginning. – Or yet another interpretation is as follows. *Salute no one on the way*, that is, because one shares *the same way*, but rather because one shares *the same way of life*. From this it is manifest that salvation comes to those who imitate the Saints and do not merely converse about them. So Matthew 7:21 reads: "Not everyone who says to me, 'Lord, Lord,' will enter the kingdom of the heavens, but the person who does the will of my Father in heaven."

11. (Verse 5). Third, with regard to *being courteous and peaceful* the text adds: *And*[35] *into whatever house you enter, first say: Peace to this house*, so that it may be clear that you are men who love and proclaim peace, according to what Isaiah 52:7 has: "How beautiful on the mountains are the feet of the person who announces and preaches peace." The Lord *effected* this peace, according to what Colossians 1:20 says: "Effecting peace through the blood of his cross," etc. The Lord also *bequeaths* peace. John 14:27 reads: "Peace I bequeath to you, my peace I give you." The Lord *announced* peace. John 20:19 has: "Jesus stood in their midst and said to them: Peace be with you." The Lord *commanded* and *brought the good news* of peace, as it is said in Ephesians 2:17: "Coming, he announced the good news of peace to you who were far off and peace to those who were near."

---

[35] On p. 255, n. 11 QuarEd correctly mention that the Vulgate does not have *Et* ("and").

12. (Verse 6). And since they may possibly be afraid that their offer of peace may be in vain, the text adds: *And if a son of peace be there,* that is, *a son of peace* according to eternal foreknowledge. Concerning such it is said in John 11:51–52 that "Jesus died . . . so that he might gather the sons of God who had been dispersed." Of these it is said in 2 Timothy 2:19: "The Lord knew who are his." Such are the sons of peace, for it is said in Matthew 5:9: "Blessed are the peacemakers, for they will be called sons of God." – In such a person the word of preaching takes effect. So the text continues: *Your peace will rest upon him,* that is, the peace proclaimed by you. Wherefore, Isaiah 66:2 says according to the other translation: "Upon whom will my Spirit rest if not upon the humble and rest-filled person?"[36] For the peace of Christ which is announced rests upon those predestined by God,[37] according to what Acts 13:48 has: "As many as had been destined for eternal life believed." And John 10:26–27: "You do not believe because you are not of my sheep. My sheep hear my voice." – Therefore, it is beneficial to speak the gospel of peace to *the predestined.* And since it is also beneficial to speak to those *who have foreknowledge,* the text adds: *But if not, it will return to you,* according to what the Psalm says: "My prayer will return to my bosom" (34:13). And this is so, because works of religion and charity are always beneficial to

---

[36] On p. 256, n. 3 QuarEd have a helpful note about the provenance of Bonaventure's reading of Isaiah 66:2 here. It seems that Bonaventure selected the Septuagint rather than the Vulgate because the former had *quietum* ("rest-filled"). And he adds *spiritus meus* ("my Spirit") which neither the Septuagint nor the Vulgate has.

[37] On p. 256, n. 2 QuarEd quote the Glossa Interlinearis which they state is from Bede who borrowed from Gregory the Great: "*And if there is a son of peace there,* predestined to life, the heavenly word that he hears will succeed." See Homily 17, n. 6 of GGHG in PL 76:1141BC. For Bede's commentary, see CCSL cxx, p. 215. The Glossa Interlinearis is a faithful conveyer of the tradition.

the one performing them and return to the one performing them, according to what Sirach 17:18–19 says:
"The alms of a man are like a purse on his person, and
will preserve the grace of a man like the apple of his
eye. And afterward he will rise up and will render them
their reward, to everyone upon their own head."

13. (Verse 7). Fourth, with regard to *steadfast maturity*
the text adds: *And remain in the same house*, as mature
men, lest perchance you be deemed unstable. So Sirach
21:25 reads: "The foot of a fool arrives with ease in the
house of his neighbor." Therefore, Bede says: "It is out of
place for the preacher to run from house to house and
change the laws of hospitality."[38] – And since they might
think that hospitality is to be varied according to the
food provided them, the text continues: *eating and drinking what they have* without *distinguishing* between
foods, as 1 Corinthians 10:27 states: "Eat whatever is
set before you and ask no question for the sake of conscience." Also without *rejecting* certain foods, according
to what 1 Timothy 4:4–5 has: "Every creature of God is
good, and nothing is to be rejected that is accepted with
thanksgiving. For it is sanctified by the word of God and
prayer." Further without requisitioning certain food,
according to what Sirach 31:21 says: "If you are sitting
among many, do not reach out your hand first of all nor
be the first to ask for a drink." – And since they could
think that it was not licit for them to be fed from some-

---

[38] For Bede's opinion, see CCSL cxx, p. 196 where he is commenting
on Luke 9:4 and borrowing verbatim from Ambrose. See Bonaventure's commentary on Luke 9:4 (#8) above where he quotes Ambrose
almost word for word. For Ambrose's opinion, see CCSL xiv, p. 197:
... *alienum a praedicatore regni caelestis adstruens cursitare per domos et inuiolabilis hospitii iura mutare* ("... adding that it is out of
place for the preacher of the heavenly kingdom to run from house to
house and change the laws of inviolable hospitality").

one else's substance, the text continues: *For the laborer deserves his wages*, not only at home for remuneration, but also on the road for sustenance. So 1 Corinthians 9:14 reads: "The Lord directed that those who preach the gospel should gain their living from the gospel." And Galatians 6:6 has: "And let the person who is instructed in the word share all good things with his teacher." So it is said in 1 Corinthians 9:11: "If we have sown spiritual things for you, it is not a great matter if we reap your carnal things."[39] And the Apostles proves his point that such a laborer is worthy of his reward in 1 Corinthians 9:4–14 by means of authoritative sources and many arguments, as is manifest there. Since the laborer is worthy of his food, he need not change his place of hospitality to obtain it. – So in conclusion of this section the text adds: *Do not go from house to house*, lest you appear to be vagrants, lest you appear to be like that wandering woman, about whom Proverbs 7:10–11 says: "She was talkative, wandering, not bearing to be quiet, not able to abide still at home." Such people are the heretics. So 2 Timothy 3:6 has: "Of such are they who make their way into homes and captivate disgraceful women who are burdened with sins." The preachers of truth must not be like this. So Ambrose states: "The preacher is not to migrate from house to house with a vagrant's facility, so that the charitable give and take between host and guest may be preserved with constancy and lest the necessity which unites one as friends be easily dissolved."[40]

---

[39] On p. 256, n. 7 QuarEd accurately indicate that Bonaventure has adjusted the Vulgate: "If we have sown for you spiritual things, is it a great matter if we reap from you carnal things?"

[40] On pp. 256–257, n. 10 QuarEd indicate that Ambrose's opinion comes to Bonaventure via the Glossa Ordinaria. The two textual variants they provide indicate that copyists had trouble figuring out the exact referents of "charity" and "friendship" in this quotation. I

Luke 10:8–16
SPECIAL FORMATION CONCERNING DIFFERENT AUDIENCES

14. *And into whatever city you enter.* After his description of the common formation of the disciples the Evangelist adds here words of *special formation* concerning different audiences. And since some were prepared *to receive* them, such as the faithful, others *to repulse* them, such as the non-believers, whose sin stemmed from contempt for divine grace and scorn for apostolic authority, this section has four items. In the first *formation with regard to the faithful* is set forth. In second place is *formation relative to the rebellious* where verse 10 reads: *And into whatever city you enter, and they do not receive you.* The third deals with *a rebuke against those who contemn* where verse 13 has: *Woe to you, Chorazin,* etc. The fourth concludes with *the authentication of the preachers* where verse 16 says: *The person who hears you,* etc.

Concerning formation of an audience of believers two things are introduced. The first is *acceptance of a temporal stipend.* The second concerns *the communication of a spiritual benefit.*

15. (Verse 8). So the first instruction concerns *acceptance of a temporal stipend*: *And into whatever city you enter,* that is, to preach the truth, as it is said in Jonah 3:4 that "Jonah began to enter[41] the city a one day's journey and cried out." And so must these stir up the city upon their entry by proclaiming the divine word, in accordance with what is said of the disciple Philip in Acts 8:5–6:

---

have offered an intelligible translation. For Ambrose's actual words, see CCSL xiv, p. 236.

[41] On p. 257, n. 3 QuarEd correctly state that the Vulgate has *in* ("into").

"He went down to the city of Samaria and preached Jesus[42] to them. And the crowds gave heed to the things spoken by Philip." – And since it is characteristic of believers to listen attentively to the divine words, the text adds: *And they receive you,* namely, through faith and love as messengers of Christ. For Matthew 18:5 says: "The person who receives one such little child in my name receives me."[43] Now the person receiving the preacher accepts his teaching with meekness and patience, according to what is said in James 1:21: "With meekness receive the ingrafted word which is able to save your souls." – And because corporal nourishment can be received from those who are receiving spiritual teaching, the text continues: *Eat what is set before you,* that is, to relieve necessity, so that you can more vigorously labor according to what the Psalm has: "You will eat the labors of your hands. And blessed are you, and may it go well with you" (127:2). Wherefore, 1 Corinthians 9:17 says this: "It is a stewardship entrusted to me." The Glossa states: "Therefore, we must not evangelize, so that we may eat. But we must eat, so that we may evangelize. Therefore, food is not the good we desire, but a necessity that is added."[44]

---

[42] The Vulgate reads *Christum* ("the Christ").

[43] See the parallel in Luke 9:48.

[44] On p. 257, n. 5 QuarEd state that this is the Glossa Ordinaria which comes from Book II, chapter 16, n. 53–54 of Augustine's *Commentary on the Lord's Sermon on the Mount.* See, n. 54 in *Saint Augustine: Commentary on the Lord's Sermon on the Mount with Seventeen Related Sermons,* translated by Denis J. Kavanagh, FC 11 (New York: Fathers of the Church, 1951), p. 160: "For instance, we ought not to preach the Gospel in order that we may eat, but we ought to eat in order to be able to preach the Gospel. For, if we preach the Gospel in order that we may eat, we esteem the Gospel as of less value than food; in that case, our good would be in the eating, and our need would be in the preaching of the Gospel."

16. And note that the text reads: *What is set before you*, and to do this with cheerfulness. For Proverbs 15:17 has: "It is better to be invited to herbs with love than to a fatted calf with hatred." So eat *what is set before you*, not what you yourselves might prepare. He says this to avoid gourmandizing, about which Seneca writes: "Into the belly luxurious things pile together, as if heaps of them are of benefit. What's the point of taking in these things? Isn't the person going to lose all the things he has ingested?"[45] And therefore, it is said in Sirach 2:4: "Accept all that will be brought to you." But this applies especially to the poor, so that they may be satisfied with ordinary food when they are hungry. For it is said in Proverbs 27:7: "A soul that is hungry will take even bitter for sweet." And Job 6:7 has: "The things that my soul would not touch before, now through anguish are my food."

17. (Verse 9). Now secondly, about *the communication of a spiritual benefit* the text reads: *And cure the sick who are there.* And this by the power of the Holy Spirit conferred on them. Concerning this power 1 Corinthians 12:9–10 says: "To another the gift of healing in the one Spirit; to another the working of miracles." The Lord gave this power to his lesser disciples to confirm their teaching. So Jerome states: "Since no one would believe inarticulate people from the country who were promising

---

[45] On p. 257, n. 7 QuarEd mention Seneca's Epistle 114 (alias 115) *in fine* as a possible source for this quotation. See Epistle 114, n. 26–27 in LCL: "Look at our kitchens, and the cooks, who bustle about over so many fires; is it, think you, for a single belly that all this bustle and preparation of food takes place? . . . But nothing will give you so much help toward moderation as the frequent thought that life is short and uncertain here below." In his commentary on Luke 10:4 (#8) above Bonaventure also quoted Seneca "loosely." Was Bonaventure using a handbook of quotations from Seneca?

them the kingdom of heaven, Christ gives them the power to perform miracles."[46] He had earlier bestowed the gift of this power to the Apostles in Luke 9:1 above: "He gave them power over all the demons and to cure diseases."[47] But he commands them here, so that they may use the gift received according to what is said in 1 Peter 4:10: "According to the gift that each has received, administer it to one another," etc. – And since bodily healing had been ordained for the illumination of the mind, the text adds: *And say to them: The kingdom of God will be at hand*[48] *for you.* In this kingdom are enclosed, as was explained above, *the truth of the teaching, the goodness of grace,* and *sublimity of glory.*[49] And the Interlinearis says: "The kingdom of God is Christ, or eternal life, or knowledge of the scriptures."[50] And *it has arrived* in such a way that he was among us, according to what is said in Luke 17:21 below: "The kingdom of God is among us." It had truly arrived, when he was already present, of whom it is said in Revelation 19:16 that "he had[51] written on his garment and on his thigh:

[46] On p. 257, n. 9 QuarEd state that Jerome's opinion is found in Book I of his commentary on Matthew 10:7–8. See Hugh of St. Cher, p. 192v, k, who gives this very same quotation from Jerome.

[47] Luke 9:1 reads in full: "Then having summoned the Twelve Apostles, he gave them power and authority over all the demons and to cure diseases."

[48] On p. 258, n. 1 QuarEd indicate that Hugh of St. Cher, Blessed Albert, Gorranus, and Lyranus also read the future. The Vulgate, however, has *appropinquavit* ("has come and therefore is at hand for you").

[49] See Bonaventure's commentary on Luke 9:2 (#3) for the same realities: truth, grace, and glory.

[50] On p. 258, n. 2 QuarEd say that they have been unable to locate this Glossa Interlinearis. They give Blessed Albert's commentary on Luke 10:9: "But the Glossa *Interlinearis*, which is *magisterial*, says that the kingdom of heaven is either Christ, or eternal life, or Scripture."

[51] The Vulgate has *habet* ("has") while Bonaventure has *habebat* ("had").

King of kings and Lord of lords." *Into you*, that is, into those who received the word of God through faith, about whom Revelation 5:10 says: "You have made us a kingdom for our God, and we will reign over the earth."[52] And through the grace of faith, according to what Colossians 1:13 has, "he has rescued us from the power of darkness and transferred us into the kingdom of his beloved Son."[53] – So it is patent how the preachers must deport themselves in relationship to believers, for they had to receive a stipend for their sustenance and had to administer the gifts of healing and instruction. Therefore, those who do not administer these spiritual benefits are less worthy to receive corporeal assistance. Wherefore Gregory says: "What are we teachers to say about these things, who receive an ecclesiastical office to go on ahead of Christ, but use our mouths to eat and not to preach?"[54] And Bernard writes: "They will come before the tribunal of the judge where there will be harsh allegations and grave accusations from the poor against them who lived off their stipends and did not cleanse them of their sins."[55]

---

[52] Bonaventure has adjusted Revelation 5:10 which reads: "You have made them a kingdom and priests for our God, and they will reign over the earth."

[53] On p. 258, n. 4 QuarEd rightly point out that the Vulgate reads *dilectionis suae* ("his beloved") whereas Bonaventure has *caritatis suae* ("his beloved").

[54] On p. 258, n. 5 QuarEd cite Book XXII c. 22, n. 53 of Gregory's *Moralia*. See Hugh of St. Cher, p. 191v, i for the exact same citation as Bonaventure has.

[55] On p. 258, n. 6 QuarEd indicate that this quotation is not from Bernard of Clairvaux, but from *Declamationes de Colloquio Simonis cum Jesu, Ex S. Bernardi sermonibus collectae* of Geoffrey the Abbot. Has Bonaventure modified the text which can be found in PL 184:448D: "They will come, they will come to the tribunal of Christ. The grave complaint and harsh accusation of the people will be heard (against those), who lived off their stipends and did not cleanse them of their sins." See Bonaventure's commentary on Luke 9:23 (#38)

18. (Verse 10). *Into whatever city you enter.* After providing formation concerning preaching to believers, the Evangelist gives *formation about those who rebel against the preaching.* He makes two points. The first is *the testimony of the truth of the Gospel.* The second is *the threat of a severe judgment.*

So with regard to the first point, *the testimony of the truth of the Gospel,* it is said: *Into whatever city you enter,* to preach the truth, according to what Acts 17:1–2 says: "They came to Thessalonica, where there was a synagogue of the Jews. Paul . . . went in to them . . . and reasoned with them from the scriptures." – *And they do not receive you,* to listen to the truth, which is the fitting response to preachers, as is said in 3 John 8–9: "We ought to receive such as these that we may be fellow workers for the truth. I would have written perhaps to the church, but Diotrephes, who loves to have the first place among them, does not receive us." – *Go out into its streets,* in witness to the truth, on account of what is said in Matthew 10:27: "What I tell you in darkness, speak in the light. And what you hear whispered, preach from the rooftops."[56]

19. (Verse 11). *Say: Even the dust from your city that cleaves to our feet, we shake off against you,* on account of your contempt for the truth which is an extremely detestable sin, according to what John 15:22 has: "If I had not come and spoken to them, they would have no sin." And so as an indication of how detestable this sin is, the text says *to shake the dust off,* as Peter says to Simon in

---

above where he also used this source under the name of "Bernard." See Hugh of St. Cher, p. 191v, i for the identical quotation from "Bernard" that Bonaventure has. Both Bonaventure and Hugh have these quotations in the same sequence.

[56] See the parallel in Luke 12:3.

Acts 8:20: "May your money go to destruction with you."[57] – *But know this, that the kingdom of God will be at hand*, that is, the truth of the Gospel, according to what Matthew 24:14 reads: "This Gospel of the kingdom will be preached in the whole world for a witness to all nations." Thus, no one can be excused because of ignorance. And so that this may occur publicly, he commands that *they shake the dust in the streets*. About this Jerome says that he gives this command "as testimony that their preaching came to this city."[58] And so they have no excuse for their non-belief.

20. Now according to *the spiritual understanding, the feet of the Apostles* are the affections of the preachers, to which dust customarily adheres in three ways.[59] There is *vainglory*, about which the Psalm says: "It brings down my glory to the dust" (7:6). And also *indignation and impatience*. Micah 7:17 says this about them: "They will lick the dust like a snake." And then, too, there are *cupidity and avarice*. Concerning them Sirach 27:5 has: "As when one sifts with a sieve, the dust will remain." – The first kind of dust sticks to the feet of the preachers when *they are praised*. But it is shaken off through a consideration of who one is, according to what Matthew 10:20 says: "It is not you who are speaking." And 1 Corinthians 12:3 reads: "No one says:[60] Jesus is Lord,

---

[57] Perhaps, a better reference would be Acts 13:51: "But they (Paul and Barnabas) shook off the dust of their feet in protest against them and went to Iconium."

[58] On p. 258, n. 13 and on p. 219, n. 9 QuarEd give Book I of Jerome's Commentary on Matthew 10:4 as a reference for this quotation. See Hugh of St. Cher, p. 192v, m for the same quotation from Jerome with two slight variations.

[59] Compare what Bonaventure says on Luke 9:5 (#9) above where he only mentions "vainglory."

[60] The Vulgate reads *potest dicere* ("can say") whereas Bonaventure has *dicit* ("says").

except through the Holy Spirit." And 1 Corinthians 4:7 states: "What do you have that you have not received?" Therefore, Sirach 10:9 has: "Why are you proud,[61] earth and ashes?" – The second kind of dust adheres when *they are not received*. But this type of dust is cast off through *remembrance of Christ*, who said in John 15:20: "Remember the word that I have spoken to you: No servant is greater than his master. If they have persecuted me, they will persecute you," etc. – The third kind of dust sticks when *presents are offered*, which blind the eyes of the leaders, according to what Baruch 6:16 reads: "Their eyes are filled from dust from the feet of those who are entering." But this dust is shaken off through *recollection of our death*. Jerome says: "The person who always thinks about his death contemns everything with ease."[62] And 1 Timothy 6:7 reads: "We brought nothing into the world. It is certain that[63] we can take nothing out."

21. (Verse 12). Second, relative to *the threat of severe judgment* the text continues: *I say to you that it will be more tolerable for Sodom on that day than for that city.* From this one infers the magnitude of *the punishment*. For it is said in the Epistle of Jude 7 that "Sodom and Gemorrah and the neighboring cities . . . were made an example undergoing the punishment of eternal fire." Wherefore, the Lord was most powerfully angry with them, as is said in Genesis 19:2 that "The Lord rained upon Sodom and Gemorrah brimstone and fire. . . . And he destroyed these cities and all the region about." From

---

[61] On p. 259, n. 1 QuarEd correctly mention that the Vulgate has *Quid superbit terra et cinis?* ("Why is earth and ashes proud?")
[62] On p. 259, n. 4 QuarEd refer to Jerome's Epistle 140 (alias 139), n. 16 and his commentary on Sirach 11:8.
[63] The Vulgate reads *quia* ("that") while Bonaventure has *quod* ("that").

this the magnitude of *the sin* is also apparent, because contempt for the truth is a greater sin than the sexual passion of the flesh. – Now the reason for this is that the inhabitants of Sodom and Gemorrah *had been offered so great a grace.* And according to what is said in Luke 12:48 below: "To the one to whom much has been given, much will be required of him." So Hebrews 2:2–3 reads: "For if the word spoken by angels proved to be valid . . . how will we escape if we neglect so great a salvation, which was first announced by the Lord and was confirmed unto us by those who heard him?" – Another explanation concerns *the deeper knowledge of the truth.* So Gregory says: "Where greater knowledge has been given, there the transgressor will be liable for a greater sin."[64] For it is said in James 4:17: "The person who knows how to do good, and does not do it, commits a sin." – And that the greatest punishment is due those who contemn the truth, is obvious from what is said in Romans 1 about those who "although they knew God, did not glorify him as God" (verse 21), that "God has given them up to a reprobate sense" (verse 28b). And the reason given for this is that "they have resolved against possession of the knowledge of God" (verse 28a).

22. (Verse 13). *Woe to you, Chorazin,* etc. Here in third place is added *the rebuke against those who contemn,* who are shown to be needing the Lord's rebuke and culpable of damnation for two things, namely, on account of *hardness of heart* and on account of *self-exaltation.* Hardness of heart rendered them *impenitent* and self-exaltation made them *arrogant.*

---

[64] On p. 259, n. 8 QuarEd cite Book XVIII c. 11, n. 18 of Gregory's *Moralia.* Bonaventure's quotation captures the gist of what Gregory is saying.

So *rebuking them for their hardness of heart*, he says: *Woe to you, Chorazin! Woe to you, Bethsaida!* which were two cities in Galilee where he had performed many of his signs, and still hardness had remained in them.[65] – For this reason the text continues: *For if in Tyre and Sidon had been worked the miracles that have been worked in you*, that is, if the Lord had shown such miracles before their destruction – which the Lord threatened through prophet Ezekiel "You, son of man, take up a lamentation for Tyre" (27:2) and "You are reduced to nothing, and you shall never be any more"[66] (27:36) – they would not have been destroyed, and this, because they would have repented."[67] – So the text continues: *they would have repented long ago, sitting in sackcloth and ashes*, as the Ninevites did, about whom Jonah 3:5 says: "They proclaimed a fast and put on sackcloth from the least to the greatest."[68]

23. And note that he mentions three things which sum up perfect penitence, scilicet, *sackcloth, ashes*, and *sitting*. For in the penitent there should be *sorrow* from a consideration of a divine offense, and this in *sackcloth*. *Fear* from a consideration of wrath, and this in *ashes*, which project the image of death. There should be *shame* in consideration of how basely one has sat at the feet of

---

[65] On p. 259, n. 10 QuarEd provide a long quotation from the Glossa Ordinaria, which, however, does not seem to be the base for Bonaventure's commentary.

[66] On p. 259, n. 11 QuarEd correctly indicate that Vulgate reads: *Ad nihilum deducta es et non eris usque in perpetuum* while Bonaventure has: *Ad nihilum redacta es et non eris usque in sempiternum*. The English translation is virtually the same.

[67] This involved sentence is very untypical of Bonaventure's style.

[68] On p. 259, n. 12 QuarEd rightly indicate that the Vulgate reverses the order as it reads: "from the greatest to the least."

Christ as a disciple, and this in *sitting*.[69] And wherefore, Jerome says that "ashes and sackcloth are the weapons of penitents."[70] And so Jeremiah 6:26 reads: "O daughter of my people, gird yourself with sackcloth and sprinkle ashes on yourself. Utter for yourself a mourning, as for an only son, a bitter lamentation." And on account of the shame of humiliation, which must accompany this action, it is said in Jeremiah 13:18: "Say to the king and to the queen: Humble yourselves, sit down. For the crown of your glory has come down off your head."[71] Therefore, if they would have performed penitence such as this, they would not have had such a hard heart and consequently such a harsh sentence.

24. (Verse 14). And thus it adds: *But it will be more tolerable for Tyre and Sidon at the judgment than for you.* For, in accordance with what is said in Luke 12:47 below, "the servant who knew his master's will . . . and did not do it . . . will be beaten with many stripes." Now the reason for this is extreme hardness in the face of very

---

[69] This is my paraphrastic translation of Bonaventure's *sequelae sive vilitatis*. It is no wonder that the Vat. manuscript changed *sequelae* into *culpae*. See p. 260, n. 2 of QuarEd.

[70] On p. 260, n. 1 QuarEd cite Jerome's commentary on John 3:5: "Sackcloth and fasting are the weapons of penitents, the aides of sinners." They also provide helpful parallels from Book VIII of Jerome's Commentary on Ezekiel 27:28–29 and his Epistle 130 (alias 8), n. 10. In his commentary on Luke 7:38 (#66) above Bonaventure states that the penitent soul must experience shame, fear, and sorrow.

[71] On p. 260, n. 3 QuarEd quote the Glossa Ordinaria (from Bede) apud Lyranum on Luke 10:13: "*In sackcloth* signifies the harsh memory of prickly sin, with which those on the left side are clothed on the day of judgment. *In ashes* refers to the consideration of death through which the mass of all humanity is reduced to dust. *In sitting* refers to the humiliation of one's own conscience. So the prophet (Psalm 126:2) says: *Rise up, after you have been sitting*, that is (1 Peter 5:6): *You have humbled yourselves under the mighty hand of God*, etc." For Bede's commentary, which the Glossa follows very closely, see CCSL cxx, pp. 217–218.

great benefits. So it is said in Romans 2:4–5: "Do you not know that the goodness of God is meant to lead you to repentance? But according to your hard and unrepentant heart you are storing up for yourself as treasure wrath on the day of wrath and of the revelation of the just judgment of God." For it is said in Sirach 3: "A hard heart will have evil on the last day" (verse 27), "the sinner will add sin to sin" (verse 29).

25. (Verse 15). Secondly, *rebuking them for their self-exaltation*, he says: *And you, Capernaum, having been exalted to the heavens*, namely, through arrogance, *you will be thrust down into hell* by divine sentence. Wherefore, Obadiah 1:4 reads: "Even if you were exalted like an eagle and built your nest in the stars, I will bring you down from there." And Job 20:6–7: "If his pride climb into[72] heaven and his head touch the clouds, in the end he will be destroyed like a dunghill." Now it is said that Capernaum *was exalted* because of the many miracles that had been performed in it. It was proud that he worked more miracles there than in other cities. For it is said in Luke 4:23 above: "How many things we have heard that you performed in Capernaum, do here also." Therefore, they were first exalted because of the gifts of divine grace, but afterward were justifiably thrust down on account of pride. And this had been predicted in Isaiah 9:1: "At the first time the land of Zabulon and the land of Nephtali were raised up," namely, by previous miracles, "and at the last time the way of the sea was oppressed,"[73] that is, cast down by judgment because of

---

[72] On p. 260, n. 4 QuarEd accurately indicate that the Vulgate reads *ad* ("to") whereas Bonaventure has *in* ("into").

[73] In his commentary on Luke 4:31 (#65) above Bonaventure also uses this quotation from Isaiah 9:1, but with a different application.

their sins, as the Glossa explains at this point.[74] And therefore, divine gifts are to be received with fear and great reverence. As Gregory says, "when gifts are increased, accountability for the gifts also increases."[75]

26. (Verse 16). *The person who hears you hears me.* Here in the fourth place is joined the authentication of the preachers. For the text shows that they are authentic both on account of the authority of *Christ as Mediator* and also on account of the authority of *the supreme ruler.*

So he first authenticates them by *the authority of Christ as Mediator* where the text has: *The person who hears you hears me.* For they themselves were acting in the person of Christ. Whence the Apostle says in 2 Corinthians 2:10: "For even I, if I have forgiven anything, have forgiven[76] it in the person of Christ for your sakes." And in 2 Corinthians 13:3 he says: "Are you seeking a proof that it is Christ who speaks in me?" And therefore, it is said in 1 Thessalonians 2:13: "And you, when you heard

---

[74] On p. 260, n. 6 QuarEd refer to the Glossa Interlinearis (from Jerome) on Isaiah 9:1: "*At the first time,* of the Lord's incarnation, *the land of Zabulon and Nephtali was raised up,* the burden of sin having been alleviated . . . *and at the last time was oppressed,* and gravely afflicted since many remained in error." They go on to quote the Glossa Ordinaria apud Lyranum on Luke 10:15: "*And you, Capernaum,* etc. One interpretation is: You were exalted, arrogantly resisting my preaching. Another is: You were exalted by my residing among you and my signs and wonders, and therefore you are subjected to a more severe punishment because you refused to believe in them."

[75] On p. 260, n. 7 QuarEd refer to Homily 9, n. 1 of GGHG as the source. With one slight adjustment Bonaventure follows Gregory perfectly. See PL 76:1106A.

[76] For some reason Bonaventure skips *quod donavi* ("what I have forgiven") from the Vulgate. I have supplied these two words to effect a smoother translation.

and received the word of God from us, you welcomed it not as a human word, but, as it truly is, the word of God." So when a person hears the disciples of Christ, Christ is heard. And similarly when they are met with contempt, Christ is contemned. – And wherefore, the text continues: *The person who rejects you rejects me.* Thus, Ezekiel 3:7 reads: "The house of Israel will not listen to you, because they will not listen to me." And Matthew 25:45 intimates this when it says: "As long as you did not do it for one of these least ones, you did not do it for me." And so the Apostle said in 1 Thessalonians 5:19–20: "Do not extinguish the Spirit. Do not reject prophesies," that is, true preaching.

27. Secondly, he authenticates them by *the authority of the supreme ruler* where the text reads: *The person*[77] *who rejects me rejects him who sent me*, both because of *the entrusted authority* and because of *consubstantiality.*[78] So John 5:23 reads: "The person who does not honor the Son does not honor the Father, who sent him." And therefore, it follows that if anyone rejects the Apostles, he rejects Christ. And the person who rejects Christ rejects God. Thus, the person who rejects the Apostles rejects God. And this is no small sin. For this reason Isaiah 33:1 says: "Woe to you who are rejecting. . . . Will you not also be rejected? . . . When you are wearied and cease rejecting, you will be rejected." So great is the authority of preachers. When they are welcomed, God is

---

[77] On p. 261, n. 1 QuarEd correctly indicate that the Vulgate has *autem* ("but").
[78] As Bonaventure explains in the remainder of this paragraph, he is referring to the Creed that the Son is consubstantial with the Father.

welcomed. And in their rejection God is rejected.[79] For these are the mouth of God announcing God's words, as is said in Jeremiah 15:19: "If you separate the precious from the vile, you will be like my mouth." And so as the mouth of God they must be fed and honored. And they, for their part, must especially guard their mouths from voracity and loquacity, so that what Revelation 14:4–5 says can truly be said of them: "These were purchased from among men and women, first fruits unto God and the Lamb. And in their mouth no lie was found, for they are without blemish before the throne of God."[80]

Luke 10:17–24
THE CONSOLATION OF THOSE RETURNING

28. *Now the seventy-two returned*, etc. After the sending forth of the disciples two by two and the formation of those going forth the Evangelist adds here the third point, namely, *the consolation of those returning*. Now this section has two parts. In the first part *the Lord restrains false happiness on the part of the disciples*. In the second *he invites them to genuine happiness* where verse 20 says: *Rejoice rather because*[81] *your names are written in heaven*.

---

[79] On p. 261, n. 2 QuarEd refer to Bede. See CCSL cxx, p. 218: "For without doubt the master is heard in the disciple, and the Father is honored in the Son."

[80] Bonaventure has added *ante thronum Dei* ("before the throne of God").

[81] On p. 261, n. 5 QuarEd correctly indicate that the Vulgate reads *quod* ("that") whereas Bonaventure has *quia* ("because").

Luke 10:17–20a
THE REPRESSION OF FALSE HAPPINESS

Four points are made concerning *the repression of false happiness* among the disciples. First is *the expression of* vain exaltation. Second is *the repression* of vain exaltation. Third is *the occasion* of vain exaltation. Fourth is *the prohibition* of vain exaltation.

29. (Verse 17). So the first topic is *the expression of vain exaltation* where it says: *Now the seventy-two returned with joy*, which they not only felt in their hearts, but also gave voice to in word, so that what Proverbs 15:13 says might be verified: "A glad heart makes a cheerful countenance." – For this reason the text continues: *Saying: Lord, even the demons were subject to us in your name.* In this way they gave expression to their joy at being made stronger than demons. But this happiness stemmed from a latent pride like that of the Pharisee whom Luke 18:11 below describes as saying in his prayer: "O God, I thank you that I am not like the rest of people," etc.

30. And note that some *are clearly exalted* over divine gifts like those who attribute such gifts to themselves. Concerning these Deuteronomy 32:27 says: "My mighty hand,[82] and not the Lord, has done all these things." Against these Deuteronomy 9:4 has: "When the Lord will have destroyed the nations in your sight, say not in your heart: On account of my righteousness has the Lord brought me into this land."[83] – Now some *are*

---

[82] As QuarEd correctly mention on p. 261, n. 8, the Vulgate reads *manus nostra excelsa* ("our mighty hand").

[83] Bonaventure has made at least three minor modifications to the Vulgate text. For example, he reads *Dominus* ("Lord") for *Dominus deus tuus* ("the Lord your God").

clearly brought down. Of these Luke 17:10 below says:
"When you have done everything well, say that we are
unprofitable servants."[84] Such a person was Paul, who
says of himself in 1 Corinthians 15:9–10: "I am the least
of the Apostles and not worthy to be called an Apostle. . . . But by the grace of God I am what I am, and his
grace in me has not been fruitless, but has abounded,"
etc.[85] – But some are *partly brought down* as they give
thanks, *partly exalted* as they exalt inappropriately, like
these disciples who rejoiced at the subjection of the demons, but attributed this not to themselves, but to the
name of the Lord when they said: *in your name*. They
are like that Pharisee of Luke 18:11. Wherefore, there
was something *commendable* in their conduct, namely,
that they returned to the fount of graces, acknowledging
the graces that had received from him and rendering
thanks to this same person. And this in accordance with
what is said in Qoheleth 1:7: "Unto the place from
whence the rivers come, they return to flow again." And
Job 38:35 reads: "Can you send lightnings, and will they
go, and upon their return say to you: Here we are?"
Concerning this the Glossa says: *"Lightnings burst
through the sky* when preachers shine brilliantly with
miracles and instill fear of the supernal in the hearts of
subjects; *upon their return say: Here we are*, because
they acknowledge that whatever they have mightily
done comes not through their own strength, but from
God's power."[86] Such are the men of perfection in whose

---

[84] Bonaventure's text varies from the Vulgate which I translate:
"When you have done everything that was commanded you, say: We
are unprofitable servants."
[85] It seems that Bonaventure has turned the Latin adverb *abun-
dantius* ("more abundantly") into a verb *abundavit* ("has abounded").
In any case, *abundavit* is not found in the Vulgate.
[86] On p. 261, n. 11 QuarEd indicate that this is the Glossa Ordinaria
(from XXX chapter 2, n. 6 of Gregory's *Moralia*). They note that the

person it is said in Isaiah 26:12: "You have wrought all our works in us,[87] O Lord." And the Psalmist says: "Not to us, O Lord, not to us, but to your name give the glory" (113:9). – But there was something *reprehensible* in their conduct, namely, that they were being exalted by the great extent of their power. This is manifest in what they said: *Demons are subject to us.* This is against what Sirach 11:4 reads: "Be not exalted in the day of your honor, for the works of the Most High alone are wonderful. And his works are glorious, and secret, and hidden." And this is what Bede says: "It is good that they confess, but because they are exalted about their working of miracles, they are frightened by Christ's example and called to humility."[88]

31. (Verse 18). Second, he addresses *the repression of vain exaltation* when he says: *and he said to them: I was watching Satan fall as lightning from heaven*, as if the Lord were saying: Do not be exalted at divine benefits, lest you fall to the ground with the proud angels. 2 Peter 2:4 reads: "If God did not spare the angels who sinned, but dragged them down by infernal ropes to Tartarus and delivered them over to be tortured." Supply: God will not spare you, if you sin through pride. Wherefore, Bernard says: "The Lord did not spare the proud angels. How much less will he spare you, rottenness and

---

original text has *auditorum* ("of listeners") whereas Bonaventure has *subditorum* ("of subjects").

[87] On p. 261, n. 12 QuarEd rightly mention that the Vulgate has *nobis* ("for us") while Bonaventure has *in nobis* ("in us").

[88] On p. 262, n. 1 QuarEd state that this is the Glossa Ordinaria on Luke 10:17. For Bede's comment see CCSL cxx, p. 218. Bede is actually commenting on Luke 10:18: the disciples are to be frightened by Satan's fall.

worms!"[89] – Now *he fell like lightning*, that is, quickly, brutally, and irrevocably. So through his example others may be warned not to seek after exalted things, in the quest of which Lucifer fell into the depths, according to what Isaiah 14 says: "How have you fallen, O Lucifer, who rose in the morning?" (verse 12). "Who said in your heart: I will ascend into heaven. I will exalt my throne above the stars of God" (verse 13). "Yet you will be brought down to hell, into the depth of the pit" (verse 15). And therefore, Romans 11:20–21 has: "Do not ponder exalted things, but fear. For if God has not spared the natural branches, perhaps he may not spare you either." – By giving this example the Lord represses in a marvelous manner pride in the disciples, as if he were saying what Proverbs 17:16 has: "The person who makes his house high," namely, with self-exalting Lucifer, "seeks a downfall" with that same individual. Wherefore, Bernard, speaking of ambitious persons, says: "Follow your leader. Multiply prebends.[90] Speed on to the episcopacy. Aspire to be archbishop. Slowly you ascend, but you will not descend slowly. *I saw Satan fall as lightning from heaven.*"[91] And so Seneca gives the op-

---

[89] On p. 262, n. 3 QuarEd have pointed me to Bernard's "First Sermon on the Lord's Advent,", n. 2. See SBOp 4.162. Bonaventure's quotation is almost verbatim.

[90] See Beryl Smalley, *The Gospels in the Schools c. 1100 – c. 1280* History Series 41 (London: Hambledon, 1985). On p. 142 Smalley discusses the disputed question of multiple sources of income for clerics and bishops and says of Hugh of St. Cher: "Hugh defended the thesis that no man could hold two benefices without committing mortal sin, if one of them sufficed to provide him with food and clothing."

[91] On p. 262, n. 6 QuarEd state that this quotation is not from Bernard of Clairvaux, but from *Declamationes de Colloquio Simonis cum Jesu, Ex S. Bernardi sermonibus collectae* of Geoffrey the Abbot, XXI, n. 25. See PL 184:451D. Bonaventure's quotation captures the gist of the original, but is hardly verbatim. See Hugh of St. Cher, p. 193q for a quotation that is virtually the same as Bonaventure's:

posite advice: "Bring yourself down to small things, from which you cannot fall."[92] So Proverbs 18:12 says: "Before it is crushed, the heart of a person is exalted. And before it is glorified, it is humbled." For the sentence of the judge in Luke 18:14 is: "Everyone who exalts himself will be humbled, and everyone who humbles himself will be exalted."

32. (Verse 19). In third place is *the occasion for vain exaltation* where the text reads: *Behold, I have given you power to tread upon serpents and scorpions*, scilicet, with regard to *corporal* snares, in accordance with what is said in Genesis 3:15: "She will crush your head, and you will lay a snare for her heel." *And over all the might of the enemy*, with regard to *spiritual* snares. Of these Ephesians 6:12 says: "Our wrestling is not against flesh and blood, but against the principalities and the powers, against the rulers of the world . . . on high."[93] – *And nothing will harm you*, because of heavenly protection, according to Mark 16:17–18: "In my name they will cast out demons. They will speak in new tongues. They will pick up serpents. And if they drink any deadly thing, it will not harm them." And this power which God had granted them could be the occasion for presumption.

"Act now, follow your leader. Multiply prebends. Speed on to the Archdiaconate. Aspire to be bishop. Slowly you ascend, but you will not descend slowly. I saw Satan fall as lightning from heaven." The editors also refer to Bernard's Sermon 2, n. 6 and Sermon 4, n. 3 on the Lord's Ascension for additional illumination.

[92] On p. 262, n. 7 QuarEd give Epistle 94 (alias 95) *in fine* as a general reference to this quotation. They also quote, as a general reference, Seneca's *Hercules furiens*, Act 1, verses 199–201.

[93] In this quotation Bonaventure has an extraordinary way of referring to scripture. I use his Latin: *"Non est nobis colluctatio adversus carnem et sanguinem, sed adversus principes et potestates, adversus mundi rectores"* etc.; usque ibi *"in caelestibus."* This looks like a "bookish" rather than an aural quotation.

This is in accordance with what is said about Hezekiah whose prayers God answered with miracles. 2 Chronicles 32:24–25 reads: "Hezekiah prayed to the Lord, and he heard him and gave him a sign. But he was not grateful in response to the benefits he had received. For his heart was exalted, and wrath was enkindled against him and against Judah and Jerusalem." – Wherefore, a multitude of divine gifts was the occasion of ruination for many, as is said of Lucifer in Ezekiel 28: "You were the seal of resemblance, full of wisdom and perfect in beauty" (verse 12). And further on verse 17 says: "Your heart was exalted." And so "you sinned, and I cast you out from the holy[94] mountain of God and destroyed you, etc." (verse 16). And therefore, a certain holy man used to say that it is a great grace not to have a divine gift. For all these external divine gifts are nothing but temptations,[95] and whoever is exalted externally must fear what Job 30:22 has: "You have exalted me and set me as it were upon the wind. You have mightily dashed me down."

33. (Verse 20). The fourth and final point is *the prohibition of vain exaltation.* The text continues: *But do not rejoice in this that the spirits are subject to you.* For joy such as this is like *the joy of the proud* in their self-promotion and rejection of others and is not fitting for true Saints according to Sirach 8:8: "Don't rejoice in the death of your enemy." And Job 31:29 reads: "If I had rejoiced at the downfall of the person who hated me." So *do not rejoice,* for such joy is *ruinous,* according to what Proverbs 14:13 has: "Mourning seizes upon the

---

[94] On p. 262, n. 12 QuarEd are correct to mention that the Vulgate does not have *sancto* ("holy").
[95] QuarEd give no hint of who the "certain wise man" might be. In any case, the wise man plays upon the meanings of *gratia* ("grace, benefit, gift").

conclusion of joy." – Such is the joy concerning a transitory matter, according to what Job 20:5 says: "The joy of the hypocrite lasts but a moment." And again Job 21:12–13 has: "They rejoice at the sound of the organ. They spend their days in good things, but in a moment they go down to hell." Wherefore, the Lord did not want his disciples to rejoice in miracles, but rather in torments and insults, according to what Matthew 5:11–12 reads: "Blessed are you when people curse you and persecute you. . . . Rejoice and exalt, because your reward is great in heaven."[96] And this is even what the Apostles did, according to what Acts 5:41 says: "The Apostles departed from the presence of the Sanhedrin rejoicing that they had been considered worthy to suffer disgrace for the name of Jesus." *Therefore, do not rejoice in this that the spirits are subject to you*, although this power has been divinely granted, lest it be an occasion of pride and consequently of a downfall. For this reason Augustine says that "the Lord used to say to his disciples: *Learn from me*, not to raise the dead, not to walk on water, but *because I am meek and humble of heart*."[97] For they should not rejoice in miracles, but in humility.

---

[96] Again Bonaventure's quotation seems "bookish": *"Beati estis, cum maledixerint vobis homines et persecuti vos fuerint"* etc.; et post: *"Gaudete et exsultate, quoniam merces vestra copiosa est in caelis."*

[97] On p. 263, n. 4 QuarEd give three references to this quotation from Augustine. None are the same as the one Bonaventure uses, especially since they do not have "to walk on water." See Augustine's *De Sancta Virginitate* (*On Holy Virginity*) chapter 35, n. 35 in *Saint Augustine: Treatises on Marriage and Other Subjects*, translated by Charles T. Wilcox et al., FC 15 (New York: Fathers of the Church, 1955), p. 185: "He . . . does not say: 'Learn from Me to make the world, or to raise the dead,' but 'for I am meek and humble of heart.'" See also Sermon 69, n. 2 in *The Works of Saint Augustine, Part III – Sermons*, Volume III: Sermons 51–69 (Brooklyn: New City Press, 1991), p. 235: *"Take my yoke upon you, and learn from me* (Mt 11:29), not how to construct the world, not how to create all things, visible and invisible, not how to perform miracles in the world, and raise the dead; but

Luke 10:20b–24
THE SAVIOR'S INVITATION TO GENUINE HAPPINESS

34. *Rejoice rather because*[98] *your names*, etc. After the Savior curtailed vain joy in the disciples, he now, in a second point, *invites them to genuine happiness and joy.* And indeed he does this by proposing a fourfold cause or reason for joy. For he shows that there will be joy for the disciples concerning God's *infallible prescience, irreprehensible providence, incomprehensible potency, desirable presence.*[99] And in these four they had exceedingly great reasons for being exalted.

First, there was joy concerning God's *infallible prescience.* With regard to this the text reads: *Rejoice rather, because your names are written*, in the book of life, *in heaven.* This book is called *the book of life*, for what is written in it *are alive*, according to what John 1:3–4 says: "What has been made was life in him." Another interpretation is this: according to what is written therein is a person predestined to life. Wherefore, the final judgment will transpire according to this book, as it is said in Revelation 20:12: "The books were opened, and another book was opened, which is the book of life." Indeed, in this book the names of evil people are not found to be definitively written, according to what the Psalm says: "Let them be blotted out of the book of the living, and with the just let them not be written"

---

because I am meek and humble of heart (Mt 11:29)." And the same words of Augustine's Sermon 69, under the title of "Sermon 10 on the Words of the Lord," occur as Lesson 7 at the Third Nocturn for the Feast of St. Matthias in the Roman Breviary (February 24).

[98] The Vulgate has *quod* ("that") while Bonaventure has *quia* ("because").

[99] In my translation I have tried to imitate Bonaventure's verbal playfulness.

(68:29). This is indeed said, not because this book may be changed, but because many seem to be *written* in it according to actual and present justice, who will appear to be *not written* in it according to divine prescience. Therefore, since good that is both interminable and infallible only belongs to those who are definitively good and saved, the disciples are right to rejoice about this and not about the gift of working miracles which both the good and the evil may enjoy.[100] So the names of evil people are not *written in heaven*, but rather *in the earth*, according to what Jeremiah 17:13 has: "Those that depart from you will be written in the earth."[101] As a sign

---

[100] In #34–35 Bonaventure is dealing with the intractable problem of human free will and divine foreknowledge/predestination. I follow the guidance provided by QuarEd on p. 263 notes 6 and 10 and quote some helpful passages from Bonaventure's *Breviloquium*. See *The Works of Bonaventure II, The Breviloquium*. Translated by José de Vinck (Paterson: St. Anthony Guild, 1963). On pp. 58–59 de Vinck translates Part I, Chapter 8, n. 1–4: ". . . in its awareness of all that is to come about God's wisdom is called prescience or foresight; in its awareness of what God Himself will do, it is called providence; in its awareness of what is to be rewarded, it is called pre-election; and in its awareness of what is to be condemned, it is called reprobation. . . . It is called . . . Book of Life as being the principle of all that is pre-elected and reproved. In respect to things as they return to Him, God is the Book of Life. . . . And since God's wisdom knows the contingent infallibly, freedom and indetermination of the [created] will are compatible with pre-election and foreknowledge. This should be understood as follows. The first Principle, because He is first and supreme, has a knowledge that is utterly simple and perfect. On account of this utter perfection, He knows all things most distinctly in all their actual and possible states. Thus, He knows the good as deserving of approbation, the evil, of reprobation." See also *Breviloquium* Part II, Chapter 1 where Bonaventure interprets "the Book of Life" as the incarnate Word.

[101] It seems to me that Bonaventure is basing some of his interpretation on that of Bede, who also refers to Jeremiah 17:13. See CCSL cxx, p. 219. On p. 263, n. 9 QuarEd refer to Jerome's commentary on Jeremiah 17:13: "*They will be written in the earth*, deleted from the book of the living. . . . The reason is manifest why they are written in

of this reality the Lord, confuting the perfidy of the Pharisees, who were strangers to the kingdom of the heavens, "wrote with his finger in the earth," as it is said in John 8:6.

35. And note that divine knowledge is called *a book*, but knowledge of *a single item* is called *a book plain and simple*. And in this book everything and everyone are written, according to what the Psalm says: "Your eyes saw my imperfect being, and in your book all will be written" (138:16). And there is the knowledge of *approbation*, and this is called *the book of life*, and in this book none are written according to the truth except those who are definitively good. And about this Exodus 32:31–32 has: "Either forgive them this trespass...or strike me out of the book which you have written." Concerning this the Glossa says that "he was secure in saying this, knowing, that he could not be struck (from the book)."[102] For he is speaking about something written on the basis of divine prescience, not on the basis of actual and present justice.

36. (Verse 21). Second, he shows that one should rejoice in *irreprehensible providence*. With regard to this the text continues: *In that very hour he rejoiced in*[103] *the Holy Spirit*, namely, with spiritual joy which must be in the Holy Spirit, not in the flesh, according to what Romans

the earth, for *they have abandoned* the fountain of life, the Lord, or *the fountain of living waters*, the Lord."
[102] On p. 263, n. 11 QuarEd cite the Glossa Interlinearis (from Augustine's *Questions on Exodus*, q. 147): "Truly, he was secure in saying this because he will not be struck (from the book)." They go on to quote Augustine: "Truly, he was secure in saying this...so that, since God would not strike Moses from his book, he would forgive the people for this sin."
[103] On p. 264, n. 1 QuarEd correctly indicate that the Vulgate does not have *in* ("in").

14:17 says: "The kingdom of God does not consist in food and drink, but in justice and peace and joy in the Holy Spirit." Thus the glorious Virgin also states in Luke 1:47 above: "My spirit exalts in God, my savior." – And in this he laid down for his disciples the manner of rejoicing and at the same time gave expression to the reason for their exaltation as he continues: *I praise you, Father, Lord of heaven and earth.*[104] Namely, I give praise that you are not only creator through power, but also governor through providence, according to what Jeremiah 23:24 has: "I fill heaven and earth." And Isaiah 66:1 states: "Heaven is my throne, and the earth my footstool." Now to this provider of all things praise is offered by a confession of *praise*, for confession is not only of *sin*, according to what James 5:16 says: "Confess your sins to one another," but also of *genuine faith*. About this Romans 10:10 has: "With the heart a person believes unto justice, but with the mouth confession is made unto salvation." And also of *divine praise*, according to what Hebrews 13:15 says: "Let us offer up a sacrifice of praise . . . that is, the fruit of our lips praising his name." And the Psalm reads: "Let us praise the Lord, for he is good," etc. (105:1). And in this way instruction is given here on how to offer *praise* to God as governor.

37. Christ also praises God for his *providence*. For this reason the text adds: *that you have hidden these things from the wise and prudent and have revealed them to little ones.* For it happens according to the judgment of divine providence that "God resists the proud, but gives grace to the humble," as is said in James 4:6. And the Psalm has: "The Lord is high and looks upon the humble. And the high he knows from afar" (137:6). So *these*

---

[104] On p. 264, n. 2 QuarEd rightly mention that the Vulgate reads *dixit* ("he said") before *confiteor* ("I praise").

things, that is, the mysteries of our redemption, *he has hidden from the wise and prudent of the world*, who consider themselves to be *wise* in divine matters and *prudent* in temporal concerns, according to what is said in 1 Corinthians 1:19: "I will destroy the wisdom of the wise, and the prudence of the prudent I will reject." And therefore, 1 Corinthians 1:20 continues: "God has turned to foolishness the wisdom of this world."[105] And wherefore, Isaiah 5:21 reads: "Woe to you who are wise in your own eyes and prudent in your own conceits." For from such people are the divine mysteries hidden, but *are revealed to little ones*. So the Psalm says: "The declaration of your words gives light and understanding to little ones" (118:130). – And note that "he does not say to *the foolish and dull minded*, but to *the little ones*, that is, the humble, so that he may show that he is not condemning intellectual acumen, but pride's tumor," as the Glossa says.[106] Wherefore, Bernard states: "Humility is the key to knowledge,"[107] according to what Proverbs 11:2 says: "Where humility is, there is wisdom."

38. And since providence's judgment is irreprehensible, the text adds: *Yes, Father, for such was your good pleasure*, as if to say: It is just, for it pleases you, for as the Glossa says: "Something unjust cannot please a just

---

[105] In the Vulgate this sentence is a question and fits very well into Paul's high rhetoric at this point.

[106] On p. 264, n. 8 QuarEd state that this is the Glossa Ordinaria (from Bede). See CCSL cxx, p. 220 for Bede's involved Latin, which the Glossa has simplified.

[107] On p. 264, n. 8 QuarEd maintain that the opinion which Bonaventure cites as that of St. Bernard is attributed to Bede by Hugh of St. Cher in his commentary on Luke 11:52. See CCSL cxx, p. 245: "The key to knowledge is the humility of Christ." See CCSL cxx, p. 220 for Bede's commentary on Luke 10:21: "*You have taken away the key of knowledge*, that is, the humility of the faith of Christ."

person."[108] Therefore, he thought it sufficient to give this reason and did not wish to provide another one. There are three explanations for this. Either because the reason given is *the most sufficient and principal one*, according to what Exodus 33:19 has: "I will have mercy on whom I will, and I will be merciful to whom it will please me." And Romans 9:18 reads: "He has mercy on whom he will, etc."[109] Or in order *to curb curiosity*, lest we dare to scrutinize divine judgments. So the Glossa says: "From this we receive a lesson in humility, lest we temerariously scrutinize the divine counsels."[110] For it is said in Proverbs 25:27: "The person who searches after Majesty will be overwhelmed by glory." Or in order to *show that divine providence is to be praised in all its deeds* and is entirely irreprehensible in everything, according to the Psalm: "The Lord is just in all his ways and holy in all his works" (144:17). – Therefore, one must rejoice and exalt in God's irreprehensible providence and not subject it to presumptuous ratiocinations. For as Gregory says: "Divine judgments are not to be disputed rashly, but to be venerated with awesome silence."[111]

39. (Verse 22). Third he shows that one must rejoice at his *incomprehensible power* where the text says: *All things have been delivered to me by my Father*. For by saying that *everything* – infinitely – *has been delivered*, he shows that his power is *universal*, according to what

---

[108] On p. 264, n. 9 QuarEd state that this is the Glossa Interlinearis on Luke 10:21. See CCSL cxx, p. 220 where Bede has the same wording, but sets it in a larger context.

[109] In Romans 9:15 Paul quotes Exodus 33:19, the same passage that Bonaventure has just cited.

[110] On p. 264, n. 11 QuarEd mention that this is the Glossa Ordinaria. It is almost verbatim from Bede. See CCSL cxx, p. 220.

[111] On p. 264, n. 13 QuarEd refer to XXXII *Moralia* chapter 1, n. 1: "For divine judgments, since they are unknown, are not to be disputed by means of audacious speeches . . . to be venerated."

John 1:3 says: "All things were made through him," that is, through the Word. And again John 17:10 reads: "All things that are mine are yours, and yours are mine." By adding *by my Father*, he indicates that this power is *natural*, according to what John 5:19 says: "Whatever the Father does, the Son does all[112] these things in like manner." In both of these he simultaneously shows *equality* and *immensity*. So the Glossa says: "When you hear *all things*, you acknowledge omnipotence. When you hear *delivered*, you confess belief in the Son, to whom by nature of one substance all things are rightly his own and not granted through grace as a gift."[113] And from this it is manifest that the power of the Son is immense and incomprehensible. – And thus the text continues: *And no one knows[114] who the Son is except the Father*, that is, there is no intellect that perfectly comprehends the Son except the Father's. And therefore, this does not exclude the Holy Spirit, but only a created intellect, which cannot comprehend him since he is immense. Wherefore, Job 11:7–8 reads: "Perchance you will comprehend the steps of God and will find out the Almighty perfectly? He is higher than heaven, and what will you do?," etc.

40. And since the Son is incomprehensible, he could comprehend the Father. For this reason the text adds: *and who the Father is except the Son*. Supply: No one knows. For as John 1:18 states: "No one has ever seen

---

[112] Bonaventure has adjusted this quotation, especially by adding *omnia* ("all").

[113] On p. 265, n. 2 QuarEd state that this is the Glossa Ordinaria, taken from Bede, who follows Ambrose. See CCSL xiv, p. 237 and CCSL cxx, p. 220.

[114] On p. 265, n. 3 QuarEd correctly state that the Vulgate reads *scit* ("knows") while Bonaventure has *novit* ("knows").

God except the only-begotten,[115] who is in the bosom of the Father, he has narrated him." – Since he himself alone comprehends the Father, he alone can reveal him. And so the text adds: *and to whom the Son wishes to reveal.* For the Son is the Wisdom and Word of the Father, who as Speaker manifests himself through his Word. So Wisdom 9:17 has: "Who will know your thought unless you give wisdom . . . from on high?" So Chrysostom says: "Philosophers contend with one another in their search for God and acknowledge that they have found nothing more than that God is unknowable. They are like the person who mistakenly undertakes to navigate an unnavigable ocean. When he discovers that it is impossible to complete the journey, he is compelled to return back home the same way he had come. Thus it is with those who began in ignorance and ended in ignorance."[116] And the reason for this is that they were not disciples of Jesus Christ, who is the truth.[117] Nor did they have the Spirit, of whom John 16:13 says: "When he, the Spirit of truth, has come, he will teach you all the truth."

41. (Verse 23). Fourth, he shows that there should be joy in *his desirable presence.* With regard to this he adds: *And turning to his disciples, he said: Blessed are the eyes that see what you see.* So you can fittingly rejoice, because you see me both in mind and body, when Abraham rejoiced who saw only by faith, according to John

---

[115] On p. 265, n. 5 QuarEd accurately indicate that the Vulgate reads *unigenitus Filius* ("only-begotten Son").

[116] On p. 265, n. 6 QuarEd refer to Chrysostom's Homily 28 on Matthew 11:25 and indicate that Bonaventure has considerably abbreviated Chrysostom's comments. See Hugh of St. Cher, p. 194u where Hugh's quotation of Chrysostom is identical to that of Bonaventure with one exception: Bonaventure reads *cum* ("when") whereas Hugh has *dum* ("when").

[117] See John 14:6: "I am the way, the truth, and the life."

8:56: "Abraham, your father, exulted that he was to see my day. He saw it and rejoiced." – And therefore, as a figure of this it is said to Solomon in 1 Kings 10:8: "Blessed are your men and blessed are your servants, who stand before you always and listen to your wisdom." This is spoken of Solomon as a figure of Christ, as Christ says of himself in Matthew 12:42: "Behold, a greater than Solomon is here." Wherefore, this was a special gift.

42. (Verse 24). And consequently the text continues: *But[118] I say to you that many prophets and kings have desired to see what you see, and have not seen it.* Those who are exalted in knowledge and power have desired *the presence* of Christ, according to what Haggai 2:8 has: "The desired of all nations will come." Therefore, because of intense desire it is said in Isaiah 64:1: "O that you would rend the heavens and come down!" And Numbers 24:17, 23 reads: "A star will arise out of Jacob, and a scepter will spring up from Israel. . . . Alas, who will live when God will do these things?" Do not be amazed, for Esther says to the great king in the person of Christ: "You, my Lord, are exceedingly admirable, and your face is full of graces."[119] And wherefore, they were desirous of seeing the presence of Christ. – They also desired *to hear his teaching*, and so the text adds: *and to hear what you hear, but they have not heard*, namely, my words. For as it is said in Hosea 10:12: "The time for seeking the Lord has arrived, when he will come who is teaching[120] you justice." For this was a superlative bene-

---

[118] On p. 265, n. 10 QuarEd correctly indicate that the Vulgate reads *enim* ("for").

[119] Esther 15:17. In his commentary on Luke 1:38 (#70) above Bonaventure also quotes Esther 2:17 and uses "Assuerus," which I have translated here by "great king."

[120] On p. 265, n. 13 QuarEd accurately mention that the Vulgate reads *docebit* ("will teach").

fit, that is, to hear God speaking, not through a creature subject to him, but in his own person united to a creature. And commemorating this benefit, the Apostle says in Hebrews 1:1–2: "God, who at sundry times and in diverse manners spoke in times past to the fathers through the prophets, last of all in these days has spoken to us by his Son."[121] *Blessed* is the person who hears these words with humility and obedience according to what is said in Luke 11:28 below: "Blessed are those who hear the word of God and keep it." So blessed are those, who through faith have seen and heard Christ on their journey of life, according to what Proverbs 8:34 reads: "Blessed is the person who hears me, and who watches daily at my gates, and waits at my door posts." But *most blessed* are those who will see in the homeland of heaven, according to what Revelation 19:9 says: "Blessed are those who are called to the marriage banquet of the Lamb."

Luke 10:25–42
THE FORM OF LIVING

43. *And behold, a certain lawyer,* etc. After the Evangelist has described the form of preaching, here in a second point he presents *the form of living.* Now a person may be informed about the right way of living in a twofold manner, namely, by *word* and *example.* Therefore, for the purposes of formation the Evangelist first sets forth *the divine commandment* and secondly adds *human example* where verse 38 says: *Now it came to pass as they were on their journey, that he entered,* etc.

---

[121] Bonaventure (or QuarEd) concludes the quotation from Hebrews 1:1–2 with *novissime, etc.* ("last of all, etc.") and seems to presuppose that his audience will supply these verses' christological punch line.

Now since *the formation provided by a commandment* only has binding force for the one who comprehends its meaning, the Evangelist first indicates that it is a *commandment that regulates life*. Secondly, he adds *an illustration which aids* comprehension where verse 30 has: *Now looking up,*[122] *Jesus.* – Now concerning the articulation of *the regulative commandment* four items are introduced: *the inquisition for the truth* that is salvific, *the acquisition of the truth* that was sought, *the approbation of the truth* that was found, *investigation of the truth* that was approved.

Luke 10:25–29
THE COMMANDMENT THAT REGULATES ONE'S LIFE

44. (Verse 25). First, then, with regard to *the inquisition for the truth that saves*, the text says: *And behold, a certain lawyer, an expert in the law, got up to test him.* This man *was* an expert and *regarded* himself as an expert. And since he *regarded* himself as an expert, he did not require of himself that he should learn. Rather his responsibility was to test others as is customary for the proud, according to what Sirach 13:14 says of the rich person: "By much talk he will test you." But again, since he *was* an expert, it was suitable and proper that he raise questions.[123] Therefore, the text adds: *and he said:*

---

[122] On p. 266, n. 5 QuarEd indicate that Bede, Hugh of St. Cher, Bl. Albert, St. Thomas, and Lyranus also read *suspiciens* ("looking up"). The Vulgate reads *suscipiens* ("receiving/accepting"). Douay Version omits this word altogether. See Bonaventure's commentary on Luke 10:30 (#52) below.

[123] On p. 266, n. 6 QuarEd quote the Glossa Interlinearis (from Ambrose): "*And behold, a certain lawyer, an expert in the law,* adhering to the words of the law, but ignorant of its power." See CCSL xiv, p. 237.

Master, what must I do to gain eternal life? He calls him
Master, for by this designation he refers to Christ as the
one to answer questions put to him, in accordance with
what is said in Matthew 22:16: "Master, we know that
you are truthful and teach the way of God in truth."
Wherefore, since Christ was professed as having the
teaching authority for salvation, the lawyer raised a
question about the truth of salvation.[124] In Matthew
19:16 it is said that a young man raised a similar question: "Good Master, what should I do[125] to have eternal
life?" These raised their questions in a serious manner
and not out of curiosity, for they did not ask about deeds
already performed, but about deeds to be done to merit
salvation according to what Sirach 3:22 has: "Think always on the things that God has commanded you and be
not curious about God's many works." So these people
were seeking after the way that leads to life, according
to the counsel of Jeremiah 6:16: "Stand along the ways,
and see and inquire of the ancient ways which is the
good way. And walk in it, and you will find refreshment
for your souls." For these are the ways that the Lord
teaches according to Isaiah 48:17: "I am the Lord who
teaches you profitable things."[126]

---

[124] On p. 266, n. 10 QuarEd refer to the Glossa Ordinaria apud
Lyranum (from Bede) on Luke 10:25: "The lawyer uses the Lord's
own words to test him, for he said in verse 20: *Rejoice, for your
names are written in heaven.* But in his testing he shows how true
the Lord's confession is in which he praises the Father and says: *You
have hidden these things from the wise*, etc." See CCSL cxx, p. 221 for
proof of how faithfully the Glossa follows Bede's thought.
[125] While Bonaventure reads *quid faciam* ("what should I do"), the
Vulgate has *quid boni faciam* ("what good work should I do").
[126] This is an excellent example of a truncated quotation from scripture. In my opinion Bonaventure's point would be made stronger if
he quoted all of the second portion of Isaiah 48:17: "I am the Lord
your God who teaches you profitable things, who governs you in the
way that you walk."

45. (Verse 26). Second, relative to *the finding of the truth that was sought*, the text continues: *But he said to him: What is written in the Law? How do you read?* From this it is obvious that the Master of truth was a friend of the Law, according to what Matthew 5:17 reads: "Do you think that[127] I have come to destroy the Law or the Prophets? I have not come to destroy, but to fulfill." In saying this, the Savior provides a *captatio benevolentiae* for the lawyer by showing him that he, too, is one who loves the Law. He also *arouses his attention* since he sends him to the Law as authentic scripture. Further, he sows the seeds of *docility* in the lawyer as he lays out a way to find the truth, and this, indeed, happens by reading the divine law. Whence John 5:39 says: "You search the scriptures, in which you think you have eternal life." For this is the way of coming to the truth and through the truth to life. So Baruch 4:1–2 has: "This is the book of the commandments of God, and the law that is forever. All who keep it, will come to life. But they who have forsaken it, to death. Convert, Jacob, and take hold of it," etc.

46. (Verse 27). And this way led him to the truth. For which reason it is added: *But[128] he answered and said: You shall love the Lord your God with your whole heart and with your whole soul and with your whole strength and with your whole mind.* This is found in Exodus 6:5: "You shall love the Lord your God with your whole heart," etc. In this commandment the legislator reduced all the commandments to one. The total form of living is encompassed in this word, according to what is said in

---

[127] On p. 266, n. 11 QuarEd rightly indicate that the Vulgate reads: *Nolite putare quoniam* ("Do not think that").

[128] On p. 266, n. 13 QuarEd accurately mention that the Vulgate omits *autem* ("But").

Matthew 22:40: "On these two commandments depends the whole Law and the Prophets."[129]

47. But there seems to be a contradiction, for here it is said that *the lawyer* gives the answer. But in Matthew 22:37 it is said that *Christ* is the one who answers.[130] Here there are *four* conditions whereas Matthew has *three*. – But it is clear that the question in Luke comes from a different occasion than the one in Matthew, as Augustine intimates in his *Harmony of the Gospels.* There he says that first Christ gave the answer as Matthew has it, and then the lawyer approved what Christ had said by repeating his answer as Luke states. And what both had is narrated by Mark 12:29–34.[131] And thus it is patent that Mark lays the foundation of concord between Matthew and Luke.[132]

48. Nevertheless, there still seems to remain a discrepancy concerning *the conditions for loving.* For it is said in Deuteronomy 6:5: "You shall love the Lord your God with your whole heart and with your whole soul and

[129] It is only in #49 below that Bonaventure will come to the second commandment of love of neighbor found in Luke 10:27.

[130] Matthew 22:37 has: "Jesus said to him: You shall love the Lord your God with your whole heart, and with your whole soul, and with your whole mind."

[131] In Mark 12:28–34 both Jesus and one of the scribes quote the commandments of love of God and love of neighbor. Mark 12:34 concludes: "And Jesus, seeing that he had answered wisely, said to him: 'You are not far from the kingdom of God.' And no one after that ventured to ask him questions."

[132] In Book II, chapter 73, n. 141–142 of his *Harmony of the Gospels* Augustine considers the discrepancies between Matthew, Mark, and Luke. In summarizing Augustine's solution, Bonaventure makes his own contribution: "And thus it is patent that Mark lays the foundation of concord between Matthew and Luke." Is Bonaventure a harbinger of the two-source hypothesis as a solution to the Synoptic Problem?

with your whole power."[133] But Luke has added *with your whole mind*, and Matthew omits *with your whole strength*.

From this it is to be understood that the perfect way of loving God demands that we refer to God all *thoughts, affections*, and *works*. And these three are mentioned in Deuteronomy 6:5 in the Law. But because *thoughts* are conceived in the heart and mentioned in the mind, Matthew adds here: *with your whole mind*, through which is the explanation of the Law. And since the person refers to God what is interior, namely, the act of memory, understanding, and will and consequently also refers to God his external actions, the phrase *with all your strength* is contained in these three.[134] Thus for greater clarification Luke adds this same phrase, namely, *with your whole strength*. Mark does likewise. – Another explanation is this. The phrase *with your whole strength* modifies the three other conditions and so the meaning is that found in Augustine: *You shall love the Lord your God with your whole heart,* namely, with your intellect without error. *With your whole soul*, that is, with your will without nay-saying. *With your whole mind*, that is, with your memory without forgetting. And *with your whole strength,* scilicet, with your complete power without holding anything back.[135] – Another interpretation is

---

[133] I have translated *fortitudine* by "power" to distinguish this noun from the one used in the parallel passage in Luke 10:27. There Luke uses *viribus* ("strength").

[134] On p. 267, n. 5 QuarEd cite Codex H here to shed some extra light of Bonaventure's involved thought: "And since the person who refers actions, thoughts and affections (to God) acts according to all the strength of his soul. . . . "

[135] QuarEd do not provide quotation marks for Augustine's text. On p. 267, n. 7 QuarEd indicate that they have sought over the years for the source of this quotation from Augustine, but in vain. See Opera Omnia 1:81, n. 8 and 3:613, n. 7 for the results of their earlier

provided by Bernard: "*With your whole heart*, that is, wisely; *with your whole soul*, that is, tenderly; *with your whole mind*, that is, strongly."[136] And in this *with all your strength* is encompassed. – Another explication is the following. *With your whole heart*, that is, vigilantly, according to what The Song of Songs 5:2 says: "I sleep, and my heart is vigilant." *With your whole soul*, that is, ardently, in accordance with what The Song of Songs 5:6 has: "My soul melted when he spoke." *With your whole strength*, that is, constantly, according to what The Song of Songs 8:6–7 states: "Love is strong as death, jealousy as hard as hell. The lamps thereof are the lamps of fire and flames. Many waters cannot quench love, nor can floods drown it." *With your whole mind*, that is, unceasingly, according to what Deuteronomy 8:11 reads:

---

quests. In this note they point to two helpful parallels. The Glossa Interlinearis on Matthew 22:37 reads: "*You shall love the Lord your God with your whole heart*, that is, with your intellect, so that you leave no place for error in your confession of the Divinity. *And with your whole soul*, that is, with your will, so that you will nothing contrary to God. *And with your whole mind* that is, in your memory, so that you do not forget God." In PL 217:616D–617A we read in Pope Innocent III's "Sermon V for the Common of One Martyr": "Through this supreme love the saints love God 'with their whole heart, with their whole mind, and with their whole soul' (Matthew 22). "With their whole mind,' that is, they love the Father with their memory without forgetting. 'With their whole heart,' that is, they love the Son with their intellect without error. 'With their whole soul,' that is, they love the Holy Spirit without nay-saying." My search of Hugh of St. Cher, p. 194v, a indicates that Bonaventure's quotation of Augustine is very close to that of Hugh.

[136] On p. 267, n. 8 QuarEd list the results of their empty search for this "quotation" from Bernard of Clairvaux. I single out Bernard's Sermon 20, n. 4 on The Song of Songs as a likely parallel. SBOp 1.116–117 reads: "Learn from Christ, O Christian, how you should love Christ. Learn how to love tenderly (*dulciter*), to love prudently (*prudenter*), to love strongly (*fortiter*). . . . Therefore, let us love affectionately (*affectuose*), circumspectly (*circumspecte*), and intensely (*valide*)." See Hugh of St. Cher, p. 194v, a for a quotation of Blessed Bernard that is virtually identical to that found in Bonaventue.

"Take heed and beware, lest at any time you forget the Lord your God." And Tobit 4:6 has: "All the days of your life keep God in mind." And thus it is clear that the third and fourth conditions are so very close to one another that at times one is included in the other.

From all the aforementioned conditions it is to be understood that in as far as they refer to *the totality of what we are able to do here below* they fall under the category of commandment and deal with the state of the journey. In as far as they refer to *the totality of consummation* they deal with the state of the heavenly homeland and strongly demonstrate that the conditions of the destination obligate those on their journey there. Therefore, through this commandment the entire human person is ordained to God in his entirety, and as a consequence is ordained to himself.[137]

49. And since he also has to be ordained to his neighbor, the text continues: *and your neighbor* – supply the verb *love* – *as yourself*. This second commandment is found in Leviticus 19:18 where it is said: "You shall love your friend as yourself." According to the Septuagint translation this passage reads: "You shall love your neighbor as yourself." That is, *from the source* you love yourself, namely, from love that is affective and effective. Or *in whom* you love yourself, that is, in God. Or *on whose account* you love yourself, scilicet, on account of God. Or *to what end* you love yourself, that is, for grace in the pre-

---

[137] On p. 268, n. 1 QuarEd refer to Book III d. 27 a. 2 q. 6 of Bonaventure's Commentary on the Sentences. See Opera Omnia 3:613–615 for Bonaventure's full discussion of "Whether we are obliged to love God with our whole heart, our whole soul, and our whole mind." On pp. 614–615 he quotes Bernard that one must love God "tenderly and wisely and strongly." He also quotes Augustine that one must love God "without error, without nay-saying, and without forgetting."

sent life and glory in the future. Or *how* you love your-self, that is, above material things and your own body and inferior to God. For the person who loves his neigh-bor in such a way, that person is the true observer of the Law.[138] Wherefore, Romans 13:9 reads: "The person who loves his neighbor has fulfilled the Law."[139]

And truly he must love his neighbor as himself on ac-count of *the conformity of nature.* Thus, Sirach 13:19 has: "Every animal loves its like. So also every person the one who is near to[140] him." Also on account of *the unity of grace,* according to what Ephesians 4:25 says: "Speak the truth, each one with his neighbor, because we are members of one another." Also, on account of *eternal reward,* for Ephesians 4:4 states: "One body and one Spirit, even as you were called in the one hope of your calling." – Therefore, in order to commend this love God willed that we be born from one father, Adam, that we be redeemed by the same blood, namely, by the blood

---

[138] On p. 268, n. 3 QuarEd observe: "Cardinal Hugh in his commen-tary on Luke 10:27 also presents the five aforementioned exposi-tions." Bonaventure's and Hugh's expositions are virtually identical. See Hugh of St. Cher, p.194v, e: *Idest, ex quo, scilicet, ex charitatis affectu, & effectu. Item in quo teipsum, scilicet, in Deo. Item propter quod teipsum, scilicet, propter Deum, Item ad quod teipsum, idest, ad gratiam in praesenti, & gloriam in futuro. Item quomodo teipsum, scilicet, supra res, & corpus proprium, & citra Deum. Qui sic diligit proximum, legem implevit, Rom. 13.c* ("That is, from the source, scili-cet, from affective and effective love. Likewise, in which you love yourself, scilicet, in God. Likewise, on whose account you love your-self, scilicet, on account of God. Likewise, to what end you love your-self, that is, for grace in the present life and glory in the future. Likewise, how you love yourself, scilicet, above material things and your own body and without losing God. The person who loves his neighbor in such a way has fulfilled the Law, Romans 13c[9]."

[139] Romans 13:9 reads: "And if there is any other commandment, it is summed up in this saying: 'You shall love your neighbor as yourself.'"

[140] Bonaventure is playing here on two meanings of *proximus,* "neighbor"; "the one near to a person."

of our Lord Jesus Christ, that we be recompensed with the same reward. The Psalmist says: "Jerusalem, which is built as a city, which is compact together" (121:3).

50. (Verse 28). Third, concerning *approbation of the truth that is found* the text continues: *And he said to him: You have answered rightly.* For he pronounced a word of rectitude, which is a word of love, according to what The Song of Songs 1:3 has: "The righteous love you." Another view. You have responded in accordance with the rule of wisdom as Proverbs 8:8–9 reads: "All your[141] words are just. There is nothing wicked or perverse in them. They are right to those who understand and just to those who find knowledge." – And since one ought to live in accordance with the rule of rectitude, the text adds: *Do this, and you will live.* For according to James 1:23: "If anyone is a hearer of the word and not a doer," etc.[142] And Romans 2:13 says: "The hearers of the Law are not just in the sight of God, but the ones who do the Law will be justified." And truly *you will live*, because you will come to eternal life as Matthew 19:17 states: "If you want to enter into life, keep the commandments." Wherefore, John 13:17 reads: "If you know these things, blessed will you be if you do them."

51. (Verse 29). Fourth, regarding *the investigation of the truth that is approved* the text continues: *But he, wishing to justify himself*, that is, to show that he was just. "For, as the Interlinearis says, he thought that he was standing not in the presence of God, but of a human

---

[141] On p. 268, n. 6 QuarEd rightly mention that the Vulgate reads *sermones mei* ("my words").
[142] This is an excellent example of Bonaventure's expectation that his listeners/readers would continue with James 1:23b–24: ". . . he is like a man looking at his natural face in a mirror. For he looks at himself and goes away and presently forgets what kind of man he is."

being,"[143] according to what Luke 16:15 below has: "You
are they who declare yourselves just in the sight of human beings, but God knows your hearts," etc. – Another
interpretation of *willing to justify himself* is this: To
prepare for justification which occurs through faith and
acknowledgment of the truth, according to what Romans
3:28 says: "But we reckon that a person is justified by
faith independently of the works of the Law." So he
needed to understand the truth that was being handed
over to him. – For which reason the text adds: *He said to
Jesus: Who is my neighbor?* So that he might understand the commandment according to what Hosea 10:12
reads: "The time for seeking the Lord has arrived, when
he will come who will teach you justice."[144] So he is
seeking diligently for the meaning of *neighbor*, for in
Scripture many different meanings are given to it. Here
are the meanings: a neighbor by *kinship*, according to
what the Psalm has: "My friends and my neighbors have
drawn near and stood against me" (37:12). And again
the Psalm says: "As a neighbor and as our brother, so did
I please," etc. (34:14). A neighbor by *religion*. Sirach 15:4
states: "She (Wisdom) will exalt him among his neighbors." A neighbor by *compassion* or a display of beneficence according to what Luke 10:36–37 below says:
"Which one, in your opinion, was neighbor to him who
fell among the robbers? But he said: He who had compassion on him." A neighbor by *natural assimilation*, in
accordance with what Sirach 13:19 states: "Every ani-

---

[143] On p. 268, n. 9 QuarEd mention that this is the Glossa Interlinearis on Luke 10:29 and quote its next sentence: "He did not recognize
the one, whom he called Master, as his neighbor."
[144] See Bonaventure's commentary on Luke 10:24 (#42) above where
he also quotes Hosea 10:12. On p. 268, n. 11 QuarEd quote the
Glossa Ordinaria on Luke 10:29: "No one is closer to a person than
God. . . . But every non-believer and tempter has neither God nor a
human person as a neighbor."

mal loves its like. So also every person the one who is near to him."[145] And Augustine says: "With the word *neighbor* every human person is understood."[146] – And therefore, since there was a doubt and there were multiple understandings of what the word "neighbor" meant, the matter had to be investigated not only for the sake of this lawyer, but also for the benefit of the faithful, who are to observe the aforementioned commandment which is the consummation of the commandments.[147]

Luke 10:30–37
A PARABLE ILLUMINES THE COMMANDMENT OF LIFE

52. *But looking up, Jesus said.* After presenting the commandment directive of how to live, the text now provides *an illustration that stimulates us to understand*, and does so through a parable. And the phrase, *But, looking up, Jesus* commences this part and shows that the person who wishes to comprehend the truth must

---

[145] In his commentary on Luke 10:27 (#49) above Bonaventure also quotes Sirach 13:19.

[146] On p. 269, n. 1 QuarEd refer to a number of passages from Augustine. I take three. They quote Augustine's Sermon 90, n. 7: "Every human person is your neighbor." They also quote his Enarrationes in Psalm 118 sermon 8, n. 2: "Indeed, every human person is neighbor to all human beings. . . . " Finally, they allude to Book I chapter 30, n. 31–32 of his *De Doctrina Christiana*. This latter passage deals explicitly with Luke 10:30–37 and will be quoted by Bonaventure in his commentary on Luke 10:36–37 (#60) below. Hugh of St. Cher, p. 194v, e comments: *Nomine autem proximi intelligitur omnis homo, ut dicit August.* ("But with the word *neighbor* every human person is understood, as Augustine says").

[147] On p. 269, n. 2 QuarEd rightly refer to Romans 13:9: "And if there is any other commandment, it is summed up in this saying: You shall love your neighbor as yourself." In his commentary on Luke 10:27 (#49) above Bonaventure also alludes to Romans 13:9.

look upwards from whence true light shines. Isaiah 60:1 has: "Arise, be enlightened, O Jerusalem," etc., for Sirach 1:5 says: "The word of God on high is the fountain of wisdom." Now in this parable four items are introduced. The first deals with *the person who is needy because of his misery*. The second concerns *the person who looks away because of his hardness of heart* where verse 31 says: *It happened that a certain priest*, etc. The third treats *the person who comes to aid a person because of his clemency* where verse 33 reads: *But a Samaritan*, etc. The fourth item is *the teaching that flows from the parable* where verse 36 states: *Which of these three, in your opinion*, etc.

Concerning *the person who is needy because of his misery* the Evangelist introduces two considerations. The first is *the removal of good*, and the second is *the infliction of evil*.

53. (Verse 30). Then, first, relative to *the removal of good* the text has: *A certain man was going down from Jerusalem to Jericho, and he fell in with robbers, who stripped him*. So perhaps, they did this because *he was alone*. The text mentions this when it says: *A certain man*, so that what Qoheleth 4:10 states appears to be true: "Woe to the person who is alone. For when he falls, he has no one *to lift him up*." Rather such a person finds *those who rob him*. Thus, this man could say what Job 19 has: "He has stripped me of my glory and has taken the crown from my head" (verse 9). "Robbers[148] have come together and have made a way for themselves through me" (verse 12). He fell among these robbers, perhaps, on account of *the loneliness of the road*, where robbers are accustomed to hide, according to Jeremiah

---

[148] The Vulgate reads *latrones eius* ("his robbers").

3:2: "You used to sit along the ways, waiting for them like a robber in a lonely place."[149]

54. Second, with regard to *the infliction of evil* the text continues: *And beating him, they went their way, leaving him half-dead*, as if to say that *they had wounded* him to the point of death, according to what is said of robbers in Proverbs 1:16: "Their feet run to evil and make haste to shed blood." And the Psalmist has: "Their mouth is full of cursing and bitterness. Their feet are swift to shed blood" (13:3). Not only *did they beat* him, lest perchance he report them, but as it is said of Ishmael in Jeremiah 41:7: "Ishmael, son of Nethaniah, killed the men coming to Gedaliah, he and the men who were with him around the center of the pit." And he did this, lest they report him as is the case here.

55. (Verse 31). *But it happened that a priest*, etc. After a description of the person who was needy through a doubly miserable condition, the text introduces *a person who looks away because of his hardness of heart*. Now this person is displayed in two characters, namely, one who is *superior* and another who is *inferior* in ecclesiastical dignity. – First, then, with regard to the person who is *superior*, the text says: *But it happened that a priest was going down the same way*. Now it was the priest's responsibility to teach and observe the Law of God in accordance with what Malachi 2:7 states: "The lips of a priest will guard knowledge, and they will seek the law from his mouth." Further, they should be holy according to what Leviticus 10:3 has: "I will be made

---

[149] On p. 269, n. 7 QuarEd quote from Jerome's Letter 108, n. 12: "Paula went straight down the road to Jericho, recalling the man in the Gospel who had been injured. . . . [She saw] the place called Adomim, which is interpreted *of blood*, because much blood was shed there because of the frequent assaults of the robbers."

holy in those who approach me, and I will be glorified in
the sight of all the people." Wherefore, it was the most
grave obligation of the priests to guard the law of God,
especially with regard to mercy. This one, however, did
not guard the law because of his hardness of heart. –
Whence the text continues: *And when he saw him, he
passed by*, not heeding what Deuteronomy 22:4 reads:
"If you see your *brother's* ass or ox to have fallen down
in the way, you shall not look away, but you shall lift it
up with him." This man *looked away from his brother* on
account of avarice.[150] What Jeremiah 6:13 says had already been verified: "From the least of them up to the
greatest all are given to avarice. And from the prophet
up to the priest, all are guilty of deceit." And in a similar
way Isaiah 1:23 says: "The princes are faithless, companions of thieves," etc.[151]

56. (Verse 32). Second, concerning the *inferior* person
the text has: *Likewise, a Levite also, when he was near
the place and saw him, passed him by*. And this person
did not attend to what Sirach 7:38–39: "Be not wanting
in comforting those who weep. And walk with those who

---

[150] This interpretation is found neither in Ambrose nor in Bede. See
Hugh of St. Cher, p. 194v, k: "I respond. Jews are by nature avaricious, and clerics even more avaricious, as they are wont to always
receive and never give, even though it is said in Acts 20g[35]: It is
more blessed to give than to receive. And these, namely, the priest
and Levite were Jews and clerics, and therefore it is no wonder that
they passed by without showing mercy." On p. 195h Hugh comments:
"In this the avarice of all clerics and priests is noted, for neither the
priest nor the levite is moved to compassion towards the needy and
infirm man." Hugh then has a long quotation from Jeremiah
6:12–13. It seems clear that Bonaventure is indebted to Hugh for his
interpretation here.
[151] It seems that Bonaventure's main reason for quoting Isaiah 1:23
is found in what follows: "Your princes are faithless, companions of
thieves. They all love bribes; they run after rewards. They judge not
for the fatherless, and the widow's cause does not come to them."

are mourning. Let it not be troublesome to you to visit the sick." It was troublesome for this Levite, for, when he was near the place and saw him, he did not want to visit him. This Levite was not similar to Tobit, who in Tobit 4:7, taught his son: "Do not turn your face away from any poor person." But this Levite turned his eyes away from this poor man, who was naked and wounded and a member of his own people. And this behavior is more reprehensible in priests and Levites than in other persons. For which reason Hosea 6:6 states: "I desired mercy and not sacrifice, and the knowledge of God more than holocausts." Therefore, this lawyer is said to have stated in Mark 12:33: "To love one's neighbor as oneself is a greater thing than all holocausts and sacrifices."

57. (Verse 33). *But a certain Samaritan*, etc. In the third place is introduced *the person who comes to aid another because of his clemency*. There is a twofold effect to the mercy this person extends, namely, *care for his infirmity* and *alleviation of his neediness*.

First, then, with regard to *mercy that cares for his infirmity* the text says: *But a certain Samaritan, as he journeyed, came upon him and seeing him*, with the eye of his benignity and the need to show him the greatest love, *was moved with mercy*, so that he could say what Job 30:25 states: "I wept heretofore for him that had been afflicted, and my soul had compassion on the poor." And again Job 31:18 has: "From my infancy mercy grew up with me."

58. (Verse 34). And since genuine mercy manifests itself in deed, the text continues: *And he went up to him*, uniting him to himself, and thus putting into effect his affections for him as his neighbor. *He bound up his wounds, pouring on oil and wine*, so that *the oil* might

ease his pain, *the wine* might sterilize his wounds, and *the bandages* might aid healing. And this work was that of the good physician, according to what Sirach 38:7 says: "By these things he will cure and will allay their pain, and the dealer in ointments will make soothing concoctions and will formulate restorative ointments." Proverbs 21:20 reads: "There is a treasure to be desired, and oil in the dwelling of the just." – And because this injured man was in need not only of medication, but also of means of transport and hospitality and food, the text adds: *And setting him on his own beast,* as a means of transport, *brought him to an inn,* for hospitality, *and took care of him,* by giving him food. And thus he fulfilled what Isaiah 58:7 says: "Break your bread with the hungry and bring the needy and homeless into your home," etc.[152]

59. (Verse 35). Second, relative to *the mercy that alleviates his neediness* the text says: *And the next day he took out two denarii and gave them to the innkeeper.* He took out a little money, for perhaps he had little, according to what Tobit 4:8–9 reads: "To the extent that you can, be merciful. If you have much, give abundantly. If you have little, take care to bestow even a little willingly." – And since, however little the money might be, there was a great will to share it, the text adds: "*And he said: Take care of him. And whatever more you spend, I, on my way back, will repay you.* From this it is obvious that his mercy was integral, and not like that of those about whom it is said in Hosea 6:4: "Your mercy is like a morning cloud and like the dew that burns off in the

---

[152] Isaiah 58:7 continues: ". . . When you see a person naked, cover him and despise not your own flesh." This sentence surely applies to the man who was stripped, left half-dead, and aided by the Samaritan.

morning." But about him could truly be said what the
Psalm has: "He shows mercy and lends all the day long,
and his seed will be in blessing" (36:26). And indeed, for
according to what is said in Proverbs 19:17: "The person
who has mercy on the poor is lending to the Lord, and
he will give him his reward."

60. (Verses 36–37). *Which one of these three, in your
opinion*, etc. Here in the fourth place occurs *the teaching
drawn from the parable*, and this has two sections. The
first deals with *learning on an intellectual level*. The
second concerns *an appeal to the affections*.

First, with regard to *learning on an intellectual level* it
is said: *Which of these three, in your opinion, proved
himself neighbor to him who fell among the robbers?*
This he asks of him, so that he might elicit the truth
from his own mouth. And he is successful. – So the text
continues: *And he said: The person who showed him
mercy.* But two of these were of the same nation, but the
other was a foreigner. Therefore, the name of *neighbor*
is to be extended not only to those near, but also to those
far away. Thus, Bede says: "According to the literal
sense it is clear that the person who was a foreigner to
this Jerusalemite and showed him mercy was more a
neighbor to him than the priest and Levite of the same
nation."[153] It is also obvious that *neighborliness* is more
centered on natural love and compassion than on carnal
kinship. Wherefore, Ambrose writes: "Kinship does not
make a neighbor, but mercy, a mercy which is according
to nature. For nothing is so much in accordance with

---

[153] On p. 270, n. 9 QuarEd state Bonaventure is actually quoting verbatim the Glossa Ordinaria on Luke 10:36, which in its turn is based on Bede. See CCSL cxx, p. 224.

nature than to assist one who shares the same nature."[154] It is also manifest from this that "with the word *neighbor* is understood everyone, who is needful of mercy or can show mercy," and thus "everybody."[155] And the intellect of the lawyer was thus enlightened by wonderful instruction. For if the Lord had given a straightforward response to the lawyer's question, the lawyer would scarcely have believed it. Therefore, the Lord most wisely elicited the truth from his own mouth and formed him in this truth more by means of question and answer than by means of pronouncing opinions. In this he gives a lesson on how one must satisfactorily deal with the proud.

61. Second, with regard to *an appeal to the affections* the text continues: *And Jesus said to him: Go and do in like manner*, so that you may extend mercy to every person, if you desire to be truly merciful, for, as Sirach 18:12 says: "The mercy of God is upon all flesh," that is, the mercy that proceeds from God. For God's mercy extends itself to all. Wherefore, Luke 6:35–36 above has: "You will be children of the Most High, for he is kind towards the ungrateful and evil. Be merciful, therefore, as your heavenly Father is merciful." – But genuine mercy does not reside solely in the affections, but also *produces ef-*

---

[154] Bonaventure's quotation is almost verbatim. See CCSL xiv, p. 241: *Non enim cognatio facit proximum. Sed misercordia, quia misericordia secundum naturam; nihil enim tam secundum naturam quam iuuare consortem naturae* ("For kinship does not make a neighbor, but mercy, for mercy is according to nature. For nothing is so much in accordance with nature than to assist one who shares the same nature").

[155] See Bonaventure's commentary on Luke 10:29 (#51) above and the notes there for more information about Bonaventure's dependence on Augustine for the meaning of "neighbor." This quotation is not found in so many words in Book I, chapter 30, n. 31 of Augustine's *De Doctrina Christiana*.

fects. Therefore, the text reads: *And you, do in like manner*. Thus Galatians 6:9–10 states: "In doing good, let us not grow tired. For in due time we will reap, if we do not slack off. Therefore, while we have time, let us do good to all." And in this the law of God is fulfilled, when a neighbor who is needy in whatsoever a way is assisted not only in word and mind, but also in deed. And this in accordance with what Galatians 6:2 says: "Bear one another's burdens, and thus you will fulfill the law of Christ," which consists in love of neighbor as Romans 13:8 has: "The person who loves his neighbor has fulfilled the Law." – Wherefore, such is the teaching drawn from the parable according to its *literal* sense.

62. But further teaching may be elicited from this parable according to *the spiritual sense*, so that *the person in need* on account of his sorry condition may be understood to be *the human race*, which in Adam the sinner *went down from Jerusalem to Jericho*, that is, from paradise into the world, and *fell in with robbers*, that is, into the power of the demons, who *stripped* him of God's gifts and *wounded* him in his natural faculties. And *they left him half-dead*, for having taken away *the likeness*, *the image* alone remained,[156] so that what the Psalm has

---

[156] Passages from Bonaventure's *Breviloquium* help explain Bonaventure's thinking here. See *The Works of Bonaventure II: The Breviloquium,* translated by José de Vinck (Paterson: St. Anthony Guild Press, 1963), 104 where de Vinck translates Part II, chapter 12, n. 1: "From this we may gather that the universe is like a book reflecting, representing, and describing its Maker, the Trinity, at three different levels of expression: as a trace, every creature; the aspect of image, in the intellectual creatures or rational spirits; the aspect of likeness, only in those who are God-conformed. Through these successive levels, comparable to the rungs of a ladder, the human mind is designed to ascend gradually to the supreme Principle who is God." In Part V chapter 1, n. 3 Bonaventure describes how grace restores God's image in the human soul. On p. 182 de Vinck translates: "Because this inpouring, rendering the soul deiform,

could truly be said: "The human person, when he was in a honorable position, did not understand. He has been compared to senseless beasts," etc. (48:21). And again the Psalm says: "Surely man has passed by in an image" (38:7).[157] Further, that *image was stripped* on account of turning away from life and *wounded* because of turning towards death, according to what Jeremiah 2:13 has: "My people have done two evils. They have forsaken me, the fountain of living water and have dug for themselves cisterns that can hold no water." Therefore, *he is stripped and wounded*, according to what Lamentations 5:16–17 reads: "The crown has fallen from our head. Woe to us, for we have sinned. Therefore is our heart sorrowful. Therefore have our eyes become darkened."

---

comes from God, conforms to God, and leads to God as an end, it restores our spirit as the image of the most blessed Trinity. . . . " See Opera Omnia 5:230, 252.

[157] On p. 271, nn. 4 and 8 QuarEd list the authors whose lead Bonaventure followed in explicating the spiritual sense of the parable of the Good Samaritan. From the list, which includes Ambrose, Bede, and the Glossa Ordinaria, I highlight Homily 34 on Luke 10:25–37 by Origen (d. 254/255) which had great influence in the history of interpretation in its Latin translation by Jerome. I quote from Homily 34, n. 3–4 in the translation of Joseph T. Lienhard, *Origen: Homilies on Luke, Fragments on Luke,* FC 94 (Washington, D.C.: Catholic University of America Press, 1996), p. 138: "3. One of the elders wanted to interpret the parable as follows. The man who was going down is Adam. Jerusalem is paradise, and Jericho is the world. The robbers are hostile powers. The priest is the Law, the Levite is the prophets, and the Samaritan is Christ. The wounds are disobedience, the beast is the Lord's body, the *pandochium* (that is, the stable), which accepts all who wish to enter, is the Church. And further, the two *denarii* mean the Father and the Son. The manager of the stable is the head of the Church, to whom its care has been entrusted. And the fact that the Samaritan promises he will return represents the Savior's second coming. 4. All of this has been said reasonably and beautifully. But we should not think that it applies to every man."

63. Now *the person who passed by with hardness in his heart* was *the righteousness of the law*, which displayed neither mercy nor medicine. This was well signified in Exodus 17:12 where it is said: "The hands of Moses were heavy." Wherefore, the Glossa of Bede says: "*The priest proclaims the law of God.* Indeed, the Law went down into the world through Moses and did not convey any health to men and women. *The Levite* came down, who manifests the type of the Prophets, but this person cures no one, for the Law exposed sins, and he passed by, for he grants no forgiveness."[158] And this had been well designated in 2 Kings 4 in the staff of Elisha which he sent to raise up the dead boy, but "it effected no voice nor sensation."[159] Wherefore, it had become a staff more useful for beating than curing. So it is said in Hebrews 10:28: "A person who makes void the Law of Moses dies without any mercy on the word of two or three witnesses."

64. Now *the person extending assistance out of mercy* is rightly understood to be Christ the Lord, for *Samaritan* means guardian.[160] Moreover, he himself is the person of

---

[158] On p. 271, n. 6 QuarEd state that this is the Glossa Ordinaria. See CCSL cxx, p. 223 where in his commentary on Luke 10:31–32 Bede says something vaguely similar to what the Glossa has. Bede, in turn, is dependent upon Augustine. See PL 35:1340: "But *the priest* and *the Levite*, who, when they saw him, passed by, signify the priesthood and ministry of the Old Testament, which could not effect salvation."

[159] In 2 Kings 4:8–37 the story is told of Elisha and the Shunammite woman. Elisha sends his servant Gehazi ahead with his staff, so that he might lay it upon the face of the dead boy. And in verse 31 we read of the ineffectiveness of Elisha's staff, for it did not raise up the dead son of the Shunammite.

[160] Origen's Homily 34, n. 5 reads in Lienhard's translation: "The name means 'guardian.' He is the one who 'neither grows drowsy nor sleeps as he guards Israel' (Psalm 121:4). . . . The Jews had said to him, 'You are a *Samaritan*, and you have a demon' (John 8:48).

whom the Psalm says: "Unless the Lord guards the
city," etc. (126:1). And Isaiah 21:11 reads: "Guardian,
how is the night going?" For "behold, the one who is Israel's guardian will neither slumber nor sleep" (Psalm
120:4). – This person *came upon the wounded man*, for
as Philippians 2:7 states: "He was made in human likeness and in form found as a man." He came, I say, "in
the likeness of sinful flesh," as it is said in Romans 8:3.
– And coming to the wounded person, he did three
things for him. He applied *medications*, and this
through *the grace of the Sacraments*, which bring about
rubbings and anointings that heal the wounds of sins.
This did not come about before the coming of the Savior,
according to what Isaiah 1:6 states: "There are wounds
and bruises and swelling sores which are not bound up
nor healed with medicine nor soothed by oil." But this
was done after the coming of Christ. Wherefore, 1 Peter
2:24 says: "Who himself bore our sins in his body upon
the tree . . . in his stripes we were healed.[161] – He also
used his own means of *conveyance*, and this through *the
grace of the virtues and gifts*, through which we are conveyed to *the inn* of the Church, according to what the
Psalmist says: "Blessed is the person, whose help is
from you. In his heart he has disposed to ascend by
steps in the valley of tears. . . . For the lawgiver will
give a blessing. They will go from virtue to virtue"
(83:6–8). And this, indeed, happens in *the inn* of the
Church. Wherefore, the Psalm continues: "I have chosen
to be an outcast in the house of God rather than to dwell

Though he denied having a demon, he was unwilling to deny that he
was a Samaritan, for he knew that he was a guardian." On p. 271, n.
8 QuarEd refer to three sermons by Augustine for this interpretation. Hugh of St. Cher, p. 195x interprets the Samaritan as "a
guardian": "Now the Samaritan, who is interpreted to be a guardian,
is Christ the Lord."

[161] The Vulgate reads *sanati estis* ("you were healed").

in the tabernacles of sinners. For God loves mercy and truth; the Lord will give grace and glory" (83:11–12). – He supplied *nutriment*, which happens through the teaching of the two testaments, which is understood to occur in the offering of *the two denarii*, which *he gave to the innkeeper*, that is, to the Prelate whose responsibility it is to administer the teaching of Christ. And his explanation of this teaching is the meaning of *to pay over and above*. Whence Sirach 45:6 reads: "And the Lord gave Moses a heart to understand[162] the commandments and the law of life and instruction in order to teach Jacob his covenant and Israel his judgments." To these the Lord *will repay all they have spent over and above* when he will return on the day of judgment according to what is said in Daniel 12:3: "Those who instruct many to justice (will shine) as stars for all eternity." Matthew 25:21 reads: "Well done, good and faithful servant. Because you have been faithful over a few things, I will set you over many," etc.[163]

---

[162] I give a short indication of a textual problem that is not mentioned by QuarEd. The Vulgate reads *Et dedit illi coram praecepta, legem vitae* ("And God gave him in his presence commandments, the law of life"). Bonaventure's text takes *coram* ("in his presence") to be two words *cor ad* ("a heart to understand").

[163] Matthew 25:21 ends with: ". . . Enter into the joy of your master."

Luke 10:38–42
A HUMAN EXAMPLE ILLUSTRATES THE FORM OF LIFE[164]

65. *Now it came to pass as they were on their journey,*
etc. After the Evangelist has transmitted the form of life
by means of the divine commandment, he now in a second section hands it on by means of *a human example.*
Thus, the Glossa of Bede states: "Having given a discourse on love of God and of neighbor, he sets forth an
example of both."[165] For here he introduces on the literal
level *an example of perfection,* an example of the active
and the contemplative lives, and *of a comparison between both.* Wherefore, this passage has two parts. In
the first *a rational comparison* is set forth while in the
second *a judicial determination* is given where verse 41
has: *And the Lord answered and said.*

Now concerning *the rational comparison* four points
are made. First is *being in the company of the divine
presence.* Second is *the leisure of the contemplative life.*
Third is *the exercise*[166] *of the active life.* Fourth is *quar-
reling between the two of them.*

---

[164] See Giles Constable, *Three Studies in Medieval Religious and Social Thought* (New York: Cambridge University Press, 1995), pp.
1–141 ("The Interpretation of Martha and Mary"). Cf. also Atanasio
Matanic, "La pericope di Lc. 10, 38–42, spiegata da Ugo di St.-Cher:
Primo esegeta degli Ordini Mendicanti († 1263)," *Divinitas* 13 (1969):
715–724. See further *The Life of Saint Mary Magdalene and of her
Sister Saint Martha: A Medieval Biography,* translated and annotated by David Mycoff, Cistercian Studies Series 108 (Kalamazoo:
Cistercian Publications, 1989). The original text for this Biography is
found in PL 112:1431–1508.
[165] On p. 272, n. 4 QuarEd mention that this is the Glossa Ordinaria.
See CCSL cxx, p. 225 for what Bede actually says.
[166] I have translated *exercitium* with "exercise" as in "spiritual exercises." "Exercise" connotes activity that is not random, but planned.

66. (Verse 38). The first point, then, deals with *being in the company of the divine presence* where the text has: *Now it came to pass as they were on their journey that he entered a certain village,* either on account of *preaching the kingdom of God,* according to what is said above in Luke 8:1: "He was journeying through towns and villages, proclaiming the good news of the kingdom of God," or on account of *seeking hospitality,* according to what is said above in Luke 9 that the Samaritans refused to extend hospitality to him and his disciples and that "they went to another village."[167] John 11:1 has more to say about this village: "Now a certain man was sick, Lazarus of Bethany, the village of Mary and Martha, his sisters."[168] In this village, I say, he found hospitality. – For which reason the text continues: *And a certain woman, named Martha, welcomed him into her house,* namely, as someone poor and needy. Wherefore, to such people he will say in the judgment what Matthew 25:35 has: "I was a stranger, and you took me in," that is, to those similar to Martha who is like Job, of whom Job 31:32 says: "The stranger did not stay outside my door. My door was open to the traveler." And in receiving that hospitality he was present *bodily,* as he is present *spiritually* to those engaged in the contemplative and the active lives, according to what Revelation 3:20 states: "I stand at the door and knock. If anyone . . . opens the door for me, I will come in to him and will have supper with him." For it is said in Proverbs 8:31: "My delights were to be with the children of men." Wisdom 8:16 states the human perspective: "When I go into my house, I will repose myself with her. For her

---

[167] See Luke 9:53 and 9:56.

[168] On p. 272, n. 7 QuarEd correctly indicate that the Vulgate reads: *de castello Mariae et Marthae sororis eius* ("of the village of Mary and Martha, her sister").

conversation has no bitterness, and her company has no tedium."[169]

67. (Verse 39). Second, relative to *the leisure of the contemplative life* the text adds: *And she had a sister called Mary*, who was perfect in the leisure of contemplation. So the text says: *who also, seating herself at the Lord's feet, was listening to his word*. Indeed, this was the leisure of this woman: *To be intent on the Lord, to have time for the Lord, to sit with the Lord,* and *to be quiet in the Lord's presence*.[170] Thus, it is said in John 11:20 that "Mary *was sitting* at home," and doing so *at his feet*.[171] For Deuteronomy 33:3 has: "Those who draw near to his feet will receive of his teaching." The meaning of *sitting at his feet* is humility, which must be present in contemplative men, for they will abound in the fruits of devo-

---

[169] On p. 272, n. 9 QuarEd cite the Glossa Ordinaria on Luke 10:38: "When Jesus entered into the house, a life of iniquity, if it ever existed there, fled. Two innocent ways of life remained, one laborious, the other leisurely, and in the middle of them was the fountain of life himself." Throughout his interpretation of Luke 10:38–42 Bonaventure will be drawing upon Augustine's Sermons 103 and 104. The Glossa Ordinaria bases its comments on Sermon 104, n. 4. I use the translation of Edmund Hill in *The Works of Saint Augustine* Part III – Sermons; Volume 4: Sermons 94A–147A (Brooklyn: New City Press, 1992), p. 83: "As for a wicked kind of life, it was entirely wanting in that household, to be found neither with Martha nor with Mary. If such ever had been there, it fled when the Lord came it. So there remained in that house, which welcomed the Lord, two kinds of life in two women; both innocent, both praiseworthy; one laborious, the other leisurely; neither criminally active, neither merely idle. Both innocent, both, I repeat, praiseworthy; but one laborious, as I said, the other leisurely; neither criminally active, which the laborious kind has to be beware of; neither merely idle, which the leisurely kind has to avoid. So there were in that house these two kinds of life, and the very fountain of life himself."

[170] I have spelled out Bonaventure's more cryptic: *Domino intendere, vacare, sedere, et tacere.*

[171] It may be niggling on my part, but John 11:20 states that while Mary was sitting at home, Jesus was talking with Martha outside.

tion according to what the Psalm says: "You send forth springs in the valleys," etc. (103:10). Now the person who sits in a humble manner is flooded with the tears of compunction according to what Jeremiah 15:17 states: "I sat alone, for you have filled me with bitterness." And this is the office of the contemplative soul, namely, to spend time in the tears of compunction and devotion.[172] Wherefore, this Mary, the exemplar of contemplation, is almost always described as weeping, scilicet, in Luke 7:38 above, where it is said that "standing behind the feet of the Lord, she began to bathe his feet with her tears," etc. And see John 11:32–33 where it is said that "When Mary came to where Jesus was and saw him, she fell at his feet. . . . When, therefore, Jesus saw her weeping, he groaned in spirit." And John 20:11 reads: "Mary was standing outside the tomb weeping." And the first tears are those of *compunction*. the second of *compassion*. The third are of *loving devotion*. Contemplatives must have all three as they sit at the feet of the Lord.[173]

68. (Verse 40). Third, with regard to *the exercise of the active life* the text continues: *But Martha was busy about much serving*. And this was good activity which

---

[172] On p. 273., n. 2 QuarEd call attention to Augustine's Sermon 104, n. 3. I modify Hill's translation on p. 83: "She was sitting at the feet of our head. The more humble her position, the more plentiful her gains. For water flows down into the lowliness of the valley. It runs off the swelling height of the hill."

[173] Bonaventure presents a marvelous exegesis on "Mary" as contemplative through the catchword of "weeping." The weakness of his interpretation is that the gospel texts he cites mention three different women. The woman of Luke 7:36–50 is unnamed. The woman of John 11:32–33 is Mary of Bethany. The woman of John 20:1–19 is Mary of Magdala.

avoided idleness,[174] according to the counsel of the wise man in Qoheleth 9:10: "Whatsoever your hand is able to do, do it earnestly. For neither work nor reason nor wisdom nor knowledge will be in hell, whither you are hastening." Martha was always doing some work. Thus it is said in John 12:1–2 that "Jesus came to Bethany. And they made him a supper there, and Martha served." – And note that the text says that *she was busy*, that is, she had enough to do,[175] *with much serving*, to show that in her serving there was perfection and a fitting way of acting according to the counsel of Blessed Peter in 2 Peter 1:10: "Brothers, busy yourselves even more, so that by your good works you can make your calling and election sure." For the work of serving especially pleases the Lord, and in this a person especially imitates Christ, as it is said in Luke 22:27 below: "But I am in your midst as he who serves." And again Matthew 20:28 has: "the Son of Man did not come to be served, but to serve." Wherefore, such serving is pleasing and honorable before God and worthy of reward, according to what John 12:26 has: "If anyone serves me, my Father will honor him."

69. Fourth, concerning *the quarrel between the two of them*, the text adds: *Martha stood and said: Lord, is it no concern of yours that my sister has left me to serve alone?* Here Martha, who is working, complains about Mary who is idle, as if she could not bear the burden of the work alone, according to what Moses says in his complaint to the Lord in Numbers 11:14: "I alone am not able to bear all these people, because it is too heavy for

---

[174] *Otium* can mean "leisure" (of contemplation) and can also mean "idleness."

[175] On p. 273, n. 7 QuarEd give evidence that *satagere* ("to be busy") comes from *satis* and *agere*. So Martha had enough to do. 2 Peter 1:10 uses *satagere* in connection with "doing" and "good works."

me." Thus Martha, too, because of the weight of the burden was asking for Mary's assistance, knowing that what Galatians 6:14 has pertains to the law of Christ: "Bear one another's burdens." Therefore, she was on secure ground in seeking Christ's decision to get her sister's help. – For this reason the text adds: *Tell her, therefore, to help me*, so that she may act according to the counsel of the Apostle in Galatians 5:13: "Through the love of the Spirit[176] serve one another." And Ephesians 4:2 reads: "Bearing with one another in love." – In this quarrel Mary is silent. And Gregory gives the reason for this: "Mary does not respond, but commits to the judge her case to remain at leisure. For if she would prepare a discourse in her defense, she would abandon her intention of listening."[177] For the role of contemplatives is not to contend, but rather to keep silent and to listen and to mediate, according to what Lamentations 3:28 has: "He will sit by himself and remain quiet." Thus Job 4:12 reads: "Now a word was spoken to me in

---

[176] The Vulgate does not have *Spiritus* ("Spirit"). I have taken the liberty of taking *Spiritus* as a genitive.

[177] On p. 273, n. 12 QuarEd state that this quotation comes from the Glossa Ordinaria, which, in turn, stems from Augustine's Sermon 103, n. 3. In PL 38:614 Sermon 103 chapter 2, n. 3 reads: *Non respondente illa, sed tamen praesente, judicat Dominus. Maria causam suam tanquam otiosa judici maluit committere, nec in respondendo voluit laborare. Si enim pararet respondenti sermonem, remitteret audiendi intentionem* ("When Mary does not reply, although she is present, the Lord renders his judgment. Mary preferred to commit to the judge her case of remaining at leisure and did not want to engage in the labor of responding. For if she would prepare a discourse in her defense, she would abandon her intention of listening"). Compare Bonaventure's Latin: *Maria non respondet, sed causam suam tanquam otiosa iudici committit. Si enim pararet respondendi sermonem, remitteret audiendi intentionem.* In any case, the quotation is from Augustine, not from Gregory. Hugh of St. Cher, p. 196v, g attributes this quotation to the Glossa.

private, and by stealth, as it were, I caught[178] the meaning of its whisper." Now Mary lost nothing by keeping silence, because the Lord assumed her cause and defended her. Therefore, Bernard says: "In every case the Lord speaks up for Mary, either when she is criticized by the Pharisee, in Luke 7:39 above, or when she is rebuked by her sister, as in this passage, or by the disciples, as it is said in Matthew 26:8–13."[179]

70. But Martha complains sometimes, by *proposing her office for others*, and then the complaint is reprehensible. Wherefore, the Glossa states: "Martha speaks for those people who, still inexperienced in divine contemplation, give voice to and spread abroad the opinion that the only work pleasing to God is fraternal love. And therefore, they assert that all who want to be dedicated to Christ must be taken up with this work."[180] – Sometimes she complains by *stating that the leisure of Mary is preferable*. Thus, Bernard says: "Do you think that in the house in which Christ is received, the voice of murmuring may be heard?" And he adds: "Happy is the house

---

[178] On p. 273, n. 13, QuarEd rightly indicate that the Vulgate reads *suscepit auris mea* ("my ear heard").

[179] On p. 273, n. 14, QuarEd point to Bernard's Sermon 3, n. 2 for the Feast of the Assumption of the Blessed Virgin Mary. Sermon 3 has the subtitle "Concerning Mary and Martha and Lazarus." See SBOp 5.239–40: *Vide praerogativam Mariae, quem in omni causa habeat advocatum. Indignatur siquidem Pharisaeus, conqueritur soror, etiam discipuli murmurant: ubique Maria tacet, et pro ea loquitur Christus* ("Look at the prerogative of Mary that she has him as an advocate in every instance. If the Pharisee is indignant, if her sister complains, even if the disciples murmur, in every case Mary is silent and Christ speaks up for her"). Apparently neither Bernard nor Bonaventure noticed that the woman in Luke 7 and the woman in Matthew 26 were unnamed.

[180] On p. 274, n. 1 QuarEd identify the Glossa as the Ordinaria. With two slight variations this quotation is taken verbatim from Bede. See CCSL cxx, p. 226.

and blessed is the congregation in which Martha complains about Mary."[181] And the reason for this is that *the
contemplative life* per se is without a doubt to be chosen.
But Martha, that is, *the active life*, is by necessity to be
supported. So Jacob chose Rachel, but according to what
was necessary, he first took Leah, as it is said in Genesis 29:17–30. – Therefore, it was licit for Martha to com-
plain *that she might be like Mary*, for she was humble.
But if she complains that *she is not helping her*, that
stems from weakness. And if she complains that Mary
sometimes wanted to help and *she herself did not want
her*, that stems from impiety. For such a complaint impedes the law of love.[182]

71. (Verse 41). *And the Lord answered and said.* After
the rational comparison the Evangelist mentions *the
judicial sentence* and makes four points: *the humiliation
of the active life, the commendation of the contemplative
life, the promulgation of the decision*, and *the assignation
of the reason*.

So first, about *the humiliation of the active life* the text
continues: *Martha, Martha, you are anxious and troubled*

---

[181] These two sentences are virtually verbatim from Bernard's
"Sermo Tertius in Assumptione Beatae Mariae, De Maria et Martha
et Lazaro," n. 2. See SBOp, 5.239.

[182] On p. 274, n. 4 QuarEd quote what Bernard, a very active and
contemplative abbot, has to say in his "Sermo Tertius in Assumptione
Beatae Mariae, De Maria et Martha et Lazaro," n. 2. I modify the
translation of *SBSermons* 3, pp. 237–238: "But, on the other hand, it
would certainly be shameful and even sinful on the part of Mary to
envy Martha. For where in the Gospel do we find Mary complaining
of Martha and saying to the Lord, 'My sister has left me alone in the
enjoyment of contemplative repose?' God forbid it, my dearest brethren, God forbid it, I say, that he who has leisure for God should aspire to the tumultuous life of the brothers charged with official duties." "Brothers charged with official duties" is my translation of
fratrum officialium. See SBOp 5.299.

about many works. He repeats her name *Martha*, in order that he might prompt her to consider her own deficiency and this by attending to the divine word. As it is said of Moses in Exodus 3:4 that: "when the Lord saw that Moses was coming forward to see, he called to him out of the midst of the bush and said: Moses, Moses." And the Lord, wishing to get the attention of sinners, repeats his appeal in Jeremiah 22:29: "O earth, O earth, hear the word of the Lord."[183] And so now that he has gotten Martha's attention, he points out that she has a triple deficiency, namely, *anxiety* in thought, *being troubled* in affection, and *being divided* in action. And all these things prevent us from totally directing ourselves to God. – So excessive *anxiety* is to be avoided, according to what Philippians 4:6 says: "Have no anxiety, but in every prayer . . . let your petitions be made known to God." And 1 Peter 5:7 has: "Cast all your anxiety upon him, because he cares for you." – *Being troubled* is also to be avoided. Thus, John 14:1 states: "Let not your heart be troubled. You believe in God. Believe also in me." Wherefore, Isaiah 42:4 says of Christ: "He will not be sad nor troublesome." For the troubled eye is not fit for seeing. – *Division* is also to be avoided. So Sirach 11:10 reads: "Son, don't get involved in many deeds." – And the active life has these disadvantages, but not the contemplative. Thus, 1 Corinthians 7:33–34: "The man who is married is anxious about the things of the world, how he may please his wife, and he is divided. And the unmarried woman and the virgin think about the things of the Lord that she may be holy in body and in spirit. Whereas she who is married thinks about the things of

---

[183] On p. 274, n. 5 QuarEd quote the Glossa Ordinaria: "*Martha, Martha*, the repetition of the name is a sign of love or perhaps, a way of getting her attention so that she might listen more carefully." The Glossa is indebted to Augustine's Sermon 103, n. 3. See PL 38:614.

the world." – Therefore, the anxious action is humiliating as it manifests its disadvantages and deficiencies.

72. (Verse 42). Second, relative to *the commendation of the contemplative life* the text reads: *But one thing is necessary*, namely, the kingdom of God. If a person has this, nothing is lacking. So Matthew 6:33 has: "Seek first the kingdom of God . . . , and all these things will be given you besides." And the Psalmist says: "One thing I have asked of the Lord. This I will seek after" (26:4). But this is the blessed life that is adherence to God which the contemplative enjoys, and in whose person it is said in the Psalm: "But it is good for me to adhere to God" (72:28). And this is that one thing that is necessary, for "the person who adheres to the Lord is one spirit (with him)," as it is said in 1 Corinthians 6:17.[184] The person who has this one thing has every good. Therefore, a figure of this is found in Tobit 10:5: "Having all things together in you alone, we ought not to let you go away from us." And Wisdom 7:11 reads: "All good things came to me together with her," etc. And therefore, the Lord said to Moses in the person of the contemplative man in Exodus 33:19: "I will show you all good."

73. Third, with regard to *the promulgation of the judgment* the text says: *Mary has chosen the best part*,[185] namely, because she chose one thing. As Augustine says: "But she preferred *one thing* to many, because *one thing* does not come from many. Rather *many things* are

---

[184] On p. 274, n. 11 QuarEd refer to the Glossa Interlinearis (from Bede): "*But one thing is necessary*, to adhere to God continually." The Glossa quotes Bede exactly. See CCSL cxx, p. 226 where Bede quotes Psalms 72:28 and 26:4, the same Psalms that Bonaventure cites.
[185] In what follows I will translate *pars* by *part*, even though in some contexts the better translation is "portion."

from one. Many are the things that have been made. But there is one who made them. . . . The things that he made are very good. How much better is he who made them."[186] By all means God is the best absolutely. And this is the part chosen by the contemplative soul. Thus Lamentations 3:24–25 has: "The Lord is my part, said my soul. Therefore, I will wait for him. The Lord is good to those that hope in him, to the soul that seeks him." And the Psalmist says: "How good God is to Israel, to those who are of a right heart" (72:1). I say, *very good* and the best. Wherefore, the contemplative soul like Mary says in the Psalm: "I cried to you, O Lord, and said: You are my hope, my part in the land of the living" (141:6). This part the contemplatives have already chosen, by contemplating and desiring it. Thus, in the person of the contemplative it is said in Deuteronomy 3:25: "I will cross over and will see this best land . . . and this fine mountain and the Lebanon." And on account of love for this part the contemplative soul wanted to possess nothing in this land except neediness alone, according to what the Psalm says: "For better is one day in your courts than a thousand elsewhere. I have chosen to be an outcast in the house of my God" (83:11). For, as it is said in Matthew 13:44: "The kingdom of the heavens is like a treasure hidden in a field, which the person who finds it hides," etc.

74. Fourth, regarding *the assignation of a reason* the text continues: *Which will not be taken away from her.* The Glossa says: "There is no censure of the part of Martha, because it also is good. Rather the reason Mary's part is praised as best is inferred from: *It will*

---

[186] On p. 275, n. 1 QuarEd refer to Augustine's Sermon 104 chapter 2, n. 3. See PL 38:617. Augustine alludes to Genesis 1:31: "And God saw all the things that he had made. And they were very good."

not be taken away from her.[187] "Look at this from another angle and understand that the part that Martha
has chosen will be taken away, for the multiplicity of
labor passes away, but the unity of love remains."[188] And
this is the reason why Mary's part is absolutely better
and preferable, for the contemplative life commences
here and is completed in the future. This is designated
in the figure of John, according to what is said in John
21:22: "If I wish him to remain so," like contemplation
once begun remains, "until I come," when contemplation
will be perfected at my coming. And since it remains

---

[187] On p. 275, n. 5 the QuarEd state that this is the Glossa Ordinaria
from Bede, who follows Ambrose and Gregory the Great. For Bede,
see CCSL cxx, p. 226. For Ambrose's minimal influence on Bede, see
CCSL xiv, p. 242. For Gregory the Great, See Book II, Homily 2, n. 9
of his *Homilies on Ezekiel the Prophet.* Cf. *Sancti Gregorii Magni
Homiliae in Hiezechihelem Prophetam,* ed. Marcvs Adriaen, CCSL
cxlii (Turnhout: Brepols, 1971) 231: *Ecce pars Marthae non reprehenditur, sed Mariae laudatur. Neque enim bonam partem elegisse
Mariam dicit, sed optimam, ut etiam pars Marthae indicaretur bona.
Quare autem pars Mariae sit optima, subinfertur cum dicitur: Quae
non auferetur ab ea* ("Behold, Martha's part is not censured, but
Mary's is praised. For it does not say that Mary has chosen the good
part, but the best, so that Martha's part is also judged good. But the
reason why Mary's part is best is inferred from what is said: It will
not be taken away from her").
[188] On p. 275, n. 6 QuarEd try to identify the source of this quotation.
They state that Codex H adds: "As the Glossa, namely, the Glossa
Ordinaria apud Lyranum, says in following Augustine's Sermon 104
Chapter 2, n. 3." They also mention as a source Bede's commentary
on Luke 10:42, where he is dependent upon Gregory the Great.
Augustine seems to be at the base of Bonaventure's quotation. See
PL 38:617: *Transit labor multitudinis, et remanet charitas unitatis.
Ergo quod elegit, non auferetur ab ea. A te autem quod elegisti: utique
hoc sequitur, utique hoc subintelligitur: a te quod elegisti auferetur*
("The multiplicity of labor passes away, and the unity of love remains. Therefore, what she chose will not be taken away from her.
But from you what you have chosen – indeed, this follows and is inferred – from you what you have chosen will be taken away"). Gregory the Great adds nothing beyond what is found in the previous
note.

longer, it is better, as the Apostle says of love in 1 Corinthians 13:8: "Love never fails." And from this he concludes that love is the greatest.[189] The same is the case
with the contemplative life. Therefore, Bede in the
Glossa states: "Who begins to be on fire with love here
when she sees him whom she loves, will be more aflame
with love there."[190] Isaiah 31:9 has: "The Lord's fire is in
Zion and his furnace in Jerusalem." Whence, seen from
such a perspective,[191] the contemplative life is to be preferred, according to what 2 Corinthians 4:18 states: "We
do not contemplate the things that are seen, but those
that are not seen. For the things that are seen are temporal, but the things that are not seen are eternal."

75. On account of this consideration *the contemplative
life*, seen by itself, is highly desirable, because it is better
and to be preferred on its own merits. For it is more secure, more pleasant, and more stable. Nevertheless, *the
active life* is not to be despised, and should occasionally
be preferred, depending on place and time, because it
precedes contemplation, is more painful, and more fruitful. For it is useful for the one engaged in it and for oth-

---

[189] See 1 Corinthians 13:13.

[190] On p. 275, n. 8 QuarEd state this is the Glossa Ordinaria apud
Lyranum. For Bede's comments, see CCSL cxx, p. 226. Bede, in turn,
borrowed from Book II, Homily 2, n. 9 of Gregory the Great's Homilies on Ezekiel the Prophet. As a matter of fact, Bonaventure's quotation makes more sense when its base in Bede is seen. CCSL cxx, p.
226 reads: *Cum praesenti ergo saeculo uita aufertur actiua contem-
platiua autem hic incipitur ut in caelesti patria perficiatur quia amoris ignis qui hic ardere inchoat cum ipsum quem amat uiderit in
amore amplius ignescit* ("Therefore, the active life is taken away
with the present age, but the contemplative begins here, so that it
may be completed in the heavenly homeland. For the fire of love
which begins to burn here when she sees him whom she loves will be
more aflame with love there").

[191] This is my rendition of *quantum est de se*.

ers.[192] – And this was well designated in Jacob's two wives, namely, Rachel and Leah,[193] one of whom designates the active life and the other contemplative life. Thus, the spouse compels his bride sometimes to go out to action, according to what is said in The Song of Songs 2:14: "Let your voice sound in my ears," etc. So if it becomes a question of what is *better*, contemplative life is better *simpliciter*, according to what Gregory says in Book VI of his Moralia: "Great are the merits of the active life, but the merits of the contemplative life are greater."[194] For *Mary has chosen the best part which will not be taken away from her.* – But if it becomes a question of *what should be chosen*, occasionally *the active life is to be chosen.* This is the case with the imperfect man who must first exercise himself in the field of the active life or when someone is obligated to engage in the works of the active life because of precept or by office. And so at times a doubt can arise as to which is to be preferred, according to what Philippians 1:21–24 has: "To me to live is Christ and to die is gain. But if to live in the flesh

---

[192] In their quest for background to this highly condensed paragraph QuarEd on p. 275, n. 10 point to Book I, Homily 3, n. 13 of Gregory the Great's *Homilies on Ezekiel the Prophet.* Their parallel is not very enlightening.

[193] See Genesis 29:18–30:24.

[194] On p. 275, n. 11 QuarEd cite as sources for Bonaventure's thought: Book VI, chapter 37, n. 55–61 of Gregory the Great's *Moralia*; Book I, Homily 3, n. 9ff and Book II, Homily 2, n. 10ff of Gregory the Great's *Homilies on Ezekiel the Prophet.* On p. 275, n. 12 they refer to Book VI, chapter 37, n. 61. See *S. Gregorii Magni Moralia in Iob Libri I–X.* Ed. Marcvs Adriaen. (CCSL cxliii; Turnhout: Brepols, 1979), p. 331 for Book VI, chapter 37, n. 61: *Sed Marthae cura non reprehenditur. Mariae uero etiam laudatur, quia magna sunt actiuae uitae merita, sed contemplatiuae potiora* ("But Martha's care is not censured. But the care of Mary is also praised, for great are the merits of the active life, but the merits of the contemplative life are greater"). As one can see, Bonaventure's quotation is almost verbatim from Gregory's *Moralia.*

is my lot, this means for me fruitful labor. And I do not know what to choose. Indeed I am hard pressed from both sides, desiring to depart and to be with Christ, a lot by far the better. Yet to stay in the flesh is necessary for your sake." – Thus, it is necessary for spiritual men sometimes to go out, sometimes to come in, sometimes to ascend, sometimes to descend, as Jacob saw in Genesis 28:12.[195]

76. Now this Gospel text is customarily read on the Feast of Mary's Assumption,[196] either because its ending is most fitting for Mary where it says: *Mary has chosen the best part for herself,*[197] *which will not be taken away from her.* For although this was said in the literal sense about Mary Magdalene, nonetheless it is more true of the Blessed Virgin Mary. Wherefore, Bernard says: *"Mary has chosen the best part for herself.* Surely, *the best.* Conjugal fecundity is good, but virginal chastity is better. But entirely the best is virginal fecundity or fecund virginity. This is Mary's privilege, and it will not be given to another, for *it will not be taken away from her."*[198] – Or another reason is this: In this Gospel reading the perfection of the active and contemplative lives

[195] Genesis 28:12 reads: "And Jacob saw in his sleep a ladder standing upon the earth, and the top thereof touching heaven, and also the angels of God ascending and descending by it." On p. 276, n. 1 QuarEd helpfully suggest John 10:9 as a parallel: "I am the door. If anyone enter by me, he will be safe and will go in and out and will find pastures." They also refer to passages from Gregory the Great and Bernard of Clairvaux.

[196] See Hugh of St. Cher, p. 196a, where he mentions in six very brief points why Luke 10:38–42 is fittingly read for Solemnity of Mary's Assumption.

[197] The Vulgate does not have *sibi* ("for herself").

[198] On p. 276, n. 3 QuarEd give as the source for this quotation Bernard's Fourth Sermon, n. 5 on the Assumption of the Blessed Virgin Mary and rightly point out that Bernard has *quia* ("for") after *Optimam plane* ("Surely the best"). See SBOp 5.248.

is described in the two sisters. Both of these lives were found most perfectly in the Virgin. For what had been given to these two sisters in a partial way, was given whole and entire to Mary. Whence Jerome says: "To others it was given in a partial way, but to Mary a plenitude of grace was infused all together at the same time."[199] – Another interpretation maintains that here the discussion is about a twofold reception of Christ: *corporal* and *spiritual*. *Corporal* in Martha's hospitality in the external house. *Spiritual* in Mary's hospitality in the interior house. And this twofold reception occurred most perfectly in Mary, who received him in *the bridal chamber of her body*, carried him, and fed him, and educated him, and assiduously served his needs. She also received him in *the bridal chamber of her heart* by seeing him, and believing in him, loving him, and imitating him. And for *both of these* she was blessed. Thus, Luke 11:27–28 below has: "Blessed is the womb that bore you. . . . Blessed are those who hear the word of God and keep it." Wherefore, Augustine says: "Mary was more blessed in accepting the faith of Christ than in conceiving the flesh of Christ. . . . For her maternal relationship would have done Mary no good unless she had borne Christ more happily in her heart than in her flesh."[200]

77. There is also another interpretation. Now there are three things emphasized here: divine *hospitality*, divine *ministry*, divine *intimacy*. And these three are found

---

[199] On p. 276, n. 4 QuarEd refer to Epistle 9 chapter 5 "Ad Paulam et Eustochium, de Assumtione B. Mariae Virg." (among the works of Jerome) as the source for Bonaventure's quotation and mention some variant readings.

[200] On p. 276, n. 7 QuarEd refer to Chapter 3, n. 3 of Augustine's *De sancta virginitate*. I have used the translation of John McQuade in *Saint Augustine, Treatises on Marriage and Other Subject*, FC 27 (New York: Fathers of the Church, 1955), p. 146.

most perfectly in the Virgin Mary: *hospitality* in the town, *ministry* in Martha, and *intimacy* in Mary.

Fittingly, the Virgin Mary, when she received Christ, was *a town fortified by towers of virtues* and elevated. Her first tower was *the strength of discipline,* of which The Song of Songs 4:4 says: "Your neck is as the tower of David, which is built with bulwarks. A thousand bucklers hang from it." For the Virgin Mary could not be overcome by any vice. – The second tower is *the righteousness of discernment,* about which The Song of Songs 7:4 states: "Your nose is as the tower of Lebanon, that points to Damascus," where the discernment of good and evil is sensed. – The third tower was *an abundance of devoted love,* concerning which The Song of Songs 8:10 reads: "I am a wall, and my breasts are like a tower," on account of the tender loving devotion in which she excelled. So these three towers were built by the Holy Spirit through grace over the three powers of the soul. The first over *the irascible.* The second over *the rational.* The third over *the concupiscible.* – And from these the Virgin was a fitting castle to receive the beloved Son of the Father, who was the power and wisdom of the Father,[201] for the Virgin was *most strong, most prudent,* and *most loving.*

78. Now *serving* there was *Martha,* who served the Lord *faithfully,* and *humbly,* and *courageously.* Fittingly Mary, too, although she was his mother, made herself handmaid and servant, according to what Luke 1:38 above says: "Behold, the handmaid of the Lord, be it done to me according to your word." So she was designated by that good woman, Abigail, who, when she was

---

[201] On p. 276, n. 9 QuarEd rightly indicate that Bonaventure is alluding here to 1 Corinthians 1:24.

requested to become David's wife, offered herself as a servant. 1 Samuel 25:41 reads: "Behold, let your servant be a handmaid, to wash the feet of your[202] servants." Such a person was the Virgin Mary because of her outstanding humility. Therefore, she said this about herself: "He has regarded the humility of his handmaid."[203] And this is what Augustine says: "Everyone, who thinks clearly, understands that Mary was Christ's servant by her conspicuous works and by most firm and truthful faith. For without doubt she showed herself as his servant, who bore him in her womb, and having given birth to him, nourished and cherished him. And as the Gospel says, *she laid him in a manger*, and fleeing from Herod, she went down to Egypt and took care of him during his entire infancy with a mother's devoted love."[204]

79. It is also fitting that Mary be seen as *one who shares the same roof* and *one who contemplates*. For she herself, like the other Mary, stood by Christ, according to what John 19:25 says: "There were standing by the cross of Jesus his Mother and his Mother's sister, Mary of Cleophas, and Mary Magdalene." For she was the Virgin, who *was closest to him*, and therefore accepted his words and reserved them for others. For it is said in Luke 2 above: "Mary kept all these words."[205] Thus, she was rightly designated by *the ark of the Lord's covenant*, about which Hebrews 9:4 says: "In which was a golden

---

[202] The Vulgate reads *domini mei* ("of my lord").

[203] Luke 1:48.

[204] On p. 276, n. 12 QuarEd state that this quotation comes from Pseudo-Augustine's *Liber de Assumtione B. Mariae Virg.* chapter 7. There are some four variants between "Augustine's" text and that of Bonaventure. See Luke 2:7 and Matthew 2:13–15 for the Gospel passages "Augustine" refers to. For comparison purposes see PL 40:1146.

[205] This sentence occurs in Luke 2:19 and 2:51.

urn containing the manna," which means much *devoted love*.[206] Further by "the rod of Aaron," which means great *righteousness in virtue*. Moreover, by "the tablets of the covenant," which means "through great knowledge of the contemplation of truth." – And she was also the greatest contemplative. Thus, Bernard says: "Blessed Mary has penetrated the most profound abyss of divine wisdom to a degree that is almost incredible, so that we can say of her that she is immersed in inaccessible light as utterly as is possible to any created nature not deified by hypostatic union."[207] And Bede states: "What did she not know about God, in whom God's wisdom was hidden and in whose womb he fashioned a body for himself?"[208]

80. And thus it is clear how this Gospel reading was appropriate for the Virgin's Assumption not through human invention, but through divine inspiration. For the Holy Spirit encapsulated in this Gospel praise for the Virgin regarding the multitude of her prerogatives. And all these privileges come together at the end of this reading: *Mary has chosen the best part, which will not be taken away from her.* For Mary chose the best part both

---

[206] In what follows Bonaventure will exegete the meaning of the remaining items in the Holy of Holies: rod of Aaron and tablets of the covenant.

[207] On p. 277, n. 2 QuarEd refer to Bernard's "Sermon for the Sunday within the Octave of the Assumption of the Blessed Virgin Mary,", n. 3. I have modified the translation of *SBSermons* 3, pp. 261–262. See SBOp 5.264. QuarEd rightly indicate that the phrase, "inaccessible light," stems from 1 Timothy 6:16.

[208] On p. 277, n. 3 QuarEd give the results of their search for the source of this quotation. Cardinal Hugh says that Gregory is the source. See Hugh of St. Cher, p. 196v, k where Hugh's quotation from "Gregory" agrees verbatim with the quotation Bonaventure attributes to Bede. QuarEd state that both Anselm and Paul the Deacon have this interpretation. Who borrowed from whom? In any case, Bede is not the source. See CCSL cxx, p. 226.

in grace and in glory. For as Jerome says: "Just as no man is good in comparison to God, so too no woman is found to be perfect in comparison to the Lord's Mother, in as much as a woman's outstanding character is proven by virtues."[209] Therefore, among women she alone is *best* through every kind of superabundance. For which reason "no one similar has been seen before or after her."[210]

---

[209] On p. 277, n. 5 QuarEd refer to pseudo-Jerome's "Letter 9 to Paula and Eustochium, de Assumtione B. Mariae Virg." chapter 16 and indicate that Bonaventure's text varies from that of pseudo-Jerome.

[210] On p. 277, n. 6 QuarEd indicate that Bonaventure is quoting Book IV of Bede on Luke 11:27 where Bede, in turn, is quoting Sedulius' *Paschal. Carm.* II, 68. See CCSL cxx, p. 237.

LUKE 11

1. *And it came to pass as he was praying in a certain place*, etc. After handing over to his disciples the form of teaching and of living, Christ, in this section, gifts them with *the form of praying*, through which the grace of understanding and of right living is sought. Now this section has three parts. The first provides an *example* of Jesus at prayer. In the second *Jesus teaches his disciples how to pray*, where verse 2 says: *And he said to them: When you pray*, etc. Finally he adds *motivation* for prayer where verse 5 has: *And he said to them: Which of you*, etc.

Luke 11:1
JESUS AS AN EXAMPLE OF PRAYER

Concerning *the example of prayer* two items are mentioned. The first is *the Lord's careful attention to prayer*, and the second is *the disciples' quickness in imitating him.*

2. (Verse 1). First, with regard to *the Lord's careful attention to prayer,* it is said: *And it came to pass while[1] he was praying in a certain place. In a certain place,* that is, in a solitary and remote place, because such locations are suitable for prayer, according to what Matthew 6:6 has: "But when you pray, go into your room, close the door, and pray to your Father in secret." Now the Lord prays *to show us his true humanity,* according to what is said in Luke 22:43 below: "Falling into an agony, he prayed the more earnestly." And *to support us in our weakness,* according to what Hebrews 5:7 has: "He was heard because of his reverent submission in all things"[2] and according to what Romans 8:26 says: "We do not know what we should pray for, as we ought. But the Spirit himself," that is, of the Lord Jesus, "helps us in our weakness."[3] And finally *to give us an example of perfect virtue.* As it is said in Matthew 26:41: After he had prayed, he said to the disciples themselves: "Watch and pray that you may not enter into temptation."[4] Further, he was *frequently* in prayer in order to teach that one must pray always, according to what 1 Thessalonians

---

[1] On p. 277, n. 10 QuarEd correctly indicate that the Vulgate reads *cum* ("as/when"), not *dum* ("while").

[2] Bonaventure has added *in omnibus* ("in all things"). I have followed the Confraternity translation in rendering *reverentia* by "reverent submission."

[3] This is almost a verbatim quotation from the Vulgate. Bonaventure, though, has put Romans 8:26b before Romans 8:26a.

[4] Bonaventure refers to Matthew here, and not to Luke 22:40, 46 which also has: "Pray that you may not enter into temptation." QuarEd on p. 277, n. 12 call their readers' attention to the Glossa's Ordinaria (from Bede) on Luke 11:1: "The Savior is often portrayed as praying for the purpose of introducing his disciples to the practice of prayer." See CCSL cxx, pp. 226–227 for the basis of the Glossa' quotation.

5:17 reads: "Pray without ceasing." Moreover, he prayed *for a long time*, as it was said in Luke 6:12 above: "It came to pass and he continued all night in prayer." And while the text may mention here that he was praying *in a certain place* to show that a remote place is necessary for those who pray, it is silent about *the time* of prayer. And this shows that prayer is suitable to all times, according to what is said below in Luke 18:1: "They must always pray and not lose heart" and in Sirach 18:22: "Let nothing hinder you from praying always."

3. Second, concerning *the disciples' quickness to imitate Christ*, this is said: *When he ceased, one of his disciples said to him: Lord, teach us to pray.* Rightfully did the disciples ask the Lord how they themselves should pray, lest they might ask for something that was against his will. For this reason Wisdom 9:13–14 says: "Which man or woman can know the counsel of God? Or who can think what the will of God is? For the thoughts of mortals are fainthearted, and our counsels uncertain." Therefore, *teach us to pray*, for you are our Lord. Thus Isaiah 48:17 reads: "I am the Lord who teaches you beneficial things." – And that this instruction must be oral is shown by the disciples' request for similar treatment: *Just as John also taught his disciples.* For to know how to pray to God pertains to the teaching of piety, because the principal object of prayer is to worship God. Thus the Prophet used to say in the Psalm: "I will enter your house, I will worship," etc. (5:8). And Chrysostom says: "The soul offers its single–minded prayer as spiritual tribute from its depths. For to pray is a great dignity. Scarcely has it proceeded from one's mouth that the angels take it into their hands and present it to God, as the angel said in Tobit 12:12: 'I offered

your prayer to God,'" etc.[5] – So prayer is presented to us as highly to be esteemed, because by means of it the attainment of every good and the removal of every evil is sought for. For this reason Tobit 12:8–9 says: "Prayer with fasting is good, and almsgiving is greater than the laying up of treasures. For almsgiving liberates from death, and likewise purges sins and makes one find mercy and eternal life."

Luke 11:2–4
JESUS TEACHES HIS DISCIPLES HOW TO PRAY

4. (Verse 2). *And he said to them: When you pray,* etc, After the example of Jesus at prayer the text continues with *Jesus teaching his disciples how to pray.* In this *the form of invocation* is given first. Then follows *the form of petition* where verse 2 says: *Hallowed be your name.*

Now with regard to *the form of invocation* the text reads: *And he said to them: When you pray, say: Father,* that is, first invoke the Father. *Say,* I interpret, not with your voice alone, but also with your heart, lest perhaps what Isaiah 29:13 states may be said of you: "This people honors me with their lips, but their heart is far from me."[6] *Say,* not only with your heart, but also with your voice, because vocal prayer is acceptable to God, ac-

---

[5] On p. 278, n. 4 QuarEd mention that Chrysostom's interpretation comes from his Homily 13 on Matthew 6:5, that Bonaventure abbreviates Chrysostom considerably, and that the Vulgate of Tobit 12:12 has *Domino* ("to the Lord") rather than *ante Deum* ("to God"). The editors, however, fail to note that Hugh of St. Cher has the exact same quotation from Chrysostom. See Hugh of St. Cher, p. 197c.

[6] The Vulgate of Isaiah 29:13 reads: *Populus iste ore suo et labiis suis glorificat me. Cor autem eius longe est a me* ("That people glorifies me with its mouth and its lips, but its heart is far from me").

cording to the Psalmist: "I will praise the Lord exceedingly with my mouth" (108:30). And this because it helps *to stir up one's memory, to arouse one from drowsiness, to enkindle one's desire, to bolster one's obedience, to express one's joy,* and *to give a good example.* – Now we invoke the name of *father.* For God is *father* by reason of *the creation of nature,* according to what Ephesians 3:15 says: "From whom all fatherhood in heaven and on earth is named." So, too, Malachi 2:10: "Have we not all one father?" God is also *father* by reason of *the bestowal of grace.* Romans 8:15 reads: "You have received a spirit of adoption as sons, by virtue of which we cry out: Abba! Father." And Galatians 4:6 has: "And because you are sons, God has sent the Spirit of his Son crying: Abba! Father." Further, God is *father* by reason of *the consummation of glory,* according to what Jeremiah 3:19 has: "You will call me father, and you will not cease to walk after me." Thus in the name *father,* God is understood as the creator of nature, the bestower of grace, and the consummator of glory.[7] And through these considerations we are led to understand who the God is, to whom alone we must make our petitions.

---

[7] In a personal communication (July 5, 1999) Bonaventurian expert Fr. Zachary Hayes, O.F.M. told me: ". . . this understanding of the Father as source, support, and goal of all creation and history is pervasive in his theology. He refers to the Father with the term *'primitas,'* arguing that while God is first with respect to all outside God, there is a deeper firstness within God in that mystery called Father. It is also referred to as *'plenitudo fontalis.'* From here all things, within (the second and third persons) and without (creation and grace) flow and return. In the text at hand, the idea appears in the triad of: Creator of nature (creation), dispenser of grace (history of salvation), and consummator of glory (final goal of history)." The most helpful parallel to Bonaventure's use of Jeremiah 3:19 here is found in his commentary on Luke 9:59 (#106) above, where he interprets Jesus' command, "Follow me" by "as a son follows his father. Jeremiah 3:19 has. . . . "

5. But when Matthew, whose version of the Our Father is found in Matthew 6:9–13, depicts this prayer as given to *the Apostles*, to whom the Lord used to explain everything, he explicitly touches on these three points. For he says: *Father*, in reference to creation; *our*, in reference to grace; *who are in heaven*, in reference to glory. But Luke expresses this prayer as handed over to *the lesser disciples*, and therefore given in a more implicit manner. However, both agree on the invocation of the name *father*, so that men and women may be inspired by this one name to *reverence* and *confidence*. For without these two wings prayer does not get off the ground. Now the name *father* engenders *reverence* as Malachi 1:6 says: "'The son honors the father. . . . If then I be a father, where is my honor?' . . . says the Lord of hosts." And Sirach 3:13 reads: "The glory of human beings stems from the honor of their fathers." At the same time it engenders *confidence*, according to what Isaiah 49:15 has: "Can a woman forget her infant, so as not to have pity on the son of her womb? And if she should forget, yet I will not forget you." And as Luke 11:13 below says: "If you, evil as you are, know how to give good gifts to your children, how much more will your heavenly Father," etc. And Bernard says: "The prayer, which has the sweet name of father, gives me confidence that all my petitions are to be granted."[8]

6. *Hallowed be thy name.* After the invocation there follows *petition*. Now there are three principal petitions in

---

[8] This quotation is based on Bernard of Clairvaux' Sermon 15.1.2. Bonaventure universalizes the petitions from the six of the Matthean Our Father to all petitions, invoked under the name of "father.' See SBOp 1.83 for Bernard's text: *Mihi dictatur oratio, cuius principium, nomine dulce paterno, sequentium obtinendarum petitionum praebet fiduciam.* See Hugh of St. Cher, p. 197v, e for the identical quotation that Bonaventure has.

this prayer. And in this Matthew and Luke are in agreement. But they differ in their explication of these petitions, for Matthew, as mentioned above in #5, gives the petitions in more explicit detail. For this reason Matthew has seven petitions whereas Luke has five. Yet in Luke's five petitions Matthew's seven are implicit.

7. Now *the distinction, order,* and *sufficiency* of these petitions are as follows. From God the Father three things are sought. The first and principal is *the consummation of glory.* The second is *the preservation of grace.* The third is *the forgiveness of sin.* And these three are arranged according to the grade and order of greater dignity. – Now for *the consummation of glory* two concur, namely, perfect *knowledge* and perfect *reverence.* And the first two petitions deal with these. – And for *the preservation of grace* the continual supply of heavenly nourishment suffices. And this is sought in the third petition. – For *the forgiveness of sin* two things come together, namely, *remission of sin* and *the elimination of punishment.* And these are asked for in the final petitions.

But since *the perfection of reverence* deals not only with affect, but also with effect, Matthew adds a third petition to the first two, namely, "Thy will be done." – Moreover, since *the elimination of punishment* is concerned not only with repulsing temptations, but also with the elimination of afflictions and tribulations, Matthew adds a seventh petition to the last two petitions: "But deliver us from evil."[9] – And in this way is evidenced *the sufficiency* of the petitions from the vantage point of each evangelist.

---

[9] On p. 279, n. 7 QuarEd write: "Cf. Glossa ordinaria apud Lyranum on Luke 11:2, which comes from Bede, who, in turn, follows

8. *The noble character* of this prayer is also obvious. Although it is most short, it contains in itself all prayer and everything to be asked for. For the petitioner either seeks *the removal of evil* or *the bestowal of good*. If petition is for the removal of *evil*, then it deals either with the evil of *sin* or with the evil of *punishment*. Or it concerns the evil *we suffer*, or the evil *we do*. And so there are two petitions. But the evil of *punishment* can be subdivided. There is *the occasion of sin*, and thus is *temptation*. There is *the reason for punishment*, and thus is *tribulation*. Concerning these there arise the last two petitions. Now if we petition for something *good*, there is *eternal* and there is *temporal* good. And if *eternal*, it concerns either *the intellect* or *the affections*. And thus there are two petitions. But *affection* has to be ordered according to *majesty* and *goodness*. And so that petition brings about the first division, which in turn has a triple subdivision. But if a *temporal* good is sought, then it deals either with *the mind* or with *the body*. But since a *corporeal* good must not be desired except in view of a *spiritual* good, both Luke and Matthew have one petition about each. – And in this way *the sufficiency* of the distinctions between the pairs that are opposed to one another and balance one another is clear. Further, *the harmony* between the evangelists is patent. And finally, *the congruity* of their diversity is obvious.[10]

9. So according to Luke there are five petitions, *ordered* according to greater or lesser nobility. In the first, petition is made for perfect *knowledge* or wisdom in intel-

---

Augustine, Enchiridion chapter 115f., n. 30." On Bede, see CCSL cxx, p. 227. For Augustine, cf. PL 40:285–286.
[10] On p. 279, n. 10 QuarEd say: "Cf. Alexander of Hales, S. p. IV. q. 10 tr. de Officio missae, p. II. #4, where the things which occur here and which follow are more fully treated. There, too, reference is made to the teachers who have written about the Lord's Prayer."

lect. In the second for perfect *reverence* in affection. In the third for *sufficiency* in food. In the fourth *forgiveness* in guilt. In the fifth *victory* in conflict. – And in these five petitions are contained Matthew's seven petitions, and through them the seven virtues, the seven gifts, the seven beatitudes, and *all* petitions. Thus the Glossa says this about what Matthew 6:13 has: *Deliver us from evil*; "There is nothing missing from these seven petitions of what pertains either to the present or the future life."[11]

10. Therefore, first with regard to *knowledge* or wisdom in *intellect* it says: *Hallowed be thy name*, that is, may *your name* shine forth as holy, that is, may knowledge of you be manifest. Thus the Psalm says: "In Judea God is known; in Israel God's name is great" (75:2). And this knowledge begins with grace, but is consummated in glory. About it Malachi 1:11 says: "From the rising of the sun to its setting my name is great among the Gentiles. And in every place a sacrifice is made, and a pure oblation is offered to my name." And this will be verified in glory when, according to Jeremiah 31:34: "No more will a man teach his neighbor or his brother, saying: 'Know the Lord.' For all will know me from the least of them even to the greatest, says the Lord."

11. And note that God's name is sanctified *in us* by means of a threefold knowledge, for God's name is always holy *in itself*. First is the knowledge by which God is known through faith, according to what Hebrews 11:6 says: "The one who approaches God must believe *that God exists*." – The second type of knowledge realizes *what God is not*. Concerning this knowledge Augustine writes:

---

[11] On p. 279, n. 11 QuarEd state that this is the Glossa Ordinaria apud Lyranum.

"You understand a great deal, if you understand what God is not."[12] – The third kind of knowledge is that of God *as God is*. About this 1 Corinthians 13:12 has: "Now I know in part, but then I will know just as I have been known." – The first kind of knowledge liberates from *foolishness*, about which the Psalmist says: "The fool said in his heart that there is no God" (13:1). – The second from *idolatry*, which worships what is not God. About this 1 Corinthians 8:4–6 states: "As for food sacrificed to idols, we know that there is no such thing as an idol in the world and that there is no God but one. For even if there are what are called gods, whether in heaven or on earth (for indeed there are many gods and many lords), yet for us there is only one God, the Father from whom are all things," etc. – The third liberates us from *all wretchedness*. And that will be in the heavenly homeland, when the gift of wisdom and peace, through which we are called children of God, will be completed. And then the name of God will be holy in us. 1 John 3:2 reads: "Beloved, now we are the children of God. And it has not yet appeared what we will be. We know that, when he appears, we will be similar to him, because we will see him just as he is." Therefore, perfect *knowledge* makes us similar, and perfect *similarity* makes us sons, and perfect *sonship* makes us worthy of sanctification by the divine name. So Chrysostom says: "The name of God is sanctified in us when, knowing that God is holy, we stand in awe and take great care lest by chance we vio-

---

[12] On p. 280, n. 2 QuarEd refer to Augustine's work *On the Trinity* VIII. c. 2, n. 3 as the major source of Bonaventure's quotation and give the Latin text, which accords with that of CCSL 1, p. 270. See *Saint Augustine, The Trinity* VIII c. 2, n. 3, translated by Stephen McKenna, FC 45 (Washington: Catholic University of America, 1963), p. 246: "For it is a part of no small knowledge if we aspire from this depth to that height, namely, if before we can know what God is, we can already know what He is not."

late the holiness of his name in us."[13] Now this will happen, when we will totally give ourselves over to God and when no distraction will cloud our minds. And that will take place in glory, as the Psalm says: "I will sing praise to you in the sight of the angels. I will worship towards your holy temple, and I will give glory to your name on account of your mercy and truth. For you have magnified your holy name above all" (137:1–2).[14]

12. Second and with regard to perfect *reverence in affect*, the text continues: *Thy kingdom come.* For when God *reigns* perfectly in us, then we are entirely subject to him, which will be in the end, according to what 1 Corinthians 15:24–28 says: "Then comes the end, when he delivers the kingdom of God the Father. . . . But he must reign, until he has put his enemies[15] under his feet. . . . When all things are made subject to him, then the Son himself will also be made subject to him who subjected all things to him, so that God may be all in all." But this reign, by which God reigns among the Saints, makes even these *Saints* to reign and to be

---

[13] On p. 280, n. 5 QuarEd refer to Chrysostom's Homily 14 on Matthew 6:9 (*Opus Imperfectum*). Se PG 56:711 for the base of this quotation which ends with *per opera nostra mala* ("through our evil deeds"). I am unable to find this quotation in Hugh of St. Cher's commentary on the Matthean and Lukan versions of the Our Father.

[14] On p. 280, n. 6 QuarEd point to a parallel thought in Augustine's *De Civitate Dei* XXII c. 30, n. 4. See CCSL xlviii, p. 865. See *Saint Augustine, The City of God Books XVII–XXII*. Translated by Gerald G. Walsh and Daniel J. Honan, FC 24 (New York: Fathers of the Church, 1954), 509: "And we ourselves will be a 'seventh day' when we shall be filled with His blessing and remade by His sanctification. In the stillness of that rest we shall see that He is God....Only when we are remade by God and perfected by a greater grace shall we have the eternal stillness of that rest in which we shall see that He is God. Then only shall we be filled with Him when He will be all in all."

[15] The Vulgate reads *omnes inimicos* ("all [his] enemies").

kings, according to what Revelation 5:9–10 says: "You have redeemed us for God with your blood, out of every tribe and tongue and people and nation, and have made them for our God a kingdom and priests, and we will reign over the earth." This is the kingdom to be petitioned and to be desired. Of it the Psalmist says: "Your kingdom is a kingdom of all ages" (144:13). And Revelation 11:15 reads: "There were loud voices in heaven, saying: 'The kingdom of this world has become that of our Lord and Christ, his Son, and they will reign forever and ever. Amen.'"[16] – Through the advent of this kingdom God does not gather additional power, but perfect obedience among men and women. And therefore, Matthew adds these words after this petition: "Thy will be done, on earth as it is in heaven." For earthly creatures do not perfectly obey God as do heavenly ones. And the Lord suggested as much in John 18:36: "My kingdom is not of this world." And this because the devil reigns in those who obey him, according to what Ephesians 6:12 has: "They are the world rulers of this darkness." But in the final judgment his power will be stripped away, when the entire world will be made subject to God, according to what Daniel 7:14 reads: "And he gave him power, and glory, and a kingdom. And all peoples, tribes and tongues will serve him."

13. (Verse 3). Third with regard to *sufficiency in food* the text adds: *Give us this day our daily bread*. The petition here is primarily for the bread of *spiritual* nourishment. Thus Matthew 6:11 has: "Give us today our 'superstan-

---

[16] The Vulgate has *Factum est regnum huius mundi Domini nostri et Christi eius. Et regnabit in saecula saeculorum* ("The kingdom of this world has become that of our Lord and of his Christ. And he will reign forever and ever").

tial' bread."[17] But since not only is spiritual nourishment prayed for, but also everything that is necessary for present existence, the Church is accustomed to say the Lord's Prayer according to its Matthean form and to substitute the Lukan *daily* for the Matthean *supersubstantial*. And by doing this, it shows that it is seeking whatever is necessary for the nourishment of this life, and that is what is meant by *this day*. Thus Jerome says in his own way that whether *this day* or *supersubstantial* is said, they both accord with the Hebrew meaning. For in Hebrew one word, that is, *sogolla*, conveys both meanings.[18] In the same way, among us *daily* means both breads, namely, spiritual and corporeal, because both are necessary for us daily. And both are to be received from God's hands daily, and therefore both are the objects of our daily petition. And this is what Bede says in the Glossa: "It says *daily* bread, for it is necessary that soul and flesh be given this, whether spiritually or bodily or to be received in both ways."[19]

14. So note that a fivefold bread is petitioned for. The first is *nourishment for present existence*, concerning which Sirach 29:28 says: "At the beginning of life water, bread, and clothing are necessary." – The second type of

---

[17] On p. 280, n. 12 QuarEd cite Peter Comestor, *Historia scholastica in Evang.* c. 49: "Christ, who is supersubstantial, that is, above all substances, and is our bread on the altar. Or there are two words involved: *super* and *substance* . . . that is, Christ, who pertains to the faithful, and thus is necessary over and above and besides bread."
[18] On p. 281, n. 1 QuarEd quote the pertinent passage from Book I of Jerome's Commentary on Matthew 6:11. A full discussion of the rarest of rarest Greek words, *epiousios*, which lies behind the Latin translated by *daily* and *supersubstantial* can be found in Fitzmyer, pp. 904–906.
[19] On p. 281, n. 2 QuarEd state that this is the Glossa Ordinaria apud Lyranum. See CCSL cxx, p. 227, where Bede is actually quoting extensively from Augustine (PL 40:285-286).

bread is *understanding of Sacred Scripture*, about which
Lamentations 4:4 has: "The little ones have asked for
bread, but there was no one to break it for them." – The
third type of bread is *the Sacrament of the Eucharist*, of
which Wisdom 16:20 reads: "You gave them bread from
heaven prepared without labor and which had in it all
that is delicious and the sweetness of every taste." And
John 6:52 says: "The bread, which I will give, is my flesh
for the life of the world." – The fourth is *the assistance of
grace*, concerning which the Psalmist has: "Men and
women ate the bread of angels" (77:25). And Luke 14:15
below reads: "Blessed is that person who will eat bread
in the kingdom of God." – The fifth is *the homage of obedience*, about which it is said in John 4:34: "My food is to
do the will of my Father, who is in the heavens."[20] Also
with regard to this 1 Kings 19:6 and 8 have: "Elijah
looked, and behold there was at his head a hearth cake,"
by means of whose strength he walked and came "to the
mountain of God, Horeb." – With these breads the Lord
refreshes us. And this was designated in John 6:9–10,
where it is said that from five loaves of bread he satisfied 5,000 people. And for each of these, petition is always to be made, according to what is found a little later
in John 6:34: "Lord, always give us this bread."

15. (Verse 4). Fourth, with regard to *forgiveness of sin*
the text has: *And forgive us our sins*, and this concerning *the obligation of repayment*. And this is why in Matthew 6:12 sins are called *debts*. For sins make us debtors to those whom we cannot repay. So the Psalmist
says: "The sinner will borrow and not pay back" (36:21).

---

[20] On p. 281, n. 6 QuarEd point out how the clause "who is in the
heavens" stems from Matthew 7:21 and 12:50. The matching clause
in the Vulgate of John 4:34 reads *eius qui misit me* ("of him who sent
me").

These are *the debts*, to which the Sunamite woman was obligated, according to 2 Kings 4:1–7, and which she could not repay until Elisha multiplied oil for her. Through *the oil* of the mercy of Christ our sins are repaid and forgiven. – But since "judgment is without mercy to the person who does not show mercy," according to what is said in James 2:13, the text continues with this condition: *As we also forgive everyone indebted to us.* Indeed, this condition is necessary in asking for forgiveness of sins. For which reason Sirach 28:2–3 reads: "Forgive your neighbor if he has harmed you. And then shall your sins be forgiven you when you pray. Man to man reserves anger, and does he seek remedy from God?" As if to say, he seeks for remedy from God in vain. So too Matthew 6:14–15 has: "If you forgive men and women their offenses, your heavenly Father will also forgive you your offenses. But if you do not forgive them, neither will your heavenly Father forgive you your offenses." For a similar reason Matthew 18:23–35 proposes the parable about the wicked servant, which ends with these words: "So also your[21] heavenly Father will do to you, if you do not each forgive your brothers from your hearts." And this is rightly said, for whoever flees from the law of clemency falls into the law of justice, about which Luke 6:37–38 above says: "Forgive, and it will be forgiven you. . . . For with what measure you measure, it will be measured to you." The Lord put this condition here to show that what is said in Judith 9:16 is true: "The prayer of the humble and the meek have always pleased you," but never that of the proud and the oppressors. So Isaiah 1:15 says: "When you multiply prayer, I will not listen. For your hands are full of blood." So Chrysostom writes: "If the person who is harmed prays in vain unless he forgives, what do you

---

[21] The Vulgate has *meus* ("my").

think happens to the prayer of the person who is not harmed, but harms and oppresses others through his unjust actions? But the person who does not pray as Christ taught is not his disciple. Nor does the Father listen to a prayer which the Son did not teach. For the Father understands the meaning of the words of his Son and does not accept what human arrogance excogitates, but what Christ's wisdom articulates."[22]

16. Now on the fifth point which deals with *victory in conflict* the text says: *And lead us not into temptation*, that is, do not permit us *to be led* and be conquered.[23] For, as it is said in James 1:13–14: "God is no tempter to evil. . . . But everyone is tempted by being drawn away and enticed by his own passion." – And note that the petition is not made *not to be tempted,* because temptation proves a person, according to what the Psalm has: "Prove me, Lord, and tempt me" (25:2). And Sirach 34:9–10 states: "The person who has not been tempted knows little."[24] But the petition is *not to be overcome or conquered by temptation*, but to conquer and triumph. This is only to be sought because of *faith in divine help*, about which 1 Corinthians 10:13 reads: "God is faithful and will not permit you to be tempted beyond your strength, but with the temptation will also give you a way out that you may be able to bear it." We should also make petition because of the recognition of our

---

[22] On page 282, n. 2 QuarEd refer to John Chrysostom's Homily 14 on Matthew 6:12 (*Opus Imperfectum*) as the source for this quotation. See PG 56:714 for the basis of Bonaventure's quotation. I am unable to find this quotation in Hugh of St. Cher's commentaries on the Matthean and Lukan versions of the Our Father.

[23] On p. 282, n. 3 QuarEd cite the Glossa Interlinearis on Matthew 6:13: "The one who is led into temptation is broken by it."

[24] On p. 282, n. 4 QuarEd indicate how Bonaventure has contracted Sirach 34:9–10 into one short verse.

weakness, according to what Nehemiah 20:12 says: "Our God, as for us we don't have strength enough to be able to resist this multitude, which rushes violently upon us. But as we know not what to do, we can only turn our eyes to you." Therefore, Chrysostom has: "Let them acknowledge that they are weak, and let the recognition of their weakness extinguish the reason for their boasting,"[25] for, according to what is said in 1 Maccabees 3:19, "victory in war does not come from the numbers of one's army, but strength comes from heaven."

17. Now since temptation is a *tribulation*, according to what James 1:12 has: "Blessed is the man who endures temptation," it follows that the person who is freed from every evil of *temptation* is consequently freed from the evil of *tribulation*. Therefore, it is not necessary to mention the additional: *Deliver us from evil*, as if it were a completely different petition, but is to be explained as implicitly contained in the single petition that Luke has. And this is what Bede says in the Glossa: "So that anyone might know that in not being led into temptation he is being freed from evil."[26] – So Luke ends the prayer with the word, *temptation*, which shows that there is a doubt about one's status or concern about a failure. And therefore, Luke does not conclude with *Amen*, which is an indication of the certitude that the prayer has been heard. But Matthew concludes with *the*

---

[25] QuarEd on p. 282, n. 7 state that this quotation comes from John Chrysostom's Homily 14 on Matthew 6:13 (*Opus Imperfectum*) and is almost verbatim. See PG 56:714. I am unable to find this quotation in Hugh of St. Cher's commentaries on the Matthean and Lukan versions of the Lord's Prayer.

[26] On p. 282, n. 9 QuarEd mention that this quotation from the Glossa Ordinaria actually stems from Augustine's *Enchiridion de fide, spe et caritate*, chapter 116, n. 30. See CCSL cxx, p. 228 where Bede is quoting Augustine.

liberation from all evil of punishment, and this includes death, about which 1 Corinthians 15:26 says: "And the last enemy to be destroyed is death." And after this there is certitude of salvation. So Matthew concludes with *Amen*, which is a sign of the certitude at that time. – But since we do not come to this certitude in this present life, the *Amen* is said silently and *sota voce* by the priest while everything else during Mass is said in a loud voice. – There are other reasons for the fittingness of this, but these are sufficient for the present.

Luke 11:5–13
JESUS GIVES MOTIVATION FOR PRAYER

18. *And he said to them: Which of you*, etc. After giving Jesus' example of prayer and his teaching on how to pray, the Evangelist mentions here in a third point *motivation for prayer*, which inspires the disciples to pray frequently and faithfully. And this section has two parts. In the first *frequent prayer* is proposed. In the second *faithful prayer* where verse 11 has: *But who of you asks his father*, etc. For *negligence* and *lack of faith* are the greatest desiccants of the fruit of prayer.

Concerning *motivation for frequency in prayer* two points are made. The first is a *similitude that persuades*. The second is a *teaching that informs* where verse 9 reads: *And I say to you: Ask, and it will be given to you.*

Now with regard to *the similitude that persuades* one to frequent prayer, three considerations are given. The first is *the opportunity that knocks*. Second *the difficulty of refusing*. Third *the importunate petitioning*. From this similitude it is shown how very effective importunate and continual prayer is.

19. (Verse 5). So first, relative to *the opportunity knocking* the text has: *Which of you will have a friend*, etc. In this instance the sentence is being read as *interrogative*, but the Glossa wants it to be read as *declarative*: "Who, that is, *anyone*, or *if someone*."[27] Nevertheless, this is said in order that the preciousness of a true friend may be demonstrated, according to what Sirach 6:15–16 states: "Nothing can be compared to a faithful friend, and no weight of gold and silver is able to counterbalance the goodness of his fidelity. A faithful friend is the medicine of life and immortality. And those who fear the Lord will find him." – Therefore, to this friend he faithfully recurs, and so the text continues: *and he will go to him in the middle of the night*. For, as it is said in Proverbs 17:17, "the person who is a friend loves at all times, and a brother is proven in a situation of distress." – And to such a friend one trustingly expresses one's need. For which reason the text adds: *and he will say to him: Friend, lend me three loaves of bread*. And this by reason of the law of *common devotion and love to a fellow human being*, of which it is said in Isaiah 58:7: "Break and share your bread with the hungry." And Qoheleth 11:1 reads: "Cast your bread upon the running waters."[28]

20. (Verse 6). But there is also the law of *the special fidelity of friendship*. On account of this the text adds: *For a friend of mine has just come to me from a journey, and I have nothing to set before him*.[29] And therefore, I am

---

[27] On p. 283, n. 1 QuarEd state that this is the Glossa Interlinearis.

[28] Perhaps Qoheleth 11:1b–2 help explain Bonaventure's reason for this quotation: ". . . for after a long time you will find it again. Give a portion to seven and also to eight. For you do not know what evil will be upon the earth."

[29] On p. 283, n. 5 QuarEd rightly mention that Bonaventure's text varies in two ways from the Vulgate. The Vulgate reads *quoniam*

bound to him by the fidelity of friendship, and through this bond you are also obligated to me. Whence Sirach 22:28–29 states: "Remain faithful to a friend in his poverty, so that you may also rejoice in his prosperity. In the time of his trouble remain faithful to him, so that you may also be heir with him in his inheritance."

21. (Verse 7). Second, concerning *the difficulty of refusing* the text has: *And he from within should answer and say: Do not disturb me*, scilicet, by disturbing one who is resting and rousing him from sleep, as Abner said to David in 1 Samuel 26:14: "Who are you, who is crying out and disturbing the king?"[30] And that this was a great disturbance is shown by an additional problem: *The door is already shut, and my children are with me in bed*, that is, children who must be loved tenderly. Thus Isaiah 8:18 says: "Behold, I and my children, whom the Lord has given me," that is, children whose love cannot be neglected, according to what Isaiah 49:15 has: "Can a woman forget her infant, so as not to have mercy on the child of her womb?"[31] – Therefore, the text adds: *I cannot get up and give to you*. And this did not entirely take away any possibility, but set forth the difficulty, as if he were saying what Elijah said to Elisha in 2 Kings 2:10: "You have asked for a difficult thing." And so he says: *I cannot*, that is, I cannot conveniently nor easily. As the king of Israel answered the king of Syria

("Since") whereas Bonaventure has *quia* ("For"). The Vulgate has *ante illum* ("before him") while Bonaventure reads *ante eum* ("before him").

[30] The words "disturbing the king" are not found in the Hebrew or Septuagint of 1 Samuel 26:14. On p. 283, n. 6 QuarEd refer to the Glossa Interlinearis: "*Do not disturb me.* I must not be disturbed by your entreaties, for *the door is already shut*, etc."

[31] Throughout this section I have followed the inclusive language practice of the Douay Version, which generally translates *filii* as "children."

in 1 Kings 20:9: "Everything for which you send your servant in the beginning, I will do. But I cannot do this thing."[32]

22. (Verse 8). Third, with regard to *the importunate petitioning*, the text reads: *And if he should persevere in knocking*,[33] through his petitions, not conquered by shame, nor exhausted by weariness nor broken by desperation, but as a true friend, according to what Sirach 22:26–27 states: "Although you have drawn a sword on a friend, do not despair. For there may be a returning to the friend. And if you have turned a sour face to your friend, do not fear."[34] And since "unrelenting toil conquers all,"[35] the text adds: *I say to you, although he will not get up and give it to him because he is his friend*, that is, moved by the truth of love, which from time to time grows lukewarm among friends. For this reason it is said in 1 John 3:18: "My dear children, let us not love in word, neither with the tongue, but in deed and in truth." Therefore, if he is not won over by an abundance of love, he is conquered by importunate insistence. – On account of this the text continues: *Because of his relent-*

---

[32] On p. 283, n. 8 QuarEd quote Book I, chapter 11 of Aristotle's *De Caelo:* "Now the impossible can be taken in two ways. For it is either to be taken *simpliciter*...or because (something cannot be done) *easily* nor quickly nor well."

[33] The Vulgate does not have *Et si ille perseveraverit pulsans* ("And if he should persevere in knocking").

[34] Sirach 22:27b continues: ". . . for there may be a reconciliation." On p. 283, n. 9 QuarEd quote the Glossa Interlinearis: *"And if he should persevere in knocking*, not intimated by shame, but forced by necessity."

[35] On p. 283, n. 10 QuarEd refer to Book I verse 145 of Virgil's *Georgics* as the source of this quotation. In the LCL translation I use, the reference is to verses 145–146.

lessness[36] *he will get up and will give to him whatever he needs.* An example of this is proposed in Luke 18:1–8 below about the judge and the widow, who harassed him. So it is said there that "the judge did not want to hear[37] her for a long time. But after this he said within himself: Even though I do not fear God nor even respect human beings, yet because she[38] is bothering me, I will vindicate her, lest by her coming she finally beat me black and blue." An example of this is also found in Judges 14:17 concerning Samson and his wife. When she asked him before, he did not want to indicate the answer to the riddle. But "she wept before him the seven days of their wedding feast. And finally, on the seventh day, since she was troublesome to him, he expounded the meaning of the riddle."[39]

23. Now according to *the spiritual understanding* Christ is understood by this *friend*, of whom Sirach 6:14 says: "A faithful friend is a strong defense. And the person who has found him has found a treasure." About this John 15 has: "No longer do I call you servants . . . but I have called you friends" (verse 15) and again: "You are my friends," etc. (verse 14). – And about this friend who *comes at night*, that is, *during the silence of the night*, as Nicodemus came, about whom it is said in John 3:2 that "he came to Jesus at night," there are two interpretations. First, this occurred because there should be the knocking of prayer during the secret silence of night, according to what Isaiah 26:9 reads: "My soul has

---

[36] I have translated *improbitatem* in the same way *improbus* was rendered in the quotation above from Virgil: "relentlessness," "unrelenting."
[37] The Vulgate does not have *audire* ("to hear").
[38] The Vulgate has *haec vidua* ("this widow").
[39] See Judges 14:1-20 for the entire story. I have taken the liberty of giving an explanatory translation of Judges 14:17.

desired you in the night." And Lamentations 2:19 has: "Arise . . . at night, at the beginning of the watches. Pour out your heart like water," etc.[40] A second interpretation is that *at night* means *in trouble*, according to what Hosea 6:1 states: "In their trouble they will rise early to me." And the Psalm says: "Call upon me in the day of trouble, and I will deliver you," etc. (49:15).[41] – *"The friend who comes from a journey* is our heart," according to what is said in the Glossa, "which, as often as it wanders about seeking after temporal things, goes away from us."[42] Pleasure causes this friend to travel about, but trouble brings it back, according to what is said of the prodigal son in Luke 15:11–32 below, who went away on account of dissipation, but returned out of need. So Hosea 2:6–7 reads: "I will hedge up your way with thorns, and I will stop it with a wall. . . . And you will say: I will go and return to my first husband, because I was better[43] off then than now." – He *has come back*,[44] when he returns to interior matters, according to what Isaiah 46:8 says: "Return, you transgressors, to

---

[40] Lamentations 2:19a concludes with: "...before the face of the Lord." In order to make his point more sharply, Bonaventure has eliminated *lauda* ("give praise") as the second word of this verse.

[41] On p. 284, n. 2 QuarEd refer to Bede. See CCSL cxx, p. 228: "Therefore, the friend to whom he comes in the middle of the night is understood to be God himself, whom we must petition in time of trouble and ask for three loaves of bread, that is, understanding of the Trinity, through which the labors of this present life are supported." In his turn Bede borrows from Augustine. See PL 35:1341–1342.

[42] On p. 284, n. 3 QuarEd state that this is the Glossa Ordinaria (from Bede) apud Lyranum on Luke 11:5–6. See CCSL cxx, p. 228 for Bede's commentary which the Glossa accurately presents.

[43] On p. 284, n. 4 QuarEd correctly mention that the Vulgate has *bene* ("well") rather than *melius* ("better").

[44] Bonaventure seems to be interpreting "the friend who comes in the middle of the night" with the prodigal son who came back to his senses (see Luke 15:17) and came back home.

your heart." But he found it empty of the consolation of spiritual nutriment.[45] Thus, it is said of sinners in Lamentations 2:12: "They said to their mothers: Where is corn and wine? when they fainted away as the wounded in the streets of the city, when they breathed out their souls in the bosoms of their mothers." "And the joy of our heart has stopped. . . . Woe to us, because we have sinned."[46]

24. Now the fact that this famished friend *asks for three loaves of bread from his true friend* means, in the interpretation of Bede and Augustine,[47] the understanding of the Trinity or the names of the three persons, so that he may find nutriment in knowledge of God alone. Wherefore, Exodus 24:11 reads: "They saw the Lord and ate and drank." And Sirach 15:3 says: "She (Wisdom) will feed him with the bread of life and understanding and will give him the water of salutary wisdom to drink." – Another interpretation is that *the three loaves of bread* are faith, hope, charity, by which threefold virtue is nourished in the soul.[48] About these Luke 15:17 below

---

[45] On p. 284, n. 5 QuarEd point to Bede's commentary. See CCSL cxx, p. 228: "Indeed, he has returned and desires to be refreshed with heavenly food, for, having come back to his senses, he is beginning to meditate on supernal and spiritual matters."

[46] Lamentations 5:15–16.

[47] On Bede, see CCSL cxx, p. 228 where Bede merely states that the three loaves of bread mean "the understanding of the Trinity." On p. 284, n. 7 QuarEd point to two places in Augustine: his Sermon 105 chapter 3, n. 4 and Letter 130 chapter 8, n. 15. Hill's translation of Sermon 105, n. 4 on p. 90 is: "But when you get hold of the three loaves, that is of the food contained in the understanding of the Trinity, you have got everything to live on yourself and something to feed others on. . . . It's bread, and it's bread, and it's bread; God the Father, God the Son, God the Holy Spirit."

[48] On p. 284, n. 8 QuarEd refer to Augustine's Sermon 105, chapter 4, n. 5 where he hints that the three loaves refer to faith, hope, and charity. They also refer to Bernard of Clairvaux' Sermon "In Roga-

says: "How many hired men in my father's house have bread in abundance," etc. Concerning these 1 Samuel 10:3 has: "When you come to the oak of Tabor, three men, who are going up to the Lord[49] in Bethel, will meet you: one carrying three kids, another three loaves of bread, and another a flask of wine," so that in these the unity of grace and the trinity of virtues might be understood and through which the image of God is reformed in the soul.[50] – But this petition *is not immediately heard* by Christ, but must be made with great insistence. For *the sinful soul* is not at all fit to receive such great gifts. So Matthew 15:26 reads: "It is not fair to take the children's bread and give it to the dogs." It is true that such insistence is required even if a person is already *a child of God*, lest the bread go stale, for the child always needs to be hungry for this bread, according to what Sirach 24:29 has: "Those who eat me will hunger for more." Another view is that through insistent petitions we may be more worthy and more disposed. Therefore, Augustine says in his "Letter to Proba

tionibus: De tribus panibus," n. 2. See SBOp 5.122–123: "But I believe that the three loaves of bread that we should ask for are the loaves of truth, charity, and fortitude. . . . So, friend, lend me three loaves, so that I may understand, so that I may love, and so that I may do your will."

[49] The Vulgate reads *Deum* ("God").

[50] On p. 284, n. 8 QuarEd supply a number of references to Bonaventure's Opera Omnia. See his *Breviloquium*, Part I, chapter 4 in Opera Omnia 5.256. I modify the translation of José de Vinck in *The Works of Bonaventure II The Breviloquium* (Paterson: St. Anthony Guild Press, 1963), 194: "As human beings, in the first creation, resembled God through a trinity of powers with unity of essence, so in the recreation they resemble God through a trinity of habits with unity of grace. Through these, the soul is carried straight up to the supreme Trinity in a way corresponding to the appropriated attributes of the three Persons: faith, through belief and assent, leads to the supreme Truth; hope, through trust and expectation, to the loftiest Height; charity, through desire and love, to the greatest Good."

about Praying to God": "He wants our desire to be exercised through our prayers, so that we can receive what he is preparing to give."[51]

25. (Verse 9). *And I say to you.* After mentioning the persuasive similitude, the Evangelist supplies *the teaching that informs* about the frequency of prayer and draws it from the aforementioned similitude. First, he exhorts *the disciples*, and then *all in general*.

So relative to *the exhortation to the disciples*, the text has: *And I say to you*, namely, as one who does not lie, for, as Numbers 23:19 states, "God is not like human beings, that he should lie, nor like a son of man, that he should be changed. Therefore, has he said something, and will not do it?" Thus, the Glossa reads: "The one who promises and does not deceive has provided great hope."[52] – Wherefore, he admonishes them to insistent and frequent prayer, when he says: *Ask, and it will be given to you. Seek, and you will find. Knock, and it will be opened for you.* Something similar is found in Matthew 7:7. About this passage Augustine says: "I thought that the manner in which these three differ from one another should, in fact, be explained accurately. But it is far better to refer to all of them as one most insistent petition. Indeed, he showed this where he included all of them in the same passage: *How much more will your Father give*

---

[51] On p. 284, n. 10 QuarEd refer to Augustine's Epistle 130 (alias 121), chapter 8, n. 17. In this section of his letter Augustine has much to say to the Roman lady Proba about prayer in Luke 11 & 18.

[52] On p. 284, n. 12 QuarEd state that this is the Glossa Ordinaria and is based on Bede's commentary on Luke 11:9. See CCSL cxx, p. 229: "The one who promises and does not deceive has provided and is providing great hope."

good things to those who ask him"[53] So the Lord wants to say what is said straightforwardly in 1 Thessalonians 5:17: "Pray without ceasing." And Colossians 4:2 reads: "Persist in prayer."

26. But multiple distinctions can be made with the result that *to ask* pertains to an action of the mouth; *to seek* to an action of heart; *to knock* to an action of labor. So ask *with your mouth, and it will be given to you.* Isaiah 62:6–7 reads: "You that are mindful of the Lord, do not keep silent . . . until he establish and make Jerusalem praiseworthy on the earth." And Isaiah 30:19–20 has: "At the voice of your cry, the moment he hears you, he will answer you. And the Lord will give you bread," etc. And Isaiah 65:24 says: "It will come to pass that before they call, I will hear, while they are still speaking."[54] – Further, *seek* with your heart, *and you will find*. Thus, Jeremiah 29:13 has: "You will seek me, and you will find me when you will seek me with all your heart." And Wisdom 1:1–2 states: "Seek him in simplicity of heart. For he is found by those who do not tempt him." – *Knock* through labor. For the person who knocks uses his hand to make an appeal. So the Psalm reads: "At night lift up your hands to the holy places" (133:2).

---

[53] On p. 285, n. 1 QuarEd refer to Book I, chapter 19, n. 9 of Augustine's *Retractationes*. His quotation is almost verbatim. Augustine clinches his argument based on Matthew 7:11 by saying: "For he did not say: to those asking and seeking and knocking." I have based my translation on that of Mary Inez Bogan, *Saint Augustine, The Retractations,* FC 60 (Washington: Catholic University of America Press, 1968), 85. In Bogan's numbering this is chapter 18. Augustine is correcting his *De Sermone Domini in Monte Libri Duo*. See *Sancti Avrelii Avgvstini Retractationvm Libri II*, ed. Almut Mutzenbecher, CCSL lvii (Turnhout: Brepols, 1984), 61.

[54] In its totality Isaiah 65:24 reads: "And it will come to pass that before they call, I will hear. While they are still speaking, I will hear." Bonaventure has not quoted the final *ego audiam* ("I will hear").

And again the Psalm says: "In the day of my trouble I sought God, with my hands lifted up[55], and I was not deceived" (76:3).

27. Another possible way of distinguishing is by reason of *the thing asked for*. *Ask* for forgiveness. *Seek* grace. *Knock* for glory, according to what Zechariah 10:1 says: "Ask the Lord for rain in the late season, and the Lord will make it snow and will send rain showers and will give grass in the field for every single person." *He will give snow* to extinguish the noxious growth through forgiveness. And *rain showers* to make the earth bountiful through grace. And *he will give grass in the field for every single person* by adorning and clothing them with glory. – Another way of interpreting is by means of *the persons asking*. *Ask*, you beginners, whose responsibility is to receive. *Seek*, you *who are making progress*, whose responsibility is to find. *Knock*, you perfect, whose responsibility is to enter. So it is said to *the beginners* in Philippians 4:6: "Let your petitions be known to God." To *those making progress* the Psalmist says: "Seek the Lord, and be strengthened. Seek his face always" (104:4). To *the perfect* Isaiah 26:2 says: "Open the gates, and the just nation will enter."[56] – Another interpretation is that it deals with *the ways of arriving at wisdom*, as Augustine distinguishes: "One does not arrive at wisdom except, as the Lord teaches, by asking, seeking, knocking, that is, by praying, reading, weeping."[57] So

---

[55] The Vulgate reads *manibus meis nocte contra eum* ("with my hands lifted up at night towards him").

[56] The Vulgate reads *ingrediatur gens iusta* ("let the just nation enter").

[57] On p. 285, n. 8 QuarEd point to Augustine's Letter 21, n. 4 as the source for this quotation. Either Bonaventure or his source made an adjustment in the first part, for the original text says nothing about "arriving at wisdom." See PL 33:89: *Quomodo autem hoc fieri potest,*

ask by praying. James 1:5 reads: "If any of you lacks
wisdom, let him ask from God . . . and it will be given to
him." *Seek* by reading in the book of Scripture and of
creation. The Song of Songs 3:2 has: "In the streets and
the broad ways I will seek him whom my soul loves."
Knock by weeping, as John did as it says in Revelation
5:4: "I wept much, for no one was found worthy to open
the book." And the text continues afterwards that John
saw that the book had been opened by the Lamb that
was slain.[58] – Another interpretation is that of the
Glossa which makes a distinction between *the ways of
arriving at glory*: "Ask by praying; *seek* by right living;
knock by persevering."[59] – Another interpretation comes
from the Glossa on Matthew 7:7: "*We ask* by faith, going
to Christ through it. *We seek* by hope, by which we attain to the interior. *We knock* by charity, as we perspire
in our labors, so that we may attain what we ask and
seek for. First, you must ask, so that *you may have*.
Next you must seek, so that *you may find*. You must
contemplate what you have found, so that *you may enter*."[60]

---

*nisi quemadmodum ipse Dominus dicit, petendo, quaerendo, pulsando;
id est orando, legendo, plangendo?* ("But how can this happen, except,
as the Lord himself says, by asking, seeking, knocking, that is, by
praying, reading, weeping?").

[58] See Revelation 5:6–8.

[59] On p. 285, n. 10 QuarEd state that this is the Glossa Interlinearis
on Luke 11:9 and go on to say that in his *Catena Aurea* on Matthew
7, n. 4 Thomas Aquinas attributes this opinion to Remigius. This
seems to be Remigius of Auxerre (d. 908), who commented on Matthew's Gospel. See *S Thomae Aquinatis Catena Aurea in Quatuor
Evangelia*, Volumen Primum complectens Expositionem in Mat-
thaeus et Marcum (Turin: Marietti, 1888), 130.

[60] On p. 285, n. 11 QuarEd state that this is the Glossa Ordinaria apud
Lyranum, which attributes this interpretation to Augustine. They
also refer their readers to "Paschas. Radbert., IV. in Matth. 7, 7."

28. (Verse 10). Second, with regard to *the exhortation given for all* the text reads: *For everyone who asks receives,* if he asks *devotedly.* So the Lord intimates this in John 15:16: "If you ask the Father for anything in my name, he will give it to you,"[61] that is, for your salvation. Otherwise, he does not give it. Wherefore, James 4:3 says: "You ask, and you do not receive, for you ask in a wrong way, so that you may spend it upon your passions."[62] So Chrysostom says: "If you ask for temporal things, why should he supply you with such things, which he commands you to spurn if you possess them?"[63] – *And the person who seeks finds,* provided, however, that the person seeks *in a fitting manner and diligently,* according to what Deuteronomy 4:29 states: "When you seek the Lord your God,[64] you will find him, if, however, you seek him with all your heart and all the affliction of your soul." And 1 Chronicles 28:9 reads: "If you seek God,[65] you will find him. But if you forsake him, he will cast you off forever." But some do not seek at times in a

---

[61] This is not exactly what the Vulgate says: *Ut quodcumque petieritis Patrem in nomine meo det vobis* ("that whatever you ask the Father in my name he may give you").

[62] On p. 285, n. 12 QuarEd refer to the Glossa Interlinearis on Matthew 7:8: *"For everyone who asks,* devotedly and perseveringly, *receives.* It follows that the person who does not receive did not ask in the right way."

[63] On p. 285, n. 13 QuarEd refer to Chrysostom's Homily 43, n. 2 on John: "He set forth in the Lord's Prayer neither dominion nor riches nor glory nor power, but everything that would prove useful for our soul. Nothing terrestrial, but everything celestial. If, therefore, we are commanded to abstain from the present things of this life, how miserable we will be, if we ask God for those things, which if we have, he commanded that we reject, so that he may free us from cares. . . . " See Hugh of St. Cher, p. 200v, h for a quotation from Chrysostom that is virtually identical to that of Bonaventure.

[64] Bonaventure has adjusted the text to his purpose by eliminating the Vulgate's *ibi* ("there"), that is, "When you seek the Lord your God there, you. . . . "

[65] The Vulgate reads *eum* ("him").

fitting manner, and therefore, they do not find. So Hosea 5:6 has: "With their flocks and with their herds they will go to seek the Lord and will not find him." And the reason for this is that they were seeking the Lord *with their flocks*. John 7:34 says: "You will seek me, and will not find me," for they were seeking after him with an evil intent to destroy him. – *And to the person who knocks, it will be opened*, if the person knocks *persistently until the end*, according to what Matthew 10:22 reads: "The person who has persevered to the end will be saved." To such a person is opened the door of glory, about which Revelation 11:19 states: "The temple of God in heaven was opened." And Revelation 4:1 has: "Behold, a door standing open in heaven." This door will be opened, when what Matthew 25:34 has will be said: "Come, you blessed, possess," etc.[66]

29. *But which one of you*, etc. After providing motivation for frequent prayer, the Evangelist adds here *motivation for faithful prayer*, and does so by showing *the generosity* of God the Father in hearing us. So in this part he first sets forth the generosity of *a human father* with respect to his child. Secondly, he concludes to the generosity of *the heavenly Father* in our regard where verse 13 reads: *Therefore, if you, evil as you are*, etc.

---

[66] On p. 286, n. 3 QuarEd cite the Glossa Ordinaria on Matthew 7:8: "In order to teach constant perseverance, diligent seeking, faithful entreating, he adds: *For everyone, who seeks, receives*, etc. Earlier he taught what we should ask for, namely, the kingdom. Here we should ask for confidence, so that we pray without hesitation. He does not deny himself to those who seek him, who spontaneously offers himself to those who do not seek him. And those who seek him will find him, who offers himself to those who do not seek him, so that they might find him. And the one, who cries out: *Behold, I stand at the door and knock* (Revelation 3:20), will open to those who knock."

Now he shows *the generosity of a human father* through the means of food and the avoidance of something harmful. And he does this according to a threefold distinction of food, that is, whether the food is from *the earth, water,* or *air.* The first deals with grain. The second with seafood. The third with fowl.

30. (Verses 11–12). So concerning *asking for grains and vegetables,* the text states: *Which of you asks his father for a loaf of bread,* for your nourishment, *will he hand him a stone?,* namely, to injure you. For human beings are sustained by loaves of bread, according to the Psalm: "Bread strengthens the human heart" (103:15). But human beings are smashed by stones, according to what Matthew 21:44 has: "The person who falls on this stone will be broken to pieces. But upon whomever it falls, it will grind him to powder." – With regard to *asking for seafood,* the text continues: *Or a fish, will he hand him a serpent?* Human beings are nourished by fish. Thus Luke 24:41–42 below reads: "Have you anything here to eat? But they offered him a piece of broiled fish and a honeycomb." But human beings are killed by serpents. Wherefore, Numbers 21:6 has: "The Lord sent among the people fiery serpents." And the people died from snake bite. – Relative to *asking for fowl,* the text says: *or if he asks for an egg,* namely, to eat, *will give him a scorpion?* to poison him? For eggs feed us while scorpions kill us, as experience clearly proves. Indeed, it is plain what the literal meaning of these verses is and the comparisons found therein.

31. Now here is *the spiritual meaning of what* is to be asked for. So Augustine in his "Letter to Proba about Praying to God" says that faith is designated by *the fish,*

hope by *the egg*, and love by *the loaf of bread*.⁶⁷ – For it
is right that asking for *bread* be understood as a petition
for *love*. Thus Augustine says: "Love is meant by *bread*.
For the greatest of all goods is love, and among foodstuffs
the usefulness of bread is superior to all."⁶⁸ Another interpretation is that love like bread nourishes and
strengthens. So The Song of Songs 8:6 states: "Love is
strong as death." Wherefore, the Sacrament of love is
handed over under the species of bread. Another interpretation is that without bread every table is empty. So
too, every heart without love.⁶⁹ Therefore, 1 Corinthians
13:2–3 reads: "If I do not have love, I am nothing. . . . It
profits me nothing." As Augustine says: "To this is contrasted *a stone*, for hard hearts reject love."⁷⁰ So by a
stone *hardness* is designated, according to what Ezekiel
36:26 has: "I will take away the stony heart out of your
flesh, and I will give you," etc.⁷¹ And Luke 3:8 above
reads: "God is able out of these stones," etc.⁷²

32. It is also fitting as Augustine says that *"faith* be understood by the fish either on account of the water of
baptism, for faith remains whole amidst the storms of

---

⁶⁷ On p. 286, n. 9 QuarEd refer to Augustine's Letter 130 (alias 121),
chapter 8, n. 16. In his commentary on Luke 11:8 (#24) above
Bonaventure cited this same letter.
⁶⁸ On p. 286, n. 10 QuarEd state that this quotation, too, is from
Augustine's Letter 130, chapter 8, n. 16 and point to Augustine's
allusion to 1 Corinthians 13:13.
⁶⁹ On p. 286, n. 12 QuarEd refer to Book II, question 22 of
Augustine's *Questions on the Gospels*: "Love is understood by *bread*
because it is the strongest emotion and so necessary that without it
all things are nothing, just as a table without bread is barren. Contrary to it is the hardness of the heart, which he compared to a
stone."
⁷⁰ On p. 286, n. 13 QuarEd indicate that Bonaventure is still quoting
from Augustine's Letter 130, chapter 8, n. 16.
⁷¹ Ezekiel 36:26 concludes with ". . . a heart of flesh."
⁷² Luke 3:8 concludes with: ". . . to raise up children to Abraham."

this world."[73] 1 John 5:4 says: "This is the victory that overcomes the world, our faith." And Hebrews 11:33 states: "By faith they conquered kingdoms." Or, as Bede says: "Since a fish is born, lives, and is nourished under the cover of the waters, so too is faith drawn from the hidden Scriptures, lives in the recesses of the heart, and remains hidden."[74] Wherefore, Hebrews 11:1 reads: "Faith is the substance of things to be hoped for, the evidence of things that are not seen." – As Augustine says: "To this is contrasted *a serpent*, who, through venomous craftiness persuaded human beings not to believe in God."[75] Thus, Qoheleth 10:8 states: "The person who destroys a hedge," that is, the defense provided by Sa-

---

[73] On p. 287, n. 1 QuarEd state the Bonaventure continues to quote from Augustine's Letter 130, chapter 8, n. 16. They also mention his Sermon 105, chapter 4, n. 6. In the translation of Hill (III/4), p. 91, we read: "We can take the fish as being faith. A certain holy man said, and it is my pleasure to say, 'Loyal faith is a good fish.' It lives in the waves, and is not broken or dissolved by the waves. A loyal faith lives among the trials and tempests of this world; the world rages, faith remains entire."

[74] On p. 287, n. 2 QuarEd try to make sense of this compact "quotation" and provide three parallels. First is Bede's Book II of Homilies on the Gospels, section 1, homily 8 on the greater litanies. I quote from the translation of Lawrence T. Martin and David Hurst, *Bede the Venerable, Homilies on the Gospels,* Book Two Lent to The Dedication of the Church, Cistercian Studies Series 111 (Kalamazoo: Cistercian Publications, 1991), 130: "By the fish, faith that is *not insincere* is represented. Just as a fish is born, lives, and is nourished beneath a covering of water, so also faith which is in God, and which seeks the joys of the other life through the weeping and tears of the present one, is begotten invisibly in the heart, is consecrated by the invisible grace of the Spirit through the water of baptism, [and] is nourished by the invisible help of divine protection so that it may not fail." Their second reference is Bede's homily on Luke 11:11 in Book III of his homilies: "The fish is faith in invisible things . . . or because it is taken from invisible places." Thirdly, they quote the Glossa Interlinearis on Matthew 7:10: "*Or if a fish*, invisible faith hidden among the waters of the Scripture."

[75] On p. 287, n. 3 QuarEd again refer to Augustine's Letter 130, chapter 8, n. 16.

cred Scripture, "a serpent will bite him," that is, the infidelity of diabolical error.

33. Further, it is fitting that *hope* is understood by *the egg*. Thus, Augustine says; "*Hope* is meant by *the egg*, for the life of the chick is not yet manifest, but is future. It is not yet seen, but it is still hoped for. *For hope that is seen is not hope*,"[76] as it is said in Romans 8:24. And just as the chick in the egg develops until it is perfect and the egg shell is broken, so too does the perfection of beatitude follow upon hope. Therefore, 1 Corinthians 13:10 reads: "When that which is perfect has come, that which is imperfect will be done away with." – As Augustine notes: "The opposite of this is *the scorpion*," that is, *despair*, which forces one to look behind and harms one from that side. "For the tail of the scorpion is to be avoided, for it is sharp and poisonous."[77] Wherefore, the person who attempts to destroy one's hope of life is a scorpion, for Ezekiel 2:6 has: "You are among destroyers and dwell among scorpions." – Therefore, *the spiritual sense* of the text at hand is this: If a person asks for the bread of *the love* of the Holy Spirit, the fish of *faith* and the egg of *hope*, God will not give these to the petitioner. Rather God will remove from the petitioner the stone of *obduracy*, the serpent of *infidelity*, and the scorpion of

---

[76] On p. 287, n. 4 QuarEd refer to Letter 130, chapter 8, n. 16.

[77] On p. 287, n. 6 QuarEd refer to Letter 130, chapter 8, n. 16 See *Saint Augustine, Letters,* Volume II, 83-130. Translated by Sister Wilfrid Parsons, FC 18 (New York: Fathers of the Church, 1953), 389: ". . . and the scorpion is opposed to it because whoever hopes for eternal life forgets the things that are behind and stretches himself forth to those that are before, since it is dangerous for him to look backward, and he is on guard against the rear of the scorpion, which has a poisoned dart in its tail."

despair.[78] Through divine help these are far removed from holy men.

34. (Verse 13). *Therefore, if you, who are evil,* etc. After he has detailed the generosity of a carnal father, he concludes by an argument *from the lesser to the greater* to a consideration of *the Spiritual Father.* For if good is communicative, then the good that is greater is more communicative and the good that is the greatest is the most communicative.[79] Therefore, if the carnal father communicates a good to his child who asks him, how much more earnestly will the heavenly Father give to the person who petitions him. And this is what the text says: *But if you, evil as you are, know how to give good gifts to your children.* Bede comments: "He calls *evil those who love this world.*"[80] But these are doubly evil on account of the evil of sin, for Sirach 11:10 says: "If you are rich, you will not be free from sin." And Augustine states: "Every rich person is either iniquitous or the heir of someone who was iniquitous."[81] – Another inter-

---

[78] On p. 287, n. 7 QuarEd indicate that two manuscripts had difficulty with the text that the editors judged genuine (as the *lectio difficilior*). Manuscript Vat. omitted "Holy Spirit" after "love" and for "God will not give them to the petitioner. Rather God will remove" read "God will give them to the petitioner and will remove." Manuscript B read: "God will give them to the petitioner, and not only this, but God will remove."

[79] On p. 287, n. 8 QuarEd point ever so briefly to two works of Pseudo-Dionysius: *The Celestial Hierarchy,* chapter 4, n. 1 and *The Divine Names,* chapter 4, n. 1f.

[80] Cf. CCSL cxx, p. 229 for what Bede says about Luke 11:13: "How do evil people give good things? But he called those who still loved this world evil and sinners."

[81] On p. 287, n. 10 the closest the QuarEd can come to a source in Augustine for this quotation is his *Enarrationes in Ps.* 48. Sermon 1, n. 12: "Make for yourself *friends of the mammon of iniquity* [Luke 16:9]. Perhaps, that which you have acquired you have acquired through iniquity. Or perhaps, this itself is the iniquity that you have possessions and another has nothing or that you abound and another

pretation is that he calls *the Apostles themselves evil*, who are said to be *evil* in comparison to divine goodness. Thus, Mark 10:18 has: "No one is good but God only." And Isaiah 64:6 reads: "All of us have become like an unclean person, our righteousness like the cloth of a menstruous woman." And Job 25:5–6 says: "The stars are not pure in his sight. How much less human beings," etc.[82] Wherefore, Gregory states: "Often our righteousness, when examined by divine righteousness, is unrighteousness. And the deed that shines brightly in the eyes of the doer is sordid in the determination of the judge."[83] – Another interpretation is they were *evil* on account of *venial sins*, without which the present life is not led. So it is said in Ephesians 5:16: "Making the most of your time, for the days are evil." For, according to what is said in Genesis 47:9: "The days of the pilgrimage of

---

has nothing, etc." The editors go on to mention that this interpretation is found verbatim in Jerome's Letter 120, chapter or question 1: "Wherefore, this common interpretation seems to me to be the most true: But the rich person is iniquitous or the heir of someone who was iniquitous." See Hugh of St. Cher, p. 201a whose quotation from Augustine is virtually identical to that of Bonaventure.

[82] Job 25:5–6 has: "Behold, even the moon does not shine, and the stars are not pure in his sight. How much less human beings that are rottenness, and the son of man who is a worm?"

[83] On p. 287, n. 12 QuarEd refer to Book V, chapter 11, n. 21 of Gregory's *Moralia*. On p. 287, n. 11 QuarEd direct their readers to take a look at what Bede has to say on Luke 11:13. See CCSL cxx, p. 230: "The Apostles . . . are called evil, for nothing by itself is lasting, immutable, and good but the Deity alone." See also Bede's Book II of Homilies on the Gospels, section 1, homily 8 on the greater litanies. I quote from the translation of Lawrence T. Martin and David Hurst, p. 132: "His disciples were good, as far as human judgment can see; he calls them 'evil' because there is surely no one in this life who is capable of being free from moral faults, as Solomon states when he says: *'There is not a just person on earth, who does good and does not sin'* (Qoheleth 7:21)."

my life . . . are few and evil."[84] For, according to what is
said in 1 John 1:8, "If we say that we have no sin, we are
liars.[85] And the truth is not in us." Thus it seems less
true that good comes from evil, but rather that good
comes from good.

35. And so he comes to the conclusion: *How much more
will your heavenly Father give the Good Spirit to those
who ask him?* Indeed, he will certainly give, because
James 1:17 has: "Every best gift and every perfect gift is
from above." This *Good Spirit* is the Holy Spirit, in
whom all gifts are given.[86] About whom Wisdom 7:7
says: "I called upon God, and the spirit of wisdom came
upon me." And a little later Wisdom 7:11 states: "All
good things came to me together with her." And 1 Corinthians 12:8 reads: "To another through the Spirit is
given," etc. And subsequently 1 Corinthians 12:11 has:
"One and the same Spirit works all these things, allot-
ting to everyone as he wills." This Spirit is given to *those
who ask* and want him, according to the Psalm: "I
opened my mouth and drew in the Spirit" (118:131).
Jeremiah 2:24 reads: "A wild ass accustomed to solitude
in the desire of his heart and breathed in the wind of his
heart." For the spirit of the saints longs for this Spirit.
Romans 8:26 has: "It is the Spirit who pleads," etc.

---

[84] A more complete text of Jacob's statement in Genesis 47:9 is: "The
days of the pilgrimage of my life are a hundred and thirty years, few
and evil...."
[85] On p. 287, n. 13 QuarEd correctly mention that the Vulgate reads
ipsi nos seducimus ("we deceive ourselves").
[86] On p. 288, n. 2 QuarEd point us to Bede's comments on Luke
11:13. See CCSL cxx, p. 230: ". . . he shows that the Holy Spirit is the
plenitude of the good gifts of God." They also refer their readers to
Book I, distinction 18 (article 1) question 1 of Bonaventure's Commentary on the Sentences. See Opera Omnia 1:323–324 where the
question is: "Whether the Holy Spirit is the gift, in which all other
gifts are given?"

Luke 11:14–21:38
THE FALSEHOOD OF JESUS' JEWISH ADVERSARIES IS REFUTED IN
FOUR DIFFERENT WAYS

36. *And Jesus*[87] *was casting out a demon*, etc. As mentioned at the beginning of this commentary, Luke's Gospel has four parts. The first deals with Christ's *nature*. The second with Christ's *teaching*. And this second part commenced in chapter four above and has two sections in accordance with the dual task of the wise person, namely, through his teaching "not to be fallacious about the things he knows and to expose the one who is fallacious."[88] So the first part dealt with the truth to be manifested for the disciples' formation and information whereas the second part concerns the falsehood to be refuted in confuting Jesus' Jewish adversaries.

Now that the first section has been completed, the second begins here. This section has a fourfold division. In the

---

[87] On p. 288, n. 4 QuarEd correctly indicate that the Vulgate does not have *Iesus* ("Jesus"). But they incorrectly note that Bede reads "Jesus." See CCSL cxx, p. 231. On Bonaventure's determination that Luke's Gospel has four parts, see #23 of his Preface and his commentary on Luke 1:4 (#7) above.

[88] See Bonaventure's commentary on Luke 4:1 (#1) above. I repeat here the pertinent footnote on Luke 4:1. QuarEd on p. 88, n. 11 cite Aristotle's *De sophisticis elenchis* chapter 1 (see 165a) as the reference for this quotation and provide the pertinent Latin text: "*Est autem, ut unum ad unum dicamus, in unoquoque opus sapientis non mentiri quidem ipsum de quibus novit, mentientem autem manifestare posse.*" In *The Works of Aristotle* Volume I, translated into English under the editorship of W. D. Ross (London: Oxford University Press, 1928), #165a reads: "To reduce it to a single point of contrast it is the business of one who knows a thing, himself to avoid fallacies in the subjects which he knows and to be able to show up the man who makes them." In my translation I have taken the Latin *sapientis*, not as "of one who knows," but in the specific sense as "of the wise person." For Bonaventure Jesus is not simply "one who knows," but the wisdom teacher.

first part Christ confutes *the deceitfulness* of the Jews. In the second their *lack of mercy* where Luke 15:1 below reads: *Now the publicans and sinners were drawing near to him to listen to him.* In the third their *curiosity* where Luke 17:20 below has: *But having been asked by the Pharisees,* etc. In the fourth their *incredulity* where Luke 19:29 below reads: *And it came to pass when Jesus*[89] *drew near,* etc.

Luke 11:14–14:35
THE DECEITFULNESS OF THE JEWS WHO FALSELY JUDGE CHRIST'S MIRACLES IS REFUTED IN TWO WAYS

Now in confuting *the deceitfulness of the Jews,* he first confutes the deceitfulness of those who falsely judge Christ's miracles relative to their *efficient cause.* Secondly, there is a confutation relative to *the time* of the miracle where Luke 13:10 below reads: *Now he was teaching in their synagogues*[90] *on the Sabbath.*

Luke 11:14–13:9
CHRIST REFUTES THE JEWS' DECEITFULNESS AND FALLACY AND INSTRUCTS HIS DISCIPLES

This first section has a twofold division. First is *the confutation of the deceitfulness and fallacy of the Jews.* Second is Christ's *instruction to his disciples on how they must avoid these* where Luke 12:1 below has: *Now when immense crowds,* etc.

---

[89] On p. 288, n. 6 QuarEd accurately mention that the Vulgate does not read *Iesus* ("Jesus").

[90] On p. 288, n. 7 QuarEd rightly indicate that the Vulgate reads *in synagoga eorum sabbatis* ("in one of their synagogues on the Sabbath").

Luke 11:14–54
CHRIST CONFUTES THE DECEITFULNESS OF THE JEWS[91]

The first section, which comprises the present chapter, is divided into three parts. In the first Christ confutes the fallacy of *those who blaspheme*. In the second the fallacy of those who *were putting Christ on trial* or were disbelieving where verse 29 below says: *Now the crowds were gathering*. In the third the fallacy of *those who were pretending* where verse 33 below reads: *No one lights a lamp*. The first of these is *in word*, but the second is *in spirit*. And the third consists *in any sign whatsoever*.

Luke 11:14–28
THE FALLACY OF THOSE BLASPHEMING IS REFUTED IN A THREEFOLD MANNER

Now to refute *the fallacy of those blaspheming* three items are introduced. For first is *the expression of the Jewish deception*. Second is *the rejection of the deception expressed* where verse 17 has: *But he, seeing their thoughts*, etc. Third is *the commendation of the truth shown* where verse 27 says: *Now it came to pass while*[92] *he was saying these things*, etc. – Concerning *the expression of Jewish deception* the Evangelist explains three things. First is *the grounds for divine praise*. Second is *the blasphemy of human deception*. Third is *the controversy joined to this strife*.

---

[91] At certain points, e.g., Bonaventure's quotation from Chrysostom in his commentary on Luke 11:32 (#68) below, medieval anti-Judaism is reflected. This translator does not condone such views.

[92] On p. 288, n. 10 QuarEd accurately say that the Vulgate reads *cum haec diceret* ("as he was saying these things") whereas Bonaventure reads *dum haec diceret* ("while he was saying these things").

Luke 11:14–16
THE EXPRESSION OF JEWISH DECEPTION

37. (Verse 14). Now first with regard to *the grounds for divine praise* the text says: *And Jesus was casting out a demon, and it was dumb.* In this event there are simultaneously two miracles, indeed, even three. Wherefore, Bede says in the Glossa: "Matthew even says that this demoniac was blind. So the Lord performed three miracles, for *the blind* sees, *the mute* speaks, *the possessed* is liberated."[93] And in this was *the basis for divine praise* both on the part on the man cured and on the part of those present. For which reason the text continues: *And when he had cast out the demon, the dumb man spoke, and the crowds marveled.* And thus was fulfilled what Isaiah 35:5–6 states: "Then the eyes of the blind will be opened, and ears of the deaf will be unstopped. Then will the lame man leap like a hart, and the tongue of the mute will be free." Now such great miracles became simultaneously the cause for *wonder* and *praise,* according to what Sirach 43:31–32 has: "The Lord excites terror and is exceedingly great, and his power is wonderful. Glorify the Lord as much as you are able. He will yet far exceed, and his magnificence is marvelous." So truly these were able to say what Mark 7:37 reads: "He has done all things well, and has made both the deaf to hear and the dumb to speak."

38. But according to *the spiritual understanding the demon* is sin, which makes a person *deaf* to hear the truth, *blind* to see the truth, and *mute* to confess the

---

[93] On p. 288, n. 11 QuarEd state that this is the Glossa Ordinaria on Luke 11:14 and that Bede is following Book II of Jerome's commentary on Matthew 12:22. The Glossa follows Bede almost verbatim. See CCSL cxx, p. 231.

truth. So Chrysostom says: "O wickedness of the demon! Having gone into both openings, by which a person was going to believe, the demon has closed them, that is, *hearing* and *sight*." And a third, that is, *the tongue*, lest people confess their faith.[94] Therefore, it is said in Isaiah 41:26: "There is no one who proclaims, there is no one who preaches nor is there anyone who hears my words."[95] And again Isaiah 42:18–19 has: "Hear, you *deaf*. And you *blind*, see that you may behold. Who is blind, but my servant? And who is deaf, but the one to whom I have sent my messengers?" Such a person is also *mute* to confess faith. So Sirach 15:9 reads: "Praise from the mouth of a sinner is not seemly."

39. And note that human beings are given speech for three purposes, namely, *to praise God, to edify their neighbor,* and *to accuse themselves*. This threefold speech is taken away by a threefold demon. A spirit of *voluptuousness* removes the first according to what Isaiah 1:15 states: "When you multiply your prayers, I will not listen to them. For your hands are full of blood."[96] – The spirit of *avarice* removes the second, for it makes people think only of themselves, according to what Matthew 25:18 has: "The one who had received one talent went away and dug in the earth. . . . " – The spirit of *pride* takes away the third, for it does not permit a person to accuse himself, according to the Psalm:

---

[94] On p. 289, n. 3 QuarEd refer to Homily 40 (alias 41), n. 3 on Matthew. The editors also cite the first words of Hugh's quotation from Chrysostom, but fail to notice its significance. See Hugh of St. Cher, p. 201f for the basis of Bonaventure's quotation from Chrysostom.

[95] Bonaventure has made two modifications of the Vulgate. For *praedicens* ("forthtells") he has *praedicans* ("preaches"). For *sermones vestros* ("your words") he has *sermones meos* ("my words").

[96] It is not immediately clear how this quotation accords with the sin of *luxuria* ("voluptuousness").

"Because I was silent, my bones grew old" (31:3). And Jeremiah 2:35 reads: "Behold, I will contend with you in judgment, because you have said: I have not sinned." – Concerning this threefold demon Revelation 16:13 says: "I saw three unclean spirits like frogs issuing from the mouth of the beast and from the mouth of the dragon and from the mouth of the false prophet." – The first demon is cast out by *fasting*, according to what Matthew 17:20 has: "This kind of demon is cast out only by fasting."[97] The second is cast out by *memory of the Lord's passion*, according to what Tobit 6:8 states: "If you put a little piece of its heart upon coals, the smoke thereof drives away all kinds of demons," etc.[98] The third by *prayer*. 1 Samuel 16:23 reads: ". . . David took his cithara and played with his hand. And Saul was refreshed and was better. For the evil spirit departed from him."[99]

40. (Verse 15). Second, relative to *the blasphemy of human deception* the text has: *But some of them said: By Beelzebub, the prince of demons, he casts out demons.* And this was a great blasphemy because what was done by the Holy Spirit was attributed to a malign spirit. So it is said immediately after this text in Matthew 12:31: "Every kind of sin and blasphemy will be forgiven hu-

---

[97] On p. 289, n. 7 QuarEd correctly indicate that the Vulgate reads *orationem et ieiunium* ("prayer and fasting").

[98] In Tobit 6:1–9 at the angel's directive Tobit catches a fish, feeds on it, and saves up its heart, gall, and liver for useful medicines. It is not obvious how Tobit 6:8 is related to the memory of the Lord's passion.

[99] On p. 289, n. 8 QuarEd make the non-judgmental statement that what Bonaventure says about the triple use of speech, the threefold demon and the threefold remedy are substantially the same as the interpretations of Hugh of St. Cher on Luke 11:14. See Hugh of St. Cher, p. 201h. Bonaventure also "borrows" from Hugh the two scripture quotations of Isaiah 1:15 and Tobit 6:8, which do not accord with his normal way of using scripture.

mans, but blasphemy against the Spirit will not be forgiven." They burst forth into this blasphemy out of envy.
So Chrysostom comments: "The Pharisees did not attack
Christ when he said great things, but only when he effected saving cures among people." "For envy does not
care about what is said, but only that it is said." "For
envy is not some inferior evil. For the adulterer completes his sin in a brief time while the envious person
never shuts up."[100] – And since this blasphemy stems
from wickedness and envy, it is fitting that this gospel
passage is read when the story of Joseph is sung on the
Third Sunday of Lent.[101] For just as Joseph's brothers
called him *the creator of dreams*[102] out of envy, so too
these said that Christ was *the invoker of demons*. And
they gave greatest expression to their envy by using the
term *Beelzebub*. For this idol was infamous. Wherefore,
it is said in 2 Kings 1:2 that "Ahaziah sent his messengers, saying: Go and consult Beelzebub, the god of Ek-
ron." And Bede in the Glossa says: "The Jews maintained that in this image the prince of demons dwelt.
They were saying that Jesus casts out demons through

---

[100] On p. 289, n. 10 QuarEd provides texts from Homily 40 (alias 41),
n. 3 on Matthew, Homily 41 (alias 42), n. 1, and Homily 40 (alias 41),
n. 3 respectively for these quotations. Bonaventure's "quotations" are
accurate as to sense, but are not verbatim. See Hugh of St. Cher, p.
201v, l, who quotes these same three passages from Chrysostom in
wording that is almost identical with that of Bonaventure.

[101] I wonder whether the liturgy's interpretation of Genesis 37:2–20
by means of Luke 11:14–26 prompted Bonaventure to determine that
the Pharisees acted out of envy. In any case, the readings at Matins
for the Third Sunday of Lent are as follows: Genesis 37:2–20 for I
Nocturn; from the Book of St. Ambrose on holy Joseph for II Nocturn; Luke 11:14–28 and Homily of St. Bede the Venerable, Book 4,
chapter 48 on Luke 11 for III Nocturn. Hugh of St. Cher p. 201v, l
comments: "Behold, when this gospel passage is read, the story of
how Joseph was sold because of his brothers' envy is sung on the
Third Sunday of Lent."

[102] This phrase is not found in Genesis 37.

its power."[103] And thus in the text it is said: *by the prince of demons.* Another interpretation is that the name of this idol was ridiculous. For when they were saying *Beelzebub*, they were really saying *man of flies.* The Jews were calling him by this name in a derisory manner, as it is said in the Glossa: "on account of the bloody filth which was immolated in his temple."[104] So they uttered such a blasphemy against him, which is also found in John 8:48 where it is said: "Are we not right in saying that you are a Samaritan and have a demon?"

41. (Verse 16). Third, concerning *the controversy joined to this strife* the text adds: *And others, to test him, demanded from him a sign from heaven.* They did not seek a sign of this nature in order to trust in him like believers, but in order to oppose him like rebels, in accordance with what the Savior says in Matthew 22:18: "Why do you test me, you hypocrites?" And the Psalm has: "Your fathers tested me," etc. (94:9). And this is evil, as it is said in 1 Corinthians 10:9: "Neither let us test Christ, as some of them tested and perished by the serpents." Now they were seeking *a sign from heaven,* like *the thunder* during the time of Samuel in 1 Samuel 12:18 or like *the emission of fire* during the time of Elijah in 1 Kings

---

[103] On p. 290, n. 1 QuarEd state that this is the Glossa Ordinaria on Luke 11:15.

[104] On p. 290, n. 2 QuarEd mention that this is the Glossa Ordinaria and provide a long quotation from it and other references. See also Fitzmyer, p. 920: "This (name) seems to have been a deliberate caconymic, a (polemical) distortion of the foregoing name to depreciate the pagan god, making it 'Lord of the Flies.'" The basis of Bonaventure's double interpretation is found in Bede. See CCSL cxx, p. 232: "Therefore, Belzebub is the lord of the flies, that is man of flies or who has flies. It is interpreted this way because of the filth coming from the immolated blood of this most foul cult. Or they called him by the name of the prince of demons."

18:38 and 2 Kings 1:10[105] or like *the regression of the sun* during the time of Hezekiah in 2 Kings 20:9–11. – But seeking a sign was proper to the Jews either through *habituation* as 1 Corinthians 1:22 reads: "The Jews seek signs, and the Greeks wisdom."[106] And therefore, Peter, the apostle to the Jews, was powerful in signs, but Paul, the apostle to the Gentiles, was powerful in wisdom. Or they sought for signs because of their *incredulity* and *hard-heartedness*, according to what Stephen said in Acts 7:51: "Stiff-necked and uncircumcised in heart and ear, you always oppose the Holy Spirit." Wherefore, Chrysostom says: "Always *learning* by means of a sign is never to be able to make progress. So always *seeking the witness* of a sign is never to be willing to believe."[107] And this is indeed true, for when they had sufficient evidence on earth, they should not seek signs from heaven. Therefore, John 10:25 states: "The works that I do in the name of my Father, they themselves bear witness concerning me."[108]

42. But *in a spiritual sense* the Lord gave *signs on the earth*, namely, the signs of *humility and poverty*, ac-

---

[105] Bonaventure makes reference to two different occasions.

[106] On p. 290, n. 5 QuarEd indicate that Bonaventure also quoted this passage in his commentary on Luke 1:18 (#30) above. In both instances Bonaventure's quotation varies from the Vulgate which reads: *Iudaei signa petunt et Graeci sapientiam quaerunt* ("The Jews ask for signs, and the Greeks seek wisdom").

[107] On p. 290, n. 7 QuarEd refer to Chrysostom's Homily 30 on Matthew 12:31 (*Opus Imperfectum*). Bonaventure's quotation does not match Chrysostom's text word for word. However, Bonaventure's quotation exactly matches Cardinal Hugh's citation of Chrysostom. See Hugh of St. Cher, p. 201v,b. Chrysostom builds upon 2 Timothy 3:7: "always learning, yet never attaining to the knowledge of the truth."

[108] On p. 290, n. 8 QuarEd rightly mention that the Vulgate for the last words of this quotation are: *haec testimonium perhibent de me* ("these bear witness concerning me").

cording to what Luke 2:12 above says: "This will be sign for you: You will find an infant wrapped in swaddling clothes." But many do not believe in this sign. Such are the proud and ambitious who seek Christ not in the humility of the cross, but with an appetite for honor and praise. And nonetheless it is said in Matthew 24:30: "Then the sign of the Son of Man will appear in the heaven," etc. But the proud contradict this sign, according to what Luke 2:34 above reads: "This child is destined . . . as a sign that will be contradicted.," for the status of humility did not please them, but rather that of dignity. So the Psalm says: "They have set up their ensigns for signs" (73:4), that is, ensigns of pride and lust, according to what Wisdom 2:9 says: "Let us leave signs of our joy everywhere." They do not want to follow without these signs. So the Psalmist says: "Our signs we have not seen," etc. (73:9).[109]

Luke 11:17–26
REJECTION OF THE DECEPTION EXPRESSED

43. *But he, seeing their thoughts, said to them.* After the expression of the Jewish deception the text continues here with *the rejection of the deception expressed.* There are three sections. The first deals with *the rejection of the falsehood.* The second with *the approbation of the truth* where verse 21 says: *When the strong man, fully armed, guards his courtyard.* The third with *the repro-*

---

[109] On p. 290 QuarEd do not mention that much of Bonaventure's commentary on Luke 11:16 (#41–42) is found in the commentary of Hugh of St. Cher, p. 201v, b.

bation of the deceitfulness where verse 24 reads: *When the unclean spirit has gone from*[110] *the person*, etc.

The discussion of *the rejection of the falsehood* follows this order. First, he makes the deduction that there is a *manifest impossibility*. Second, he shows that there is a *false improbability*. Finally, he displays *the infallible truth*.[111]

44. (Verses 17–18). So first he shows that there is *a manifest impossibility*, when he says: *Every kingdom divided against itself is brought to desolation.* By this he intends to make the following argument: Every divided kingdom, by the very fact that it is divided in itself, is destroyed. But if one demon casts out another, Satan is divided in himself. Therefore, his kingdom does not survive. It follows, therefore, that Satan himself would be destroying his own kingdom and taking away his *power*[112] and dominion. But this is a manifest impossibility. And it follows from the words of the Pharisees. Therefore, it was manifestly false. So he sets forth *the major premise* of this reason when he says: *Every kingdom divided against itself is brought to desolation, and house will fall upon house.* And this is indeed per se known and true, for division is the cause of ruination. So the reason for the thing predicated is in the subject. And this is what Jerome says: "Through harmony small things grow, while through disharmony the greatest

---

[110] On p. 290, n. 12 QuarEd accurately indicate that the Vulgate reads *de homine* ("out of the person") whereas Bonaventure has *ab homine* ("from the person").

[111] In his exegesis Bonaventure will be treating Luke 11:17–18 as a syllogism with a major premise, a minor premise, and a conclusion.

[112] Here Bonaventure plays on the root for "possibility" and "impossibility," namely, *posse* ("power").

things will come to ruin."[113] For unity is the cause of
salvation, and division of perdition according to what
Hosea 10:2 says: "Their heart is divided, now they will
perish." And Proverbs 28:2 reads: "On account of the
sins of the land it has many rulers."[114] An example of
this is found in those building the tower in Genesis 11:
Although they were "of one tongue" (verse 1), "the Lord
divided[115] them from that place into all lands. And they
ceased building" (verse 8). So in the final stage of the
world its unity will be destroyed as it is said in Luke
21:10–11 below: "Nation will rise against nation, and
kingdom against kingdom. And there will be great
earthquakes," etc. – Then he adds *the minor premise*
and says: *If, then, Satan is*[116] *divided against himself*,
that is, is fighting against himself. He gives this *as a
condition*, for it follows from the aforementioned words
of the scribes and Pharisees, but in itself it is not true.
For Satan is in harmony with Satan in doing evil. So
Job 41:6–8 states: "His body is like molten shields, shut
close up with scales pressing upon one another. One is
joined to another, so that no breath of air can come between them. They stick to one another, and they hold
one another fast and shall not be separated."[117] Wherefore, the Psalm has: "The kings of the earth rose up, and
the princes met together against the Lord," etc. (2:2). –
After this he sets forth *the conclusion* when he says:

---

[113] On p. 291, n. 1 QuarEd refer to Book II of Jerome's commentary
on Matthew 12:26. They also refer interested readers to Opera Omnia 5.195, n. 3 for additional sources for this quotation.
[114] Hugh of St. Cher, p. 201v, e has the same quotation from Jerome
and quotes Hosea 10:2 and Proverbs 28:2. Bonaventure does not borrow Hugh's citation of Micah 7:6.
[115] The usual translation of *divisit* is "scattered," but Bonaventure's
context requires "divided."
[116] On p. 291, n.4 QuarEd rightly indicate that the Vulgate has *et*
("also"), that is, "If, then, Satan is also divided. . . . "
[117] In Job this is the description of Leviathan.

How will his kingdom stand? Although this is stated as
a question, it is impossible to sustain the position that
Satan himself is casting himself out of his kingdom. For
the reign of Satan lies among the wicked and sinners.
Job 41:25 has: "He himself is king over all the children
of pride." And therefore, the Apostle says in Romans
6:12: "Let not sin reign in your mortal body." – Finally,
he adds *the proof of the minor premise from their own
words*, for these were the reason for their entire false
inference. So the text continues: *Because you say that I
cast out demons by Beelzebub.* For if what you say is
true that Satan is casting out Satan, then his empire is
divided, and because of this is headed to perdition. And
in this way the argument is formulated in Matthew
12:26: "If Satan casts out Satan, he is divided against
himself. How then will his kingdom stand?" – It is thus
clear how he makes the deduction from their words that
they are stating a manifest impossibility.

45. (Verse 19). Second, he leads them to a *false improbability* when he says: *Now, if I cast out demons by Beelzebub.* By means of this statement he wants to formulate the following reasoning: If I cast out demons by the
power of the demons, and if I have given power to your
children to cast out demons[118] – this is his unarticulated
presupposition – therefore, they are casting out demons
by the prince of the demons. But this is false and im-
probable both according to their opinion and according
to the witness of the Apostles themselves. Therefore,
what the Pharisees are putting forward is false, and
what the Apostles are bearing witness to is true. There-

---

[118] Here Bonaventure takes with utmost seriousness the belief that
Jesus Christ was Son of God and that what God did the Son did.

fore, *they will be your judges.*[119] – Now in this argumentation *the proposition*, which they are making, is set forward in the words: *But if I cast out demons by Beelzebub*, that is, according to your claim in verse 15 above: *By Beelzebub he is casting out demons.* – *The conclusion* comes next, which they do not concede, in the words: *By whom do your children cast out demons?* As if he were saying: It follows that they are casting them out by Beelzebub, which, however, they do not concede. Wherefore, Bede comments: "He calls *the children* of the Jews Apostles, who among the other gifts, which they had accepted from the Lord, received the gift of even expelling demons. And they attributed their power to expel not to the devil, but to God."[120] – Now he adds *the refutation* to which they subject themselves when he says: *Behold, they will be your judges*, for what you in your blasphemy are stating as false they are testifying to as true, according to what Isaiah 43:9–10 reads: "It is true. You are my witnesses, says the Lord." And they are not only *witnesses* on account of their assertion of the truth, but also *judges* on account of the perfection of the truth, according to what Matthew 19:28 has: "You, who have left

---

[119] It seems to me that Bonaventure's commentary makes better sense if it is compared to that of Hugh of St. Cher, to whom he seems to be indebted. Hugh of St. Cher, p. 202a comments on Luke 11:19: "*Bede*: as if to say: If the expulsion of the demons performed by the exorcists among your children is attributed to God and not to the devil, why doesn't the same work performed by me have the same cause? Or according to *Augustine and Bede*: The Apostles are their children, who, among other miracles, expelled demons. The Jews did not attribute this expulsion to the devil, but to God. But they attributed the same expulsion performed by Christ to the demons. Whence it is manifest that they were being moved by envy." And Hugh concludes his exegesis with a quotation from Isaiah 43:9–10, one of the scripture passages also quoted by Bonaventure.

[120] On p. 291, n. 11 QuarEd indicate that these words are found in the Glossa Ordinaria on Luke 11:19. See CCSL cxx, p. 233 for the actual words of Bede.

all things and have followed me . . . will sit on twelve
thrones, judging the twelve tribes of Israel."[121] For these
are the ones of whom Isaiah 3:14 says: "The Lord will
come in judgment with the ancients of his people."[122] He
calls the more perfect ones *the ancient ones*, according to
what Wisdom 4:8 states: "Venerable old age is not that
of a long time nor counted by the number of years. For
the understanding of a person is gray hair. And a spotless life is old age."

46. (Verse 20). Third comes the reduction to *the infallible truth* in the words: *But, if I cast out demons by the
finger of God. But* means "certainly." *If* means "since."
By the finger of God means "the Holy Spirit." So it is
said in Matthew 12:28: "If I cast out demons by the
Spirit of God." For the Holy Spirit is called *the finger of
God*, as it is said in Exodus 8:19: "This is the finger of
God." Now the reason for this is that the Son is called
the arm of the Father, according to what Isaiah 53:1
reads: "To whom is the arm of the Lord revealed?" He is
also said to be *the hand*, according to what the Psalmist
says: "Put forth your hand from on high" (143:7).[123] And
the reason for this is that just as the person who works
with his arm is also making things with his hand, so too
the Father made everything through the Son, as it is
said in John 1:3: "Everything was made through him."
Now the Holy Spirit proceeds from the Father and the
Son, just as the finger from the body and the arm, and is

---

[121] Bonaventure introduces the clause "left all things" from Luke
18:28. It is not found in Matthew 19:28.
[122] Isaiah 3:14 can also be interpreted to mean that God will come to
judge the ancients of his people.
[123] Hugh of St. Cher, p. 202d also quotes Matthew 12:28, Exodus
8:19, Isaiah 53:1, and Psalm 143:7. This seems another indication
that Bonaventure has borrowed scripture quotations from Hugh, his
elder contemporary.

connatural and consubstantial with them, and therefore is rightfully called *finger* in the scriptures.[124] Another interpretation sees the hand as *one* and the fingers as *distinct and different.* Thus from the one Spirit come forth different gifts, as it is said in 1 Corinthians 12:11: "All these things are the work of one and the same Spirit, who distributes to everyone as he wills."[125] – Therefore, since I cast out demons in this Spirit, *truly the kingdom of God has come upon you,* that is, kingly power, which protects us, the devil having been expelled, according to what John 12:31 reads: "Now is the judgment of the world. Now will the prince of this world be cast out." – And note that the text has: *The kingdom of God has come upon you.* For the kingdom of God comes upon us through *grace,* according to what is said in Luke 17:21 below: "The kingdom of God is within you."[126] But we will come into that kingdom through *glory,* when it will be said to us: "Come, blessed of my Father, receive the kingdom."[127]

47. And note that this is a necessary consequence. For there is no middle ground. Either a human being is under the power of God or under that of the devil. So if the power of the devil is cast out of a person, it follows that divine power is introduced. – In #39 above it was shown that a threefold evil spirit was cast out of a person[128] and replaced with a threefold gift of the divine Spirit.

---

[124] On p. 292, n. 3 QuarEd state that Jerome hints at this interpretation in Book II of his commentary on Matthew 12:28. See also Bede in CCSL cxx, p. 233.

[125] On p. 292, n. 4 QuarEd call attention to what seems to be a weak source in Bede. See CCSL cxx, p. 233.

[126] Contemporary translations generally render the Greek as "The kingdom of God is among you." See NAB and NRSV.

[127] Matthew 25:34 within Jesus' parable of the sheep and the goats.

[128] Namely, voluptuousness, avarice, and pride.

That is, the spirit of *holiness*, about which Wisdom 1:5 says: "The Holy Spirit of discipline will flee from the deceitful." The spirit of *poverty*, about which Matthew 5:3 has: "Blessed are the poor in spirit." And the spirit of *humility*, concerning which Isaiah 66:2 states: "Upon whom will I have respect, but the person who is poor and contrite in spirit?" – In the Psalm the Prophet petitioned for this threefold Spirit: "Create a clean heart in me, O God, and renew a *right* spirit within me. . . . Do not take your *holy* Spirit from me. . . . Strengthen me with a *foundational*[129] spirit" (50:12–14). In this passage the threefold spirit occurs: *the right spirit* refers to poverty; *the holy spirit* refers to purity; and *the foundational spirit* refers to humility. The person who has this spirit has justice towards *himself, neighbor*, and *God* or has the spirit *within, outside*, and *above* and thereby has peace and joy, and therefore has within himself the kingdom of God. For, according to what Romans 14:17 says: "The kingdom of God does not consist of food and drink, but in justice and peace and joy in the Holy Spirit."

48. (Verse 21). *When the strong man, fully armed, guards his courtyard.* After he has rejected the falsehood, here in a second point *he affirms the truth*. In this approbation he proceeds in the following order. First, he sets forth the *preparatory* truth. Second, he adds the *principal* truth. Finally, he subjoins the *corollary* truth.

Now first as he sets forth *the preparatory truth*, he says: *When the strong man, fully armed, guards his courtyard,*

---

[129] The translation "foundational" seems the best way to render *principalis* in this context.

everything[130] *that he possesses is undisturbed.* This is per
se obvious. For peaceful possession derives from the
strength of the possessor, which does not allow someone
less powerful to assail him. For this devil is *the strong
man,* about whom it is said in Job 41:24: "There is no
power upon earth that can be compared to him who was
made to fear no one." And Habakkuk 1:12 reads: "Lord,
you have appointed him for judgment and have made
him strong, so that you might correct." This is the *one
fully armed,* according to what is said in Job 41:6: "His
body is like molten shields." And since he has such great
power and arms, a feeble human being is unable to
mount any attack against him. By all means, *he holds
his possessions in peace,* for he has no fear of losing
them, according to what Gregory says: "He has no need
to repulse those over whom he feels he is in control by
peaceful right."[131] And this is *the peace of sinners,* relative to which the Psalmist says: "I was zealous concerning the wicked, seeing the peace of sinners" (72:3).
And Matthew 10:34 reads: "I have not come to send
peace, but a sword." Therefore, by this he intends to say
that the strong man is not cast out by someone less
strong. Therefore, if no earthly power prevails against
the power of the devil, but only heavenly power, then
the power that casts out demons is not from the earth,
but from heaven, not human, but divine.

49. (Verse 22). Second, he adds *the principal truth* which
now has persuasive power when he states: *But if a*

---

[130] On p. 292, n. 13 QuarEd accurately observe that the Vulgate does
not read *omnia* ("everything"). In his Admonition 27.5 Francis of
Assisi refers to Luke 11:21.
[131] On p. 293, n. 1 QuarEd refer to Book XXIV, chapter 11, n. 27 of
Gregory's *Moralia.* Hugh of St. Cher, p. 202k quotes the same passage from Gregory and says that what the devil possesses is "all sinners."

stronger than he comes over and overcomes him. Stronger than the devil is divine power, namely, our Christ. 1 Corinthians 1:23–24: "We say that Christ is the power of God and the wisdom of God."[132] And again: "That the weakness of God is stronger than human beings."[133] And therefore, Job 9:19 has: "If strength be called for, God is most strong." And wherefore, it is said in Isaiah 9:6: "He will be called Wonderful, Counsellor, God the strong." This one *comes over*, that is, he comes from above, according to what John 3:31 reads: "The one who comes from heaven is over all."[134] Now this one *conquers* the devil as someone less strong, according to what is said in John 16:33: "Take heart. I have conquered the world." Whence although he appears to be conquered, nevertheless he conquers, for by dying he has come back to life. And this is designated in Jeremiah 46:12: "The strong has stumbled against the strong, and both have fallen together." For Christ has conquered bodily, temporally, and visibly whereas the devil is conquered everlastingly, totally, and irreparably. So it is said in Revelation 5:5–6: "Behold, the lion of the tribe of Judah, the root of David, has conquered to open the book....And I saw in the midst of the throne and of the four living creatures. . . a Lamb standing, as if slain." Behold, he conquered because he was slain. Therefore, what is said in 1 Corinthians 15:55, 57 can be said to the devil: "O death, where is your victory? . . . Thanks be to God, who has given us the victory through our Lord Jesus."[135]

---

[132] Bonaventure has *dicimus* ("we say") whereas the Vulgate has *praedicamus* ("we preach").

[133] 1 Corinthians 1:25.

[134] I have translated *superveniens* as "comes over" to bring out Bonaventure's play on *super* ("over"). Hugh of St. Cher, p. 202m quotes this same passage from John 3:31.

[135] 1 Corinthians 15:57 ends with "our Lord, Jesus Christ."

50. And since he conquered him by *the passion*, he despoiled him by *the resurrection*. So the text continues: *He will take away all his weapons that he relied on.* And he did this, when he broke asunder the gates of hell, according to the Psalm: "Because he has broken gates of brass and burst iron bars" (106:16). And again the Psalm says: "He will destroy the bow and break the weapons. And he will burn the shield in the fire" (45:10). The devil makes these *weapons* for himself from human beings through their consent, according to what Romans 6:13 reads: "Do not yield your members to sin as weapons of iniquity." – Another interpretation is that the diabolical *weapons* are the diverse machinations of temptations by which they prevailed over human beings.[136] And of these *he has been deprived* through Christ's victory in the resurrection and *despoiled* in the ascension. – Whence the text adds: *and he will divide his spoils.* And indeed he did this when he made *vessels of mercy* from *vessels of wrath*.[137] And this was done in *the ascension*, according to what Ephesians 4:8 has: "Ascending on high, he has led captivity captive and given gifts to men and women." Now our Emmanuel has accomplished this. Isaiah 8:3 says: "Call his name: Hasten, take away the spoils, make haste to take away the prey." Now *the prey* pertains to the strong devil, according to what Isaiah 49:24–25 has: "Will the prey be taken away from the strong? Or can

---

[136] On p. 293, n. 8 QuarEd call attention to Bede's interpretation. See CCSL cxx, p. 234 for Bede's commentary on Luke 11:22: "The weapons upon which this strong one wickedly relied are the evils of spiritual cunning and deceit. Indeed, his spoils are the men and women deceived by him. Christ the victor distributed these spoils as a trophy of his triumph, for having led captivity captive he gave gifts to men and women, namely, ordaining certain ones as apostles, others as evangelists, some as prophets, and still others as pastors and teachers."

[137] On p. 293, n. 9 QuarEd are correct to point to Bonaventure's allusion here to Romans 9:22–23.

that which has been taken by the mighty be saved? For thus says the Lord: Verily, even what was captured by the strong will be taken away." And Hosea 13:15 states: "The Lord will carry off the treasure of every desirable vessel." – A figure of this occurred beforehand in David, of whom 1 Samuel 30:26 says that having returned from the fall of Amalek and after the Amalekites had been despoiled, he distributed the spoils and "sent gifts to the elders of Judah and his neighbors."[138] – And note that Christ is said *to distribute the spoils of the devil*, for, although he himself had liberated all, he nevertheless also assigned a portion of this glory to different preachers, who are themselves *the despoilers of Egypt* in Exodus 12:36.[139] From this, then, it is obvious the casting out of the demons was accomplished by Christ, not through diabolical power nor by human power, but through the Holy Spirit. And this is the principal truth.

51. (Verse 23). Third, relative to *the corollary truth*, the text reads: *The person who is not with me is against me*. And men and women, because the devil has them as his possession, repudiate Christ and do so according to what 2 Corinthians 6:15 says: "What harmony is there between Christ and Belial?" – And since no one can resist his strength, the text continues: *The[140] person who does not gather with me scatters*. For according to what is said in Job 9:4: "Who has resisted him and has had peace?" For Christ's duty is to gather, according to what

---

[138] A translation of the actual Vulgate text is: "he sent gifts of the spoils to the elders of Judah, his neighbors."

[139] Exodus 12:36 occurs in the narrative of the events around the Exodus: "And the Lord gave favor to the people in the sight of the Egyptians, so that they lent unto them. And they despoiled the Egyptians."

[140] On p. 293, n. 14 QuarEd correctly indicate that the Vulgate reads *Et qui* ("And the person").

John 11:51–52 states: "He was to die...so that he might gather into one the children of God who had been scattered abroad." And Isaiah 11:12 reads: "He will gather the fugitives of Israel and will assemble the dispersed of Judah from the four quarters of the earth." The Psalm has: "He will gather together the dispersed of Israel" (146:2). But the duty of the devil is to scatter, according to what John 10:12 says: "The wolf seizes and scatters the sheep." Therefore, it is best to enter into the sheepfold of the Lord, who cannot be overcome by a stronger one, as it is said in John 10:29: "What my Father has given me is greater than all, and no one is able to snatch them out of my hand."[141]

52. (Verse 24). *When the unclean spirit*, etc. After the rejection of the falsehood and the approbation of the truth the Evangelist adds here *the reprobation of deceitfulness*, whose origin lies in a malignant spirit, according to what John 8:44 says: "He is a liar and its father," that is, the father of lies and deceit. So the Savior reproves the deceitfulness of the Pharisees, whose *beginning, development,* and *ending* he shows to be effected in them through a malignant spirit and does this with regard to *the exit, return*, and *entry* of the malignant spirit. For *it exits* on account of the detestation of uncleanness, *returns* through the pretense of justice, but *enters* through the profundity of wickedness.[142]

---

[141] To complete Bonaventure's thought, I have given the second part of this verse.

[142] In the last two sentences Bonaventure's word playfulness is almost extreme: *originem, progressum, consummationem; egressum, regressum, ingressum; egreditur per detestationem immunditiae, regreditur per simulationem iustitiae, ingreditur per profundationem nequitiae.*

So first, with regard to *the exit* of the unclean spirit through *detestation of uncleanness* the text has: *When the unclean spirit has gone from a person,*[143] namely, through genuine penitence, according to what Zechariah 13:2 reads: "I will take away the false prophets and the unclean spirit from the earth." But to accomplish this abstinence and insistent prayer are necessary, through which the exterior and the interior are cleansed. And then the unclean spirit exits, according to what Matthew 17:20 states: "This kind of demon[144] is cast out only by prayer and fasting." – And since the devil always desires to seduce good people, whenever he is expelled from others, the text continues: *he roams through arid and*[145] *waterless places in search of rest. Arid and waterless places* are places where carnal propensities and concupiscence do not thrive, according to the Psalmist: "In a desert land where there is no road and no water, thus in a holy place I have appeared to you" (62:3) in Jerome's exposition.[146] On this account the Virgin Mary, since she had no trace of concupiscence whatsoever, is said to be *rock of the desert.* Isaiah 16:1 reads: "Send forth, O Lord, the lamb, the ruler of the earth, from the

---

[143] Again Bonaventure reads *ab homine* ("from a person") whereas the Vulgate has *de homine* ("out of a person"). See also Bonaventure's commentary on Luke 11:16 (#43) above and the footnote there.

[144] On p. 294, n. 5 QuarEd correctly indicate that the Vulgate does not read *daemonii* ("of demon").

[145] On p. 294, n. 6 QuarEd accurately mention that the Vulgate does not read *arida et* ("arid and").

[146] On p. 294, n. 7 QuarEd tackle the source of this quotation. In reality, Jerome interprets the world as the desert on account of sinners. The more informative parallel stems from Book XXXIII, chapter 3, n. 8 of Gregory's *Moralia* where he is interpreting Matthew 12:43–44: "For since the time of the flood, *the arid and waterless places* are the hearts of the just, which are dried up from every drop of carnal concupiscence through rigorous discipline."

rock of the desert, to the mountain of daughter Zion."[147]
The devil *roams about* these places *in search of rest*,
that is, with the intent to erect a shade of negligence
and a fountain of insolence among them, so that he can
rest there. Now in such a place *he finds rest*, according
to what Job 40:16 says: "He sleeps under the shade, in
the covert of the reed, and in moist places."[148] And Ezekiel 29:3 reads: "Behold, I come against you, . . . great
dragon, who recline in the midst of the rivers." Now the
devil only rests in those, in whom he has found an efflu-
ence of concupiscence. But since he cannot find such in
holy men, who have disciplined and chastised themselves, he does not come to rest in them, but flees, according to what James 4:7 has: "Resist the devil, and he
will flee from you."

53. Secondly, relative to *the return* under *the pretense of
justice*, the text adds: *and finding none*, that is, rest, *it
says: I will return to my house from which I exited.*[149] He
calls the house *his own* because he had not yet been

---

[147] On p. 294, n. 8 QuarEd refer to Book III, distinction 3, part 1, article 2, question 3, conclusio 3 of Bonaventure's Sentences Commentary. See Opera Omnia 3:78 and note 5 where Bonaventure states
that Jerome interprets "the rock of the desert" of Isaiah 16:1 to be
Ruth, but he himself maintains that it refers to the mother of God.
[148] On p. 294, n. 10 QuarEd note the influence of Bede on Bonaventure's interpretation. See CCSL cxx, p. 235 on Luke 11:24: *"To search
for rest and not finding it*, for the devil flees from chaste minds and
can only find an agreeable rest for himself in the hearts of the perverse. Whence the Lord says of him: *He sleeps under the shadow, in
the covert of the reed, and in moist places*. That is, 'the shadow' refers
to darkened consciences; 'the covert' refers to those who are bright on
the outside, but empty inside; 'in moist places' indicates hypocrites
who have lascivious and voluptuous minds."
[149] On p. 294, n. 11 QuarEd correctly indicate that the Vulgate reads
unde exivi ("whence I exited"); a normal English translation would be
"which I left." But I am translating *exivi* by "I have exited" to prepare for Bonaventure's later points.

fully expelled from it. And to such a house the devil returns. A figure of this occurs in Isaiah 37:34: "By the way, which Sennacherib," that is, Satan, "used in coming, by that will he return."[150] With justification does he call *the house* of sinners *his own,* for the sinner "who has committed a sin is the slave of sin," as it is said in John 8:34. And through this he does not have rights over himself, but is the slave of the devil. Therefore, Proverbs 5:9–10 has: "Give not your honor to strangers and your years to the cruel, lest strangers be filled through your powers and your labors be in another man's house."

54. (Verse 25). But the appearance of goodness and justice leads the expelled demon back to this house. And for this reason the text continues: *And when he has come to it, he finds it swept clean and decorated,*[151] not *interiorly*, as the Prophet says in the Psalm: "I exercised and swept my spirit" (76:7). And again the Psalm says: "All the glory of the daughter of the king is within" (44:14). Thus he does not find the interior of the house *swept and decorated*, but *the outside*, as Luke 11:39 below says: "Now, you Pharisees, you clean the outside of the cup and the dish, but within you are full of robbery and wickedness." And Matthew 23:27 has: "Woe to you, who are like whitened sepulchers," etc." Such cleanness is not sufficient for the Holy Spirit, who not only seeks to dwell in a clean body, but also in a holy soul. So Wisdom 1:4 reads: "Wisdom will not enter into a malicious soul nor dwell in a body subject to sins." And therefore, we are invited to both. Isaiah 1:16 states: "Wash yourselves, be clean," etc. But that cleanness, which is only

---

[150] On p. 294, n. 11 QuarEd rightly call attention to Bonaventure's two variants from the Vulgate. The Vulgate begins the verse with *In via* ("On the way") and does not read "Sennacherib."
[151] The Vulgate does not have *et ornatam* ("and decorated"). This expression stems from Matthew 12:44.

external, leaves the house empty of the grace of the Holy Spirit, and thus subject to occupation by the devil. So noting this, Matthew 12:44 says: "He finds the place *unoccupied*, swept clean and decorated," *unoccupied*, namely, by grace and virtue. Wherefore, Chrysostom says: "Those bereft of virtue will easily be occupied by the actions of the devil."[152] And therefore, Jerome comments: "Always do something good, so that the devil may find you occupied."[153]

55. (Verse 26). Third, concerning *entry* by *the profundity of iniquity* the text says: *And then he goes and takes seven other spirits more evil than himself, and they enter in and dwell there.* These *seven spirits* are counterfeits, which imitate the virtues in form and deceive people. They are, therefore, more evil than manifest vices and display greater perversity of evil, as Augustine says: "Counterfeit equity is not equity, but double iniquity."[154]

56. So note *three* groups of seven spirits.[155] The first is *good* and encompasses the seven gifts, about which

---

[152] On p. 295, n. 3 QuarEd cite the opinion of Chrysostom in his Homily 43 (alias 44) on Matthew, n. 3: "...but also these were void of all virtue, and were more easily invaded by the demons than before." Hugh of St. Cher, p. 202v,h has the same wording in his quotation from Chrysostom as Bonaventure.

[153] On p. 295, n. 4 QuarEd quote Jerome's Letter 125 (alias 4), n. 11: "Do some kind of work, so that the devil will always find you occupied." Bonaventure's quotation is quite accurate.

[154] On p. 295, n. 6 QuarEd refer to Augustine's *Enarrationes* on Psalm 63, n. 11. Hugh of St. Cher, p. 202v, k has the selfsame quotation as Bonaventure.

[155] On p. 295, n. 9 QuarEd intimate that Bede's commentary has laid the foundation for Bonaventure's. See CCSL cxx, p. 235: "Wherefore, the seven spirits that have entered are rightly said to be more evil than he, for not only are these seven vices contrary to the seven spiritual virtues, but they also through hypocrisy make themselves counterfeit virtues." The editors go on to say that Cardinal Hugh of

Isaiah 11:2–3 says: "The spirit of the Lord will rest upon him: the spirit of wisdom and of understanding, the spirit of counsel, and of fortitude, the spirit of knowledge, and of godliness. And he shall be filled with the spirit of the fear of the Lord."[156] – The second is *evil* and encompasses the seven spirits of iniquity, that is, the seven capital vices which are opposed to the seven gifts. For voluptuousness is opposed to *wisdom*, gluttony to *understanding*, avarice to *counsel*, sloth to *fortitude*, anger to *knowledge*, envy to *godliness*, and pride to *fear of the Lord*. And about these it is said in Mark 16:9 that seven demons had been cast out of Mary Magdalene.[157] – The third group encompasses the seven counterfeit spirits, which the Lord calls *more evil spirits*, for under the guise of holiness they deceive the innocent. Of these Proverbs 26:25 states: "There are seven iniquities in his heart." Hypocrisy, which is counterfeiter of the gifts of the Holy Spirit, impels all these. In Matthew 23:13–29 the Lord gives a sign of this by making seven exclamations to the hypocrites, warning them by means of *woes*. He adds an eighth *woe*, but it is not joined with the designation, *the hypocrites*.[158] Therefore, these *more evil spirits* are securely at home, for the more an evil ap-

---

St. Cher also talks about three groups of spirits in his commentary on Luke 11:26. See Hugh of St. Cher, p. 202v, m where a close scrutiny will indicate how greatly Bonaventure was dependent on Hugh's exegesis, e.g., both quote Augustine and Matthew 23.

[156] Bonaventure merely quotes the first words of Isaiah 11:2-3, that is, the first two gifts. For clearer understanding I have cited all of Isaiah 11:2-3.

[157] Here Bonaventure repeats the common and erroneous medieval opinion that Mary Magdalene was a great sinner. Mary Magdalene was cured of an illness, whose power was so great that it was indicated by the number of completeness, that is, seven. Briefly, one looks in vain in the Gospels for any proof that Mary of Magdala was a greater sinner than the rest of us, her brothers and sisters in the flesh and in the faith.

[158] See Matthew 23:16.

pears to be minimal, the less it is reproved and becomes more securely at home. Isaiah 13:21 reads: "Wild beasts will rest there, and their houses will be filled with dragons, and ostriches will dwell there, and the hairy ones will dance there," where the monstrosities of the vices are found.

57. And since the stronger the hold the devil has on a person the worse off and in greater slavery that person is, the text continues: *And the last state of that person is worse than the first.* Either this occurs on account of *a relapse*. Concerning such John 5:14 reads: "Behold, you are cured. Sin no more, lest something worse happen to you." And 2 Peter 2:21 has: "It were better for them not to have known the way of justice than having known it, to turn back from the holy commandment delivered to them."[159] So Chrysostom comments: "The punishment of the later vices is more severe."[160] Or this occurs on account of *the duplication of iniquity*, with counterfeiting effects, according to what Sirach 7:3 states: "Do not sow iniquity in the furrows of injustice,[161] and you will not reap them sevenfold." From this it is obvious that the Pharisees are not only convicted of *falsehood*, but also reproved for their *deceitfulness*.

Now these things can be given *an allegorical interpretation* referring to the Jews and Gentiles, according to Bede's interpretation which is sufficiently well picked

---

[159] I have given the quotation in its entirety whereas Bonaventure was content to write: "It were better for them not to have known, etc."
[160] On p. 295, n. 13 QuarEd provide this simple reference: Homily 43 (alias 44) on Matthew, n. 4.
[161] Bonaventure's text diverges from the Vulgate in two ways. The Vulgate reads *mala* ("evils") whereas Bonaventure has *iniquitatem* ("iniquity"). The Vulgate has *iniuriae* ("injustice") while Bonaventure has *iniustitiae* ("injustice").

up by the Glossa on Luke 11:24: *It has gone out from the Jews*, etc.[162]

Luke 11:27–28
COMMENDATION OF THE TRUTH PROVEN

58. (Verse 27). *Now it came to pass*, etc. After the expression of Judaic deception and the reprobation of the deception expressed, the Evangelist adds here *a commendation of the truth proven*. And indeed this was fitting, so that, the truth having been manifested, Truth himself, manifesting himself as the truth, might be manifestly praised before the entire multitude. Now in the description of this commendation three things are introduced. First is *the condition of the person giving praise*. Second is *the expression of divine praise*. Third is *the approbation of the praise expressed*.

First, then, with regard to *the condition of the person giving praise*, the text has: *Now it came to pass while*[163] *he was saying these things*, namely, to confute falsehood, *that a certain woman from the crowd lifted up her voice and said to him*, for the commendation of the truth and the refutation of the Pharisees. In this matter a twofold condition is noted in the person giving praise, that is, *strength* and *littleness. Strength* is noted in this that *she lifted up her voice*, according to what Isaiah 40:9 says: "Lift up your voice with strength . . . raise your voice, do not be afraid." *Littleness* in this that she is *a certain*

---

[162] On p. 295, n. 15 QuarEd state that this is the Glossa Ordinaria. For Bede's interpretation of Luke 11:26 see CCSL cxx, pp. 235–236. Bede, in turn, is dependent upon Jerome's commentary on Matthew; see PL 26:86B–87A, Hugh of St. Cher, p. 202v, d-n also engages in the Jews/Gentiles allegorical interpretation.

[163] The Vulgate has *cum* ("as") while Bonaventure has *dum* ("while").

woman, neither named nor noble, but from the crowd, so that what the Psalm says might be fulfilled: "The poor and needy will praise your name" (73:21).[164] From this it is clear that the person who praises the divine name must not be timid, so that she does not dare to give praise. Nor must she be haughty, so that she is embarrassed to give praise. Rather she must be strong and humble. Wherefore, since certain people *were silent* out of *fear* and others *were blaspheming* out of *arrogance and haughtiness*, this humble and strong woman was not *silent* with the fearful and did not revile with the blasphemers. So the Glossa says: "With great confidence she confesses the Son of God among the blasphemers."[165] Therefore, they could say to her what Matthew 15:28 states: "O woman, great is your faith," which has made you so strong that what Proverbs 31:10 has may be said: "Who will find a strong woman?" In you has been verified what Sirach 26:24 states: "As everlasting foundations upon a solid rock, so are the commandments of God in the heart of a holy woman."

59. Secondly, concerning *the expression of divine praise* the text continues: *Blessed is the womb that bore you.* Through this she praises Christ, the Son of God, lifting up the commendation of her praise from the perspective of Mary's beatitude, as if she were saying: Blessed is the woman who bore so good a son. And rightly so, for it was fitting for the female sex to give such praise, but not only for women, but also for men. For in Luke 1:48

---

[164] On p. 296, n. 2 QuarEd gives two references to a longstanding tradition that this woman was either Martha or Martha's servant, who was named either Stella or Marcella. There is no basis for such speculation in Luke 11:27.

[165] On p. 296, n. 4 QuarEd state that this is the Glossa Interlinearis on Luke 11:27 and that it ultimately comes from Bede. See CCSL cxx, p. 236 for Bede's original text of which the Glossa has given the gist.

above the Virgin said: "Henceforth all generations will call me blessed."

60. And note that she blesses the womb of the Virgin and does so, for she bore the Son of God for nine months and six days. These six days count for one month. Wisdom 7:1–2 reads: "In the womb of my mother I was made[166] to be flesh in the time of ten months." Therefore, in praise of the Virgin it is said in The Song of Songs 7:2: "Your womb is like a heap of wheat," for Christ was the grain of wheat, according to what is said in John 12:24–25.[167] And by this wheat her womb became full, and therefore she is *blessed* on account of *three privileges*. For, as Bernard says, "she was made fruitful without corruption, heavy with child without bother, brought forth her child without pain."[168] Isaiah 66:8 says: "Who has ever heard of such a thing? And who has seen anything like it?" – Or she is blessed on account of *three miracles*. The first miracle is the coming together of things that are infinitely separate from one another. For God became man there. The creator, a creature. The immense one, a small one. The Word, an infant. The eternal one, a temporal being, according to what John 1:14 has: "And the Word became flesh."[169] And Jeremiah

---

[166] The Vulgate has *figuratus sum* ("I was fashioned") whereas Bonaventure reads *factus sum* ("I was made"). In the notes on p. 296 QuarEd give no indication of why Bonaventure mentions nine months and six days.

[167] John 12:24–25 reads: "Amen, amen, I say to you, unless the grain of wheat falls into the ground and dies, it remains alone. But if it dies, it bears much fruit."

[168] On p. 296, n. 8 QuarEd refer to Bernard's "Sermo in Dominica infra Octavam Assumptionis,", n. 7. See SBOp 5.267. The quotation is not quite exact, for Bernard has *fecunda* ("fecund") in place of Bonaventure's *fecundata* ("made fruitful").

[169] On p. 296, n. 9 QuarEd refer to two of Bernard's sermons where he engages in theological rhetoric about similar contrasts. See, e.g., "Sermo Secundus in Nativitate," n. 4 in SBOp 4.253–254.

31:22 reads: "The Lord will make a new thing upon the earth: a woman will encompass a man." – The second miracle is this that the one who fashioned the womb was fashioned in a womb.[170] Wherefore, the Psalm says: "Glorious things are said of you, city of God....A man was born in her, and the Most High himself has established her" (86:35). What Sirach 43:2 says can be interpreted in her regard: "A wonderful vessel, the work of the Most High." – The third miracle is that the one who contains all things is contained in this womb. He is contained there, "whom the entire world does not contain."[171] Wherefore, the church chants: "For you have borne in your womb him whom the heavens cannot contain."[172] Therefore, Isaiah 45:15 has: "Truly, you are a hidden God."[173]

61. Not only does the woman bless the Virgin for bearing a child, but also blesses *her breasts* for providing nourishment where the text has: *and the breasts that nursed you*, that is, may they be blessed. From this it is to be understood that he was nursed solely from the breasts of the most blessed Virgin. This was designated

[170] On p. 296, n. 10 QuarEd cite Augustine's Sermon 291, n. 6: "He was fashioned in you who made you. He was fashioned in you, through whom you were made, etc."
[171] On p. 296, n. 11 QuarEd give as the base for this quotation two references to *Missale Romanum*: 1) The graduale for the feast of the Visitation of the Blessed Virgin Mary; 2) The votive Mass, *Salve*, for the Blessed Virgin.
[172] On p. 296, n. 11 QuarEd cite the responsory to the sixth reading during Nocturn II at Matins for the feast of the Lord's Nativity.
[173] On p. 296, n. 11 QuarEd refer to Augustine's Sermon 128, n. 2: "God, who is and who was, became. The creator, a creature. The one who is immense is contained . . . the incomprehensible one becomes comprehensible." Their final words on this passage is: "Cardinal Hugh also has these three miracles." See Hugh of St. Cher, p. 203g to appreciate to what a great extent Bonaventure is indebted to his Dominican Cardinal contemporary for his exegesis..

in Moses, who refused to be nursed by an Egyptian woman, as it is said.[174] And therefore, a Hebrew woman was sought, namely, his own mother, as it is said in Exodus 2:7–8. Now this designates the Virgin Mary, whose breasts Christ sucked, according to what The Song of Songs 8:1 says: "Who will give you to me as my brother, sucking the breasts of my mother," etc. Therefore, he joined these two together in order to show that the Virgin Mary was the true and perfect mother of Christ, for she not only begot him, but also brought him up. And as she truly educated him, she, therefore, truly begot him. And in this refutation is made, as it is said in the Glossa, of the impiety of the Manichees and others who say that he came out of the womb with an ethereal body.[175] Wherefore, Bede says: "From the same source flows both milk for nourishing and semen for procreating children. Therefore, from the semen of the Virgin, according to the physicians,[176] he could be conceived who could be nourished by her milk."[177]

---

[174] On p. 297, n. 1 QuarEd refer to Flavius Josephus' *Jewish Antiquities* Book II, chapter 9, n. 5 (224–227) as the source for this interpretation. The pertinent passage in H. St. J. Thackeray's translation in LCL, p. 263 runs: "And so Thermuthis (the king's daughter) ordered a woman to be brought to suckle the infant. But when, instead of taking the breast, it spurned it, and then repeated the action with several women. . . . Therefore, the infant, gleefully as it were, fastened upon the breast, and, by request of the princess, the mother was permanently entrusted with its nurture."

[175] On p. 297, n. 2 QuarEd cite the Glossa Ordinaria (from Bede) on Luke 11:27: "Here Mary is praised who bore the Lord. And the wickedness is confounded of both the present Jews and the future heretics, who deny Christ's true humanity. For she confesses the true Son of God against the blasphemous Jews and gives witness that he is a true human son, consubstantial with his mother. For unless he were one flesh with his mother, in vain would the womb and breasts of the Virgin be blessed."

[176] A very illuminating discussion of "ancient medical representations of the female body" and of "the products of nutrition: semen, menses, and milk" can be found in Teresa M. Shaw, *The Burden of the Flesh:*

62. (Verse 28). Thirdly, about *the approbation of the praise expressed* the text continues: *But he said: Rather, blessed are they who hear the word of God.* He did not say this in a contradictory way, but rather by adding something more. As if he were saying: Not only is the womb *blessed* that bore me, the Word made flesh, but *more blessed* is the person who accepts the word that I proffer. Whence Mary was not only *blessed* because she bore Christ in the flesh, but indeed was *more blessed* because she most perfectly bore him in her mind, according to what Augustine says: "Mary was more blessed in conceiving the faith of Christ than the flesh of Christ."[178] For blessed is everyone, who hears and obeys, according to what John 13:17 has: "If you know these things, blessed will be you be if you do them." – And therefore, the text adds: *and keep it.* And so James 1:22 reads: "Be doers of the word and not hearers only." By this saying Christ did not want to be praised for carnal kinship per se. For it is said to the Jews in Luke 3:8 above: "Do not say: We have Abraham as our father," etc. Rather for *a spiritual kinship*, for the union of minds is more holy than the union of bodies.[179] And therefore, since his mother and brothers were seeking him in Matthew 12:50, he said: "Whoever does the will of my Father in heaven, he is my brother, sister, and mother." And on account of this the Virgin Mary was praiseworthy in her conception because he conceived *by*

Fasting and Sexuality in Early Christianity (Minneapolis: Fortress, 1998), pp. 64–78. In brief, both women and men produced semen.

[177] This seems to be a summary of Bede's commentary. See CCSL cxx, pp. 236–237.

[178] On p. 297, n. 3 QuarEd refer to Augustine's *Liber de Sancta Virginitate*, chapter 3, n. 3.

[179] On p. 297, n. 4 QuarEd refer to the comment of Ambrose on Luke 8:21. See CCSL xiv, p. 187: "Nor are the parents wrongfully set aside, but unions of minds are thought to be more religious than those of bodies."

faith. And so Elizabeth said to her in Luke 1:45 above: "Blessed is she who has believed, because the things promised her by the Lord will be accomplished." – From this a wonderful commendation of the truth is manifest. This truth makes all who cling to it blessed, not just those who share *carnal kinship*, like the Virgin Mary, but also those who cling to it by *spiritual love*, like any holy soul. For as Augustine says: "Blessedness consists in the joy that comes from the truth."[180] The persons who hear, love, and do the truth are those who will come to this joy, according to what Sirach 24:30–31 states: "The persons who hear me will not be confounded,[181] and those who work by me will not sin, and those who explain me will have life everlasting."

63. Now *spiritually* it is to be noted here that *the woman from the crowd* presents a type of the Law, which commends *carnal generation*, according to the promise made to Abraham in Genesis 15:5: "Look up to heaven and number the stars, if you can. And he said to Abraham: So shall your seed be." And to David in the Psalm: "The Lord has sworn truth to David, and he will not make it void: of the fruit of your womb I will set upon your throne" (131:11).[182] And in Romans 9:5: "From the fathers is the Christ according to the flesh." But *Christ* functions as a type of grace and of the spirit, who verily commends *a spiritual generation*, according to what

---

[180] On p. 297, n. 6 QuarEd refer to Book X, chapter 23, n. 33 of Augustine's *Confessions:* "Indeed, blessed is a life that consists of the joy that comes from the truth."

[181] Bonaventure has changed the Vulgate's singular subject ("he") into a plural ("they") and has thereby given all three clauses a plural subject. Hugh of St. Cher, p. 203i also quotes this passage from Sirach.

[182] I have taken the liberty of quoting all of Genesis 15:5 and Psalm 131:11. Bonaventure merely writes: "Look up to heaven, etc." and "of the fruit, etc." respectively.

Matthew 12:48 says: "Who is my mother and who are my brothers?"[183] – *The spiritual conception* of this generation happens first *through faith*, as in the unity of the church. John 7:38 reads: "The person who believes in me, as the scripture says," etc.[184] As a sign of this the Virgin Mary conceived through faith. Luke 1:45 has: "Blessed is she who has believed." – Now *the birth* transpires *through work*. Sirach 24:42 states: "I said: I will water my garden of plants," etc.[185] But those who believe and do not perform any works are like those, of whom Isaiah 37:3 says: "The children have come to the point of being born, and there is no strength to bring them forth." – *Nursing* happens *in love and contemplation*. The Song of Songs 1:1 reads: "Let him kiss me with the kiss of his mouth, because your breasts are better than wine," etc. And Proverbs 5:19 has: "Let her be your dearest hind and most agreeable fawn," etc.[186] – And thus in these three *the reception of grace, the work of the active life*, and *the consolation of the contemplative life* are intimated. And all this is summarized in "faith which works through love."[187] Only those who have this faith will be blessed.

---

[183] Bonaventure seems to provide a cross reference to his earlier quotation of Matthew 12:50 in #62: "For whoever does the will of my father in heaven is my brother and sister and mother."

[184] Here is my translation of the continuation of John 7:38: ". . . from the womb of that person there will flow rivers of living water." I puzzle over why Bonaventure so drastically truncates his scripture quotations in #63.

[185] If one reads Sirach 24:42 in its entirety and checks the variant readings of the Vulgate, one finds that the final clause of Sirach 24:42 can be translated: "and I will water abundantly the fruits of my birth." This clause fits hand in glove with the point Bonaventure is making.

[186] The next clause of Proverbs 5:19 makes Bonaventure's point: "Let her breasts inebriate you at all times."

[187] Galatians 5:6.

Luke 11:29–32
THE FALLACY OF THOSE WHO ARE DISBELIEVING

64. (Verse 29). *And as the crowds were gathering together*, etc. After the Savior had confuted the fallacy of those who were blaspheming or disparaging him, he in a second point confutes *the fallacy of those who are disbelieving*, who under the guise of studiousness were seeking signs to satisfy their curiosity. Now this fallacy of the incredulity of the Jews is confuted in a threefold way. For first this nation is accused of being *reluctant to believe*. Second, *lukewarm to learn*. Third, *frigid to do penance*.

Therefore, in the first point this nation is accused of being deceitful and incredulous, that it is *reluctant to believe*, when the text says: *And as the crowds were gathering together, he began to say: This generation is an evil generation.* For *the crowds were gathering together*, that is, they came to him for various reasons: Some to listen to his teaching; some to see miracles; some to have their hunger relieved; some to have their health restored; some to hatch plots; others to pay homage, according to the diverse types of persons who are mentioned in the Gospel.[188] But these, as the Glossa says, were coming "to see the wonderful things which they had heard were done by him,"[189] and which they

---

[188] See a similar list in Hugh of St. Cher, p. 203v, a. For more detail about Bonaventure's use of Hugh of St. Cher in his commentary on Luke 11:29-32 see Robert J. Karris, "Bonaventure's Commentary on Luke: Four Case Studies of his Creative Borrowing from Hugh of St. Cher," *Franciscan Studies* 59 (2001): 133-236, esp. pp. 134-163, 228-230.

[189] On p. 298, n. 2 QuarEd state that this is the Glossa Interlinearis. They go on to cite the Glossa Ordinaria on Matthew 4:25: "The crowd was made up of four kinds of people. Namely, some on account of the heavenly mystery, like the disciples; some to seek a cure for an illness; some because of his fame and their curiosity, wanting to expe-

wanted to see, not out of the zeal of faith, but rather out of evil intent and curiosity and error. And therefore, the text continues: *This generation is an evil generation.* And it is said in Matthew 12:39: "An evil and adulterous generation seeks a sign." For it is an *evil* and *adulterous* generation on account of infidelity and idolatry. So what Proverbs 30:11 says fits it: "There is a generation that curses its father and does not bless its mother." And also what Deuteronomy 32:20 has: "It is a perverse generation and unfaithful children." For their infidelity is clear from their question of curiosity. For which reason the text continues: *it seeks a sign,* namely, a sign from heaven. The Glossa comments: "As if those things which they had seen, were not signs."[190] – And the signs given them on account of their incredulity were not of a heavenly nature, but earthly, not spiritual, but sensuous. *Heavenly* signs are denied them, but they are granted *earthly* ones. Therefore, the text continues: *And no sign will be given it but the sign of Jonah the prophet.*[191] To be sure, he said this, not because he would not give other signs. See how in John 11:39–44 it is said that he raised Lazarus who had been dead for four days. And in John 12:28 it is said: "And a voice from heaven sounded for him."[192] And John 20:30 says: "Many other signs he worked in the sight of all, which are not written in their book."[193] And finally, there is the sign in Luke 23:45:

---

rience whether it were true what was being said; others out of envy, wanting to accuse him and catch him in something."

[190] On p. 298, n. 4 QuarEd state that this is the Glossa Interlinearis, from Book II of Jerome's commentary on Matthew 12:38.

[191] The Vulgate does not have *prophetae* ("the prophet").

[192] On p. 298, n. 5 QuarEd indicate Bonaventure's divergence from the Vulgate's *Venit ergo vox de caelo* ("Therefore, a voice from heaven came"). Bonaventure may have thought of Mark 1:11: "And a voice sounded from heaven."

[193] A translation of the Vulgate of John 20:30 may help readers to see where Bonaventure's quotation differs: "Many other signs Jesus also

"The sun was darkened" at his death. But all the other signs have meaning only for believers, for example, that the God who suffered and died was raised on the third day. A figure of this occurred beforehand in the prophet Jonah. And therefore, in John 2 to the Pharisees who were asking: "What sign do you show us, because you are doing these things?" (verse 19) he said: "Destroy this temple, and in three days I will raise it up. . . . But he was speaking of the temple of his body" (verses 19, 21). – And a figure of this occurred beforehand in *Jonah*, whom the fish vomited forth on the third day, and therefore, the Ninevites believed what had been entrusted to Jonah.[194]

65. (Verse 30). For which reason he adds: *For just as Jonah was a sign to the Ninevites, thus*[195] *will the Son of Man be to this generation.* For Jonah was a sign to the Ninivites not only by word, but also by the miracle performed because, having been thrown into the sea and swallowed by the fish, he returned on the third day to the realm above. Through this he signified Christ who suffered, died, and was raised. Therefore, in Matthew 12:40 a sign of this kind is applied: "For just as Jonah was in the belly of the fish for three days and three nights, so will the Son of Man be in the heart of the earth." Therefore, the people who do not believe this sign

---

worked in the sight of his disciples, which are not written in this book."

[194] On p. 298, n. 7 QuarEd rightly point to Jonah 2:1, 9; 3:5 as the references for Bonaventure's use of the Jonah story. The Ninevites, however, knew nothing of Jonah's being swallowed and vomited forth by a large fish.

[195] On p. 298, n. 8 QuarEd correctly indicate that the Vulgate reads *ita erit et* ("so also will be") whereas Bonaventure has *sic erit* ("thus will be").

are more hardhearted than the Ninivites, nor are the signs of the Lord in any way beneficial to them.

66. (Verse 31). Secondly, the generation of the Jews is accused of being *lukewarm in learning*, as the text says: *The queen of the South will rise up in the judgment with the men of this generation.* From this it is clear that the resurrection will be universal, not only for the good, but also for the evil. But the resurrection will be for judgment, according to what John 5:28–29 states: "All who are in the tombs will hear the voice of the Son of God...and will come forth," etc.[196] And since the evil ones will be condemned by means of a comparison with those who are better, the text adds: *and will condemn them.* Bede says: "Not by the power of judgment, but by means of a comparison with someone who has acted better."[197] And what follows shows her goodness: *for she came from the ends of the earth to hear the wisdom of Solomon,* according to what is said in 2 Chronicles 9:1: "When the queen of Sheba heard of the fame of Solomon, she came to try him with hard questions in Jerusalem." Something similar is said in 1 Kings 10:1–10. Wherefore, the queen was *praiseworthy* in a threefold manner. First, she was moved by *the fame* of Solomon. Second, she came from *remote territory*. Third, she came to a person who was of *the same rank*. – On the contrary, this people were *blameworthy* in three ways. He notes this when he

---

[196] Bonaventure's point is actually contained in the rest of John 5:29: "And they who have done good will come forth unto resurrection of life, but those who have done evil unto resurrection of judgment."
[197] Bonaventure's quotation is verbatim from Bede. See CCSL cxx, p. 238. On p. 298, n. 11 QuarEd cite the words that the Glossa Ordinaria adds to these words of Bede: "For, having left her kingdom, she came into Judea to hear a man who was famous for his wisdom, but the Jews do not listen to the wisdom of God conversing with them, but blaspheme him."

says: *And behold, a greater than Solomon is here*. For by using the word *behold*, he indicates that Christ *was known* not only by his words, but also by sight, according to what Baruch 3:38 reads: "Afterwards he was seen on the earth," etc. By adding the word *here*, he shows that he was not absent, but *present*, so that what Deuteronomy 30:11 has could be rightly said to them: "The commandment that I command you today is not . . . far from you." Indeed, by saying *a greater than Solomon*, he shows that not only is he to be believed as a wise man, but as *the beginning and fountain of all wisdom*, according to what John 8:25 has: "I am the beginning, who is speaking to you."[198]

---

[198] Bonaventure quotes John 8:25 five times in his commentary on Luke's Gospel: Luke 7:14 (#25), Luke 8:15 (#22), Luke 9:35 (#65), Luke 22:44 (#51). I make four points about Bonaventure's extraordinary quotation of John 8:25. First, Jesus' statement is a response to the question of the Jews: "Who are you?" Second, the Vulgate reads: *Principium quia et loquor vobis*, which may be translated as "What I have said to you from the beginning" or by "Why do I speak to you at all?" Third, Bonaventure's text reads: *Ego principium, qui et loquor vobis* ("I am the beginning, who is speaking to you"). Bonaventure's text is distinctive in two major ways, for he has *Ego* ("I") and reads *qui* ("who"). This second reading of "who" loses some of its distinctive character when one notes that *qui* ("who") is a textual variant for *quia* ("what") in the Vulgate. Fourth, Bonaventure's exposition of John 8:25 in his Commentary on St. John's Gospel sheds some wondrous light on his interpretation of this verse. I translate Opera Omnia 6:361: "First, for he is the creator. For which reason the text says: *Jesus said to them: Beginning*, that is, I am the creating beginning. For all things have received their existence through him, as it is said above in John 1:1: "In the beginning was the Word" and again "All things were made through him" (1:3). – He is also the teacher – *who is speaking with you* (8:25). Hebrews 1:2 states: "In these last days he has spoken to us through a Son, whom he established as heir of all things and through whom he created the world." In a similar way the Lord answered the question of the Samaritan woman: "I am the one who is speaking with you" (John 4:26). And the blind man in John 9:37 below. – He is also judge, even though he is not now speaking words of condemnation, but of instruction and invitation." Even though Bonaventure does not read *ego* ("I") in his interpreta-

67. For Christ was greater than Solomon by reason of his *power*, *knowledge*, and *justice*. Therefore, what this Psalm says is very fitting for him: "O God, give to the king your judgment" (71:1).[199] The Jews believed this Psalm to have been composed in praise of Solomon, when it was said therein: "He will rule from sea to sea" (verse 8). And again: "His name outlasts the sun, and in him all the tribes of the earth will be blessed" (verse 17). Solomon was a *temporal* peacemaker, but Christ an *eternal*. Isaiah 9:7 reads: "His rule will be multiplied." He was *wise*, but Christ is *Wisdom*. 1 Corinthians 1:24 has: "Christ, the power and wisdom of God." And Colossians 2:3 says: "In whom are hidden all the treasures of wisdom and knowledge." He *effected justice*, but he was *justice itself*. 1 Corinthians 1:30 states: "who has become for us God-given justice." etc.

Wherefore, through a comparison by reason of seven preeminent characteristics the queen of the South will judge the unbelieving Jews. For the queen: She, of the *weak sex*, comes *from a remote territory, with difficulty, having left her kingdom, with gifts, to a mere man, known only by reputation*, as is expressly garnered from 1 Kings 10:1–10. But for the Jews: *men* who contemn and despise *Christ present, freely revealing himself, unique, beneficent, God and man, proved by miracles.*[200]

---

tion of John 8:25 in his Johannine commentary on this verse, it is clear that he presupposes it. In sum, in the five times he uses John 8:25 in his commentary on Luke's Gospel Bonaventure supplies *ego* ("I"), so that his listeners and readers will know that Jesus is the beginning: "I am the beginning who is speaking to you."

[199] On p. 299, n. 4 QuarEd indicate that Psalm 71 bears the title *In Salomonem* ("about Solomon").

[200] On p. 299, n. 7 QuarEd mention that Cardinal Hugh proposes the same seven preeminent characteristics. See Hugh of St. Cher, p. 203v, n: "For seven reasons the queen of the South condemns the Jews. First, because she is a woman, and they are men. Second, be-

68. (Verse 32). Thirdly, the generation of Jews is accused because it is *frigid in repenting* where the text says: *the men of Nineveh will rise up in the judgment with this generation and will condemn it* and will do so on account of their repentance and the impenitence of the Jews. For through a comparison with those who are better they are accused of being less good. – For which reason the text continues: *For they repented at the preaching*[201] *of Jonah*. Jonah 3:5 reads: "The men of Nineveh believed in the Lord[202] and proclaimed a fast and put on sackcloth." And this despite the fact that Jonah was unknown to them and had preached for a few days. Furthermore, he was merely human and had performed no miracle. – But Christ showed greater things than these to the Jews. Therefore, the text adds: *And behold, a greater than Jonah is here.* For Christ was not only man, but also and truly God, which he showed by the magnitude of his miracles. He did not preach for a few days, but for three years. Therefore, the hardness of the unbelieving Jews is greatly condemned. So Chrysostom says: "Within three days the Ninevites became God's people, although they had not had prophets. Within the three days of the crucifixion the Jews became the people

---

cause she came from afar, and they had him present. Third, because she came with difficulty and spent much, and they had him revealed free of charge. Fourth, because she left her kingdom, and there are in their own land. Fifth, because she came with gifts, and they denied the beneficence of Christ. Sixth, because she came to a mere man, and they came to God and man. Seventh, because she knew Solomon by reputation only, and they despised the one approved by many miracles."

[201] On p. 299, n. 8 QuarEd correctly indicate that the Vulgate reads *ad praedicationem* ("at the preaching") whereas Bonaventure has *in praedicatione* ("at the preaching"), a reading he shares with Hugh of St. Cher, Blessed Albert, St. Thomas, and Lyranus.

[202] The Vulgate has *in Deo* ("in God").

of the devil. The former escaped imminent vengeance; the latter have suffered the most atrocious vengeance."[203]

69. It is thus clear how the error of the Jews, who were seeking signs to test him, is exposed by these examples, so that they might not remain in the hardness of their non-belief. Now the Jews, who were heeding the Law and the Prophets and were seeing Christ and not believing in him, are being censured by means of the comparison with the queen of Sheba and the Ninevites. Thus clerics and learned men can be censured in comparison with women and lay people. For the clerics perceive Christ in the Scriptures and touch him with their

---

[203] On p. 299, n. 9 QuarEd refer to Chrysostom's Homily 30 on Matthew 12:41 (*Opus Imperfectum*). A comparison with the actual text of Chrysostom's Homily 30 in PG 56:789 and the text of Chrysostom quoted by Hugh of St. Cher, p. 203v, f indicates that Bonaventure was probably indebted to Hugh for his quotation of Chrysostom. The *Opus Imperfectum* reads: *Illi, qui semper fuerunt populus diaboli, intra dies tres facti sunt populus Dei; isti, qui semper videbantur populus Dei, intra dies tres, crucifixo Christo, facti sunt populus satanae. Et illi quidem personam ignorantes, et rem incredibilem audientes, et conversionis suae signa et virtutes quaerere debuerunt ab eo, quibus et persona idonea praedicantis et praedicationis indubitabilis veritas monstraretur* ("These, who were always the people of the devil, became the people of God within three days. The others, who always seemed to be the people of God, Christ having been crucified, became the people of Satan. And those, who truly did not know the person and were hearing an incredible thing, should have asked him for signs and miracles before they converted. To the others were shown a person suitably equipped to preach and the truth of indubitable preaching"). Hugh's text reads: *Chr. Ninivitae intra tres dies facti sunt populus Dei, qui tamen prophetas non habuerunt, Judaei intra tres dies crucifixionis Domini, facti sunt populus diaboli. Illi evaserunt vindictam imminentem, isti pertulerunt atrocissimam* ("Chr. Within three days the Ninevites became God's people, although they had not had prophets. Within the three days of the crucifixion of the Lord the Jews became the people of the devil. The former escaped imminent vengeance; the latter have suffered the most atrocious vengeance").

hands in the Sacraments, and nevertheless believe in him and venerate him less than women and lay people.[204] So now we can say what Matthew 21:31 has: "The publicans and harlots are going before you," etc.[205] And again Augustine in his Book of Confessions states: "The unlearned are seizing heaven, and we with our learning are being submerged in hell."[206] – By these examples all Christians can also be censured, for they are tardy in hearing the word of God and doing penance for their sins. To excuse themselves, they demand the signs of miracles, when, however, they have before their eyes Christ crucified, so that Galatians 3:1 can be said to them: "O foolish Galatians! Who has bewitched you to not obey the truth, before whose eyes Christ has been ordained among you as crucified?"[207] – So possessing and seeing the sign of the cross of Christ, we must not be

---

[204] See the similar comments by Hugh of St. Cher, p. 203v, r: "Morally. Clerics are designated by the Jews, and women and lay people by the queen and the Ninevites. The latter come from a great distance with much labor to hear sermons, but the former, who are present on the spot, contemn them. Wherefore, Chrysostom says: 'The queen of the South will rise up with Christians and will condemn them, for she came from the ends of the earth, and Christians don't want to come from their homes or from the streets, where they are loitering, to hear Christ. Further, many leave the church where Christ is teaching, and offend Christ, the only teacher.'"

[205] Matthew 21:31b reads: "Jesus said to them: 'Amen I say to you, the publicans and harlots are entering the kingdom of God before you.'"

[206] On p. 299, n. 11 QuarEd cite Book VIII, chapter 8, n. 19 of Augustine's *Confessions*: "The unlearned are rising up and are seizing heaven. And we with our learning, but without a heart, behold, where we are rolling around in flesh and blood." The last words of Bonaventure's "quotation" diverge considerably from Augustine's text.

[207] Bonaventure's text of Galatians 3:1 is unique because it reads "Christ" alone rather than "Jesus Christ" and follows two variant readings, to wit, "to not obey the truth" and "has been ordained." See Vulgate, p. 1804. A translation of the standard Vulgate text is: "O foolish Galatians! Who has bewitched you, before whose eyes Jesus Christ has been depicted as crucified?"

like the Jews: *reluctant* in believing, *lukewarm* in listening, and *frigid* in repenting and doing good in comparison to the queen of the South and the Ninevites, lest we be condemned by the Lord.

Luke 11:33–54
CHRIST REFUTES THE FALLACY OF THE HYPOCRITES

70. *No one lights a lamp*, etc. After the Savior has confuted the fallacy of the blasphemers and unbelievers or tempters, he confutes in this section *the fallacy of the hypocrites*. Now this section has two parts. In the first *he commends the simplicity of a right intention*. In the second, however, *he confutes the deceitfulness of wicked hypocrisy* where verse 37 reads: *And after he had spoken, a Pharisee asked him,*[208] etc.

So in *commending the simplicity of a right intention*, he introduces three matters, namely, *a rational similitude, an adaptation of the similitude*, and *praiseworthy instruction*.

Luke 11:33–36
CHRIST COMMENDS THE SIMPLICITY OF A RIGHT INTENTION

71. (Verse 33). So first, *a rational similitude* is introduced where the text has: *No one lights a lamp and puts it in a hidden place nor under a bushel. Lamp* means a carrier of light or a vessel containing light, and is either material or spiritual, but not hidden. For a material lamp that is hidden does not give off light, but is entirely useless.

---

[208] On p. 300, n. 6 QuarEd correctly mention that the Vulgate reads *illum* ("him") while Bonaventure has *eum* ("him").

But something similar does not occur with a spiritual lamp. So Sirach 20:32–33 says: "Wisdom that is hidden, and treasure that is not seen, what profit is there in them both? Better is the man who hides his folly than the person who hides his wisdom."[209] And therefore, this lamp must not be hidden, but must be manifested. – So the text continues: *but upon the lamp stand,* namely, he places it, *so that they who enter in may see the light.* Now the higher the lamps are placed, the much more brightly do they shine. And therefore, they must be placed *upon the lamp stand* as upon an elevated place, according to the vision of Zechariah 4:2: "I have looked, and behold, a golden lamp stand...and the seven lights thereof upon it."[210]

72. (Verse 34). Secondly, there is *the adaptation of the similitude* where the text says: *The lamp of your body is your eye.* For the corporal eye is the lamp of *the material body,* because it rules, directs, and illumines the entire body. But the spiritual eye, that is, the intention, is the lamp of *the spiritual body,* that is, the congeries of good works.[211] For the intention is said to be *eye* and *lamp.*

---

[209] Bonaventure used this same quotation in his commentary on Luke 8:16 (#23) above. Bonaventure differs most significantly from the Vulgate of Sirach 20:33 in that he has the singular ("man") whereas the Vulgate has the plural ("they"). See the parallel in Sirach 41:18: "Better is the man who hides his folly than the man who hides his wisdom."

[210] The full pertinent text of Zechariah 4:2 reads: "I have looked, and behold a golden lamp stand, and its lamp upon the top of it, and the seven lights thereof upon it."

[211] On p. 300, n. 7 QuarEd provide three very useful parallels. They quote the Glossa Interlinearis: "*The lamp of your body,* that is, of all your actions, *is your eye,* that is, the intention of your mind." They also quote the Glossa Interlinearis on Matthew 6:22 where *the entire body* is called "the congeries of virtues or all one's actions." Their most important parallel is to Book II of Augustine's *De Sermone Domini in Monte,* chapter 13, n. 45. I quote the salient passage from

Eye, in as far as it is illumined by God for the direction of the entire person. *Lamp*, in as far as it directs every action, thought, and affection, as though "it is directing on the way of peace" the steps of the person and shining "on those who sit in darkness and in the shadow of death," according to Luke 1:79 above. – For it is the property of a lamp to illumine, and therefore, the word of God is said to be *a lamp*, according to the Psalmist: "Your word is a lamp to my feet and a light to my paths" (118:105). With regard to *things to be believed*. 2 Peter 1:19 has: "We have the word of prophecy, surer still, to which you do well to attend, as to a lamp shining in a dark place." With regard to *things to be done* because of commandments. Proverbs 6:23 reads: "The commandment is a lamp, and the law a light." *The preacher* is said to be *a lamp*.[212] John 5:35 says: "He was the lamp, burning and shining." Philippians 2:15 states: "Among these you shine like stars in the world." It is said to be *the gift of the Holy Spirit*. Exodus 25:37 has: "You shall also make seven lamps and set them upon the lamp stand," that is, the seven gifts of the Holy Spirit upon Christ. It is also said to be *a work*. Luke 12:35 below reads: "Let your loins be girt about and your

---

the translation of Denis J. Kavanagh, *Saint Augustine: Commentary on the Lord's Sermon on the Mount with Seventeen Related Sermons,* FC 11 (New York: Fathers of the Church, 1951), 153–154: "Therefore, in this passage (Matthew 6:22–23) we ought to understand the eye as the intention with which we perform all our actions. If this intention be pure and upright and directing its gaze where it ought to be directed, then, unfailingly, all our works are good works, because they are performed in accordance with that intention. And by the expression, *'whole body,'* he designated all those works, for the Apostle also designates certain works as our *'members* – works which he reproves and which he orders us to mortify."

[212] On p. 300, n. 10 QuarEd cite Book XXX chapter 25, n. 77 of Gregory's *Moralia*: "Now by lamp the light of preaching is meant."

lamps burning."[213] It is also said to be *the intention*, which, if it is *deceitful*, is extinguished, according to what Job 18:6 states: "The light will be dark in his tabernacle, and the lamp that is over him, will be extinguished." But if it is *just*, it illumines the entire body of good works.[214] – Wherefore, *the lamp*, first of all, fittingly refers to *the word of God* and *the gift of the Holy Spirit*. And through this it appropriately refers to *the intention of the heart*, and from there descends in *the eloquence* of true preaching and in *the work* of a holy way of life. So it is applied to these according to a certain type of analogy. Thus, *the light of a just intention* operates in the middle, accepting things from the superior and reverberating in the entire congeries of deeds.[215]

73. For which reason he adds: *If your eye be simple*, that is, the just intention, *your whole body will be full of light*. For as Ambrose says: "Intention stamps its name on your work."[216] From this it is clear that he understands *the eye of the heart*, whose most laudable disposition is *simplicity*, according to what 1 Chronicles 29:17 has: "I know, O Lord, that you test hearts and love simplicity." Now an eye is said to be *simple* that intends a single, highest, and indivisible good. So it is said of Job in Job 1:1 that "he was a man, simple and upright." And such people love God, according to what The Song of Songs

---

[213] On p 300, n. 12 QuarEd refer to Book XXVIII chapter 3, n. 12 of Gregory's *Moralia* and to Homily 13, n. 1 of GGHG.

[214] On p. 300, n. 13 QuarEd refer to Book XIV chapter 8, n. 10 of Gregory's *Moralia*.

[215] In #72 Bonaventure is indebted to Hugh of St. Cher, p. 204a, who interprets "the lamp" as the word of God, preachers, John, one's intention, gifts of the Holy Spirit, works, empty glory, prosperity. Hugh also uses most of the same scripture quotations that Bonaventure does.

[216] On p. 301, n. 2 QuarEd refer to Book I, chapter 30, n. 147 of Ambrose's *De Officiis*.

1:3 states: "the upright love you." And the Song of Songs 4:9 reads: "You have wounded my heart, my sister, my spouse . . . with one of your eyes and with one hair of your neck," that is, in the unity and simplicity of an upright intention, which alone pleases God. And since such people do whatever they do *out of charity*, everything is upright and good and shining, according to what Ephesians 5:8–9 has: "Walk as children of the light. But the fruit of the light is in all goodness and justice and truth." And since nothing proceeds from a heart thus illumined *except works of light*, as "a good tree cannot produce bad fruit," nor light darkness, nor contrariwise a bad tree produce good fruit.[217]

74. And therefore, he adds: *But if it be evil, your entire*[218] *body will be full of darkness.* For an evil eye corrupts the will and makes it evil. But once it has been corrupted, its works are also corrupt. Therefore, Sirach 14 reads: "The evil of the envious is wicked, and he turns away his face," namely, from God "and despises his own soul" (verse 8). And a little later Sirach 14:10 has: "An evil eye is toward evil things." So when the intention is corrupted, it deviates from the way of light and stumbles in the darkness, according to Sirach 11:16: "Error and darkness are created for sinners." Since the intention is darkened and corrupted, the deed is darkened and corrupted. So the Glossa comments: "If the intention that precedes an action is perverse, an evil deed follows, even though it seems to be just."[219] And so it is said that *the body is full*

---

[217] Bonaventure has an incomplete sentence here as he seems to have gotten caught up in interpreting Luke 11:34 by means of Matthew 7:18.

[218] On p. 301, n. 5 QuarEd accurately indicate that the Vulgate does not read *totum* ("entire").

[219] On p. 301, n. 7 QuarEd quote the Glossa Interlinearis (from Bede) on Luke 11:34: "If the intention that precedes is perverse, an evil

of darkness, which indeed is the work of sin. About this Romans 13:12 says: "Let us lay aside the works of darkness." – In this way, therefore, the similitude of the lamp is being adapted. Just as the lamp upon the lamp stand is bright and the one under the measure is dark and just as no one, having lighted a lamp, "puts it under the measure, but upon the lamp stand," so the simple intention directed upwards is bright and the intention directed downwards is crooked, evil, and dark. Therefore, people must not proceed in their actions with duplicity and hypocrisy, but rather with light and with simplicity of intention. For Proverbs 11:5 reads: "The justice of the upright will direct his way, and the wicked will fall by his own wickedness."

75. (Verse 35). In third place is *praiseworthy instruction*. The text reads: *Take care, therefore, that the light in you is not darkness*, that is, lest the intention through which you must be light be obscured by the darkness of vices. Now he is addressing those who have converted to him. About these the Apostle says in Ephesians 5:8: "You were once darkness, but now you are light in the Lord. Walk, then, as children of the light," so that you may be children of that light "that enlightens every person coming into this world" (John 1:9). Do not be *children of those people*, about whom John 3:19 says: "The light has come into the world, and people loved the darkness rather than the light. For their works were evil." Therefore, since an evil intention corrupts the entire work, he teaches that it is specially to be avoided and says: *Take care*, etc.[220]

---

deed will follow, even if sometimes it seems to be just." See CCSL cxx, p. 239 for Bede's opinion that the Glossa follows quite faithfully.
[220] On p. 301, n. 9 QuarEd cite the Glossa Interlinearis on Luke 11:35: "The intention itself, which is the light of the soul, is blackened by the vices of darkness."

76. (Verse 36). But again, since *the intention* cannot be full of light, unless a good *action* is present, the text adds: *If, then, your entire body is full of light, having no part in darkness,* namely, with the result that there is no wickedness in intention nor in thought nor in affection nor in speech nor in action, which are parts of our total being and of our meritorious or blameworthy conduct. – So if in these there is no impurity from any quarter, what follows will be true: *it will all be illumined, as when a bright lamp illumines you,* that is, your conscience, according to the prophetic plea: "Since you illumine my lamp, O Lord, my God, illumine my darkness," according to what Psalm 17:29 has.[221] God will also enlighten you *to build up the church of Christ,* according to the commandment of the Lord in Matthew 5:16: "So let your light shine before men and women that they may see your good works and give glory to your Father, who is in the heavens."[222] God will also enlighten you *to confute the wickedness of another,* according to what Philippians 2:15–16 has: "Be . . . blameless . . . in the midst of a depraved and perverse generation, among whom you shine like stars in the world, holding fast to the word of life." God will also enlighten you *to have divine knowledge,* according to what Sirach 2:10 says: "You who fear the Lord, love him, and your hearts will be enlightened." God will also enlighten you *to see divine glory.* Tobit 13:13 reads: "You will shine with a glorious light," etc.

---

[221] On p. 302, n. 1 QuarEd cite the Glossa Interlinearis (from Bede): ". . . if you do good with a good intention, not having on your conscience any trace of an evil thought." For Bede's original see CCSL cxx, p. 240.

[222] On p. 302, n. 2 QuarEd cite the Glossa Interlinearis (from Bede): ". . . You will be gifted with the gift of light both here and in the future." This is a verbatim quotation from Bede, but occurs as the last words of an eight-line long conditional sentence. See CCSL cxx, p. 240.

Luke 11:37–54
CHRIST CONFUTES THE DECEITFULNESS OF WICKED HYPOCRISY

77. *Now after he had spoken, a Pharisee asked him to dine*, etc. After the Evangelist had commended the simplicity of an upright intention, in this part *he confutes the deceitfulness of wicked hypocrisy*. Now this part has two sections. The first part deals with *a rebuke of duplicity*. The second concerns *the threat of misfortune* where verse 42 says: *Woe to you, Pharisees*, etc. – Concerning *the rebuke of duplicity* three things are mentioned. First is *the wickedness of Jewish hypocrisy*. Second is *the severity of the rebuke*. Third is *the gentleness of a loving admonition*.

Luke 11:37–41
CHRIST REBUKES DUPLICITY

78. (Verse 37). So first, with regard to *the wickedness of duplicity* on the part of the Pharisees the text says: *Now after he had spoken, a Pharisee asked him to dine with him.* By doing this, he displayed an exterior piety in relieving the need of Christ, about which he himself says in the Psalm: "But I am a beggar and poor" (39:18). To relieve his hunger Christ accepted alms, not only accepted, but also begged, even when he was still twelve years old, as Bernard says in a certain Sermon: "When Jesus was twelve years old," etc. Bernard asks: Who gave Jesus food during the three days and answers: "So that you might take on all the misfortunes of human life and might conform yourself to our poverty in everything, you were begging alms at the gates as one of a crowd of the poor. Who will allow me to share in those morsels you begged or to be fed with the leftovers of that divine

food?"[223] 2 Corinthians 8:9 reads: "He became poor for us," etc.[224] The Glossa on that passage has: "Don't be ashamed in your mendicancy to approach him who became poor for us."[225] So to alleviate his neediness he accepted alms not only from good people, but also from bad ones. Whence the text continues: *And he went in and reclined at table.* – By doing this, he gave us a lesson that private sinners are not to be avoided. And that alms may be licitly accepted from evil people, so that they may become good, provided that they do not give these from someone else's property or from things wrongfully acquired. And that sinners are to be won over by benevolence.[226] And that we must be gracious to our enemies and detractors as Christ was with the person with him at table, although he knew in his heart that he despised and condemned him.

79. (Verse 38). For which reason the text continues: *But the Pharisee began to reflect within himself and say*, that

---

[223] On p. 302, n. 8 QuarEd provide clues for tracking down the source of this quotation about Luke 2:42. See *Aelredi Abbatis Rievallis Tractatus de Jesu Puero Duodenni*, n. 6 in PL 184:853D–854A. Aelred's treatise is found among the works of St. Bernard of Clairvaux. Bonaventure's quotation is almost verbatim.

[224] On p. 302, n. 9 QuarEd correctly state that the Vulgate reads *propter vos* ("for your sake") rather than Bonaventure's *pro vobis* ("for you").

[225] On p. 302, n. 9 QuarEd cite the Glossa Ordinaria: "Therefore, don't be ashamed in your mendicancy to approach him, who, clothed in our poverty when he made himself poor, enriched us." They also refer to Augustine's Sermon 36, chapter 2, n. 3–4.

[226] On p. 302, n. 10 QuarEd have called my attention to a parallel in Hugh of St. Cher, p. 204v, c where he raises the question of whether Jesus was going against his own teaching in Matthew 10b[13] that his disciples should only remain with someone who is worthy. Hugh gives three responses: "First, so that he might give an example that alms, which are necessary for life, can be accepted from evil people. Second, because he was not openly evil. Third, that some were to be become better on account of his presence."

is, to search after the reason and cause, *why he had not baptized*,²²⁷ that is, washed according to the Jewish custom, *before dinner*, and because of this he judged him to be unclean and a person who held the ancestral traditions in contempt. So similarly the Pharisees are said to have objected to the Lord and his disciples in Matthew 15:2: "Why do your disciples transgress the tradition of the elders? For they do not wash their hands when they take food." Now this was important to the Jews. Therefore, it is said in Mark 7:3–4: "But the Pharisees and all the Jews do not eat without frequently washing their hands, maintaining the tradition of the elders. And when they come from the market, they do not eat without washing first." And the reason for this was that they placed the greatest emphasis on preserving bodily cleanliness. Wherefore, from this a twofold hypocrisy is shown in the Pharisee. First, because he was impiously judging internally the person whose bodily needs he was piously taking care of externally. Second, because he was zealous for bodily cleanliness and did not attend to spiritual cleanliness. And therefore, he was a hypocrite both in the sight of human beings and God. Against his action Sirach 1:36–37 says: "Come not to the Lord with a double heart, and don't be a hypocrite in the sight of human beings."

80. (Verse 39). Second, relative to *the severity of the rebuke* on the part of the Teacher, the text adds: *And the Lord said to him: Now you Pharisees clean the outside of the cup and dish. Cup* is a vessel for drinking, *dish* one for eating. And the Pharisees and the Jews especially cleaned these vessels, for they thought that they would defile themselves through the uncleanness of vessels. So

---

²²⁷ I have retained this literal rendition of *baptizatus*, so that Bonaventure's explanatory clause will make greater sense.

it is said in Mark 7:4 that "many things have been handed down to them to observe: washing of cups and pots and copper vessels." Indeed, since, as Ambrose says: "The cup is a glass vessel, and the dish an earthen one."[228] And since both are easily broken, they rightfully designate the fragility of the human body. About such fragility the Pharisees are especially intent, having neglected a clean conscience. And this was reprehensible. For it is said in Isaiah 1:16: "Wash yourselves. Be clean. Remove the evil of your devices from my eyes."[229] And Jeremiah 4:14 reads: "Wash your heart from wickedness, O Jerusalem, that you may be saved." This the Pharisees did not observe. – For which reason the text adds: *But within you are full of robbery and wickedness*, and therefore, unclean and abominable. So what Micah 6:12 has might be said of them: "Her rich men were filled with iniquity, and those who lived within her were telling lies." Sirach 1:40 states: "You have come to the Lord wickedly, and your heart is full of guile and deceit."[230] For you simulate outside what you do not have inside. And this is not only *wickedness*, but also *foolishness*. For, having neglected the better things of the human person, they paid attention only to the worse.

81. (Verse 40). So the text continues: *Foolish ones! Did not he who made the outside*, namely, the body, *also*

---

[228] On p. 303, n. 3 QuarEd cite the Glossa Ordinaria: "*Cup*, glass vessel; *dish*, earthen from the earth. Through this the fragility of the human body is symbolized, through which they pretend holiness and simulate justice. They washed what was outside, but were most wicked inside." See CCSL xiv, p. 248 for Ambrose's comments which are distantly related to those of the Glossa.

[229] Hugh of St. Cher, p. 204v, g also cites Isaiah 1:16.

[230] On p. 303, n. 5 QuarEd cite the Glossa Interlinearis: "*Now you, Pharisees, what is outside*, etc., You preserve externally the cleanness of the flesh. *But what is inside you*, etc., you retain the turpitude of the soul."

make what[231] *is inside?*, namely, the spirit. At the same
time *the heresy of the Manichees* is condemned, who attributed the spirit to God as its creator, and the body to
the devil, even though it is said in Genesis 2:7 that "the
Lord God formed man of the slime of the earth and
breathed into his face the breath of life."[232] *The hypocrisy
of the Pharisees* is also confuted, who were busily
pleasing God through the purification of the body alone,
although the Lord had made both, and was specially the
creator of the soul, according to what Qoheleth12:7 says:
"The spirit returns to God, who gave it." And the Lord
gives himself the principal name of *God of souls*. Ezekiel
18:4 states: "All souls are mine, says the Lord, as the
soul of the father, so also the soul of the son is mine."
And therefore, his chief desire is the cleanness of the
souls. And to such he promises his presence, according
to what Matthew 5:8 has: "Blessed are the clean of
heart, for they will see God." And so the Pharisees, who
did not care about this, were like fools. So Chrysostom
says: "God does not praise the cleanness of bodies nor
condemn dirt. Nevertheless, if you accept as true that
God hates dirt on vessels, how much more does he hate
dirt on consciences?"[233] Therefore, capital attention must
be given to this: without a clean conscience nothing is
clean. Titus 1:15 reads: "All things are clean for the

---

[231] On p. 303, n. 6 QuarEd correctly mention that the Vulgate reads
id quod ("that which").

[232] On p. 303, n. 6 QuarEd call their attention to Bede's comments.
See CCSL cxx, p. 241: "The one, he says, who created both natures of
humans, desires both to be cleaned. This against the Manichees, who
maintain that only the soul was created by God, but that the flesh by
the devil."

[233] On p. 303, n. 8 QuarEd cite the pertinent section of Chrysostom's
Homily 44 on Matthew 23:25 (*Opus Imperfectum*) and indicate that
Bonaventure's quotation omits some words. Bonaventure's quotation
of Chrysostom, however, is almost verbatim with that found in Hugh
of St. Cher, p. 204v, f.

clean. However, for the defiled and unbelieving nothing is clean, but their minds and consciences are defiled."

82. (Verse 41). Thirdly, with regard to *the gentleness of the admonition* on the part of the physician the text adds: *Nevertheless, give that which remains as alms. What remains,* that is, the remedy that is left to be done, so that through *alms you may purge your iniquity.* "For penance is the second plank that is left after shipwreck."[234] – And in this sense *alms* is to be taken here. This is clear from what follows: *And*[235] *all things will be clean for you.* It is impossible that all things be made clean through the distribution of one single external alms. What is called here a gift of alms is *whatever work of mercy that is ordained by rank,* which first begins with the person himself, according to what Sirach 30:24 has: "Have mercy on your own soul, pleasing God."[236]

---

[234] On p. 303, n. 10 QuarEd refer to Jerome's Letter 130, n. 9.

[235] On p. 303, n. 11 QuarEd rightly mention that the Vulgate has *et ecce* ("and behold").

[236] Hugh of St. Cher, p. 204v, k has the same quotation. The combination of *ordinare/ordinate* ("to ordain by rank") and Sirach 30:24 is often found in discussions of almsgiving. See Rabanus Maurus, *Liber secundus De Clericorum Institutione,* chapter 28 in PL 107:340CD; Bede, CCSL cxx, p. 242 on Luke 11:41: *Qui enim uult ordinate dare elemosinam a se ipso debet incipere et eam sibi primum dare. Est enim elemosina opus misericordiae uerissimeque dictum est: Miserere animae tuae, placens Deo. . . .* ("For the person who wants to give alms in a manner ordained by rank must begin with himself and give alms to himself first of all. For almsgiving is a work of mercy in the most true sense: Have mercy on your own soul, pleasing God. . . . "). Gunther, *De Oratione, Jejunio et Eleemosyna,* Liber Tertius Decimus: De Eleemosyna, chapter 1 in PL 212:210D has only the quotation from Sirach 30:24. The Latin word *ordinare/ordinate* is almost a technical term in discussions of almsgiving. Authors do not want to give the impression that a person may commit murder and gain the effects of almsgiving by a mere external one-time act. Repentance and personal conversion must rank first. See the superb statement by Rabanus Maurus in PL 107:340D: "Therefore, a person

People bestow this mercy on themselves when they purge themselves from vices through penance. For otherwise they are cruel to themselves, according to the Psalm: "The person who loves iniquity hates his own soul" (10:6).[237] – Another interpretation looks at alms *properly so called* and takes *Give that which remains as alms* to mean "from what is left over." This interpretation addresses *the form* of alms in accordance with 2 Corinthians 8:13: "I do not mean that the relief of others should become your burden."[238] And after treating the form of alms, the text goes on to mention its *efficacy*: *And all things are clean to you*, for alms disposes one to grace, by which the entire soul is made clean. And for this reason it is said in 1 Timothy 4:8: "Compassion[239] is profitable in all respects, since it has the promise of the present life as well as of that which is to come."

83. Now although it may be said that *alms are profitable for three things* principally, Scripture shows that alms have a *sevenfold* efficacy.[240] First, because *it cleanses*

---

exercises the art of mercy well and in a manner ordained by rank who does not permit himself to be lacking in good works and a holy way of life and the fruits of virtues, and then in as far as possible, either in spiritual things or in bodily things, does not stop helping his neighbors."

[237] On p. 303, n. 12 QuarEd refer to a parallel in Augustine's Sermon 106, chapter 3, n. 4.

[238] This passage occurs in Paul's appeal to the Corinthians to give from their surplus to aid the poor Christians in Jerusalem. Hugh of St. Cher, p. 204v, i has the same quotation.

[239] In the Pastoral Epistles *pietas* is normally translated as "godliness," but Bonaventure seems to quote 1 Timothy 4:8 for one specific meaning of *pietas*, namely, "compassion" to those in need.

[240] There are many parallels between what Bonaventure lists as "seven effects" and what Hugh of St. Cher calls "multiple effects" and goes on to list twelve. See Hugh of St. Cher, pp. 204v-205k. If I compare Bonaventure's seven effects with Hugh of St. Cher's twelve effects, I arrive at the following results: Bonaventure's 1 = Hugh's 4; B 2 = H 2; B 3 = H 3; B 4 = H 5; B 5 = H 7; B 6 = H 6; B 7 = H 12.

from sin, as the present passage shows. And Sirach
3:15–17 states: "Alms given to a father will not be forgotten. . . . Your sins will melt away like ice in warm
weather." – Second, because *it frees from eternal punishment*. Tobit 4:11 reads: "Alms deliver from all sin and
from death and does not suffer[241] the soul to go into
darkness." – Third, because *it delivers from transitory*[242]
punishment. Daniel 4:24 says: "Redeem your sins with
alms."[243] – Fourth, because *it mitigates the desire of evil
concupiscence*. Sirach 3:33 reads: "Water quenches a
flaming fire, and alms resist sins."[244] – Fifth, because *it
grants victory over the enemy*. Sirach 29:15–17 states:
"Shut up alms in the heart of the poor, and these will
address God earnestly on your behalf. . . . They will
fight against your enemy better than the shield of the
mighty and the spear."[245] – Sixth, because *it preserves
grace*, according to what Sirach 17:18 has: "The alms of
a man are like a purse on his person, and will preserve
the grace of a man like the apple of his eye."[246] – Seventh, because *it provides assurance of arriving to glory*.
Tobit 4:12 says: "Alms will be a great assurance before
the most high God to those who give them." – These
seven effects are those of alms, which are manifested
both *bodily* and *spiritually*.

---

[241] On p. 304, n. 4 QuarEd correctly mention that the Vulgate reads
patietur ("will not suffer").
[242] One would expect "eternal" to be balanced by "temporal," but
Bonaventure writes *transitoria*.
[243] Daniel 4:24 reads in its entirety: "Wherefore, O king, let my counsel be acceptable to you, and redeem your sins with alms and your
iniquities with works of mercy to the poor. Perhaps, he will forgive
your offences."
[244] Hugh of St. Cher, p. 204v, h has the same quotation.
[245] In the modern edition of the Vulgate Sirach 29 does not have
verses 16–17. That is, Bonaventure is quoting from the Vulgate of
Sirach 29:15 and 18.
[246] Bonaventure uses this same quotation in his commentary on Luke
6:11 (#23) above.

84. The works of *bodily mercy*[247] are designated by this verse: "I visit. I give to drink. I give to eat. I liberate. I clothe. I invite into my house. I bury."[248] These actions, with the exception of the last, are examined at the judgment in Matthew 25:31–46. But the last one is treated in Tobit 2:1–9. – Now for alms to have these effects, *simplicity in heart* is necessary first of all.[249] So Matthew 6:3 says: "But when you give alms, don't let your left hand know," etc. – Second, *discernment in selection*, according to what Sirach 12:1 has: "If you are doing good, know to whom you are doing it." – Third, *compassion in affection*. Isaiah 58:10 reads: "When you pour out your soul to the hungry . . . then will your light rise up in darkness." And Job 30:25 states: "I formerly wept for the person who was afflicted, and my soul had compassion on the poor." – Fourth, *gentleness in speech*. Sirach 18:16 says: "Will not the dew assuage the heat? So also a good word is better than a gift." – Fifth, *cheerfulness on the face*. Sirach 35:11 has: "In every gift show a cheerful countenance." The Psalmist states: "Happy is the person who shows mercy," (111:5). – Sixth, *a gift of a fitting quantity*. Tobit 4:8–9 reads: "According to your ability be merciful. If you have much, give abundantly," etc.[250] – Seventh, *speed in performing the deed* and displaying it. Proverbs 3:28 has: "Do not say to your friend:

---

[247] Our contemporary argot is "corporal works of mercy."

[248] The Latin is: *Visito, poto, cibo, redimo, tego, colligo, condo.* Hugh of St. Cher, p. 204v, k has this same verse and goes on to give a scripture citation for each verb.

[249] In #84 Bonaventure is heavily indebted to Hugh of St. Cher, p. 205A (top left column). Hugh begins his exposition with: "Now there are many things that adorn alms. The first is compassion of heart. Isaiah 58:10 says...." If one follows Bonaventure's numbering of the seven conditions and applies it to the seven adornments of Hugh of St. Cher, this sequence results: 3, 4, 5, 6, 2, 7, 1.

[250] Tobit 4:9 concludes with: ". . . if you have little, take care even so to bestow willingly a little."

Go and come back again," etc.[251] – And then alms has its source in the entire person, and therefore, is acceptable and pleasing to God.[252]

Luke 11:42–54
THE THREAT OF MISFORTUNE

85. *But woe to you Pharisees*, etc. After the rebuke against duplicity *a threat of misfortune* is added here against hypocrites and the double-minded. In Matthew 23:13–39 this further determination is added: "Woe to you, scribes and Pharisees, hypocrites!" And since these two types of persons, namely, the Pharisees and the scribes, feign religion in a special way, he launches his attack against these two groups. In Matthew he attacks both together whereas here he distinguishes between the two. So this section has two parts. In the first part the threat of *woe is made against the Pharisees* themselves. In the second against *the scribes* or lawyers where verse 45 reads: *but one of the lawyers, answering, said*, etc.

Now *the threat* of eternal damnation is thrice voiced against *the Pharisees* for a threefold reason, namely, on account of *negligence, arrogance*, and *fraudulence*, for there was *negligence* in the omission of good, *arrogance* in the commission of evil, *fraudulence* in the occultation of evil and the manifestation of good.

---

[251] Proverbs 3:28 concludes with: ". . . and tomorrow I will give to you, when you can give at the present moment."

[252] On p. 304, n. 12 QuarEd engage in understatement: "Cardinal Hugh has something similar." For even greater detail of Bonaventure's borrowing from Hugh as both exegete Luke 11:41, see Robert J. Karris, "Bonaventure's Commentary of Luke: Four Case Studies of his Creative Borrowing from Hugh of St. Cher," *Franciscan Studies* 59 (2001): 163-181, 230-232.

Luke 11:42–44
WOES AGAINST THE PHARISEES

86. (Verse 42). So first, *the Pharisees* are threatened with eternal punishment on account of *negligence*, through which their intention is minimal and their omission maximum. And this, for he says: *But woe to you Pharisees*, who[253] pay tithes on mint and rue and every herb, as if you are greatly intent on fulfilling the divine commandments. Thus in Luke 18:12 below the Pharisee praised himself: "I pay tithes of all that I possess." But, nevertheless, they were not justified by this because they omitted the most important things. Therefore, the text continues: *and disregard all judgment*[254] *and the love of God*, that is, justice and mercy. And this is what God especially requires, according to what Micah 6:8 states: "I will show you, O human, what is good and what the Lord requires of you. Verily, to do judgment and to love mercy." And the text calls this *love*. Zechariah 7:9 has: "Judge with true judgment and show compassion and mercy, each one with his neighbor."[255] Thus, that there be *justice* with regard to oneself, and *love* or mercy relative to one's neighbor. – Another interpretation is that *judgment* refers to the divine *commandment*, according to what the Psalm says: "The commandments of the Lord are true, justified in themselves," etc. (18:10). Then *love* is said to be *the goal of the commandment* and its fulfillment. 1 Timothy 1:5 reads: "The goal of the commandment is love," etc. – Yet

---

[253] On p. 305, n. 1 QuarEd correctly indicate that the Vulgate reads *quia* ("for") rather than *qui* ("who"). They also mention that Cardinal Hugo, Gorranus, and Lyranus read *quia*.

[254] On p. 305, n. 2 QuarEd rightly mention that the Vulgate simply reads *iudicium* ("judgment").

[255] On p. 305, n. 2 QuarEd correctly state that the last words of the Vulgate text are *cum fratre suo* ("with his brother").

another interpretation is that *judgment* refers to *the judicial commandments*, according to what Exodus 21:1 has: "These are the commandments which you are to set before them. If you buy a Hebrew servant," etc. *Love* refers to *the ethical commandments*. Thus, Romans 13:8–9 reads: "The person who loves his neighbor has fulfilled the Law. For...you shall not kill," etc.[256] Therefore, he is rebuking them because they have abandoned *the judicial* and *ethical commandments*, which they should have been greatly solicitous to fulfill, in favor of *the ceremonial commandments*. – And therefore, he adds: *But these things you ought to have done*, namely, justice and love first and foremost. So Hosea 6:6 says: "I desire mercy and not sacrifice, and knowledge of God rather than holocausts." – *while not leaving the others undone*, for, as Sirach 19:1 states, "the person who contemns small matters will fall little by little." And Qoheleth 7:19 has: "The person who fears God neglects nothing."

87. (Verse 43). Second, he asserts this *threat* against *arrogance*, when he adds: *Woe to you Pharisees, because you love the front seats in the synagogues*, with regard to *the ambition to get honors*. Wherefore, the Glossa says: "He rebukes their arrogance, because they were desirous of the first places."[257] But this place of honor is not to be sought after. So Sirach 7:4 states: "Seek not from a human an exalted office nor from the king the seat of

---

[256] Romans 13:9 in its entirety reads: "For you shall not commit adultery. You shall not kill. You shall not steal. You shall not covet. And if there is any other commandment, it is summed up in this saying: You shall love your neighbor as yourself."

[257] On p. 305, n. 6 QuarEd cite The Glossa Interlinearis (from Ambrose): "He rebuked their arrogance, because they are desirous of the first places." See CCSL xiv, p. 249 for Ambrose's text: "He rebuked the arrogance and the vainglory of the Jews, since they are desirous of the first places at a banquet."

honor." For such a seat is not one of true *excellence*, but rather of *pestilence*, according to the Psalm: "Blessed is the man . . . who does not sit in the chair of pestilence" (1:1). But the scribes and the Pharisees were sitting in the chair of honor. Nonetheless, they were unworthy of it, because their words were not matched by fitting actions. So it is said in Matthew 23:2–3: "The scribes and Pharisees have sat on the chair of Moses. Do what they say. Do not act according to their works."[258] – And since *a desire for praise* follows the quest for honor, the text continues: *and greetings in the market place*, that is, praise in the sight of many people, so that they might seem to be more honorable to others. Wherefore, Matthew 23:6–7 reads: "They love greetings in the market place and to be called 'Rabbi' by people." So they are denounced here, for they were seeking vainglory. For the sake of this glory they were not even courageous enough to profess an acknowledged truth, in accordance with what John 12:42–43 says: "Even among the rulers many believed in Jesus, but because of the Pharisees they did not profess it, lest they should be put out of the synagogue. For they loved human glory more than the glory of God." – From this it is clear that we must entirely contemn praise and honors like Christ and not seek them like the Pharisees. From those who love these things, as Jerome says, are not disciples of Christ, but a scribe and a Pharisee.[259] For Christ, when they wanted to make him king, "fled into the mountain," as John 6:15

---

[258] Bonaventure's quotation of Matthew 23:3 is not verbatim. Matthew 23:3 says: "All things, therefore, that they command you, observe and do. But do not act according to their works, for they talk but do nothing."

[259] On p. 305, n. 10 QuarEd cite Book IV of Jerome's commentary on Matthew 23:5: "Therefore, whoever does something like this to be seen by men and women, is a scribe and a Pharisee."

says. When he was being praised, he sought out the desert for prayer, as Luke 5:16 above has.

88. (Verse 44). Third, he repeats *the threat*, but this time against *fraudelence* when he says: *Woe to you, who*[260] *are like monuments whose contents are not apparent*, that is, what kinds of things are inside, because fetid and unclean matters are inside, but on the outside things are beautiful. Wherefore, he adds: *over which people walk unaware*. Such are the hypocrites, who, although they are evil inside, seem to be perfect on the outside. Therefore, it is fitting that they are called *tombs*, according to the Psalmist: "Their throat is an open tomb. They dealt deceitfully with their tongues" (5:11). And so they are not *children of the Bridegroom*, but completely opposed. For The Song of Songs 1:4 reads: "I am black, but beautiful." But these are white, but stink. Thus, they are rightfully called *tombs*. So Matthew 23:27 has: "Woe to you, scribes and Pharisees, hypocrites! For you are like whited sepulchers, which outwardly appear beautiful to people, but within they are full of the bones of the deceased and of all uncleanness." Therefore, Chrysostom says: "The bodies of the righteous are called *temples*, but the bodies of sinners are called *tombs*, for there is a dead soul within. For it should not be considered alive when it has effected nothing living, that is, spiritual, in the body." And a little later Chrysostom continues: "Speak up, O hypocrite, if the good is to be good, why do you not want *to be* what you want *to appear* to be? But what it is shameful *to appear* to be is more shameful *to*

---

[260] The Vulgate reads *quia* ("because") rather than Bonaventure's *qui* ("who").

be. So either be what you appear to be or appear to be what you are."[261]

From these words of the Lord one can gather who are the people who must be judged to be *hypocrites*, that is, those in whom *negligence, arrogance,* and *fraudulence* rule. Now these are those who prefer the minimum to the maximum, the transitory to the eternal, the sham to the authentic. But the prerogative of judging these is not that of any person whatsoever, but of Christ, who looks into the heart, according to what 1 Corinthians 4:5 has: "Do not judge before the time, until the Lord comes, who will bring to light the things hidden in darkness," etc. For the Lord does not reprove obvious and evident goodness, but sophistical and non-existent goodness.

Luke 11:45–54
WOES AGAINST THE LAWYERS

89. *But one of the lawyers, responding,* etc. After having uttered the threat of woe to the Pharisees, here he levels a second woe, against *the lawyers,* and this for three reasons. First, on account of their *slothfulness* against the truth of life. Second, on account of their *perfidy* against the truth of justice where verse 47 reads: *Woe to you, who build the tombs.* Third, on account of their *fallacy* against the truth of teaching where verse 52 has:

---

[261] On p. 306, n. 1 QuarEd refer to Homily 45 on Matthew 23:27 (*Opus Imperfectum*) and indicate that Bonaventure has noticeably abbreviated Chrysostom's text. In this first section of #88 Bonaventure is heavily dependent on Hugh of St. Cher, who also quotes Psalm 5:11, The Song of Songs 1:4, and Chrysostom. See Hugh of St. Cher, p. 205l.

Woe to you, lawyers, who[262] *have taken away the key of knowledge*. For this threefold truth should especially be in teachers of the Law, but in the lawyers there was nothing but hypocrisy.

Therefore, in threatening hell on account of *slothfulness*, he first treats their *show of authority* and then deals with *the threat of disaster*.

90. (Verse 45). So first, concerning *a show of authority* on the part of the lawyer the text says: *But one of the lawyers*, who obviously seemed to himself to be an expert, according to what Isaiah 5:21 says: "Woe to you who are wise in your own eyes and prudent in your own conceits." And since such seem to themselves to be learned and great, they consider it an affront to be rebuked by someone. For which reason the text adds: *Answering, he said to him: Teacher, in saying these things you are insulting us also*. He would not say this, unless he felt in his conscience that he had similarly transgressed. But out of pride he did not want to be rebuked. Wherefore, what Romans 2:19–21 has could be said to him: "You are confident that you are a guide to the blind, a light to those who are in darkness, an instructor of the unwise, a teacher of children....Therefore, you who teach others do not teach yourself?" They think that sound teaching is *an insult*, for, as it is said in Proverbs 18:2, "a fool does not receive the words of wisdom, unless you say the things which are close to his heart." And truly, such a person is foolish who is wont to think himself learned, for Proverbs 26:12 states: "Have you

---

[262] On p. 306, n. 5 QuarEd correctly indicate that the Vulgate reads *quia* ("because") whereas Bonaventure reads *qui* ("who"). They also mention that *qui* is the reading of Hugh of St. Cher, St. Thomas in his *Catena Aurea* on Luke, chapter 11, n. 12, Gorranus, and Lyranus.

seen a man wise in his own conceit? There will be more hope for a fool than for him."

91. (Verse 46). Second, relative to *the threat of disaster* on account of his slothfulness to do good, it is said: *And he said: Woe to you lawyers*, that is, the woe of eternal damnation. And the reason for this is that they say much, but do little. – Therefore, the text continues: *Because you load men and women with burdens, which they cannot bear*, that is, superstitious and useless precepts and traditions, so Acts 15:10 can rightly be said of them: This is a burden "that neither we nor our fathers have been able to bear."[263] Therefore, Matthew 23:4 reads: "They bind together heavy and oppressive burdens and lay them on the shoulders of men and women." That is, burdens that someone is not bound to carry, but they say they are bound. – And because they have imposed these burdens and *teach* them, but do not *carry* them by observing them, the text adds: *And you yourselves do not touch the burdens with one of your fingers.*

92. Note this significant detail that it says: *You do not touch with one of your fingers*. It does not say: *You do not carry*, for such could be the excuse of not being strong enough. Frequently a teacher gives instruction about something that he *cannot* do. Indeed, his teaching is not to be contemned if he *wants* to do something, for the will is reckoned to him as the deed. So 1 Samuel 30:24 states: "Equal will be the portion of him who went down to battle and of him that remained with the burdens of baggage. And they will divide alike." And this is said on behalf of men, who had striven to the point of exhaustion. But it is clear that the person who does not want to raise a finger to the burdens does not want to

---

[263] Hugh of St. Cher, p. 205q also quotes this passage.

engage in any work. And such a person, whether the burden is imposed by a teacher or by a prelate, is entirely reprehensible and is not an imitator of Christ, about whom it is said in Acts 1:1: "Jesus began to do and to teach." Therefore, against these people Deuteronomy 25:13 reads: "You shall not have different weights in your bag."[264] And Proverbs 20:10 says: "Different weights and different measures. Both are abominable before God."[265] But this occurs when a person is merciful to himself and hard on his neighbor or subject. When a person bears nothing, but imposes everything to be borne by others. Whence Chrysostom says: "Do you want to appear to be and to be holy? Be austere in your own life, but benign towards others. Let people hear you commanding little things and doing weighty deeds."[266]

93. (Verse 47). *Woe to you, who build*, etc. After he had rebuked them with a woe for the sin of sloth in not leading a truth-filled life, he launches a second woe against them concerning *the sin of perfidy against the truth of justice*, which transpired in the impious persecution of the just. Two points are made. First, *that sin is shown to be grave*. Second, *the punishment for that sin is grave*.

Therefore, concerning *the gravity of the sin* the text says: *Woe to you, who build the tombs of the prophets,*

---

[264] Deuteronomy 25:13 concludes with: ". . . a greater and a less."

[265] Hugh of St. Cher, p. 205v, a also quotes Deuteronomy 25:13 and Proverbs 20:10.

[266] On p. 307, n. 1 QuarEd refer to Homily 43 on Matthew 23:4 (*Opus Imperfectum*). Hugh of St. Cher, p. 205v, a also quotes this passage and much more of Chrysostom's tirade about priests who impose a harsh penance on penitents in confession: "If God is benign, why should the priest be austere? Do you want to appear holy? Be austere in your own life, but benign towards others. Let people hear you commanding little things and doing weighty deeds."

pretending to be pious in fact, but executing impiety in soul, as their fathers did. – For which reason the text adds: *But your fathers killed them,*[267] namely, as the impious kills the just. Wherefore, in Acts 7:52 Blessed Stephen said: "Which one of the prophets did not your fathers persecute? And they killed those who foretold the coming of the Righteous One." And also these, although they might feign otherwise, were, nonetheless, their imitators.

94. (Verse 48). For which reason he says: *But you truly give witness that you approve of the deeds of your fathers,* that is, you agree that these things were the deeds of your fathers. So Matthew 23:31 reads: "You are witnesses against yourselves that you are the children of those who killed the prophets." – Therefore, the text adds: *For they indeed killed them, but you build their tombs.* And in this way through sign and word they were witnesses that their fathers killed them. And indeed *they were simulating* that they disapproved of this through their signs and works. Thus, Matthew 23:29–30 has: "You adorn the tombs of the just and say: If we had lived in the days of our fathers, we would not have been their accomplices." But *they were approving* now by a similar action and purpose that they, like their fathers, were persecutors of the good. And from this they were witnesses that they were in agreement with the deeds of their fathers. Wherefore, Jerome comments: "You are witnesses against yourselves. For by your deeds you are giving witness that you are imitators of the fathers, whose crimes you are denouncing with your words."[268]

---

[267] On p. 307, n. 2 QuarEd correctly indicate that the Vulgate reads *illos* ("them") while Bonaventure reads *eos* ("them").

[268] On p. 307, n. 5 QuarEd cite Book IV of Jerome's *Commentary on Matthew* 23:29–30: "He argues against them with a most shrewd syllogism that they are the children of murderers, while they obtain

So Acts 7:51 says: "Stiff-necked and uncircumcised in heart and ear, you always oppose the Holy Spirit. As your fathers did, so you do also."

95. (Verse 49). And since the evil, which they were fomenting in their heart, with God's permission was to be manifested in deed, the text adds: *For this reason also the wisdom of God has said*, "that is, has established from eternity,"[269] or Christ himself has established and foreseen it, who is "the power of God and the wisdom of God."[270] Or *he said*, that is, he foretold it by prophetic voice. – *I will send them prophets and apostles. And some of them they will put to death and persecute*, according to what Jeremiah 7:25–26 says: "I have sent to you all my servants the prophets from time to time, rising up early and sending. They have not hearkened to me, but[271] they have not inclined their ear and have hardened their neck and have done worse than their fathers." This has been verified in them, who *have killed* not only the prophets, but also *the Lord himself*. So in Acts 3:14–15

a reputation for goodness and glory from the people by building the tombs of the prophets whom their ancestors killed. They say: If we have lived at that time, we would not have done what our fathers did. But even if they are saying this with their mouth, they are saying by their deed of building an ambitious and magnificent monument to the memory of those who were murdered that they do not deny that the prophets were slain by their fathers." See Hugh of St. Cher, p. 205v, d where he quotes Jerome and virtually uses the same words that Bonaventure does: "You are witnesses against yourselves. For by your deeds you are giving witness that you are imitators of your fathers, whose crimes you are denouncing with your words."
[269] On p. 307, n. 7 QuarEd state that this is the Glossa Interlinearis.
[270] 1 Corinthians 1:24. On p. 307, n. 7 QuarEd refer to the interpretations of Bede and Ambrose. For Bede, see CCSL cxx, p. 244: "He says that he himself is the wisdom of God. For he is the power of God and the wisdom of God as the apostle says." For Ambrose, see CCSL xiv, pp. 249–250: "Who is wisdom except Christ? For in Matthew you have: *Behold, I send you prophets and wise men*" (23:34).
[271] The Vulgate has *et* ("and") rather than Bonaventure's *sed* ("but").

Peter says to them: "But you disowned the Holy and Righteous One and asked that a murderer be given to you. But the author of life you killed." They killed him, and all *his witnesses* were persecuted. For James was killed, and Peter apprehended as Acts 12:2–3 states. They also persecuted Paul and Barnabas with the result that they went over to the Gentiles as Acts 13:50 and Acts 14:5–6 portray. And all the disciples were also scourged as Acts 5:40 says.

96. (Verse 50). Second, relative to *the gravity of the punishment* the text says: *that the blood of all the prophets is required*. For *it is required* by punishment. So the Psalm says: "For by requiring their blood, he has remembered," etc. (9:13). And Genesis 9:5–6 reads: "From the hand of a man and of his brother I will require the life of men and women. Whosoever shall shed human blood, that person's blood will be shed." – Wherefore, *blood is required*, that is, the punishment by shedding of blood. For which reason the text adds: *that has been shed from the foundation of the world*, that is, from the beginning until the end. It says: *required of this generation*, as if to say that the punishment for all the blood shed by the holy men will be upon this generation, for they shed the blood of him who was "The Holy of the Holy Ones," namely, Christ, as Daniel 9:24 says. And subsequently Daniel 9:26 reads: "Christ will be slain, and the people who deny him will not be his people." Wherefore, they said in John 19:15: "We have no king but Caesar." And Matthew 27:25 has: "His blood upon us and upon our children." – Another interpretation: This verse means that they may be punished as an example to others, since, although they saw that evil in others was punished, they did not amend their ways. So Chrysostom comments: "Why does God punish the sins of others in them, who alone suffered such things, al-

though they were not the only ones to sin? It is like this situation: Although many servants have sinned, only one is beaten for his own sin. One alone endured for all the punishment of scourging that had been promised to all."[272] Now the reason why the punishment fell heavily on them is given by the same John Chrysostom: "For, he says, you have heard of the punishment meted out to Cain and to other evildoers. And if you have not amended your life because of their example, you will experience more severe punishments, and what happened to the former ones will come upon you."[273]

97. (Verse 51). And therefore, he gives an example taken from the witness of Scripture: *from the blood of Abel unto the blood of Zechariah*. For *Abel* was the first just man killed by his brother, according to what is said in Genesis 4:8. Now *Zechariah* was that Zechariah who was the son of Jehoiada, who was killed by king Joash, who had accepted many good things from Zechariah's father, according to the historical account found in 2

---

[272] On p. 308, n. 2 QuarEd cite the pertinent passage from Chrysostom's Homily 46 on Matthew 23:35 (*Opus Imperfectum*). Bonaventure has provided a summary of Chrysostom's commentary. In reality Bonaventure has modified the version of Chrysostom's comments found in Hugh of St. Cher, p. 205v, l: "Therefore, why does God punish the sins of others in them, who alone suffered such things, although they were not the only ones to sin? It is like this situation: Although many servants have sinned, only one is beaten for his own sin. And he seems to have been beaten for all, because he alone endured what had also been promised to others."

[273] On p. 308, n. 3 QuarEd cite Chrysostom's Homily 74, n. 2 on Matthew and indicate that Chrysostom says far more than Bonaventure's summary of two sentences. In truth Bonaventure has modified the version of Chrysostom's comments found in Hugh of St. Cher, p. 205v, l: "As if he were saying: you have heard of the punishment meted out to Cain and to other evildoers. And you have not amended your life because of their example. Wherefore, you will experience more severe punishments, and what happened to the former ones, which you did not fear, will come upon you."

Chronicles 24:22. However, this man was not the last to be killed, but his death correlates well with the first person slain. "For Abel was a shepherd of sheep and was murdered in a field. But Zechariah was a priest and was murdered in the court of the temple. These designate the two orders of martyrs, namely, the laity and those who perform the office of the altar."[274] – So he designates the exact location of the death of this one when he adds: *who was slain between the altar and the temple*, that is, he was killed between the temple and the altar of holocaust. "For there were two altars in the temple: one inside, namely, the altar of incense, the other outside, that is, the altar of holocaust," according to what is read in Exodus 35:15–16.[275] And between this and the temple Zechariah was slain by the Jews, according to what is written in 2 Chronicles 24:21–22: "They gathered against him and stoned him at the king's command in the court of the house of God....When he was dying, he said: May the Lord see and requite it." He said this, keeping in mind the equity of divine justice, which does not let anything go unrequited.

98. To accentuate its infallibility he repeats the future punishment and says: *Yes, I say to you, it will be required of this generation*, so that through the demonstrative pronoun, "this," there might be a determination of the evil generation. For the Glossa of Bede says: "All evil people are one generation, one city, one body of the devil

---

[274] On p. 308, n. 5 QuarEd mention that this quotation is taken from the Glossa Ordinaria (from Bede) on Luke 11:51. For Bede, see CCSL cxx, p. 245. Hugh of St. Cher, p. 206d quotes much of Bede and the Glossa Ordinaria, but without attribution.
[275] On p. 308, n. 6 QuarEd indicate that Bonaventure's quotation is taken from the Glossa Ordinaria apud Lyranum and is based on Book II of Bede's homilies, section one, Homily 13 for the Vigil of St. John the Baptist.

just as all good people are one body, one generation of God."[276] Therefore, what Proverbs 30:14 says can be understood of this iniquitous generation: "A generation that has swords for teeth and grind with their jaw teeth, so that they may devour the needy from the land and the poor from among men and women." This is the generation, from which punishment will be required. But in this punishment it will be especially required of the Jewish nation, for perfidy was consummated in them.[277] So Chrysostom says: "Just as God promised to *good people* through many generations that Christ would come, but bestowed him as a gift to the last holy ones, so too what God threatened to *evil people* through individual generations God has now rendered to the final generation. For never was such *grace* given to men and women as that which came in Christ or has such *destruction* come upon impious people as upon the Jews."[278] Thus, they could very well say what Genesis 42:21–22 states: "We deserved to suffer these things, for we have sinned against our brother. . . . Behold, his blood is required."[279]

---

[276] On p. 308, n. 7 QuarEd state that this is the Glossa Ordinaria and indicate that Bede is following Book IV of Jerome's commentary on Matthew 23:35–36. The quotation is not taken from Bede's commentary on Luke, however. Hugh of St. Cher, p. 205v, l writes: "Note that through this demonstrative pronoun ("this") there is no determination of a generation of the Jews, for not all were killed by the Jews. But the Glossa specifies that by this generation is meant a generation of evil doers: For all evildoers are one generation, as Bede says."

[277] This translator does not accord with this blast of medieval anti-Judaism.

[278] On p. 308, n. 9 QuarEd refer to Chrysostom's Homily 46 on Matthew 23:35 and observe that the original text is much longer. As far as I can determine, Hugh of St. Cher does not quote this passage from Chrysostom in his commentary on Luke 11:51.

[279] The reference is to the decision of Joseph's brothers to sell him into slavery.

99. (Verse 52). *Woe to you lawyers*, etc. Here for the third time he repeats a *woe*. This time it concerns *fraudulence against the truth of teaching*. And since evil doers and deceivers are proficient in doing the worst things, first comes *the threat of hell*. Second is added *the obduracy of iniquity*.

First, then, concerning *the threat of punishment* on account of a lack of truth in teaching the text has: *Woe to you lawyers! who*[280] *have taken away the key of knowledge*, that is, relative to their office of dispensing instruction. Now this key of knowledge is principally about Christ, the supreme teacher: "For one is your teacher, Christ," according to what is said in Matthew 23:10. And about this Isaiah 22:22 reads: "I will lay the key of the house of David upon his shoulder, and will open," etc.[281] The scribes have taken this away, feigning that they are teaching in a right manner. But in fact they were not teaching rightly, for they were neglecting themselves and were impeding others.

100. For which reason the text adds: *You have not entered yourselves, and those who were entering you have hindered.* For they themselves *were not entering*, for, although they had the words, they did not have the deeds. Wherefore, what Romans 2:21 says could be applied to them: "You who teach others, do you not teach yourself? You who preach that people should not steal, do you steal?" And since they only had words, *they could not enter*. Matthew 7:21 has: "Not everyone who says to me: Lord, Lord, will enter into the kingdom of the heav-

---

[280] On p. 309, n. 1 QuarEd rightly state that the Vulgate reads *quia* ("because"). They mention that Cardinal Hugh, St. Thomas in his *Catena Aurea* on Luke chapter 11, n. 13, Gorranus, and Lyranus read *qui* ("who").

[281] Hugh of St. Cher, p. 206f also quotes this passage.

ens," etc. Therefore, they did not enter by words alone.
And *they also impeded others* by their evil example.[282]
Whence what Jeremiah 50:6 states is verified: "My people has become a lost flock. Their pastors have led them
astray," namely, from the right way or by *evil example*
or *false teaching*, according to what Lamentations 2:14
says: "Your prophets have seen false and foolish things
for you. And they have not exposed your iniquity to you,
so that they might excite you to penance. But they have
seen for you false revelations and banishments." For
from false revelations almost all distorted consciences
are formed, through which people are cast out from the
reign of God and are prohibited from entering it. Therefore, Chrysostom comments: "The Law and the Prophets
openly preached the coming of Christ, but they closed
this door of understanding by perverse expositions."[283]
And so they were impeding people from entering, calling
them away from the path of truth by word and example.
Proverbs 3:27 talks about a different manner of acting:
"Do not prevent the person who is able from doing good.
If you are able, do good yourself."

101. (Verse 53). Secondly, with regard to *obduracy of
iniquity* the text says: *Now after he had said these things
to them, the Pharisees and the lawyers began to press him
hard.* In doing this, they show that their hearts were
obdurate and impervious in hearing the divine word, so
that it is manifested that what Isaiah 6:10 says is veri-

---

[282] On p. 309, n. 4 QuarEd call attention to Bede's commentary. See
CCSL cxx, p. 245: "Every teacher who edifies his listeners by his
word, but scandalizes them by his example does not himself enter
the kingdom of God and does not permit those who could enter it to
do so."
[283] On p. 309, n. 6 QuarEd refer to Chrysostom's Homily 44 on Matthew 23:14 (*Opus Imperfectum*). Hugh of St. Cher, p. 206i has the
very same quotation.

fied in them: "Blind the heart of this people, and close their eyes, and make their ears hard of hearing."[284] And Matthew 13:15 states: "The heart of this people has been hardened, and with their ears they have been hard of hearing."[285] – Not only was there obduracy towards the truth in them, but also *attacks against the truth*. Wherefore, the text continues: *to provoke him to speak on many matters*, as if that most pure mouth would say something evil or false. Thus was verified what Amos 5:10 states: "They hated him who rebuked them in the gate and abhorred him who spoke perfectly." And so Proverbs 9:7 reads: "The person who teaches one who scorns brings injury upon himself," for he resorts to insults on account of the truth he has heard.

102. (Verse 54). And since it is not sufficient for obstinate wickedness to insult the person it hates, but also to endeavor to plot his demise, the text adds: *setting traps for him and plotting to seize upon something out of his mouth, so that they might accuse him.*[286] For they did not dare to kill him openly for fear of the crowds, but wanted to kill him secretly out of hatred for the truth heard. Wherefore, John 8:40 says: "Why are you seeking to kill me, one who has spoken the truth to you?"[287] They were seeking to do this cautiously and maliciously. Thus, Matthew 22:15 has: "The Pharisees went out and took counsel how they might trap Jesus[288] in his speech."

---

[284] Isaiah 6:10 reads: "Blind the heart of this people, and make their ears hard of hearing, and close their eyes."
[285] Matthew 13:15 is quoting from Isaiah 6:10.
[286] On p. 309, n. 9 QuarEd correctly mention that the Vulgate reads *eum* ("him") while Bonaventure's text has *illum* ("him").
[287] Bonaventure has added *Quid* ("Why") and changed the Vulgate's declarative sentence into a question.
[288] The Vulgate reads *eum* ("him"). Hugh of St. Cher, p. 206m also quotes Matthew 22:15 and reads *Jesum* ("Jesus") rather than *eum* ("him").

LUKE 12

Luke 12:1–59
CHRIST GIVES INSTRUCTION ON HOW TO AVOID THE FALLACY HE
HAS JUST REFUTED

1. *Now when immense crowds had gathered together*, etc.
After the Lord has reproved the deceit of wicked hypocrisy in the Pharisees, here *he cautions his disciples about
the hypocrisy reproved.* And since *fear* evilly humbling or
love evilly inflaming causes duplicity of this kind,[1] this

---

[1] On p. 309, n. 11 QuarEd provide a helpful parallel to Bonaventure's
strange expressions in Augustine's commentary on Psalm 79, n. 13.
See *Sancti Avrelii Avgvstini Erarrationes in Psalmos LI–C,* CCSL
xxxix (Turnhout: Brepols: 1956), 1117–1118 where Augustine is
commenting on "Things burned with fire and dug up": "Therefore,
my brothers, love and fear lead to every deed done justly. Love and
fear lead to every sin. In order to do good, you love God and you fear
God. But in order to do evil, you love the world and you fear the
world. . . . Indeed, love inflames. Fear humbles. Therefore, sins of
evil love have been ignited by fire. Sins of evil fear have been dug up.
Good fear humbles, and good love inflames. . . . Just as all righteous
deeds are done with good fear and good love, so too are all sins committed out of evil love and evil fear."

section is divided into two. In the first he warns the disciples to beware of *duplicity that arises from timidity*. In the second of *duplicity that arises from cupidity* where Luke 12:13 has: *Now one of the crowd said to him*, etc.

Luke 12:1–12
INSTRUCTION ON HOW TO AVOID DUPLICITY ARISING FROM TIMIDITY

Now this first part has four sections. In the first he *gives instruction about avoiding deceit*. In the second he *strengthens them to repel timidity* where verse 4 has: *But I say to you, my friends*, etc. In the third he *requests them to preserve the truth* where verse 8 reads: *But I say to you: Everyone who acknowledges me*, etc. In the fourth he *instills assurance in them* where verse 11 states: *Now when they bring you before the synagogues*. And these sections correspond to one another, for the last two match the first two.

Luke 12:1–3
INSTRUCTION ON HOW TO AVOID DECEIT

Now he teaches his disciples *to avoid deceit* with instruction that is solemn and credible. *Solemn*, I say, because of *the immensity of the crowd*, and *credible* on account of *the certitude of the source*.

2. (Verse 1). First, then, with regard to *the immensity of the crowd to which he gives a celebrated admonition* the text says: *Now when immense crowds had gathered together, so that they were treading on one another*. And this was so, for each one wanted to get close to him. Either *to experience salvific healing*, as in Luke 6:19 above:

"All the crowd was trying to touch him," etc. Or *to receive his teaching*, as in Luke 15:1 below: "The publicans were approaching Jesus," etc. Or *to see the kindness* of the Christ himself, as it is said by figure in Job 29:25: "And although I sat as a king, with the army standing about, yet I was a comforter to those who mourned." In the presence of so great a multitude his teaching was solemn. – For this reason the text continues: *He began to say to his disciples*, openly, for the truth does not need hiding places, according to what John 18:20 says: "I have spoken openly to the world. I have always taught in the synagogue and in the temple," etc. And this was fitting for Christ's teaching in confutation of the Pharisees' malice, which always sought out hiding places. For "contraries are cured by contraries,"[2] and darkness is expelled by light.

3. On account of this the text adds: *Beware of the leaven of the Pharisees, which is hypocrisy*. That is, beware that you do not become hypocrites like the Pharisees, whose life and teaching because of their malice and deceit are said to be *leaven*, for they corrupt *imperceptibly*. Hosea 7:4 reads: "The city rested a little from the leaven[3] till the whole was leavened." It also corrupts *totally*, as it is said in 1 Corinthians 5: "A little leaven ferments the whole lump" (verse 6), and verse 7 adds: "Purge out the

---

[2] On p. 310, n. 6 QuarEd provide some parallels. Aristotle, n. *Ethics*, Book II, chapter 3: "Medications were customarily applied by contraries." Homily 32, n. 1 of GGHG reads in PL 1232D–1233A: "But the heavenly physician uses medicaments to oppose each and every one of the vices. For as in the art of medicine heat cures cold and cold cures heat, so too does our Lord set forth his preaching to oppose sins, so that he prescribes continence for luxuriousness, largess for stinginess, meekness for anger, and humility for arrogance."

[3] On p. 310, n. 7 QuarEd correctly indicate that the Vulgate has a different reading: *a commixtione fermenti* ("from the mingling of the leaven").

old leaven, so that you may be a new dough." Now this is *the old leaven* that consists of *fraudulence in teaching* and *malice in living*.[4] So 1 Corinthians 5:8 continues: "Not with the leaven of malice and wickedness, but with the unleavened bread of sincerity and truth." To this leaven he is recalling them in this verse. And of this there is a figure in Deuteronomy 16:4: "Nothing leavened shall be seen within all your boundaries,"[5] for this simulation and hypocrisy must be removed far away from all our deeds, and especially from *spiritual dedication*. Leviticus 2:11 states: "Every offering that is made to the Lord shall be made without leaven." From *bodily affliction*. Deuteronomy 16:3 says: "Seven days you shall eat the bread of affliction without leaven." From *the preaching of the divine word*. Exodus 23:18 has: "You shall not sacrifice the blood of a holocaust upon leaven."[6]

4. So Scripture teaches that this vice is to be avoided as the most corruptive. But although it is most corruptive, it is, nevertheless, not a capital sin, because its corruption stems from another cause. For *hypocrisy* takes it origin from vainglory, and this, in turn, comes from pride. And therefore, hypocrisy is fittingly compared to *leaven*. For just as leaven inflates, and by inflating renders a thing empty and thus corrupts, so too pride, by

---

[4] Hugh of St. Cher, p. 206p also quotes Hosea 7:4 and 1 Corinthians 5:6 and 5:7.

[5] On p. 310, n. 9 QuarEd accurately mention that the Vulgate reads: *Non apparebit fermentum in omnibus terminis tuis* ("No leaven shall be seen within all your borders").

[6] On p. 310, n. 10 QuarEd rightly indicate that the Vulgate reads *sanguinem victimae meae* ("the blood of my victim"). What this quotation has to do with "the preaching of the divine word" escapes this translator. Hugh of St. Cher, p. 206p provides a clue as he also quotes Exodus 23:18: "You shall not sacrifice the blood of a holocaust upon leaven, that is, by perversely teaching, and a hypocrite shall not communicate in the body and blood of Christ."

inflating a person, leads to the emptiness of glory, and this emptiness leads to corrupting falsehood. Wherefore, this leaven is avoided by the truth of *voluntary humiliation, internal boasting, external marking,*[7] according to what 2 Corinthians 1:12 says: "Our boast is this, the testimony of our conscience, that in simplicity of heart and godly sincerity and not in fleshly wisdom, but in the grace of God, we have conducted ourselves in this world."

5. (Verse 2). Secondly, with regard to *the certitude of the source that gives credible information* the text adds: *But there is nothing concealed that will not be disclosed, and nothing hidden that will not be made known*, so that by *concealed* is meant *knowledge* hidden in the mind and by *hidden* is meant *delight* hidden in the affections. Both of which are manifest to God, according to what Jeremiah 17:10 states: "I am the Lord, who scrutinizes the heart and the interior parts,[8] who gives to every one," etc. The Psalmist says: "It is God who scrutinizes hearts and the interior parts" (7:10).[9] And therefore, since it is Christ's prerogative to manifest and reveal all hidden matters in the judgment, according to Wisdom 6:4: "Power is given you from the Lord and strength from the Most High, who will examine your works and will scrutinize your thoughts" and according to 1 Corinthians 4:5: "The Lord will come who will bring to light

---

[7] Bonaventure seems to be carried away by the word play, *humiliationis, gloriationis, signationis*, and does not communicate his meaning clearly.

[8] "The interior parts" are the seat of the affections. The Vulgate reads: *Ego Dominus, scrutans cor et probans renes* ("I am the Lord, who scrutinizes the heart and proves the interior parts").

[9] On p. 311, n. 1 QuarEd quote the Glossa Interlinearis on Luke 12:2: ". . . iniquity will be disclosed, and your intention, which is known now only to God, will be known by all."

the matters hidden in darkness and will manifest the counsels of hearts," etc.,[10] all evils are, therefore, to be avoided, no matter how secret they may be.[11] For all things will become manifest in the judgment.

6. (Verse 3). And what is more, things done in hiding will also become manifest to all and lead to greater shame. For which reason the text adds: *For what you have said in darkness will be said in the light.* He says this about a manifestation with respect to *sight*. An example of this occurs with David in 2 Samuel 12:12 where the Lord said to David through Nathan: "You have done this deed secretly, but I will do this thing in the sight of all Israel and in the sight of this sun."[12] For the light of the sun makes all things clear to sight. – Now with regard to a manifestation with respect to *hearing* the text says: *And what you have whispered into the ear in inner rooms will be preached on the rooftops*, that is, with all listening. Indeed, this will happen in the judgment, namely, when, according to John 5:28, "all, who are in the tombs, will hear the voice of the Son of God." And then the whisperings of slander will be made manifest, according to Wisdom 1:8–9: "The person who speaks unjust things cannot be hidden. Neither will the chastising judgment pass him by. For inquiry will be made into the thoughts of the ungodly," etc. And therefore, this counsel is given in Qoheleth 10:20: "In your thoughts do not utter a detraction against the king,

---

[10] Hugh of St. Cher, p.206v, b also has these two quotations, but in reverse order. This is, he quotes 1 Corinthians 4:5 first and then Wisdom 6:4.

[11] On p. 311, n. 2 QuarEd give a simple, direct, and true assessment of this sentence: "The sentence is unbecomingly constructed."

[12] On p. 311, n. 3 QuarEd correctly mention that the Vulgate reads differently: "For you have done it secretly, but I will do this thing in the sight of all Israel and in the sight of the sun."

and in the secret of your private room do not speak evil of a rich man, for the birds[13] of the heaven will carry your voice."[14]

7. Therefore, on account of the judgment that will make all things manifest in the future, all hypocrisy should be avoided in the present age. Sirach 1:37–39 reads: "Be not a hypocrite in the sight of men and women . . . lest God reveal your secrets and cast you down in the middle of the congregation." – And note that this is the most noble reason for which hypocrisy should be avoided, namely, the universal and full disclosure of interior matters. This is especially opposed to the simulation of the hypocrites. But this disclosure will come about through Christ, "who is the brightness of the Father's[15] glory and the image of his substance, upholding all things by the word of his power" (Hebrews 1:3). And since he is the innermost brightness, it is his prerogative to disclose all things. Sirach 23:28 reads: "The eyes of the Lord are far brighter than the sun, beholding round about all human ways and the bottom of the deep and peering into human hearts," etc. Since he is the living Word, all things are patent to him. And he exposes all things as the Word. Hebrews 4:12–13 says: "The Word of God is living and efficient and sharper than any two-edged sword, extending even to the division of soul. . . . There is no creature hidden from his sight." And therefore, Christ is the judge, because he will disclose all things in the judgment and is said to come "like lightning," and "to descend at the voice of the Archan-

---

[13] The Vulgate reads the singular *avis* ("a bird").

[14] Hugh of St. Cher, p. 206v, d also quotes this passage.

[15] On p. 311, n. 8 QuarEd rightly indicate that the Vulgate does not read *paternae* ("the Father's").

gel."[16] For he will reveal all things to all in the most clear manner.[17]

Luke 12:4–7
CHRIST STRENGTHENS HIS DISCIPLES TO REPEL TIMIDITY

8. (Verse 4). *But I say to you, my friends*, etc. After he had given instruction about avoiding deceit, here in his second point *he strengthens his disciples to repel timidity.* Now in doing this, he offers a twofold consideration. The first is *the punishment of hell*, into which no human person has power to cast. The second is *general foresight*, which no human person can flee. The first considers divine *power*. The second has divine *providence* in mind. And the first one instills genuine *fear* while the second genuine *hope*. And both of these are medicines against worldly fear.

So the first consideration calls the disciples away from fear of men and women, for *they have no power over the punishment of hell*, which is the only thing to be feared. On this account the text says: *But I say to you, my friends*, that is, who love me and are loved by me, according to what John 16:27 says: "The Father himself loves you, because you have loved me," etc. He says to such people: *do not be afraid of those who kill the body, and after that have nothing more that they can do.*[18] Do

---

[16] The references are to Matthew 24:27 and 1 Thessalonians 4:16.

[17] A comparison between Bonaventure's commentary here and those of Ambrose, Bede, and Hugh of St. Cher reveals that Bonaventure's stress on Christology is his own hallmark.

[18] On p. 312, n. 2 QuarEd correctly mention that Vulgate's word order for the last three words is *amplius quid faciant* whereas Bonaventure reads *quid amplius faciant*. I have made no attempt to reflect this difference in a wooden translation.

not fear *the punishment of bodily death*, because it is partial and of short duration. Wherefore, Isaiah 51:12 reads: "Who are you that you are afraid of a mortal human being and of a son of man, who will wither away like grass?" And 1 Maccabees 2:62 states: "Do not fear the words of a sinful man, for his glory is dung and worms," etc. So since their power is transitory, it is not to be feared, nor their punishment. Therefore, Seneca says: "Death, exile, mourning, sorrow are not punishments, but life's taxes. . . . I am prepared to pay what I must where the money-lender demands my money."[19] And Chrysostom comments: "If we are going to die with no purpose after a little while, why do we not die before that little while in God's cause with glory? If you have received an ox or a horse on loan, you immediately set to work and say: Perhaps, it will be taken away from me tomorrow. Why do you not do this while you are in your body?"[20] – They are not to be feared in the spirit, *because they happen in the flesh* and therefore as it were *outside*,

---

[19] On p. 312, n. 3 QuarEd refer to *Excerpt. e libris Senecae, II. de Remediis fortuitorum* and state that Bonaventure's first sentence comes from the end of Seneca's discussion and that his second sentence comes from the beginning of Seneca's discussion. Alas, they give no more detailed bibliographical information. In any case, it seems clear that Bonaventure borrowed this quotation from Cardinal Hugh. See Hugh of St. Cher, p. 206v, h where the sentence is integral: "*Sen.* Death, exile, mourning, sorrow are not punishments, but life's taxes, which I am prepared to pay when I must where the money-lender demands my money."

[20] On p. 312, n. 4 QuarEd refer to Chrysostom's Homily 25 on Matthew 10:28 and state that Chrysostom's text is far more expansive. Bonaventure's quotation is taken almost verbatim from Cardinal Hugh. See Hugh of St. Cher, p. 206v, i: "If we are going to die with no purpose after a little while, why do we not die before that little while in God's cause with glory, so that we may do willingly what is going to happen of necessity? And below: If you have received an ox or a horse on loan, you immediately set to work and say: Perhaps, it will be taken away from me tomorrow. Why do you not do this while you are in your body?"

as with clothing, in accordance with what is said in 2 Corinthians 5:4: "We do not wish to be unclothed, but rather clothed over." Therefore, Chrysostom observes: "On account of the soul God made the body, and the enemy is greatly envious of this soul and persecutes it. But the body is the soul's vestment. Therefore, just as if someone tears the vestment of another, the person himself indeed suffers injury, but does not experience a loss in his nature, so too the soul suffers the pain of murder, but does not experience a loss in its nature."[21] Wherefore, *bodily* punishment is not to be feared nor the person who inflicts it. But *spiritual* punishment is especially to be dreaded, and he alone who inflicts it.

9. (Verse 5). On account of this the text continues: *But I will show you whom you shall fear*, so that through fear of this person you may shun evil, according to what Jeremiah 10:5–7 has: "Do not fear those things which can neither do evil nor good. . . . Who will not fear you, O King of the nations?," etc. – So in order that we may not fear worldly power, we ought to fear divine power. For which reason the text says: *Fear him who, after he has killed, has the power to cast into hell.* So the Psalm says: "Let all the earth fear the Lord, and let all the inhabitants of the world be in awe of him" (32:8). – And since fear of this kind is specially useful and even neces-

---

[21] On p. 312, n. 5 QuarEd refer to Chrysostom's Homily 25 on Matthew 10:28. See the previous note. Bonaventure is heavily indebted to Cardinal Hugh. See Hugh of St. Cher, p. 206v, n: "On account of the soul God made the body, and the enemy is greatly envious of this soul and persecutes it. Christ came on account of this soul. But the body is the soul's vestment. Wherefore, 2 Corinthians 5:4 states: 'We do not wish to be unclothed, but rather clothed over. Therefore, just as if someone tears the vestment of another, the person himself indeed suffers injury, but does not experience a loss in his nature, so too the soul suffers the pain of murder, but does not experience a loss in its nature."

sary, he repeats: *Yes, I say to you: Fear this person.*
Therefore, Isaiah 8:13 states: "Sanctify the Lord of hosts
himself. And let him be your fear, and let him be your
dread." And Jeremiah 5:22 reads: "Will you not then fear
me? And will you not repent at my presence?"

10. (Verse 6). Secondly, he calls them away from fear of
men and women, because *they can do nothing against
the general protection of God.* Relative to this the text
has: *Are not five sparrows sold for a dipondius?* The
name "dipondius" here refers to money which consisted
of two obols or ases.[22] So Bede comments: "A dipondius
is a weight consisting of two ases. An as is to weights
what one is to numbers. When there are *two ases*, this is
called a *dipondius.*"[23] This is neither in agreement or in
disagreement with what is said in Matthew 10:29: "Are
not two sparrows sold for an as?" For, as we see, since
five eggs are sold for one denarius, two are had for an
obol.[24] Therefore, a sparrow sells for a very small price,
and a great number would be purchased for one de-

---

[22] "Obol" is a Greek term while "as" is Latin and is taken as a loan
word from the Greek "assarion." A "dipondius" was one-eighth of a
denarius, which was the daily wage. See John J. Rouisseau; Rami
Arav, *Jesus and His World: An Archaeological and Cultural Dictionary* (Minneapolis: Fortress, 1995), p. 57 for the very helpful
"Equivalence Table" in their article on "Coins and Money."
[23] On p 312, n. 8 QuarEd state that this is the Glossa Ordinaria on
Luke 12:6. See CCSL cxx, p. 247 where Bede merely says: ". . . it is a
type of smallest weight, composed of two ases." See Hugh of St. Cher,
p. 206v, o: "Beda. A dipondius is a weight consisting of two ases. An
as is to weights what one is to numbers. When there are *two ases*, this
is called a *dipondius.* That is, the property that oneness has among
numbers, as has the same among weights." Bonaventure has abbreviated the quotation from "Bede" that he found in Hugh of St. Cher.
[24] This is a very strange sentence, for an obol is one-sixteenth of a
denarius. Bonaventure seems to make a hash out of what Hugh of
St. Cher, p. 207p has: "As you see, that if five eggs cost an obol and if
someone only wants to buy half an obol's worth, he is only given two
eggs."

narius.[25] Nonetheless, not even the tiniest sparrow is without divine protection. – Therefore, the text continues: *And yet none of these is forgotten before God.* By all means, it is governed by divine providence, according to what Wisdom 11:25 says: "You love all things that exist, and you hate none of the things you have made. For you did not produce anything hating it." Nor does this contradict what 1 Corinthians 9:9 has: "Is it for oxen that God has care?"[26] For the first case deals with the care of *special* providence, by which God leads along the way of eternal salvation. The second instance stands for the *general* providence of governance and preservation, about which the Psalmist says: "Who gives beasts their food and to the young ravens that call upon him" (146:9).[27] – And note that he says: *Yet not one of them is forgotten before God.* He uses a few words, but says volumes, for nothing happens to them without the ordination of divine providence. So Matthew 10:29 reads: "Yet not one of them falls to the ground without your Father's leave." And truly sparrows fall to the ground most readily. Whence they are said to suffer from "falling sickness" or epilepsy. And therefore, he most powerfully sets them forth as an example of something that is evident to all. From this one can infer *from the lesser* to the

---

[25] If you follow Matthew's pricing, you get 32 sparrows for your denarius. If you follow Luke's pricing, you get 40 sparrows for your denarius.

[26] Hugh of St. Cher, p. 207a also quotes this passage, but interprets it differently than Bonaventure.

[27] On p. 312, n. 11 QuarEd give a number of references to discussions on divine providence in Bonaventure. See, for example, Book I, distinction 39, chapter 4 of Bonaventure's Commentary on the Sentences in Opera Omnia 1:683: "That God knows all things both always and simultaneously."

greater, namely, how divine providence cares for men and women in a special way.[28]

11. (Verse 7). The text gives expression to divine providence as it continues: *Yes, the very hairs of your head are all numbered.* This means that God's greatest care goes to human beings. So Bede says: *"Yes, the very hairs,* so that I do not have to say anything about the rest of the body, for even the minute particles of the body are preserved by God's providence."[29] So there is not so much a reference to a knowledge of *numbers* here, as to the most caring conservation, for not a hair from the bodies of the saints who are suffering can perish. Therefore, Luke 21:18 below states: "Not a hair of your head will perish." Thus, God's care for us is so great, that not a hair from our head can be taken away without his consent. Wherefore, we ought not to be anxious out of fear, according to what 1 Peter 5:7 says: "Cast all your anxiety upon God, for God cares for you." – And he draws this conclusion: *Therefore, do not be afraid, for you are of more than many sparrows,* "that is, of more value."[30] In saying this, he simultaneously arrives at the conclusion and gives the reason for the inference of an *argument from lesser to greater.* For if God cares for the lesser

[28] On p. 313, n. 1 QuarEd cite the Glossa Interlinearis: ". . . but all things are under God's providence. How much more you made in the image of God." See CCSL cxx, p. 247 for the source in Bede's commentary of the Glossa's observation.

[29] On p. 313, n. 2 QuarEd state that this is the Glossa Interlinearis. A check of CCSL cxx, pp. 247–248 reveals that Bede makes no such comment. See Hugh of St. Cher, p. 207b: *"Bede.* So that I do not have to say anything about the rest of the body, for even the smallest particles of the body are preserved by God's providence."

[30] On p. 313, n. 4 QuarEd state: "As it is said in the Glossa Interlinearis: *Therefore, do not be afraid*: cast all care upon him, among whom not a hair will perish. *You are of more than many sparrows,* of more value, because you are rational beings, because you are eternal beings. Cf. Bede, IV on Luke 12:7." For Bede, see CCSL cxx, p. 248.

thing, how much more intensely for the greater thing. And if God's care is focused on us, we should not fear the world. Now we are of greater value than brute creatures, than birds, for we are rational creatures, and we are so because we have been made in God's image. For which reason all others are subject to men and women. Genesis 1:26 says: "Let us make man to our image and likeness . . . and let him have dominion over the birds of heaven," etc. And therefore, humans are most directly under God's protection, and especially righteous persons and the friends of God. And therefore, he does not need any perishable help. So Genesis 15:1 has: "Do not fear, Abram. I am your protector, and your reward exceedingly great." As if to say: Do not fear, for when you suffer anything, aid will be at hand. Further, you cannot suffer anything without the recompense of a reward, as long as you adhere to me.

Luke 12:8–10
CHRIST URGES HIS DISCIPLES TO PRESERVE THE TRUTH

12. (Verse 8). *But I say to you: Everyone*, etc. After he has stirred his disciples to avoid deceit and to repel timidity, here in a third point he urges them *to preserve the truth*. For veracity of confession is against the deceit of hypocrisy. Now he deals with this in a twofold manner. First, by suggesting *the equity of divine judgment*. Second, by suggesting *the unpardonableness of the sin of blasphemy*. Through the first he admonishes them *to confess the truth*. Through the second *to shun falsity*.

Therefore, he first admonishes them *to confess the truth* on account of *the equity of divine judgment* when he says: *But I say to you: Everyone who acknowledges*[31] *me before men and women.* The pronoun, *me*, reveals the person in two natures, that is, who confesses me to be true God and man, not only saying it *with the heart*, according to what 1 Corinthians 12:3 states: "No one can say: Jesus is Lord, except through the Holy Spirit." But also expressing it *with the mouth*, according to what is said in Romans 10:10: "With the heart a person believes unto justice, and with the mouth confession is made unto salvation." Not only *with the mouth*, but also *with deeds*, contrary to the hypocrites and evil Christians, about whom Titus 1:16 reads: "They confess that they know God, but by their deeds they deny God." Against these Matthew 7:21 says: "Not everyone who says to me: Lord, Lord," etc. And therefore, 1 John 3:18 states: "Let us not love in word, neither with the tongue, but in deed and in truth." – The person who confesses in this manner confesses completely, namely, with heart, mouth, and deed.[32] About such a person the text says: *The Son of Man will also acknowledge him before the angels of God*, namely, that this person is one of his, according to what Matthew 25:34 has: "Come, blessed of my Father, take possession of the kingdom."[33] Therefore, what Proverbs 11:25 says is verified: "The soul that blesses will be enriched."

---

[31] Throughout this paragraph Bonaventure will play off the dual meanings of the verb *confiteor*, that is, "I acknowledge; I confess."

[32] See Hugh of St. Cher, p. 207e–f where Hugh also quotes Romans 10:10 and 1 Corinthians 12:3 and speaks of a confession and acknowledgment that is "with heart, mouth, and deed."

[33] See Hugh of St. Cher, p. 207h where Hugh also quotes Matthew 25:34 and gives the reason for the quotation: "The Son of Man will also acknowledge him before the angels of God, namely, that he is blessed of his Father."

13. (Verse 9). So the equity of retribution relative to *those confessing* is clear, and it remains now to show the equity with regard to *those denying*. The text continues: *But whoever denies me before men and women will be denied before the angels of God*, when, that is, the Lord will say what Matthew 25:12 has: "I do not know you," etc.[34] So Luke 9:26 above reads: "Whoever is ashamed of me and my words, of him will the Son of Man be ashamed," etc.[35] And the equity of divine judgment requires this. Of this equity 1 Samuel 2:30 says: "The person[36] who glorifies me, I will glorify. But those who despise me will be despised." – And note that the person who acknowledges the truth which Christ has taught is confessing Christ either in faith or in deeds. But the person who denies that teaching has the consequence of also denying Christ. The person who says that Christ's teaching is false is saying that Christ is consequently a liar, and by this is saying that he is not God, but a deceiver.

14. And note that *the confession* of Christ's name has great recompense, for the acknowledgment by which Christ will acknowledge those who acknowledge him will be *probative, honorific*, and *salvific*, for Christ is king, judge, and pontifex. His acknowledgment will be *public, magnificent*, and *perpetual*, but ours will be slight and momentary.[37] And similarly, his *denial* is to

---

[34] Matthew 25:12 is the conclusion of the parable of the ten virgins.

[35] On p. 314, n. 1 QuarEd cite the Glossa Interlinearis: "*But whoever denies*, out of fear*, me* to be God or man, *before men and women*, where the confession of my name must be proffered, *will be denied before the angels of God*, and will not be led to the vision of the Father, which the saints enjoy."

[36] The Vulgate reads *quicumque* ("whosoever").

[37] On p. 314, n. 3 QuarEd indicate that Cod. H had trouble with this lame comparison and added *occulta* ("hidden").

be understood from the contrary and becomes manifest in the judicial pronouncement: "Come, blessed" and "Depart, accursed."[38] – Therefore, this is a most excellent message which raises our minds to the Truth. Now the reason for this is that the Truth speaks truthfully. Therefore, he cannot deny himself nor the person who acknowledges him, nor acknowledge that he is a liar nor that he is against himself. Wherefore, 2 Timothy 2:12–13 reads: "If we deny[39] him, he will also deny us. If we are faithless, he remains faithful. He cannot deny himself."

15. (Verse 10). Secondly, he warns them *to shun falsehood* on account of *the unpardonableness of blasphemy,* which, although it is forgivable if done out of ignorance, is, however, unpardonable when done out of firmly determined malice. For which reason the text adds: *And everyone who speaks a word against the Son of Man, it will be forgiven him. Who speaks a word against the Son of Man* refers to a person who charges him with falsehood, *having been deceived by ignorance.* And such ignorance can obtain forgiveness. Wherefore, *it will be forgiven him* does not refer to an *action,* for not all repent, but to a *suitability,* for ignorance is the excuse.[40] Now a sin committed out of ignorance is said to be *against the Son.* And in this way Paul blasphemed, and therefore obtained mercy. 1 Timothy 1:13 reads: "I was[41] a blasphemer and persecutor and bitter adversary, but I ob-

---

[38] See Matthew 25:34 and 25:41 respectively.
[39] The Vulgate reads *negabimus* ("we will deny") while Bonaventure has *negaverimus* ("we would deny").
[40] Bonaventure seems to be invoking the scholastic distinction between "act" and "potency." The person who blasphemes out of ignorance has the possibility of being forgiven, but may not actually be forgiven.
[41] The Vulgate reads *qui prius fui* ("I formerly was").

tained mercy, because I acted ignorantly, in unbelief." –
But this is not what the person does who blasphemes
out of firmly determined malice. For which reason the
text adds: *but to the person who blasphemes against the
Holy Spirit, it will not be forgiven. The person who blasphemes against the Holy Spirit* is the person who resists
the truth out of firmly determined malice and says unworthy things of God. And it is said of such a person
that *it will not be forgiven,* not because such a person
never obtains forgiveness, but because such a person *is
unsuitable* for forgiveness. For this sin *has no hint of an
excuse.* Wherefore, Richard says: "Somebody blasphemes
out of coercion, this person sins against the Father.
Somebody out of deception, this person sins against the
Son. Somebody out of wickedness alone, this person sins
against the Holy Spirit. Now it is the most wicked kind.
In it wickedness increases to its height, when someone
delights in blaming God. Therefore, what else does the
spirit of blasphemy seem to be except the desire to censure God? Therefore, because this evil has *no hint of excuse* in it, it doesn't deserve to receive forgiveness."[42]

---

[42] On p. 314, n. 8 QuarEd refer to Richard of St. Victor's *Tractatus de
spiritu blasphemiae* and continue: "We note that the sentences
quoted here do not occur in the same order in the original text." The
original text is found in PL 196:1185D–1192C. The first part of
Bonaventure's quotation is loosely based on 196:1190A whereas the
second part stems from 196:1188A. But we don't have to go to Richard of St. Victor's work, for Bonaventure based his quotation on Cardinal Hugh. Hugh of St. Cher, p. 207v, b comments: "*Rich. de S.
Vict. . . .* Somebody blasphemes out of coercion, this person sins
against the Father. Somebody out of deception, this person sins
against the Son. Somebody out of wickedness alone, and this is the
worse species, against the Holy Spirit. Now it is the most wicked
kind. And in it wickedness increases to its height, when someone
delights in blaming God and boasts in it. Therefore, what else does
the spirit of blasphemy seem to be except the wish and desire to censure God? The spirit of blasphemy breathes hatred of God. The Holy
Spirit inspires love of God. Therefore, because this evil has no hint of

16. Such a person is also unsuitable for forgiveness, for *he is assailing the divine grace*, through which a person is prepared for repentance. Therefore, such a person is suitable for unrepentance. And if a person remains in that state, his sin will never be forgiven. Thus Bede says: "The person, who does not recognize the grace of the Holy Spirit, which inspires repentance and returns one to communion, persevering in an unrepentant heart, will be in an unpardonable condition since this condition is now not human, but diabolical."[43] And concerning such blasphemy, which has *final unrepentance* joined to it, there is truly never any forgiveness. So it is said in Matthew 12:32 that "it will not be forgiven him, neither in this world nor in the world to come." – Nevertheless, such a person is unsuitable for a third reason, for, although this sin is ascribed to the Holy Spirit by means of appropriation, such a sinner is showing *the greatest dishonor to the entire Trinity*. For the person who knowingly and craftily attacks salvific truth and with firm wicked intent is the greatest *despiser* of divine power, the greatest *calumniator* of divine truth, the greatest *persecutor* of the highest good, "has run up against God with his neck raised up and is armed with a bull's neck," according to what Job 15:26 says. Wherefore, since such *contempt, calumny*, and *persecution* can only come from an obdurate heart and since unrepentance and the unpardonable nature of the sin are the bedfel-

---

excuse in it, it doesn't deserve to receive exculpatory forgiveness. . . ."

[43] On p. 314, n. 9 QuarEd state that this opinion of Bede is found in the words of the Glossa Ordinaria on Luke 12:10. I do not find this "quotation" in Bede's extensive commentary on Luke 12:10. See CCSL cxx, pp. 248–250.

lows of obduracy, blasphemy against the Holy Spirit is not forgiven.[44]

Luke 12:11–12
Christ Offers Assurance in the Face of Persecution

17. (Verse 11). *But when they bring you before the synagogues*, etc. Here in a fourth point he exhorts them *to have assurance against pusillanimity*. Now he does this in a twofold manner, namely, *by removing anxiety about the danger* and *by conferring certitude about aid*.

So he first *removes anxiety about the danger* when he says: *But when they bring you before the synagogues and the magistrates and the authorities*. In saying this, he hints that his disciples will suffer tribulations from the Jews and the Gentiles. Thus, this is said in Matthew 10:17 in greater detail: "For they will hand you over to councils and in synagogues," etc.[45] So the Psalm says: "The kings of the earth stood up," etc. (2:2).[46]

18. And note that the text enumerates three types of persons, before whom men and women fear to speak, namely, before *many people*, before *learned experts*, and before *the great*. Before *many people* when he says: *In*

---

[44] On p. 315, n. 1 QuarEd refer readers to Book II. distinction 43, article 2, questions 1–2 of Bonaventure's Commentary on the Sentences for more enlightenment on Bonaventure's dense teaching here. See Opera Omnia 2:986–991.

[45] Bonaventure's point about the greater detail in Matthew 10:17 is found in what Bonaventure obscures by his "etc." Matthew 10:17 reads: ". . . for they will hand you over to councils and will scourge you in their synagogues."

[46] Psalm 2:2 reads: "The kings of the earth stood up, and the princes met together, against the Lord and against his Christ." See Acts 4:26 where Psalm 2:2 is also quoted.

synagogues. Against such fear Job 31:34 states: "If I have been afraid at a very great multitude and the contempt of kinsmen has terrified me." Before *learned experts,* the text has: *the magistrates.* Acts 5:26 reads: "Then the magistrate went off with the officers and brought the Apostles."[47] Before *the great,* where the text has: *and the authorities.* Romans 13:3 states: "Do you wish not to fear the authority? Do what is good." The first group is not to be feared, because "there are more with us," as 2 Kings 6:16 says.[48] Nor the second group, because there are wiser people among us, and because Acts 6:10 has: "They were not able to withstand the wisdom and the Spirit who spoke."[49] Similarly neither the third group. 1 John 4:4 reads: "You have overcome them, because greater is he who is in you than he who is in the world."

19. And since there is danger in speaking in front of a crowd that watches every word and since danger leads to fear, and fear to anxiety, and anxiety to an unsettled mind, and an unsettled mind to disorder, and disorder is the occasion for impatience and spiritual ruin, Christ calls them away from useless anxiety and says: *Do not be anxious how or wherewith you will respond,* that is, "to those who are interrogating you" maliciously, *or what you will say,* namely, "to those who want to learn."[50] By

---

[47] On p. 315, n. 4 QuarEd indicate that the manuscript tradition of Bonaventure's quotation is corrupt. Acts 5:26 reads: "Then the magistrate went off with the officers and brought them (the Apostles) without violence, for they feared the people lest they should be stoned."

[48] These are the words of the prophet Elisha.

[49] These are the words of Stephen.

[50] On p. 315, n. 6 QuarEd state that Bonaventure is quoting the Glossa Interlinearis here: "*Do not be anxious how,* about the manner of proceeding, *or wherewith,* about the manner of finding suitable words, *you may respond,* to those wishing to learn."

saying this, he does not take away the anxious solicitude *which is the desire for learning*, but that of *curiosity*. About this Philippians 4:6 states: "Have no anxiety, but in every prayer and supplication with thanksgiving let your petitions be made known to God," for, as James 1:5 says, "if any of you lacks wisdom, let him ask it of God," etc. And this is especially to be done in a situation of need, where no elaborate words or profound statements are required, but the sheer and simple truth of faith, expressed in great constancy and fervor. This is in accordance with what is said in 1 Corinthians 2:4: "Our preaching was not in the persuasive words of human wisdom," etc. Also he does not intend to draw a person away from *the study of the truth*, since he himself says in John 5:39: "Search the Scriptures, in which you think that you have eternal life."[51] But his purpose is to persuade people, when they are in the danger of death, not to trust in their ingenuity. For when people rely on their ingenuity, their inventiveness is poor, their judgment falls short, and they frequently miss the mark. For which reason Proverbs 3:5 reads: "Trust in the Lord with all your heart, and do not rely on your own cleverness."

20. (Verse 12). Secondly, he confers *certitude about aid* when he says: *For the Holy Spirit will teach you in that very hour what you ought to say.* Now this Spirit is the best teacher, for the Spirit teaches men and women *to understand* and *to express themselves in a refined manner*. Relative to the first point it is said in Job 32:8: "The inspiration of the Almighty gives understanding." And John 16:13 has: "But when he, the Spirit of Truth, comes, he will teach you all the truth," for, as it is said

---

[51] It seems clear that Bonaventure is taking *Scrutamini* as an imperative, "Search," rather than as an indicative, "You search."

in 1 Corinthians 2:10: "The Spirit searches all things, even the deep things of God." Relative to the second point it is said in Wisdom 10:21: "Wisdom opened the mouth of the dumb," etc.[52] And Matthew 10:20 reads: "It is not you who are speaking, but the Spirit of your Father."[53] Therefore, the Apostle said in 2 Corinthians 13:3: "Are you seeking for a proof of the Christ who speaks in me?" – Now concerning these two Luke 21:15 below states: "I will give you utterance and wisdom which all your adversaries will not be able to resist or gainsay." And 1 John 2:27 says: "The anointing teaches you about all things."[54] Wherefore, Bernard says: "Reading is good, but better is anointing, which *teaches about all things.*"[55] For the anointing teaches love of God and neighbor, and on this "depend the whole Law and the Prophets," according to what is said in Matthew 22:40. Also, all *the wisdom of philosophy*, as Augustine

---

[52] Bonaventure's point may be found more readily in the second part of Wisdom 10:21: ". . . and made the tongues of infants eloquent."

[53] On p. 315, n. 12 QuarEd cite the Glossa Interlinearis: *"For the Holy Spirit will teach you*, etc., for your words will proceed not from your ingenuity or skill, but from the grace of the Holy Spirit."

[54] 1 John 2:20 is helpful to grasp Bonaventure's meaning: "But you have an anointing from the Holy One, and you know all things." 1 John 2:27 reads in its entirety: "And as for you, let the anointing that you have received from him, dwell in you. And you will have no need that anyone teach you. But as his anointing teaches you concerning all things and is true and is no lie, even as it has taught you, abide in him."

[55] On p. 316, n. 1 QuarEd point their readers to *Declamationes de Colloquio Simonis cum Jesus, Ex S. Bernardi sermonibus collectae* of Geoffrey the Abbot, Chapter 15 "De quatuor virtutibus." The quotation Bonaventure cites can be found in PL 184:447B: "Therefore, reading is useful. Learning is useful. But much more necessary is the anointing, for it alone teaches about all things." In his commentary on Luke 9:23 (#38) above Bonaventure quoted from chapter 2 of this same work.

says: "Here is physics, ethics, and civics."[56] The Holy Spirit, by making the soul adhere to God, even makes it God's intimate friend, to whom God reveals secrets. John 15:15 reads: "But I say to you, my friends." Now the fervor of the Spirit elevates the soul above itself, where it hears and sees secret things, as happened to Paul according to 2 Corinthians 12:4, and to Ezekiel as Ezekiel 3:12 says: "The Spirit took me up," etc., and to John as Revelation 1:10 states: "I was in the Spirit," etc.

Luke 12:13–59
INSTRUCTION ON TWO KINDS OF SOLICITUDE

21. *Now someone out of the crowd said to him*, etc. After he had deterred them from deceit coming from human timidity and from timidity itself, he deters them from *cupidity* in this section. And this section has two parts. In the first one *he restrains them from the solicitude that is avarice*. In the second *he stirs them to solicitude that is providence* where verse 35 reads: *Let your loins be girt*, etc.

---

[56] On p. 316, n. 2 QuarEd provide a lengthy quotation from Augustine's Letter 137, chapter 5, n. 17. In this section of his letter Augustine deals with the twofold commandment of love, but doesn't say in so many words what Bonaventure quotes him as saying. I have adapted the translation of Sister Wilfrid Parsons in *Saint Augustine Letters, Volume III (131–164)*, FC 20 (New York: Fathers of the Church, 1953), p. 33–34: "Herein is physics, since all the causes of all natures are found in God, the Creator. Herein is ethics, since the good and honorable life is formed in no other way than by loving what ought to be loved as it ought to be loved, that is, God and our neighbor. Herein is logic, since there is no other truth and light for the rational mind than God. Herein is civics, the praiseworthy security of the state, for the best city is erected and safeguarded on no other foundation than the bond of faith and unbreakable concord."

Luke 12:13–34
ABOUT THE SOLICITUDE THAT IS AVARICE

In his curbing of *the solicitude that is avarice*, he makes four points. First, he provides *a discursive teaching*. Second, he cites *a frightful example* where verse 16 has: *But he spoke to them a parable*, etc. Third, he makes *an unassailable argument* where verse 22 states: *And he said to his disciples*, etc. Fourth, *he promises the things that are desired* where verse 29 reads: *And as for you, do not seek what you will eat*, etc.

Luke 12:13–15
DISCURSIVE TEACHING AGAINST AVARICE

His *discursive teaching* against the solicitude that is avarice has three components. First is *the silencing of an avaricious petition*. The second aims *to dissuade people from avarice*. The third *assigns a reason* for this teaching.

22. (Verse 13). First, then, relative to *the silencing of an avaricious petition* the text has: *Now someone out of the crowd said to him: Master, tell my brother to divide the inheritance with me*. Truly, he was *from the crowd*, because *he was solicitous about the earth*, according to what Isaiah 29:4 says: "Your speech will be muttered out of the earth," etc. He also spoke against himself when he called him *master*. For Christ did not profess to be a teacher who taught how to acquire and divide temporal goods, but rather on how to abandon such things. To the young man who asked: "Good master, what shall I do to gain eternal life?" he responded: "If you desire to

be perfect, go and sell," etc.[57] Therefore, Christ did not teach how money might be increased, but how want might be preserved. – He also speaks against himself, when he desires *to be divided from his brother*, with whom he should be joined. But this question came from self-love, which divides what is joined.[58] This is what the devil, not the Lord, especially does. Hosea 13:15: "He will divide the brothers."[59]

23. (Verse 14). And since, as Bede says in the Glossa, "Christ is not a God of dissension, but of peace and unity,"[60] he rejects the aforementioned petition. The text

---

[57] Bonaventure's quotation is an idiosyncratic combination of Matthew 19:16, 21 and Luke 18:18, 22

[58] On p. 316, n. 11 QuarEd refer to Book XI, chapter 15, n. 19–20 of Augustine's *De Genesi ad litteram*. I employ the translation of John Hammond Taylor, *St. Augustine, The Literal Meaning of Genesis*, Volume II Books 7–12, ACW 42 (New York: Newman, 1982), pp. 146–147: ". . . *Avarice is the root of all evils*, if we understand 'avarice' in the general sense of the word, that is, the attitude by which a person desires more than what is due by reason of his excellence, and a certain love of one's own interest, his private interest, to which the Latin word *privatus* was wisely given, a term which obviously expresses loss rather than gain. . . . But St. Paul, in using the word, intended to go from the special to the general meaning and wished avarice to be understood in the broad sense of the word when he said, *Avarice is the root of all evils*. For it was by this vice that the Devil fell, and yet he certainly did not love money, but rather his own power. . . . Opposed to this disease is charity, who *seeks not her own*, that is, does not rejoice in her own (*privata*) excellence....There are, then, two loves, of which one is holy, the other unclean; one turned towards the neighbor, the other centered on self; one looking to the common good...."

[59] See Hugh of St. Cher, p. 207v, m: "Therefore, to divide a community is the office of the devil, not of Christ. Hosea 13:4: He will divide between the brothers, namely, the infernal one, that is, the devil."

[60] On p. 316, n. 12 QuarEd state that this is the Glossa Ordinaria on Luke 12:14. For Bede, see CCSL cxx, p. 250: "The Lord denies that he is the one who divides men and women. He had come to offer them peace with himself and with the angels. For he is not a God of dissension, but of peace."

reads: *But he,* namely, Jesus, *said to him: Man, who has appointed me judge or arbitrator over you?,* that is, a judge over lawsuits and a divider of properties. The Glossa reads: "He is disdained to be a judge over lawsuits and an arbiter over properties, who possesses judgment over the living and the dead and the assessment of merits."[61] It is indeed true as it is said in the Psalm that "He has been appointed[62] king by him over Zion, his holy mountain" (2:6) and that "all things have been placed in his[63] power" (Esther 13:9). But since God had sent him to communicate spiritual matters, he refused to descend to dividing material things, suggesting by this what is said in 2 Timothy 2:4: "No one serving as God's soldier entangles himself in worldly affairs." – And note that Christ calls him *man,* an animal and a brute, on account of *love for earthly matters* and a *lawsuit over a division of property.* Wherefore, 1 Corinthians 3:3 has: "Since there are jealousy and strife," etc.[64] And the Psalm states: "O you children of men, how long will you be dull of heart?" (4:6). So in this a silencing of the avaricious petition is taught.

24. (Verse 15). Second, about *dissuading people from avarice,* the text adds: *And he said to them: Take heed*

---

[61] On p. 316, n. 14 QuarEd state that this is the Glossa Ordinaria apud Lyranum and is based on Ambrose. For Ambrose's interpretation, see CCSL xiv, p. 255. The major difference between Bonaventure's quotation and the interpretations of the Glossa and Ambrose lies in one verb. Bonaventure reads *dedignatur* ("he is disdained") whereas the other two read *dignatur* ("he is granted"). Hugh of St. Cher, p. 207v, m quotes Ambrose's interpretation and has the verb *dignatur.*

[62] The Vulgate reads *ego constitutus sum* ("I have been appointed").

[63] The Vulgate reads *tua* ("your").

[64] Bonaventure's point is made by a quotation of all of 1 Corinthians 3:3: "Since there are jealousy and strife among you, are you not carnal, and walking as mere men?" See also 1 Corinthians 2:14: "But the animal man does not perceive the things that are of the Spirit of God. . . . "

and guard yourselves from all avarice. Take heed, namely, so that you are careful, and *guard yourselves,* so that you are cautious. Ephesians 5:15 reads: "Take heed, brothers, that you walk cautiously, not as unwise, but as wise," etc. For *providence* makes people guard themselves against dangers, into which a person may fall for the sake of avarice. 1 Timothy 6:9–10 has: "Those who seek to become rich fall into temptation and a snare of the devil[65] and many useless and harmful desires, which plunge men and women into destruction and damnation. For cupidity is the root of evils," etc.[66] Thus it blinds a person, which was signified in the blinding of Tobias by the dung of the swallows in Tobit 2:11.[67] And therefore, he says: *Take heed,* namely, be eternally vigilant, *and guard yourselves from avarice,* which seeks temporal goods, according to what 2 Corinthians 4:18 has: "While we look not at the things that are seen, but at the things that are not seen. For the things that are seen are temporal, but the things that are not seen are eternal." And since the desire for any transitory good whatsoever, namely, for money and power and honor, can be termed *avarice,* he says: *guard yourselves against all avarice.*[68]

---

[65] The Vulgate does not have *diaboli* ("of the devil").

[66] The Vulgate reads *omnium malorum* ("of all evils").

[67] Swallows have positive and negative symbolism. Positively, they are symbols of rebirth, harmony and domestic contentment. Herbert Friedmann, *A Bestiary for Saint Jerome: Animal Symbolism in European Religious Art* (Washington: Smithsonian Institution Press, 1980), p. 298 refers to the negative symbolism: ". . . in the Low Countries in the fifteenth century . . . it came to signify lewdness, because of a tale that the young birds, while still in the nest, were blinded by their own excrement. This led to moralizing along the following line: 'As the swallow is blinded by its own excrement, thus do the unchaste' fall into sin and error." Perhaps, in Bonaventure's circle the moralizing went: "As the swallow is blinded by its own excrement, thus do the avaricious fall into sin and error."

[68] On p. 317, n. 4 QuarEd refer to Book XI, chapter 15, n. 19 of Augustine's *De Genesi ad litteram.* See note 58 above.

Isaiah 33:14–15 reads: "Who could dwell with the eternal flames?[69] . . . The person who casts aside avarice by false accusations and shakes his hands free of all bribes."

25. Third, concerning *the assignment of a reason or cause,* the text adds: *For it is not in an abundance of any kind, his life does not consist in what he possesses.*[70] That is, the life of any person does not consist *in abundance. Abundance,* I say, *of the things he possesses.* That is, no one on account of the abundance of his riches can live longer. The Psalm has: "They[71] will leave their riches to strangers, and their tombs will be their houses forever" (48:11–12). And Job 27:19 reads: "The rich man, when he falls asleep, will take nothing with him," etc. And the Psalm says: "They have slept their sleep. And all the men of riches have found nothing in their hands" (75:6). Wherefore, *abundance* does not prolong one's life, but often shortens it. Sirach 8:3 states: "Gold and silver have destroyed many." And Acts 8:20 has: "May your money go with you into perdition." And therefore, it ought to be destroyed, lest it destroy its possessor. Sirach 29:13 says: "Lose your money for your brother and friend, and hide it not under a stone to be lost."

Luke 12:16–21
CHRIST GIVES A FRIGHTFUL EXAMPLE AGAINST AVARICE

26. (Verse 16). *But he spoke a parable to them, saying,* etc. Here he provides a second teaching against the anxiety that is avarice through *a frightful example.* He

---

[69] The Vulgate reads *Quis poterit habitare de vobis cum igne devorante?* ("Who of you could dwell with devouring fire?").

[70] The first part of this verse in the Vulgate is elliptical.

[71] In the original Psalm "they" refers to "the senseless and the fool."

makes three points: *the occasion* of useless security, *the conception* of useless security, *the elimination* of useless security.

So relative to *the occasion of useless security* stemming from an abundant harvest, he says: *The land of a certain rich man brought forth abundant crops.* For the goods of the rich customarily issued from an abundance of temporal fruits. The Psalm says: "Their storehouses full, flowing out of this into that. Their sheep," etc. (143:13).[72] Wherefore, Job 21:7–9 reads: "Why do the wicked live, elevated and strengthened by riches? . . . Their houses are secure and peaceable, and the rod of God is not upon them."

27. (Verse 17). And since riches make people so secure that they become anxious and restless, the text adds: *And he began to take thought with himself, saying: What will I do, for I have no room to store my crops?* Qoheleth 4:7–8 states: "There is another vanity that I saw under the sun. There is but one, and he has not a second . . .[73] and yet he does not cease to labor. Neither are his eyes satisfied with riches." Indeed, they are certainly anxious. Qoheleth 5:11 says: "The fullness of the rich does not allow him to sleep."

28. (Verse 18). And the reason for this is that he is constrained *to think.* And so the text adds: *And he said: I will do this. I will pull down my barns and build larger ones. And therein I will store up all my grain and my goods.* The Glossa says: "Behold, great anxiety springs

---

[72] Psalm 143:13 reads in full: "Their storehouses full, flowing out of this into that. Their sheep fruitful in young, abounding in their goings forth."

[73] Bonaventure has abbreviated to the point of obscurity. The full text reads: "he has not a second, neither son nor brother."

from avarice,"[74] and causes what had been constructed
to be destroyed and replaced by new buildings. For although the barns were full, vain cupidity sought new
storehouses. Qoheleth 5:9 has: "The avaricious person
will not be satisfied with money," etc. And Sirach 14:9
reads: "The eye of the avaricious person is insatiable. In
his portion of iniquity he will not be satisfied."[75] His
barn was full, but his heart was empty. The reasons for
this are multiple. Only God can fill the soul which is capable of receiving the Trinity.[76] Temporal goods do not
enter the heart except through apparent similarity.
They increase concupiscence. They do not make the soul
better. Further, they are of an entirely different nature,
like the differences between an angel and a bodily place
or the soul and a bodily treasure. Moreover, the soul,
since it has quantity not by mass, but by power, is not
filled by material quantity, but by an amount of power
like the grace of the Holy Spirit – Wisdom 1:4–5 and
Acts 2:4.[77]

---

[74] On p. 317, n. 11 QuarEd indicate that this is the Glossa Interlinearis and cite a broad parallel from Book XV, chapter 22, n. 26 of the
Moralia of Gregory the Great.

[75] I have translated this quotation according to the punctuation given
by QuarEd. Sirach 14:9 may be translated in full as: "The eye of the
avaricious person is insatiable in his portion of iniquity. He will not
be satisfied till he consume his own soul, drying it up."

[76] On p. 318, n. 1 QuarEd cite the author of *Liber de Spiritu et anima*
(among the works of Augustine), chapter 27: "For it pertains only to
the Trinity to enter and fill a nature or a substance which the Trinity has created." They also refer to Basil, Homily "in illud Lucae *De-
struam horrea mea* etc. (alias Homil. 6 in Ditescentes), n. 1–2."

[77] Bonaventure is engaging in a rapid philosophical discussion here
about the nature of the soul. Wisdom 1:4–5 reads: "For wisdom will
not enter into a malicious soul, nor dwell in a body subject to sins.
For the Holy Spirit of discipline will flee from the deceitful and will
withdraw himself from thoughts that are without understanding.
And he will not abide when iniquity enters." Acts 2:4 has: "And they
will all filled with the Holy Spirit and began to speak in foreign
tongues, even as the Holy Spirit prompted them to speak." On p. 318,

29. (Verse 19). Now secondly, concerning *the conception of useless security* through a foolish promise the text continues: *And I will say to my soul,* that is, to my sensual nature.[78] John 12:25 has: "The person who loves his soul loses it." – *Soul, you have many good things stored up for many years.* Revelation 3:17 states: "You say that I am rich and have grown wealthy and have need of nothing," etc.[79] Zechariah 11:5 has: "Blessed be the Lord. We have become rich." – And since an abundance with security gives birth to the evil of moral depravity, the text adds: *Take your ease.* Behold, *negligence.* Qoheleth 4:5–6 says: "The fool folds his hands together . . . and says: Better is a handful with ease than both hands full with labor and vexation of mind." *Eat.* Behold, *gluttony.* Sirach 11:19 reads: "I have found my ease, and now I will eat of my goods alone." *Drink,* to the point of *drunkenness.* Against this Proverbs 23:20–21 states: "Do not attend the feasts of the great drinkers . . . because they who give themselves to drinking and club together will be consumed." *Be merry.* Behold, *wantonness.*[80] James 5:5 says: "You have feasted upon earth, and you have nourished your hearts on dissipation."[81] These are the vices that the rich were accustomed to. Amos 6:1–6 says: "Woe to you who are wealthy in Zion . . . who sleep upon beds of ivory and are wanton

---

n. 2 QuarEd refer to Augustine's *De quantitate animae,* chapter 3, n. 4–5.

[78] See Hugh of St. Cher, p. 208k: "And I will say to my soul. Gl. that is, to my sensual nature."

[79] Revelation 3:17 continues with: ". . . and does not know that you are the wretched and miserable and poor and blind and naked one."

[80] See Hugh of St. Cher, p. 208o–r: "Take your ease: negligence or sloth. Eat: gluttony. Drink: drunkenness. Be merry: dissipation." That is, Hugh has a skeletal interpretation whereas Bonaventure's is typically expanded by scripture quotations.

[81] James 5:5 is addressed to the rich and ends with "on the day of slaughter."

on your couches, who eat the lambs from the
flock ... drinking wine in bowls and are anointed with
the finest oil." Now the cause of this wantonness is useless security, which the soul stupidly conceives, or *by
promising* itself a long temporal life through *presumption*, according to what Isaiah 28:15 says: "We have entered into league with death and have made a pact with
hell. When the overflowing scourge will pass through, it
will not come upon us." Or *by showing contempt* through
despair. Isaiah 22:13 has: "Let us eat and drink, for tomorrow we will die."

30. (Verse 20). Thirdly, with regard to *the elimination of
useless security* through the equity of a divine sentence,
the text continues: *But God said to him*. The Glossa has:
"God's *word* to the man is a sudden rebuke and restrains
him from his evil machinations."[82] – For which reason
the text adds the sentence: *Fool, this night they will demand*[83] *your soul of you*. 1 Thessalonians 5:3 reads:
"When they will say: Peace and security, then sudden
destruction will come upon them." He calls him *a fool* on
account of his earthly wisdom, for 1 Corinthians 1:20
says: "God has turned to foolishness the wisdom of this
world." The fool is the person who does not foresee future
dangers. Qoheleth 2:14 states: "The eyes of a wise man
are in his head. The fool walks in darkness." For, uncer-

---

[82] On p. 318, n. 8 QuarEd state that this is the Glossa Ordinaria
from Bede. The Glossa is almost verbatim with Bede, for whose text
see CCSL cxx, p. 251. Hugh of St. Cher, p. 208s has almost the
same text as Bonaventure, but says that it comes from Bede. Here
are the Latin texts. Bonaventure: *Dicere Dei ad hominem est pravas
eius machinationes subita animadversione compescere*. Bede: *Haec
Deo ad hominem dicere est prauas eius machinationes subita ani-
maduersione compescere*. Hugh: *Bed. Dicere Dei ad hominem, &
pravas ejus machinationes subita animadversione compescere*.
[83] On p. 318, n. 9 QuarEd correctly mention that the Vulgate reads
repetunt ("they demand").

tain about the future, he sleeps secure. Proverbs 27:1 gives contrary counsel: "Boast not for tomorrow, for you do not know what the next day may bring forth." And James 4:14 has: "What is our[84] life? It is a mist that appears for a little while." Ambrose comments: "There are no goods that a person can take with him. Mercy is the sole companion of the dead."[85] So 1 Timothy 6:7 says: "We brought nothing into this[86] world, and certainly we can take nothing out." And Job 20:20–22: "When he had things he coveted, he was unable to possess them. . . . When he shall be filled, he shall be in straits. . . . And every sorrow shall fall upon him."[87]

31. (Verse 21). And since this sentence is common for all avaricious people, the text adds: *So is everyone*[88] *who lays up treasure for himself, and is not rich as regards God. He lays up treasures for himself* refers to the person who multiplies treasures for himself on earth. The Psalm says: "He lays up things and does not know for whom he will gather them" (38:7). But *to be rich as regards God* refers to the person who abounds in merits and the works of piety. 1 Corinthians 1:5–7 reads: "In all things you have been enriched in him...so that you lack no grace." Therefore, it is said in Matthew 6:19–20: "Do not lay up for yourselves treasures on earth, where rust and moth consume . . . but lay up for yourselves treasures in

---

[84] The Vulgate has *vestra* ("your").

[85] On p. 318, n. 11 QuarEd state that Ambrose's interpretation is cited according to the Glossa Ordinaria. For Ambrose's exegesis, see CCSL xiv, p. 255: "For neither can we take with us our possessions. Virtue is the only companion of the dead. Only mercy accompanies us."

[86] The Vulgate does not have *hunc* ("this").

[87] Hugh of St. Cher, p. 208u cites Job 20:20–22, Job 27:19, and 1 Timothy 6:7.

[88] On p. 318, n. 12 QuarEd accurately mention that the Vulgate does not have *omnis* ("everyone").

heaven, where neither rust nor moth consume, nor thieves break in and steal."[89] – Now *hope* makes us *rich as regards God*. We have this hope in God, according to what 1 Peter 1:3–4 has: "He has begotten us again . . . unto a living hope, unto an incorruptible inheritance . . . reserved in heaven." Now this hope is rooted in poverty. So 2 Corinthians 6:10 states: "As poor, yet enriching many; as having nothing, but possessing all things." Such a person was Paul. Thus, he writes in Philippians 4:18: "I have all and more than enough." Christ has made us such. Therefore, 2 Corinthians 8:9 says: "He became poor for your sakes, that by his poverty you might become rich." Wherefore, he says to such people: "Blessed are the poor in spirit, for theirs is the kingdom of the heavens" (Matthew 5:3).[90]

Luke 12:22–28
CHRIST GIVES AN UNASSAILABLE ARGUMENT AGAINST AVARICE

32. *And he said to his disciples*, etc. Here in a third way he deters them from the anxiety that is avarice *by an unassailable argument*, which is drawn from the three genera of creatures. First, from *rational* creatures. Second, from *sensitive* creatures where verse 24 reads: *Consider the ravens*. Third, from *vegetable* creatures where verse 27 says: *Consider the lilies of the field.*[91]

---

[89] On p. 319, n. 1 QuarEd cite the Glossa Ordinaria: "The person who is rich as regards God is the one who, contemning transitory things, has given them to the poor. His expectation is the Lord. Whose sum and substance, that is, the possession of his conscience, by which he is sustained and flourishes, lies with God, not with earthly purses."

[90] Bonaventure's Franciscan christological orientation is evident here, as he roots hope in the Lord's poverty for us.

[91] On p. 319, n. 5 QuarEd correctly indicate that the Vulgate does not have *agri* ("of the field") and mention that the parallel passage in Matthew 6:28 has "of the field."

So, first, from the *rational* creature he fashions the following argument: The person who gives what is greater will give what is less. But the soul is more than food and the body more than clothing. Therefore, the one who has given soul and body will give food and clothing. Therefore, it is not necessary to be anxious about these. In this reasoning process he first gives his *principal conclusion* in advance and then adds *the proof*.

33. (Verse 22). So in the first place he gives his *principal conclusion* in advance when he says: *Therefore, I say to you: Do not be anxious for your soul, what you will eat, nor for your body, what you will put on*,[92] that is, don't be anxious about food and clothing, which are most necessary for life. Be anxious much less over other things that pertain to the present life. Philippians 4:6 has: "Have no anxiety, but in every prayer and supplication with thanksgiving let your petitions be known to God." – And note that he does not prohibit anxiety, which stems from *care for the soul*, but that which issues from *distrust of God*, as if God does not care about us. To the contrary is what 1 Peter 5:7 states: "Cast all your anxiety upon God, because he cares for you." And the Psalmist says: "Cast your care upon the Lord," etc. (54:23). And Ambrose comments: "It is shameful for a person, who is fighting for the kingdom, to care about food or about clothing. For the king knows how to feed, nourish, and clothe his family."[93]

---

[92] The Vulgate does not read "your" soul nor "your" body. See Matthew 6:25 which has "your soul" and "your body."

[93] In his commentary on Luke 12:31 in CCSL xiv, p. 258 Ambrose writes: "Certainly, it is shameful for men, who are fighting for the kingdom, to care about food. The king knows how to feed, nourish, clothe his family." Hugh of St. Cher, p. 208v, b comments: "*Ambrose in the Glossa.* It is shameful for a person to care about food, or about clothing who is fighting for a kingdom, that is, for a temporal king in

34. (Verse 23). Then he adds *the proof*, when he says: *The soul is greater than food, and the body greater than clothing*. From this it follows: The one who gave the greater will also supply what is less. Ambrose has: "It is absurd for us to think that a supply of food be lacking to us, who are receiving the continual substance of life from God."[94] For the soul and body are constitutive parts of a human being, for whose sake all creatures have been made, according to what Genesis 1:26 says: "Let us make man to our image and likeness . . . and let him have dominion over the birds of the air," etc. Therefore, Chrysostom has: "God made all things for the sake of man, but man for his own sake. God made all things in wisdom, but man not only in wisdom, but also according to his own wisdom."[95] Thus, Wisdom 6:8 reads: "He made the little and the great, and cares equally for all." And Augustine in his *De agone christiano* states: "God cares for Angels and for rational souls by himself, but he governs all the others through them."[96] – And note that in

---

the literal sense, or for the eternal kingdom. The temporal king, or the eternal, knows how to feed, nourish, clothe his family." Did Bonaventure abbreviate Hugh?

[94] Bonaventure's quotation is virtually the same as that found in CCSL xiv, p. 256.

[95] On p. 319, n. 10 QuarEd refer to Chrysostom's Homily 16 on Matthew 6:26 (*Opus Imperfectum*), and indicate that Bonaventure's text abbreviates much. See Hugh of St. Cher, p. 208v, c where this quotation appears almost verbatim: "Wherefore, Chrysostom: God made all things for the sake of man, but man for his own sake. And *below*. God made all things in wisdom, but man not only in wisdom, but also according to his own wisdom."

[96] On p. 319, n. 11 QuarEd cite Augustine's *De agone christiano*, chapter 8, n. 9. I use the translation of Augustine's *The Christian Combat* by Robert P. Russell in *Saint Augustine: Christian Instruction, Admonition and Grace, The Christian Combat, Faith, Hope and Charity*, 4 (New York: CIMA Publishing Co., 1947), p. 325: "God exercises a direct Providence over holy, rational creatures (whether the most exalted and excellent of the angels, or men who serve Him wholeheartedly), but rules everything else by means of these. Ac-

his comparison he rightly prefers the soul to food and
the body to clothing, for the soul gives vigor to the body
by animating it, and the body is like the soul's clothing
which appears on the outside. Therefore, if God provides
vigor for the body through the soul's enlivening, how
much more steadfastly does God provide a sufficiency of
life-sustaining nourishment. Again, if God provides the
clothing of the body for the soul, how much more readily
the covering of external clothing.[97]

35. (Verse 24). *Consider the ravens.* Here he takes up the
argument from *the sensitive creature.* And first, *he sets
forth his example.* Then he makes his *argument.*

So he proposes *an example* to be considered and says:
Consider the ravens. They neither reap nor sow. Behold,
they do not engage in the practice of work.[98] *They have
no cellar,* to store their wine. *Nor barn,* to hold their
grain. Behold, they do not have a storeroom. *And God
feeds them.* Behold, they lack nothing. The Psalm says:
"Who gives beasts their food and to the fledglings of ra-

---

cordingly, it was also possible for the Apostle to say in all truth: 'For
God has no care for oxen.'" Two further points need to be made.
Augustine uses Luke 12:5–6, 24, 27 in his interpretation. See Hugh
of St. Cher, p. 208v, c whose quotation of Augustine is virtually identical to that of Bonaventure: "*Augustine de Agone Christiano.* God
cares for Angels and for holy rational souls by himself; he governs all
the others through them."

[97] On p. 319, n. 12 QuarEd cite a passage from Ambrose that introduced the quotation Bonaventure used earlier in this section #34.
See CCSL xiv, pp. 255–256: "Therefore, since the soul is clothed with
the garment of the body and the body is enlivened by the vigor of the
soul, it is absurd. . . . "

[98] On p. 320, n. 1 QuarEd call attention, in dealing with textual matters, to Bonaventure's apparent dependence on Ambrose here. See
CCSL xiv, p. 256: "For if divine providence bestows the needed
nourishment for the birds of the heaven, who engage in no practice of
cultivation and have no crop from the abundance of a harvest. . . . "

vens that call upon him" (146:9) – And note that he sets
forth the example of ravens rather than that of other
birds. And one reason for this comes from their extraordinary gluttony. So it is said in Genesis 8:6–7 that "from
the window of the ark Noah sent forth a raven, which
went forth and did not return." And the reason for this
is that it fell upon a carcass.[99] A second reason is found
in the nature of the raven. The raven does not feed its
young in the beginning, because it does not think they
are hers until it sees that they are black.[100] Job 38:41
reads: "Who provides the raven with its food, when her
young ones cry out to God, wandering about, because
they have no food?" Therefore, it is fitting that *ravens*
can stand for the other birds.[101] Matthew 6:26 has:
"Look at the birds of the heaven, for they do not sow,"
etc.[102]

---

[99] On p. 320, n. 2 QuarEd cite Augustine's *Questions on Genesis*,
question 15 which deals with the question of what happened to the
raven who flew out from the ark and never returned. Augustine answers: "It is conjectured by many that the raven could have fallen
upon a carcass, which the dove by nature flees from."

[100] On p. 320, n. 3 QuarEd quote extensively from Book XXX, chapter
9, n. 33 of Gregory's *Moralia* to provide a parallel. A search on the
internet turned up "The Aberdeen Bestiary Project, Folio 37r of Aberdeen University Library." This medieval text from the time of
Bonaventure has this to say about the raven: "It is said that when its
young have been hatched, the bird does not feed them fully until it
sees that they have black feathers similar to its own. But after it has
seen that they are of dark plumage and has recognized them as of its
own species, it feeds them more generously."

[101] On p. 320, n. 4 QuarEd cite the Glossa Interlinearis on Luke 12:24:
"*Consider the ravens.* Matthew: *birds.* Therefore, here the species
stands for the genus."

[102] Hugh of St. Cher, p. 208v, d also quotes Matthew 6:26, Psalm
146:9, and Job 38:41 in his explication of the meaning of the ravens.
It seems to me that Bonaventure has obtained his second reason by
summarizing Hugh's longer interpretation.

36. Then *he draws out his argument* by adding: *Of how much more value are you than they?* The Glossa reads: "On account of reason and the immortality, that is promised you, you are of more value."[103] 1 Corinthians 9:9–10 states: "Is it for oxen that God has care? . . . For these things were written for our sakes." – But since someone could argue the contrary position that we are due more care than ravens because of the excellence of our reason, he shows that this is nothing. For if our bodily stature does not *increase* through human thought, but through divine determination, the same thing also holds for *an increase in food.*

37. (Verse 25). For which reason he adds: *But which of you by thinking about it can add to his stature a single cubit?* As if he were saying: Not one, because this does not pertain to the power of a human person thinking, but is the work of God bringing forth. So it is said in 2 Maccabees 7:22: "I do not know how you were formed in my womb. Nor did I give you . . . life, nor did I myself frame the limbs of every one of you." And 1 Corinthians 15:38 has: "God gives it a body, even as he wills, and to each of the seeds a body of its own." Therefore, the Philosopher also says that "it is the nature of all existing things to have a limit and a principle of size and increase."[104] Therefore, if these minimal matters are not within human control, but have been constituted in the

---

[103] On p. 320, n. 5 QuarEd indicate that this is the Glossa Interlinearis and intimate that it is based on Book I of Jerome's commentary on Matthew 6:26.

[104] On p. 320, n. 8 QuarEd point to Book II, chapter 4 of Aristotle's *De Anima.* The Greek text can be found in Book II, chapter 4 #416a. See *Aristotelis Opera Omnia Graece et Latine . . . Volumen Tertium* (Paris: Firmin-Didot, 1927), 449 #(8): *At eorum omnium quae natura constant, est finis et ratio, tam magnitudinis quam accretionis* ("But it is the nature of all things that exist to have a limit and principle, both of size and of increase").

control of divine providence, how much less other matters.

38. (Verse 26). So he adds: *Therefore, if you are not able to do even a very little thing, why are you anxious about the rest?* As if he were saying: It's useless and foolish. Bede says: "Leave the body to be clothed by him, who made it come to this stature."[105] – However, this reason does not seem to be valid, for, although we should not be anxious about *increasing our stature*, nonetheless we can and should be anxious about *nutriment*. For although *the augmentative* power of our bodies is not subject to our will and reason, nothing, however, impedes the *nutritive* power except when it is necessary to do so because of one's regimen and foresight.

Nonetheless, the answer to this is that the reasoning is sound. For, if human beings ought not control and care for those things which have been committed to *the providence of nature,* by like reasoning neither should they be concerned about those things committed to *heavenly providence.* – Again, just as human beings cannot lengthen their bodies, so too they cannot prolong the end of their lives which the Lord has established. –

---

[105] On p. 320 QuarEd indicate that this quotation actually comes from the Glossa Interlinearis. For Bede's more involved statement, see CCSL cxx, p. 253. Since Bede is actually quoting from Augustine, I use Denis J. Kavanagh's translation in *Saint Augustine, Commentary on the Lord's Sermon on the Mount with Seventeen Related Sermons*, FC 11 (New York: Fathers of the Church, 1951). His translation of Book II, chapter 15, n. 51 on p. 158 reads: "Your body can also be clothed by the providence of Him through whose power and dominion it has come to pass that your body should be brought to its present stature." See Hugh of St. Cher, p. 209b: *"Beda.* Therefore, leave the body to be clothed by him, who makes it come to this stature." It seems that Bonaventure is adapting the quotation of Bede he found in Hugh's commentary.

Finally, if we must not be anxious about our bodies' stature, but be content with the height the Lord has granted us, why don't we behave similarly about external nourishment?

39. (Verse 27). *Consider the lilies*, etc. In his third point he *develops an argument from vegetable nature*. And first, he sets forth *a sensible similitude*, and then adds his *adaptation*.

So he first sets forth *a similitude* when he says: *Consider the lilies of the field*,[106] *how they grow. They neither toil nor spin*. Ambrose comments: "A clear comparison. Lilies do not require, like other flowers, any cultivation from farmers."[107] Wherefore, they grow not by human industry, but by divine command, which had been given from the beginning of the world. Genesis 1:11 reads: "Let the earth bring forth the green herb." – And since the work of the Most High Artificer is more excellent than every work of human art, the text adds: *Yet I say to you that*[108] *not even Solomon in all his glory was arrayed like one of these*. And yet Solomon was most attentive to the grand appearance of his clothes and marshaled together will, industry, and means to adorn himself. Wherefore, it is said of him in 1 Kings 10:4–5: "When the queen of Sheba saw all the wisdom of Solomon and the apartments of his servants and the order of his ministers and their apparel...she no longer had any spirit in her." And this, because he had most expertly ordained all things according to human industry. But

---

[106] The Vulgate does not have *agri* ("of the field").

[107] On p. 321, n. 1 QuarEd state that Ambrose's interpretation is taken from the Glossa Ordinaria. For Ambrose's more involved commentary, see CCSL xiv, p. 257.

[108] On p. 321, n. 3 QuarEd correctly indicate that the Vulgate does not read *quia* ("that").

nevertheless, they could not equal the works and the industry of nature, which is God's work. Thus, Bede says: "What purple of kings, what tapestry can be compared to flowers?"[109]

40. (Verse 28). Then after the similitude he adds *its adaptation* and infers a *conclusion: But if the grass which today is in the field and tomorrow is thrown into the oven,* that is, quickly dries up. The Psalm says: "Let them be like grass on tops of houses, which withers before it is plucked up" (128:6). And James 1:11 reads: "The sun rises with a burning heat and parches the grass. And its flower falls, and the beauty of its appearance perishes." *God so clothes,* namely, with beauty, adornment and grace: "The color of the flower is said to be its clothing."[110] – *How much more you, O you of little faith?,* that is, how much more will he clothe you, even if you have a modicum of faith, for both by reason of nature and by reason of faith you surpass them. Wherefore, it is said in Matthew 14:31 to Peter, who is doubting the Lord's omnipotence during the storm at sea: "O you of little faith, why did you doubt?" The person has *little faith* in the rule of paternal providence whose daily fear is that he will die of hunger. The Psalm says: "They did not believe in God nor trusted in God's salvation. . . . God commanded the

---

[109] See CCSL cxx, p. 253: "And truly, what silk, what purple of kings, what tapestry can be compared to flowers?" See Hugh of St. Cher, p. 209e: *"Bede.* What purple of kings, what tapestry can be compared to flowers?"

[110] Bonaventure gives no reference to this quotation. On p. 321, n. 7 QuarEd cite the Glossa Ordinaria on Luke 12:27: "The color of the flower is said to be its clothing, as it is said: Shame covered him [cf. Psalm 68:8: Shame covered my face]." I wonder whether Bonaventure's source is not Hugh of St. Cher, p. 209e: *"Bede.* What purple of kings, what tapestry can be compared to flowers? The color of the flower is said to be its clothing, as it is said in common speech. Shame covered him. *Psalm* 68. Shame covered my face."

clouds from above and opened the doors of heaven, and manna rained down upon them to eat," etc. (77:22–24). Therefore, if someone is of the true faith, that person believes that heavenly providence governs all things.[111] God's providence exercises greater care and must exercise such care over the more precious, more worthy, and more lasting of creatures, over rational creatures rather than non-rational and vegetative creatures. And even for these lesser creatures God's providence is such that they lack nothing. Therefore, how much more is it to be believed that God will care for those things that pertain to the governing of humans who are more precious, superior, and more worthy than all the other creatures. For they are rational and are made in the image of God. Therefore, this reasoning is unassailable, for, if someone says anything against it, he destroys the governance of divine providence and the order of the universe. And therefore, such a person not only has little faith, but also has a perverse opinion.

Luke 12:29–34
CHRIST DETERS FROM AVARICE BY PROMISING THE THINGS THAT ARE DESIRED

41. (Verse 29). *And as for you, do not seek what you shall eat.* Here in a fourth point he deters them from the anxiety that is avarice by *promising the things that are desired.* He introduces three points. For he dissuades them from the anxiety that is avarice and covetousness by promising *a sufficiency of provisions for the journey,*

---

[111] On p. 321, n. 10 QuarEd indicate that this section is corrupt "in Vat. et codd." I have taken the liberty of fashioning short sentences for the sake of some clarity.

great excellence of reward,[112] and *a superabundance of treasure.*

So first, he dissuades them from the anxiety that is avarice and covetousness *by promising a sufficiency of provisions for the journey* and says: *And as for you, do not seek what you shall eat or what you shall drink,* namely, as the covetous and ceaselessly inquisitive seek, so that they may abound and become haughty. – Therefore, he adds: *And do not exalt yourselves,*[113] on account of the acquisition of earthly things.[114] 1 Timothy 6:17 has: "Charge the rich of this world not to be haughty or to trust in the uncertainty of riches."[115] For to search for earthly things in such a manner is not fitting for heavenly men and women, but for earthly ones.

42. (Verse 30). Therefore, he adds: *For after all these things the nations of the world seek,* for they have worldly wisdom. Baruch 3:23 says: "The children of Hagar who sought after wisdom that is of the earth, the merchants of Midian and Teman." But heavenly men do not have to be intent on these matters, for they belong to the family of the Most High Father. – So the text continues: *But your Father knows that you need these things.* And there

---

[112] Bonaventure uses the rare word *superexcellentia*. Rather than translate this by "superexcellence," I have used "great excellence."

[113] Modern English translations, based on the very rare Greek verb, *meteorizomai*, read: "And do not keep on worrying" (NRSV). The Vulgate reads *Et nolite in sublime tolli.*

[114] On p. 321, n. 13 QuarEd helpfully refer to Augustine's Sermon 61, chapter 9, n. 10. I use the translation of Denis J. Kavanagh, *Saint Augustine, Commentary on the Lord's Sermon on the Mount with Seventeen Related Sermons,* FC 11 (New York: Fathers of the Church, 1951), p. 283: "Charge them what? (1 Timothy 6:17). Charge them most especially not to be proud. Riches beget nothing else so much as pride....The worm of riches is pride."

[115] Hugh of St. Cher, p. 209p also quotes 1 Timothy 6:17.

is no doubt that *he can* provide them. Romans 10:12 has: "There is the same Lord of all, rich towards all who call upon him." There is also no doubt that *he wants to.* Isaiah 49:15 states: "Can a woman forget her infant, so as not to have pity on the son of her womb?," etc.[116] And therefore, those who want to set off for the heavenly homeland are not forsaken on the journey for lack of food.

43. (Verse 31). For which reason he adds: *But seek first the kingdom of God,* as your principal purpose, *and all these things will be given to you,* as provisions for the journey. For the one who is disposed to give *the kingdom* without hesitation will not deny *food.* The one who is prepared to give eternal goods will not deny temporal goods. Therefore, Augustine comments: "The Lord shows that temporal things are not to be sought as our goods, even though they are necessary. But the kingdom of God is to be sought, and in it we find the reason for which we do everything."[117] So our anxiety must not be focussed on obtaining food, but on obtaining the eternal kingdom. Romans 14:17 reads: "The kingdom of God does not consist in food and drink, but in justice and peace and joy in the Holy Spirit." Chrysostom says: "The kingdom of God is *recompense.* Justice is *the way,* by which we come to the kingdom."[118] – And note that this promise is ex-

---

[116] Isaiah 49:15 concludes with: "...and if she should forget, yet I will not forget you."

[117] On p. 322, n. 4 QuarEd refer to Book II, chapter 16, n. 53 of Augustine's *Commentary on the Lord's Sermon on the Mount* and state that Bonaventure's quotation is actually taken from Glossa Ordinaria on Matthew 6:33. Hugh of St. Cher, p. 209v, c has: "*Augustinus.* Here he plainly shows that temporal things are not to be sought as our goods, even if necessary. But the kingdom of God is to be sought, and in it we find our reason, for which we do everything." Did Bonaventure find his quotation of Augustine in Hugh?

[118] On p. 322, n. 6 QuarEd cite Chrysostom's Homily 16 on Matthew 6:33 (*Opus Imperfectum*): "*The kingdom of God* is the recompense for

ceedingly just, for the person who seeks *the kingdom and its justice* is God's *servant*, God's *friend* and God's *son*. Romans 8:14 reads: "Those who are led by the Spirit of God, they are the sons of God." Now God does not keep things away from his servant, friend, and son, so that he does not provide for him those things that are necessary. To think otherwise of God is most perverse. For such a person belongs to God. Such a person is possessed by God, and therefore has, as a consequence, the things that God possesses. Wherefore, the Apostle says in 1 Corinthians 3:22–23: "All things are yours, and you are Christ's, and Christ is God's."

44. (Verse 32). Secondly, he dissuades from the anxiety that is avarice *by promising a great excellence of reward* and says: *Do not be afraid, little flock*. The words, *little flock*, are used to distinguish them from *the multitude of the reprobates*. Matthew 20:16 says: "Many are called, but few are chosen." Another interpretation is that they are *little* by reason of *their own insignificance*. 1 Corinthians 1:26 has: "Consider your own call, brothers, that there were not many wise according to the flesh, not many mighty," etc. Yet another interpretation is that they are *little* by reason of *voluntary humility*. Ezekiel 34:31 states: "But you men and women are my flocks, and I am your God."[119] For God is the God of the humble. Sirach 3:21 reads: "God is the power of God alone, and

---

good deeds and bad deeds. On the other hand, *justice* is the path of piety, by which one journeys to the kingdom." Hugh of St. Cher, p. 209v, b comments: "*Chrysostom*. The kingdom of God is recompense, justice is the way, by which one journeys to the kingdom." It seems that Bonaventure quoted Chrysostom's text from Hugh.

[119] Bonaventure's text is strange. Ezekiel 34:31 reads: "But you are my flocks, the flocks of my pasture are men and women. And I am the Lord your God, says the Lord God."

God is honored by the humble."[120] And to such people
God promises the kingdom in Matthew 19:14: "Let the
little children...come to me. For of such is the kingdom
of the heavens."[121] – Therefore, he adds: *For it has
pleased your Father to give you the kingdom.* Proverbs
29:23 says: "Glory will uphold the humble in spirit." And
Job 22:29 states: "The person who has been humbled
will be in glory." Now this great excellence of the promised kingdom leads to *hope*, and by instilling hope, leads
to *assurance*, and through this it takes away *the pusillanimity*[122] *of fear* and *the burning desire of avarice.* 2
Corinthians 6:10 reads: "As poor, yet enriching many, as
having nothing, yet possessing all things." For only that
kingdom is the true possession of the heart, which fills
the heart and cannot be taken away, for it is inside.
Luke 17:21 below says: "Behold, the kingdom of God is
within you."

---

[120] On p. 322, n. 10 QuarEd give some rationale for Bonaventure's
first and third interpretation by calling their readers' attention to
Bede's commentary. See CCSL cxx, p. 254: "He calls them a little
flock of the elect either on account of a comparison with the greater
number of the reprobate or rather on account of the fervor of humility." Bede then goes on in this eight-line sentence to explain the humility involved in being so small in number, etc. In this context it is
important to note that in his interpretation of this passage Hugh of
St. Cher quotes both Ezekiel 34:31 and Bede. See Hugh of St. Cher,
p. 209v, e: "*Ezekiel* 34g[31]. You are my flocks, the flocks of my pasture are men and women, and I am your God. Little, as *Bede* says, is
used either in comparison with the greater number of the reprobate
or rather on account of the fervor of humility, through which humility the Church grows, through which humility it arrives at the kingdom."
[121] Hugh of St. Cher, p. 209v, h also quotes Matthew 19:14: "Let the
little children come to me, and do not prevent them, for of such is the
kingdom of the heavens."
[122] Bonaventure's word play here is on the stem *pusill-*, which stands
behind the "little" (*pusillus*) of "little flock" and is manifest in pusillanimity.

45. And note that the Father is pleased *to give the kingdom of glory* to the little ones, that is, the poor in spirit.[123] Wherefore, Matthew 5:3 has: "Blessed are the poor in spirit, for theirs is the kingdom of the heavens." For such *desire eternal things.* Proverbs 10:24 reads: "To the righteous their desire will be given." And the Psalm says: "The Lord has heard the desire of the poor" (9:17), because *they despise temporal things.* Matthew 19:29 states: "Who have left father or mother . . . will receive a hundredfold," etc. *They embrace spiritual things.* Galatians 5:25–26 reads: "If we live by the Spirit, let us also walk by the Spirit. Let us not become covetous of vainglory." – In like manner it has pleased the Father *to grant them forgiveness.* Judith 9:16 says: "The prayer of the humble and meek has always pleased you," namely, to grant forgiveness. Exodus 33:19 has: "I have mercy on whom I will have mercy."[124] – It has pleased the Father *to give grace.* Isaiah 42:1 states: "Behold, my servant, I will uphold him, my elect," etc.[125] – It has pleased the Father *to give wisdom.* Matthew 11:25 reads: "You have hidden these things from the wise and clever and have revealed them to little ones." – It has pleased the Father *to give eternal glory*, as in this verse: *Do not be afraid, little flock*, etc. The Psalm says: "The Lord takes pleasure

---

[123] It seems that Bonaventure is borrowing the interpretation of "the kingdom" found in Hugh of St. Cher and adapting it to his Franciscan interpretation on the role that poverty plays in discipleship. See Hugh of St. Cher, p. 209v, g: "To give you the kingdom of doctrine, grace, glory."

[124] On p. 323, n. 1 QuarEd rightly indicate that Bonaventure's reading is not that of the Vulgate, which has *Miserebor cui voluero* ("I will have mercy on whom I will"). They call attention to Romans 9:15: "I will have mercy, upon whom I have mercy." In his commentary on Luke 10:21 (#9) above Bonaventure quotes the Vulgate accurately.

[125] Bonaventure's point about "giving grace" may be found in what all of Isaiah 42:1 says: "Behold, my servant, I will uphold him, my elect. My soul delights in him. I have given my spirit upon him, and he will bring forth judgment to the Gentiles."

in those who fear him, and in those who hope in his mercy" (146:11).

46. (Verse 33). Thirdly, he dissuades from the anxiety that is avarice *by promising a superabundant treasure* for abandoning worldly treasure when he says: *Sell what you possess and give alms*, that is, distribute your goods to the poor, according to what Matthew 19:21 has: "Go and sell all[126] that you have and give to the poor." – And since it is difficult to sell and give without recompense, the text adds: *Make for yourselves purses that do not grow old.* Sirach 17:18–19 reads: "The alms of a man are like a purse with him and will preserve the grace of a person like the apple of his eye. And afterward he will rise up and will render them their reward, to every one upon their own head." – And since this reward is the most opulent, that is contained in these *purses*, he adds: *a treasure unfailing in the heavens. You are making* is to be understood behind this text, and this happens through almsgiving. Wherefore, Tobit 12:8–9 says: "Prayer with fasting and alms is good and greater than to amass treasures of gold. For alms delivers from death . . . and makes[127] one attain eternal life." – And he shows that this heavenly treasure is *unfailing.* Since it cannot be taken away *by thieves*, cannot be *destroyed directly by itself*, the text continues: *where neither thief draws near nor moth destroys.* Chrysostom notes: "All the good things of the world are subject to one of three dissolutions. For either they grow old of themselves, or they are consumed by the debauchery of their owners, or are stolen by strangers through deceit, force, or calumny."[128] And

---

[126] "All" (*omnia*) is not found in Matthew 19:21, but in the parallel passage of Luke 18:22.

[127] The Vulgate reads *faciet* ("will make").

[128] On p. 323, n. 7 QuarEd refer to Chrysostom's Homily 15 on Matthew 6:19 (*Opus Imperfectum*). See Hugh of St. Cher, p. 209v, o:

therefore, on earth it is impossible to have a treasure that is unfailing. Therefore, those who want an unfailing treasure should distribute their earthly treasures, so that their treasures may abound in heaven. The Psalm reads: "He distributed and gave to the poor. His justice remains forever and ever" (111:9). Thus, Augustine comments: "The Lord did not command that we should lose our treasures, but shows us the place where we should put them."[129]

"*Chrysostom.* All the good things of the world are subject to one of three dissolutions. For either they grow old of themselves. Hebrews 8d[13]: Everything that is obsolete and has grown old is near its dissolution. Or they are consumed by the debauchery of their owners, etc. James 4a[9]: Act now, you rich, weep, sobbing in your misery, etc. Or are stolen by strangers through deceit, force, or calumny, for all who through iniquity hasten to make the goods of others their own are called thieves. John 10a[8]: Whoever have come are thieves and robbers." If Bonaventure has based his quotation of Chrysostom on that of Hugh, why has he omitted the references to Scripture? Bonaventure's interpretive style was to interpret Scripture by Scripture. The pertinent section of Chrysostom's commentary is found in the spurious work, *Opus Imperfectum.* See PG 56:719: *Omnia bona mundi triplex interitus tollit. Aut enim a semetipsis veterascunt, et tineant, sicut vestimenta: aut ipsis dominis luxuriose viventibus comeduntur, sicut caeterae facultates : aut ab extraneis vel dolo, vel vi, vel calumniis, vel quolibet alio iniquo modo diripiuntur. Quia omnes fures dicuntur, qui per iniquitatem festinant aliena facere sua* ("All the good things of the world are subject to one of three dissolutions. For either they grow old of themselves, and are eaten by moths, like clothes. Or they are consumed by their owners living debauchedly, like other faculties. Or are stolen by strangers either by deceit or by force or by calumnies, or by whatever iniquitous manner. For all who through iniquity hasten to make the goods of others their own are called thieves").
[129] On p. 323, n. 8 QuarEd refer to Augustine's Sermon 86 (alias 43 De Diversis), chapter 1, n. 1. See PL 38:524: "For it is not as avaricious non-believers think: Our God wanted us to abandon our things. If what has been commanded us is well understood, and piously believed, and devoutly accepted, he did not command us that we should lose our goods, but shows us the place where we should put them." See Hugh of St. Cher, p. 209v, n: "*Aug.* The Lord did not command that we should lose our treasures, but shows us the place where we

47. (Verse 34). But great effort has to be expended where the treasure is located, for there, too, will one's reason be located. Therefore, he adds: *For where your treasure is, there also will be your heart. Treasure* is that which the reason loves principally, according to what Matthew 13:44 reads: "The kingdom of the heavens is like a treasure hidden," etc. But where the thing that is loved principally is located, there will reason dwell. So Bernard says: "The soul is more truly where it loves than where it is animating."[130] And therefore, where your treasure is, there too is your heart. Bede comments: "If your heart is fixed on the earth, it is downward. If in the heavens, it is fixed on Christ. For it is a necessary rule that where the treasure one loves has gone, there, too, affective thought will follow."[131] And since the wise person has treasure in heaven and the foolish on earth, Qoheleth 10:2 has: "The heart of the wise person is in his right hand, and the heart of a fool is in his left hand,"

---

should put them." It seems that Bonaventure has quoted Augustine verbatim from Hugh.

[130] On p. 323, n. 10 QuarEd cite Bernard's *De Praecepto et dispensatione*, chapter 20, n. 60: "For our spirit is more present not where it is animating, but where it loves. . . . Finally, where your treasure is, there is your heart (Matthew 6:21)." See SBOp 3.292.

[131] On p. 323, n. 11 QuarEd give the source(s) of this quotation as follows: "Cardinal Hugh attributed this opinion to Chrysostom (see his Homily 20 [alias 21] on Matthew, n. 3). But Gorranus attributed it to the Glossa Ordinaria where it occurs verbatim. Its beginning is taken from Bede, who is following Book I of Jerome's commentary on Matthew 6:21)." See Hugh of St. Cher, p. 210p: "If on earth, the heart is downward. If it is in the heavens, it is fixed on Christ. For it is a necessary rule that where the treasure one loves has gone, there, too, affective thought will follow." As far as I can tell from consulting Bede's commentary in CCSL cxx, p. 255, he has no substantial words in common with Bonaventure. See Augustine's Homily 86, chapter 1, n. 1 in PL 38:524: "Therefore, if one's things are buried in the earth, the heart seeks the lowest things. But if one's things are kept in heaven, the heart will be above."

etc.[132] 2 Corinthians 4:18 reads: "While we look not at the things that are seen, but at the things that are not seen. For the things that are seen are temporal, but the things that are not seen are eternal." For this treasure that is *visible* and earthly consists in *money*.[133] But the *invisible* treasure consists in wisdom. Wisdom 7:11, 14 state: "All good things came to me together with her. . . . For she is an infinite treasure to men and women. When they use this treasure, they become sharers in God's friendship."

48. And note that this treasure, which consists of wisdom, *begins with reverential fear.* Isaiah 33:6 says: "Riches of salvation, wisdom and knowledge; the fear of the Lord is his treasure." And *it grows and makes progress* in *studious discipline.* Matthew 13:52 reads: "Every scribe instructed in the kingdom of the heavens," etc. *It is preserved* by *a holy conscience.* Luke 6:45 above has: "The good person from the good treasure of his heart," etc. *It is consummated* in *sublime glory.* Matthew 19:21 states: "If you want to be perfect, go, sell all[134] that you have . . . and you will have treasure in heaven." – And such people are mentioned here. Wherefore, he promises to the poor *food for the journey, a kingdom of excellence,* and *a treasure of abundance.* For the poor are wont to be afflicted and despised and poor for the name of our Lord Jesus Christ.

---

[132] Hugh of St. Cher, p. 210p also quotes this passage.

[133] Bede (CCSL cxx, p. 255), and Hugh of St. Cher (p. 210p), follow Jerome's interpretation (PL 26:45CD), and mention gluttony, lust, lasciviousness as well as avarice (money).

[134] Matthew 19:21 does not have *omnia* ("all") whereas the parallel in Luke 18:22 does.

Luke 12:35–59
ENCOURAGEMENT ABOUT THE ANXIETY THAT IS PROVIDENCE

49. *Let your loins be girt about,* etc. After he has deterred them from the anxiety that is avarice, here, in a second point, he urges them to *the anxiety that is providence,* lest anyone might think that he wanted to remove all anxiety from the human heart. Now he urges them to this type of anxiety through a consideration of the two comings. First, he considers *the second coming* which will be terrifying. Secondly, he treats *the first coming* which was amiable where verse 49 reads: *I have come to cast fire on the earth.*

Luke 12:35–48
ENCOURAGEMENT THROUGH CONSIDERING THE SECOND COMING

This first part has two sections. In the first he urges *all generally* to the anxiety of vigilance. In the second he gives *special consideration to prelates* where verse 41 has: *But Peter said to him.*

Luke 12:35–40
CHRIST URGES ALL TO THE ANXIETY THAT IS VIGILANCE

In his *general leading of all* to a consideration of the anxiety that is vigilance he proceeds in this order. First, he sets forth *the manner of vigilance.* Secondly, he adds *the motivation* where verse 37 says: *Blessed are those servants,* etc. Thirdly, he introduces *an incentive* where verse 39 states: *But of this be assured,* etc. The first of these deals with *merit.* The second with *reward.* The third with *imminent danger.*

Now concerning *the manner of vigilance* the Evangelist introduces the two points which the Lord urges upon his disciples, namely, *an unimpeded promptness in the body* and *an anxious expectation in the heart.*

50. (Verse 35). First, then, relative to *unimpeded promptness in body* he says: *Let your loins be girt about,* etc. Like a person unincumbered, who has been girt about to make progress on the journey, like a person unimpeded, who restrains the carnal desires in himself. Wherefore, Gregory writes: "Voluptuousness for the principal sex is designated by the word *loins.*"[135] Job 40:11 says: "His strength is in his loins," etc.[136] "Therefore, *we gird about our loins,* when we restrain the voluptuousness of the flesh through continence. But since it is not sufficient not to do evil, unless someone also strives to strenuously engage in good works, he immediately adds: *and your lamps burning in your hands.* Indeed, we have lamps burning in our hands when we show the example of our light of good deeds to our neighbors."[137] For it is fittingly said that *lamp* means the divine commandment. Proverbs 6:23 reads: "The commandment is a lamp, and the law a light," etc. This lamp is *in the hand,* when the commandment is being

---

[135] On p. 324, n. 5 QuarEd refer to Homily 13, n. 1 of GGHG. See note 137 below.

[136] Job 40:11 continues: ". . . and his force in the navel of his body."

[137] On p. 324, n. 5 QuarEd point to Homily 13, n. 1 of GGHG. See PL 76:1123D–1124A. Bonaventure puts Gregory's quotation from Job 40:11 in a different place and restricts Gregory's reference to both male and female voluptuousness. Other than these two adaptations his quotation is fairly verbatim. See CCSL cxx, p. 256 where Bede also quotes from Gregory's homily on Luke 12:35–40. See Hurst, pp. 151–152 where Gregory's Homily 13 is renumbered as Homily 20. Hugh of St. Cher, p. 210d quotes Job 40:11 in its entirety and then quotes Gregory's interpretation: "He says loins on account of men, and navel on account of women, as *Gregory* says."

fulfilled. Proverbs 31:18–19 states: "Her lamp will not be extinguished in the night. She had put out her hand to strong things," etc. And Matthew 5:16 says: "Let your light shine before men and women, so that they may see your good works," etc. – And note that just as the lamp hides the light from the wind, but not from sight, so too are good works compared to the lamp. For "so must the deed be in public, while the intention remains in secret."[138] In this way a person wants to give an example of virtue to others while at the same time he is not seeking the gift of transitory favor.[139]

51. (Verse 36). Secondly, concerning *the anxious expectation in the heart* the text continues: *And you yourselves like people waiting for their master's return from the wedding*, that is, when he will come in judgment, descending from the heavens. So Gregory states: "The Lord went away to the wedding when after his resurrection he joined himself as the new man to the multitude of angels. He will return when he is manifested to us through the judgment."[140] Wherefore, the good must always wait for him. Philippians 3:20 has: "We await a

---

[138] On p. 324, n. 7 QuarEd indicate that this quotation comes from Homily 11, n. 1 of GGHG. See PL 76:1115B. Bonaventure's quotation is almost verbatim. As a matter of fact, Gregory's entire sentence helps explain Bonaventure's next sentence. Hurst, p. 63 translates this part of what he calls Homily 9 as follows: "We must let our work be in the open in such a way that our intention remains secret. Then we provide an example to our neighbors from our good work, and yet by the intention by which we seek to please God alone we always choose secrecy."

[139] On p. 324, n. 8 QuarEd provide an extensive note on a textual variant here and how both variants – *munus* ("gift") and *nummus* ("coin") – resonate with interpretations of Gregory.

[140] On p. 324, n. 9 QuarEd refer to Homily 13, n. 2 of GGHG. See PL 76:1124B. Bonaventure has made some adaptations to Gregory's interpretation, e.g., he has shortened "after rising from the dead and ascending into heaven" to "after his resurrection."

Savior, the Lord Jesus Christ," etc. And this expectation
is not *vain*. Proverbs 17:8 reads: "The expectation of the
person who waits is a very attractive jewel." This expectation is also not *drowsy*. The Psalms states: "Expect the
Lord and act courageously" (26:14). – And therefore,
the text adds: *so that when he comes*, "hastening to the
judgment,"[141] *and knocks*, through the affliction of infirmity, *they may straightaway open for him* with intimate desire. Revelation 3:20 says: "Behold, I stand at
the door and knock. If anyone . . . opens the door to me, I
will come in to him," etc. Bede comments: "The person
who doesn't want to open the door to the judge who
knocks is the one who, afraid to see him mad whom he
has disdained, is frightened to leave his body. The person who opens the door is the one who has been happily
and securely waiting and who rejoices at approaching
death."[142] The Song of Songs 5:2,5 has: "The voice of my
beloved knocking . . . I rose up to open to my beloved,"
etc.[143]

52. And it should be noted here that this Gospel is read
on the feasts of Confessors, because they are given a triple commendation. That is, with regard to *restraining*

---

[141] On p. 324, n. 11 QuarEd indicate that this is the Glossa Interlinearis which continues its interpretation with: "*and knocks*, designat-
ing by sicknesses that death is near, *straightaway opens to him*,
happy to receive him." They give the accurate intimation that this
interpretation is based on Homily 13, n. 3 of GGHG. See PL
76:1124C.

[142] On p. 324, n. 12 QuarEd state that this quotation stems from
Bede who is quoting Homily 13, n. 3 of GGHG. The quotation itself
comes from the Glossa Ordinaria. See PL 76:1124C for Gregory's
more extended commentary which is what Bede quotes. See CCSL
cxx, p. 256.

[143] Hugh of St. Cher, p. 210v, d quotes Bede, James 5:9, Revelation
3:20, The Song of Songs 5:2, and the Glossa of Bede. Hugh's quotation of the Glossa of Bede agrees word for word with that of
Bonaventure.

evil in girting their loins; with regard to *doing good* in carrying a lamp, and with regard to *expecting the best* in the similitude of the people waiting for their master. Further, in accordance with the three things mentioned in Micah 6:8: "I will indicate to you, O human, what is good . . . to do judgment" with respect to yourself, "to love mercy" with respect to your neighbor, "and to walk solicitously with your God" with respect to God.

53. Now to achieve the goal that *evil be completely absent* in us, *our loins must be triply girt*. First, *touches* of the carnal loin, about which the Psalm says: "My loins are filled with illusions, and there is no health in my flesh" (37:8). And these are girt about with the cincture of *chastity*. Isaiah 32:11–12 reads: "Gird your loins. Mourn for your breasts," etc. – Secondly, *the affection* of the carnal loin by the cincture of strong *virtue*. Job 40:2 states: "Gird up your loins like a strong man."[144] And Jeremiah 1:17 has: "Gird up your loins, rise up and speak to them." – Thirdly, *the thought* of the carnal loin by the cincture of *truth*. 1 Peter 1:13 says: "Having girded up the loins of your understanding, be sober," etc.[145]

54. Now to achieve the goal of having *the good in us shine completely, the lamp of a righteous intention must be carried*. Luke 11:34 above had: "The lamp of your body is your eye." – Further, the lamp of *true preaching* must be carried. The Psalm says: "Your word is a lamp for my feet" (118:105). Sirach 48:1 reads: "Elijah . . . rose up like a fire, and his word burnt like a torch." – Moreover,

---

[144] I have tried to capture Bonaventure's word play on *virtus* ("virtue") and *vir* ("man") through use of the adjective "strong."

[145] See Hugh of St. Cher, p. 210d where he also quotes Psalm 37:8, 1 Peter 1:13, Isaiah 32:11–12, Job 38:2 (= Job 40:2), and Jeremiah 1:17, but does so to make points other than those made by Bonaventure.

the lamp of *integrity of life*. John 5:35 says: "He was a lamp, burning and shining."[146] And the Psalmist has: "There I will bring forth a horn for David. I have prepared a lamp for my Christ" (131:17).[147]

55. Finally, to achieve the goal of having *desire inflamed completely, Christ must be faithfully waited for*. Habakkuk 2:3 states: "If he makes a delay, wait for him, for he will surely come," etc.[148] – Further, he must be expected *with joy*. Proverbs 10:28 reads: "The expectation of the just is joy," etc. – Moreover, he must be expected *vigilantly*. Job 14:14 says: "All the days in which I am now in warfare, I expect until my change comes." And in this way the servants are expecting "their master, when he returns from the wedding." – Thus the blessed Confessors are perfectly praised according to what Titus 2:12–13 has: "We may live temperately and justly and

---

[146] The reference is to John the Baptist.

[147] Psalm 131:17 originally referred to "my anointed." On p. 325, n. 8 QuarEd observe: "Cardinal Hugh also makes a threefold distinction of the lamp." I elaborate on their observation. Hugh of St. Cher, p. 210b takes the first lamp to be that of "the light of erudition" and illustrates it with a quotation from Matthew 5:14. He takes the second lamp to be "the ardor of compassion" and illustrates it with quotations from 2 Corinthians 11:29, Sirach 48:1, John 5:35, and Blessed Bernard. The third lamp is "manual assistance" and is illustrated by Proverbs 31:20. On a second level of interpretation of the three lamps, Hugh considers the first to be "a pure intention of the mind" and supports this view by quoting Luke 11:34 and the Glossa. The second lamp is "the word of preaching" and is supported by quotations from Psalm 118:105, Proverbs 31:18, and Romans 15:18. The third lamp is "the example of integrity of life" and is illustrated by Psalm 131:17 and John 1:4. While borrowing some terminology and Scripture quotations from Hugh, Bonaventure has rewritten these materials for his reflections on the fitting nature of this gospel passage for the feast of Confessors.

[148] In Habakkuk 2:3 one waits for "a vision" (*visus*). I have changed "vision" to "him" to accommodate Bonaventure's interpretation. The Vulgate has *illum* ("him") while Bonaventure has *eum* ("him").

piously in this world, expecting the blessed hope and glorious coming of God," etc.[149]

56. (Verse 37). *Blessed are those servants*, etc. In his second point he brings up *the motivation for careful vigilance.* And it is twofold, namely, *the blessing of those who keep vigil* without *ceasing* and without any *exception.*

So relative to *the blessing of those who keep vigil without ceasing*, he says: *Blessed are those servants, whom the master, on his return, shall find vigilant.* Proverbs 8:34 has: "Blessed is the person who listens to me and keeps daily vigil at my gates." And therefore, Sirach 39:6 reads: "The just will give his heart to keep early vigil," etc. The Lord blesses such people. Job 8:5–6 states: "If you rise early and petition . . . the Almighty . . . he will immediately keep vigil with you and will make the dwelling of your justice peaceful." – So he adds: *Amen, I say to you that he will gird himself*, "preparing himself for recompense."[150] The Psalm says: "The Lord has reigned. He has clothed himself with beauty," etc. (92:1).[151] *And he will make them recline at table*, namely, at the eternal banquet. Ezekiel 34:15 states: "I will feed my sheep, and

---

[149] Titus 2:13 concludes with "glorious coming of our great God and our Savior Jesus Christ."

[150] On p. 325, n. 13 QuarEd cite the Glossa Interlinearis, which is taken from Homily 13, n. 4 of GGHG: *"He will gird himself*, preparing himself for recompense. *And will make them recline at table*, to be refreshed by eternal beatitude. Our reclining is to rest in the kingdom." See PL 76:1125: "He will gird himself, that is, he will prepare for recompense. And he will make them recline at table, that is, to be refreshed in eternal rest. Indeed, our reclining is to rest in the kingdom."

[151] Psalm 92:1 reads in its entirety: "The Lord has reigned. He is clothed with beauty. The Lord is clothed with strength and has girded himself."

I will make them lie down."[152] – *and coming over he will minister to them* with a most generous sharing. *Coming over*, that is, effecting a passing over. Sirach 24:26 has: "Come over to me all you who desire me," etc. For *from Christ* and *through Christ* we come over *to Christ*, namely, from the glory of the body to the glory of the soul, and from this to the glory of the Deity. For which reason John 10:9 reads: "I am the door. If anyone enter by me, that person will be saved." And John 14:6 states: "I am the way, the truth, and the life."[153] Now Christ is said *to minister*, because he will always give them the matter of the actual joy of unfailing sustenance. Revelation 7:16–17 says: "They shall neither hunger or thirst any more . . . for the Lamb, who is in the midst of the throne, will shepherd them and will guide them to the fountains of the waters of life." Revelation 19:9 has: "Therefore, blessed are they who are called to the Lamb's marriage supper," where the Lamb without blemish will be *spouse, food, Lord*, and *servant*. The Psalmist says: "They will be inebriated with the abundance of your house, and you will make them drink of the torrent of your pleasure" (35:9). He himself *will serve* and *will invite*, according to what The Song of Songs 5:1 states: "Eat, friends, and drink and be inebriated, dearly beloved."

---

[152] See Hugh of St. Cher, p. 210v, g–h: "g. I say to you that he will gird himself] preparing himself for recompense. Ps. 92: The Lord has reigned. He is clothed with beauty, etc. h. And he will make them recline at table] that is, to be refreshed in eternal beatitude. *Bede*. Our reclining is to rest in the kingdom. Ezekiel 34d[15]: I will feed my sheep, and I will make them lie down, says the Lord God."

[153] On p. 325, n. 14 QuarEd cite Homily 13, n. 4 of GGHG: "*Coming over* now, the Lord ministers to us, for he will fill us with the brightness of his light. Truly it is said *to come over*, since he returns from judgment to the kingdom. Or certainly the Lord *comes over* to us after the judgment, for he lifts us up from the form of humanity into the contemplation of his Divinity." See PL 76:1125A.

57. (Verse 38). Now with respect to *the blessing upon those who are completely vigilant* he adds: *And if he comes in the second watch or if he comes in the third*[154] *and finds them so, blessed are those servants.* And note here that *the three watches* are understood to be the three stages of present life, that is, *childhood, youth,* and *old age.* Therefore, the Glossa of Bede says: "He calls them watches in a similitude that stems from watchmen at night. The first watch is the guard of childhood, the second of youth, and the third of old age. If someone neglected to watch during *childhood,* that person should not yet despair. If that person was negligent during *youth,* he may at least finally repent *in old age,* for the faithful Lord patiently waits for our repentance."[155] Isaiah 30:18 reads: "Therefore, the Lord waits that he may have mercy on you. And therefore he will be exalted in sparing you. For God is the God of judgment. Blessed are all they who wait for him."[156] – And note that in Mark 13:35 it is suggested that there are *four* watches according to the way watchmen divide up the hours: "Watch," he says, "for you do not know when the Lord[157]

---

[154] On p. 326, n. 3 QuarEd correctly mention that the Vulgate has *in tertia vigilia* ("in the third watch").

[155] On p. 326, n. 4 QuarEd indicate that this is the Glossa Ordinaria on Luke 12:38 and state that the original text is much longer. They also mention that Bede is following Homily 13, n. 5 of GGHG. For Bede's far more involved interpretation, see CCSL cxx, p. 257. For Gregory, see PL 76:1125BC.

[156] Hugh of St. Cher, p. 210v, n also cites Isaiah 30:18. Immediately before his citation, however, he has an interpretation that sounds very much like that of the Glossa of Bede: "The first watch is the guard of childhood. The second is the guard of adolescence. The third is the guard of youth. The fourth is the guard of old age. Therefore, if someone neglects the first and second watch, let him not despair, because our faithful judge is still waiting up until the third watch. Wherefore, Isaiah 30:18. . . . "

[157] On p. 326, n. 6 QuarEd accurately indicate that the Vulgate reads *dominus domus* ("master of the house"). By eliminating "of the house,"

is coming: in the evening, or at midnight, or at cockcrow, or early in the morning." And *these watches* are understood to be the four stages in which a human person enjoys free will: the first and the last and two intermediary stages. The one in full maturity, the other in decline.[158] By this it is suggested that the Lord accepts our vigilance at every hour without exception, but especially the vigilance that commences with our youth. Lamentations 3:27 reads: "It is good for a man when he has borne the yoke from his youth."[159] And nevertheless, he does not refuse even the last watch of the old. Wherefore, it is said in Matthew 14:25 that "in the fourth watch of the night he came to his disciples, walking upon the sea." Therefore, no hour whatever is unprofitable, but it is most profitable *to watch*. Luke 21:36 below says: "Watch, praying at all times, that you may be accounted worthy to escape all these things that are to come, and to stand before the Son of Man," etc.

58. (Verse 39). *But of this be assured*, etc. Here in a third place he adds *an incentive for keeping watch* and does so in two points, namely, *by proposing a parabolic example* and *by concluding with his principle of how to be anxious.*[160]

Bonaventure has insured the reading of *dominus*, not as "master," but as "Lord."

[158] On p. 326, n. 6 QuarEd quote the opinions of Theophylactus and Blessed Albert on these four watches. They differ from each other and from the interpretation of Bonaventure.

[159] Hugh of St. Cher, p. 210v, n also quotes Mark 13:35 and Lamentations 3:27.

[160] On p. 326, n. 9 QuarEd cite the Glossa Interlinearis on Luke 12:39–40: "*But of this be assured*, he proves by a simile that they must keep watch. *Because . . . you must be ready . . .* after the similitude he provides an exhortation." They say that the interpretation of the Glossa Interlinearis is based on Homily 13, n. 5 of GGHG.

Therefore, he first *proposes a parabolic example* by saying: *But of this be assured, that if the head of the house had known at what hour the thief was coming, he would certainly have kept watch*, namely, to guard the house, lest a thief furtively steal something. – Therefore, he says: *he would not let his house be broken into*. And if he knew what hour to suspect, he would never leave his house unguarded. Otherwise, he would be caring for his family not in a wise, but in a foolish way. Take the example of Ishbaal, about whom 2 Samuel 4:5–6 says that "Ishbaal was sleeping upon his bed at noon. And the portress, who was sifting wheat, had fallen asleep. Now Rechab and Baanah, his brother, . . . secretly went into the house and stabbed him in the groin and fled."[161] Thus it also happens *spiritually* to the person who is negligent in vigilantly guarding his house. Wherefore, Gregory says: "While the portress was asleep, Ishbaal is killed, for, when protective care and discernment have ceased, he had opened the way for the evil spirits to kill the soul."[162] And therefore, the spiritual man counters this by saying what Isaiah 21:8 has: "I am upon the watchtower of the Lord, standing continually by day. And I am at my watch, standing for whole nights." And so 1 Peter 5:8 reads: "Be sober and watchful, for your adversary the devil," etc.[163]

59. (Verse 40). Then he concludes by giving his principle of how to be anxious. *You also must be ready, because*

---

[161] There seems to be some reduplication in this story, for 2 Samuel 4:7 goes on to narrate that they not only killed Ishbaal, but also beheaded him and fled with his head. Hugh of St. Cher, p. 211o also quotes 2 Samuel 4:5–6, but allegorizes the elements of the quotation as he mentions them, e.g., Rechab is death, and Baanah is the devil.

[162] On p. 326, n. 12 QuarEd refer to Book I, chapter 35, n. 49 of Gregory's *Moralia*.

[163] Hugh of St. Cher, p. 210v, o also quotes this passage.

at an hour that you do not expect, the Son of Man will come.[164] The Glossa says: "The Lord always wanted us to be ignorant of our final hour, so that it may always be expected, and so that we should always be prepared for it."[165] Thus, Matthew 24:36 reads: "of that day and hour no one knows," etc.[166] And 1 Thessalonians 5:2, 4 states: "The day of the Lord will come like a thief in the night. . . . But you, brothers, are not in the dark, that that day should overtake you like a thief."[167] And Qoheleth 9:12 says: "Human beings do not know their own end, but like fish are captured by the hook . . . so men and women are taken in the evil time."[168] Thus it is with those who do not prepare themselves. Therefore, it is said in Sirach 5:8–9: "Do not delay in converting to the Lord,[169] and do not defer it from day to day. For his wrath will come of a sudden and in the time of vengeance he will destroy you."[170] Wherefore, Alcuin comments: "It is dissolute to think of converting tomorrow

---

[164] The Vulgate reads *venit* ("is coming").

[165] On p. 326, n. 14 QuarEd state that this is the Glossa Ordinaria, taken from Bede, who bases his interpretation on that of Homily 13, n. 6 of GGHG. For Gregory's interpretation see PL 76:1126BC: "Indeed, our Lord wanted our final hour to be unknown to us, so that it might be always waited for, so that, since we could not anticipate it, we might be prepared for it without ceasing." See CCSL cxx, p. 257 where Bede follows Gregory's interpretation verbatim. Hugh of St. Cher, p. 211c also quotes the Glossa and has the exact same wording as Bonaventure.

[166] Hugh of St. Cher, p. 211c also quotes this passage.

[167] Hugh of St. Cher, p. 210v, c also quotes 1 Thessalonians 5:2, but not 5:4.

[168] Hugh of St. Cher, p. 211c quotes this passage, but also quotes the part that Bonaventure skipped, that is, "and like birds are caught in the snare."

[169] The Vulgate reads *Deum* ("God"). Hugh of St. Cher, p. 210v, n also has *Dominum* ("Lord").

[170] Hugh of St. Cher, p. 210v, n also quotes this passage.

and to put off converting today."[171] And Seneca writes: "Any day whatsoever of our life ought to be regulated as the final day."[172] Therefore, for the reason that we should always be prepared, the Lord wanted us to be ignorant of the hour of our death and of the day of judgment. "For nothing is more certain than death, but nothing is more uncertain than the hour of death."[173] Thus, Sirach 38:23 reads: "Remember my judgment. For yours will also be so. Yesterday for me, and tomorrow for you." And of the hour of judgment it is said in Matthew 25:6, 10: "At midnight a cry arose: Behold, the bridegroom is coming . . . those virgins who were prepared went in with him to the marriage feast, and the door was closed." Gregory says: "O, if taste could be with the palate of the heart, what surprise it would have at the words *The bridegroom is coming!*, what sweetness at

---

[171] On p. 327, n. 2 QuarEd refer to Alcuin's *De Virtutibus et Vitiis Liber*, chapter 14. Hugh of St. Cher, p. 210v, n has this same quotation in exactly the same words. See PL 101:623B where Alcuin writes: *Dissoluta et paralytica [Ms. periculosa] cogitatio est, de crastina cogitare conversione, et hodiernam negligere* ("It is dissolute and paralyzing [Mss. dangerous] to think of converting tomorrow and to put off converting today").

[172] On p. 327, n. 3 QuarEd cite Seneca's Epistle 12, n. 7. I use the LCL translation on p. 71: "Hence, every day ought to be regulated as if it closed the series (of days), as if it rounded out and completed our existence." There is one substantial verbal contact between Bonaventure and Seneca, namely, *ordinandus est* ("ought to be regulated"). Hugh of St. Cher, p. 210v, n has this same quotation in exactly the same words right after his quotation of Alcuin.

[173] On p. 327, n. 4 QuarEd say that this quotation comes from Anselm, *Meditatio* 7, chapter 1. See PL 158:741A: "Nothing more certain than death. Nothing more uncertain than the hour of death." The editors go on to quote Smaragdus, "Summarium in Epist. et Evangel. (Smargdo additum) in Natali Sanctorum plurim. Evang. Luc. 12., n. 3": "Death is certain. The day is uncertain. More uncertain is the hour. Therefore, let the wise person look after his soul."

They went in with him to the marriage feast!, what bitterness at *The door is closed!*"[174]

Luke 12:41–48
CHRIST URGES THE PRELATES TO BE VIGILANT

60. (Verse 41). *Now Peter said to him.* After he had urged all generally to be vigilant, here he singles out *the prelates* for special attention. And he does so in this order. For first *he commends vigilance on the part of the prelates.* Secondly, *he denounces insolence* where verse 45 says: *But if that servant says to himself,* etc. Thirdly, *he heavily attacks negligence* where verse 47 has: *But that servant who knew,* etc.

Now in *commending vigilance to the prelates,* he first commends it with regard to the privilege of *merit.* Secondly, he commends it relative to *the excellence of reward* where verse 43 reads: *Blessed is that servant.*

He demonstrates the first in his response to Peter's question where the text states: *But Peter said to him: Lord, are you speaking this parable to us or*[175] *to all?* He asks well and usefully, so that he may know to what he

---

[174] On p. 327, n. 5 QuarEd state that this quotation comes from Homily 12, n. 4 of GGHG. See PL 76:1120C where Gregory's opening gambit is slightly different than Bonaventure's: "O, if taste could be in the palate of the heart, what surprise it would have when it is said. . . . " In his commentary on Luke 12:40, "The Son of Man will come," Hugh of St. Cher, p. 211d quotes: Matthew 25:6, Augustine, 2 Corinthians 1:12, Sirach 13:30, and Gregory. His quotation of Gregory's opening words are: "O, if you would taste in the palate of the heart. . . . " His next words match those of Bonaventure's quotation verbatim.

[175] On p. 327, n. 9 QuarEd rightly mention that the Vulgate reads *an et* ("or also").

is obligated. Sirach 3:22 reads: "Think always on the things which God has commanded you." And especially those things are to be learned which are spoken in parables. Proverbs 1:5–6 has: "The wise person will listen and will become wiser. . . . He will understand a parable and its interpretation, the words of the wise and their enigmas."

61. (Verse 42). On a superficial level it does not seem that the Lord answers Peter's question. But upon closer examination he is giving a perfect answer, intimating that the aforementioned parable about vigilance pertains to *everyone generally*, but *to prelates in a special way* when he says: *But the Lord said: Who, do you think, is the faithful and prudent steward?* He calls prelates *stewards*. 1 Corinthians 4:1 states: "Let people so account us as servants of Christ and stewards of the mysteries of God." It is difficult to find that such people are faithful. Wherefore, 1 Corinthians 4:2 has: "Now here it is required among stewards that a person be found faithful." And Proverbs 20:6 states: "Many people are called merciful, but who will find a faithful man?" *Who, do you think, is the faithful steward?* In *purpose*. 1 Timothy 1:12–13 reads: "I have obtained the mercy of God in order that I may be faithful."[176] And Revelation 2:10 says: "May you be faithful until death." *And prudent, in election.* Proverbs 14:35 has: "A wise servant is acceptable

---

[176] On p. 327, n. 11 QuarEd accurately mention that this is not the Vulgate reading. It seems that Bonaventure has combined 1 Timothy 1:13 with 1 Timothy 1:12. 1 Timothy 1:12–13 reads: "I give thanks to Christ Jesus our Lord, who has strengthened me, because he counted me faithful in making me his minister. For I formerly was a blasphemer, a persecutor and a bitter adversary, but I have obtained the mercy of God because I acted ignorantly, in unbelief." The editors wisely refer to 1 Corinthians 7:25: "as one who has obtained mercy from the Lord in order that I may be faithful."

to the king." Thus, Proverbs 27:23 states: "Be diligent to recognize the countenance of your cattle, and consider your own flocks."

62. *Whom the master has set*[177] *over his family*, through entrusted authority. Hebrews 5:4 says: "No one takes the honor to himself, but the person is called by the Lord as was Aaron." The Psalm has: "But I have been set up as king by him over Zion, his holy mountain" (2:6). – *in order to give them their ration of grain in due time*, by communicating sound doctrine. Qoheleth 8:5 reads: "The heart of a wise person understands time and response," etc. He is also attentive to the capacity of his listeners. Therefore, the text has: *ration*. Gregory says: "According to the quality of the hearers ought the discourse of teachers to be fashioned, so as to suit all and each for their several needs, and yet never deviate from the skill of providing common edification."[178] We have an example of this in Joseph, who was established in the land of Egypt to dispense grain. Genesis 41:37–57 tells of Joseph's *faithfulness* and *prudence*, *authority* and *vigilance* or diligence. – And since these were the qualities found in holy prelates, this gospel is sung at Lauds of the office of Confessors and Pontiffs, who were outstanding and commendable in the four qualities just mentioned. – And about these four it is said in the Glossa of Bede: "How rare is the individual who *serves the Lord for the Lord's sake*, who feeds the sheep of Christ not for lucre, but for the love of Christ. Who is *prudent*, providing for himself in the future. *Whom he has set up*,

---

[177] The Vulgate reads *constituet* ("will set").
[178] On p. 327, n. 14 QuarEd refer to Book XXX, chapter 3, n. 12 of Gregory's *Moralia* and to the Prologue of Book III of his *Liber Regulae Pastoralis*. I have based my translation on that found in NPNF2, Volume 12, p. 24. Hugh of St. Cher, p. 211h quotes Gregory in the selfsame words found in Bonaventure's quotation.

that is, how rare is the person who *is called by God like Aaron* instead of pushing himself forward, and who feeds the sheep *rather than himself.*"[179] Therefore, because of *the lack of fidelity* Malachi 1:10 states: "Who is there among you who closes my doors and kindles the fire on my altar gratis?" And Philippians 2:21 has: "They all seek their own interests," etc.[180] Further, few are *prudent.* Thus Isaiah 24:2 reads: "As with the people, so with the priest." And Hosea 4:6 states: "Since you have rejected knowledge, I will also reject you,[181] lest you should function as my priest." Moreover, few are *divinely constituted.* Wherefore, Hosea 8:4 says: "They have reigned, but not by me." Similarly, there are few *whose goal is the welfare of the flock.* Thus, Ezekiel 34:2–3 has: "Woe to the shepherds of Israel, who fed themselves. Should not the flocks be fed by the shepherds?," etc.[182] Therefore, it is significant that he begins with *Who, do you think?* on account of the rarity and difficulty and costliness through which such persons excel in the privilege of merit.[183]

---

[179] On p. 328, n. 2 QuarEd state that this is the Glossa Ordinaria, that St. Thomas (*Catena Aurea* on Matthew 24, n. 13) attributes the quotation simply to the Glossa, that Gorranus in his comments on Luke 12:42 attributes it to St. Jerome, and that there is an implicit allusion to Hebrews 5:4 in the quotation. For Bede's very dissimilar commentary, see CCSL cxx, pp. 258–259.

[180] Hugh of St. Cher, p. 211v, e also quotes Malachi 1:10 and Philippians 2:21.

[181] The Vulgate reads *repellam te* ("I will reject you") whereas Bonaventure has *repellam et ego te* ("I will also reject you").

[182] Ezekiel 34:3 continues: "You consumed the milk, and you clothed yourselves with wool. And you killed that which was fat, but you did not feed my flock."

[183] On p. 327, n. 10 QuarEd suggest that Bonaventure may be influenced in this section by Bede's commentary. See CCSL cxx, p. 258 for Bede's commentary on Luke 12:42: "Truly when he says, *Who, do you think, is,* he is suggesting the difficulty, not the impossibility, of advancing in virtue. The Psalmist says: *Who is wise and will keep these things?* The answer is not 'no one,' but rather it is a 'rare individ-

63. (Verse 43). Secondly, with regard to *the excellence of the reward* he adds: *Blessed is that servant, whom his master, when he comes, will find so doing.* Matthew 25:21 reads: "Well done, good and faithful servant," etc. *So doing,* that is, *faithfully, prudently* and *vigilantly* according to what 1 Peter 4:10 says: "According to the gift each has received, administer it to one another as good stewards of the manifold grace of God." And Chrysostom comments: "These things were said about speech and power, about money and about every type of stewardship entrusted to each person. For each person ought to use the things he has for the common good, whether wisdom or rule or riches, not for the harm of those who have them."[184]

64. (Verse 44). Now *the perfect fruit of glory* is given for the use of this grace. About this glory the text continues: *Truly I say to you that he will set him over all that he*

---

ual.'" Note that at the end of #62 that Bonaventure talks about the "rarity and difficulty" of being a faithful steward.

[184] On p. 328, n. 7 QuarEd refer to Chrysostom's Homily 77 (alias 78) on Matthew, n. 3. Hugh of St. Cher, p. 211v, k comments: "That is, faithfully, humbly, prudently, distributing in a useful manner the Lord's grain to his family. *Chrysostom.* These things were said about speech, about power, about money...." With the exception of one extra *de* ("about") Hugh's quotation of Chrysostom is identical to that of Bonaventure. See PG 58:706 for Chrysostom's actual words: *Haec autem non de pecunii tantum dicta sunt, sed etiam de verbo et de virtute, de donis et dispensatione cuique commissa. Haec parabola magistratibus quoque optime competat. Quisque enim omnia, quae sua sunt, ad communem utilitatem conferre debet. Sive sapientiam habeas, sive principatum, sive divitias, sive quidvis aliud, ne ad detrimentum conservorum, neve ad perniciem sit tuam* ("But these things were not said of money only, but also about speech and about power, about gifts and a stewardship entrusted to each. This parable is also most fitting for magistrates. For each person must dispose of all that he has for the common good. Whether you have wisdom, or rule, or riches or anything whatsoever, and not to the detriment of those who have these things. Let it not be to your harm").

possesses, "over the joys of the heavenly kingdom," "not that they alone may have eternal joys, but before all the rest, both on account of their lives and also on account of their care of the flock."[185] Thus, 1 Peter 5:2,4 states: "Presbyters, feed the flock of God that is among you. . . . And when the prince of the shepherds appears, you will receive the unfading crown of glory." Wherefore, Chrysostom says: "When the people do good, each one of them will be recompensed for the good he has done, but the priest for the good deeds of all."[186] 1 Thessalonians 2:19 reads: "What is my[187] hope or joy or crown of glory, if not you before our Lord Jesus Christ at his coming?"[188]

65. (Verse 45). *But if that servant says to himself*, etc. After he had commended vigilance and foresight or care on the part of prelates, he now *excoriates insolence*. Indeed, he does so by *making clear the enormity of the sin* and by *threatening a severe judgment*.

---

[185] On p. 328, n. 8 QuarEd state that these quotations are from the Glossa Interlinearis and Ordinaria and are taken from Bede. See CCSL cxx, p. 259 for Bede's commentary: "That is, over all the joys of the heavenly kingdom, not in such a way that they alone may have dominion over these, but that they may enjoy their eternal possession more abundantly than all the other saints." Hugh of St. Cher, p. 211v, l reads: "*Bede*. He may have the joys of the heavenly kingdom, not that he alone may have eternal joys, but before all the rest, both on account of his life and also on account of his care of the flock."

[186] On p. 328, n. 10 QuarEd refer to Chrysostom's Homily 52 on Matthew 24:25 (*Opus Imperfectum*). Bonaventure's quotation is virtually identical to that found in PG 56:926: *Et bene agente populo, unusquisque quidem pro suo bono remuneratur, sacerdos autem pro bonis omnium*. The quotation of Chrysostom found in Hugh of St. Cher, p. 211v, l is verbatim with that found in Bonaventure.

[187] The Vulgate has *nostra* ("our").

[188] After his quotation of Chrysostom's Homily 52, Cardinal Hugh has one line of commentary and then adds a quotation from 1 Thessalonians 2:19, where he reads "our hope," etc. See Hugh of St. Cher, p. 211v, l.

So first, with regard to *making the enormity of the sin clear* he says: *But if that servant says to himself: My master delays his coming.* The Glossa has: "On the contrary, if he hides from himself that the judgment is coming shortly and promises himself that he is secure," according to what Ezekiel 12:22 states: "What is this proverb that you have in the land of Israel which says: The days will be prolonged, and every vision will fail?"[189] And 2 Peter 3:3–4 reads: "Deceitful scoffers will come, people walking according to their own lusts, saying: Where is the promise of his coming? For since the fathers fell asleep, all things continue as they were from the beginning of creation." – And since such a thought engenders security, and security brings forth contempt, and contempt iniquity, he adds: *and begins to beat the boys and handmaids*, namely, by scandalizing the little ones, when, however, he should be nurturing them by word and example.[190] On account of this Isaiah 3:15 says: "Why do you consume my people and grind the faces of the poor?" And this is a grave sin. 1 Corinthians 8:12 reads: "When you sin against the brothers and wound their weak consciences, you sin against Christ." And especially when they sin against the little ones. Matthew 18:6 states: "Whoever scandalizes one of these little ones who believe in me, it were better for him," etc.[191] – And

---

[189] On p. 328, n. 12 QuarEd state that this is the Glossa Interlinearis and refer their readers to Book IV of Jerome's commentary on Matthew 24:48–49 where he also quotes Ezekiel 12:22. Hugh of St. Cher, p. 211v, m also quotes Ezekiel 12:22.

[190] On p. 328, n. 14 QuarEd cite the Glossa Interlinearis: "*And begins to beat*, to incite them to vices or to mangle the consciences of the weak by an evil word or example. *Boys and handmaids*, the weaker they are because of age or sex, the more easily they come to ruin." See CCSL cxx, p. 259 for the basis of this interpretation in Bede's commentary.

[191] Matthew 18:6 continues: ". . . to have a great millstone hung around his neck and to be drowned in the depths of the sea."

since *concupiscence* is the mother of perfidy, the text adds: *and to eat and to drink and to get drunk*, namely, doing the will of the flesh, according to what Isaiah 28:7 says: "The priest and the prophet have been ignorant on account of drunkenness.[192] They are swallowed up in wine. They have gone astray in drunkenness." And this is especially inappropriate for pastors and prelates, among whom the spirit of wisdom and understanding should reign. Malachi 2:7 has: "The lips of a priest will guard knowledge, and they will seek the law from his mouth." But on the contrary as Isaiah 56:10–11 reads: "His watchmen are all blind. They are all ignorant: dumb dogs unable to bark, seeing vain things and loving dreams. And most impudent dogs, they never had enough," etc.

66. (Verse 46). Secondly, relative to *the threat of a severe judgment* he adds: *The master of that servant will come on a day he does not expect, and at an hour he does not know*. Deuteronomy 32:35 has: "The day of destruction is at hand, and the time is hastening to come." And Zephaniah 1:14 reads: "The great day of the Lord is near, near and exceedingly swift."[193] And although it is *near*, he, nevertheless, comes unexpectedly to worldly people. Thus, Qoheleth 9:12 states: "Men and women do not know their own end. But like fish are taken with the hook, and like birds are caught with the snare, so too are men and women taken in the evil time when it will suddenly come upon them." – And since a grave judgment is in store for those who contemn the judge, the text adds: *and will cut them asunder*, namely, from fellowship with the good, according to what Matthew 25:33 has: "He will set the sheep on his right hand, but the

---

[192] Hugh of St. Cher, p. 211v, p quotes the first sentence of Isaiah 28:7.
[193] Hugh of St. Cher, p. 211v, m also quotes Zephaniah 1:14.

goats on his left."[194] *And make him share the lot of the unfaithful,* namely, those who have already been judged.[195] John 3:18 says: "The person who does not believe is already judged." And this rightly, for it is said in 1 Timothy 5:8: "If anyone does not take care of his own and especially of his household, he has denied the faith and worse than an unbeliever."[196] This *lot* is very dire, according to what the Psalm has: "Fire, brimstone, storms of winds[197] will be the lot of their cup" (10:7). And Revelation 21:8 reads: "As for the cowardly and unbelieving, and abominable and murderers, and fornicators and sorcerers, and idolaters and all liars, their lot will be in the pool that burns with fire and brimstone." From this it is patent that just as there is a great reward for good prelates, so too there will be a very great punishment for the reprobates. Wisdom 6:6–7 states: "A most severe judgment will occur for those who bear rule.[198] For to the person who is little, mercy is granted. But the mighty will suffer mighty torments."

67. (Verse 47). *But that servant,* etc. After he had urged them to vigilance and excoriated insolence, here in a third point *he heavily attacks negligence.* He does this in a twofold manner, namely, by reason of *greater knowledge* and by reason of *entrusted authority.*

---

[194] Hugh of St. Cher, p. 211v, t alludes to Matthew 25:32.

[195] On p. 329, n. 6 QuarEd cite the Glossa Interlinearis: *"And will cut him asunder,* by segregating him from the consort of the faithful, and by associating him with those who did not have faith. For the person who does not care for his own denies the faith and is worse than an unbeliever [1 Timothy 5:8]." See CCSL cxx, p. 260 for the commentary of Bede that stands behind the Glossa's interpretation.

[196] Hugh of St. Cher, p. 211v, t refers generally to 1 Timothy 5a without citing any verse(s).

[197] The Vulgate has *ignis et suphur et spiritus procellarum* ("fire and brimstone and storms of winds").

[198] Hugh of St. Cher, p. 211v, y quotes Wisdom 6:6 only.

First, then, concerning *the gravity of negligence* by reason of *greater knowledge,* he says: *But that servant who knew his master's will,* through the gift of knowledge. 1 Corinthians 8:1–2 states: "Knowledge puffs up, but love builds up. If anyone thinks that he knows something, he has not yet known as he ought to know." – *and has not prepared himself,*[199] to receive the gift of grace. Proverbs 16:1 has: "It is the task of men and women to prepare the soul," etc. So 1 Samuel 7:3 says: "Prepare your hearts for the Lord." – *and did not act according to his will.* Supply: through the vice of his own negligence. James 4:17 reads: "The person who knows the good and does not do it commits a sin."[200] – *will be beaten with many stripes,* that is, through the severity of the divine sentence. Wherefore, 2 Peter 2:21 states: "It were better for them not to have known the way of truth," etc.[201] And Romans 1:21, 24 has: "Who, although they knew God, did not glorify him as God. . . . For which reason God has given them up to the desires of their hearts, to uncleanness, so that they dishonor their own bodies among themselves." And the reason for this is stated by Gregory: "Where the gift of knowledge is greater, there the transgressor is subjected to a more severe punishment."[202] Therefore, even ignorance excuses.[203]

---

[199] On p. 329, n. 12 QuarEd correctly mention that the Vulgate does not read *se* ("himself") and state that Cardinal Hugh, Blessed Albert, St. Thomas (*Catena Aurea* on Luke, chapter 12, n. 12), and Lyranus read *se* ("himself").

[200] Hugh of St. Cher, p. 212y also quotes James 4:17.

[201] The Vulgate has *viam justitiae* ("the way of justice") while Bonaventure has *viam veritatis* ("way of truth"). Hugh of St. Cher, p. 211v, y also quotes 2 Peter 2:21 and reads *viam veritatis* ("the way of truth").

[202] On p. 329, n. 14 QuarEd refer to Bonaventure's commentary on Luke 10:12 (#21) above where he also quoted this statement from Book XVIII, chapter 11, n. 18 of Gregory's *Moralia.*

[203] On p. 329, n. 14 QuarEd show how two of the manuscripts had difficulty with this blanket statement about "ignorance."

68. (Verse 48). For which reason the text adds: *Whereas he who did not know it*, through a lack of knowledge, *and did things deserving of stripes*, by committing a sin, *will be beaten with few*, through a mitigation of the divine sentence.[204]

And note that it is *simple* ignorance that is an excuse, according to what 1 Timothy 1:13 states: Behold, "I obtained the mercy of God because I acted out of ignorance." And Luke 23:34 below reads: "Father, forgive them, for they know not what they are doing." There is also a different type of ignorance, *intentional* ignorance, about which the Psalm says: "He did not want to understand that he might do good things" (35:4). Such will be severely punished. Thus, 1 Corinthians 14:38 has: "Whoever ignores will be ignored." And Hosea 4:14 says: "The people that does not understand will be beaten." And Bede says this in the Glossa, because Proverbs 28:9 states: "The person who turns away his ear from listening to the law, his prayer will be an abomination."[205]

---

[204] On p. 329, n. 15 QuarEd cite the Glossa Interlinearis: "*Whereas he who did not know it*. This not knowing refers to the person who wants to understand, but is unable."

[205] On p. 330, n. 3 QuarEd quote the Glossa Ordinaria on Luke 12:48: "*Ambrose*: Many, thinking that they will be beaten with fewer stripes if they are ignorant of what they must do, turn away their ears from hearing the truth. But since they could know if they wanted to apply themselves, they are judged not as ignorant people, but as contemners." The editors note that Hugh of St. Cher also attributes this Glossa to Bede and that this interpretation already occurs in Book XV, chapter 45, n. 51 of Gregory's *Moralia*. There are striking parallels between Bonaventure's interpretation in this paragraph and that of Cardinal Hugh. See Hugh of St. Cher, p. 212a: "Whereas he who did not know it], that is, who did not know in a simple way and not out of contempt for learning. For many do not want to learn, because they think that they are to be punished less if they sin out of ignorance. Of these 1 Corinthians 14:38: Whoever ignores, will be ignored. Hosea 4:14: The people that does not understand will be beaten. *Glossa Bedae*: Many, thinking that they have fewer people

And the Psalm reads: "Their madness is according to the likeness of a serpent, like the deaf asp that stops her ears," etc. (57:5)

69. Secondly, with regard to *the gravity of negligence* by reason of *entrusted authority* the text continues: *But of everyone to whom much has been given*, namely, in an office, *much will be required*. Therefore, Gregory says: "When his gifts increase, the responsibility of accounting for them also grows greater. Everyone must be more humble, then, and more ready to serve, as a result of his office, the more he sees that he will be constrained to render an account of them."[206] Luke 16:2 below says: "Render an account of your stewardship."[207] – Wherefore, the text continues: *and of him to whom they have entrusted much*, "namely, divine judgments,"[208] or Father and Son and Holy Spirit. *They will demand the more*, that at the future universal judgment. Matthew 25:19 reads: "Then after a long time the master of those servants came and settled accounts with them." Thus, from prelates, to whom the care of their subjects has been entrusted, the Lord requires not only their own souls, but also the souls entrusted into their care. For which reason it is said in Hebrews 13:17: "Obey your superiors

---

beating them if they are ignorant of what they must do, turn away from hearing the truth. But since they could know if they wanted to apply themselves, they will be judged not as ignorant people, but as contemners. Proverbs 28:9: The person who turns away his ears from listening to the law, etc."

[206] On p. 330, n. 4 QuarEd refer to Homily 9, n. 1 of GGHG. I have based my translation on that of Hurst, p. 127. In Hurst's numbering this is Homily 18. See PL 76:1106AB. Bonaventure's quotation is virtually identical with Gregory's text.

[207] Hugh of St. Cher, p. 212f also quotes this passage.

[208] On p. 330, n. 5 QuarEd state that this interpretation is from the Glossa Interlinearis (taken from Bede). For Bede's interpretation, see CCSL cxx, p. 260 line 1175. See Hugh of St. Cher, p. 212g: "And to whom much has been given,] that is, divine judgments."

and be subject to them. For they keep watch as having to render an account of your souls." For to each one of them is said what 1 Kings 20:39 has: "Guard this man. And if he slips away, it will be your soul for his soul."[209] And Jeremiah 13:20–21 states: "Where is the flock that was given to you, your beautiful cattle? What will you say when he will visit you? For you have given them teaching against you and have given them instruction against your own head?" And therefore, in Acts 20:28 Paul said to the leaders at the birth of the Church: "Take heed to yourselves and to the whole flock, in which the Holy Spirit has placed you as bishops to rule the Church of God, which he has purchased with his own blood." And Ezekiel 34:10 reads: "Behold, I myself . . . will require my flock from their hand, and I will cause them to cease from feeding the flock any more. Neither will the shepherds feed themselves any more."[210]

Luke 12:49–13:9
CHRIST URGES VIGILANCE FROM A CONSIDERATION OF THE FIRST ADVENT AND CENSURES NEGLIGENCE

70. (Verse 49). *I have come to cast fire on the earth*, etc. After he had urged them to vigilance through consideration of the second coming, he now stirs them to vigilance through *consideration of the first coming*. And this part has two sections. In the first *he stirs them to vigilance* by showing the efficacy of the first coming. In the second *he rebukes the foolishness and negligence of the Jews* where verse 54 says: *But he also said to the crowds*, etc.

---

[209] Hugh of St. Cher, p. 212h also quotes this passage.
[210] On p. 330, n. 6 QuarEd cite Bede on Luke 12:48. See CCSL cxx, p. 260: "But *much* will be required of him to whom the care of feeding the Lord's flock has also been entrusted with his own salvation."

Luke 12:49–53
The efficacy of Christ's first coming prompts vigilance

Therefore, in expressing *the efficacy of the first coming to stir up vigilance*, he points out that he has come for three purposes, namely, *to send forth the fire of love, to bring about the remedy which is the passion*, and *to effect a separation from carnal affection*.

First, then, relative to *the sending of the fire of love* through the efficacy of the first coming, he says: *I have come to cast fire on the earth*, namely, the fire of *divine* love. This love is compared to fire in The Song of Songs 8:6: "Love is strong as death, jealousy as hard as hell. Its lamps are lamps of fire," etc.[211] But *carnal* love is like an *infernal* fire. Job 31:12 reads: "It is a fire that devours to the point of destruction." And Sirach 3:33 states: "As water quenches a fire," etc. But *spiritual* love is like a *heavenly* fire. Lamentations 1:13 has: "From above he has sent fire into my bones," etc.[212] The Lord *sends* this *by communicating his teaching*. The Psalmist says: "Your word is exceedingly refined by fire" (118:140). And Jeremiah 23:29 reads: "Are not my words like a fire . . . and like a hammer that breaks the rock into pieces?" Likewise, *by pouring out grace*. Deuteronomy 4:36 has: "From heaven he made you hear his voice . . . and upon earth he showed you his most intense fire." Moreover, *by inflaming for justice*. Sirach 48:1 says: "Elijah rose up like fire," since the fire of divine zeal was in him. About this zeal Zephaniah 3:8 states: "With the fire of my zeal the whole earth will be

---

[211] On p. 330, n. 11 QuarEd refer to Ambrose's interpretation of "fire" and two of Gregory's and intimate the uniqueness of Bonaventure's interpretation. Hugh of St. Cher, p. 212k interprets the fire as illuminating, warming, and strengthening the earth.

[212] Hugh of St. Cher, p. 212k also quotes this passage.

devoured." Therefore, it was fitting that at his word fire descended from heaven upon the sacrifice, as 1 Kings 18:38 says, and upon the captain and his fifty men, as it is said in 2 Kings 2:10 : "If I be a man of God, let fire descend from heaven," etc. – And since this fire is sent in vain unless it burns, the text adds: *And what will I but that it be kindled? Meditation upon present benefits enkindles* this fire. The Psalm reads: "My heart grew hot within me, and in my meditation a fire will flame forth" (38:4). And Luke 24:32 below has: "Were not our hearts burning within us?" Furthermore, *by remembering the past.* Leviticus 6:12 says: "The fire on my[213] altar shall always burn, and the priest shall feed it, putting wood on it every day in the morning," etc. Finally, *by looking ahead meditatively for future promises.* Proverbs 30:5 says: "Every word of God is fire tried and is a buckler to those who hope in him."

71. (Verse 50). Secondly, concerning *the accomplishment of the remedy of the passion* the text adds: *But I have a baptism to be baptized with.* Note that the passion of Christ is said to be *a baptism,* for in his blood we are purified as in the baptismal laver. Revelation 7:14 reads: "These are they who have come out of the great tribulation and have washed their robes . . . in the blood of the Lamb." So Hebrews 9:13–14 states: "If the blood of goats and bulls and the sprinkled ashes of a heifer sanctify the unclean unto the cleansing of the flesh, how much more will the blood of Christ . . . cleanse our[214] conscience," etc. Christ was baptized with this baptism, for his entire body was colored red by this blood. Isaiah 63:1–2 has: "Who is this who comes from Edom, with dyed garments from Bosrah? . . . Why, then, is your ap-

---

[213] The Vulgate does not read *meo* ("my").
[214] The Vulgate reads *vestram* ("your").

parel red, and your garments like those who tread in the winepress?" – And note that the passion of Christ is compared to *a baptism*, as it is here, because it was *universal*. The Psalm says: "You have washed all your waves over me" (87:8). – Further, it is compared to *a cup*. Matthew 26:39 reads: "Father, if it is possible, let this cup pass away from me." Because it was *voluntary*. Matthew 20:22 states: "Can you drink of the cup, of which I am about to drink?" – Moreover, since it was *most cruel* and painful, it is compared to *the winepress*. Isaiah 63:3 says: "I have trod the winepress alone, and from the Gentiles there was not a man with me."

72. Therefore, Christ was baptized with this baptism, not because he lacked any necessity, but because of an abundance of love. Therefore, the text continues: *And how constrained I am*. That is, *constrained* by the love that holds dominion over the heart. Ephesians 2:4 reads: "God, who is rich in mercy, by reason of the very great love wherewith he has loved us." – And note that love *constrains by the power of attraction*. John 3:16 states: "God so loved the world, that he sent his only begotten Son." Jeremiah 31:3 has: "I have loved you with an everlasting love. Therefore, I have attracted you, taking pity on you." Wherefore, Hugh says: "It is a mighty power that you wield, O love. You alone could draw God down from heaven to earth. O how strong a bond is yours, whereby both God was able to be bound and the one bound in this way destroyed the bonds of iniquity! I do not know that there is anything that I could say more to your praise than that you drew God down from heaven and lifted human beings from earth to heaven."[215] So Hosea 11:4 reads: "I will draw them

---

[215] On p. 331, n. 13 QuarEd refer to Hugh of St. Victor's *De Laude Caritatis*. See PL 176:974BC. Bonaventure's quotation is verbatim

with the cords of Adam, in the bonds of love." – Further, love *expands by spreading far and wide its benevolence.* The Psalm says: "Your commandment is exceedingly broad" (118:97). 2 Corinthians 6:11 has: "Our heart is wide open." – *It overflows with extraordinary power to unite.* The Song of Songs 8:5 states: "Who is this who comes up from the desert, flowing with delights?" John 4:13–14 reads: "The person who drinks . . . in him will come about a fountain of water, springing up unto life everlasting." – *It is inclined to fitting condescension.* Galatians 2:20 says: "Who loved me and handed himself over for my sake." – On account of these four characteristics Ephesians 3:17–18 has: "being rooted and established in love, you may be able to comprehend with all the saints," etc.[216] – And since this love was manifested so completely in the passion, he says: *until it is accomplished,* namely, in the pouring forth of blood.[217] Revelation 1:5 states: "Who loved us and washed us from our sins in his blood." And 1 John 3:16 reads: "In this we have come to know the love of God that he laid down his life for us."[218] And so it was that Christ was thirsty on the cross. John 19:28,30 reads: "Jesus, knowing that all things were now accomplished, that the Scripture might

---

with the major exception that he reads *hoc* ("in this way") rather than *homo* ("the human being"). Hugh writes: " O how strong a bond is yours, whereby both God was able to be bound and the human being, who was bound, destroyed the bonds of iniquity!" I have based my translation on *Hugh of St. Victor, The Divine Love: The two treatises* De Laude Caritatis *and* De Amore Sponsi ad Sponsam, translated by A Religious of C.S.M.V, Fleur de Lys Series of Spiritual Classics (London: Mowbray, 1956), p. 18.

[216] Ephesians 3:18–19 continues: ". . . what is the breadth and length and height and depth, and to know Christ's love which surpasses knowledge. . . . "

[217] On p. 331, n. 17 QuarEd cite the Glossa Interlinearis: *"Until it is accomplished,* the passion itself."

[218] Bonaventure combines 1 John 3:16 and John 10:11 and makes modifications to each quotation.

be fulfilled, said: I thirst. . . . Therefore, when Jesus had taken the wine, he said: It is consummated. And bowing his head, he gave up[219] his spirit."

73. (Verse 51). Thirdly, about *effecting a separation from carnal affection* the text adds: *Do you think that I have come to give peace upon the earth?*, namely, worldly peace. He did not come to bring this type of peace, but to take it away, for this is an *evil* peace, concerning which Isaiah 28:15 says: "We have established[220] a covenant with death and have made a pact with hell." – A just man rejects this peace. In the Psalm it is said: "I was zealous against the wicked, seeing the peace of the sinners" (72:3). Because such a peace is a *wicked* peace. Deuteronomy 29:19 reads: "I will have peace and will walk in the wickedness of my heart." – It is a *false* peace. Jeremiah 6:14 states: "They healed the injury to the daughter of my people shamelessly, saying: Peace, peace. But there was no peace." – And a *momentary* peace. 1 Thessalonians 5:3 has: "When they will say: Peace and security, even then sudden destruction will come upon them." – It is a *deceptive* peace. Jeremiah 9:8 states: "With his mouth a person speaks peace with his friend, and secretly lays snares for him." – It is a *disturbing* peace. In his canticle of Isaiah 38:17 Hezekiah sings: "Behold, in peace is my bitterness most bitter."[221]

---

[219] On p. 331, n. 18 QuarEd correctly indicate that the Vulgate reads *tradidit* ("he handed over") whereas Bonaventure has *emisit* ("gave up"). They also point to Matthew 27:50 which reads *emisit* ("gave up").

[220] On p. 332, n. 2 QuarEd rightly mention that the Vulgate reads *Percussimus* ("We have struck") while Bonaventure has *Pepigimus* ("We have established").

[221] Hezekiah goes on to sing in Isaiah 38:17: "But you have delivered my soul that it should not perish. You have cast all my sins behind your back."

Sirach 41:1 reads: "O death, how bitter is your remembrance to a person who has peace in his possessions."

74. This worldly peace is *inimical to true peace*. For the peace of Christ is *the good* peace. Luke 2:14 above says: "On earth peace to men and women of good will." Therefore, the Apostle writes: "Grace and peace to you."[222] It is *true* peace. Romans 14:17 states: "The kingdom of God is justice and peace and joy." – It is *lasting* peace. John 14:27 says: "Peace I leave to you, not as the world gives, do I give to you." – It is *directive* peace. Luke 1:78–79 has: "Because of the loving kindness . . . wherewith God has visited us...to direct our feet into the way of peace." – It is *consoling* peace. John 16:33 reads: "That in me you may have peace. In the world you will have affliction." Philippians 4:7 states: "May the peace of God which surpasses all understanding guard your hearts and your minds." – Therefore, since it is entirely contrary to worldly peace – and two contraries cannot exist at the same time[223] – this peace can only be effected by the author of peace by the annihilation of the counterfeit peace.

75. Therefore, the text continues: *No, I tell you*, that is, I assert to you that I have not come to bring peace, but separation, according to what Isaiah 52:11 has: "Depart, depart. Go out from here and touch no unclean thing." And 2 Corinthians 6:17 says: "Go out from among them, be separated, says the Lord." And Matthew 10:35 reads: "For I have come to set a man at variance with his fa-

---

[222] On p. 332, n. 7 QuarEd sagely observe that this greeting occurs at the beginning of almost all of Paul's letters. See Romans 1:7; 1 Corinthians 1:3; 2 Corinthians 1:2, etc.

[223] On p. 332, n. 11 QuarEd cite Book II, chapter 4 (c. 14) of Aristotle's *Periherm.*: "But contraries cannot happen to be in the same place at the same time."

ther," etc. And the reason for this is given in Matthew 10:37: "The person who loves father or mother more than me is not worthy of me." And therefore, Luke 14:26 below states: "If anyone comes to me and does not hate father and mother and wife and children and brothers and sisters, yes, even his own life, he cannot be my disciple."

76. (Verses 52–53). And therefore, the text adds: *For henceforth in one house five will be divided*, that is, separated from carnal affection. And according to what Deuteronomy 33:9 has: "Who has said to his father and to his mother: I do not know you. And to his brethren: I know you not. And their own children they have not known. These have kept your word and observed your covenant." – And he adds *the manner* of separation: *three against two, and two against three will be divided*, that is, persons, who would especially seem to be joined by bonds of the flesh, will be separated by the spirit of charity from carnal love. Do not wonder that this takes place through the divine word, for Hebrews 4:12 states: "The word of God is living and efficacious and keener than any two-edged sword, extending even to the separation of soul and spirit, of joints also and of marrow, and a discerner of thoughts," etc.[224] – And he adds *the manner and an example*: *Father against son, and son against father*,[225] namely, *will be divided*. Chrysostom says: "God alone is the father of souls. One shows fleshly obedience to carnal fathers, holiness of the soul to the spiritual father."[226] This will not be limited to the

---

[224] Hugh of St. Cher, p. 212v, a also quotes this passage. It is also found in the *Opus Imperfectum*. See PG 56:768 and note 226 below.

[225] On p. 332, n. 16 QuarEd accurately indicate that the Vulgate reads *suum* ("his").

[226] On p. 332, n. 16 QuarEd refer to Chrysostom's Homily 26 on Matthew 10:27 (*Opus Imperfectum*). See PG 56:769: *Solus autem Deus*

male gender, but also to women. Thus, the text continues: *Mother against daughter, and daughter against
mother, mother-in-law against her daughter-in-law, and
daughter-in-law against her mother-in-law.*

77. And note that the Lord sets forth *five persons* and
mentions *six relationships*: father and son, mother and
daughter, daughter-in-law against mother-in-law. For
one person is mother and mother-in-law at the same
time.[227] And he mentions two men and three women either because women are more prone to division because
of their instability or because many men are effeminate
and carnal rather than spiritual. Thus, 1 Corinthians
11:30 says: "This is why many among you are infirm
and weak, and many sleep."[228] It happened in this way
literally, as he says, after his preaching. So the Glossa of

---

*omnium animarum sanctarum Pater est. Reddite ergo unicuique
quod suum est. Carnalibus patribus praebete carnis obsequium,
spiritualibus autem patribus animae sanctitatem* ("But God alone is
the father of all holy souls. Therefore, render to each one what is his
due. Show fleshly obedience to carnal fathers, but to spiritual fathers
the holiness of the soul"). Hugh of St. Cher, p. 212v, c reads:
*Chrysostom. Solus Deus animarum pater est, carnalibus patribus
praebe carnis obsequium, spirituali vero patri animae sanctitatem*
("God alone is the father of souls. Show fleshly obedience to carnal
fathers, but the holiness of the soul to the spiritual father"). It seems
that Hugh of St. Cher is Bonaventure's source rather than the *Opus
Imperfectum*.
[227] On p. 333, n. 1 QuarEd cite Book VII of Ambrose's commentary on
Luke 12, n. 137. See CCSL xiv, p. 261: "For who are the five people
when the subject of the verse seems to be six persons: father and son,
mother and daughter, mother-in-law and daughter-in-law? The same
mother who is mentioned can also be the mother-in-law, for she is
the mother of the son and the mother-in-law of his wife, etc."
[228] Bonaventure's medieval bias against women is manifest here.
Moreover, his reasoning in this passage is somewhat hard to follow.
He seems to quote 1 Corinthians 11:30 because it refers to the consequences of divisions at the Last Supper: sickness and the sleep of
death.

Bede has: "After the baptism of the passion, after the coming of fire, the entire world was divided against itself. Each and every house contained believers and nonbelievers, those fighting against the faith and those fighting for the faith,"[229] according to what Zechariah 8:10 states: "I have divided all men and women, each one against his neighbor."[230] And Sirach 33:15 reads: "Look upon all the works of the Almighty: two against two and one against another."[231] Matthew 10:21 has: "But brother will hand over brother to death, and the father his son. And children will rise up against parents and put them to death."

78. *Spiritually*, "every person is the home either of God or of the devil."[232] According to the evil peace that is in the person, a peace that stems from sin, the father is *the devil*. John 8:44 states: "You are from the devil as father." But *the flesh* is mother and daughter-in-law. Ezekiel 16:3 says: "Your father was an Amorite, and your mother a Hittite," that is, garrulous. But the son *is divided* against father and mother and mother-in-law when he abandons the desires of the flesh and renounces

---

[229] On p. 333, n. 2 QuarEd state that this is the Glossa Ordinaria on Luke 12:51. This interpretation is loosely based on that of Bede. See CCSL cxx, pp. 261–262.

[230] On p. 333, n. 3 QuarEd correctly indicate that the Vulgate reads *Dimisi* ("I have dismissed") whereas Bonaventure has *Divisi* ("I have divided") and go on to mention that Hugh of St. Cher also reads *Divisi* ("I have divided"). See Hugh of St. Cher, p. 212v, e.

[231] The Vulgate reads *duo duo, unum contra unum* ("two against two, one against another") while Bonaventure reads *duo contra duo, et unum contra unum* ("two against two, and one against another"). See Hugh of St. Cher, p. 212v, e where he has this quotation immediately after the one from Zechariah 8:10 and has the same wording as Bonaventure.

[232] On p. 333, n. 4 QuarEd cite Book VII of Ambrose on Luke 12, n. 138. See CCSL xiv, p. 261: "The house is one, and the person is one. For each house is either of God or of the devil."

the devil and his pomps and is separated from them by baptism. Wherefore, the Psalm has: "For my father and my mother have abandoned me, but the Lord has taken me up" (26:10).[233] To effect this division one must be born anew. John 3:5 reads: "Unless a person is born again of water and the Holy[234] Spirit, he cannot enter into the kingdom of God." For the fire of divine love and the baptism both of fire and the flowing of water and of blood separate all people from the enemies of their household.[235] And this is the efficacy of the first advent.

Luke 12:54–13:9
CHRIST REBUKES NEGLIGENCE

79. (Verse 54). *But he said to the crowds*, etc. After he has urged them to vigilance, here in a second point *he rebukes the negligence* which does not take advantage of the grace which is the coming of Christ. And this section has two parts. In the first *he censures negligence with respect to acknowledging this grace*. In the second *negligence with regard to doing penance* where Luke 13:1 says: *Now there came at the very time[236] some*, etc. For Christ came to confer grace and to preach penance.

---

[233] In his "moral" interpretation Cardinal Hugh also quotes Ezekiel 16:3 and Psalm 26:10. See Hugh of St. Cher, p. 212v, e. See also QuarEd p. 333, n. 4.

[234] The Vulgate does not have *Sancto* ("Holy").

[235] On p. 333, n. 6 QuarEd sagely indicate that Bonaventure is alluding to Matthew 10:36: "And a person's enemies will be those of his own household."

[236] On p. 333, n. 8 QuarEd accurately indicate that the Vulgate reads *ipso in tempore* ("in that very time") whereas Bonaventure reads *ipso tempore* ("at that very time"). They also mention that Hugh of St. Cher and Lyranus also have *ipso tempore* ("at that very time"). See Hugh of St. Cher, p. 213v.

Luke 12:54–59
Christ Rebukes Negligence in Acknowledging Grace

Now *he censures negligence relative to acknowledging grace* and does so for three reasons, namely, on account of the warning of *external judgment, internal judgment,* and *the verdict of a superior.*

So, first, concerning *the warning of external judgment,* on account of which negligence in acknowledging grace is reprehensible, the text has: *But he also said to the crowds: When you see a cloud rising in the west, you say at once: A shower is coming,* that is, a rain shower, *and so it will come to pass,*[237] for this is a sign, since heaven is being covered by a cloud, that rain is being prepared for the earth. The Psalm says: "Who covers the heaven with clouds and prepares rain for the earth" (146:8).

80. (Verse 55). *And when you see the south wind, you say: There will be a scorching heat, and thus*[238] *it comes to pass.* Job 37:17 reads: "Are not your clothes hot, when the south wind blows upon the earth?"

81. (Verse 56). And since from these sensible observations men and women are led to understand those things that these were neglecting to consider, he adds: *You hypocrites, you know how to judge the face of the sky and*

---

[237] On p. 333, n. 10 QuarEd correctly mention that the Vulgate reads *fit* ("it comes to pass") and that Hugh of St. Cher and Lyranus agree with Bonaventure in reading *fiet* ("it will come to pass"). They also provide a lengthy quotation from Book XIII, chapter 10, n. 2–4 of Isidore's *Etymologia* about the relationship between *nimbus* and *nubes,* both of which mean "cloud" and are used by Bonaventure in his commentary.

[238] On p. 333, n. 11 QuarEd rightly mention that the Vulgate lacks *ita* ("thus").

of the earth, but how is it that you do not judge this time?[239] And therefore, he calls them *hypocrites*, for they were professing knowledge of the Scriptures like Catholics, rather than knowledge of the nature of things and of the stars like astrologers. But in reality they were paying more heed to the latter rather than to the former. And this is hypocrisy in Christian religion, to be more solicitous about the things of nature than about the things of grace. Wherefore, Augustine says: "More praiseworthy is the intellect that takes note of its own weakness rather than the one that scrutinizes the constellations of the heavens and the depths of the earth."[240] Therefore, Sirach 3:22 reads: "Think always on the things that God has commanded you, and be not curious about many of God's works." Therefore, these are reprehensible, who take pains to consider the time of this rain and neglect to consider the time of grace, since through these sensible realities they can be led to spiritual realities. So they have abandoned the heavenly fatherland for the sake of the road thereto, and the face of the Lord for the sake of the Lord's footprints. Against these people Augustine in the second book of his *De Libero Arbitrio* says: "Woe to these who have abandoned you as their leader and wander about in your footprints, who love your signs instead of you and forget what you are indicating by your signs."[241]

---

[239] On p. 333, n. 12 QuarEd cite Bede on Luke 12:56. See CCSL cxx, p. 263: "This *time*, this is either the first or second coming of the Lord. For about both he had said many things beforehand."

[240] On p. 334, n. 1 QuarEd cite the author of spurious *Liber de Spiritu et Anima*, chapter 50. See PL 40:816: "Indeed, more praiseworthy is the intellect that takes note of its misery, rather than the one, having ignored its misery, scrutinizes the movements of the stars and the natures of things." Hugh of St. Cher, p. 213b provides a quotation from pseudo-Augustine that is identical to Bonaventure's.

[241] On p. 334, n. 3 QuarEd refer to Book II, chapter 16, n. 43 of Augustine's *De Libero Arbitrio*. See *Sancti Avrelii Avgvstini Contra*

82. On account of which it is to be understood that *the cloud* suggests the flesh of Christ. Isaiah 19:1 says: "The Lord will ascend upon a swift cloud and will enter into Egypt."[242] – *The appearance of a cloud rising from the west* designates the flesh of Christ rising and ascending.[243] The Psalmist says: "Who ascends upon the west, the Lord is his name" (67:5). – *The descent of the cloud and of rain* designates the descent of the Holy Spirit after Christ's ascension. 1 Kings 18:44–45 reads: "A little cloud arose out of the sea like a human foot. . . . And there fell a great rain."[244] – *The blowing of the south wind* refers to the wind of the Holy Spirit coming upon the disciples. The Song of Songs 4:16 states: "Arise, O north wind, and come, O south wind, blow through my garden." This happened, as Acts 2:2 says, when "suddenly there came a sound from heaven as of a vehement wind blowing." – *The heat that follows* refers to the fervor of love, which has brought to fruition all the harvests of the Church. Proverbs 10:5 says: "The son who gathers in

---

Academicos, De Beata Vita, De Ordine, De magistro, De Libero Arbitrio, ed. W. M. Green, CCSL 29 (Turnhout: Brepols, 1970), p. 266: *Vae qui derelinquunt te ducem et oberrant in uestigiis tuis, qui nutus tuos pro te amant te obliuiscuntur quid innuas. . . .* ("Woe, who abandon you as their leader and wander about in your footprints, who love your signs instead of you, forget what you are indicating by your signs"). Bonaventure's quotation is almost verbatim. It is important to note that earlier in this same paragraph when Bonaventure quoted Augustine from Hugh of St. Cher he merely said "Augustine." Now when he knows the source firsthand, he is happy to identify it.

[242] On p. 334, n. 4 QuarEd cite Jerome's commentary on Isaiah 19:1: "Some refer this entire prophecy to the time of the Savior, when he entered *upon a swift cloud*, that is, the human body that he has assumed from the Virgin, etc."

[243] On p. 334, n. 5 QuarEd cite Bede. See CCSL cxx, p. 263 where Bede is quoting Augustine (PL 35:1342): "*A cloud rising in the west*, signifies his flesh rising from death. For from him the rain of evangelical preaching was poured upon all lands. *South wind* before the heat means the lesser tribulations before the judgment."

[244] Hugh of St. Cher, p. 212v, g also quotes this scripture passage.

the harvest is wise, but the son who snores the summer away is a son of confusion," etc.

83. *Morally*, now, the words *a cloud rising in the west* are understood as the sorrow of compunction, born from the recollection of death. *Rain* means a flood of tears. *The blowing south wind* is devotion that brings joy. *Heat* refers to devotion that inflames the heart. Tobit 3:22 reads: "After a storm you restore calm, and after tears and weeping you pour in exultation."[245] – Therefore, this is the order of the descent of grace into our heart. For first we humans consider our end and death, and then we bring forth sorrow. After that we break into tears. That is then followed by consolation. Finally, we are inflamed with love. So in Luke 7:38 above it is said of the penitent sinful woman that "standing behind at the feet of the Lord, she began to bathe his feet with her tears...and anointed them with ointment."

84. (Verse 57). Secondly, he deals with *the warning of the internal judgment: Now, why even by yourselves do you not judge what is right?*, as if he were saying: Even if you neglect the external warning, may you not neglect the internal one. So Sirach 31:18 states: "Judge the things of your neighbor by yourself,"[246] that is, by your natural court of justice.[247] For a natural court of justice

---

[245] Hugh of St. Cher, p. 212v, g also quotes Tobit 3:22.

[246] The Vulgate reads *Intellege proximi tui ex te ipso* ("Judge of the disposition of your neighbor by yourself"). Bonaventure's imperative is *Cognosce* ("Judge"). Hugh of St. Cher, p. 213c quotes Sirach 31:18: *Intellige* (sic) *quae sunt proximi tui ex teipso* ("Judge the things of your neighbor by yourself").

[247] On p. 334, n. 11 QuarEd cite the Glossa Interlinearis (from Bede): "*But why even by yourselves*, from natural reason, *do you not judge what is just*, that I am God and will come in judgment." On p. 334, n. 12 they quote Origen's Homily 35 on Luke: "Unless the power to

is inserted into human beings, by which they are directed to see and choose. The Psalm says: "The light of your countenance, O Lord, is signed upon us" (4:7). And Isaiah 46:8 has: "Return, you transgressors, to your heart." For therein it is dictated what is just. And between all the things that are just, the natural reason dictates the choice. Even Antiochus recognized this as he said in 2 Maccabees 9:12: "It is just to be subject to God, and a mortal human being[248] should not think himself equal to God." Therefore, this is the most important decision about justice that any person should make, namely, God is to be worshipped and Christ to be honored and the gift of the Holy Spirit is to be received with reverence. For John 5:23 says: "The person who does not honor the Son does not honor the Father," etc. It is also just to decide that "God will judge the world in justice"[249] and that by judging ourselves we anticipate that judgment. For as 1 Corinthians 11:31 states: "If we judged ourselves, we should not thus be judged," etc. Therefore, our conscience naturally murmurs against us, and it itself also testifies that our evil deeds will not remain unpunished. And therefore, it prompts us that we must be solicitous to merit divine grace. Romans 2:14–15 reads: "When the Gentiles, who have no Law, do what the Law prescribes,[250] these having no Law of this kind are a law unto themselves. For they show the work of the Law written in their hearts, with their conscience bearing witness to them," etc.

---

judge what is just had been inserted into us by nature, the Savior would never had said: *But why even by yourselves*, etc."

[248] The Vulgate does not read *hominem* ("human being").

[249] Psalm 95:13.

[250] It is amazing that in this discussion Bonaventure's quotation lacks the key word, *naturaliter* ("by nature"). The opening gambit of Romans 2:14 reads: "When the Gentiles, who have no Law, do by nature what the Law prescribes. . . . "

85. (Verse 58). Thirdly, concerning *the warning about the edict from a superior* the text continues: *But when you are going with your adversary on the way to the ruler.* Bede says: "Our *adversary* on the way is the word of God which is contrary to our carnal desires in the present life."[251] Our *ruler* is Christ. Isaiah 32:8 has: "The ruler will devise those things that are worthy of a ruler." To this ruler the word of God directs us in *a triple way.* There is *the way of innocence,* about which the Psalm says: "The person who walks in the undefiled way, this one served me" (100:6). There is the way of *repentance.* Exodus 8:27 reads: "We will go a three days' journey in solitude."[252] There is the way of *wisdom.* Proverbs 4:11 has: "I will show you the way of wisdom. I will lead you by the paths of justice."[253] – The Prophet prayed that these ways be shown to him, saying: "Show me your ways."[254] Now he shows these *by example.* John 14:6 says: "I am the way, the truth, and the life." He shows *by word.* Isaiah 30:21 states: "You will hear the words of your preceptor: This is the good way. Walk in it."[255] He

---

[251] On p. 335, n. 2 QuarEd refer to Book IV of Bede's commentary on Luke 12:58 and state that Bede is following Augustine's Sermon 9, chapter 3, n. 3 and Sermon 109, chapter 3, n. 3. They also list three other parallels. For Bede, see CCSL cxx, p. 264. Bonaventure's quotation is virtually verbatim. Hugh of St. Cher, p. 213e provides most of this quotation, but does not cite it as stemming from Bede.

[252] The Vulgate reads *Via trium dierum pergemus in solitudine* ("We will go on a way of three days in the wilderness"). I have translated Bonaventure's text in a penitential modality.

[253] On p. 335, n. 3 QuarEd state the Cardinal Hugh also proposes this triple way. See Hugh of St. Cher, p. 213h where he also quotes Proverbs 4:11 and Exodus 8:27.

[254] Psalm 24:4.

[255] On p. 335, n. 4 QuarEd correctly indicate that the Vulgate of Isaiah 30:21 is dissimilar and reads: *Et aures tuae audient verbum post tergum monentis: Haec via, ambulate in ea* ("And your ears will hear the word of one admonishing you from behind your back: This is the way. Walk in it"). Hugh of St. Cher, p. 213h quotes Isaiah 30:21 in his interpretation of the second way, that of "repentance."

also shows it by *a gift divinely inspired*. Wisdom 10:10 reads: "The Lord[256] led the just through right ways and showed him the kingdom of God."

86. Now since the word of God directs us along the right way, along which carnality refuses to go – and reason must believe more strongly in the word of God than in carnal suggestion – the text adds: *take pains to be free of him*, by fulfilling *the commandments*, by avoiding *things prohibited*, by hoping in *the promises*, and by being afraid of *the threats*. The person who does these things is secure from the adversary.[257] Sirach 36:9 has: "Extol the adversary and crush the enemy." For the person who extols the divine word crushes the enemy, that is, the flesh, the world and the devil.[258] Bede says: "Since in this life you are preparing yourself to view the pleasing face of the judge, let not contempt for the word of God accuse you. Although the word of God is contrary to your flesh, nonetheless it was given to you in the womb itself as a guardian for this journey."[259] – Therefore, he adds:

---

[256] In the context of Wisdom 10:10 the subject is "wisdom," not "the Lord." In his interpretation of "the way of wisdom" Hugh of St. Cher on p. 213h quotes John 14:6, Psalm 106:4, Proverbs 4:11, Psalm 24:4, and Wisdom 10:10.

[257] On p. 335, n. 5 QuarEd refer to Bede. See CCSL cxx, p. 264: "From whom (the adversary which is the word of God) the person is freed who is humbly subject to his commandments."

[258] See Hugh of St. Cher, p. 213i: "Take pains to be free of him] by fulfilling the commandments, by avoiding things prohibited, by hoping in the promises, by being afraid of threats. The person who does these four things, is secure from the adversary, that is, the divine word. About this Sirach 36:9 says: Extol the adversary, and crush the enemy, that is, exalt the divine word. And thus you will crush the threefold enemy, that is, the world, the flesh, and the devil."

[259] On p. 335, n. 7 QuarEd merely state that this quotation is taken from the Glossa Ordinaria. See CCSL cxx, p. 264 where Bede gives some inkling of the meaning of this involved sentence: "For the person who contemns the word of God will be held as a sinner in the

lest he deliver you to the judge, that is, to Christ. Acts
10:42 states: "He it is who has been appointed as judge
of the living and of the dead," etc. – *and the judge to the
exactor*, that is, the devil, who demands punishment for
sin.[260] Job 3:18 reads: "They have not listened to[261] the
voice of the exactor." – *And the exactor cast you into
prison*, namely, into hell. Isaiah 24:22 says: "They will
be gathered together as in the gathering of one bundle
into the pit, and they will be shut up there in prison,"
for this punishment is irremediable.[262]

87. (Verse 59). Therefore, he adds: *I say to you: You will
not come out from there until you have paid the very last
mite*,[263] that is, never, because you will never pay it. Bede
comments: "He always pays by suffering punishments
for sins, but never obtaining forgiveness."[264] Thus, *until*

---

examination by the judge." Hugh of St. Cher, p. 213 does not have
this quotation.

[260] On p. 335, n. 9 QuarEd quote the Glossa Interlinearis: *"To the
exactor*, the devil, who demands punishment for the guilty who is in
the state of the sin the devil suggested."

[261] On p. 335, n. 9 QuarEd correctly indicate that the Vulgate reads
audierunt ("listened to") while Bonaventure reads *exaudierunt* ("listened to").

[262] On p. 335, n. 10 QuarEd cite the Glossa Interlinearis: *"Into the
prison*, of hell."

[263] On p. 335, n. 11 QuarEd accurately mention that the Vulgate reads
donec etiam novissimum minutum reddas ("until you have paid even
the very last mite"). That is, Bonaventure's text does not read *etiam*
("even").

[264] On p. 335, n. 12 QuarEd refer to Book IV of Bede's commentary on
Luke 12:59, but say that Bonaventure is actually quoting the Glossa
Ordinaria. See CCSL cxx, p. 264 for Bede's interpretation which provides the base for the Glossa. See Hugh of St. Cher, p. 213r: "The
Glossa of Bede: He always pays, suffering punishments for sins, but
never obtaining forgiveness." Hugh of St. Cher will follow this quotation immediately with one from Augustine and one from
Chrysostom. These quotations are the very same ones that Bonaventure will use in this paragraph #87.

does not set down a terminus here, just as it does not establish such in this passage: "The Lord said to my Lord: Sit at my right hand until I make your enemies your footstool."[265] Augustine writes: "*Until* does not signify the terminus of the punishment, but that you are always paying and never paying it off in full."[266] And it is said *to pay off the last mite in full*, since reprobates are punished not only for great sins, but also for small ones.[267] Chrysostom says: "If at any time you were condemned and thrown into prison, then not only for serious sins, but also for the idle word you have spoken, punishments will be laid upon you."[268] Into these pun-

---

[265] I have quoted all of Psalm 109:1 instead of Bonaventure's abbreviated version. On p. 335, n. 12 QuarEd quote the Glossa Interlinearis: "*Until*, this is, never, as in *Until I put*, etc."

[266] On p. 335, n. 13 QuarEd cite Book I, chapter 11, n. 30 of Augustine's *De Sermone Domini in Monte*. See *Sancti Avrelii Avgvstini De Sermone Domini in Monte Libros Duos*. Ed. Almut Mutzenbecher, CCSL xxxv (Turnhout: Brepols, 1967), 32: . . . *semper non esse exiturum, quia semper soluet nouissimum quadrantem, dum sempiternas poenas terrenorum peccatorum luit* (". . . will never come out, for he is always paying the last farthing while he is suffering everlasting punishments for earthly sins." See Hugh of St. Cher, p. 213r: "Augustine. *Until* in this passage does not signify the end of the punishment, but that you are always paying and never paying it off in full." It seems that Bonaventure is quoting Augustine from Hugh of St. Cher.

[267] On p. 335, n. 14 QuarEd cite the Glossa Interlinearis (from Bede): "*You have paid the last mite*, that is, you will be punished for the smallest sins." See CCSL cxx, p. 264.

[268] On p. 335, n. 14 QuarEd refer to Chrysostom's Homily 11 on Matthew 5:25 (*Opus Imperfectum*). See PG 56:693: *Si semel condemnatus fueris missus in carcerem, jam non solum de gravibus peccatis, sed etiam pro verbo otioso, quod loquutus es, id est, si Racha alicui dixisti, pro eo sunt exigenda a te supplicia* ("If at any time you were condemned and thrown into prison, then not only for serious sins, but also for the idle word you have spoken, that is, if you have said 'Racha,' punishments must be laid upon you for them"). See Hugh of St. Cher, p. 213r: "Wherefore, Chrysostom: If at any time you were condemned and thrown into prison, then not only for serious sins, but also for the idle word you have spoken, punishments must be

ishments are cast headlong those who do not keep the divine words, which dispatch men to divine grace and to Christ. Thus John 5:39 reads: "Search the Scriptures. . . . It is they that bear witness to me."

88. Therefore, from these considerations it is obvious that human negligence in recognizing and receiving God's grace is inexcusable. To draw people to God's grace he employs a triple warning, namely, that of the book of *creation, conscience,* and *Scripture* which are like three witnesses.[269] One of these is *external,* another *internal,* and the third as it were, *supernal.* Wherefore, as it is said in Hebrews 2:1–3: "We ought the more earnestly observe the things that we have heard, lest perhaps we drift away. For if the word spoken by angels proved to be valid, and every transgression and disobedience received a just punishment, how will we escape if we neglect so great a salvation?"

---

laid upon you." Bonaventure seems dependent upon Hugh of St. Cher rather than directly upon *Opus Imperfectum.*

[269] On p. 336, n. 1 QuarEd refer to Book IV, distinction 43, article 3, question 1 of Bonaventure's *Commentary on the Sentences* and to Part II, chapters 11 and 12 and Part VII, chapter 1 of Bonaventure's *Breviloquium* for more detail on "the threefold book." See Opera Omnia 4:896–897, Opera Omnia 5:229–230, Opera Omnia 5:281–282 respectively.

LUKE 13

Luke 13:1–9
CENSURE OF NEGLIGENCE IN DOING PENANCE

1. *Now there came in that very time some who*, etc. Above he censured negligence relative to acknowledging grace. Here he rebukes negligence relative to *engaging in the work of repentance*. And he does this in a threefold manner. First, through *the example he has heard about*. Second, through *the example he has seized upon* where verse 4 reads: *like those eighteen*, etc. Finally, through *the example he had invented or thought up* where verse 6 has: *But he spoke this parable*.

Luke 13:1–3
CENSURE OF SUCH NEGLIGENCE THROUGH AN EXAMPLE CHRIST HAS HEARD ABOUT

In developing the example *he had heard about*, he proceeds in this fashion. First, *the cruelty of the punishment* is proposed. Second, *the enormity of their sins* is negated. Third, he draws a conclusion about *the necessity of repenting.*

2. (Verse 1). Thus, *the narrative of a cruel punishment* is mentioned: *Now there came at that very time some who told him about the Galileans,* namely, harsh and terrible things, which they were especially prone to recite. Wherefore, the text adds: *whose blood Pilate had mingled with their sacrifices,* according to history. Josephus narrates that there was a certain person in Galilee who gave himself out to be the Messiah promised in the Law. And many of the Galileans were following him. He had indicated to them a day on which he would ascend into heaven from Mount Gerizim while they looked on. But Pilate, seeing that he had seduced many from the tetrarchy of Herod, feared lest after these he would lead astray many from his own tetrarchy. Therefore, when the day had been indicated and those whom he had led astray were worshipping him and offering sacrifices to him, Pilate quickly intervened and killed them in the midst of their sacrifices. And among those he killed was the person who was giving himself off as the Christ.[1] So

---

[1] On p. 336, n. 5 QuarEd have a long footnote on this passage. The basis in Josephus for Bonaventure's commentary is Josephus' *Jewish Antiquities* XVIII 4.1 (#85–87). LCL translates the Greek, which seems to be faithfully followed by the Latin translation QuarEd provide: "The Samaritan nation too was not exempt from disturbance. For a man who made light of mendacity and in all his designs catered to the mob, rallied them, bidding them go in a body with him to Mount Gerizim, which in their belief is the most sacred of mountains. He assured them that on their arrival he would show them the sacred vessels which were buried there, where Moses had deposited them. . . . Many prisoners were taken, of whom Pilate put to death the principal leaders and those who were most influential among the fugitives." Obviously, this passage has nothing to do with Galileans, the supposed Messiah and his ascension, and blood mingled with sacrifices. At the end of their note QuarEd simply note: "St. Bonaventure, Cardinal Hugo, and Blessed Albert base their narration

from this can be understood what Acts 5:36–37 says: "Some time ago there rose up Theudas, claiming to be somebody, and a number of men, about four hundred, joined him. He was slain, and all his followers were dispersed. . . . After him rose up Judas the Galilean . . . and he drew people after him. He, too, perished, and all his followers were scattered abroad." And the punishment was indeed harsh, because they were delivered over to an horrendous death *quickly, violently*, and *in numbers*.

3. (Verses 2–3). Secondly, relative to *negating that their sin was of greater enormity*, the text adds: *And he answered and said to them: Do you think that these Galileans were worse sinners than all the other Galileans, be-*

---

on Peter Comestor, *Historia scholastica*, In Evangelia, chapter 94." See PL 198:1585D: "For a certain person, saying that he was the Son of God, had seduced many of the Galileans. After he had led them to Gerizim, he told them that he would ascend into heaven in their presence. While they were making sacrifices to him, Pilate intervened, slew him and everyone else, for he feared that he would also lead astray the Judeans." Bonaventure's summary of Josephus is very similar to that of Cardinal Hugh. See Hugh of St. Cher, p. 213v, c: "It is doubtful who these Galileans were, for the Gospel history gives no determination. Josephus says, and it is found in his *Histories* that there was a certain person in Galilee who gave himself out to be the son of God, the Messiah promised in the Law. And many of the Galileans were following him as his adherents, whom he had seduced. And he had indicated to them a day on which he would ascend into heaven from Mount Gerizim while they looked on. But Pilate, seeing that he had seduced many from the tetrarchy of Herod, that is, of Galilea, feared lest after these he would lead astray those from his own tetrarchy, namely, the Jerusalemites. Therefore, when on the day indicated they were on Mount Gerizim, and those whom he had led astray were worshipping him and offering sacrifices to him, Pilate quickly intervened and killed them in the midst of their sacrifices. And among others he killed the son of God." Fitzmyer, pp. 1006–7 observes: "The incident to which Luke refers is not mentioned elsewhere either in the gospel tradition or in other ancient writers. . . . Luke's picture of Pilate in this episode is not contradicted by the brutal person depicted in Josephus' writings."

cause they suffered such things? For this is what people, who judge by externals, are often wont to believe.[2] However, one should not judge by externals. – Thus, the text continues: *I tell you, No,* that is, I assert that they were not worse sinners. So one should not judge rashly, but rather be fearful. For God's judgments are secret. Wherefore, Qoheleth 8:10 states: "I saw the wicked buried, who, when they were still alive,[3] were in the holy place and were praised in the city as people of just deeds." And Qoheleth 8:14 then reads: "There are just people, to whom evils happen, as though they had done the works of the wicked. And there are wicked people, who are as secure, as if they had done the deeds of the just." And again Qoheleth 9:2 has: "All things are kept uncertain for the time to come, because all things equally happen to the just and the wicked, the good and the evil, the clean and the unclean, those who offer victims and those who despise sacrifices." And so it is said in 1 Corinthians 4:5: "Do not pass judgment before the time, until the Lord comes, who will both bring to light the things hidden in darkness and make manifest the counsels of hearts." For as Gregory says: "The judgments of God are not to be disputed rashly, but to be venerated with awesome silence."[4]

4. Third, concerning *the conclusion of the necessity of repentance* the text has: *But unless you repent, you will all perish in a similar manner.* Sirach 2:21–22 reads: "Those who fear the Lord keep his commandments and

---

[2] On p. 336, n. 7 QuarEd helpfully point to 1 Samuel 16:7: "For human beings look at appearances, but the Lord looks into the heart."

[3] The Vulgate reads: *Vidi impios sepultos qui etiam cum adviverent* ("I saw the wicked buried, who also when they were living").

[4] See Bonaventure's commentary on Luke 10:21 (#38) above where he uses the same "quotation" from Book XXXII, chapter 1, n.1 of Gregory the Great's *Moralia.*

will have patience even until his visitation, saying: If we do not do penance, we will fall into the hands of the Lord and not into human hands." But as it is said in Hebrews 10:31: "It is a fearful thing to fall into the hands of the living God," for the Psalm says: "Unless you be converted, he will brandish his sword," etc. (7:13). And Sirach 5:8–9 states: "Delay not to be converted to the Lord and defer it not from day to day. For his wrath will come suddenly, and in the time of vengeance he will destroy you."

5. And note that there are twelve reasons why a person *perishes*, as garnered from the Scriptures:[5]

First, on account of the failure of *repentance*, as is the case here: "Unless you repent, you will all perish in the same manner." And Luke 15:17 states: "How many hired men in my father's house have bread in abundance, while I am perishing here with hunger?" Contrariwise, it is said in 2 Peter 3:9: "For your sake God[6] is long-suffering, not wishing that any should perish, but that all should turn to repentance."

Second, on account of a lack of *foresight*. Job 4:20 reads: "Since no one understands, they will perish for ever." Contrariwise, it is said in Sirach 23:7: "Hear, O children, the discipline of my mouth, and those who keep it will not perish through their speech," etc.[7]

Third, on account of a lack of *patience*. Matthew 26:52 has: "All those who take up the sword will perish by the sword." The Psalm says: "The sinner will see and will be

---

[5] As far as I can tell, Hugh of St. Cher has nothing similar.
[6] The Vulgate reads *Dominus* ("the Lord").
[7] In the Vulgate the subject of the second clause is singular.

angry," etc. (111:10).[8] Contrariwise, the Psalmist states: "The poor person will not be forgotten to the end. The patience of the poor will not perish forever" (9:19).

Fourth, on account of a lack of *innocence*. The Psalm has: "The swords of the enemy have utterly failed. . . . Their memory has perished with a noise" (9:7). Contrariwise, Job 4:7 reads: "Remember, I pray you, which innocent person ever perished or when were the just destroyed?"

Fifth, on account of a lack of *clemency*. The Psalm says: "You have rebuked the Gentiles, and the wicked person has perished" (9:6). John 11:50 reads: "It is expedient for you[9] that one person die for the people instead of the entire nation perishing."

Sixth, on account of a lack of *wisdom*. Baruch 3:28 states: "Since they did not have wisdom, they perished through their folly." Contrariwise, Proverbs 24:14 has: "When you have found wisdom, you will have hope in the end, and your hope will not perish," etc.

6. Seventh, on account of a lack of *faith*. 1 Corinthians 10:9 says: "Let us not tempt Christ, as some of them tempted and perished by the serpents." Contrariwise, John 3:14–15 reads: "The Son of Man must be lifted up, so that everyone who believes in him, may not perish, but may have life everlasting."
Eighth, on account of a lack of *love*. 2 Thessalonians 2:10 states: "To those who are perishing, for they have not accepted the love of truth that they might be saved."

---

[8] The key word "perish" occurs at the end of this verse. Psalm 111:10 reads in its entirety: "The sinner will see and will be angry. He will gnash with his teeth and pine away. The desire of the wicked will perish."
[9] The Vulgate reads *nobis* ("for us").

Contrariwise, it is said in John 17:12: "Not one of them has perished except the son of perdition," etc.

Ninth, on account of a lack of *truth*. Proverbs 19:5 reads: "A false witness will not go unpunished, and the person who speaks lies will perish."[10] Proverbs 21:28 has: "A lying witness will perish."

Tenth, on account of a lack of *peace and unity*. 1 Corinthians 10:10 says: "Do not murmur as some of them murmured and perished at the hands of the destroyer." And Numbers 16:33 has this about the schismatics who murmured against the Lord: "And they went down alive into hell, the ground closing upon them, and they perished."

Eleventh, on account of a lack of *liberality*. Qoheleth 5:12–13 reads: "Riches, collected to the harm of their owner, have perished with very great affliction,"[11] that is, they were made to perish. And 1 Timothy 6:9 states: "Those who want to become rich fall into temptation and a snare of the devil[12] and many useless and harmful desires, which plunge people into destruction and damnation."

Twelfth, on account of a lack of *humility*. Sirach 8:18 has: "The foolhardy person goes according to his own will, and you will perish together with his folly." Contrariwise,

---

[10] On p. 337, n. 12 QuarEd rightly indicate that the Vulgates reads *non effugiet* ("will not escape") for Bonaventure's *peribit* ("will perish").

[11] On p. 337, n. 14 QuarEd correctly mention that the Vulgate has a slightly different text: *divitiae conservatae in malum domini sui. Pereunt enim in afflictione pessima* ("Riches stored up to the harm of their owner. For they perish with the most wretched affliction").

[12] The Vulgate lacks *diaboli* ("of the devil").

Matthew 18:14 says: "It is not the will of your Father . . . that a single one of these little ones should perish." John 10:27–28 reads: "My sheep hear my voice, . . . and I give them everlasting life, and they will never perish."

Luke 13:4–5
CENSURE OF NEGLIGENT REPENTANCE BY AN EXAMPLE CHRIST HAS SEIZED UPON

7. (Verse 4). *Like those eighteen upon whom*, etc. In this instance *he censures negligence in repenting by means of an example he has seized upon*, that conforms to the example he has heard about. He first sets forth *the gravity of the punishment*, then *he negates the profundity of iniquity*, and finally *draws the conclusion about the necessity of repentance*.

So first, with regard to *the gravity and horrible nature of the sudden punishment*, he says: *Like those eighteen upon whom the tower of Siloam fell and killed them*. These eighteen were Jerusalemites, who had literally built the tower near Siloam and were crushed by the ruination of the tower, as if of a sudden, but this occurred by the just judgment of God. For Proverbs 17:16 reads: "The person who makes his house high is seeking his own ruination," etc.

8. (Verses 4–5). Secondly, relative to *the negation of the profundity of iniquity* he adds: *Do you think that they were more guilty than all the other dwellers in Jerusalem*, for they alone were punished? – *No, I tell you*, for certainly there were many other sinners in it. Jeremiah 5:1 has: "Go about through the streets of Jerusalem and see and consider and seek in its broad places whether you

can find a man who exercises judgment and seeks faith.
And I will be merciful unto it."

9. Thirdly, concerning *the conclusion about the necessity
of repentance* this is subjoined: *But if you do not have
repentance, you will all perish in the same manner.*[13] *In
the same manner* – not relative to corporal punishment,
but relative to spiritual and hellish punishment. For as
the tower fell upon these, thus upon all reprobates falls
that *cornerstone*, about which Matthew 21:44 speaks:
"And the person who falls upon this stone will be broken
to pieces, but upon whomever it falls, it will grind him
to dust."[14] Now this stone, which grew into a mountain,[15]
is rightly called *a tower* because of its strength and
height. Proverbs 18:10 says: "A very strong tower is the
name of the Lord."[16] This tower crushes those reprobates
in judgment, according to what Sirach 27:3 reads: "Sin
will be crushed with the sinner," etc. And then they will
perish with their sins. Jeremiah 10:15 states: "Their
deeds are vain and worthy of derision. In the time of
their visitation they will perish." Such are those who
neglect the works of repentance and contemn the cross
of Christ. 1 Corinthians 1:18 says: "Indeed, the word of
the cross is foolishness to those who are perishing, but

---

[13] On p. 338, n. 3 QuarEd accurately mention that the Vulgate reads
Sed nisi poenitentiam egeritis ("But unless you repent") whereas
Bonaventure reads *Sed si poenitentiam non habueritis* ("But if you
do not have repentance").

[14] Luke 20:18 contains the same saying. On p. 338, n. 4 QuarEd helpfully call attention to Bede's commentary. See CCSL cxx, p. 265: "It
is not for naught that the number is ten plus eight – the Greeks use
the letters I and H for these numbers – for the name Jesus in Greek
begins with these two letters."

[15] On p. 338, n. 5 QuarEd call their readers' attention to Daniel 2:35:
"But the stone that struck the statue became a great mountain and
filled the whole earth."

[16] See Hugh of St. Cher, p. 213v, k who also cites Matthew 21:44 and
Proverbs 18:10.

to those who are saved it is the power of God unto salvation," etc.[17]

10. Now note that human beings are wont to be punished for ten reasons. Namely, for the purpose of *purgation*, as in the case of Miriam, the sister of Moses. Numbers 12:10 has: "Miriam appeared white as snow with leprosy," etc. – For *proving*, as in the case of Job. Job 2:7 reads: "Satan went forth from the presence of the Lord and struck Job with a very grievous ulcer from the sole of his foot even to the top of his head." – For *humbling*, as in the case of Paul. 2 Corinthians 12:7 states: "There was given me a thorn for the flesh, a messenger of satan, to buffet me," namely, "lest the greatness of the revelations should puff me up." – For *the glorification of divine power*, as in the case of the man born blind. John 9:3 has: "Neither has this man sinned nor his parents, but so that the works of God may be manifested in him," etc. – For *the commemoration of divine clemency*, as in the case of the father of John the Baptist. Luke 1:20 above says: "Behold, you will be dumb and unable to speak until the day," etc. – For *the manifestation of divine judgment*, as in the case of Herod. Acts 12:23 reads: "An angel of the Lord struck him," etc. And also in the case of Antiochus in 2 Maccabees.[18] – For *the punishment of parents*. Exodus 20:5 states: "I am God, jealous, pun-

---

[17] The last part of Bonaventure's quotation of 1 Corinthians 1:18 differs from the Vulgate which reads: *his autem qui salvi fiunt, id est, nobis, virtus Dei est* ("but to those who are saved, that is, to us, it is the power of God"). On p. 338, n. 7 QuarEd suggest Bonaventure's last words, that is, *in salutem* ("unto salvation") may be derived from Romans 1:16: "For it is the power of God unto salvation for all who believe."

[18] Acts 12:23 says this of the arrogant Herod: "But immediately an angel of the Lord struck him down, because he had not given the honor to God. And he was eaten by worms and died." The author of 2 Maccabees 9 is much more descriptive.

ishing the sins of the fathers upon their children upon
the third and fourth generation that hate me."[19] For this
reason the children of Sodom were destroyed in Genesis
19:25. – For *the terror of others.* Proverbs 19:25 says:
"The wicked person having been scourged, the foolish
person will be wiser." Thus it is that these were punished, about whom these verses speak, so that others
may be filled with terror. – For *an example to posterity.*
Tobit 2:12 reads: "God permitted this trial to happen to
him, so that an example of patience might be given to
posterity. – For *the detestation of crimes*, as in the case
of Dathan and Abiram. Numbers 16:31–32 has: "The
earth broke asunder under their feet, and opening its
mouth, devoured them," etc.[20] Thus also in the case of
Gehazi. 2 Kings 5:27 reads: "The leprosy of Naaman will
stick to you and to your seed forever." And so also in the
case of Ananias. Acts 5:3 says: "Why has satan tempted
your heart that you should lie to the Holy Spirit," etc.[21]
In this it is shown to what extent one must abhor division, simony, and apostasy. Therefore, these people
were immediately punished in this manner.[22]

---

[19] Bonaventure's text literally reads: "Exodus 20:5 states: I am God,
jealous, punishing the sins, etc."
[20] I have expanded Bonaventure's quotation of Numbers 16:32 by
adding "devoured them."
[21] Bonaventure is content to write: "'Why has satan tempted your
heart,' etc."
[22] On p. 338, n. 16 QuarEd indicate that Cardinal Hugh has eleven
reasons for punishment. See Hugh of St. Cher, p. 213v, k: *Undecim
enim causis aliquis punitur praesenti poena. Primo ad ejus purga-
tionem, ut Maria soror Moysi. Numbers 12c[10]. Item ad proba-
tionem, ut Job 1 & 2. Item ad punitionis continuationem, ut Herodes,
Acts 12d[23]. Item ad defensionem superbiae, sive ad humilitatis con-
servationem, ut Paulus 2 Cor 12b[7]. Item ad Christi glorificationem,
ut caecus, Joan. 9a[3]. Item ad posteriorum exemplum, ut Tob 2b[12].
Item ad terrorem malorum. Prov 19b[25]. Flagellato pestilente, etc.
Item ad parentum punitionem. Exodus 20a[5]. Ego sum Deus zelotes,
etc. Item ad sobrietatem. Eccl 31e[2]. Infirmitas gravis, etc. Item ad*

Luke 13:6–9
CENSURE OF NEGLIGENT REPENTANCE BY AN EXAMPLE CHRIST HAS THOUGHT UP

11. (Verse 6). *Now he spoke this parable: A certain man had a fig tree*, etc. Here in the third place he presents an example *he had thought up* or invented about a fruitless fig tree that is to be cut down. Under this metaphor three things are understood about the soul, which neglects repentance, namely, *the defect of negligence* in not bearing fruit, *the sternness of the sentence* in threatening, and *the usefulness*[23] *of repentance* in remedying the situation.

---

majorem cautelam, ut pueri Sodomitae, Gen 19[25], qui si vixissent, pejores essent, etc. gravius punirentur. Item ad habendum memoriam Dei, ut Zacharias pater Joannis, sup. 1b[20]. Ut probet, aut puniat, aut purget, aut tueatur; Aut Christi pateat gloria, poena datur. Ut sit in exemplum terror, vel poena parentum: Ut sit sobria mens, cauta, memorque Dei ("For someone receives punishment at the present time for eleven reasons. First, for the purpose of his *purgation*, as in the case of Miriam, the sister of Moses. Numbers 12:10. Further, for *proving*, as in Job 1–2. Likewise, punishment follows upon an action, as in the case of Herod, Acts 12:23. Further, to prevent pride or to preserve humility, as in the case of Paul. 2 Corinthians 12:7. Moreover, for the glorification of Christ, as in the case of the blind man, John 9:3. Further, for an example to posterity, as in Tobit 2:12. Likewise, to instill terror in the wicked. Proverbs 19:25: The wicked person having been scourged, etc. Moreover, for the punishment of parents. Exodus 20:5 states: I am God, jealous, etc. Moreover, for the sake of sobriety. Sirach 31:2 says: Grievous sickness (makes the soul sober). Likewise, to provide a greater warning, as in the case of the children of Sodom, Genesis 19:25, who, if they had lived, would have been worse, etc., and would be punished more severely. Further, to keep God in memory, as in the case of Zechariah, father of John, in Luke 1:20 above. In order to prove or punish or purge or warn or to manifest Christ's glory, punishment is given. In order that terror or the punishment of parents may set an example, so that the mind may be sober, circumspect, and mindful of God"). Hugh's last two sentences are actually printed in verse form.

[23] In his commentary on Luke 13:8 below Bonaventure will talk about *the necessity* of repentance.

So first, relative to *the defect of negligence in bearing fruit* the text says: *A certain man had a fig tree planted in his vineyard,* that is, to receive its fruit, which, however, negligence took from him. – Wherefore, the text continues: *And he came, seeking fruit thereon and found none.* By *vineyard* is understood the ecclesiastical congregation. Isaiah 5:7 states: "The vineyard of the Lord of hosts is the house of Israel." By the *unfruitful fig tree,* which is full of leaves, is understood the soul, which refuses repentance because of negligence. Joel 1:7 reads: "He has laid waste my vineyard and has peeled off the bark of my fig tree. He has stripped it bare and cast it away. Its branches are made white." This fig tree is full of *leaves* when it is full of verbiage to excuse itself. Genesis 3:7 says: "They sewed together fig leaves, and made aprons for themselves."[24] And this merited the Lord's curse. Matthew 21:19 has: "Seeing a fig tree...he found nothing on it but leaves. And he said to it: May no fruit ever come from you. . . . "[25]

---

[24] On p. 339, n. 3 QuarEd refer to Ambrose and Bede and summarize their interpretations thus: "For them *the vineyard* mainly refers to the house of Israel. But *the fig tree* refers to the synagogue, and generally to the nature of the human race." See CCSL xiv, p. 269–271 and CCSL cxx, pp. 265–266. The editors also refer to Homily 31, n. 2 of GGHG. See PL 76:1128C: "What does the fig tree represent if not human nature? . . . Third, the master of the vineyard comes to the fig tree, because by expecting, admonishing, and visiting he made demands on the nature of the human race before the law, under the law, under grace."

[25] On p. 339, n. 5 QuarEd cite the Glossa Ordinaria (from Ambrose) on Luke 13:6: "At the beginning of the human race Adam and Eve, after they had sinned, *made aprons for themselves,* out of the leaves of the fig tree. Therefore, the leaves of the fig tree are understood to be sins. Now they were under the fig tree as under the shadow of death, about which it was said (Isaiah 9:2): They who sat under the shadow of death, light has risen for them." See CCSL xiv, p. 271.

12. (Verse 7). Secondly, concerning *the sternness of the sentence in threatening* the text continues: *Now he said to the vine-dresser: Behold, for three years now I have come, seeking fruit on this fig tree, and I find none.* By *three years* are understood childhood, adolescence, and youth. During these times someone may neglect to engage in repentance, according to what Job 24:23 says: "God has given him space for repentance, but he abused it through pride." *The cultivator of this vineyard* is the preacher and especially the prelate, about whom 1 Corinthians 3:6 reads: "I have planted. Apollos has watered." Thus Augustine in his *Against the Five Heresies* says: "Where are you, O good farmers? What are you doing? Why are you resting? And you see how the earth is filled with so many wicked people. Here thorns, here spiny plants, here hay spring up. Burn the thorns. Tear up the spiny plants. Cut down the hay. And sow good seed. Let storms not terrorize you. Even if iniquity flourishes, nonetheless let your love grow fervent. Sow during the storms that you will reap during the harvest," etc.[26] – It is fitting that such a negligent farmer is threatened with the severity of divine judgment. For which reason the text adds: *Cut it down, therefore. Why*

---

[26] On p. 339, n. 7 QuarEd refer to chapter 6, n. 8 of this spurious work of Augustine and note that it was already known to Bede. See PL 42:1108. This work is known as *Tractatus Adversus Quinque Haereses sive Contra Quinque Hostium Genera.* Bonaventure's quotation is virtually identical with that in PL 42:1108. See Hugh of St. Cher, p. 214z, who in his *moraliter* section quotes this self-same passage from "Augustine." Hugh's quotation, however, in comparison to Bonaventure's is both abbreviated and expanded: "'Where are you, O good farmers? What are you doing? Why are you resting? And you see how the earth is filled with so many wicked people. Here thorns, here spiny plants, here hay spring up. Burn the thorns. Tear up the spiny plants. Cut down the hay. And sow good seed. . . . But to whom do I say this? Oh, where are you, fountains of tears, by means of which I may speak to these farmers? Some are dead. Others have fled. The land has been handed over into the hands of the impious."

does it still encumber the ground? That is, denounce it
as a tree to be cut down, according to what John the
Baptist said in Matthew 3:8–10: "Bring forth fruit worthy of repentance. . . . For even now the axe is laid at
the root the trees. Every tree that is not bringing forth
good fruit will be cut down and thrown into the fire."[27]
And Paul in Romans 2:4–5 states: "Do you not know
that the goodness of God is meant to lead you to repentance? But according to your hardness and impenitent
heart you are treasuring up for yourself wrath on the
day of wrath and of the revelation of the just judgment
of God." And David in the Psalm says: "Therefore, God
will destroy you forever. He will pluck you out and remove you from your dwelling place and your root from
out of the land of the living" (51:7).

13. (Verse 8). Thirdly, about *the necessity of repentance
to remedy the situation* the text adds: *But he answered
him and said: Sir, let it alone also this year*, that is,
during the time of old age, *till I dig around it and manure it*, that is, until I make it call to memory its fragility and iniquity. For *the person digs* who humbles himself. Isaiah 2:10 says: "Enter into the rock. Hide in the
ditch from the face of the fear of the Lord and from the
glory of his majesty." And 2 Kings 3:16 reads: "Make the
channel of this torrent full of ditches." Wherefore, the
Glossa comments: "Indeed, *a ditch* goes deep, and a rebuke, since it reveals the mind to itself, humbles."[28] The
person who recalls sin to mind is the one who *spreads
manure*. So the Glossa of Bede reads: "*Until I spread
manure*, that is, I will recall to mind the evils and

---

[27] See the parallel in Luke 3:8–9.
[28] On p. 339, n. 12 QuarEd state that this is the Glossa Ordinaria,
based on Homily 31, n. 5 of GGHG, which is also followed by Bede.
On Bede, see CCSL cxx, p. 267. On Gregory, see PL 76:1229CD.

abomination which he has committed, and I will arouse the grace of compunction with the fruits of good deeds as from the abundance of the manure."[29] "For sins are said to be manure. So Joel 1:17 states: *The beasts have rotted in their dung.*"[30] And Lamentations 4:5 has: "Those that were raised in scarlet have embraced dung."[31] Recognition of these matters makes the soul fruitful. So Isaiah 38:15 says: "I will recount to you all my years in the bitterness of my soul." And Jeremiah 31:21 reads: "Set up a watchtower for yourself. Make bitterness for yourself." Now just as a tree gives fruit, when manure is spread around it, so too the soul, when it recalls its sins.

14. (Verse 9). So he adds: *Perhaps, it will bear fruit,* supply: then leave it alone. This is also figurative speech, in which the necessary words are not mentioned. But nevertheless, it is a common way of speaking.[32] – *But if not, then afterwards cut it down,* that is, by the mature sword of judicial sentence. Canonical Jude 12–13 reads: "Unfruitful trees, autumnal, twice dead, . . . for which the storm of darkness is reserved[33] forever." – Another interpretation. *You will cut it down,* by death. Deuteronomy 20:20 has: "But if there are trees that do not bear

---

[29] On p. 339, n. 13 QuarEd indicate that this is the Glossa Ordinaria. Hugh of St. Cher, p. 214u has a more full citation of "Bede."

[30] On p. 339, n. 14 QuarEd cite Homily 31, n. 5 of GGHG. See PL 76:1229D: "For the sins of the flesh are called dung. Therefore, it is also said through the prophet: *The beasts have rotted in their dung* (Joel 1:17)."

[31] Hugh of St. Cher, p. 214v, u also quotes Lamentations 4:5.

[32] On p. 340, n. 2 QuarEd refer to this as aposiopesis or a sudden breaking off in the middle of a spoken thought.

[33] On p. 340, n. 3 QuarEd accurately indicate that the Vulgate reads *servata est* ("has been preserved") whereas Bonaventure has *reservatur* ("is reserved").

fruit, but are wild . . . you will cut them down."[34] And Job 4:20 states: "From morning until evening they will be cut down. And since no one understands, they will perish forever."

15. And note that there are six ages for human beings like six years, namely, *infancy, childhood, adolescence, youth, decline, and old age*.[35] During the *first* age the Lord does not seek fruit on account of the defect of free will. But during the *second* he requires it in some way, that is, during *childhood*, more so during *adolescence*, and especially during *youth*. But he expects to find negligence often even to *old age*. And then finally at the end, he offers a severe judgment upon the negligent.

16. Now this can be interpreted *allegorically* about the synagogue, in which the Lord *sought fruit* during *the three intermediate ages of the world*. It was during this time that the synagogue flourished, and the Lord is still expecting its repentance.[36] Another interpretation.

---

[34] The Vulgate reads the imperative *succide* ("cut them down") while Bonaventure has the future *succides ea* ("you will cut them down").

[35] On p. 340, n. 5 QuarEd refer to paragraph 2 of the Prologue of Bonaventure's *Breviloquium*, to collation 15, n. 12ff. and collation 16, n. 2ff. of his *Collations on the Six Days of Creation*. I have followed José de Vinck's guidance in translating *senectus* by "decline" and *senium* by "old age."

[36] On the "intermediate ages" see *The Works of Bonaventure V: Collations on the Six Days*, translated by José de Vinck (Paterson: St. Anthony Guild, 1970), 224 on Collation 15.14–16: "And in the course of the third age, which extends from Abraham to David, the Synagogue began to flourish with Abraham, through the circumcision performed in his flesh....And in the fourth age, or time, which extends from David to the Babylonian captivity, the reign of kings and the priesthood became strong and flourished like the two [major] lights, and the prophets were stars. . . . So also in the fifth age, that is, from the Babylonian exile to Christ, the Synagogue began to fail and to become old and lost its authority."

During the threefold time, namely, of the Patriarchs, Judges, and Kings, and finally *he waited* for repentance during the time of the Prophets. And since it had not converted at their words, it *was cut down* at the time of Christ's coming.

Another interpretation. These three years refer to the time of *the threefold law*, that is, of nature, of Scripture, and of grace. But these things are sufficiently expounded in the Glossa.[37]

17. Now according to *information about horticultural practices* it is to be noted *spiritually* that *an unfruitful tree is cut down*, especially one that doesn't bear fruit in the course of a three year period. This fittingly refers to the person who is negligent in performing the works of virtue. And indeed, human negligence is rightly censured by a *fruitless fig tree*. First, the fact that the fig tree has many and large leaves is a special rebuke to the person whose negligence is manifested in his great verbiage. Sirach 4:34 reads: "Be not hasty with your tongue and slack and remiss in your deeds." Contrariwise, Hosea 10:1 states: "Israel, a vine full of branches, its fruit is pleasing to it." – Second, the fact that the leaves of the fig tree are similar to the human hand is a special censure of the person who invites others to do the work. Romans 2:21 says: "You who teach another do not teach

---

[37] On p. 340, n. 8 QuarEd provide rich parallels: "Namely, *Ordinaria* (from Ambrose, VII on Luke 13, n. 166) apud Lyranum on Luke 13:7. Also confer the Glossa Ordinaria on Luke 13:6. Ambrose's words are: He came to Abraham. He came to Moses. He came to Mary. That is, he came in a sign. He came in the Law. He came in the body. We recognize his coming through his benefits, etc. Cf. Augustine Sermon 110 (alias 32 De Verbis Domini) c. 1, n. 1: *The fig tree* is the human race. *The period of three years* are the three times: one before the Law, one under the Law, the third under grace. See Homily 31., n. 2f. of GGHG."

yourself," etc. Contrariwise, Acts 1:1 has: "Jesus began
to do and to teach," etc. – Third, the fruit of the fig tree
is sweet. Therefore, its absence justly designates negligence, and its presence designates a deed of virtue,
which is sweet and exceedingly delectable. "For that
person alone is guiltless who contains this and enjoys
it."[38] – Now there are deeds of virtue that are sweet at
the beginning of virtue, more sweet to the person making
progress on the way of virtue, and most sweet to the
person who is already perfect in virtue. For this reason
Judges 9:13 says: "How can I forsake my sweetness and
my most sweet fruits and go to be promoted among the
other trees?"[39]

18. Now the fig tree is said to have *the most sweet fruit*
to designate the three kinds of fruit. For some are *sweet*
like the fruits of repentance. Some are *more sweet* like
the fruits of justice. But some are *most sweet* like the
fruits of wisdom. The Lord seeks these three types of
fruit during the three years since there is a threefold
state of virtue. For the fruit of *repentance* is sought from
beginners, the fruit of *justice* from the proficient, but the
fruit of *wisdom* from the perfect.

So first, during *the first year* the Lord requires *the fruit
of repentance*, about which Luke 3:8 above has: "Bring
forth fruits befitting repentance." Now this fruit consists

---

[38] On p. 340, n. 11 QuarEd refer to Aristotle, II. Ethic. c. 3.
[39] Bonaventure's text of Judges 9:13 differs somewhat from the Vulgate: *Numquid possum deserere vinum meum quod laetificat Deum
et homines et inter ligna cetera commoveri?* ("Can I forsake my vine
which gives joy to God and human beings and be promoted among
the other trees?). See Hugh of St. Cher, p. 213v, l where he also
quotes Judges 9:13: *Nunquid possum deserere dulcedinem meam,
fructusque suavissimos, etc.* ("Can I forsake my sweetness, and my
most sweet fruits, etc.").

of three things. First, by *eliminating superfluity*. Jeremiah 2:7 reads: "I brought you into the land of Carmel to eat of its fruit and its good things." *Carmel* is interpreted as the knowledge and practice of circumcision and designates eliminating superfluity.[40] – Second, by *mortification of the flesh*. John 12:24 states: "Unless the grain of wheat falls into the ground and dies," etc. – By *purification of the mind*. Isaiah 27:9 has: "The iniquity of the house of Jacob will be forgiven, and this is all its fruit, that its sin took away."

19. During *the second year*, namely, in the state of those who are proficient, the Lord requires *the fruit of justice*. About this Philippians 1:10–11 says: "So that you may be upright without offense . . . filled with the fruit of justice through Jesus Christ to the glory and praise of God." – *Harmony* is the beginning or sower of this fruit. James 3:18 has: "Now the fruit of justice is sown in peace by those who make peace." Job 22:21 reads: "Be at peace, and thereby you will have the best fruits." – *Clemency makes it manifest and advances it.* The Psalm says: "He will be like a tree, which is planted near the running waters," etc. (1:3).[41] Thus the Psalm again states: "By the fruit of their grain, wine, and oil they are multiplied" (4:8). – *Patience preserves* it. James 5:7 has: "Behold, the farmer waits for the precious fruit of the earth, being patient," etc. Hebrews 12:11 reads: "All discipline is for the present a matter not for joy, but for sorrow. But afterwards it yields the most peaceful

---

[40] On p. 341, n. 1 QuarEd refer to Jerome's *Liber Interpretationis Hebraicorvm Nominvm* on 3 Kings. See CCSL lxxii, p. 110: "Carmel means very delicate or soft or knowledge and practice of circumcision."
[41] I complete Bonaventure's quotation of Psalm 1:3a: "...which will bring forth its fruit in due season."

fruit."[42] But *perseverance gives shelter to it.* Luke 21:29 below states: "Behold the fig tree and all the trees. When they send forth fruit, you know that summer is near." In the last chapter of Proverbs this is said about the strong woman: "with the fruit of her hands she has planted a vineyard" (31:16).

20. In *the third year* he requires *the fruit of wisdom*, about which Proverbs 3:14 has: "Its fruits are the premier and purest."[43] Further, this fruit is *most beautiful* to look at. Deuteronomy 33:13–14 has: "Of the blessing of the Lord be his land...of the fruits brought forth by the sun and moon." – *The most fragrant* to smell. Sirach 24:23 reads: "As the vine I have brought forth a pleasant fragrance, and my flowers are the fruits of honor and decency." The Song of Songs 4:13 says: "Your plants are a paradise of pomegranates with the fruits of the orchard," etc. – *Most flavorful* to taste. The Song of Songs 2:3 states: "I sat under the shadow of the one whom I had desired, and his fruit was sweet to my palate." And The Song of Songs 5:1 has: "Let my beloved come into his garden and eat the fruit of his apple trees," etc. – *Most precious* to possess. Proverbs 8:19 reads: "My fruit is better than gold and a precious stone, and my blossoms than choice silver." – *Everlasting* in duration. Wisdom 3:15 says: "The fruit of good deeds is glorious, and the root of wisdom never fails." For wisdom commences here and endures everlastingly.

---

[42] I translate all the Vulgate of Hebrews 12:11: "But all discipline seems for the present to be a matter not for joy, but for sorrow. But afterwards it brings forth the most peaceful fruit of justice to those who have been exercised by it."
[43] Bonaventure seems to be following a variant reading of Proverbs 3:14. A translation of the Vulgate is: "her (Wisdom's) fruits are better than premier and purest gold."

Now since the Lord requires of the tree that he had planted in its first state the fruit of *repentance*, and that is of a *threefold manner*, in the second the fruit of *justice*, and that is of a *fourfold manner*, in the third the fruit of *wisdom*, and that is of a *fivefold manner*, he, therefore, is requiring twelve fruits from the tree he has planted. As a figure of this it is said in Revelation 22:2: "On both sides of the river was the tree of life, bearing twelve fruits, yielding its fruit according to each month and its leaves for the healing of the nations."

Luke 13:10–14:35
CHRIST REFUTES HIS OPPONENTS WHO ARGUE THAT HE WORKS HIS MIRACLES AT THE WRONG TIME

21. *Now he was teaching in one of their synagogues*, etc. This section, in which the Savior confutes the deceitfulness of the Jews who calumniate him, is divided into two parts, in accordance with the twofold manner in which they unjustly attack Christ's miracles. That is, from the aspect of their *efficient cause* and from the perspective of *the circumstances of time*. The first part has already been dealt with. This verse inaugurates the second part.[44]

In its turn this part is divided into two according to two occasions. In the first he refutes *during an assembly* those who unjustly attacked Christ's miracles which he performed on the Sabbath. But in the second he confutes them *during a banquet* where Luke 14:1 reads: *And it came to pass when he entered*, etc.

---

[44] See the detailed outline at Bonaventure's commentary on Luke 11:13 (#35–36) above.

Luke 13:10–35
CHRIST REFUTES HIS OPPONENTS DURING AN ASSEMBLY

The first part has a twofold division. For first, *he confutes* those who were saying that miracles should not be performed on a Sabbath. Second, given the same occasion of the assembly, *he shows* that good deeds are to be performed without interruption where verse 18 has: *What is the kingdom of God like?*

Luke 13:10–17
CHRIST ARGUES AGAINST HIS OPPONENTS THAT THE SABBATH IS A TIME FOR PERFORMING MIRACLES

Now concerning *the confutation* of those who are calumniating Christ for his miracles the Evangelist proceeds in this fashion. First, he sets forth *the performance of the miraculous cure.* Second is added *the rebuke from Jewish superstition* where verse 14 states: *But the ruler of the synagogue,* etc. Third is *the confutation of the objection raised* where verse 15 reads: *But the Lord answered him.* Fourth comes *the acknowledgment of glorious victory* where verse 17 says: *As he said these things, they were put to shame,* etc. – Now about *the performance of the miraculous cure* three things are mentioned, namely, *the solemnity of the day* and *the gravity of the longstanding illness* and *the powerfulness of the instantaneous miracle.*

22. (Verse 10). So first, relative to *the solemnity of the sacred day* it says: *Now he was teaching in one of their synagogues on the Sabbath.* – Note that the Lord was teaching on the Sabbath *to preserve the custom of the Jews.* Acts 15:21 says: "Moses for generations past has had his preachers in every city in the synagogues where

he is read aloud every Sabbath." – Another interpretation
is *to publicize his teaching*, for on a solemn day they
were together and were more intent on the word of God.
John 18:20 reads: "I have always taught in the synagogue . . . where all the Jews gather." – Still another interpretation is that the Sabbath was *a day of quiet*, and
he had come to announce peace and quiet. So Ephesians
2:17 states: "And coming, he announced the good news
of peace to you who were far off, and of peace to those
who were near." – Yet another interpretation is that the
commandment about the Sabbath, which was directed
towards love, was eminently a *figure of the time of grace*,
during which this commandment obtains, namely: "This
is my commandment that you love one another" (John
15:12). – Another interpretation is *to preserve order*, for
restoration had to begin here where *creation* was ended.
It is said in Genesis 2:2–3 that "on the seventh day God
ended the work he had made . . . and blessed it on the
seventh day," etc.[45] – Another interpretation is *to provide instruction* that the person intent on acquiring wisdom must cease from everything according to what
Sirach 38:25 says: "Write down wisdom during a time of
leisure."[46] – There is also a seventh reason: *To show that
he is Lord of the Law and of the Sabbath*, as he performs
miracles on the Sabbath. John 5:17–18 states: "My Father works even until now, and I work. This, then, is

---

[45] Bonaventure implies what Genesis 2:2 says explicitly: God rested
on the seventh day. In trying to make sense of Bonaventure's interpretation here, QuarEd on p. 342, n. 6 refer to Book IV of Ambrose's
commentary on Luke 4, n. 58. See CCSL xiv, p. 127: "'On the Sabbath' signifies that the works of the Lord's restorative medicine have
begun, so that from now on a new creation has begun where what
had been the old creation beforehand has ceased."

[46] On p. 342, n. 7 QuarEd cite the Glossa Ordinaria (from Ambrose)
on Luke 13:10: "*On a Sabbath* he teaches and raises up the woman
bent down, for through the word of his preaching he leads the erect
from temporal things to eternal and to the rest of the resurrection."

why the Jews were seeking[47] to kill him, for he not only broke the Sabbath, but also called God his own Father, making himself equal to God."

23. (Verse 11). Second, with regard to *the gravity of the longstanding illness* the text continues: *And behold, there was a woman, who for eighteen years*, indicating *the duration* of the sickness, *had had a sickness caused by a spirit.* Sirach 10:11–12 has: "A long sickness is troublesome to the physician.[48] The physician makes short shrift of a brief sickness." – *And she was bent over*, with regard to *the weightiness* or gravity of her sickness, according to what that person was lamenting: "I have become miserable and bent over even to the end," etc.[49] – *And utterly unable to look upwards*, because of *the continual nature* of the illness, according to what Lamentations 1:14 says: "God has delivered me into a hand, from which I am unable to stand up."

24. Now this *long-lived incurvation* can be understood as the sickness of *avarice* and cupidity, which inclines the heart to temporal things. The Psalm has: "They have set their eyes bowing down to the earth" (16:11). And the demons seek this. Isaiah 51:23 reads: "Bow down, so that we may go over."[50] – This infirmity of being bowed down had lasted for *eighteen years*, that is, throughout the entirety of life. For as Jerome says: While all other vices become decrepit in old people, only avarice is ever young.[51] And it is said of the avaricious person in Qo-

---

[47] On p. 342, n. 7 QuarEd accurately indicate that the Vulgate reads *magis quaerebant* ("were more intently seeking").

[48] Bonaventure follows a variant reading. See Vulgate, p. 1041.

[49] Bonaventure cites Psalm 37:7 in this different manner.

[50] See Hugh of St. Cher, p. 214v, i where he also quotes Isaiah 51:23.

[51] QuarEd do not put this citation in quotation marks, and on p. 342, n. 11 they say that it comes from "Sermon 48 ad Fratres in eremo

heleth 2:23: "All his days are full of sorrow and miseries. Even at night his mind has no rest." And Hosea 7:9 reads: "Strangers have devoured his strength, and he knew it not. But gray hairs also spread over him, and he was ignorant of his status." – Further, this sickness *does not allow her to look upwards*. So it is said in Matthew 6:21: "Where your treasure is, there also is your heart."[52] And the Psalm has: "Fire has fallen on them," namely, the fire of cupidity, "and they have not seen the sun," (57:9) lest they be mindful of, etc.[53]

25. (Verse 12). Third, relative to *the powerfulness of the instantaneous miracle* the text adds: *When Jesus had seen[54] her,* namely, with *the eye of compassion.* The Psalmist says: "Because the Lord has looked forth from his high sanctuary . . . that he might hear the groans of those in fetters, that he might release the children of the slain" (101:20–21). And 2 Kings 20:5 reads: "I have heard your plea. I have seen your tears." – *And he said to her: Woman, you are delivered from your infirmity,* through *the promise of truth.* Since he was certain of what was to happen, he used the past for the immediate future. Numbers 23:19 states: "God is not like a human being,

---

(among the works of Augustine)" which reads: *Omnia in homine senescunt vitia, sola avaritia iuvenescit* ("All vices grow decrepit in a person; only avarice is ever young").

[52] See Hugh of St. Cher, p. 214v, i where he also quotes Matthew 6:21.

[53] It seems that Bonaventure is reflecting Homily 31, n. 6 of GGHG. See PL 76:1230C: "Every sinner, thinking about earthly matters and not considering heavenly ones, cannot look upwards. For while the sinner is following inferior desires, the sinner is curved downwards from the rectitude of the mind and always sees those things about which he is incessantly thinking."

[54] On p. 343, n. 1 QuarEd correctly mention that the Vulgate reads *videret* ("saw") whereas Bonaventure has *vidisset* ("had seen").

that he might lie. . . . Thus has he said something and will not do it? Has he spoken, and he will not fulfill it?"

26. (Verse 13). *And he laid his hands on her, and immediately she was made straight and glorified God*, relative to *the effect of Christ's power*. Qoheleth 8:3–4 reads: "God will do everything that pleases him, and his word is full of power." Now therefore, *he laid his hands*, so that he may show that he is the hand through which the Almighty works all things and through which he restores everything. Isaiah 59:1 says: "Behold, the hand of the Lord is not shortened, so that it cannot save." And in Numbers 11:23 the Lord said to Moses: "Is the hand of the Lord unable? Presently you will see whether my word will come to pass or not." And therefore, Sirach 36:6–7 has: "Renew your signs and work miracles, glorify your hand and your right arm."

27. And note that he says four things here about the incurvation of this woman, which the Lord accomplishes in *the salvation of any faithful soul*. For first, *he saw* her, predestining her. Wisdom 4:15 states: "His regard is upon his chosen." – Now second, *he called* her, attracting her attention externally. Matthew 9:13 reads: "I have not come to call the righteous, but sinners." And Proverbs 9:3 says: "Wisdom has sent her maids to invite to the tower and to the walls of the city." – Third, *he laid his hand* on her, justifying her. Ezekiel 3:14 has: "I went away in bitterness in the indignation of my spirit, for the hand of the Lord was with me, strengthening me." And Luke 1:66 above states: "For the hand of the Lord was with him." – Fourth, *she rose up*, glorifying God. 1 Samuel 2:8 reads: "He raises up the needy from the dust and lifts up the poor from the dunghill, that he

may sit with princes and hold the throne of glory."[55] –
About these four something similar is said in Romans
8:30: "Those whom he predestined he also called. And
those whom he has called he has justified. And those
whom he has justified he has also magnified."[56]

28. (Verse 14). *But the ruler of the synagogue*, etc. Here
in the second place he adds *the rebuke from Jewish superstition*. He makes two points. First is *the commotion of
inordinate zeal in the heart*. Second is *the simulation of
ordinate zeal in word*.

So first with regard to *the commotion of inordinate zeal
in the heart* the text has: *But the ruler of the synagogue,
indignant that Jesus had cured on the Sabbath,*[57] *said*,
as if to say that his response had its roots in the indignation of his heart. Now this indignation sprang from a
presumption of justice. Wherefore, only *"true* justice
breathes compassion, but *false* justice indignation."[58]
Now this false justice was a zealous observer of the Law

---

[55] On p. 343, n. 6 QuarEd cite the Glossa Interlinearis (from Bede) on
Luke 13:12–13: *"When Jesus saw her*, predestining her through
grace. *He called*, etc., illuminating her through teaching. *And he laid
his hand on her*, helping her by spiritual gifts. *And immediately she
was made straight*, to glorify God, up until the end persevering in
good works." The Glossa Interlinearis is almost verbatim from Bede.
See CCSL cxx, p. 268.
[56] On p. 343, n. 9 QuarEd rightly indicate that the Vulgate reads
glorificavit ("glorified") whereas Bonaventure has *magnificavit*
("magnified"). They also note that the reading *magnificavit* is already found in a commentary on Romans among the works of Ambrose and also in Peter Lombard, Hugh of St. Cher, and Lyranus.
[57] On p. 343, n. 11 QuarEd accurately mention that the Vulgate
reads *Sabbato* ("on the Sabbath") while Bonaventure reads *in Sabbato* ("on the Sabbath").
[58] Bonaventure is quoting Homily 34, n. 2 of GGHG. See PL
76:1246D. He also quoted this passage in his commentary on Luke
9:43 (#81) above. See the note there.

of the Sabbath, but it was a foolish zeal. Romans 10:2–3 reads: "They have zeal for God, but not according to knowledge. For, ignorant of the justice of God and wishing[59] to establish their own, they have not submitted to the justice of God." Thus a foolish presumption engenders *zeal*, and zeal *indignation*, and indignation *transgression of the divine law*, according to what is said in Proverbs 29:22: "The person who is easily stirred up to indignation is more prone to sin."[60] So the person who is foolishly zealous for the law is the person who destroys the law. For which reason Galatians 1:13–14 states: "Beyond all measure I persecuted the church of God and ravaged it . . . showing much more zeal for the traditions of my fathers," etc.[61]

29. Second concerning *the simulation of ordinate zeal in word* the text continues: *He said to the crowd: There are six days on which one ought to work.*" Behold, *here is an allegation of the truth.* Exodus 20:9–10 says: "Six days shall you labor and shall do all your works. But on the seventh day is the Sabbath of the Lord." – *On these, therefore, come and be cured.* Behold, *a show of piety.* Wherefore, what is said of pretenders in 2 Timothy 3:5 fits him: "Having a semblance of piety, but disowning its power." – When he says: *And not on the Sabbath.* Behold, *a display of holiness,* for he showed himself as being *holy* in wanting to preserve the Sabbath as *holy* in accordance with Leviticus 23:3: "Six days shall you work.

---

[59] On p. 343, n. 13 QuarEd correctly indicate that the Vulgate reads *quaerentes* ("seeking") whereas Bonaventure reads *volentes* ("wishing").

[60] Bonaventure reads the singular *peccatum* ("sin") while the Vulgate has *peccata* ("sins").

[61] On p. 343, n. 13 QuarEd cite the Glossa Interlinearis: "*But the ruler of the synagogue, indignant, said,* as one zealous for the letter of the Law."

The seventh day, since it is the rest of the Sabbath, will be called *holy.*" Wherefore, the Jews said in John 9:16: "This man is not from God, for he does not observe the Sabbath." But the observance of the holy day on the part of the ruler of the synagogue is rather for *the simulation of justice* than its *fulfillment* according to what Isaiah 1:13–14 reads: "The new moons and the Sabbaths and other festivals I will not abide. . . . My soul has hated your first days of the month and solemnities." And the reason for this is that they served for superstition rather than for devotion. So Lamentations 1:7 has: "The enemies have seen her and have mocked her Sabbaths."

30. (Verse 15). *But the Lord answered him and said,* etc. Here in the third place the text conjoins *the confutation of the proposed objection* on two levels. First, by means of an *example from their own tangible praxis.* Second, by introducing a *discursive argument.*

So first he sets forth *the tangible example* and says: *But the Lord answered him and said: Hypocrite!*[62] As *Lord,* he answers, for it is said in Matthew 7:29 that "he was teaching as one having power." And he did this especially when he was censuring others, as this individual whom he calls *hypocrite.* For he saw what was hidden inside this man. So 1 Corinthians 4:4 reads: "The one who judges me is the Lord." For he knew the hidden matters of the heart, and greatly hated the vice of hypocrisy. Therefore, Sirach 1:37–39 states: "Be not a hypocrite in the sight of men and women . . . lest . . . God reveal your secrets and cast you down in the middle of the synagogue," as he did to this person, whom he confutes and convicts by means of an evident and perceivable exam-

---

[62] On p. 344, n. 5 QuarEd correctly indicate that the Vulgate reads the plural *Hypocritae* ("Hypocrites").

ple. – And wherefore, he adds: *Does not each one of you on the Sabbath*[63] *loose his ox or ass from the manger and lead it forth to water?* The Glossa has: "Fittingly he calls the pretenders *hypocrites*, who, although they aspire to be seen as teachers of the people, are not afraid to postpone the cure of men and women in favor of the care of cattle."[64] In these matters what Isaiah 57:1 says is fulfilled: "The just man perishes, and there is no one who takes it into his heart." And this also seems to be fulfilled today, according to what Bernard says: "A soul perishes, and there is none who cares for it. An ass falls down, and there is someone who lifts it up."[65] Therefore, he calls the person *a hypocrite*, who, pretending to be zealous for the Law, is more concerned about cattle or money than about the soul.

31. (Verse 16). Second, he sets forth *a discursive argument* as he continues: *Now this woman, a daughter of Abraham, whom Satan has bound, behold, for eighteen years*, to whom compassion is due. Because she is of the

---

[63] On p. 344, n. 7 QuarEd correctly mention that the Vulgate reads *Sabbato* ("on the Sabbath") while Bonaventure has *in Sabbato* ("on the Sabbath").

[64] On p. 344, n. 7 QuarEd say that this is the Glossa Ordinaria from Bede. See CCSL cxx, p. 268. Bede, however, has *non puderet* ("is not ashamed") instead of the Glossa's *verentur* ("are afraid").

[65] On p. 344, n. 8 QuarEd state that Bernard's quotation comes from Book IV, chapter 6, n. 20 of his *De Consideratione* and that Bernard's original text has *reputet* ("thinks about it") whereas Bonaventure (and Hugh) have *curet* ("cares"). The changes are more than this. See SBOp 3.464: *Cadit asina, et est qui sublevet eam; perit anima, et nemo qui reputet* ("An ass falls down, and there is someone who lifts it up. A soul perishes, and there is no one who thinks about it"). See Hugh of St. Cher, p. 215a who has this sequence: quotation from Bede (which is what Bonaventure calls Glossa), quotation from Isaiah 57:1, quotation from Blessed Bernard. Bonaventure agrees verbatim with Hugh in the last two quotations. In his quotation from Bede Hugh uses the singular, e.g., "hypocrite."

weaker sex. 1 Peter 3:7 says: "Husbands . . . paying honor to the woman as to the weaker vessel." And since she is weak from the demon's possession. Therefore, Matthew 15:22 reads: "Have pity on me, son of David, for my daughter is sorely beset by a demon." Since she also was of the seed of Abraham, whom God had chosen for himself. Thus, Matthew 15:24 says: "I was not sent except to the lost sheep of the house of Israel." – So from these opportune reasons a very strong case is built that the cure of the woman must not be delayed because of the Sabbath. – So the text continues: *Ought not she be loosed from this bond on the Sabbath?* Indeed, she certainly ought to be loosed, for it was the opportune time. First, since it is infinitely clear that greater care must be shown for the salvation of a human person than for a brute animal. For this reason 1 Corinthians 9:9 has: "Is it for the oxen that God has care?" Second, since the Sabbath was established not to the detriment of men and women, but rather for the salvation of the human race. So John 7:23 reads: "If a man receives circumcision on the Sabbath so that the Sabbath[66] may not be broken, are you indignant with me because I made a whole man well on the Sabbath?" Third, since all *servile* works are avoided on the Sabbath. Thus, Leviticus 23:8 states: "You will not do any servile work on it," but does not ban *spiritual* works. So Matthew 12:5 has: "Have you not read in the Law that on the Sabbath the priests in the temple break the Sabbath and are guiltless?" So *divine and miraculous* works are not forbidden. Therefore, John 5:17 says: "My Father works even until now, and I work." And John 9:4 reads: "I must work . . . while it is day." Also works that are *necessary to maintain health*

---

[66] On p. 344, n. 13 QuarEd rightly mention that the Vulgate reads *lex Moysi* ("Law of Moses") where Bonaventure has *Sabbatum* ("the Sabbath").

are not forbidden, such as eating and drinking. Wherefore, neither is *healing* forbidden.

32. From this one can understand how much solicitude
and diligence one must show, so that a sinner may be
liberated from the bonds of the devil, and even, if it were
possible, without a modicum of delay. Proverbs says:
"Do not give sleep to your eyes, nor let your eyelids
slumber. Run, make haste, stir up your friend."[67] A sign
of this is found in the return of the prodigal son in Luke
15:20 below: "But while he was a long way off, his father
saw him and was moved with compassion, and ran and
fell upon his neck and kissed him." – And note that
there is no difference between a daughter of Abraham
being freed from the chain of Satan and a soul *being
freed from the guilt of sin.* Therefore, the Glossa says:
"Daughter of Abraham, every faithful soul."[68] Christ liberates this soul through the ministry of priests. Matthew 18:18 reads: "Amen, I say to you, what you loose
on earth, will be loosed also in heaven." But it has to
happen that people dispose themselves *in their inner
persons.* Isaiah 52:2 states: "Loose the bonds from around
your neck, O captive daughter of Zion." And then God
operates *from on high.* The Psalm has: "You have broken
my bonds. I will offer a sacrifice of praise to you"
(115:16–17).[69] So in this loosing *priests* work through the

---

[67] Bonaventure's quotation is from Proverbs 6:4 and 6:3c.

[68] On p. 345, n. 2 QuarEd state that this is the Glossa Ordinaria
(from Bede) on Luke 13:16. See CCSL cxx, p. 268: "The daughter of
Abraham is any faithful soul. The daughter of Abraham is the church,
gathered together into the unity of faith from both peoples. . . ."

[69] See Hugh of St. Cher, p. 215b where he quotes Psalm 115:16, then
Isaiah 52:2, and follows with a sentence that Bonaventure attributes
to the Glossa: *Unde Psalm. 115. in persona Ecclesiae dicit. Dirupisti
vincula mea. Isa. 52a[2] Solve vincula colli tui captiva filia Sion.
Filia etiam Abrahae est quaecunque fidelis anima* ("Wherefore,
Psalm 115 says in the person of the Church: You have broken my

external dispensation of the Sacrament, and *the sinner* through the inner detestation of sin, and *God* through the infusion of the grace of the Holy Spirit from on high.

33. (Verse 17). *And as he said these things,* etc. Here in the fourth place he adds *the acknowledgment of glorious victory* and makes two points, namely, *the shame of the rebellious* and *the rejoicing of the faithful.*

So first, with regard to *the shame of the rebellious* the text has: *And as he said these things, all his adversaries were put to shame.* The Glossa comments: "*Adversaries,* the scribes and the Pharisees, who cannot contradict the clear truth, but who do not want to believe because of their envy."[70] About such people Job 24:13 says: "They have been rebellious to the light. They have not known his ways."[71] Such people are not instructed, but confounded when the truth is declared. Isaiah 41:11–12 reads: "Behold, all who fight against you will be confounded and put to shame. They will be as nothing, and the men who contradict you will perish. You will seek them, and you will not find the men who rebelled against you."

34. Second, relative to *the rejoicing of the faithful,* the text continues: *And all the people rejoiced at all the glorious things that were done by him.* Bede observes: "*People,* that is, the simple and humble, who love the words of truth and miracles."[72] These rejoice in the manifesta-

---

bonds. Isaiah 52:2 has: Loose the bonds from around your neck, O captive daughter of Zion. The daughter of Abraham is also every faithful soul whatsoever").

[70] On p. 345, n. 5 QuarEd simply say that this is the Glossa Ordinaria.

[71] See Hugh of St. Cher, p. 215f where he also quotes Job 24:13.

[72] On p. 345, n. 7 QuarEd state: "Or Glossa Ordinaria on this passage."

tion of divine glory. So Isaiah 29:19 says: "Poor women and men will exult in the Holy One of Israel." *They will exult, I say, in all the things which have gloriously been done by him.* Sirach 42:16 reads: "Full of the glory of the Lord is his work."

And note that Christ's works were *gratuitous* from the perspective of *the condescension of divine dignity*, and for these one must *grateful.* Tobit 12:6 has: "Bless the God of heaven, give glory to him in the sight of all the living, because he has shown his mercy to you." They were also *glorious* relative to *the operation of power* and *the manifestation of majesty*, and for these one must *rejoice* and *exult.* The Psalm says: "Shout with joy to God, all the earth. Sing a psalm to his name. Give glory to his praise. Say to God: How terrifying are your works. . . . In the multitude of your power your enemies will speak lies to you" (65:1–2).

35. Now these matters can be expounded *allegorically* about the Church gathered from among the Gentiles, which has been *bent over* for three times six years.[73] That is, under the dictates of the law of nature, the Mosaic Law, and also the prophets. Works done in whatever one of these pertained to the six days, that is, to servile works, which were done out of fear. And these could not lift the soul upwards, for fear pressed it down, and only love lifts upwards. So Luke 1:69 above says: "He has lifted up for us a horn of salvation in the house of David." And this occurred through the spirit of charity. Ezekiel 2:2 reads: "And the Spirit entered into

---

[73] On p. 345, n. 11 QuarEd indicate that this interpretation is found in Ambrose and Bede and that the Glossa Ordinaria bases its comments on those of Bede. See CCSL xiv, pp. 274–275 and CCSL cxx, pp. 268–269.

me . . . and set me upon my feet." – This woman *is re-leased on the Sabbath* like *the ox and ass*, which are led to water. For this Church is gathered together from *Jewish* and *Gentile* people, who are referred to by *the ox* and *the ass*, in accordance with what Isaiah 1:3 says: "The ox knows its owner, and the ass its master's crib." And Isaiah 32:20 states: "Blessed are you who sow upon all waters, sending thither the foot of the ox and the ass."[74] Now the Lord has released both: *the Jews* coming to the Church out of the burden of legal servitude and *the Gentiles* out of the chains of servitude to idolatry. Ephesians 2:14–15 reads: "He himself is our peace, who made both one, and has broken down the intervening wall of the enclosure, the enmity, in his flesh. He has made void the Law of the commandments expressed in decrees, so that of the two he might create into himself one new human being, and make peace," etc. – Now by means of this release the people of the Jews who are against Christ *is confounded*, the people of the Gentiles *exults*, according to what Matthew 8:11–12 says: "Many will come from the east and from the west and will re-cline with Abraham and Isaac and Jacob. . . . But the children of the kingdom will be put forth into the dark-ness outside."[75] And this on account of rebellion. Where-fore, Acts 13:46–47 reads: "It was necessary that the

---

[74] See Hugh of St. Cher, p. 215a: "Mystically. Through these two animals the calling of two peoples is signified. Through the ox the Jewish people is signified, for it ruminates and chews its chud. Through the ass the Gentile people. These two peoples, having been loosed from the chains of sins, are led by the Apostles to water, for they are refreshed by the drink of the Sacred Scriptures from thirst and the heat of the world. Isaiah 1a[3] says: The ox knows its owner, etc. Isaiah 32d[20] has: Blessed are you who sow upon all waters, sending thither the foot of the ox and the ass."

[75] Luke 13:28–29 says something similar.

kingdom of God[76] be preached to you first. But since you reject it and judge yourself unworthy of eternal life, behold, we now turn to the Gentiles. For so the Lord has commanded us."[77]

Luke 13:18–35
GOOD DEEDS ARE TO BE DONE WITHOUT INTERRUPTION

36. *He said, therefore, What is the kingdom of God like,* etc. After he has refuted those who were falsely blaming him for miracles performed on the Sabbath, he in a second point shows that *good deeds are to be done without interruption.* And first he appealingly makes his case with *the assistance of examples from nature.* Second, by means of *a revelation of a divine decree* where verse 22 reads: *And he passed on through towns and villages.*

Luke 13:18–21
EXAMPLES FROM NATURE

So he offers his guidance through *an example* in a twofold manner. Through the first they are urged *to continually make progress in the knowledge of the truth.* Through

---

[76] The Vulgate reads *verbum Dei* ("word of God") whereas Bonaventure has *regnum Dei* ("kingdom of God").

[77] In his Sunday Sermon 3 #4 for the Second Sunday of Advent Bonaventure treats Luke 13:16. See *Sancti Bonaventurae Sermones Dominicales,* ed I. G. Bourgerol, Bibliotheca Franciscana Scholastica Medii Aevi 27 (Grottaferrata: Colelgio S. Bonaventurae, 1977), p. 150: "This woman, inclined to the earth, who could not look upwards, signifies the soul, bound fittingly by the corruption of original sin to earthly matters on account of its proneness to evil. It cannot strive for heavenly matters on account of its difficulty in doing good." See also Sermon 38 #9 for the Eleventh Sunday after Pentecost in *Sermones Dominicales,* p. 394.

the second *to make progress in the fervor of love* where
verse 20 says: *And again he said: To what will I liken.*

So in the first instance he shows *the continual growth in
the knowledge of the truth* by means of the metaphor of
the grain of mustard seed. He does so in a threefold way,
namely, with regard to *the properties* that the grain of
mustard seed has in *itself*, as *sown*, and as *fully grown*.

37. (Verse 18). First, then, concerning *the property of the
grain of mustard seed in itself*, through which it is assimilated to the knowledge of the truth, the text says:
*He said, therefore, What is the kingdom of God like, and
to what will I liken it?* Here knowledge of or teaching
about the truth is said to be *the kingdom of the heavens.*
So Bede in the Glossa comments: "The preaching of the
Gospel is the kingdom of the heavens, concerning which
another place says: *The kingdom of God will be taken
away from you, and it will be given to a people yielding
its fruits*, according to Matthew 21:43."[78] This knowledge
is fittingly said to be *the kingdom*, for truly the kingdom
of the heavens is nothing other than perfect knowledge
of divine truth. John 17:3 states: "This is eternal life that

---

[78] On p. 346, n. 4 QuarEd state that this Glossa is the Interlinearis
on Mark 4:30 and quote it: "*To what will we liken the kingdom of
God*, Bede: The preaching of the Gospel, which leads to the kingdom
of God, about which it is said (Matthew 21:43): *The kingdom will be
taken away from you*, etc." The editors go on to say that according to
both the Glossa Ordinaria and Interlinearis on Luke 13:18–19 *"the
kingdom of God* or of the heavens is understood to mean 'faith,
through which one comes to the kingdom.'" See Hugh of St. Cher, p.
215g: "Jerome. The grain of mustard seed is knowledge of the Scriptures or the preaching of the Gospel, which teaches one to come to
the kingdom of God. Therefore, it is also called the kingdom of the
heavens. Matthew 21d[34] says: It will be taken away, etc. Likewise,
according to Bede, the grain of mustard seed is said to be the faith,
by which one comes to the kingdom."

they may know you, the only true God, and him whom
you have sent, Jesus Christ."

38. (Verse 19). And while this is *sublime* and *joyous* in
the heavenly homeland, it must be *humble* and *burning*
on the journey thereto. As a designation of this reality
the text has: *It is like a grain of mustard seed.* So it is
likened to *a grain of mustard seed* because it is *small in
size* and *mighty in power* or ardor. By this it is suggested
that our knowledge must be *humble*, according to what
Romans 11:20 says: "Be not high-minded, but fear." And
Romans 12:3 has: "A person ought not to think of himself more than he ought, but to think of himself with
moderation, and according to how God has apportioned
to each one the measure of faith." For, as it is said in
Proverbs 11:2: "Where there is humility, there is also
wisdom," etc. It is also suggested that it be *burning* and
ardent. So the Glossa of Bede comments: "Knowledge of
the Scriptures is compared to *a grain of mustard seed* on
behalf of the fervor of faith or because it is said to cast
out poisons, that is, all perverse teachings."[79] So it is
said in Luke 17:6 below: "If you have faith like a grain of
mustard seed, you will say to this mulberry tree: Be up-
rooted and planted in the sea, and it will obey you."

39. Second, concerning *the property of the grain of mustard seed in as far as it is sown* the text adds: *Which a
man took and cast into his own garden.* This *garden*
stands for the Church militant. The Song of Songs 4:12
says: "My sister, my spouse, is a garden enclosed, a

---

[79] On p. 346, n. 7 QuarEd state that this is the Glossa Interlinearis.
See CCSL cxx, 269: *ob feruorem utique fidei uel quod dicatur uenena
expellere* ("indeed, on account of the fervor of faith or that it is said to
cast out poisons"). Bonaventure's reading of *pro fervore fidei* ("on
behalf of the fervor of faith") is unique.

fountain sealed up, a garden enclosed."[80] This is *the garden of pleasure* "where the seeds of the virtues grow."[81] In this garden the first thing *to be sown* is the seed of faith, but this happens through *a human being*. For the preaching of the faith is sown through human ministry. A figure of this reality is found in Genesis 2:15: "God took man and placed him in the paradise of pleasure to care for it and guard it." Such a person was Paul. 1 Corinthians 3:6 states: "I planted. Apollos watered, but God gave the growth." For it is the responsibility of humans, that is, as rational and wise, to preach the teachings of faith. Now the supreme sower of this faith was Christ, who is said to be *the man* in the manner of antonomasia, according to what the Psalm has: "Will not Zion say: The man, the man is born in her?," etc. (86:5).[82] So he also calls himself time and time again *Son of Man*, for man was in him according to the fullness of reason and in as far as perfection and infirmity go. Philippians 2:7 reads: "Being made like unto men, and appearing in the form of man." And this *man sowed* this seed, when he preached the teaching of the Gospel. Matthew 13:24 says: "The kingdom of the heavens is

---

[80] On p. 346, n. 8 QuarEd cite the Glossa Interlinearis (from Book II of Jerome's commentary on Matthew 13:32): "*A man*, God in the just person or the just man nourishes the grain of preaching in his heart. *Took*, it had qualities worthy of acceptance. *Cast into his garden*, where the fruits of the virtues grow." They also refer to Bede's interpretation. See CCSL cxx, p. 269: "The man is Christ. The garden is the church which is always his, cultivated by disciplines and endowed with gifts."

[81] See the previous note and the Glossa Interlinearis, which reads: *ubi crescunt germina virtutum* ("where the fruits of the virtues grow"). Bonaventure's Latin is: *ubi crescunt semina virtutum*. See Hugh of St. Cher 215o: *recondidit in cor suum, ubi crescunt germina virtutum* ("he hid in his heart, where the fruits of the virtues grow").

[82] Antonomasia is a figure of speech used when a name appropriate to several different things is applied to that one of them to which it is preeminently suitable.

like a man who sowed good seed in his field." The person who preaches falsehood is contrasted with this man. So Matthew 13:25 continues: "But while men were sleeping," that is, the prelates, "his enemy came and sowed weeds among the wheat," etc.

40. Third, with regard to *the property of the grain of mustard seed to grow* the text adds: *And it grew and became a large tree*. This is said about the growth of faith in the rigor of its powers. Therefore, the Glossa observes: "It grew, not like herbs, which quickly dry up and fade away, but like a tree that is long-lived and enjoys unexpected fertility."[83] Colossians 1:5–6 reads: "In the word of the truth of the Gospel which has reached you, even as it is in the whole world, both bearing fruit and growing, just as it does among you." And a little later verse 10 has: "May you walk worthy of God and please him in all things, bearing fruit in every good work and growing in the knowledge of God." Now this knowledge grows that much more tall through truth, the more deeply its roots are sunk through humility. So Isaiah 37:31 says: "That which will be saved of the house of Judah and which is left, will take roots[84] downward and will bear fruit upwards."

41. And since the knowledge of faith, as it grows within itself, redounds to the salvation of others, the text says: *And the birds of the air rested in its branches. The birds of the air* are spiritual men. Isaiah 60:8 reads: "Who are these, who fly like clouds, and like doves to their win-

---

[83] On p. 347, n. 3 QuarEd state that this is the Glossa Ordinaria (from Bede) apud Lyranum, which reads *et opima* ("and abundant") together with Bede rather than Bonaventure's *et inopinata* ("and unexpected"). See CCSL cxx, p. 270.

[84] On p. 347, n. 5 QuarEd correctly indicate that the Vulgate has *radicem* ("root") whereas Bonaventure has *radices* ("roots").

dows?" About these Proverbs 1:17 states: "A net is spread in vain before the eyes of those who have wings." By *branches* of the tree are understood the teachings of the truth proceeding from the mouth of the wise person. Thus, Wisdom says in Sirach 24:22: "I have stretched out my branches like the turpentine tree, and my branches are of honor and grace." Wherefore, *the birds of the air rest* in the branches of the growing mustard seed, for those who come to the knowledge of the truth are resting under the teaching of a faithful teacher. So the Glossa has: "*In its branches*, that is, spiritual men, who climb on high on the wings of the virtues, rest in diverse teachings."[85] – Thus, a small seed grows into the greatness of a tree through continual increase. Therefore, people who are small must continually labor in the pursuit of merit, so that they may become such a tree, whose top reaches to heaven through faith and the desire of things eternal.[86]

42. (Verse 20). *And again he said: To what will I liken,* etc. After he had set forth an example as an incentive to make continuous progress in the knowledge of the truth, here he adds *an example as an incentive to make progress in the fervor of love.* And he does this under the metaphor of *leaven.* He uses the three properties it has in the assimilation process as analogies to urge people to make

---

[85] On p. 347, n. 8 QuarEd state that this is the Glossa Interlinearis (from Bede) on Luke 13:19. See CCSL cxx, p. 270: *Rami huius arboris dogmatum sunt diuersitates in quibus animae castae quae uirtutum pennis ad superna tendere sciunt nidificare et requiscere gaudent* ("The branches of this tree are the diversity of teachings, on which chaste souls, who know how to reach for supernal matters on the wings of the virtues, are happy to build their nests and rest").

[86] See Hugh of St. Cher, p. 215v, b–c: *Et uolucres coeli] i. spirituales uiri. c. Requieverunt in ramis ejus.] idest, sententiis ejus* ("And the birds of the air] that is, spiritual men. c. They rest in its branches] that is, in his teachings").

continuous progress in love. That is, the property leaven has by *its own nature*, the property it has from *another's industry*, and the property it has from *both*.

So first, with regard to the property, which it has by *its own nature* and through which it tends to excite us to make progress in love, the text says: *And again he said: To what will I liken the kingdom of God?* And here by *the kingdom of God* is understood the love of God, for God reigns in those alone who love him. Colossians 1:13 has: "He has rescued us from the power of darkness and transferred us into the kingdom of the Son of his love."[87] For, as it is said in Romans 14:17: "The kingdom of God does not consist in food and drink, but in justice and peace and joy in the Holy Spirit."

43. (Verse 21). And since love and joy expand the heart and warm it from inside, they find an external analogy in leaven. Thus the text adds: *It is like leaven.* – And note that *leaven* sometimes refers to the corruption of peace and unity, as in Luke 12:1 above: "Beware of the leaven of the Pharisees, which is hypocrisy." And this meaning is entirely right, for leaven is old dough, corrupted by age and turning sour, which corrupts the remainder of the matter and turns it sour.[88] Therefore, it is pertinently said in 1 Corinthians 5:7: "Purge out the old leaven." – At other times ardor and love are understood by *leaven*, as here, for leaven warms the dough and induces a certain fire into it, as if from the hidden interior. So it is

---

[87] I have forgone the normal translation, "kingdom of his beloved Son," in order to accentuate the point Bonaventure is making here.
[88] See Edmon L. Rowell, "Leaven," in *Eerdmans Dictionary of the Bible*, ed. David Noel Freedman et al. (Grand Rapids: Eerdmans, 2000), p. 797: "A fermentation agent, in the Bible always leftover dough (sourdough) mixed with new dough to facilitate rising."

not incongruous that *leaven* is love.[89] Nor it is contrary
to reason that *leaven* be treated in different ways on account of its diverse properties. So Augustine says in the
third book of his *De Doctrina Christiana*: "Since things
appear to each other in many ways, we should not
imagine there is any precept that we must believe that,
because a thing has a certain analogical meaning in one
place, it always has this meaning. For example, the
Lord represented *leaven* in a *condemnatory* fashion
when he said: *Beware of the leaven of the Pharisees.* And
as an object of *praise* when he said: *The kingdom of
heaven is like a woman who hid leaven in three measures
of flour.*"[90] Now there are many and similar examples of
this kind in Scripture, as he says: "*The lion* signifies
Christ in Revelation 5:5: *The lion of the tribe of Judah
has conquered.* But it signifies *the devil* in 1 Peter 5:8:
"*Your adversary, the devil, like a roaring lion,* etc. And

---

[89] On p. 347, n. 17 QuarEd cite the Glossa Interlinearis: "*is like
leaven*, love for its ardor or holy teaching." They go on to quote Book
I question 12 of Augustine's *Questions on the Gospels*: "*The woman
means wisdom. The leaven* is love, which engenders warmth and
quickens." See Hugh of St. Cher, p. 215v, ef: *Cui simile, etc.] idest,
charitatem, vel sanctam doctrinam, quae regnare faciunt. f Simile est
fermento,] quod elevat pastam, et sapidam facit, sic charitas, et
sancta doctrina mentem elevant, et sapidas faciunt ei praesentes
tribulationes* ("To what will I liken, etc.] that is, love or holy teaching, which effects the kingdom. f. It is like leaven,] which raises up
the dough, and makes it tasty, and so love and holy teaching raise up
the mind and make present tribulations palatable to it"). For
Bonaventure's use of Hugh of St. Cher's commentary on Luke 13:20
see Robert J. Karris, "Bonaventure's Commentary on Luke: Four
Case Studies of his Creative Borrowing from Hugh of St. Cher,"
Franciscan Studies 59 (2001): 133-236, esp. pp. 181-214, 232-235.
[90] I have modified the translation by John J. Gavigan of Book 3,
chapter 25, n. 35 of *Christian Doctrine* in *Writings of Saint
Augustine* Volume 4, FC 4 (New York: CIMA Publishing Co., 1947),
144.

there are also many others."[91] The cause of this diversity is the multiplicity of properties, from which a diversity of analogies and representations arise in figures.

44. Second, concerning the property it has from *another's industry* the text continues: *which a woman took and hid in three measures of flour.* According to the literal sense, as Bede says, "*a measure* is a type of measurement customarily used in Palestine, containing a bushel and a half."[92]

And note that this *woman* is understood to be divine wisdom or the Church.[93] Proverbs 31:10 says: "Who will find a valiant woman," etc. Now *the flour* is the faithful, who are ground between two millstones, that is, a superior and an inferior, namely, fear and hope.[94] Deuteronomy 24:6 reads: "You shall not accept the inferior or the superior millstone as a pledge." From this flour issues *one bread*, which Christ kneaded into his own mystical

---

[91] This is my rendition of Book 3, chapter 25, n. 36 of Augustine's *De Doctrina Christiana*.

[92] See CCSL cxx, p. 270: *Satum genus est mensurae iuxta morem prouinciae Palestinae unum et dimidium modium capiens* ("A measure is a type of measurement customarily used in the province of Palestine, containing one and a half bushels"). Bede borrows from Jerome's commentary on Matthew 13:33 (PL 26:93C). Bonaventure's quotation is not verbatim. See Hugh of St. Cher, p. 215v, b whose quotation of Bede agrees with that of Bonaventure: *Beda: Satum ad litteram genus est mensurae juxta morem Palestinae, modium, et dimidium capiens* ("Bede says: A measure literally is a type of measurement customarily used in Palestine, containing a bushel and a half").

[93] On the woman as "wisdom" see, n. 89 above. On p. 348, n. 4 QuarEd state that both Ambrose and Bede interpret the woman as "the Church." See CCSL xiv, p. 279 and CCSL cxx, p. 270 respectively. See Hugh of St. Cher, p. 215v, h: "Woman] The Church or any faithful soul. . . . "

[94] A more literal translation would be "upper and lower millstones," but Bonaventure is beyond the literal meaning here.

body. 1 Corinthians 10:17 states: "We, although many, are one bread in Christ."[95] – But *the three measures* are *three different types of the faithful*, in whom the wisdom of God hides love for the journey, namely, good *prelates*, good people engaged in *the contemplative life*, and good people engaged in *the active life*. So the Glossa has: "Three measures, three types of people: Noah, Daniel and Job."[96] Ezekiel 14:14 says: "If Noah, Daniel or Job shall be in their midst, they would be delivered by their justice."[97] So this first exposition greatly accords with the literal sense. Bede gives many other interpretations in the Glossa, so that from his work "the multiform wisdom of God,"[98] "which was hidden in a mystery,"[99] is clear.[100]

---

[95] On p. 348, n. 5 QuarEd state that Bonaventure's interpretation of Deuteronomy 24:6 goes back to Gregory and then cite Bede's commentary. See CCSL cxx, p. 270: "We are the flour of this woman, the Church, as many times as we, through the exercise of fear and hope, are ground by the superior and inferior millstone, so that according to the Apostle we, although many, may be one bread, one body."

[96] On p. 348, n. 6 QuarEd state that this is the Glossa Ordinaria (from Augustine) apud Lyranum. In his commentary on Luke 7:16 (#31) and Luke 9:28 (#45) above Bonaventure also refers to Noah, Daniel, and Job.

[97] Bonaventure seems to have truncated Ezekiel 14:14: "And if the three men, Noah, Daniel and Job, shall be in its midst, they shall deliver their own souls by their justice, says the Lord of hosts." See Hugh of St. Cher p. 215v, i where he refers to Ezekiel 14:14, but does not quote it.

[98] Bonaventure quotes Ephesians 3:10 verbatim.

[99] 1 Corinthians 2:7 reads: "But we speak the wisdom of God in a mystery, which was hidden."

[100] On p. 348, n. 7 QuarEd indicate that the Glossa Ordinaria apud Lyranum contains six interpretations. According to my count Bede has a mere two interpretations. See CCSL cxx, pp. 270–271: Loving the Lord with one's entire heart, soul, and strength; three harvests of thirtyfold, sixtyfold, and a hundredfold which refer to the married, the continent, and virgins.

Second, *the three measures* mean *the three ways of loving*, namely, with the whole heart, with the whole soul and with the whole mind. Wherefore, the Glossa of Bede comments: "The Church hides the leaven of love in three measures of flour, because it commands that we love God with the whole heart, with the whole soul and with the whole strength."[101] Deuteronomy 6:5 reads: "You shall love the Lord your God," etc. And Matthew 22 says: "You shall love the Lord your God," etc. (verse 37). "In this commandment," etc. (verse 40).

The third way is this: *the three measures* mean *spirit* and *soul* and *body*, which make a person integral. The Glossa says: "So that the spirit and soul and body, brought into a unity, may not disagree among themselves,"[102] according to what 1 Thessalonians 5:23 states: "May your spirit and soul and body be preserved integral, without complaint at the coming of the Lord," etc.

The fourth way is this: *the three measures* are taken to be *the three powers of the soul*, which are reformed by love. The Glossa reads: "The three powers of the soul are brought back to a unity, so that we may possess wisdom through *reason*, hatred of vices through *anger*, desire for virtues through *cupidity*,"[103] according to what Micah 6:8 says: "To do judgment, to love mercy and to walk justly with your God."

---

[101] On p. 348, n. 8 QuarEd state that this is the Glossa Ordinaria. See CCSL cxx, p. 270.

[102] On p. 348, n. 9 QuarEd indicate that this is the Glossa Ordinaria (from Ambrose). See CCSL xiv, pp. 280–282. The Glossa has drastically summarized Ambrose's interpretation.

[103] On p. 348, n. 10 QuarEd state that this is the Glossa Ordinaria (from Book II of Jerome's commentary on Matthew 13:33).

45. In the fifth manner love is joined and somehow mixed with *faith in the Trinity*, so that it not only believes who the true God is, but also by believing, tends towards God. Thus, the Glossa has: "The Church mixes the faith of men and women into the three measures of flour, that is, for the sake of belief in the Father and Son and Holy Spirit."[104] So it is said of love in 1 Corinthians 13:7 that "it believes all things."

Sixth, *the three measures* stand for *the threefold harvest* to which love orders. So the Glossa observes: "These *measures* can be understood as the harvests of the seeds sown by the Lord, namely, thirtyfold, sixtyfold and a hundredfold. About these harvests Matthew 13:23 has: 'It bears fruit and yields in one case a hundredfold, in another sixtyfold, and in another thirtyfold.'"[105]

Seventh, *the three measures* of flour can be taken as *the three parts of the human race* from the three sons of Noah, disseminated throughout the entire world. About them Genesis 10:1 reads: "These are the generations of Noah: Shem, Ham, and Japheth."[106]

---

[104] On p. 348, n. 11 QuarEd state that this is a continuation of the Glossia Ordinaria (from Jerome) cited in the preceding note and that the original text reads: *Ecclesia fidem hominis tribus satis farinae miscet, etc.* ("The Church mixes the faith of men and women with the three measures of flour").

[105] On p. 349, n. 1 QuarEd state that this is the Glossa Ordinaria apud Lyranum. In his commentary on Luke 8:8 (#11) Bonaventure also uses Matthew 13:23.

[106] On p. 349, n. 2 QuarEd indicate that Hilary makes mention of this interpretation in his Commentary on Matthew chapter 13, n. 6: "Although the three measures of flour are to be referred to the sacrament of our faith, that is, to the unity of Father, Son, and Holy Spirit, I remember that many took it to refer also to the calling of three nations from Shem, Ham, and Japheth." They also make reference to Augustine's Sermon 111, chapter 1, n. 1: "The three measures of flour . . . is the human race. Recall the flood. Three remained.

Eighth, according to Hilary, *flour* is to be understood as
Scripture. The *three measures* stand for the three parts
of Scripture, that is, the Mosaic, prophetic, and evangelical. And in these the wisdom of God hid love, for, as
Matthew 22:40 says, "On these two commandments depend the whole Law and the Prophets. "[107]

Ninth is an interpretation from Ambrose: *"The woman
is the Church.* We are her *flour*, which hides the Lord
Jesus as *leaven* in our interior until the heavenly heat of
wisdom expands it."[108]

Wherefore, the others will be restored. Noah had three sons, from
whom the human race was restored." See Hugh of St. Cher, p. 215v,
i.

[107] On p. 349, n. 3 QuarEd cite Hilary's Commentary on Matthew,
chapter 13, n. 5: "The leaven is in the flour. . . . The Lord compared
himself to this. . . . But this, equally joined together with three
measures of flour, that is, the Law, the Prophets, the Gospels, he
makes all this one, etc." It is obvious that Bonaventure's quotation
barely follows Hilary. See Hugh of St. Cher, p. 215v, i: *Item tria sata
farinae sunt tres partes Scripturae, secundum Hilarum scilicet, lex,
prophetae, et Evangelium. In quibus fermentum absconditur, quia in
his tribus charitas, et sapientia docetur, et continetur* ("Further, the
three measures of flour are the three parts of Scripture, according to
Hilary, namely, the Law, the Prophets, the Gospel. In these the
leaven is hidden, for in these three love and wisdom is taught and is
contained").

[108] See CCSL xiv, p. 279: *Igitur sancta ecclesia, quae typo mulieris
istius euangelicae figuratur, cuius farina nos sumus, dominum Iesum
in interioribus nostrae mentis abscondat, donec animi nostri secreta
penetralia color sapientiae caelestis obducat* ("Therefore, the holy
church, which finds a figure in the type of this woman in the gospel,
whose flour we are, hides the Lord Jesus in the interior of our mind
until the heat of heavenly wisdom expands the deepest secrets of our
mind"). See Hugh of St. Cher, p. 215v, i: *Item secundum Ambr.
Mulier Ecclesia cujus farina nos sumus, Dominum Jesum, ut fermentum in interioribus nostris abscondit, donec ea calor caelestis sapientiae obdulcat* ("Further, according to Ambrose. *The woman*, the
Church, whose flour we are, hides the Lord Jesus as leaven in our
interior until the heavenly heat of wisdom sweetens it").

Tenth, according to Bernard, is this: *"The woman* is the Virgin Mary. *The three measures* are the threefold nature or substance in the one person of Christ, namely, flesh, soul, and divinity. The first measure is *ancient*, the second is *new*, but the third is *eternal*. Now Mary mixed these with *the leaven* of her faith and love."[109] Wherefore, Hugh states: "Since love burned in her mind with singular ardor, he performed miracles in her flesh."[110] As a figure of this it is said in Genesis 18:6:

---

[109] On p. 349, n. 5 QuarEd refer to Book V, chapter 10, n. 22–23 of Bernard's *De Consideratione*. See SBOp 3.484–486. The closest parallel occurs on p. 485: *In utero Virginis, ut sentio ego, commixtio haec et fermentatio facta est, et ipsa mulier quae miscuit, et fermentavit; nam fermentum non immerito fortasse dixerim fidem Mariae. . . . Novum: animam, quae de nihilo tunc creata creditur, cum infusa; antiquum: carnem, quae a primo usque hominum, id est ex Adam, traducta cognoscitur; aeternum: Verbum, quod ab aeterno Patre coaeternum illi genitum indubitata veritate asseritur* ("In the womb of the Virgin, in my opinion, this mixing and fermentation occurred, and she herself was the woman who mixed it and leavened it. For perhaps I might say that it is fitting that the leaven is Mary's faith. . . . New: the soul, which is believed to have been created then *ex nihilo*, and infused. Ancient: flesh, which is recognized as handed down till now from the first human, that is, from Adam. Eternal: the Word, which is stated with indubitable truth to be co-eternal with the eternal Father and born through her"). It seems that Bonaventure copied and adapted Bernard's quotation from Hugh and not from Bernard directly. See Hugh of St. Cher, pp. 215v–216 i: *Secundum B. Bern. Mulier est Maria, fermentum fides ejus, tria sata, tria in persona Christi, scilicet, caro, anima, et divinitas, sive antiquum, novum, et aeternum* ("According to Blessed Bernard. The woman is Mary. The leaven is her faith. The three measures are the three components in the person of Christ, namely, flesh, soul, and divinity or ancient, new, and eternal").

[110] On p. 349, n. 6 QuarEd indicate that this quotation is from Hugh of St. Victor's work on the Virginity of Mary, chapter 2 and that Bonaventure also quotes this passage in Collation VI #8 of his *De Donis Spiritus Sancti*. See Opera Omnia 5:485. A more exact reference is to Hugh of St. Victor's *Libellus Epistolaris de B. Mariae Virginitate* in PL 176:872A: *Nam quia in corde, quo amor Spiritus sancti singulariter ardebat, ideo in carne ejus virtus Spiritus sancti mirabilia faciebat* ("For since the love of the Holy Spirit burned in

"Abraham made haste into the tent to Sara and said to her: Hurry, mix together three measures of fine flour." And the blessed Virgin did so, for at the word of the Angel she immediately consented, saying: "Behold, the handmaid of the Lord," etc.[111]

46. So from these considerations it is obvious how the Holy Spirit has externally brought forth, through his saintly people, various understandings of one small matter. The result is that "the multiform wisdom of God"[112] may appear, a wisdom, which he hid, like a woman baker, as leaven in the measures of flour. For, as Dionysius says, the whole of mystical theology, that is, "which is hidden in a mystery,"[113] consists in ecstatic love according to a threefold hierarchic power: purgative, illuminative and perfective.[114]

---

her heart with singular ardor, it followed that the power of the Holy Spirit performed miracles in her flesh"). Bonaventure makes no reference to the Holy Spirit here or when he quotes this same passage in Opera Omnia 5:485.

[111] Luke 1:38. See Hugh of St. Cher, p. 215v, i where he also cites Genesis 18:6.

[112] Ephesians 3:10.

[113] 1 Corinthians 2:7.

[114] On p. 349, n. 9 QuarEd supply references to Dionysius. See Bernard McGinn, *The Flowering of Mysticism: Men and Women in the New Mysticism (1200–1350)*. Volume III of The Presence of God: A History of Western Christian Mysticism (New York: Crossroad, 1998), p. 371, n. 176: "Bonaventure has in mind (Dionysius') *De cael. hier.* 7.3, but the reference to ecstatic love (not found in Dionysius) is taken from Gallus. A similar text is also indicative of the characteristics of Bonaventure's Dionysianism in tying the three ways to the passion: . . . scilicet effectum purgandi, illuminandi et perficiendi (*Serm. II Dom. 2 post Pascha* in 9:296b)." On "hierarchic power," see Hayes, pp. 157–61, esp. pp. 159–60: "The third definition (of Dionysius) refers principally to the return to God through ever deeper realization of God-likeness effected through the divine influence which reaches to the human person from out of the fullness of divine love in order to lift up the creature to deiformity."

47. Third, with regard to the effect on the part of *both*, the text adds: *until all of it was leavened*. The Glossa says: "Love, hidden in the mind, must grow for so long a time until it transforms the mind to its total perfection where it loves nothing except God."[115] For just as the leaven expands more and more, so too does the love of God. So Gregory has: "The love of God is never idle. For it does great things, if it exists. But if it refuses to act, it is not love."[116] And Bernard states: "Love either makes progress or stops progressing."[117] So "love never fails,"[118] but like leaven and fire it converts the whole into its own nature. Therefore, Exodus 19:18 reads: "All mount Sinai was smoking, because the Lord had descended upon it in fire." – For the fire and heat of love commence here on the journey, but occupy the entire heart in the heavenly homeland. Isaiah 31:9 says: "The Lord has

---

[115] On p. 349, n. 10 QuarEd state that this is the Glossa Ordinaria (from Bede) on Luke 13:21. The Glossa abbreviates what Bede has in CCSL cxx, p. 271. See Hugh of St. Cher, p. 216a: *Beda. Tamdiu charitas in mente recondita crescere debet, donec mentem totam in sui perfectionem commutet, ut nihil praeter Deum diligat, recolat, quod hic incipitur, in alia vita perficetur* ("Bede says: Love, concealed in the mind, must grow for so long a time until it transforms the mind to its total perfection where it loves, contemplates nothing except God, which begins here and is perfected in the other life").

[116] On p. 349, n. 11 QuarEd refer to Homily 30, n. 2 of GGHG. See PL 76:1121B. Bonaventure's quotation is almost verbatim.

[117] On p. 349, n. 11 QuarEd refer to Bernard's Letter 254. Although Bernard does quote 1 Corinthians 13:8 in Letter 254, n. 2, he nowhere says exactly what Bonaventure quotes him as saying. See SBOp 8.156–160. See *The Letters of St Bernard of Clairvaux*, translated by Bruno Scott James (Kalamazoo: Cistercian Publications, 1998), p. 408–411. James numbers this letter 329. I quote from, n. 4 on p. 410: "If therefore to apply oneself to perfection is to be perfect, then it follows that not to wish to be perfect is to fall away. . . . If to progress is to run, when you cease progressing you cease running, and when you cease running you fall behind. From this it is evident that to cease wishing to progress is nothing else than to fall away."

[118] 1 Corinthians 13:8.

spoken, whose fire is in Zion and whose furnace in Jerusalem." So just as from the heart, which is in the middle, flows vital heat into the entire body, so too from perfect love all unions of virtuous deeds receive that ardor and vigor, by means of which they tend upwards. And as it is said, "if your eye be sound, your whole body will be full of light,"[119] so too if your heart is *aflame*, your entire body will be warm. If the heart is *divine*, the entire person is divine through deifying love, according to what the Psalm says: "My flesh and my heart have fainted away. You are the God of my heart, and God is my portion forever" (72:26).

Luke 13:22–35
THE REVELATION OF A DIVINE DECREE

48. *And he was traveling through towns*, etc. In the section just concluded the Evangelist used the guidance of an example from nature to show that good deeds must be done without ceasing. Here he makes the same point through *the revelation of a divine decree*. And he reveals this in a twofold manner. First, with regard to *the severity of the divine strictness in judging*. Second, relative to *the sublimity of the divine disposition in redeeming* where verse 31 reads: *On that same day certain Pharisees came up*.

Luke 13:22–30
THE SEVERITY OF THE DIVINE STRICTNESS IN JUDGING

Now the severity of strictness in judging is shown in a threefold manner. First, with regard to *the difficulty of*

---

[119] Luke 11:34; Matthew 6:22.

meriting. Second, relative to *the austerity in judgment*, where verse 25 reads: *But when the master of the house has entered.* Third, concerning *the disaster in punishment* where verse 28 has: *There will be weeping.* – He manifests *the difficulty*, which exists *in meriting*, in a twofold way, namely, through *an example* in deed and *a teaching* in word.

49. (Verse 22). So first, with regard to *the example*, by which he shows the difficulty of entering heaven, he says: *And as he was traveling through towns and villages, teaching and making his way towards Jerusalem.* In this, that *he was traveling and going about*, it is clear that *he was laboring* unceasingly. Wherefore, he could say what the Psalm has: "I am poor and in labors since my youth" (87:16). And he was giving an *example* to others that *they must labor.* Proverbs 6:3 states: "Run about, make haste, stir up your friend." Now in this that he was making his way *towards Jerusalem*, it is clear that he was hastening to *his passion.* So Matthew 20:18 reads: "Behold, we are going up to Jerusalem, and the Son of Man will be handed over to the chief priests and the Scribes. And they will condemn him to death." And in this he was giving an example to others that *they must endure suffering.* For 1 Peter 2:21 says: "Christ suffered for us,[120] leaving you an example that you may follow in his footsteps." Therefore, James 5:10–11 states: "Take, brothers, the prophets as an example of an evil end and of longsuffering and labor and patience. They spoke in the name of the Lord. . . . You have heard of the suffering of Job, and you have seen the death of the Lord."[121] – Therefore, from this example of the Lord, who

---

[120] The Vulgate reads *vobis* ("for you").

[121] Bonaventure has modified this quotation by adding *exitus mali et longanimitatis* ("evil end and longsuffering"). "The evil end" seems to

endured so much labor and, in the end, his passion, it is obvious that entry into heaven is difficult. So Luke 24:26 reads: "Did not the Christ have to suffer and thus enter into his glory?" And hence it is fitting to enter heaven through tribulations. Acts 14:21 has: "Through many tribulations we must enter the kingdom of God."

50. And note that these words about the example of the Lord suggest to us three things, by which a person comes to the glory of paradise, namely, good *action*, true *preaching*, and peaceful *contemplation*. *Action* is suggested by this that *he was traveling through towns and villages*. And *preaching* by the fact that *he was teaching while traveling*. *Contemplation* in this that *he was making his way towards Jerusalem*, which, through analogy, is *the vision of peace*. The Psalm says: "Jerusalem, which is built as a city. . . . For to it the tribes, the tribes of the Lord went up" (121:3–4). The first of these pertains to *prudence*, the second to *understanding*, and the third to *wisdom*. Another interpretation is that the first refers to *goodness*, the second to *discipline*, the third to *knowledge*. The Psalm has: "Teach me goodness and discipline and knowledge" (118:66).

51. (Verse 23). Second, relative to *teaching in word*, by which he responds to a question about the few who are to be saved, he adds: *But someone said to him: Lord, are only a few to be saved?* This person asked this because he had not heard the divine sentence, pronounced in Matthew 20:16: "Many are called, but few are chosen." As a figure of this, it is said in Micah 7:1: "Woe to me!

refer to the horrible deaths some of the prophets endured at the hands of their persecutors. In the light of this modification I have translated *finem Domini* not as "the Lord's purpose," but as "the Lord's death."

For I have become like the person who in autumn gleans the grapes for the vintage."[122] – Another interpretation is: The person raised this question to give Christ the occasion of teaching by word what he had shown by example.

52. (Verses 23–24). So he adds: *But he*[123] *said to them: Strive to enter by the narrow gate.* Matthew 7:14 states: "How narrow the gate and constricted the way that leads to life. And there are few who find it." This *gate* is Christ. John 10:9 says: "I am the gate."[124] He is *the way.* John 14:6 reads: "I am the way. . . . No one comes to the Father except through me." This *way is constricted,* and *the gate is narrow,* not on account of insignificant power, but on account of the strictness of modesty and the measure of justice. So Chrysostom comments: "The narrow gate is Christ, not because of insignificant power, but by reason of humility. Christ receives unto himself only those who have stripped themselves of sins and removed every burden of the world."[125] And therefore,

---

[122] Micah 7:1b reads: "There is no cluster to eat. My soul desired the firstripe figs."

[123] On p. 350, n. 11 QuarEd accurately indicate that the Vulgate has *ipse* ("he") here and Bonaventure does not.

[124] The Latin here is *ostium* whereas the Latin in Matthew 7:14 is *porta.* Both Latin words mean "gate."

[125] On p. 350, n. 13 QuarEd refer to Homily 18 on Matthew 7:13 from the *Opus Imperfectum,* which is more expansive than Bonaventure's quotation. See Hugh of St. Cher, p. 216i, where in his interpretation of the "narrow gate," Hugh quotes Acts 14:21, Matthew 7:14, Micah 7:1, and Chrysostom four times. Two of these quotations are similar to Bonaventure's materials and read: *Chrys. Porta angusta, Christus. Joan. 10b: Ego sum ostium, quod non potestis penetrare sine humilitatis ratione. Et infra: Christus in se non recipit, nisi qui se exuerint a peccatis, et deposuerint omnem sarcinam mundi, et facti fuerint subtiles, et spirituales. Diabolus latus est, quia apud illum omnia sine lege, Christus angustus, quia omnia sub lege consistunt.* ("Chrysostom: The narrow gate is Christ. John 10b[9]: I am the gate, which you cannot penetrate without a humble mind. And below he

Matthew 19:24 has: "It is easier for a camel to pass through the eye of a needle than for a rich person to enter the kingdom of the heavens."[126] Therefore, *the gate* of heaven is said to be *narrow*, because, unless people reduce their size through insignificance[127] and austerity, they cannot enter.

53. And since there are few people of such characteristics, the text continues: *For many, I tell you, will seek to enter.* The Glossa observes: "Prompted by love for salvation and rewards."[128] *And will not be able.* The Glossa says: "Frightened by the harshness of the journey," because they are not seeking with an integral and complete will. For they want to pursue Christ and do not want to follow him, according to what Proverbs 13:4 states: "The sluggard wills and wills not." Wherefore, Chrysostom says: "Unless a person wants to walk along the way, he cannot arrive at the gate. If you are not walking along the way of justice and think that you know Christ, you are deceived. It is like a person who hears that honey is sweet, but does not taste it. That person knows the name of honey, but has no experience of its pleasant taste."[129]

---

says: Christ receives unto himself only those who have stripped themselves of sins and removed every burden of the world, and have become slender and spiritual. The devil is wide, because with him all things exist without law. Christ is narrow, because all things exist with law"). It seems that Bonaventure was indebted to his elder Dominican commentator.

[126] This saying is also found in Luke 18:25.

[127] Thrice in this paragraph Bonaventure uses the term *parvitas*, which I have translated by "insignificance/insignificant."

[128] On p. 350, n. 14 QuarEd state that this quotation and the one that immediately follows are from the Glossa Interlinearis (from Bede). See CCSL cxx, p 271.

[129] On p. 351, n. 1 QuarEd state that this quotation stems from Chrysostom's Homily 18 on Matthew 7:13, taken from the *Opus Imperfectum*, which is longer. See Hugh of St. Cher, p. 216i where after quoting Proverbs 13:4, Hugh writes: *Chrys. Nisi ambulaverit quis*

So the slothful, who vacillate between willing and not willing, cannot enter. In a similar way those cannot enter who simultaneously desire the present world and God. About these Hosea 5:6 says: "With their flocks and with their herds they will go to seek the Lord, and they will not find the Lord."[130] And concerning such people it is said in Matthew 6:24: "No one can serve two masters. . . . You cannot serve God and mammon."[131] So 1 Kings 18:21 reads: "How long do you halt between two sides? If the Lord is God, follow him. But if Baal, follow him."

54. Since it is impossible to enter the kingdom of heaven with desires for earthly things and difficult to get rid of these, it is necessary to strive against desire. For this reason the text says: *Strive to enter by the narrow gate*, as if to say: It is impossible to enter with the desires that many seek. But you at least are endeavoring to enter, after having tread upon your desires. So Matthew 11:12 also has: "From the days of John the Baptist the kingdom of heaven has been enduring violent assault, and the violent have been seizing it by force." There is no objection to this that in the same chapter it is said: "My yoke is easy" (verse 30). For the heavenly gate and way are constricted for *beginners*, but wide for *the proficient* and spacious for *those who reach the goal*. On behalf of the first the Psalmist said: "For the sake of the words of your lips I have kept hard ways" (16:4). On be-

---

per viam, non potest pervenire ad portam. Si nec fuisti, nec es in via justitiae, et putas te cognoscere Christum, mentiris. Sicut qui mel audit esse dulce, non gustat, nomen mellis scit, gratiam autem saporis ignorat. This quotation is virtually the same as that of Bonaventure and merits as similar translation. Bonaventure is obviously dependent on Hugh of St. Cher here.

[130] See Hugh of St. Cher, p. 216l, where he also quotes Hosea 5:6.
[131] Luke 16:13 contains the same teaching.

half of the second: "I have run the way of your commandments, when you enlarged my heart" (Psalm 118:32). On behalf of the third: "I have been delighted in the way of your testimonies, as in all riches" (Psalm 118:14). On behalf on these three it is said in Proverbs 4:18: "The path of the just, like a shining light, goes forward and increases even to perfect day." And again afterwards: "I will lead you along the paths of equity. When you will have entered upon them, your steps will not be constricted. And when you run, you will not encounter a stumbling block."[132]

55. (Verse 25). *But when the master of the house has entered.* After he has encouraged them to make continuous progress in good deeds on account of the difficulty in meriting, here in a second point he spurs them to this goal on account of *the austerity in the future judgment.* He shows this austerity in two ways, namely, because it rejects *the supplication of petitions* and *the allegation of reasons.*

First, with regard to *the rejection of supplication* the text says: *But when the master of the house has entered and shut the door*, through judiciary strictness. Matthew 25:10 reads: "Those virgins who were ready went in with him to the marriage feast, and the door was shut." – And note that Christ is said to be *master of the house* with respect to *the just.* So Matthew 20:1 states: "The kingdom of heaven is like a master of the house, who went out early in the morning to hire laborers for his vineyard." Now he is said to be *master of the family*,[133]

---

[132] Proverbs 4:11–12. On p. 351, n. 6 QuarEd write: "Cf. Book XI, chapter 50, n. 68 (in fine) of Gregory's *Moralia* and Book II, Homily 5, n. 13 of Gregory's *Homilies on Ezekiel*."
[133] Bonaventure rings some changes on the meaning of *paterfamilias.*

because he has a large family. A figure of this is found in Job 1:3: "Job's possession was seven thousand sheep, three thousand camels, and five hundred yoke of oxen and five hundred she asses, and a family exceedingly large."[134] – This one is also *judge over the wicked*, to whom he closes the gate of mercy. So it is said in Deuteronomy 11:16–17: "Beware lest . . . you depart from the Lord. . . . And the Lord, being angry, shut up the heaven, and the rains cease coming down." – This door is open for the entire length of the way, but it is closed at the end. Ezekiel 46:2–3 has: "But the gate will not be closed until evening. And the people of the land will adore at the door of that gate before the Lord on the Sabbaths and on the new moons."[135]

56. And since the withdrawal of mercy leads men and women to a recognition of their own misery, and this in turn leads to the urgent and excessive persistence of pleas, the text adds: *And you will begin to stand outside and to knock on the door*, out of tardy repentance. Wisdom 5:2–3 reads: "Seeing it, they will be troubled with terrible fear . . . saying within themselves, repenting." And Hebrews 12:17 states: "He found no opportunity for repentance, although he had sought after it with tears." – *Saying: Lord, open for us*, through an importune supplication. Matthew 25:11 says: "Finally, the other virgins also came and said: Lord, Lord, open for us." – *And he*

---

[134] See Hugh of St. Cher, p. 216m–n, where he also cites Matthew 25:10 and Job 1:3.

[135] On p. 351, n. 11 QuarEd cite the Glossa Ordinaria (from Bede) on Luke 13:25: ". . . So *he will enter*, when he leads the entire Church to contemplate him. *He closes the door*, when he takes away an opportunity of repentance for the reprobates, who, *standing outside will knock*, that is, segregated from the just, they will in vain plead for the mercy they have contemned." See CCSL cxx, p. 271 for Bede's more expansive commentary.

will say in answer: I do not know where you come from, through final reprobation. Proverbs 1:28–29 reads: "Then they will call upon me, and I will not hear. They will rise in the morning and will not find me. For they have hated instruction and have not accepted the fear of the Lord." Wherefore, Proverbs 6:34–35 also says: "The jealousy and rage of the husband will not be sparing on the day of revenge. Nor will he acquiesce to anyone's pleas." – And note that it is said that the Lord *does not know us*, not because the Lord does not recognize us through *simple knowledge*, since it is said in Job 12:16: "The Lord knows both the deceiver and the person who is deceived." And the Psalm has: "In your book all will be written" (138:16). But because the Lord does not know them with *the knowledge of approbation*, for it is said in 2 Timothy 2:19: "The Lord knows who are his."[136] Job 8:18 states: "If one swallow him up out of his place, he will deny him and will say: I do not know you."[137]

57. (Verse 26). Second, with regard to *the rejection of alleged reasons* the text continues: *Then you will begin to say: We ate and drank in your presence*. Behold, an allegation of intimate acquaintance in *life*. *And you taught in our streets*, that is, there is an intimate acquaintance in *teaching*. Or it could first of all refer to *the miracles* that Christ performed among the Jews, when he multiplied the bread, as in John 6, and changed water

---

[136] See Bonaventure's commentary on Luke 10:20 (#35) above for a similar discussion of "simple knowledge" and "the knowledge of approbation."

[137] See Hugh of St. Cher, p. 216v, a, who also quotes Matthew 25:11, Job 12:16, 2 Timothy 2:19, Job 8:18, and writes: *Sol. Omnes cognoscit notitia simplicis cognitionis. Matt. 7d. Sed tantum bonos notitia approbationis* ("Sol. He knows all with the knowledge of simple cognition. Matthew 7d[21]. But only the good with the knowledge of approbation"). Bonaventure has borrowed much from Hugh.

into wine, as in John 2.[138] Second, relative to *teaching*. For these had seen the miracles and had heard the teaching. So Matthew 11:21 says: "Woe to you, Corazain. Woe to you, Bethsaida. For, if in Tyre and Sidon had been worked the miracles that have been worked in you, they would have repented long ago in sackcloth and ashes."[139] Thus they allege knowledge of Christ because they have known his *deeds and miracles* and have also known his *words and teaching*. Such people will be the wicked Christians at the judgment, about whom Titus 1:16 states: "They profess that they know God, but by their deeds they disown God."[140]

58. (Verse 27). And since the assertion of *knowledge* is of little value without the affirmation of *imitation and deeds*, the text says: *And he will say to you: I do not know where you are from.* Chrysostom comments: "I do not recognize my image in you. You, who carry the banner of the tyrant, cannot receive pay as my soldiers."[141] Chrysostom, however, says this, not concerning the image of *creation*, of which the Psalm says: "Human beings have passed as an image" (38:7). Rather he says it of the image of *re-creation*, about which Augustine says: "The Lord did not know them, since he did not find the character of faith and love among them."[142] Therefore, *the*

---

[138] The full references are John 6:1–15 and John 2:1–11.

[139] Luke 10:13 has the same teaching.

[140] On p. 352, n. 4 QuarEd cite a parallel from Book II, chapter 5, n. 6 of Gregory's *Moralia*.

[141] On p. 352, n. 7 QuarEd refer to Chrysostom's Homily 25 on Matthew 25:11 in the *Opus Imperfectum*, which is more extensive than Bonaventure's quotation.

[142] On p. 352, n. 8 QuarEd give a long list of possible parallels in Augustine and state that they have not found the passage Bonaventure attributes to Augustine in the works of Augustine, but in Bede's commentary on Luke 13:25, CCSL cxx, p. 272 reads: . . . *nescit eos unde sint apud quos fidei et dilectionis suae caracterem non approbat*

denial of knowledge does not look to the externals of personal relationships, which is the basis of their claim to intimate acquaintance, but only to the difference in moral conduct. Habakkuk 1:13 says: "Your eyes, O Lord, are pure . . . and you cannot look upon iniquity."[143] – So he adds: *Depart from me, all you workers of iniquity.* The Psalm says: "Depart from me, all of you who work iniquity" (6:9). – The reason for this dismissal is the distance between justice and iniquity. 2 Corinthians 6:14–15 reads: "What has justice in common with iniquity? Or what fellowship has light with darkness? What harmony is there between Christ and Belial?" So since the reprobates will be unjust and dark and Belial's men, but Christ will be *the just judge, the true light, the highest good*, he will compel the evil to descend into hell through a final judgment, saying: "Depart from me, accursed ones, into the everlasting fire which was prepared for the devil and his angels."[144] So because people will be judged not on the basis of their great knowledge,

---

(". . . he does not know where they come from, among whom he does not approve the character of his faith and love"). The editors also mention that Cardinal Hugh attributes this passage to Augustine.

[143] In this first part of his commentary on Luke 11:27 Bonaventure is heavily indebted to Cardinal Hugh. See Hugh of St. Cher, p. 216v, b: *Nescio vos unde sitis.] Beda: Fidei, et dilectionis meae characterem non approbo apud vos . . . Chrys. q.d. imaginem meam cognosco in vobis. Et inf. Non potestis meorum militum stipendia accipere, qui tyranni vexilla portatis. Item Chrys. q.d. nolo vos cognoscere, non propter extraneas personas, sed propter odibiles militias. Aug. non novit eos Dominus, apud quos characterem fidei, et dilectionis non invenit* ("I do not know where you come from.] Bede says: I do not approve the character of my faith and love among you . . . Chrysostom, as if saying: I recognize my image in you. And below: You, who carry the banner of the tyrant, cannot receive pay as my soldiers. Further, Chrysostom, as if saying: I will not recognize you, not because of your external characteristics, but because you are hateful soldiers. Augustine: The Lord did not know them, among whom he did not find the character of faith and love").

[144] Matthew 25:41.

but on the strength of their work, one must continually harken to good works. Wherefore, Romans 2:13 reads: "Not the hearers of the Law, but its doers are just before God." For which reason the Psalm says: "God has spoken once. These two things I have heard: That power belongs to God and mercy, to you, O Lord, for you render to all according to their works" (61:12–13).

59. (Verse 28). *There will be weeping*. Now here in a third point, after he has urged them to continuous progress, by indicating the difficulty in meriting and the harshness in judgment, he spurs them to this goal by manifesting *the disaster in punishment*. He also does this in a twofold manner, namely, from a consideration of *one's own downfall* and from a consideration of *the glorification of others*.

So first with regard to *the consideration of one's own downfall* the text says: *There will be weeping and the gnashing of teeth*, relative to the punishment of the senses. And the punishment of *heat* is felt from *the weeping of the eyes*, and the punishment of cold from *the gnashing of teeth*.[145] Now therefore, these two punishments are better expressed as corporal. There are a number of reasons for this. First, because these two qualities are active and very painful. For which reason Job 24:19 reads: "They will pass from the snow waters

---

[145] On p. 353, n. 1 QuarEd helpfully cite the Glossa Ordinaria (from Bede) on Luke 13:28: "*Weeping* is wont to be brought about by heat, *gnashing of teeth* by cold, for there *they will pass from the snow waters to excessive heat*." This last clause is a quotation from Job 24:19, which Bonaventure will quote shortly. The editors also refer to Book II, chapter 2 of Aristotle's *De Generatione et corruptione*. In brief, the four elements of fire, air, water, and earth are tangible in the following ways: fire is hot and dry; air is hot and moist; water is cold and moist; earth is cold and dry. Hot and cold are active whereas dry and moist are passive or susceptible.

to excessive heat."[146] Or because one has sinned twofold in one's body, namely, by concupiscence of the eyes and concupiscence of the flesh.[147] Therefore, one is punished in these. Wisdom 11:17 reads: "By what things a person sins, by these he is also tormented." Or because *tears* come from the inside whereas *gnashing of teeth* comes from the outside. And by these the universal scope of punishments is understood, especially those of the body. So the Glossa of Bede says: "Note that through *weeping*, which comes from the eyes, and *gnashing*, which deals with the teeth, is understood the genuine resurrection of the bodies of the impious."[148] But this weeping will not occur because of the restoration of the humor, but because of sorrow and moaning. Or if this does occur, it will be a wondrous reconstitution of the humor, just as it will wondrously take place in so many people who have been tortured, their bodies being animated by their spirits.

60. And since *the punishment of the senses* is joined to *the punishment of the damned*, which will be the loss of the communion of Saints in the glory of paradise, the text adds: *When you see Abraham and Isaac and Jacob*

---

[146] Bonaventure's text varies from the Vulgate which may be translated as: "Let him pass from excessive heat to the snow waters and his sin even to hell." See Hugh of St. Cher, p. 216v, i where he quotes Job 24:19: "They will pass from snow waters to excessive heat."

[147] On p. 353, n. 2 QuarEd rightly indicate that Bonaventure is alluding to 1 John 2:16: "Because all that is in the world is the concupiscence of the flesh and the concupiscence of the eyes."

[148] On p. 353, n. 3 QuarEd state that this is the Glossa Ordinaria on Luke 13:28 and stems from Book II of Bede's commentary on Matthew 8:12. Bede, for his part, is quoting Jerome. See Hugh of St. Cher, p. 216v, i: *Item per fletum oculorum, et stridorem dentium, vera resurrectio corporum designatur* ("Likewise, by the weeping of the eyes and the gnashing of teeth the genuine resurrection of bodies is designated"). Hugh, however, gives no reference to the Glossa or to Bede for this interpretation.

and all the prophets in the kingdom of God, that is, all the Patriarchs and Prophets. The first were exemplars of how to live. So John 8:39 has: "If you are the children of Abraham, do the works of Abraham." The second are exemplars in behavior and in teaching. 2 Peter 1:19 reads: "We have the word of prophecy, surer still, to which you do well to attend." Another interpretation is that *the Patriarchs* were those to whom the promise was made. *The Prophets* were those by whom promulgation of the promise was made, according to what Luke 1:70 above says: "As he has spoken through the mouths of his holy ones, the prophets from of old." And both of these have summoned and urged people that they must enter the kingdom of God. Those who are children of the flesh and have refused to be imitators of the saints will not enter, but will be excluded. – So the text continues: *But you yourselves will be cast outside*. Revelation 22:15 states: "Outside are the dogs and the sorcerers and the fornicators . . . the idolaters and everyone who loves and practices deceit."[149] As a figure of this it is said in Genesis 21:10: "Cast out the bondwoman and her son. For the son of a bondwoman will not be heir with the son of a free woman."[150] For it is said in John 8:35: "The slave does not abide in the house forever, but the son abides there forever."

61. (Verse 29). Second, with regard to *the consideration of the glorification of others*, the text continues: *And they will come from the east and west, from[151] the north and*

---

[149] Bonaventure does not have *et homicidae* ("and the murderers").

[150] Bonaventure has universalized this quotation by eliminating *hanc* ("this") and *filio meo Isaac* ("my son Isaac"). Genesis 21:10 reads: "Cast out this bondwoman and her son, for the son of the bondwoman will not be heir with my son Isaac."

[151] On p. 353, n. 8 QuarEd correctly mention that the Vulgate does not have *ab* ("from"). Rather it reads *et* ("and").

south. This concerns all the nations gathered from every part of the world. For the Jews having been rejected because of their carnality, the Lord has called together the Gentiles as spiritual children. Therefore, it is said in John 10:16: "I have other sheep that are not of this fold. And I must also bring them." These are gathered from every part of the world through the ministry of the Apostles, according to the Psalm: "Each and every nation that you have made will come and adore before you, O Lord. And they will glorify your name" (85:9). And Isaiah 43:5–6 reads: "I will bring your seed from the east, and I will gather you from the west. I will say to the north: Give them up, and to the south: Hold not back." Therefore, they are said to be gathered together from such distant regions on account of the diversity of customs, from which they are called to the unity of love and happiness. – For which reason the text adds: *And they will feast in the kingdom of God*. Isaiah 25:6 has: "The Lord . . . will make on this mountain for all people a feast of fat things, a feast of wine, of fat things full of marrow, of refined wine."

62. (Verse 30). And since this will be to the confounding of the reprobates and the glory of the elect, the text adds: *And behold, the last are those who were first, and the first are those who were last.*[152] *The first* are last because of pride whereas *the last* are first on account of humility. For it is said in Luke 18:14 below: "Everyone who humbles himself will be exalted, and everyone who exalts himself will be humbled."[153] Why is this? For the Psalmist says: "The Lord is high and has regard for the humble, and the exalted he knows from afar" (137:6). A

---

[152] On p. 353, n. 11 QuarEd correctly indicate that the Vulgate twice reads *erunt* ("will be") whereas Bonaventure has *erant* ("were").
[153] Bonaventure has inverted the contrasts in Luke 18:14.

special example of this appears in the two people, namely, the Jews, who are blinded, and the Gentiles who are elected. Romans 11:25–26 reads: "For I don't want you to be ignorant, brothers, of this mystery . . . that a partial blindness has befallen Israel until the full number of the Gentiles should enter. And thus all Israel will be saved." An example of this also appears in Judas, who was an Apostle and condemned, and the person who was a robber and was saved, as Luke 23:43 below says.[154] And by this example all are urged to a divine fear, according to what 1 Corinthians 10:12 states: "Let the person who thinks he stands take heed lest he fall."

63. So from this consideration of the future judgment we are prompted to be continuously engaged in good works on account of the aforementioned triple rationale. First, since *it is difficult to be justified in the Lord's sight* because of the difficulty in meriting. So the Psalm has: "Enter not into judgment with your servant, O Lord, for in your sight no living person will be justified" (142:2). And 1 Peter 4:18 says: "And if the just person will scarcely be saved, where will the impious and sinner appear?" – Second, because *it is impossible to be excused* on account of the harshness of the judgment. Proverbs 28:9 reads: "The person who turns away his ear from hearing the law, his prayer will become an abomination." And Job 41:3 states: "I will not spare him,[155] even

---

[154] On p. 354, n. 2 QuarEd cite the helpful commentary of the Glossa Interlinearis (from Book III of Bede's Commentary on Matthew 19:30): "*And behold, those are last who were first*, like Judas, and those who are *first*, etc. like the robber." See Hugh of St. Cher, p. 216v, qr: "q. And behold those are last who were first,] like Judas. r. And those are first who were last.] like the robber."

[155] On p. 354, n. 4 QuarEd accurately mention that the Vulgate reads *et* ("and") after the principal clause. I have given a free rendering of the rest of the verse.

though his words are powerful and wrought into a supplication." – Third, because *it is necessary to tremble* on account of the disaster of the punishment. Revelation 20:15 has: "The person who was not found written in the book of life was cast into the pool of fire and sulfur."[156] In Matthew 22:13 this is said about the person who did not have a wedding garment: "Bind his hands and feet and cast him into the darkness outside, where there will be weeping and gnashing of teeth." – And so the counsel of Wisdom in Qoheleth 9:10 is well taken: "Whatsoever your hand is able to do, do it instantly. For neither work nor reason nor wisdom nor knowledge exist in hell, whither you are hastening."

Luke 13:30–35
THE SUBLIMITY OF THE DIVINE DISPOSITION IN REDEEMING

64. *On that same day*, etc. After he had spurred them on to perform good works without ceasing on account of the severity of divine strictness in judging, here in a second point he urges them to the same goal *on account of the sublimity of the divine disposition in redeeming*. Now this section has two parts. In the first the sublimity of the divine disposition *in the redemption of the human race* is expressed. In the second *in the rejection of a rebellious people* where verse 34 says: *Jerusalem, Jerusalem*, etc.

Now *the sublimity of the divine disposition in redeeming* is manifested in a threefold manner: The intention of human beings to begin the passion of Christ *before its time was in vain*. At a fitting time Christ *will voluntarily*

---

[156] The Vulgate does not have *et sulphuris* ("and of sulfur").

assume his passion. From eternity his passion *was infallibly preordained.*

65. (Verse 31). So first it is suggested that human beings *vainly intended* to begin the passion of Christ before its time, when the text says: *On that same day certain Pharisees came up, saying to him: Depart and go away from here, for Herod wants to kill you.* This Herod was the son of the Herod who, wanting to kill the infant Jesus before the time, killed the boys of Bethlehem, according to what is said in Matthew 2:16: "Then Herod, seeing that he had been tricked by the Magi . . . sent and slew all the boys in Bethlehem." And so this son, imitator of a paternal crime, wanted to kill him before the time, as he had killed his predecessor. As it is said in Matthew 14:10: "Herod sent and had John beheaded in prison."[157] So now he wanted to do this to Christ, as an adult. And later on the nephew wanted to do this to him already glorified. So the first Herod was bad, the second worse, the third worst.[158] And all persecuted Christ, but in vain. For it is said in the Psalm: "The Lord brings to naught the counsels of the nations, and he rejects the devices of people, and casts aside the counsel of princes" (32:10). – And note that the Pharisees announced this to Christ, either because some among them were perhaps good, or because they wanted to deter Christ and send him away from them, or also because they wanted to tempt him to see whether he would de-

---

[157] See Luke 9:9: "But Herod said: John I beheaded. . . . "
[158] Bonaventure is somewhat elliptical here. In his commentary on Luke 1:5 (#8) he also discusses the three Herods: father, son, and nephew. The third Herod, Agrippa, killed James and shut Peter in prison and could thus be described as trying to kill Christ glorified by attacking the members of his body. In any case, in his commentary on Luke 1:5 Herod the Great is *infamior et inter omnes crudelior* ("the most nefarious and cruelest of the lot").

sist from preaching the truth out of fear. This latter is
the more credible, for they were wont to do this. So Matthew 22:15–16 reads: "The Pharisees left and took counsel how they might trap Jesus in his speech, and they
sent to him their disciples with the Herodians."

66. And note that according to *the mystical understanding Herod* is understood as a person glorying in skins[159]
and designates any proud and vainglorious person, who
glories in the ostentation of external works and words.
And such a person *persecuted the infant Christ* in Bethlehem, who is born as a poor person. For the vainglorious were wont to persecute the poor of Christ. So Bernard says in a certain sermon: "It is obvious to what extent evil power will harm, how an impious leader will
conform whatever subjects he has to his impiety. Plainly
the city is miserable, in which Herod rules, for it will
be . . . a participant in Herod's malice. . . . Indeed,
Herod's malice . . . is to wish to destroy a religious
movement in its infancy. . . . Therefore, if anything pertains to salvation, if anything of a religious nature rises
up, the person who resists these things . . . is persecuting the infant Savior."[160]

---

[159] See Jerome in CCSL lxxii, p. 140: *Erodes pelliceus gloriosus*
("Herod, made of skins, glorious"). It seems that these skins are to be
understood as rare and costly like ermine and mink in our society.
[160] On p. 354, n. 15 QuarEd refer to Bernard's Third Sermon, n. 3 for
the Feast of the Lord's Epiphany. See SBOp 4.305–306. I have tried
to indicate by dots the fact that Bernard's text is longer than
Bonaventure's. See Hugh of St. Cher, p. 217u where Hugh has virtually the same text as that of Bonaventure: *Unde B. Bern. Patet,
quantum noceat iniqua potestas, quomodo caput impium subjectos
quoque suae conformat impietati. Misera plane civitas, in qua regnat
Herodes, quoniam Herodianae particeps erit malitiae: Herodiana
vero malitia est, nascentem velle extinguere religionem. Si quid ergo
ad salutem pertinens, si quid religionis oritur, quicunque resistit,
cum Herode nascentem persequitur Salvatorem* ("It is obvious to what
extent evil power may harm, how an impious leader also conforms

67. (Verse 32). Second, the passion of Christ is indeed suggested *as voluntarily accepted by him* as the text adds: *And he said to them: Go and tell that fox.* He calls Herod *a fox* because of his wickedness and deceit, which, however, will not prevail against Christ's wisdom. Wisdom reads: "Wickedness does not overcome wisdom. Therefore, she reaches from end to end mightily."[161] – And since the death of Christ had not been accomplished according to the machination of human wickedness, but according to the disposition of Christ's own wisdom and will, the text adds: *Behold, I cast out demons and perform cures today and tomorrow*, through the performance of miracles. Acts 10:38 says: "He went about doing good and healing all who were in the power of the devil." – *And on the third day I am to consummate my course*, through the suffering of the passion, during which he said according to John 19:30: "It is consummated." And Hebrews 2:10 states: "For it became him, for whom are all things and through whom are all things, who had brought many sons into glory . . . to be consummated through suffering."[162] So these *three days* can be understood as the three years during which the Lord preached

---

the subjects he has to his impiety. Plainly the city is miserable, in which Herod rules, for it will be a participant in Herod's malice. Indeed, Herod's malice is to wish to destroy a religious movement in its infancy. Therefore, if anything pertains to salvation, if anything of a religious nature rises up, the person who resists these things is persecuting the infant Savior"). This translator wonders whether Cardinals Hugh and Bonaventure would have applied Bernard's interpretation to anyone who tried to snuff out the nascent Dominican and Franciscan religious movements.

[161] Wisdom 7:30–8:1. Instead of *ergo* ('Therefore") the Vulgate reads *enim* ("For").

[162] On p. 355, n. 3 QuarEd accurately indicate that the Vulgate reads *consummare* ("to consummate") while Bonaventure has *consum-mari* ("to be consummated"). I have preserved Bonaventure's train of thought by not translating *consummare* in Hebrews 2:10 by "to perfect."

and performed miracles, and this phrase also means that in the end he voluntarily suffered according to his own will. John 10:18 says: "I have the power to lay down my life[163] and the power to take it up again." So when he didn't want it to happen, no one could harm him, according to what John 7:30 reads: "No one laid hands on him, because his hour had not yet come." Therefore, fox-like wickedness could plot the death of Christ, but could not bring it about unless he himself willed it. About this Isaiah 53:7 has: "He was offered up, because he himself willed it." – And through this it is also *spiritually understood* that *the mystical body* of Christ does not suffer at the hands of impious heretics, unless it is in accordance with God's ordinance.[164] Christ understands these latter by *Herod*, attributing to him the name and characteristics of a fox.[165]

68. (Verse 33). Third, Christ's passion is suggested *as infallibly preordained from eternity.* Wherefore, the text adds: *Nevertheless, I must go my way today and tomorrow and the next day.* This favorable time did not take place out of compulsion, but according to heavenly ordinance, according to what Luke 24:25 states: "O foolish ones and slow of heart to believe in all that the prophets have spoken," etc. For God had foreseen this, according

---

[163] Bonaventure has *animam meam* ("my life") whereas the Vulgate has *eam* ("it").

[164] See Bonaventure's commentary on Luke 9:58 (#104) above: The fox is a tricky animal, intent on treachery, given to destruction and deceit, etc.

[165] On p. 355, n. 2 QuarEd cite the Glossa Interlinearis (from Augustine): "*Behold, I cast out demons,* so that men and women will condemn their sins and the errors in which they have been living. *And perform cures,* so that they may live according to my precepts, in which is true health. *Today and tomorrow and on the third day I am to consummate my course,* and I will glorify together with me in the resurrection those so prepared."

to what is said in Acts 2:23: "Him, whom you delivered up by the firm purpose and foreknowledge of God, you . . . have slain by the hands of wicked men." This the Prophets had also foretold, according to what is said in Acts 3:18: "But in this way God fulfilled what he had announced beforehand by the mouth of the prophets[166] that his Christ should suffer." During his passion he himself pointed to this favorable time of divine ordinance when he prayed, as it is said in Matthew 26:42: "My Father, if this cup cannot pass away unless I drink it, your will be done."

69. And since the divine ordinance not only preordained the time, but also the place, the text continues: *For it is not admitted that a Prophet perish outside Jerusalem. It is not admitted*, "that is, it is not fitting."[167] *Prophetic scriptures* do not admit it or *divine providence* does not allow it. This Prophet par excellence is Christ, who foreknew all future matters. About whom Deuteronomy 18:15 states: "The Lord will raise up for you a prophet like me from among . . . your brethren." And Luke 7:16 above reads: "A great prophet has risen among us." It was not fitting that he die except in Jerusalem, according to the scriptures. And because that was the kingly, magisterial, and priestly city, and Christ was the supreme king, teacher and priest. And therefore, it was not fitting that he die except in that place. So Luke 18:31 below says: "Behold, we are going up to Jerusalem, and all things that are written by the prophets about the Son of Man will be accomplished." For the Prophets had with one voice foretold this that the new law would

---

[166] The Vulgate reads *omnium prophetarum* ("of all the prophets").

[167] On p. 355, n. 8 QuarEd cite the Glossa Interlinearis: "*It is not admitted* in an absolute sense, that is, it is not fitting. Or it is not admitted to Herod."

come from Jerusalem. So Isaiah 2:3 reads: "Come, let us go up to the mountain of the Lord and to the house of the God of Jacob. . . . For the law will come forth from Zion, and the word of the Lord from Jerusalem." And Zechariah 13:1 has: "In that day there will be a fountain open to the house of David and to the inhabitants of Jerusalem for the washing of the sinner and the unclean woman." – And note that Christ was condemned in Jerusalem, but suffered outside the gate. Therefore, Hebrews 13:12 states: "Jesus, so that he might sanctify the people by his blood, suffered outside the gate."

70. Now *mystically* it is to be noted here that these three days are explained in a threefold manner by diverse interpreters: *allegorically, morally*, and *anagogically*. – The *allegorical interpretation* is this. The first day is the law of *nature*. The second is the law of *Scripture*. The third is the law of *grace*. About this Mark 8:2 says: "I have compassion on the crowd, for behold, they have already been with me for three days."[168] – Another exposition is that the first day is that of *the passion*. The second, of *the burial*. The third, of *the resurrection*. John 2:19 reads: "Destroy this temple, and in three days I will raise it up."[169] – Another exegesis is this: The first day is *the passing of the sixth age*. The second is *the repose of the souls*. But the third day, *the resurrection of the bodies*, occurs during the eighth age. Hosea 6:3 says: "He will revive us after two days. On the third day he will raise us up."[170]

---

[168] On p. 356, n. 1 QuarEd state: "This interpretation is in accord with the Glossa Ordinaria (from Bede) on Matthew 15:32."
[169] On p. 356, n. 2 QuarEd refer to Bernard of Clairvaux, "Sermo in die sancto Paschae,", n. 8.
[170] See Collation 15.17–18 in *The Works of Bonaventure V: Collations on the Six Days*, translated by José de Vinck (Paterson: St. Anthony Guild Press, 1970), p. 224: "And in the sixth age, Christ was born,

71. The *moral interpretation* is this. The first day is that
of *compunction*. The second, of *confession*. The third, of
satisfaction. Exodus 5:3 reads: "The God of the Hebrews
has called us. We will make a journey of three days into
the desert."[171] – Another exposition is this. The first day
is that of good *thoughts*. The second, of good *words*. The
third, of good *deeds*.[172] Jonah 3:4, according to the Septuagint translation, states: "Three more days, and
Nineveh will be destroyed."[173] – Another interpretation
is this. The three days are the three vows of a religious
institute, namely, *chastity, obedience,* and *poverty*.
Genesis 40:12–13 says: "There are three days, after
which Pharaoh will remember your service and will restore you to your former position."

72. The *anagogical interpretation* is as follows. The first
day is *purgation*. The second is *illumination*. And the
third is *perfection*. Luke 2:46 above says: "It came to pass
that after three days they found him in the temple." –
Another exposition is that the first day is the contem-

---

and he was crucified on the sixth day. . . . The seventh age runs con-
currently with the sixth, that is, the repose of the souls after Christ's
passion. After that comes the eighth age, the resurrection. . . ."

[171] Bonaventure seems to have conflated Exodus 5:3b with his version of Exodus 8:27a, which he also quotes in his interpretation of
Luke 12:58 (#85) above to support his view of "the way of repentance."

[172] On p. 356, n. 4 QuarEd cite Origen's Homily 3, n. 3 on Exodus: "I
understand him to be the way who said (John 14:6): *I am the way
and the truth and the life.* . . . This pertains to the mystical understanding. If (we turn) to the moral understanding also . . . we make a
journey of three days out of Egypt, if, purifying our *words, deeds,* or
thoughts (for these three are those things by which men and women
can sin), we become *pure of heart*, so that we can see God (Matthew
5:8)." The editors also refer to Bernard of Clairvaux, "Serm. 1. in
Dominica 6. post Pentec., n. 2."

[173] The Vulgate mentions "forty days." On p. 356, n. 5 QuarEd refer
to Jerome and Justin on these two readings.

plation of God in his *vestiges*. The second in his *image* or
mirror. The third in *himself*.[174] Numbers 10:33 reads:
"The ark of the Lord went before them, for three days
providing a place for the camp." – Another interpretation is that the first day is the contemplation of *the subcelestial hierarchy*. The second, of *the celestial hierarchy*.
The third, of *the supercelestial hierarchy*.[175] In the first is
the casting out of the demons. In the second is *the perfection of health*. But in the third is *the consummation of
every good*. And of this triduum Joshua 2:22 says: "The
explorers[176] came to the mountains and remained there
for three days."[177] – This *ark* is Christ, who in whatever

---

[174] See chapter 1, n. 2 of Bonaventure's *Itinerarium Mentis in Deum*,
edited by Philotheus Boehner (St. Bonaventure, New York: The
Franciscan Institute, 1998), p. 39: "By so praying, we are given light
to discern the steps of the soul's ascent to God. For we are so created
that the material universe itself is a ladder by which we may ascend
to God. And among things, some are vestiges, others, images; some
corporeal, others, spiritual; some temporal, others, everlasting; some
things are outside us, and some within. . . ."
[175] For far more detail on these "hierarchies," see Collations 20–23 of
Bonaventure's *Collations on the Six Days*.
[176] The Vulgate reads *Illi vero ambulantes* ("But these walking").
Ambulare is the Latin verb that is translated by "to go my way" in
Luke 13:33.
[177] On p. 356, n. 10 QuarEd say: "Cardinal Hugh also provides diverse interpretations of *the three days* in his commentary on Luke
13:33." In reality, Bonaventure's interpretations are very similar to
those of Hugh. They have seven scripture quotations in common, for
example. See Hugh of St. Cher, p. 217i: "And note that the Lord calls
himself a prophet, although he is the Lord. So Moses in Deuteronomy 18c[15]: God will raise for you from among your brothers a
prophet, etc. Hebrews 13b[12–13]: Jesus, so that he might sanctify
the people by his blood, suffered outside the gate. Let us, therefore,
go forth, etc. Further, this is how Today and tomorrow, etc., are interpreted. According to Bede: Today or the first day is the renuncia-
tion of vanity, on which the demons are cast out. The second is love
or the recognition of the truth, in which a cure is performed. The
third is final glorification, in which the Church will be consummated.
The first is the day of repentance. The second, of justice. The third,
of coronation. John 2d[19]: Destroy this temple, etc. Moreover, the

hierarchy of these hierarchies is the highest hierarch and our leader, so that we may come to the land of promise, which has been re-promised to us.[178] As a *figure* of this he says that he *goes his way for three days*, because he makes us always ascend on high through this triple hierarchy, unless perchance we descend to perform actions. As a figure of this it is said in Genesis 28:12 that "Jacob saw the angels of God *ascending* and *descending* on the ladder." No one saw them *standing still*. By this it is signified that persons must always make progress in doing good. For this is to approach the heavenly Jerusalem, which we do not approach by

---

first day is the natural law. The second day is the law of Moses. The third day is the law of the Gospel. Hosea 6a[3]: He will revive us after two days. On the third day he will raise us up. Furthermore, the first day is contrition. The second confession. The third satisfaction. On the first day he cast out demons, that is, sins from the heart. On the second he applies healing medicine. On the third he completes the healing. Exodus 5a[3]: The God of the Hebrews has called us, so that we may make a three day's journey into the desert. Additionally, the first day is good thoughts. The second good speech. The third good deeds. Jonah 3b[4]: Still three days, and Nineveh will be destroyed, in another translation. Again, the first day is recognition of the truth. The second love of the good. The third detesting evil. Genesis 40c[12–13]: There are still three days. After these Pharaoh will remember your service. Yet again, the first day is good behavior. The second tranquil contemplation. The third true preaching. Matthew 15d[32]: I have compassion on the crowd, for they have now been with me for three days. Finally, the first day is fasting. The second is prayer. The third is almsgiving. Tobit 12b[8]: Prayer is good with fasting and almsgiving."

[178] See Collation 3, n. 12 in *The Works of Bonaventure V: Collations on the Six Days*, p. 48. "He (the Word of God) it is who restored the hierarchy of heaven, and that below heaven which had totally fallen. Hence He must needs have touched both heaven and earth. This Hierarch had to be preeminent, endowed with awareness, acceptable to God, victorious, most generous, and just."

movements of our body, but by the affections of our heart and mind.[179]

73. (Verse 34). *Jerusalem, Jerusalem*, etc. After he had manifested the sublimity of divine ordinance in the redemption of the human race, here in a second point he turns to *the reprobation of a rebellious people*. And first he touches on *rebellion*, then on *obduracy*, and third on *desertion*.

So first with regard to *the rebellion* of this nation he says: *Jerusalem, Jerusalem, who kill the Prophets and stone those who are sent to you*. Here the idiom is to refer to the inhabitants by the city in which they dwell.[180] Acts 7:51–52 has: "Stiff-necked and uncircumcised in heart and ear, you always oppose the Holy Spirit. . . . Which of the prophets have not your fathers persecuted?" So 2 Kings 21:16 states: "Manasseh shed very much innocent[181] blood till he filled Jerusalem up to the mouth." And they did this, because they hated the truth, according to what Amos 5:10 reads: "They hated the

---

[179] On p. 356, n. 12 QuarEd cite two helpful parallels. See Letter 329, n. 5 in *The Letters of St. Bernard of Clairvaux*, translated by Bruno Scott James (Kalamazoo: Cistercian Publications, 1998), 410: "Jacob saw a ladder and on that ladder he saw angels, but none was sitting down or standing still, all were either going up or coming down. From this we can learn that in this mortal life there is no half way between going up and coming down. The soul must either increase or decrease just as the body must." This is Letter 254, n. 5 in the critical edition of Leclercq-Rochais. In Tractate 48, n. 3 of his *Tractates on the Gospel of John* Augustine writes: "The person who believes advances while the person who says No falls back. The soul is not moved by the feet, but by the affections."
[180] On p. 356, n. 14 QuarEd had a long quotation from Isidore of Seville on the meaning of metonymy.
[181] On p. 356, n. 14 QuarEd rightly indicate that the Vulgate reads *innoxium* ("innocent") while Bonaventure has *innocentem* ("innocent").

person who rebuked in the gate and abhorred the person who spoke perfectly." And this occurred because they didn't want to be accused. "For everyone who does evil hates the light and does not come to the light."[182] For which reason it is said in Ezekiel 2:3–4: "Son of man, I send you to . . . a rebellious people, who have revolted against me. . . . Their fathers have transgressed my covenant. And those to whom I am sending you are children of a stick neck and obdurate heart." And this refers to *stoning* itself.

74. Second, relative to *the obduracy* of this people the text continues: *How often would I have gathered my children together, as a mother bird gathers her young under her wings, and you would not.* In this way their obduracy appears enormous, for they refused to be softened by such great kindness. – Now Christ compared himself to *a mother bird* only with regard to the multiple characteristics she displays in her *superabundant loving dedication*. But he is compared to *a hen* on account of its *conduct*, for the hen is moved by its dedication and vigilance to its chicks, and gathers them together, and defends them with her wings against the rapacity of the hawk. Thus, too, did Christ act, during the time he was in the flesh. Therefore, Matthew 23:37 says: "How often would I have gathered your children together, as a hen gathers her young under her wings, and you would not." – He is compared to *a pelican* in his *passion*, because the pelican is brought to weep for three days over her chicks which had been killed, and afterwards to use its beak to shed its own blood, and thus bring them back to life.[183] –

---

[182] John 3:20.

[183] On p. 357, n. 6 QuarEd refer to Augustine's interpretation of Psalm 101, sermon 1, n. 8 for a helpful parallel. See NPNF 1, Volume 8: *Augustine: Expositions on the Book of Psalms*, p. 497: "These birds are said to slay their young with their beaks, and for three

In this manner Christ thrice wept for the human race. First for Lazarus: John 11:35. Second over Jerusalem: Luke 19:41 below. Third on the cross: Hebrews 5:7. And afterwards he shed his blood, by which he also gave us life. So the Psalm says: "I have become like a pelican of the desert" (101:7).[184] – Third, Christ is compared to *an eagle* in his *resurrection* and *ascension*. The eagle entices its young to tend upwards and to gaze at the sun and to fly to the highest places. And they are able to do this by sucking up his blood. So Job 39:27–30 has: "Will not the eagle mount up at your command and build its nest in the highest places? . . . Her young ones suck up blood."[185] Now this bird, although it has a rugged exterior, is, nonetheless, very dedicated in providing for its offspring. For this reason Christ, our redeemer, is fittingly likened to it. So Deuteronomy 32:10–11 states: "He led him and taught him and kept him as the apple of his eye. As an eagle, enticing its young to fly and hovering over them, he spread his wings and has taken him and carried him on his shoulders."[186] – To refuse this kindness is the height of obduracy and perfidy. For which reason Isaiah 1:4 reads: "Woe to the sinful nation, a people laden with iniquity, a wicked seed, ungracious children. They have forsaken the Lord. They have blasphemed the Holy One of Israel. They have resolutely turned their backs."

---

days to mourn them when slain by themselves in the nest: after which they say the mother wounds herself deeply, and pours forth her blood over her young, bathed in which they recover life. This may be true, it may be false: yet if it be true, see how it agrees with him, who gave us life by his blood."

[184] See the immediately preceding note for Augustine's interpretation of this verse of Psalm 101.

[185] On p. 357, n. 7 QuarEd refer to Augustine and Gregory as precursors for this strong imagery.

[186] See Hugh of St. Cher, p. 217v, g where he also refers to Deuteronomy 32:10–11 and Job 39:27–30.

75. (Verse 35). Third, concerning *the desertion* of this people the text continues: *Behold, your house will be left deserted for you.*[187] Isaiah 1:7–8 has: "Your land is deserted. Your cities are burnt with fire. . . . And the daughter of Zion will be abandoned as a covert in a vineyard and as a hut in a garden of cucumbers and as a city that is laid waste." – And since desertion is linked with obduracy in the same way that visitation is joined to dedication, the text says: *And I say to you: You will not see me until the time comes when you will say: Blessed is he who comes in the name of the Lord.* The Psalm says: "Blessed is he who comes in the name of the Lord. We have blessed you out of the house of the Lord. The Lord is God, and he has shown upon us" (117:26–27). Now this can refer to *the sight of faith,* which only gives sight to a person when that person believes that Christ is true man and true God.[188] John 9:35–38 states: "The Lord said to the man born blind: Do you believe in the Son of God? He answered and said: Who is he, Lord, that I may believe in him? And Jesus said to him: You have both seen him, and he it is who is speaking with you. And he said: I believe, Lord. And falling down, he worshipped him." – It can also refer to *the sight of glory,* to which only that person attains who blesses with both life and tongue. Isaiah 26:10 has according to the alternate translation: "Let the impious person be taken away, lest he see the glory of God."[189]

---

[187] The Vulgate does not have *deserta* ("deserted") and reads *Ecce, relinquitur vobis domus vestra* ("Behold, your house is left to you").

[188] On p. 357, n. 12 QuarEd cite the Glossa Ordinaria (from Jerome) on Luke 13:35: "Unless you do penance and confess me as the Son of the Omnipotent Father, you will not see my face in the second coming."

[189] Bonaventure refers to the Septuagint translation. See Hugh of St. Cher, p. 217v, m, who also quotes Isaiah 26:10 according to the Septuagint.

But according to our translation it is said: "In the land of the saints he has done wicked things, and he will not see the glory of the Lord."

76. And note that according to the Glossa's interpretation the reference here is *the sight during judgment*.[190] For after the sight of Christ in humility only the sight of him in majesty is to be expected. And this will be twofold: of his *Divinity* and of his *humanity. Of his Divinity*, and that will be the greatest good possible, because it will have the greatest joy joined to it. Job 33:26 reads: "He will see his face with jubilation, and he will render to men and women his justice." And Isaiah 33:17 has: "They will see the king in his splendor," etc. The other sight is of his *humanity*, and this will be common for everyone. For all will certainly see the power and dominion of Christ. Revelation 1:7 says: "Behold, he will come[191] with the clouds, and every eye will see him, even they who pierced him."[192] So the Lord wants to say that this Jewish people will not see Christ for their salvation unless it converts to faith and praises him. This is the final expectation in the last days after the full number of the Gentiles. So Romans 11:25–26 has: "A partial blindness has befallen Israel until the full number of the Gentiles should enter. And thus all Israel will be saved."[193] And

---

[190] On p. 358, n. 1 QuarEd cite the Glossa Ordinaria (from Bede, who quotes Augustine): "*When you will say*: Indeed, the crowds said this when the Lord entered Jerusalem [cf. Luke 19:38; Matthew 21:9]. But since Luke does not say that the Lord returned to Galilee afterwards, so that this might be sung to him by them, this compels a mystical interpretation of his coming in glory." See CCSL cxx, p. 274.

[191] The Vulgate reads *venit* ("he comes") whereas Bonaventure has *veniet* ("he will come").

[192] See Hugh of St. Cher, p. 217v, m who also quotes Revelation 1:7.

[193] Bonaventure is wont to redeem his medieval anti-Judaism by referring to Romans 11:25–26. See, for example, his earlier citation in

Romans 9:27 says: "Isaiah cries out concerning Israel: Though the number of the children of Israel are as the sand of the sea, the remnant will be saved." And in this the depth of the divine dispensation is manifestly apparent, which causes the Apostle to exclaim in Romans 11:33: "Oh, the depth of the riches of the wisdom and of the knowledge of God. How incomprehensible are his judgments and inscrutable his ways."

---

his commentary on Luke 13:30 (#62) above and in his commentary on Luke 19:40 (#62) below. For more detail refer to the Introduction.

LUKE 14

Luke 14:1–35

CHRIST REFUTES HIS OPPONENTS DURING A BANQUET

1. *And it came to pass, when he entered the house*, etc.
Earlier he had refuted those who had unjustly attacked
Christ's miracles during an assembly. Here he openly
confronts them *during a banquet*. For on these two occasions people are especially wont to utter slander and to
make observations, that is, during assemblies and banquets. Now this section, which comprises this present
chapter, is divided into three parts. In the first part *he
refutes the Pharisees who are observing him*. In the second *he instructs the reclining banqueters* where verse 7
reads: *But he also spoke to those invited*. And in the
third *he instructs the crowds who are following him*
where verse 25 says: *Now great crowds were going along
with him*.

Luke 14:1–6

CHRIST CONFUTES THE PHARISEES WHO WERE WATCHING HIM

Now concerning Christ's *confutation of those who are watching him* the Evangelist proceeds in this fashion. First, he describes *the Pharisees as watching.* Second, to this he joins *the unmasking of those watching him,* where verse 2 has: *And behold, there was a certain man before him who had dropsy.* Third, *the confutation of those who had been unmasked* where verse 4 reads: *And he took him and healed him.* – Now the Pharisee's watching of Christ is described in a twofold manner, namely, relative to *Christ's kindness* and *the Pharisees' malice.*

2. (Verse 1). So with regard to Christ's kindness the text says: *And it came to pass, when he entered the house of one of the rulers of the Pharisees on the Sabbath to take food.* In this action Christ's wonderful kindness is manifest. It is *great* in that he was associating with mortal human beings, although he was God. Baruch 3:36–38 states: "This is our God, and no other will be compared to him. . . ."[1] Afterwards he was seen on earth and associated with human beings." Indeed, it was *greater* in that he was associating with his persecutors. So what Ezekiel 2:6 has was fulfilled in him: "Son of man, . . . unbelievers and subversives are with you, and you live with scorpions." But his kindness is *greatest,* because his association took the form of intimate sharing of food, so that Revelation 3:20 may be fulfilled: "I stand at the door and knock. If anyone...opens the door for me, I will come in to him and will sup with him, and he with me." So through the fact that *he entered a strange house,*

---

[1] On p. 358, n. 12 QuarEd rightly indicate that the Vulgate reads *adversus eum* ("over against him") while Bonaventure has *ad eum* ("to him").

Christ's *humility* is commended. Through the fact that he entered *a Pharisee's house, love.* Through the fact that *he ate a stranger's food, the poverty* of Christ himself. And in these is shown *the highest kindness,* by which *the most high* wanted to be humbled for us, *the most just* to associate with the impious, *the most rich* to become poor among men and women. Wherefore, 2 Corinthians 8:9 says: "You know the graciousness of our Lord Jesus Christ, that, although he was rich, he became poor for our sakes, so that by his poverty we might become rich."[2]

3. Now second, concerning *the malice of those watching him* the text continues: *And they were watching him.* The Evangelist does not give *the reason,* so that he may intimate that they were watching both his *words* and his *miracles* and that they were watching him to censure and accuse him. Luke 11:53–54 above says: "The Pharisees and the lawyers began to press him...and to provoke him to speak...setting traps for him and plotting to seize upon something out of his mouth, so that they might accuse him." So John 15:20 also states: "If they have persecuted me, they will persecute you also. If they have kept my word, they will keep yours also." They were also watching his *miracles,* according to what is said in Mark 3:2: "They were watching him whether he cured on the Sabbath, so that they might accuse him." So this type of watching issued from *malice that lies in wait to ambush.* Against it Proverbs 24:15 states: "Lie not in wait, nor seek after wickedness in the house of the just nor spoil his rest." And since it is most difficult for the malicious person to desist from watching his neighbor, Proverbs 23:6–8 says: "Eat not with an envious person

---

[2] Bonaventure has changed the Vulgate's twofold *vos* ("your sakes/you") to a twofold *nos* ("our sakes/we").

and desire not his food. For like a soothsayer and di-
viner, he thinks what he knows not. Eat and drink, he
will say to you. And his heart is not with you. The food
that you have eaten, you will vomit forth, and you will
waste your pleasant conversation."

4. (Verse 2). *And behold, there was a certain man with
dropsy.* After describing the Pharisees watching Jesus,
here in a second point he depicts *the unmasking of the
watchers.* He makes three points, namely, *the sickness is
of such a nature that it is detectable, the unmasking
question,* and *concealing simulation.*

So first, concerning *the sickness that is of such a nature
that the watchers detect it,* the text says: *And behold,
there was a certain man before him who had dropsy.* Literally this *man with dropsy,* through his obvious and
grave malady, presented a way for the faithlessness of
the Jews to be unmasked and confuted. And through the
words, *and behold,* time and place are indicated, as if
the Lord had then led him into the middle of the group.
So Sirach 39:24, 26, 39 read: "The works of all flesh are
before him, and there is nothing hid from his
eyes. . . . There is no saying: What is this or what is
that? For all things will be sought in their time. . . . All
the works of the Lord are good, and the Lord will administer every good work in his due time." So this bodily
ailment was an effective means to attack and expurgate
a spiritual malady, because it was directly contrary to
it.[3] For this man with dropsy was before Jesus to im-
plore his mercy, which the Pharisees were attacking. He

---

[3] On p. 359, n. 7 QuarEd cite the Glossa Ordinaria (from Bede) apud
Lyranum on Luke 14:4: "The defect, which this man had in his body,
the Pharisees carried in their minds. And behold, he is cured bodily
in their presence, so that they may learn through this example to be
cured spiritually." See CCSL cxx, p. 275.

was imploring God's mercy, for he was *a human being*. For Sirach 18:12 states: "The mercy of God is upon all flesh."[4] And he was *a sick human being*, according to what Sirach 11:12–13 says: "There is an exhausted man who needs help, is very weak . . . yet the eye of God has looked upon him for good." And he was *before him*, because such people have recourse to God, and God condescends to such people. The Psalm has: "Because he has looked forth from his high sanctuary; from heaven the Lord has looked upon the earth" (101:20).

5. (Verse 3). Second, relative to Christ's *unmasking question* the text continues: *And Jesus responded and said to the lawyers and the Pharisees*. It is significant that the text says *responded*, since no one previously had asked anything. For he was responding to their *thoughts*, which he saw and heard, according to what Matthew 9:4 states: "When Jesus had seen their thoughts, he said: Why do you harbor evil thoughts in your hearts?" Wherefore, the Glossa says: "*Jesus responded* to the watchers who were lying in ambush,"[5] because it is said in Wisdom 1:10: "The ear of jealousy hears all things, and the tumult of murmuring will not be hidden." And so he responds to their thoughts by asking them the question, which they themselves were considering: *Is it lawful to cure on the Sabbath?* – The Pharisees are said to have posed this question to the Lord, as it is said in Matthew 12:10: "They asked him: Is it lawful to cure on the Sabbath? that they might accuse him." But Luke expresses their thoughts while Matthew expresses their words. The Lord asked this of them, for they avowed that they were lawyers. So the Glossa has: "He seeks a

---

[4] In its entirety Sirach 18:12 reads: "Human compassion is towards one's neighbor, but the mercy of God is upon all flesh."
[5] On p. 359, n. 10 QuarEd state that this is the Glossa Interlinearis.

judgment about the Law from the lawyers."[6] For which reason Malachi 2:7 reads: "The lips of the priest will guard knowledge, and they will seek the law from his mouth." And the Glossa in the same place says: "If a priest is asked about the Law, let him teach. Otherwise, he boasts of his dignity in vain, because he has not acted in accordance with it."[7]

6. (Verse 4). Third, concerning their *concealing simulation* the text adds: *But they remained silent.* So they were silent, for, seeing that they had been found out and detected, they feared to be confounded by their response. So the Glossa of Bede says: "It is fitting that they kept silent, having seen that what they might say would be said against themselves. For if it were permitted, why *are you watching me?* If it is not permitted, why *do you provide for your animals?*"[8] So they, by keeping quiet, feign ignorance, so that they might cover up their wickedness. Something similar is found in Matthew 21:25–27 where, when the Lord asked them about the origin of John's baptism, they refused to answer, lest they be convicted of incredulity.[9] So what Sirach 37:3 states could be said of them: "O most wicked presumption. Whence were you created to cover the dry earth with your malice?" Now when their flowery speech failed them, they had recourse to the darkness of ignorance and a paucity of words. Wherefore, they were silent not out of prudence, but out of that ignorance which holds hands with malice. So Sirach 20:6 reads: "There is a person who keeps silent, because he knows not what

---

[6] On p. 359, n. 12 QuarEd indicate that this is the Glossa Interlinearis.
[7] On p. 359, n. 12 QuarEd say that this is the Glossa Interlinearis.
[8] On p. 360, n. 1 QuarEd refer to the Glossa Ordinaria. I have translated *dictum* as "would be said" and thus agree with the interpretation of Strabo and Lyranus. See CCSL cxx, p. 275.
[9] See also Luke 20:1–8.

to say. There is also a person who keeps silent, knowing the proper time."[10]

7. *And he took him,* etc. After the unmasking of those watching Christ, here the Evangelist adds *the confutation of those unmasked* and makes three points: *the magnificence of the deed, the efficacy of the word, the evidence of the sign.*

So first, with regard to *the magnificence of the deed* the text says: *And he took hold of him and healed him and let him go.* In *taking hold of him,* he manifests his *humility,* for he does not disdain touching those infirm in order to teach humility. For this reason the Apostle says in Hebrews 2:16: "He never takes hold of angels, but the offspring of Abraham." By *healing him,* he shows forth his *power.* So Luke 6:19 above has: "Power went out from him and healed all." By *letting him go,* he displays his *generosity,* namely, to let him go away free. For he does not reduce him to slavery on account of the benefit conferred, but he let him go away free. The Glossa says: *"He let him go* away healed in body, so that he might participate in the salvation of souls."[11] So in Luke 8:39 Christ said to the possessed man he had healed: "Return to your house and tell all that God has done for you." Through his way of performing this miracle Christ shows forth his *humility* to confute the pride of the Jews, his *power* over against their sloth, his *generosity* and *benignity* over against their faithlessness. For they did not deign to touch the man with dropsy nor could they cure him nor did they want to liberate him.

---

[10] In his commentary on Luke 9:36 (#68) above Bonaventure quotes Sirach 20:6 in a shorter version.

[11] On p. 360, n. 6 QuarEd state that this is the Glossa Interlinearis. See Hugh of St. Cher, p. 218l who also quotes this Gloss.

8. (Verse 5). Second, relative to *the efficacy of his word* the text adds: *Then addressing them, he said: Which of you will have an ass or an ox fall into a pit,* namely, through an accident. For temporal possessions can be endangered and lost in many ways. Sometimes this happens from *the inside* through their own death like we see every day. Sometimes it comes about from *the outside* through an alien tyrannical force as in the description of Job 1:14–15: "The oxen were plowing, and the asses feeding . . . ,[12] and the Sabeans rushed in and took everything away." Sometimes it comes about through a *superior power* through pestilence. Exodus 9:3 reads: "Behold, my hand will be upon . . . your horses and asses and camels and oxen . . . a very grave pestilence."[13] Sometimes it occurs because of *a lower power*, by perishing in a hole, like here. Therefore, these possessions are not to be greatly loved, for they can be lost in so many ways.[14]

9. But nonetheless, the Pharisees greatly loved these possessions. So the Glossa notes: "In this avarice of yours you are like all people."[15] For their love of an ox or an ass made them not care about the observance of the Sabbath. So the text adds: *And will not immediately draw it up on the Sabbath?* by quickly coming to its aid.

---

[12] The Vulgate reads *juxta eos* ("beside them").

[13] These words introduce God's fifth plague against Pharaoh's disobedience.

[14] On p. 360, n. 8 QuarEd refer to Bonaventure's exegesis of Luke 12:33 (#46) above where he quotes Chrysostom: "All the good things of the world are subject to one of three dissolutions. For either they grow old of themselves, or they are consumed by the debauchery of their owners, or are stolen by strangers through deceit, force, or calumny."

[15] On p. 360, n. 9 QuarEd indicate that this is the Glossa Interlinearis (from Bede) on Luke 14:5. See CCSL cxx, p. 275. See Hugh of St. Cher, p. 218o: *Beda: Non animali, sed suae avaritiae consulens* ("Bede: Not deliberating about the fate of their animal, but about their avarice").

The Glossa says: "Not deliberating about the fate of their animal, but about their avarice."[16] And indeed, in taking this action, they do not think that they have offended against the Law. Now if the salvation of a human being is preferable to the rescue of an ass or ox, it is manifest that the Sabbath is not broken through the cure of a human being. And that is the argument from *the major premise*. For it seems that the Sabbath would be broken to a greater extent by a work that is more servile, for Leviticus 23:7 states: "You shall do no servile work on it."[17] But it is a greater servile work to free an ass or an ox than to cure a human being. Now if the person who draws an ox from the pit does not break the Sabbath, how much less does the person who cures a human being. For if a work of *avarice* does not break the Sabbath, neither does a work of *mercy*, since the work of avarice is one of servitude whereas the work of mercy is one of liberality.

10. (Verse 6). Third, concerning the *evidence of the sign* the text continues: *And they could give him no answer to these things*. The Glossa has: "Convinced."[18] For it is an evident sign that a person is convinced when he has nowhere to flee. It is no wonder that they could not respond to Christ's wisdom, since the most wise people would not be able to withstand his disciples. Luke 21:15 below reads: "I will give you utterance and wisdom which all your adversaries will be unable to withstand." And this was fulfilled in Stephen, about whom Acts 6:9–10 says: "Now there arose some from the synagogue which

---

[16] On p. 360, n. 10 QuarEd point to the Glossa Interlinearis. The words are virtually identical to those of Bede. See CCSL cxx, p. 275.

[17] See Bonaventure's commentary on the parallel passages of Luke 6:1–11 (#1–17) and 13:14–17 (#29–33) above.

[18] On p. 360, n. 12 QuarEd note: According to Gorranus this is the Glossa Interlinearis. Lyrannus does not have it. The Latin *convicti* can mean "convinced" and "condemned."

is called that of the Freemen and of the Cyrenians and of the Alexandrians and of those who were from Cilicia and the province of Asia, disputing with Stephen. And they were unable to withstand the wisdom and the Spirit who spoke."

11. Now having considered the literal sense, three things occur to us to need elucidation according to *the spiritual sense*. According to the saints these can be elicited from the aforementioned words. – First is *the illness of dropsy*,[19] whose characteristic feature, as the Glossa says, is that "the more one drinks, the more thirsty one becomes."[20] And in this it designates *every concupiscence*, which can never be satiated, and especially *avarice*, according to what Proverbs 30:16 says: "Fire never says: It is enough." So it is to be noted that, according to the ex-

---

[19] On dropsy, see Fitzmyer, p. 1041: ". . . suffering from edema, an abnormal accumulation of serous fluids in connective tissues or cavities of the body accompanied by swelling, distention, or defective circulation." On p. 361, n. 1 QuarEd quote Book IV, chapter 7, n. 23 of Isidore of Seville's *Etymologia*: "For (dropsy) is subcutaneous fluid with swelling and foul breath." See Willi Braun, *Feasting and social rhetoric in Luke 14,* Society of New Testament Studies Monograph Series 85 (Cambridge: Cambridge University Press, 1995), pp. 30–38 for evidence of dropsy as a Hellenistic metaphor for consuming passion. On p. 34 Braun quotes Stobaeus: "Diogenes compared money-lovers to dropsies: as dropsies, though filled with fluid crave drink, so money-lovers, though loaded with money, crave more of it, yet both to their demise. For, their desires increase the more they acquire the objects of their cravings."
[20] On p. 361, n. 1 QuarEd refer to the Glossa Ordinaria, which follows Augustine and Bede on Luke 14:1. See Book II, question XXIXB of Augustine's *Quaestiones Evangeliorvm*. Edited by Almut Mutzenbecher; (CCSL xlivb; Turnhout: Brepols, 1980), p. 70: "Now we rightly compare the man with dropsy to an avaricious rich person. For just as the man with dropsy, the more he swells up with inordinate fluid, the more he gets thirsty, so too the more the avaricious rich man increases the wealth which he cannot use in a good way, so too the more ardently he desires such wealth." See CCSL cxx, p. 275: "Now the man with dropsy the more he drinks, the more he gets thirsty. And every avaricious person increases his thirst, who, when he has acquired that which he seeks, desires to acquire even more."

positors,[21] dropsy appears in seven ways. – First, it is *a tumor of the body*, and by this *pride* is understood. Deuteronomy 17:13 reads: "When all the people hear it, they will fear, so that no one afterwards may swell with pride," etc. – Second is *the suppression of spiritual matters*, and in this *envy* is understood, which suppresses spiritual goods.[22] Proverbs 14:30 states: "The rottenness of the bones is envy." – Third is *foulness of breath*, by which *anger* is understood, which causes a person to spout off abusive language. The Psalm says: "Their throat is an open sepulcher. With their tongues they have acted deceitfully" (13:3). – Fourth is *swelling of the feet*, by which is understood *sloth*. Titus 1:12 has: "Cretans, always liars, evil beasts, slothful gluttons." And Wisdom 15:15 reads: "Their feet are slothful in walking." – Fifth is *a passionate thirst*, by which is understood *avarice*. Proverbs 30:16 has: "The earth is not

---

[21] See Hugh of St. Cher, p. 218q for the work of one of these expositors: "The common appearances of a person with dropsy are: tumor of the body, by which pride is noted, which is cured by the restraint of humility as had been signified. Judges 8a[3]: Since Gedeon had responded to the men of Ephraim in a humble manner, it is said: When he had said this, their spirit was appeased, with which they had swelled against him, etc. A foul mouth, the infamy of sin. Isaiah 34a[3]: Out of their carcasses will arise a stench, etc. The thirst of avarice. Job 18[9]: Thirst will burn against him. Inflamation of the genitalia, that is, voluptuousness. Colossians 2[18]: Inflated, etc. Swelling of the feet, that is, an attitude of sloth in doing good. Titus 1c[12]: Cretans, always liars, etc. Wisdom 15d[15]: Their feet are slothful in walking. The suppression of spiritual goods, by which envy is meant, which suppresses good things lest they be communicated. Against this is Wisdom 7b[13]: Which without guile, etc. Proverbs 14d[30]: The rottenness of the bones is envy. Infection of the skin, that is, the deformity of external behavior. Bernard: This form of clothing is an indication of deformity of mind and morals, etc." It is obvious that Hugh often presupposes that his audience will know the full scripture quotation, of which he cites a mere snippet. Further, it is clear that Bonaventure, as he numbers the ways in which dropsy manifests itself, is much dependent upon Hugh.
[22] The meaning seems to be that envy prompts one to neglect mentioning the good things of the Spirit others are accomplishing. See the parallel in Hugh of St. Cher, p. 218q.

satisfied with water," that is, earthly human beings with temporal opulence. And Qoheleth 5:9 says: "An avaricious person will not be satisfied with money." – Sixth is *swelling of the genitalia*, by which is designated *voluptuousness*. So the Psalmist says: "For my loins are filled with fantasies, and there is no health in my flesh" (37:8). – Seventh is *infection of the skin* or of the extremities, by which is understood *gluttony*, which deals entirely with taking care of one's skin. Philippians 3:19 states: "Their god is the belly, their glory is in their shame, they mind the things of the earth."

12. Now the second point we must consider is *the work of power*, by which is understood *the cure of spiritual sickness*. About this there are three components, namely, that *he took hold of him*, that *he cured him*, that *he let him go*. *He took hold of him*, that is, by *an infusion of grace*. Isaiah 42:6 has: "I, the Lord, have called you in justice and have taken hold of you by the hand and have preserved you." The Psalm says: "Put forth your hand from on high, take me out and deliver me from many waters," etc. (143:7). – Now *he healed him* through *the expiation of sin*. The Psalmist prays: "Who forgives all your iniquities, who heals all your infirmities" (102:3). And Matthew 1:21 reads: "He will save his people from their sins." – Truly *he let him go* through *the remission of punishment*. Matthew 18:27 states: "Moved with compassion, the master of that servant let him go and forgave him the debt." And this is what we pray for in the Lord's Prayer: "Forgive us our debts," etc.[23]

13. Now the third point to be taken into consideration is *the lesson contained in the example* of the comparison of *the ox* and *the ass* falling into the pit and being drawn

---

[23] Matthew 6:12.

out on the Sabbath. Through *the ox* and *the ass* are understood *both peoples*, namely, Gentile and Jewish, according to what Isaiah 1:3 says: "The ox knows its owner, and the ass his master's manger." For this is Gregory's exposition.[24] – Another interpretation is that by *the ox* and *the ass* are understood a *wise* man and a *stupid* man. So the Glossa on what Deuteronomy 22:10 states: "*You shall not plough with an ox and an ass together*, that is, you shall not join the stupid person with the wise person in preaching in order that they may announce the word of God with equal authority."[25] Therefore, these *fall into the pit* of concupiscence on account of original sin, and then into infernal Limbo. And this happened universally before the coming of Christ. For which reason the Psalm says: "Let not the tempest of water drown me, nor the deep swallow me up. And let not the pit shut its mouth upon me" (68:16). From this, then, the Lord *draws out on the Sabbath*, that is, on the seventh day, which is the day of Christ's burial, on

---

[24] On p. 361, n. 13 QuarEd refer to Book I, chapter 16, n. 23, Book XVII, chapter 26, n. 38, and Book XXXV, chapter 14, n. 39 of Gregory's *Moralia*.

[25] On p. 361, n. 14 QuarEd quote from the Glossa Ordinaria (from Isidore's Commentary on Deuteronomy, chapter 6, n. 2.3): "You may not join the stupid person with the wise person in preaching, lest through the person who is unable to fulfill this task you impede the person who can accomplish it. Indeed the stupid person and the wise person are well conjoined when the one commands and the other obeys, but not when they announce the word of God with equal authority." It is interesting to note that in this quotation Bonaventure is dependent upon and corrective of Hugh of St. Cher. See Hugh of St. Cher, p. 218q: *Mystice. per asinum stultus quilibet, per bovem sapiens designatur. Unde Deut. 22. Non arabis in bove simul, etc asino. Ibi Gl. idest fatuum sapienti in praedicatione non sociabis, ut aequali potestate verbum Dei annuncient.* ("The mystical interpretation. Any stupid person whatever is designated by the ass, a wise person by the ox. Wherefore, Deuteronomy 22[10]: You shall not plough with an ox and ass together. At that passage the Glossa: that is, you shall not join the stupid person with the wise person in preaching in order that they may announce the word of God with equal authority").

which rest for souls commenced, according to what Zechariah 9:11 states: "You also by the blood of your covenant have released your prisoners from the pit, in which there is no water."

Luke 14:7–24
Christ Instructs the Reclining Banqueters

14. *But he also spoke to those invited*, etc. After having successfully refuted those watching him, here in a second point Christ *teaches the banqueters*. Now this part is divided into three sections in accordance with its threefold instruction. For first, he instructs *those invited to a wedding banquet*. Second, he teaches *those invited to the banquet of a household* where verse 12 reads: *But he also said to him who had invited him*. Third, he gives instruction to *those invited to the eternal banquet* where verse 16 has: *A certain man gave a great supper*, etc. The first of these concerns the banquet of *grace*. The second the banquet of *nature*. The third the banquet of *glory*. The first is *sacramental*. The second is *material*. The third is *eternal* and *spiritual*.

Luke 14:7–11
Christ Instructs Those Invited to a Wedding Banquet

So in teaching *those invited to a wedding banquet*, by which is understood the status of the present Church, he first *reproves vanity and arrogance*. Second, *he commends humility and respect* where verse 10 states: *But when you are invited*. – Now in his *reproof of arrogance* three things are introduced, namely, *the occasion* that sets the scene for the parable; *the persuasive argument* for

censuring pride; and *the rationale* that gives the basis
for shame.

15. (Verse 7). So first, relative to *the occasion that sets
the stage for the parable* the text has: *But he also spoke
a parable to those invited.* The Glossa has: "*Parable,*
something with a mystical significance."[26] For since
anyone could draw some parallel between the Lord's
teaching and a carnal wedding banquet, the Evangelist
himself, who is guiding the interpreter, wants that
teaching to be understood in a parabolic manner. For
this was the Lord Savior's style in teaching, according to
what the Psalm has: "I will open my mouth in parables.
I will utter propositions from the beginning" (77:2). And
a parable does not carry conviction unless it is spoken at
an opportune time, according to what Sirach 20:22 says:
"A parable coming out of a fool's mouth will be rejected,
for he does not speak it at an opportune time." In contrast to the fool's action Proverbs 25:11 reads: "To speak
a word at an opportune time is like apples of gold on
beds of silver." Therefore, the text adds *the occasion of
place and time*, so that the point of this parable might
be drawn from the wedding banquet. So the text continues: *Observing how they were choosing the first places*,
namely, according to the mores of the proud, which were
indeed operative among the Pharisees. Matthew 23:6–7
states: "They love the first places at suppers and the
front seats in the synagogues and greetings in the market place." And this as a sign of honor according to what
Job 29:25 says: "If I had a mind to go to them, I sat in
the first place." For *first* is linked with *highest*. And just
as pride and ambition thrive on the inordinate appetite
of superiority, so too do they on priority. Now the proud,

---

[26] On p. 362, n. 4 QuarEd state that this is the Glossa Interlinearis
(from Bede). See CCSL cxx, p. 276.

who desire to be honored by others, seek things of this nature. Take the example of Saul in 1 Samuel 15:30: "Only honor me before the elders of my people and before Israel."[27]

16. (Verses 7–8). Now secondly with regard to *the persuasive argument to dissuade people from pride* the text adds: *He said to them: When you are invited to a wedding banquet, do not recline in the first place.* Although these words could be understood of *a carnal wedding banquet,* nevertheless the following texts themselves and their expositors require them to be understood of *a spiritual wedding banquet.* So the Glossa states: "Since, called by the preacher through the grace of faith, you have joined yourself to the members of the Church, you exult, not priding yourself on your merits as if you were more lofty than all the rest."[28] Now this wedding is not just any whatsoever, but is *the wedding of the Lamb*, about which Revelation 19:7 says: "The marriage of the Lamb has come, and his spouse has prepared herself." God the Father prepared this *wedding banquet,* according to what is said in Matthew 22:2: "The kingdom of the heavens is like a king who prepared a wedding banquet for his son." This wedding was celebrated in the bridal chamber of the virginal womb. The Psalmist sings: "He has set his tabernacle in the sun, and he is like a bridegroom coming out of his bridal chamber" (18:6). There was consummated the matrimony between the divine and human nature and consequently between Christ and the Church, according to what Ephesians 5:32 has. Speaking of matrimony, the Apostle says: "This is a

---

[27] In all honesty I must indicate, along with QuarEd on p. 362, n. 8, that 1 Samuel 15:30 begins with Saul confessing to Samuel and to God: "I have sinned."
[28] On p. 362, n. 9 QuarEd state that this is the Glossa Ordinaria (from Bede). See CCSL cxx, p. 276.

great mystery. Now I am speaking in reference to Christ and the Church."[29] – *The banquet* at this wedding consists in the reception of the Sacraments of the Church and the teachings of the Sacred Scriptures. Proverbs 9:1–3 reads: "Wisdom has built herself a house. She has hewn out her seven pillars. She has slain her victims, mixed her wine, and set forth the table.[30] And she has sent her maids to invite to the tower," etc. To this banquet *are invited* all, who are called to faith through the preaching of the truth. Matthew 22:3 says: "He sent his servants to call in those invited to the wedding feast."[31] – Thus those invited *recline and feast* on the investigation and rumination of the divine and mystical sayings. A sign of this is that heavenly food was called *manna* in Exodus 16:15 and is interpreted as "What is this?" For they must understand what they are receiving. So also in Leviticus 11:26 it is said that the animal which "does not ruminate is unclean."[32] – Now the person who *reclines in the first place* is the one who is preferred to others either in dignity of office or in the prerogatives of

---

[29] On p. 362, n. 10 QuarEd state that Bonaventure's twofold interpretation of the wedding follows that of Homily 38, n. 3 of GGHG. See PL 76:1283A–C. Gregory also quotes Psalm 18:6. On p. 362, n. 12 QuarEd cite the Glossa Interlinearis (from Bede): "*When you are invited to a wedding banquet*, the wedding, the union of Christ and the Church."

[30] On p. 362, n. 13 QuarEd correctly indicate that the Vulgate reads *mensam suam* ("her table") whereas Bonaventure simply has *mensam* ("table"). See Hugh of St. Cher, p. 218v, d who reads *mensam suam* ("her table").

[31] See Hugh of St. Cher, p. 218v, d where Hugh also quotes Matthew 22:3, Proverbs 9:1–3, and Leviticus 11:26.

[32] The Vulgate reads *erit* ("shall be") while Bonaventure (and Hugh of St. Cher, p. 218v, d) has *est* ("is"). Bonaventure is referring to a monastic tradition of munching, mumbling, and ruminating on the scriptures. See Ivan Illich, *In the Vineyard of the Text: A Commentary on Hugh's* Didascalicon (Chicago: University of Chicago Press, 1993), esp. pp. 51–65. On pp. 362–363, n. 15 QuarEd cite a long passage from Chrysostom's Homily 41 on Matthew 22:3 (*Opus Imperfectum*). See Hugh of St. Cher, p. 218v, c who quotes a long section from this same homily.

holiness or in the teaching of the truth. And to this honor no one must ascend of his own accord, because it is said in Hebrews 5:4: "No one takes the honor to himself except the person who is called by God, as Aaron was." And so Sirach 6:2 reads: "Do not extol yourself in the thoughts of your soul like a bull, lest perhaps your strength be quashed."[33] Not even *in front of others*. Thus Sirach 11:4 has: "Glory not in apparel at any time, and be not exalted in the day of your honor."

17.Third, then, comes *the rationale that gives the basis for shame*. The text continues: *lest perhaps one more distinguished than you has been invited by him*, that is, a person who is worthy of greater honor because of interior grace. The Glossa notes: "He has more grace in the eyes of the one inviting, although his graced nature is hidden to others."[34] 1 Samuel 16:7 states: "Do not look at his countenance nor on the height of his stature, because I have rejected him. I do not judge the way humans see things. For humans see the appearances, but the Lord looks into the heart."

18. (Verse 9). *And then*[35] *he who invited you and him come*, through *the disposition of grace*. Proverbs 16:2 says: "God[36] is the one who weighs the spirits." *And say to you: Make room for this man*, on account of his superior dignity. 1 Samuel 15:28 reads: "The Lord has rent your kingdom from you . . . and has given it to your neighbor who is better than you." – *And then you will*

---

[33] For some reason Bonaventure does not quote the final words of Sirach 6:2: *per stultitiam* ("by folly").
[34] On p. 363, n. 2 QuarEd indicate that this is the Glossa Interlinearis. My translation is expansive.
[35] On p. 363, n. 3 QuarEd correctly mention that the Vulgate does not read *tunc* ("then").
[36] The Vulgate has *Dominus* ("The Lord").

begin[37] *with shame to take the last place,* in evident abasement, according to what the Psalm states: "And having been exalted, I have been humbled and troubled" (87:16). And so Sirach 13:10 has: "Beware that you be not deceived into folly and be humbled." But that person *is deceived into folly,* who considers himself to be someone great. Galatians 6:3 says: "If anyone thinks himself to be something, whereas he is nothing, he deceives himself." And such a person is humbled by God's just judgment, according to what Luke 1:52 above states: "God has put down the mighty from their thrones and has exalted the humble." About this type of judgment it is said in Sirach 11:5–6: "Many tyrants have sat on the throne, and he whom no man would think on, has worn the crown. Many mighty men have been greatly brought down, and the glorious have been delivered into the hands of foreigners."[38] And wherefore, it is said in Sirach 7:4: "Seek not from a human being a pre-eminence nor from a king the seat of honor." For Proverbs 20:21 reads: "The inheritance, obtained hastily in the beginning, will be without a blessing in the end."

19. (Verse 10). *But when you are invited.* After he has censured arrogance, here *he invites them to respect.* Indeed, he does this by *prompting them to perfect humility, by noting the benefit connected with it, confirming it by divine justice.*

---

[37] On p. 363, n. 5 QuarEd accurately indicate that the Vulgate reads *incipias* ("you begin"). On p. 363, n. 3 they cite the Glossa Interlinearis: "*And come,* by showing his grace both to you and to him. *He who called both you and him,* God, who knows the hearts of each person. *Say to you: Make room for this man.* Consider yourself a minor."

[38] On p. 363, n. 7 QuarEd correctly mention that the Vulgate reads *alterorum* ("of others") while Bonaventure has *alienorum* ("of foreigners").

So first, *in prompting them to perfect humility*, he says: *But when you are invited*, to the wedding feast, *go and[39] recline in the last place*, placing yourself after all people, according to what Matthew 20:26–28 has: "Whoever wishes to become great among you will be your servant. And whoever wishes to be first among you will be your slave, even as the Son of Man has not come to be served, but to serve." So he sat in the last place. Isaiah 53:2–3 reads: "We have seen him . . . the most abject of men, a man of sorrows and acquainted with infirmity. Behold,[40] his features, hidden and despised." – As a commendation of this humility the seats of the more prominent persons are farther removed from the altar,[41] and in processions those higher in dignity come last, in imitation of Christ himself, who indeed prompted this humility when he washed the feet of all the Apostles. John 13:14–15 states: "If I, the Lord and Teacher, have washed your feet, you also ought to wash the feet of one another. For I have given you an example," etc. For "no disciple is above his teacher."[42] And therefore, the Apostle says in 1 Corinthians 9:19: "Although I was free of all, I have made myself a slave of all." And again he says in 15:9: "I am the least of the Apostles and am not worthy to be called an Apostle." And in Ephesians 3:8 he states: "To me, the very least of all saints, was given this grace." And so Peter, the prince of the Apostles, says in 1 Peter 2:13: "Be

---

[39] On p. 363, n. 10 QuarEd accurately indicate that the Vulgate lacks *et* ("and").

[40] On p. 363, n. 11 QuarEd correctly mention that the Vulgate reads *quasi* ("as if") while Bonaventure has *ideo* ("behold").

[41] On p. 363, n. 12 QuarEd call attention to Cardinal Hugh's commentary on Luke 14:7. See Hugh of St. Cher, p. 218v, c: "Through his teaching he mystically intends to persuade us on how we must choose seats in church. Therefore, the superior persons sit in the more humble seats, that is, farther removed from the altar, which, nevertheless, are now considered by custom as those of greater dignitaries."

[42] Luke 6:40. See Matthew 10:24 for the same saying.

subject to every human creature for God's sake." –
Therefore, *recline in the last place*, regarding yourself as
inferior to all.

20. But you will say: How will I truly regard myself as
worse than all, since many are worse than I am? – To
this objection Bernard in Homily 37 on The Song of Songs
says:[43] "For if each of us could clearly see the truth of
our condition in God's sight, it would be our duty to depart neither upwards nor downwards from that level,
but to conform to the truth in all things. Now, however,
since God has placed this counsel in a dark hiding place
and his word is hidden from us, so that no one knows
whether he is worthy of love or hate, it is certainly the
better and safer thing to follow the advice of him who is
Truth itself and to choose for ourselves the last place.
Afterwards, we may be led up higher from there with
honor rather than have us recede shortly, to our shame,
from the higher seat we had usurped. You run no risk,
therefore, however much you humble yourself, however
much you regard yourself as less than you are, that is,
less than Truth regards you. But the evil is great and
the risk frightening if you exalt yourself even a little
above what you are, if in your thoughts you consider
yourself of more worth than even one person whom
Truth may judge your equal or even your better. To
make myself clearer: if you pass through a doorway
which is very low, you suffer no hurt no matter how
much you bend. But if you raise your head higher than
the doorway, even by a finger's breadth, you will dash it

---

[43] Bonaventure's quotation is from Homily 37, n. 6–7, is one-column
long, and except for a few variations is identical to the critical text of
Bernard. See SBOp 2.12–13. I have based my translation on that of
Kilian Walsh, *The Works of Bernard of Clairvaux Volume Three: On
the Song of Songs II,* Cistercian Fathers Series 7 (Kalamazoo: Cistercian Publications, 1976), pp. 185–186. I have not identified the many
scripture passages Bernard weaves into his homily.

against the lintel and injure yourself. So clearly a person need not fear any humiliation, but that person should quake with fear before rashly yielding to even the least degree of self-exaltation. So, O human being, do not compare yourself to those greater or less than you, to a few or even to one person. For how do you know, O human being, but that this one person, whom you perhaps regard as the vilest and most wretched of all, whose life you recoil from and spurn as more befouled and wicked, not merely than yours, for you trust that you are a sober-living man and just and religious, but even than all other wicked people? How do you know, I say, but that in time to come, with the aid of the right hand of the Most High, he will not surpass both you and them if he has not done so already in God's sight? That is why God wished us to choose neither a middle seat nor the penultimate, not even one of the lowest rank. But he said: Sit down in the lowest place, namely, that you may sit last of all, and not presume to compare yourself, still less to prefer yourself, I say, to anyone."

21. Now second, he treats *the benefit connected* with perfect humility: *That when he who invited you comes in, he may say to you: Friend, go up higher.* The one who *has invited* us is Christ, who *comes* to us either in *inspiration*, according to what John 14:23 has: "We will come to him and will make our abode with him." Or he *comes in death*. Luke 12:36 above says: "So that when he comes and knocks at the door, they may straightway open to him." Or *he comes in the final reckoning*. Revelation 22:12 reads: "Behold, I come quickly. And my reward is with me, to render to each one according to his works." – When he comes here, he calls the humble *friends*. For Christ is the true friend, according to what Proverbs 17:17 states: "The person who is a friend loves at all times." And he recognizes the humble as friends, be-

cause such people obey him. John 15:14 reads: "You are my friends if you do the things I command you." And then he does not call them by the name of *servant*, but by that of *friend*. John 15:15 says: "No longer do I call you servants, but friends, because . . . all things that I have heard from my Father I have made known to you." – To such persons he says: *Go up higher*, that is, to superior honor and dignity. The Psalm says: "O God, your friends are made exceedingly honorable" (138:17). – And so the text continues: *Then you will be honored in the presence of those who are reclining*, that is, in the presence of all.[44] Proverbs 29:23 says: "Humiliation follows the proud, and glory will uphold the humble of spirit." The Psalmist states: "I am with him in tribulation. I will deliver him and will glorify him. I will fill him with length of days and will show him my salvation" (90:15–16). And on account of this Job 22:29 has: "The person who has been humbled will be in glory, and the person who has bowed down his eyes will be saved."

22. (Verse 11). Third, *confirming perfect humility by divine justice*, he adds: *For everyone who exalts himself*, through proud elation, according to what Job 15:12 reads: "Why does your heart elevate you, and why do you stare with your eyes, as if you were thinking great things?" – *will be humbled*, through judiciary strictness. Isaiah 2:11–17 states: "The lofty eyes of a human being will be humbled. . . . Because the day of the Lord . . . will be upon everyone that is proud and arrogant, and he will

---

[44] On p. 364, n. 11 QuarEd refer to Bede. See CCSL cxx, p. 276: "When the Lord comes, he will beatify with the name of *friend* the person he finds to be humble, and will command that person to go up higher, etc." On p. 364, n. 13 QuarEd cite the Glossa Interlinearis: "*Friend*, he acknowledges you as friend because of your humility and because you put yourself in a lower place with assurance. *Go up higher*, to the greater reward of eternal glory or here to receive the greater gifts of the Holy Spirit."

be humbled. . . . And every human loftiness will be bowed down, and the haughtiness of men will be humbled." An example of this was manifest in Lucifer. Isaiah 14:12–13 has: "How have you fallen, O Lucifer, who rose in the morning? . . . who said in your heart: I will ascend into heaven. I will exalt my throne above the stars of God."[45] And because he exalted himself, he fell. So Ezekiel 28:6–8 says: "Because your heart is lifted up like the heart of God, therefore behold I will bring upon you strangers. . . . And they will defile your beauty and will kill you and bring you down. And you will die the death of those slain." For which reason Obadiah 1:3–4 says this to the imitator of Lucifer, that is, any proud person: "The pride of your heart has lifted you up, who dwell in the cliffs of the rocks and set your throne on high. . . . Though you be as exalted as an eagle and though you set your nest among the stars, I will bring you down from there." Whence, the wise person gives this counsel in Sirach 6:2–3: "Do not extol yourself in your thought[46] like a bull, lest perhaps your strength be quashed . . . and you be left like a dry tree in the wilderness."

---

[45] In his commentary on Luke 14:11 Hugh of St. Cher quotes three of the same scripture passages that Bonaventure does. See Hugh of St. Cher, p. 218v, c: "Proverbs 29d[23]: Humbling follows the proud, that is, humiliation. Take the example of Lucifer. Isaiah 14c[12–13]. Proverbs 29[23]: And glory will upheld the humble in spirit. Take the example of David, who although he was least among his brothers became King of Israel. 1 Samuel 19c[=16:12–13]. And of Saul it is said in 1 Kings 1d[=15:17]: When you were a little child, were you not made, etc. Job 22d[29]: The person who has been humbled will be in glory, and the person who has bowed down his eyes, etc." I have corrected the two erroneous citations in this brief passage.
[46] On p. 365, n. 7 QuarEd rightly indicate that the Vulgate reads *in cogitatione animae tuae* ("in the thought of your soul") whereas Bonaventure has *in cogitatione tua* ("in your thought"). See Bonaventure's commentary on Luke 14:9 (#16) above where he also quotes Sirach 6:2, but follows the Vulgate reading.

23. In this way divine justice humbles the proud and exalts the humble. So the text adds: *And the person who humbles himself* through voluntary abjection. The Psalm says: "The Lord, the keeper of little ones, I was humbled, and he delivered me" (114:6). And 2 Samuel 6:22 reads: "I will play and demean myself more than I have done, and I will be humble in my eyes."[47] *Will be exalted* through divine glorification. An example is found in the Lord Savior. Philippians 2:8–9 states: "He humbled himself. . . . Therefore, God has also exalted him," etc. And so it is said in 1 Peter 5:6: "Humble yourselves under the mighty hand of God, so that he may exalt you in the time of visitation." And of these two it is said in the Psalm: "I will break all the horns of sinners, and the horns of the just will be exalted" (74:11). And Ezekiel 17:24 has: "All the trees of the country will know that I the Lord have humbled the lofty tree and exalted the lowly tree."

24. Now the reason for this justice and equity is that the more anyone *exalts* himself, the less *he honors God* and the less he magnifies God. And also the more a person turns away from God, the consequence follows that the less he is. Ezekiel 28:19 says: "You are brought to nothing, and you will never be any more." – Again, the more a person exalts himself, the more he raises himself over himself and therefore the more evanescent he becomes. And the more evanescent he is, the more he recedes from the truth and the less he is.[48] Therefore, the more a person exalts himself, the greater is he cast down. Job 30:22 reads: "You have lifted me up, and set

---

[47] David, who had leapt and danced before the Lord, is speaking to Michal.
[48] On p. 365, n. 12 QuarEd refer to Book XX, chapter 33, n. 65 of Gregory's *Moralia*, where, among other things, Gregory says: "For the person who adheres to the truth, in no way succumbs to vanity, etc."

me, as it were, upon the wind. And you have mightily
dashed me down." – Finally, the more a person exalts
himself, *the more he loves human glory*. And the more
he embraces this, the more he is subject to human
praise. And for this reason he is more the slave of men
and women, and he is cast down the more. The Psalm
says: "But you set them up for deception. When they
were lifted up, you cast them down" (72:18).[49]

25. Seen from a contrary perspective, the more a person
humbles himself, the more *he honors God*. Sirach 3:21
states: "Great is the power of God alone, and he is honored by the humble." The more a person honors God, the
more he draws near to God, and therefore is lifted up to
more sublime matters. – Further, the more a person
humbles himself, the more *he travels into his interior*.
And the more he is gathered together interiorly, the more
power is generated. So the more a person is humbled,
the more things are accomplished according to the
truth. So 2 Corinthians 12:9 has: "Power is made perfect
in weakness." – Finally, the more one is humbled, *the less
a person prizes earthly glory*. And the less one prizes it,
the more one tramples it under foot and the higher one
is placed above all inferior things, and so accomplishes
more. Isaiah 60:15 reads: "I will make you the pride of
the ages." – Wherefore, everyone who exalts himself, the
more he exalts himself, the greater he distances himself
from his *superiors*. And the more he distances himself
from his superiors, the more he moves away from *the
interior*, and through this action the more *he subjects
himself to his inferiors*. So the more one is lifted up, the

---

[49] On p. 365, n. 13 QuarEd cite Augustine (Enarratio on Psalm 72, n.
24): "He did not say: *He cast them down*, because they were lifted up,
not as if after they were lifted up, he cast them down. But in the very
fact that they were lifted up, they were cast down. For to be lifted up
in this way is already to fall."

farther is he cast down according to the truth and must be cast down according to divine judgment. And on the contrary, everyone who humbles himself, the more he humbles himself, the more *he draws near to his superiors*, the more *he travels into his interior*, and the more *he tramples under foot his inferiors*. So the more one humbles oneself under God, the more one is exalted by divine judgment.

Luke 14:12–15
Christ instructs those invited to the banquet of a household

26. (Verse 12). *But he said to him*, etc. After he has given instruction to those invited to the wedding banquet, here in a second point he provides instruction for *those invited to a banquet of a household*. In this instruction he first *draws the invited away from earthly geniality*, and then *draws them to divine charity*[50] where verse 13 reads: *But when you give a banquet*.

Thus *in drawing them away from earthly geniality*, he notes three aspects of this withdrawal, namely, *its occasion, the exhortation*, and *the persuasive rationale*.

So first, with regard to *the occasion* that prompts this instruction, the text says: *But he also said to him who had invited him*. So he said this to him, because his invitation provided him with the occasion of speaking about the manner to be used in extending invitations, according to what Sirach 27:13 states: "In the midst of

---

[50] On p. 366, n. 4 QuarEd indicate that they have opted for the reading *caritatem divinam* ("divine charity") instead of *curialitatem divinam* ("divine geniality").

the unwise hold your tongue until the right time." Or he
said this to him, so that he might repay with spiritual
teaching the person who was ministering bodily sustenance to him. In this way he showed that divine gifts
are to be shared, according to what 1 Peter 4:10 says:
"According to the gift that each has received, administer
it to one another."[51] – So a model is provided for the
spiritual man who partakes of bodily food that he should
dispense spiritual nourishment to his host, as is suggested in Luke 10:38–39 above: "Martha invited Christ
into her house, . . . and her sister Mary, sitting at the
feet of the Lord, listened to his word."[52] In a designation
of this the wise person says of Christ Wisdom in Wisdom
8:9: "I proposed to take her to me to live with me,
knowing that she will communicate her good things to
me and will be an encouragement to me in my thinking
and in my weariness." Further, in this a model is given
that during banquets of spiritual men spiritual teachings are to be intermingled. So there is the custom that
spiritual reading is intermingled with bodily nutriment,
on account of the word of the Lord in Deuteronomy 8:3
and Matthew 4:4: "Not by bread alone does man live,
but by every word that comes forth from the mouth of
the Lord."[53]

27. Second, concerning *the exhortation that teaches* the
text adds: *When you give a dinner or a supper: Dinner* in

---

[51] On p. 366, n. 7 QuarEd quote from Theophylactus on Luke
14:12–15: "A banquet is made up of two types of people: the invited,
and those who invite. He had led off by giving a salutary admonition
about humility to the class of those invited. . . . Now he also addresses the person who invited him and for his part showed his graciousness . . . leading him away from hosting banquets for the sake
of . . . human favor."
[52] The first part of Bonaventure's quotation is not verbatim.
[53] Deuteronomy 8:3 reads *Domini* ("of the Lord") whereas Matthew
4:4 has *Dei* ("of God").

the early part of the day and *supper* towards the end of the day.[54] – *Do not invite your friends*, for reasons of *companionship*. Matthew 5:46 reads: "If you love those who love you, what reward will you have? Do not even the publicans do that?" For it is said in Sirach 37:5: "A companion will console his friend for the sake of the belly and will take up the shield against the enemy." *Nor relatives*, for reasons of *kinship*. Sirach 18:12 has: "Human compassion extends to one's neighbors, but God's mercy to all flesh." *Nor neighbors*, for reasons of *intimate acquaintance*. On the contrary 3 John 5–6 advises: "Beloved, you are acting in accordance with faith whatever you are doing for the brethren, and that even when they are strangers, who have borne witness to your charity." *Nor brothers*, for reasons of *consanquinity*, for it is said: "Forget your people and your father's house."[55] And Deuteronomy 33:9–10 reads: "Who have said . . . to their brothers: I do not know those. . . . These keep . . . your law," etc. *Nor the rich*, for reasons of *pomposity*. For it is said in Luke 16:19 below: "There was a certain rich man who used to clothe himself in purple and fine linen and feasted every day in splendor." And later the text says that "he was buried in hell" (16:22).[56] – Now he says this, not because it is against a commandment to invite those known to oneself, for it is written in 1 Timothy 5:8: "If anyone does not take care of his own, and especially of his household, he has denied the faith and is worse than an unbeliever." And it is written of Joseph in Genesis 43 that he hosted a ban-

---

[54] On p. 366, n. 10 QuarEd cite the Glossa Interlinearis: "*When you give a dinner*, at whatever hour of the day, *or a supper*, in the evening, *do not invite your friends*, who are related to you by blood or carnal affection."
[55] All of Psalm 44:11 reads: "Hearken, O daughter, and see and incline your ear. Forget your people and your father's house."
[56] Bonaventure has five categories rather than Luke's four: friends, brothers, relatives, rich neighbors.

quet for his brothers. Rather he says this because a person involved in invitations of this kind, if he wants to merit eternal life, must not have a carnal intention, but a spiritual one, not an earthly intention, but a heavenly one, not a mercenary intention, but a gratuitous one.[57]

28. Wherefore, note that there is a *banquet that is neither good nor evil*, but part and parcel of human concourse. About this Job 1:4 reads: "His sons went and hosted banquets by houses, every one in his day." – And there is *an evil banquet*, and this is threefold: *evil, worse, worst*. The first is the banquet of *gluttony*. Romans 13:13 says: "Not in profligate living and drunkenness," etc. And Proverbs 23:20–21 states: "Attend not the banquets of great drinkers nor engage in the profligate living of those who contribute flesh to eat.[58] For they who give themselves to drinking and who consort together will be consumed." And James 5:5 reads: "You have feasted upon earth, and you have nourished your hearts on luxurious things." – The second is the banquet of *vainglory*. About this Daniel 5:1 says: "King Belshazzar gave a grand banquet for all his nobles, etc."[59] And Mark 6:21 has: "Herod on his birthday gave a banquet for the officials, tribunes, and chief men of Galilee." And during the first banquet the temple vessels of the Lord were defiled. During the second Christ's precursor was murdered. – The third is the banquet of *wickedness*. About this it is said in 2 Samuel 13:27–29 that Absalom invited his brother Ammon to a banquet, during the course of which

---

[57] On p. 367, n. 1 QuarEd quote the Glossa Ordinaria (from Bede) on Luke 14:12: "He does not indict brothers, friends, and rich people for enjoying banquets with one another as if it were a crime, but he shows that these are worthless for the reward of life, etc." See CCSL cxx, p. 277.
[58] In Jewish antiquity eating meat was a sign of festivity.
[59] The Vulgate reads *optimatibus suis mille* ("for a thousand of his nobles").

he murdered him. And it is said in 1 Maccabees 16:15–16 that "the son of Abubus gave a great banquet for Simon, and when he was inebriated, he killed him and his two sons." – There is also a *good banquet*, and it is threefold: *good, better*, and *best*. The first is a banquet of *compassion*. About this Luke 14:13 below says: "When you give a banquet, invite the poor and the crippled." – The second is the banquet of *love*. Of this The Song of Songs 5:1 speaks: "Eat, O friends, and drink, and be inebriated, my dearly beloved." – The third is a banquet of *delight*. Isaiah 25:6 states: "The Lord . . . will make unto all peoples on this mountain a banquet, a banquet of fat things, . . . full of marrow, of purified wine." – The first type of banquet is permitted. The second type is forbidden. The third is recommended.[60]

29. Third, concerning *the persuasive rationale* the text continues: *lest perhaps they also invite you in return and a recompense be made to you.* For the person who performs deeds for an earthly reward only receives an earthly and temporal recompense. For an eternal reward

---

[60] See Hugh of St. Cher, p. 218v, c where he treats six types of banquets. There is significant correspondence between Hugh's treatment and that of Bonaventure, and it is obvious that Bonaventure's exposition is more polished. Hugh writes: "A banquet of compassion for God's sake, as here. Isaiah 58d[7]: The needy and the wanderers, etc. Tobit 2a[2]: Go, and bring in others, etc. Of one's household. In this a good of nature. Job 1[4]: They gave banquets, etc. Genesis 43[16]: Joseph commanded the steward of his house, saying: Bring in, etc. Of goods, this is neither good nor evil. So here: Do not invite, etc. 1 Samuel 3d[20–21]: David made a banquet for Abner and his men who came with him. And Abner said to David: I will rise and I will gather, etc. Of gluttony. This is evil. Romans 13d[13]: Not in profligate living and drunkenness. James 5a[5]: You have feasted upon earth, etc. Luke 16e[19] below: There was a certain rich man. Proverbs 23c[21]: They who give themselves to drinking and who consort together, etc. Of treachery. 1 Kings 13e[= 2 Samuel 13:27]: Absalom made a banquet. I Maccabees 16c[16]: Ptolemy rose up, etc. Of vainglory. Mark 6c[21]: About Herod. Daniel 5a[1]: King Belshazzar gave a grand banquet, etc."

is transformed into a temporal one on account of the love of *glory*. Matthew 6:1 has: "Take heed not to perform your righteousness before men and women, in order to be seen by them. Otherwise, you will have no reward with your Father in heaven." Wherefore, Matthew says this about the hypocrites in the same chapter: "Amen, I say to you that they have received their reward" (verse 2). On account of the love of *earthliness*. So about this Exodus 1:21 says: "The midwives feared God, and God built houses for them." The Glossa says that "eternal reward was changed into a temporal reward for them."[61] On account of the love of *one's flesh and blood*. Matthew 10:37 reads: "The person who loves father or mother more than me is not worthy of me." And the reason for this is given in Matthew 6:24: "No one can serve two masters." And as Ambrose says: "Intention stamps its name on your work."[62] So the person who performs a deed for the sake of a temporal reward is stripped of an eternal reward, because heaven is not due to any work that was performed for a worldly purpose. – But contrariwise, those things which are done for God's sake, are worthy of a double reward. So 1 Timothy 4:8 states: "Godliness is profitable in all respects, since it has the promise of the present life and of future life." And there-

---

[61] On p. 367, n. 9 QuarEd state that this is the Glossa Ordinaria on Exodus 1:20, which is taken from Book XVIII, chapter 3, n. 6 of Gregory's *Moralia*. In order to understand Gregory and Bonaventure, readers should recall that in saving the Hebrew baby boys, the Egyptian midwives lied to the Egyptian king. Gregory writes: "In this recompense (*The Lord built houses for them*) it is broadly recognized that the sin of lying is rewarded. For their benignity they have a reward which could have been a recompense of eternal life for them, but was reduced to an earthly recompense because the sin of lying was mixed in, so that in their life, which they wanted to protect by lying, they are receiving a reward for the good things they did, etc."

[62] On p. 367, n. 11 QuarEd cite Book I, chapter 30, n. 147 of Ambrose's *De Officiis*: *Affectus tuus nomen imponit operi tuo* ("Your desire stamps its name on your work"). In his commentary on Luke 11:34 (#73) above Bonaventure also quotes this sentence from Ambrose.

fore, the Lord said in Matthew 6:33: "Seek first the kingdom of God and his justice, and all these things will be given to you besides." But it is said to the earthly man in Luke 16:25 below: "Son, remember that during your life you received good things and Lazarus in like manner evil things. But now he is comforted here, but you are tormented."

30. (Verse 13). *But when you give a banquet.* After he had held them back from earthly geniality, here in a second point *he urges them to divine charity.* He also does this in a threefold manner, namely, by *the commendation of fraternal compassion, the assignation of the reason bolstering the commendation, the approbation of the reason which had bolstered the commendation.*

So first, with regard to *the commendation of fraternal compassion* the text reads: *But when you give a banquet, invite the poor,* on account of a lack of external goods. Isaiah 58:7 says: "Break your bread with the hungry, and bring the needy and the wanderers into your house." And this was commanded in the Law. Deuteronomy 15:11 reads: "The poor will not be absent in the land of your habitation. Therefore, I command you to open your hand to your needy and poor brother, who lives with you in the land."[63] To this poor person you must open your hand, and especially to the just. So it is said in Sirach 9:22: "Let just men be your guests, and let your glory be in the fear of the Lord."[64] And it is said in Tobit 2:1–2: "When there was a festival and a good dinner was prepared in Tobit's house, he said to his son: Go, and bring some of our tribe who fear God, to feast with us." Thus,

---

[63] On p. 368, n. 1 QuarEd quote the Glossa Interlinearis: "*Invite the poor,* from whom you can expect nothing in the present."
[64] See Hugh of St. Cher, p. 219 g and m, where he also cites Isaiah 58:7 and Sirach 9:22.

Sirach 12:5–6 states: "Give to the good, and receive not a sinner. Do good to the humble, and give not to the ungodly."[65] – Nevertheless, this passage does not exclude the giving of alms to other poor people. These, too, should be invited, as Chrysostom makes clear in his Seventy-ninth Homily on Matthew which reads: *"As long as you did not do it for one of these least ones, you did not do it for me.*[66] The Lord says this, not only about his disciples, not only about those who have chosen the monks' way of life, but about every believer. For it is just that the person who believes in God should enjoy the respect of everyone, even if he is a servant, even if he is among those who beg in the market place. And if we despise such a person who is naked or hungry, we will hear these words," etc.[67] – *The crippled*, on account of a defect in strength. Sirach 7:39 says: "Be not slow to visit the sick. For by these things you will be confirmed in love." According to Matthew 25:36 the Lord will say: "I was sick, and you visited me." For the person who condescends to another's sickness extends to Christ what he does for the ill person. – *Lame and blind*, on account of a defect in one's members. Luke 14:21 below has: "Go out into the streets and lanes of the city and bring in here the poor and the crippled, the blind and the lame." And this is

---

[65] See Hugh of St. Cher, p. 219m, who also quotes Tobit 2:2 and Sirach 12:5–6.
[66] Matthew 25:45.
[67] On p. 368, n. 4 QuarEd cite Chrysostom's Homily (alias 80.[codd. 60], n. 1. See PG 58:718: "What do you say? They are your brothers. Why do you call them least? Behold, they are certainly your brothers, for they are humble, poor, abject. For he specially invites these to fraternity: the nobodies, those held in contempt. He does not invite only the monks, or those who dwell on the mountain tops, but individual believers, even if they are seculars, even if they are hungry, famished, naked, wayfarers. None of these are exempt from care. For baptism also makes them a brother, and sharer in the divine mysteries." Bonaventure's quotation seems like a summary. As far as I can ascertain, Hugh of St. Cher does not cite this passage from Chrysostom.

indeed right, because mercy must be extended to those in misery and assistance given to those who suffer penury. So Mark 8:2 states: "I have compassion on the crowd, for behold, they have now been with me for three days and have nothing to eat."

31. (Verse 14). Second, relative to *the assignation of the reason bolstering the commendation* the text continues: *And blessed shall you be, because they have nothing by which to repay you.* Therefore, it is necessary that someone else repay for them. Proverbs 19:17 reads: "The person who has mercy on the poor lends to the Lord."[68] What follows speaks to the immensity of the reward: *For you will be repaid in the resurrection of the just,* that is, in eternal glory. About this resurrection Revelation 20:6 says: "Blessed and holy is the person who takes part in the first resurrection." And Luke 20:35–36 below has: "Those who will be accounted worthy of that world and of the resurrection . . . will be equal to the Angels and are sons of God, since they are sons of the resurrection." In this resurrection the evil will rise to death, but the just to life. John 5:29 states: "They who have done good will come forth unto resurrection of life, but they who have done evil unto resurrection of judgment." In this judgment recompense will be given to the merciful. So Sirach 12:2 reads: "Do good to the just, and you will find great recompense. And if not from him, then certainly from God." And especially concerning almsgiving. So Matthew 25:34–35 has: "Come, blessed of my Father, take possession of the kingdom. . . . I was hungry, and you gave me to eat," etc. And thus Matthew 5:7 states: "Blessed are the merciful, for they will receive mercy." So the recompense of happiness is especially given for

---

[68] Proverbs 19:17 reads in full: "The person who has mercy on the poor lends to the Lord, and he will repay him."

works of compassion. For which reason Sirach 17:18–19 says: "The alms of a man is like a purse with him and will preserve the grace of the person like the apple of the eye. And afterward he will rise up and will render them their reward, to each one upon his head."[69] – Now the reason for this is that no one is worthy of mercy unless that person shows mercy, for James 2:13 states: "Judgment is without mercy to the person who has not shown mercy." And no one comes to eternal beatitude except by the way of mercy. The Psalm says: "Human beings and beasts you will save, O Lord. How you have multiplied your mercy, O God" (35:7–8). And again the Letter to Titus notes: "Not by the works of righteousness that we ourselves did, but according to his mercy he saved us."[70]

32. (Verse 15). Third, concerning *the approbation of the reason which had bolstered the commendation* the text says: *When one of those who were at table with him heard these things. He heard,*[71] I say, not only with his bodily ears, but also with the ear of his heart, according to what Revelation 2:7 says: "The person who has an ear, let him hear what the Spirit says to the churches." And since the person who hears in this way believes, according to what Romans 10:17 states: "Faith depends on hearing, and hearing on the word of Christ," that is, the person who comes to faith through hearing renders testimony by speaking and confessing; Job 29:11 has: "The ear that heard me blessed me, and the eye that

---

[69] Bonaventure is wont to quote Sirach 17:18. See, e.g., his commentary on Luke 6:11 (#23) above.
[70] Titus 3:5.
[71] On p. 369, n. 1 QuarEd cite the Glossa Interlinearis: "*When he heard these things,* that those who receive the poor will be blessed in the resurrection."

saw me gave witness to me," the text adds:[72] *Blessed is the person who will feast in the kingdom of God*, as if to say: Better is the recompense that will take place in the resurrection of the dead than that which is in the present, because here it is pitiful, but there it is blessed. The Psalmist says: "Better is one day in your courts than a thousand" (83:11). So Revelation 19:9 reads: "Blessed are they who are invited to the wedding banquet of the Lamb."

33. And note that the food that will be in the kingdom of God will not be fleshly, but spiritual food. And this bread is the Uncreated Word and the Incarnate Word. Truly, we eat this bread on our journey *sacramentally*, according to what 1 Corinthians 11:28 has: "Let a person prove himself, and so let him eat of that bread and drink of the cup." But in the celestial homeland we will eat *spiritually*, by seeing face to face. John 6:52 states: "If anyone eats of this bread, he will live forever."[73] For John 17:3 says: "This is eternal life that they may know you the only true God and him whom you have sent, Jesus Christ." This bread is promised to us to be eaten after our departure from this life, "when the Lord will give sleep to his beloved. Behold, the heritage of the Lord is children. The reward, the fruit of the womb."[74] For just

---

[72] I have kept this long sentence intact, so that my readers might feel how uncharacteristic it is to Bonaventure's style.

[73] On p. 369, n. 4 QuarEd helpfully refer to Augustine's Sermon 112, n. 5. See *The Works of Saint Augustine: Sermons III/4 (94A–147A) on the New Testament*, translation and notes by Edmund Hill (Brooklyn: New City Press, 1992). I modify Hill's translation on pp. 149–150: "...*Blessed is the one who eats bread in the kingdom of God*. He was sighing for it as though it were a long way off, and there was the bread itself seated in his presence. What, I mean to say, is the bread of the kingdom of God, anything but the one who says, *I am the living bread, who have come down from heaven* (John 6:41)?"

[74] Psalm 126:2–3.

as no one comes to the sleep of rest except through *six days of labor*, so too *six days of bread*, which are preparatory to that eternal food, which we will eat in the celestial homeland, precede the eating of this bread.

34. The first bread is that of *the sorrow of repentance*. The Psalm has: "My tears have been my bread day and night" (41:4). And again the Psalm says: "Rise up after you have been sitting, you that eat the bread of sorrow" (126:2). Concerning this bread it is said in Genesis 21:14 by way of a figure: Abraham gave Hagar "bread and a container of water," and she went off into the desert. – The second is the bread of *the work of justice*. Genesis 3:19 reads: "In the sweat of your face you will eat your bread." The Psalm states: "You will eat the works of your hands. Blessed are you, and it will be well with you" (127:2). – The third is the bread of *the instruction of teaching*. Matthew 4:4 says: "Not by bread alone does a human person live, but by every word that comes forth from the mouth of God." Of this bread it is said in Lamentations 4:4: "The little ones have asked for bread, and there was no one to break it for them." – The fourth is the bread of *the Sacrament of the Eucharist*, about which John 6:52 has: "The bread that I will give, is my flesh," etc. And Matthew 26:26 reads: "While they were at supper, Jesus took bread." – The fifth is the bread of *internal consolation*. 1 Samuel 30:11–12 states: "They gave the Egyptian boy bread. ... When he had eaten it, his spirit returned, and he was refreshed."[75] And Wisdom 16:20 says: "You have given them bread from

---

[75] Bonaventure has adapted 1 Samuel 30:11–12 to his purposes by, among other things, changing an "Egyptian man" into an "Egyptian boy" and by not mentioning the water, figs, and raisins that were also given to the man to eat.

heaven . . . having," etc.[76] – The sixth is the bread of *supernal contemplation*. Concerning this Genesis 49:20 reads: "Asher, his bread will be bountiful, and he will present delicacies to kings." Proverbs 9:5 says: "Come. Eat my bread and drink my wine, which I have mixed for you."[77] Sirach 15:3 has: "Wisdom will feed him with the bread of life and understanding and will give him the water of salutary wisdom to drink."

35. Through these six breads one comes to the seventh, which is found here: *Blessed is the person who will eat bread in the kingdom of God.*[78] But there are many who

---

[76] Wisdom 16:20 reads: "Instead of these things you fed your people with the food of angels and gave them bread from heaven, prepared without labor, having in it all that is delicious, and the sweetness of every taste."

[77] Wisdom is the speaker.

[78] On p. 369, n. 13 QuarEd helpfully refer to Hugh of St. Cher and Bernard of Clairvaux for parallels to Bonaventure's "seven breads." In his "Sermo Primus, Dominica VI post Pentecosten" Bernard preaches about Mark 8:1–9 and in, n. 4 mentions "the seven breads." I translate from SBOp 5:208 and quote those scripture passages that parallel Bonaventure: "The first bread is the word of God. . . . The second is the bread of obedience. . . . The third bread is holy meditation. . . . The fourth bread is the tears of those who are praying. And the fifth is the labor of repentance. Do not be amazed that I call labor or tears bread, unless perhaps what you read in the Prophet has slipped your memory: *You fed us with the bread of tears* and likewise in another Psalm: *The labors*, he says, *of your hands, for you will eat. Blessed are you , and it will be well with you.* The sixth bread is joyous social unanimity. . . . Furthermore, the seventh bread is the Eucharist, for *the bread*, he says, *which I give is my flesh for the life of the world.*" In his "Sermo Tertius in Dedicatione Ecclesiae," n. 2 Bernard mentions three breads: "The bread of tears, the bread of obedience, and the living bread from heaven." See SBOp. 5:380. See Hugh of St. Cher, 219v, p: "The bread of sorrow and repentance. Psalm 41[4]: My tears have been to me. The same [Psalm 126:2]: Rise up after you have been sitting, you that eat the bread of sorrow. Genesis 21b[14]: Abraham gave Hagar the bread of repentance and a container of water, and she went off into the desert. Of labor. Genesis 3d[19]: In the sweat of your face, etc. Psalm 127[2]: The works of your hands, etc. Of the word of God. Lamentations 4a[4]: The little ones have asked for bread, etc. Of divine consolation. 1 Samuel 30c[11–12]: When the Egyptian had eaten the bread, his spirit re-

are so miserable that they cannot pass from bread to bread. So they do not come to the bread of that heavenly banquet, for they refuse to eat the other preparatory breads. – A figure of these seven breads is found in Matthew 15:36: "Jesus, taking seven loaves of bread, blessed."[79] For by beginning with the bread of *the sorrow of repentance* one proceeds to the bread of *eternal refreshment*. The person who eats this bread will have no lack whatsoever. John 6:35 reads: "I am the bread of life. The person who comes to me will not hunger." For that person will not develop an aversion to that bread, according to what Sirach 24:29–31 states: "Those who eat me will still hunger, and those who drink me will still thirst. The person who listens to me will not be confounded. . . . Those who explain me will have eternal life."

Luke 14:16–24
CHRIST INSTRUCTS THOSE INVITED TO THE ETERNAL BANQUET

36. (Verse 16). *But he said to him.* After he had given instruction to those who had been invited to a wedding banquet and those who are inviting people to their household banquet, he now *provides instruction for those who are to be invited to the eternal banquet* by means of a parable. He makes three points. The first is *the invitation of many.* The second is *the excuses of those invited,* where verse 18 reads: *And they all with one ac-*

---

turned, etc. Of the Eucharist. John 6e[52]: The bread that I will give, etc. Of contemplation. Genesis 49c[20]: Asher, his bread is bountiful, and he will present delicacies to kings. Of eternal refreshment, as here: Blessed is the person who will eat bread in the kingdom of God. But there are many who cannot pass from one bread to another."
[79] On p. 369, n. 14 QuarEd correctly indicate that this is not an exact quotation from Matthew 15:36 and may have been influenced by Matthew 26:26.

count began to excuse themselves. The third is *the repulsion of those who contemned the invitation* where verse 21 says: *And the servant returned,* etc.

Now concerning *the invitation of many* the Evangelist introduces three things, namely, *the preparation of the eternal refreshment, the invitation of many to faith, the stirring of faith to fervor.*

So first, with regard to *the preparation of the eternal refreshment* the text says: *A certain man gave a great supper,* that is, Christ has prepared the eternal refreshment. For Christ is said to be *a certain man* in a singular sense, for he was conceived without male seed, born without his Mother suffering, free from every sin, and died for the sake of the sin of men and women. About this man it is said in the Psalm: "The man was born in her, and the Most High himself has founded her" (86:5). This man *gave a supper,* for he has prepared the highest and ultimate refreshment. So the Glossa comments: "This banquet is not said to be *a dinner,* but *a supper,* for after *the dinner,* of which Matthew treats, only *supper* remains, and after *supper* there is no more banqueting."[80] About this supper Revelation 19:9 states: "Blessed are those who are invited to the wedding supper of the Lamb." This supper is said to be *great,* because it is *too great to be estimated.* So Genesis 15:1 reads: "I am . . . your reward, exceedingly great." Because it is *unending.* Baruch 3:24–25 has: "O Israel, how great is

---

[80] On p. 370, n. 5 QuarEd refer to the Glossa Ordinaria on Luke 14:16. The Glossa follows Bede, who, for his part, quotes extensively from Homily 36, n. 2 of GGHG. See CCSL cxx, pp. 278–279 and PL 76:1267AB. Americans may have trouble understanding the ancient and medieval differentiation between "dinner" (*prandium*) and "supper" (*coena*), for we use them almost interchangeably. In Italy the 1 p.m. meal is *pranzo* ("dinner") while the 8 p.m. meal is *cena* ("supper"). While there may be some sort of relaxation after "supper," it is the last meal of the day.

the house of the Lord and how vast is the place of his possession. It is great and has no end, high and immense." Now it cannot be estimated both because of its food and because of the one who serves it – God and the supreme good. Luke 22:29–30 below says: "I appoint to you a kingdom, just as my Father has appointed one to me, so that you may eat and drink at my table in my kingdom," etc. About this the Psalm has: "They will be inebriated with the plenty of your house, and you will make them drink of the torrent of your pleasure" (35:9).

37. Second, concerning *the invitation of many to faith* the text adds: *He invited many*, to faith, for they are from every state of life and nation and age, according to what Joel 2:15–16 reads: "Sanctify a fast, call a solemn assembly, gather together the people, sanctify the congregation, assemble the elderly and gather together the little ones and those sucking at the breast." Those who are so invited are consequently called to the eternal refreshment. So 1 Peter 5:10 says: "But the God of grace, who has called us unto eternal glory in Christ Jesus, will himself perfect," etc.[81] So then *he invites many* to show his supreme liberality and benignity. But as a consequence *he chooses few*, so that he may show the severity of judgment. For this reason Matthew 20:16 has: "Many are called, but few are chosen." Therefore, this invitation of a multitude is comparable to a catch of fish in which the net takes in every kind of fish. Matthew 13:47 states: "The kingdom of the heavens is like a net cast into the sea that gathered in fish of every kind," etc.

---

[81] On p. 370, n. 8 QuarEd correctly mention that the Vulgate has *omnis gratiae* ("of all grace") and *aeternam suam gloriam* ("his eternal glory") while Bonaventure has *gratiae* ("of grace") and *aeternam gloriam* ("eternal glory").

38. (Verse 17). Third, with regard to *the stirring of the same multitude to fervor* the text continues: *And he sent his servant at supper time to tell those invited to come.* "That *servant*," as the Glossa says, "is the order of preachers,"[82] who, although they are many, are nonetheless understood under the category of *a single servant* who stands for the unity of the office. Proverbs 9:3 says this about this mission: "Wisdom sent her maids to invite them to the tower and to walls of the city." About this servant Isaiah 49:5-6 states: "And now the Lord, who formed me from the womb to be his servant, . . . says this: It is a small thing that you should be my servant to raise up the tribes of Jacob and to convert the dregs of Israel. . . . I have given you to be the light of the Gentiles, so that you may be my salvation even to the farthest part of the earth." – *The hour of the supper* is the end of the world, that is the time of the sixth age,[83] according to what 1 Corinthians 10:11 reads: "We are those upon whom the end of the world has come."[84] And

---

[82] On p. 370, n. 10 QuarEd cite the Glossa Ordinaria (from Bede, who borrows from Gregory): "The hour of the supper, the end of the world. So the Apostle (1 Corinthians 10:11): *We are those upon whom the end of the world has come.* At the time of this end a servant is sent, that is, the order of preachers, to those invited, etc." See CCSL cxx, p. 278 and PL 76:1267A. The editors also quote the Glossa Interlinearis: "*And he sent his servant,* the order of preachers." In Bonaventure's day "the order of preachers" referred primarily to the Dominicans and Franciscans.
[83] See The Prologue, n. 2–3 of *The Works of Bonaventure II: The Breviloquium*, translated by José de Vinck (Paterson: St. Anthony Guild Press, 1963), 10–11: "The sixth age, when Christ was born in the form of man who, in turn, is the true image of God, corresponds to the Sixth day, when the first man was brought to life. The seventh age, which is, for souls, eternal rest, corresponds to the Seventh Day, when God *rested from all His work of creation.* . . . The sixth (age) is called old age, for the world's sixth age ends with the day of judgment, but is enlightened with the wisdom of Christ's teachings. . . ."
[84] On p. 370, n. 11 QuarEd rightly mention that the Vulgate does not read *Nos sumus* ("We are those"). See the previous note and the quotation from the Glossa Ordinaria, which with Bonaventure has *Nos sumus* ("We are those").

1 John 2:18 has: You have heard that "it is the last hour."[85] – These servants say to those invited that *they should come to the supper. They should come,* I say, because of *internal desire and fervor,* according to what the Psalmist says: "My soul has thirsted for God, the living fountain.[86] When will I come and appear before the face of God?" (41:3). These servants must *preach,* according to what Isaiah 2:3 reads: "Come, let us go up to the mountain of God and to the house of the God of Jacob, and he will teach us," etc., for in accordance with Revelation 22:17: "and let the person who hears say: Come."[87]

39. And since nothing stirs the desire to come to God as much as a consideration of the rewards involved, the text adds: *For everything is now ready.* For *the dwelling places are ready.* John 14:2–3 reads: "In my Father's house there are many mansions. Were it not so, I would have told you, because I go to prepare a place for you. And if I go and prepare a place for you, I am coming again and I will take you to myself."[88] – Likewise, *joys are prepared and ready.* 1 Corinthians 2:9 says: "Eye has not seen and ear has not heard, nor has it entered into the human heart, what things God has prepared for those who love him." This passage has been taken from

---

[85] See Hugh of St. Cher, p. 220e where he also quotes 1 Corinthians 10:11 (with *nos sumus*) and 1 John 2:18.

[86] On p. 370, n. 12 QuarEd correctly indicate that the Vulgate reads *fortem* ("strong") while Bonaventure has *fontem* ("fountain"). The first part of Psalm 41:3 reads: "My soul has thirsted for the strong living God."

[87] On pp. 370–371, n. 13 QuarEd cite the Glossia Ordinaria (from Gregory and Bede) on Luke 14:17: "The servant is sent, that is, the order of preachers, to those invited through the Law and the Prophets, so that, aversion to food having been removed, they may prepare themselves to taste the supper, *for everything is now ready.* For Christ having been immolated, the entrance into the kingdom lies open." See CCSL cxx, p. 279 and PL 76:1267C.

[88] See Hugh of St. Cher, p. 220f, who also quotes John 14:2–3.

Isaiah 64:4: "The eye has not seen, O God, except through you, what things you have prepared for those who wait for you." – Furthermore, *the table is prepared and ready.* The Psalm says: "You have prepared a table before me, against those that afflict me," etc. (22:5). – Moreover, *the spouse* has prepared herself together with those who have been predestined to life. Revelation 19:7 reads: "The marriage of the Lamb has come, and his spouse has prepared herself." For as it is said in Matthew 25:10: "Those who were prepared enter with him to the wedding feast, and the door was shut."

40. (Verse 18). *And they all with one accord began.* After the invitation of the multitude the next point occurs here: *the excuses of those invited.* For many come to faith, who, nevertheless, do not want to attain to love on account of their inclination to vices, which they mask under the veil of an excuse.[89] – *And they all with one accord began to excuse.* The Glossa observes: "Everyone, who loves earthly matters more than heavenly, has an excuse, even while saying that he is striving for heavenly things."[90] Therefore, since there is a threefold cause of all sin,[91] which draws us away from the love of Christ, the text here introduces, via the three kinds of excuses, the three types of men and women who reject his invitation. The first of these comes from *the ambition of pride.*

---

[89] On p. 371, n. 5 QuarEd cite Homily 36, n. 2 of GGHG. See PL 76:1267A: "Who *invited many,* but few come, for they at one time subjected themselves to him out of faith, but gainsay his eternal banquet by living evilly."

[90] On p. 371, n. 6 QuarEd state that this is the Glossa Ordinaria (from Gregory). See PL 76:1263AB. See Hugh of St. Cher, p. 220g, who quotes this same passage from "Gregory."

[91] On p. 371, n. 7 QuarEd appropriately cite 1 John 2:16: "All that is in the world is concupiscence of the flesh and concupiscence of the eyes and the pride of life."

The second from *the anxiety of avarice*. The third, then, from *the lust of voluptuousness*.

41. So then relative to the first excuse, which stems from *the ambition of pride*, the text says: *The first said to him:*[92] *I have bought a country estate.*[93] This *first individual* is a proud fellow, who always wants to obtain the first place. Sirach 10:14–15 reads: "The beginning of man's pride is to fall away from God, because his heart has strayed from him who made him. For pride is the beginning of all sin." It was this man's desire *to buy a country estate*, because he is seeking nothing other than to domineer and be pre-eminent. Wherefore, Augustine writes: "In the purchase of a country estate domination and pride are noted. For to have a country estate means to subject people to yourself and is pride, the first of the vices."[94] The proud person makes this *purchase* by giving his soul over to the devil in servitude, for as Job 41:25 says: "He beholds every lofty thing, and he is king over all the children of pride." So while he is desirous of being lord over men and women, he becomes the slave of vices. And this is an especially bad deal.

---

[92] On p. 371, n. 8 QuarEd accurately state that the Vulgate reads *ei* ("to him") while Bonaventure has *illi* ("to him").

[93] I have translated *villa* by "country estate," for that more accurately conveys Bonaventure's (and Augustine's) point than the more usual "farm." In his Sermon 112 Augustine deals with a country estate or manor on which the owner employs, dominates, and bosses around many servants and thus swells his pride with illusions of power and grandeur.

[94] On p. 371, n. 9 QuarEd cite Augustine's Sermon 112, chapter 2, n. 2: "In the purchase of a country estate domineering is noted. Thus, pride is being castigated. For it is pleasurable to have a country estate, to hold onto it, to possess it, to subject the people on it to oneself, to domineer. It's an evil vice, that first vice." They conclude by saying that Bonaventure is citing Augustine by way of the Glossa Ordinaria on Luke 14:18. See Hugh of St. Cher, p. 220h, who also quotes Augustine in a version that agrees thematically, but not verbatim with Bonaventure's citation.

Therefore, such an individual confesses that he is a slave when he says: *And I must go out and see it.* Pride creates this *necessity* and causes people to be mercurial and to depart from themselves in a certain manner. Nahum 1:11 reads: "Out of you will depart one that plots evil against the Lord, contriving treachery in his mind."[95] – And since vice covers itself with *the cloak of virtue*, because the proud person wants to be seen as humble, the text adds: *I pray you, hold me excused.* The Glossa comments: "Pray for me, for I am a sinful man."[96] He humbles himself by his words, although he remains proud in his heart. So Gregory says: "When he says: *I pray you, have me excused,* that's humility sounding forth in his voice. But when *he despises the invitation to come,* that's pride in action."[97] Such people are designated by those of whom it is said in Matthew 27:29: "Bending the knee before him, they mocked him." And of such a person it is said in Sirach 19:23: "There is a person who humbles himself wickedly, and his interior is full of deceit." And of such persons the Prophet speaks in the Psalm: "Incline not my heart to evil words to make excuses upon excuses in sins" (140:4). And therefore, from an opposite perspective Proverbs 18:17 says this about the just man: "The just man is the first one to accuse himself."

---

[95] On p. 371, n. 11 QuarEd cite the Glossa Interlinearis: "*I have bought a country estate.* I have acquired it through great labor or I have accepted it at the price of the faith I have in God. *And I must go out,* from internal contemplation, *and see it,* to apply all my efforts to it."

[96] On p. 371, n. 12 QuarEd state that this is the Glossa Interlinearis, taken from Homily 36, n. 4 of GGHG. See PL 76:1268C. Gregory's words are taken out of context.

[97] On p. 371, n. 12 QuarEd state that Bonaventure cites Gregory's interpretation via the Glossa Ordinaria on Luke 14:18. See PL 76:1268C.

42. (Verse 19). Second, concerning *the second excuse*, which stems from *the anxiety of avarice*, the text says: *And another said: I have bought five yoke of oxen.* For the anxiety of avarice causes a person to seek for and deal only with earthly matters. Therefore, it is compared to the labor of oxen, whose task it is to plough and work the land. And there are said to be *five yoke of oxen* on account of the five senses oriented towards these earthly concerns. So the Glossa observes: "These *yoke of oxen* are mentioned because earthly matters are controlled by them. For oxen are oriented towards the earth."[98] They can also be said to be *a yoke* because they collar and control the neck, forcing everything towards the earth. They sell the soul for the sake of the earth. Sirach 10:3 reads: "There is no more wicked thing than to love money. For this person puts his soul up for sale; because while he is still alive, he has thrown away what is most precious." For since, as it is said in Matthew 6:21, "where your treasure is, there also is your heart,"[99] and the treasure of the avaricious person is outside himself, namely, on the earth, it follows that the most precious things of the avaricious person are thrown onto the earth. So it is necessary that he be oppressed by the yoke of servitude, for he has sold himself. Thus Sirach 27:2 has: "In the midst of buying and selling[100] one will

---

[98] On p. 372, n. 2 QuarEd state that this Glossa is not from the glosses of Strabo or Lyrannus, but from Sermon 112, chapter 3, n. 3 of Augustine: "Why are they called yoke of oxen? For through these senses the earthly things of the flesh are sought out. For oxen are oriented towards the earth," etc. Bonaventure does not mention the basic insights of Augustine: 1) the five yoke of oxen are the five senses; 2) the five senses are paired: two eyes, two ears, two nostrils; taste comes from both tongue and palate; touch is both external and internal feeling. See Hugh of St. Cher, p. 220p, who states Augustine's basic insights, but does not attribute them to Augustine.

[99] See also Luke 12:34.

[100] Bonaventure inverts the Vulgate's *venditionis et emptionis* "selling and buying."

be distressed by sins." – For avarice renders a person anxious and curious.[101] So the text continues: *And I am on my way to try them,* for the avaricious person is continually bothered with superfluities. So the Glossa comments: "It is fitting that a prying nature is designated by the five senses. While a person is investigating the life of his neighbor on the outside, he is ignorant of his own inner life. And the more the prying person knows about the stranger, the less he knows about himself."[102] – And note that love has only *one yoke,* for it reduces all solicitude to one, according to what Luke 10:42 above says: "One thing is necessary."[103] And Micah 6:8 reads: "To walk solicitously with your God," etc. And Matthew 11:30 has: "My yoke is easy," etc. And Lamentations 3:27 reads: "It is good for a man when he has borne the yoke of the Lord[104] from his youth." But inquisitiveness is concerned with *five* things in accordance with the totality of the senses. So Qoheleth 7:30 states: "God has made the human person right, and he has entangled himself with an infinity of questions." – And since the vice of cupidity and avarice cloaks itself as *a type of providence,* the text adds: *I pray you hold me excused.* But to such people can be said what Jeremiah 2:33–34 has: "Why do you endeavor to show that your ways[105] are good in search of my love, you who have also

---

[101] In what follows I have taken the liberty of translating *curiositas/curiosus* as "curious, prying, inquisitive" depending on the perceived context.
[102] On p. 372, n. 5 QuarEd state that this is the Glossa Ordinaria (from Gregory, who is followed by Bede). See PL 76:1268BC and CCSL cxx, p. 279.
[103] See Hugh of St. Cher, p. 220q, who also quotes Luke 10:42, but none of the other scripture passages that Bonaventure cites.
[104] The Vulgate does not read *Domini* ("of the Lord").
[105] On p. 372, n. 8 QuarEd correctly indicate that the Vulgate reads *viam* ("way").

taught your evils as your very many[106] ways, while on your clothing is found the blood of the souls of the poor and the innocent?"

43. (Verse 20). Third, relative to *the third excuse*, which stems from *the lust of voluptuousness*, the text continues: *And another said: I have married a wife, and therefore, I cannot come.* This *wife* is concupiscence of the flesh, about which Qoheleth 7:27 says: "I have found a woman more bitter than death, who is a hunter's snare, and her heart is a net."[107] This vice is said to be a *wife* because of the strong attachment of lust. 1 Corinthians 6:16 reads: "Do you not know that he who clings to a woman[108] becomes one body with her? For the two, it says, will be one flesh." – And so the text adds: *And therefore, I cannot come.* It does not say: *Hold me excused*, because only the sin of the flesh, which is scarcely able to pass itself off as *a type of virtue*, is least to be excused. But nevertheless, in truth it is greatly to be excused on account of the greater drive of concupiscence, according to what Romans 7:23 states: "I see another law in my members, warring against the law of my mind and making me prisoner in the servitude of sin."[109] And for such a reason he says: *I cannot come*, for as Bernard says, "Just as fire and water cannot mix, so too spiritual and carnal delights do not come together in the same person."[110] But in making such an excuse, the man lies, for, even if he be the slave of

---

[106] On p. 372, n. 8 QuarEd accurately mention that the Vulgate does not read *plurimas* ("very many").

[107] On p. 372, n. 9 QuarEd refer to Sermon 112, chapter 8, n. 6 of Augustine.

[108] On p. 372, n. 9 QuarEd correctly indicate that the Vulgate reads *meretrici* ("harlot").

[109] On p. 372, n. 10 QuarEd accurately mention that the Vulgate reads *in lege peccati* ("in the law of sin") while Bonaventure has *in servitutem peccati* ("in the servitude of sin").

[110] On p. 372, n. 11 QuarEd refer to Bernard's Letter 2, n. 10. See SBOp 7.20. Bonaventure's quotation is almost verbatim.

concupiscence, he may perform a good deed and in the actual performance of the deed possess the grace, through which he experiences *the ability* to overcome concupiscence.[111] So Romans 7:24–25 has: "Unhappy person that I am! Who will deliver me from the body of this death?" And the continuous response is: "The grace of God through our Lord Jesus Christ," for Philippians 2:13 says: "It is God who on account of his good pleasure works in you both the will and the performance." – And note here that although it is legitimate to have a wife, nonetheless on account of abuse and on account of vice associated with it *an evil thing* is understood by means of *a good thing*. For which reason even the Apostle says in 1 Corinthians 7:29: "It remains that those who have wives be as if they have none." So too the Glossa also says that "many take wives not for the sake of procreation, but for the sake of the desires of the flesh. So by this thing carnal pleasure is understood."[112] So it is not incongruous that *wife* by reason of *the sacramental bond* designates the Church, the spouse of Christ, and by reason of *lust* can designate the concupiscence of carnal pleasure.[113]

44. (Verse 21). *And the servant returned*, etc. After the invitation to the multitude and the excuses of those invited a third point is made, namely, *the repulsion of those who contemned the invitation*. About this the Evangelist introduces three issues: *the invitation to the*

---

[111] In articulating his theology of the relationship of the effects of original sin, grace, and free will, Bonaventure is severely brief.

[112] On p. 373, n. 1 QuarEd state that this is the Glossa Ordinaria (from Gregory, who is followed by Bede). See PL 76:1269A and CCSL cxx, p. 280.

[113] It is interesting to see Bonaventure deal in his age with the contemporary problem of the polyvalent nature of simile, metaphor, and symbol.

indigent, the compulsion of those neglected, and *the repulsion of those contemning.*

First, relative to *the invitation to the indigent,* which had its origin in the contempt of the others, the text says: *And the servant returned and reported these things to his master,* namely, the obduracy and rebellion of those invited. A servant reports these things, when the order of preachers does not seek its own comfort, but divine honor, so that just as he was sent by God with a commission of authority, so too may he return with purity of intention. And about such people it is said in Ezekiel 1:14: "The living creatures ran and returned like flashes of lightning." So Job 38:35 reads: "Can you send flashes of lightning, and they will go. And when they return, will they say to you: We are here?" The Glossa on this passage says: *"Lightnings burst through the sky* when preachers shine brilliantly with miracles. *Upon their return they say: Here we are,* because they acknowledge that whatever they have mightily done comes not through them, but from God."[114] Another interpretation is that *they return* to God through thanksgiving, according to what Qoheleth 1:7 states: "Unto the place from which they rivers come, they return to flow again." And since they cannot give thanks for the rebellion of those who heard, but rather lament over the abhorrence of sin, it follows that they are said *to report to the Lord,* just as it is said of the Apostles in Acts 4 that, after they have suffered maltreatment from the Jews, "they lifted up their voice with one accord to God and said: Lord, it is you who did make . . . all things, who

---

[114] On p. 373, n. 5 QuarEd state that this is the Glossa Ordinaria (from Book XXX, chapter 2, n. 8 of Gregory's *Moralia*) and discuss Gregory's original text. See Bonaventure's commentary on Luke 10:17 (#30) above where he quotes a more full version of this same Glossa.

spoke . . . through the mouth of our father David . . . : Why did the Gentiles rage" (verses 24–25). "Now, Lord, take note of their threats and grant to your servants to speak your word with all boldness" (verse 29). "When they had prayed, the place . . . was shaken" (verse 31). This shaking is to be understood as the commotion of God's wrath against the rebellion of those who had heard.

45. For this reason the text adds: *Then the master of the house was angry and said to his servant: Go out quickly into the streets and lanes of the city*, that is, engage in public preaching, according to what Proverbs 1:20–21 says: "Wisdom preaches abroad. She speaks forth in the streets. In front of multitudes she cries out; at the entrance of the gates of the city she utters her words." *This going out* is to engage in the work of preaching, according to what Matthew 13:3 states: "The sower went out to sow his seed." – And since, the proud having been rejected,[115] the humble are accepted, the text continues: *And bring in here the poor, and the crippled, and the blind, and the lame*. The Glossae provide three interpretations. In the first interpretation these words refer to *a defect in the natural order of things*. Thus, *the poor* are lacking in possessions. *The crippled* lack the power of their limbs. *The blind* have a defect in sight. *The lame* have a deficiency in walking. Looking at the literal sense, such persons are also admitted to the kingdom of the heaven.[116] 1 Corinthians 1:26–29 reads: "Consider

---

[115] On p. 373, n. 9 QuarEd cite Homily 36, n. 6 of GGHG. See PL 76:1269B: "Therefore, since the proud refuse to come, the poor are chosen."

[116] On p. 373, n. 11 QuarEd cite the Glossa Ordinaria (from Ambrose) apud Lyrannum: "He invites the poor and crippled, blind and lame, showing that *a deficiency in body* excludes no one from the kingdom, etc." See CCSL xiv, p. 284.

your own invitation,[117] brothers: that there were not many wise according to the flesh, not many mighty, not many noble. But the foolish things of the world God has chosen to put to shame the wise. And the weak things of the world God has chosen to put to shame the strong. And the base things of the world and the despised God has chosen, and the things that are not, to bring to naught the things that are, lest any flesh should glory in itself before him."

46. In another interpretation the text refers to *corrupting defects*. People are *poor* because of a lack of *grace*. *Crippled*, because of a lack of *virtue*. *Blind* because of a lack of *wisdom*. And *lame* because of a lack of *good will*. And nevertheless, God chooses and invites these, for as Matthew 9:13 says: "I have not come to call the just, but sinners to repentance."[118] So it was also said to the Pharisees in Matthew 21:31: "The tax collectors and harlots are entering the kingdom of God before you."[119]

47. In the third interpretation the text refers to *a defect in strength*. They are said to be *poor and crippled* relative to their own reputation. And indeed we understand those people to be *poor*, who place no confidence in extraordinary *opulence*. About these Proverbs 13:7 reads: "Another person is as it were poor, when he has great riches." We understand those people to be *crippled*, who

---

[117] On p. 373, n. 11 QuarEd correctly indicate that the Vulgate reads *Videte* ("See"). I have translated *vocationem* as "invitation" rather than "call" to fit the context of Bonaventure's interpretation of "those invited."

[118] The words *ad poenitentiam* ("to repentance") are not found in Matthew 9:13, but come from the parallel in Luke 5:32.

[119] On p. 373, n. 12 QuarEd cite Homily 36, n. 6 of GGHG. While the parallel to Bonaventure's interpretation is not too close, Gregory does says that sinners, too, are invited and come to the banquet. See PL 76:1269B.

place no confidence in their *strength*. 1 Corinthians 1:25: "The weakness of God is stronger than human beings." *Blind*, who place no confidence in their *knowledge*, that is, who consider themselves to be blind. So John 9:41 states: "If you were blind, you would not have sin. But now that you say, We sin, your sin remains." *Lame*, who place no confidence in their *rectitude*. So Jacob, after he had seen the Lord, is said to have come up lame in Genesis 32:31. The Lord brings such people into the banquet, that is, *the poor* through contempt of earthly opulence. The Psalm says: "God will spare the poor and the needy," etc. (71:13). *The crippled* through contempt of their self-reliance. Isaiah 40:31 has: "They who hope in the Lord will renew their strength." *The blind* through contempt of their own abilities. John 9:39 reads: "For judgment have I come into this world, that they who do not see may see," etc. *The lame* through contempt of their own righteousness. Isaiah 35:6 states: "Then will the lame leap like a hart, and the tongue of the dumb will be loosed." – And for the benefit of all these it is said in Luke 7:22 above: "The blind see, the lame walk, . . . the deaf hear, the dead rise, the poor have the gospel preached to them." For these are invited to and brought into life. – And this last interpretation seems to be more congruous than the previous ones, for "God resists the proud."[120]

48. (Verse 22). Second, with regard to *the compulsion of those neglected*, which follows the invitation of the humble, the text adds: *And the servant said: Master, your order has been carried out, and there is still room.* For there are not as many *humble* as predestined to life. There are not as many *willingly ready* for eternal life as predestined by God.

---

[120] 1 Peter 5:5.

49. (Verse 23). Thus the text continues: *Then the Master said to the servant: Go out into the highways and hedges.* By *highways and hedges*, which lie outside the city, are understood the sinners, who are outside ecclesiastical unity, and especially Gentiles. So Gregory observes: "When he invites those from *the lanes and streets*, he signifies the Jews, who knew how to observe the Law amidst urban existence. But when he invites those from *the highways and hedges*, he signifies the rustic people of the Gentiles."[121] And by means of this same reasoning *all sinners* can be understood, especially the lazy, who once invited are dragged along to do good. – So the text adds: *And compel them to come in*, namely, by the threat of eternal punishments and a display of present punishments. For, as Gregory says, "Evils, which press upon us here, compel us to run to God."[122] For this reason the Psalm says: "When he killed them, then they sought him" (77:34). Therefore, the servant of God compels these when he terrifies them by the threat of a severe judgment, according to what 2 Timothy 4:2 has: "Preach the word, be urgent in season, out of season. Reprove, entreat, rebuke," etc. – And *the reason* for this is the complement of the number of the elect. So the text continues: *so that my house may be filled*. The Glossa reads: "by the number of predestined believers, whose number will not remain unfilled."[123] Revelation 6:11 comments about this number: "Rest a little while longer, until the

---

[121] On p. 374, n. 5 QuarEd refer to Homily 36, n. 8 of GGHG and the Glossa Ordinaria apud Lyrannum on Luke 14:23. Bonaventure does not follow Gregory verbatim and may well be quoting the Glossa. See PL 76:1270CD.

[122] On p. 374, n. 6 QuarEd say that this interpretation is suggested in Homily 36, n. 9 of GGHG. In PL 76:1271A there might be a basis for Bonaventure's quotation. In his commentary on Luke 6:18 (#45) Bonaventure also quotes this passage from Gregory.

[123] On p. 374, n. 7 QuarEd state that this is the Glossa Interlinearis. See Hugh of St. Cher, p. 221b, who also quotes this Glossa.

number of your brothers . . . is filled."[124] Therefore, this *house will be filled*, when the totality of those chosen is saved. About these Revelation 7:9 says: "After these things I saw a great multitude, which no one could number." And Revelation 14:1 states: "I saw the Lamb standing upon Mount Zion and with him," etc.[125] And the canticle of Deuteronomy 32:8 has: "The Most High appointed the bounds of peoples according to the number of the children of Israel." Gregory says here that "as many men and women will be saved as angels have remained."[126] But whatever may be said about that, it is certain that the number of the elect will be *perfect*. As a figure of this it is said in Deuteronomy 33:2: "The Lord appeared from mount Paran, and with him thousands of Saints."

50. (Verse 24). Third, about *the rejection of those who contemn the invitation* the text says: *But I tell you that none of those men who were invited*, and have excused themselves, *will taste of my supper*.[127] For only the

---

[124] Bonaventure has turned third person verbs into second person ones and shortened the quotation. On p. 374, n. 7 QuarEd say that Bonaventure is quoting Revelation 6:11 from the response to the second reading from the first nocturn of Matins for the Feast of the Holy Innocents. See Hugh of St. Cher, p. 221b, who quotes Revelation 6:11 in full according to the Vulgate.

[125] Revelation 14:1 continues: "and with him a hundred and forty-four thousand having his name and the name of his Father written on their foreheads."

[126] On p. 374, n. 9 QuarEd state that Gregory's interpretation is found in Homily 34, n. 11 of his GGHG. See PL 76:1252C where Gregory quotes Deuteronomy 32:8 in his interpretation of Luke 15:1–10. Bonaventure's quotation is not exact. Hurst, p. 289 translates the pertinent passage: "We believe that as many of the human race ascend to there, as there were chosen angels who happened to remain there."

[127] On p. 374, n. 11 QuarEd cite the Glossa Interlinearis (from Gregory): ". . . even if they sometimes seek to enter through last minute repentance. So it is said (Matthew 25:12) to the foolish virgins: *Amen, I say to you: I do not know you*. Therefore, no one who has been

humble will attain to that supper. Matthew 18:3 reads: "Unless you turn and become like little children, you will not enter into the kingdom of the heavens." Wherefore, it is also said in the Psalm: "How great is the multitude of your delightfulness, O Lord, which you have hidden for those who fear you!" (30:20). For the Lord reserves it for *those who fear him*, but rejects the proud. "For if God did not spare the angels when they sinned, but by infernal ropes," etc. as it is said in 2 Peter 2:4. And later 2 Peter 2:9 has: "The Lord knows how to deliver the God-fearing from temptation, and to reserve the wicked . . . for torment." And on account of this Romans 11:20–21 reads: "Be not high-minded, but fear. For if God has not spared the natural branches, perhaps he may not spare you either." And so he says in Hebrews 2:1–3: "Therefore, we ought to observe more earnestly . . . lest perhaps we drift away. For if the word spoken by angels proved to be valid . . . how will we escape if we neglect so great a salvation?"

Luke 14:25–34
CHRIST INSTRUCTS THE CROWDS FOLLOWING HIM

51. (Verse 25). *Now great crowds were going along.* After he has confronted his detractors and given instruction to those banqueting, he here *gives instruction to those accompanying him.* Now this section is divided into two parts. In the first part he instructs *those travelling with him by explicit teaching* while in the second he uses *parabolic examples* where verse 28 reads: *For which of us wishing to build a tower,* etc. – Now he proceeds in this fashion in his teaching in *explicit words* about what

---

invited should excuse himself." See PL 76:1272BC. At best the Glossa is a paraphrase of Gregory.

is necessary to accompany Christ spiritually, namely, *the indication, principle, and completion of spiritual following.*

Luke 14:25–27
CHRIST INSTRUCTS THE CROWDS BY EXPLICIT TEACHING

So first, with regard to *the indication of spiritual following* the text says: *Now great crowds were going along with him*, as a sign of spiritual following. So the Glossa observes: *"Crowds were going along with him*, namely, captivated by the attractiveness of his preaching and his miracles."[128] So they could say what John 6:69 has: "Lord, to whom will we go? You have the words of eternal life." And note here that the Pharisees had calumniated Christ, and the crowds are accompanying him, for the person whom the proud despise the humble follow. So John 7:48–49 reads: "Has anyone of the rulers believed in him . . . ? But this crowd, which does not know the Law, is accursed." But the crowds were following Jesus as *sheep* following their *shepherd*. Matthew 9:36 states: "Seeing the crowds, Jesus was moved with compassion for them because they were bewildered and lying down like sheep without a shepherd." Furthermore, they were following him like *people* following their *king*. Matthew 21:9 says: "The crowds that went before him and those that followed shouted: Hosanna," etc. Moreover, they were following him like *disciples* following their *teacher*. Luke 5:1 above has: "It came to pass that when the crowds were pressing upon him to hear the word of God, and he was standing by Lake Gennesaret."

---

[128] On p. 375, n. 5 QuarEd state that this is the Glossa Interlinearis.

52. (Verses 25–26). Second, with regard to *the principle of spiritual following* the text adds: *And he turned to them.* He turned, I say, with *benignity.* The Psalm says: "O God, you will turn and give us life" (84:7). *He said,* in *true teaching*: *If anyone comes to me,* out of *the supererogation of righteousness.* Matthew 11:28 states: "Come to me, all you who labor and are burdened." – *And does not hate his father and mother, and wife and children, and brothers and sisters, yes, even his very life,* through *mortification of carnal affection,* according to the Psalm: "Hearken, O daughter, and see and incline your ear," etc. (44:11). *Cannot be my disciple,* through *the adoption of evangelical perfection,* about which Luke 6:40 above says: "When perfected, everyone will be like his teacher." – And the reason for this is that the principle of the spiritual life is to put off carnal affection, for 1 Corinthians 2:14 reads: "The sensual person does not perceive the things that are of the Spirit of God, for it is foolishness to him, and he cannot understand," etc. Isaiah 28:9 states: "Whom will he teach knowledge? And whom will he make understand the hearing? The ones weaned from the milk," etc., that is, separated from carnal affection.

53. So it is to be noted here that this passage does not command hatred of parents in as far as *nature* goes, for that would be impious since it is said in 1 John 3:15: "The person[129] who hates his brother is a murderer." But it commands hatred as far as *sin* goes, as Augustine says: "Men and women are to be loved in such a way that their errors are not loved."[130] About this hatred the

---

[129] The Vulgate reads *omnis* ("everyone") while Bonaventure has *qui* ("the person who").

[130] On p. 375, n. 12 QuarEd have directed me to: Prosper of Aquitaine's *Liber Unus Sententiarum ex operibus S. Augustini Delibatarum,* n. 2. See PL 51:427A: *Sic diligendi sunt homines, ut eorum non*

Psalm says: "Have I not hated them, O Lord, who hated you and languished because of your enemies? I have hated them with a perfect hatred" (138:21–22).[131] Thus, Gregory comments: "We can both love and hate at the same time, so that we both love by divine precept those related to us by blood and we deny by hatred and flight those we experience as against us in God's way."[132] So this hatred does not arise from cruelty, but from love, just as the hatred of our own soul, which we must hate, not with regard to salvation, but with regard to carnal things. So Gregory observes: "Then we hate our soul when we resist its carnal affections."[133] About this hatred John 12:25 says: "The person who hates his soul in this world keeps it unto life everlasting."[134] Augustine says: "If you have loved badly, then you have hated. If you have hated well, then you have loved. Happy are they who have hated it in keeping it that they may not destroy it in loving it."[135] This is given more full expression in Sirach 18:30–31: "Son, do not go after your lusts, but turn away from your own will. If you give to your soul

---

diligantur errores ("Men and women are to be loved in such a way that their errors are not loved").

[131] See Hugh of St. Cher, p. 221, where he also quotes Psalm 138:22.

[132] On p. 375, n. 13 QuarEd state that Gregory's interpretation comes from his Homily 37, n. 2 of GGHG and is found in the Glossa Ordinaria on Luke 14:26. See PL 76:1275D for the origin of the Glossa Ordinaria's abbreviated version of Gregory's homily on Luke 14:25–33. See Hugh of St. Cher, p. 221, where he also quotes Gregory.

[133] On p. 375, n. 14 QuarEd state that this quotation comes from the same passages indicated in, n. 132 above. See PL 76:1276A. See Hugh of St. Cher, p. 221: *Tunc bene animam nostram odimus, cum ejus carnalibus desideriis non acquiescimus, sed reluctamur, et frangimus* ("Then we well hate our soul when we do not acquiesce to its carnal desires, but we resist and break them").

[134] See Hugh of St. Cher, p. 221l, where he uses the same quotation.

[135] On p. 375, n. 14 QuarEd point their readers to Augustine's exposition of John 12:25 in his Tractate 51, n. 10. I have utilized the translation of John W. Rettig in *St. Augustine: Tractates on the Gospel of John 28–54*, FC 88 (Washington: Catholic University of America Press, 1993), p. 276.

her desires, she will make you come[136] in joy to your enemies." Therefore, just as the principle of spiritual *life* is *not to lust,* which refers to the prohibition of all evil,[137] and *to decline from evil,*[138] so too the foundation of spiritual *following* is *to decline from all carnal relationships,* be these towards oneself or towards one's parents. For which reason Ephesians 4:22 reads: "As regards your former way of life put off[139] the old man, which is being corrupted according to its deceptive lusts."

54. (Verse 27). Third, relative to *the completion of spiritual following* the text continues: *And the person who does not carry his cross,* through *perfect mortification of the flesh, and come after me,* through *a right intention, cannot be my disciple,* through *genuine imitation.* – And note that here is the *consummation* of following and being a disciple of Christ, namely, in carrying the cross, for it was there that Christ consummated his course, as it is said in John 19:17: "And bearing the cross for himself, he went forth to the place of Calvary."[140] In this cross of Christ there is the highest *humility.* Philippians 2:8 reads: "He humbled himself, becoming obedient unto death, even death on a cross." Highest *poverty,* so that in truth Christ could say what Job 1:21 has: "Naked

---

[136] On p. 376, n. 1 QuarEd rightly mention that the Vulgate does not read *venire* ("to come").

[137] On p. 376, n. 2 QuarEd helpfully refer to Romans 7:7: "For I had not known lust unless the Law had said: You shall not lust" and cite Augustine's *De Spiritu et Litteris,* chapter 4, n. 6.

[138] On p. 376, n. 2 QuarEd refer to Psalm 36:27: "Decline from evil and do good."

[139] On p. 376, n. 3 QuarEd correctly indicate that the Vulgate reads *deponere* ("to put off") while Bonaventure has *deponite* ("put off").

[140] See also Jesus' last words on the cross in John 19:30: "It is consummated." On p. 376, n. 4 QuarEd cite the Glossa Interlinearis (from Gregory): ". . . it is called cross from suffering, which must always be borne, so that the love of Christ may be manifested." The Latin for "cross" is *crux* while the Latin for "suffering" comes from the same stem, *cruciatus.* See PL 76:1277A.

came I out of my mother's womb, and naked will I return thither." Whence it is said in John 19:23 that "the soldiers, when they had crucified him, took his garments and made of them four parts." There is also the highest *austerity,* according to what the Psalm says: "They have dug my hands and my feet. They have numbered all my bones" (21:17).

55. So *to carry the cross* is to take up *humility* in heart, *austerity* in flesh, and *poverty* in suffering, against those *three capital sins* and against *the threefold excuses* of those who refused to come to the supper. This cross was *Christ's,* because Christ freely accepted it. Similarly, the person who wants to follow Christ must *freely* take up the cross, so that he may bear it of his own free will as *his own* cross, not under duress as a *stranger's* cross with the result that he is not an imitator of Christ, but rather of Simon. About Simon Mark 15:21 says: "They forced a certain Simon of Cyrene . . . to take up his cross." To this cross Christ offers us a special *invitation.* He was the first to carry it as a royal banner and sign. So Hebrews 13:12–13 states: "Christ suffered outside the gate. Let us, therefore, go forth to him," etc. Therefore, the persons who do not want to follow in this manner are not disciples of Christ, because they do not want to imitate him in the way he showed himself to us as an exemplar and teacher. Thus Galatians 5:24 reads: "Now those who belong to Christ have crucified their flesh with its passions and desires." For which reason 2 Corinthians 4:10 has: "Always bearing about in our bodies the dying of the cross,[141] so that the life of Jesus may also be made manifest in our bodies." Wherefore, Chrysostom observes: "Let no one be ashamed of the cross. Let us carry it

---

[141] On p. 376, n. 12 QuarEd accurately indicate that the Vulgate reads *Iesu* ("of Jesus") while Bonaventure has *crucis* ("of the cross").

about like a crown. Furthermore, let everything we do be done with the cross: regeneration, consecration. For this reason we inscribe the cross in our homes, on our doors, journeys, foreheads, and minds."[142] So this should be carried like a sign of the living God, about which Revelation 7:2–3 says: "I saw another angel ascending from the rising of the sun, having the seal of the living God. And he cried with a loud voice to the four angels who had it in their power to harm the earth and the sea, saying: Do not harm the earth or the sea or the trees until we have signed the servants of God[143] on their foreheads," namely, so that it may be clearly known who is a disciple of Christ.

Luke 14:28–34
CHRIST INSTRUCTS THE CROWDS IN PARABLES

56. *For which of you, wishing to build*, etc. After he has given instruction through explicit teaching to those following, here in a second point he gives instruction to the same people *through parabolic examples*. And since we have to imitate Christ in *actions* and *sufferings* – in the first we are similar to *those building*; in the second to *those going into battle* – it follows that the first item in

---

[142] On p. 376, n. 13 QuarEd refer to Chrysostom's Homily 54, n. 4 on Matthew. My check of PG 58:537 indicated that Bonaventure's quotation is a paraphrastic abbreviation. See Hugh of St. Cher, p. 221m: *Chrysost. Nullus verecundetur crucem, circumferamus eam, ut coronam. Etenim omnia, quae secundum nos sunt, per crucem perficiuntur, regeneratio, consecratio, propter hoc, in domo, in januis, in muris, in frontibus, et in mente scribimus eam* ("Let no one be ashamed of the cross. Let us carry it about like a crown. Furthermore, let everything we do be done with the cross: regeneration, consecration. For this reason we inscribe the cross in our homes, on our doors, walls, foreheads, and minds"). The main difference between Bonaventure's quotation from Chrysostom and that of Hugh is that Hugh reads *muris* ("walls") where Bonaventure has *viis* ("journeys").

[143] The Vulgate reads *Dei nostri* ("of our God").

this part deals with the parable of *the man who is build-ing*. The second adds the parable and the example of *the king going into battle* where verse 31 reads: *Or what king setting out*. In the third there is *the application of both* where verse 33 has: *So, therefore, everyone of you who has not renounced*.[144]

Concerning the parable of *the man building* three points are introduced: *the notion of the proposition to build, the provision of sufficient money, the avoidance of imminent mockery*.

57. (Verse 28). So first with regard to *the notion of the proposition to build* the text says: *For which of you, wishing to build a tower*. By *tower*, which is the tallest building, we can understand the peak of the perfection of merits, which gradually rises up from the nadir to the apex, beginning from *a foundation of fear* and pro-gressing to *the summit of deifying wisdom*. And first the tower is to be built with *the gift of fear*, about which what Micah 4:8 states can be understood: "You, O cloudy tower of the flock . . . unto you will God come,"[145] for fear renders one a little child out of consideration of the judgment. – The second tower is built with *compassion*, about which Isaiah 5:2 says: "He built a tower in the middle of the vineyard, and set up a winepress therein," because compassion arises from a consideration of suf-fering. – The third tower is built with *knowledge*. The Song of Songs 4:4 reads: "Your neck is like the tower of David, which is built with bulwarks. A thousand bucklers

---

[144] On p. 376, n. 16 QuarEd accurately mention that the Vulgate reads *renuntiat* ("does not renounce") while Bonaventure has *renuntiaverit* ("has not renounced").

[145] On p. 377, n. 2 QuarEd helpfully quote Jerome's comment on Mi-cah 4:8: ". . . Therefore, the tower is at one time that of the flock and of the people of God. . . . Now it is filthy (cloudy) and destitute . . . and unto this tower God will come, etc."

hang upon it, all the armor of valiant men," etc. This is understood of the knowledge of Sacred Scripture. – The fourth tower is built of *strength*. Proverbs 18:10 states: "The name of the Lord is a most strong tower. The just man runs to it and will be exalted." And in the Psalm it says: "You have led me, for you have been made my hope, a tower of strength" (60:3–4). – The fifth tower is built of *counsel*, about which The Song of Songs 7:4 reads: "Your nose is the tower of Lebanon, that looks towards Damascus," because counsel acts against the snares of the enemy. – The sixth tower is built of *understanding*. Concerning this The Song of Songs 7:4 has: "Your neck is like a tower of ivory. Your eyes like the fish pools of Heshbon," where it is interpreted that purity of heart and clarity of spiritual understanding are understood. – The seventh tower is built of *wisdom*, about which The Song of Songs 8:10 states: "I am a wall, and my breasts are like a tower," which is said on account of the consolation that comes from tasting the milk from the breasts of divine wisdom.[146]

---

[146] In his interpretation of the tower Bonaventure quotes scripture in an uncharacteristic way and seems dependent upon tradition. See Hugh of St. Cher, p. 221v, a, where after treating the three "evil towers" of pride, voluptuousness, and avarice, Hugh turns to the eight "good towers": "The first tower is hope in God that stems from good merits. Psalm 60[4]: My hope is a tower of strength. The cost of building this tower is one's own good merits. . . . There is also a second good tower, namely, the tower of David, that is, humility. The Song of Songs 4b[4]: Your neck is like the tower of David, which is built with bulwarks. The third tower is of ivory, that is, chastity. The Song of Songs 7b[4]: Your neck is like a tower of ivory. The fourth is the tower of Lebanon, that is, innocence. The Song of Songs 4b[=7:4]: Your nose is the tower of Lebanon, that looks towards Damascus. The fifth is the tower of the flock, that is, fraternal charity. Micah 4c[8]: And you, O cloudy tower of the flock, daughter of Zion, unto you will God come. The sixth is the tower of the vineyard, that is, the defense of the Church. Isaiah 5a[2]: The Lord planted a chosen vine and built a tower in its midst. The seventh tower is the word, that is, of sacred doctrine. The Song of Songs 8c[10]: I am a wall, and my breasts are like a tower. The eighth is a tower of strength, that is, Christ. Proverbs 18b[10]: The name of the Lord is a most strong

Now before the height of this building may be achieved, the building has need of *the building of seven virtues*. About this building Proverbs 9:1 says: "Wisdom has built herself a house, has hewn out seven pillars." Now Christ is the *founder* and *the foundation* of this building as well as its *completion*.[147] Nonetheless, the spiritual man is compared to this building. So 1 Corinthians 3:9 reads: "We are God's helpers. You are God's cultivated field. You are God's building." Therefore, everyone who proposes to ascend to the height of virtue wants to build his tower here.

58. Second, relative to *the provision of sufficient money* the text continues: *Does not*[148] *sit down first and calculate the expenses that are necessary whether he has the means to complete it? To sit down* means to probe within oneself the secrets of one's conscience.[149] Lamentations 3:28 has: "He will sit by himself and keep silent." *To calculate* is to plan ahead with careful consideration. So the Glossa states: "With diligent consideration we must plan ahead everything that we do."[150] And this is what is said in Proverbs 4:25: "May your eyes look straight ahead, and may your vision guide your steps." Now *the*

---

tower. Of these towers it is said in Psalm 121[7]: Let peace be in your strength, and abundance in your towers."

[147] On p. 377, n. 7 QuarEd refer to Bernard of Clairvaux' Sermon 52 de Diversis where the words of Proverbs 9:1 are applied to the Blessed Virgin Mary, in whom the Wisdom of the Father built himself a home and hewed out seven pillars, that is, the three theological virtues and the four cardinal virtues. See SBOp 6.274–277. If Bernard's interpretation is traditional, then Bonaventure has adapted it christologically.

[148] On p. 377, n. 9 QuarEd correctly indicate that the Vulgate reads *Non* ("not") while Bonaventure has *Nonne* ("not").

[149] On p. 377, n. 9 QuarEd quote the Glossa Interlinearis: "*Does not sit down*, being at rest from the tumult of the world."

[150] On p. 377 n 10 QuarEd state that this is the Glossa Interlinearis (from Gregory who is followed by Bede). See PL 76:1277C and CCSL cxx, p. 282.

necessary expenses are the efforts of the mind, by which a person appropriately cooperates with the grace of Christ *courageously*, according to what the Psalmist says: "Act courageously, and let your heart be strengthened, all you who hope in the Lord" (30:25). *Beneficially.* Thus, 1 Corinthians 3:2 reads: "But if anyone builds upon this foundation, gold, silver, and precious stones," etc. *Efficaciously.* Hebrews 12:15 states: "Take heed lest anyone be wanting in the grace of God," etc. *Perseveringly.* 1 Kings 7:51 has: "Solomon completed all the work he was doing in the house of the Lord." – When this building was completed, the Lord appeared to dwell therein.[151] So 1 Kings 9:1–2 says: "It came to pass that when Solomon had completed the building of the house of the Lord and the king's house and all that he desired, the Lord appeared to him." Therefore, the expenses that are sufficient to complete the building consist of a resolute will that acts *courageously, beneficially, efficaciously,* and *perseveringly.* But if anything is lacking, the Lord supplies. So Philippians 2:13 reads: "It is God who of his good pleasure works in you both the will and the completion." Therefore, the person who wants to commence a lofty work must plan ahead, if he wants to see it through, because, as it is said in Luke 9:62 above: "No one, having put his hand to the plow," etc.

59. (Verse 29). Third, with regard to *the avoidance of imminent mockery* the text notes: *Lest, after he has laid the foundation* namely, in order to proceed to a higher state in imitating Christ. And this is the meaning of *to lay a foundation.* 1 Corinthians 3:11 has: "No one can lay another foundation but that which has been laid, which is Christ Jesus." A person begins to lay this foun-

---

[151] This is not exactly what is found in 1 Kings 9:1–2, which Bonaventure immediately quotes.

dation through faith and good deeds, according to what Matthew 7:24 states: "Everyone, who hears these words of mine and acts upon them, is like the man who built his house on rock." Persons who want to follow Christ perfectly situated the foundations of their dwellings on this *rock*, according to what Jeremiah 48:28 reads: "Leave the cities and dwell in the rock, you that dwell in Moab," etc. – *and was not able to finish*, and this by persevering, like those about whom it is said in Luke 8:13 above: "They believe for a while, and in time of temptation fall away." Such are those people who destroy by their *relapses* whatever they had built of good *in the beginning*. Sirach 34:28 says: "When one builds up and another pulls down, what profit do they have except the labor?" Such are those people who are *dissolute and remiss*. Proverbs 18:9 reads: "The person who is loose and dissolute in his work is the brother of the person who demolishes his own work." – *All who see*, by looking around at perfection once begun. 1 Corinthians 4:9 says: "We have been made a spectacle to the world, both to angels and to humans."[152] For what is set up high is visible to everyone. Matthew 5:14–15 states: "A city set on a mountain cannot be hidden. Neither do people light a lamp and put it under a measure, but upon the lamp stand, so that it may give light to all in the house."

60. (Verses 29–30). *They begin to mock him, saying that this man began to build and was not able to finish*. And they do this by casting aspersions and by deriding, because it is exceedingly shameful for those who backslide and apostatize. For they are mocked by the demons. Lamentations 1:7 says: "Enemies have seen her and have mocked her Sabbaths." The spiritual man abhors such mockery. The Psalmist prays: "Neither let my

---

[152] Hugh of St. Cher, p. 221v, g also quotes this passage.

enemies mock me," etc. (24:3). These enemies deride imperfection, according to what Nehemiah 4:3 states: "Tobiah the Ammonite said: Let the Jews build. Foxes will go up and leap over their stone wall."[153] Wherefore, Ambrose observes: "In everything that we do we should consider our hidden adversaries, who lie in wait for our works. And unless we are vigilant against them, we will experience as our mockers those who try to convince us to do evil."[154] Now the person who turns his back from what he has begun is mocked for his *rashness* in presuming, *instability* in pursuing his goal, *faintheartedness* in leaving off. And this not only from the devil, but also from the world. Sirach 20:17–18 states: "A fool will have no friends and receive no thanks for his good deeds. . . . How often and how many will laugh him to scorn!"

61. (Verse 31). *Or what king setting out to engage in battle*, etc. Earlier he proposed a parable about a builder. Now he proposes a parable *about a king going into battle.* Now in this part three items are mentioned, namely, *the proposition of war, the calculation of risk,* and *the provision of relief.*

So first, relative to *the proposition of war* the text says: *Or what king setting out to engage in a war against an-*

---

[153] On p. 378, n. 8 QuarEd rightly indicate that the Vulgate has a different reading: *Aedificent, si ascenderit vulpis, transiliet murum eorum lapideum* ("Let them build. If a fox goes up, it will leap over their stone wall").

[154] On p. 378, n. 9 QuarEd indicate that this opinion is also found in Cardinal Hugh and actually occurs in the Glossa Ordinaria (from Gregory and thence Bede) on Luke 14:29. See Hugh of St. Cher, p. 221v, g, where Hugh presents this quotation from "Ambrose" in the same words as those used by Bonaventure. See PL 76:1278A for Gregory's interpretation which has a conclusion different from that of Hugh and Bonaventure. See CCSL cxx, p. 283 for a wording that is closer to that of Hugh and Bonaventure.

other king. This *king* is whoever rules himself according to the law of God. Proverbs 20:8 reads: "The king, who sits on the throne of judgment," etc.[155] And Revelation 5:10 states: "You have made us for our God a kingdom . . . and we will reign over the earth."[156] It is responsibility of this king *to engage in war*, for Job 7:1 says: "Human life upon the earth is a warfare." Now this has a triple meaning. First, that someone engages in war with the king of *pride*. About this Job 41:25 reads: "He is king over all the children of pride." Second, with the king of *justice*. Concerning this the Psalm says: "You will rule them with a rod," etc. (2:9). Third, with the king of *celestial providence*. About this Qoheleth 5:8 states: "The king reigns over all the land," etc. – Now he engages in war with *the king of pride* when he protests against it. Ephesians 6:12 reads: "Our wrestling is not against flesh and blood, but against the world-rulers of this darkness." – He also engages in war with *the king of justice* when he seeks to justify himself in the presence of God, for it is said in Jeremiah 2:35: "Behold, I will contend with you in judgment, because you have said: I have not sinned." Job also wanted to engage in this type of war when he said in Job 13:3: "I will speak to the Almighty, and I desire to dispute with God." And Jeremiah 12:1 has: "You indeed, O Lord, are just, if I dispute with you. Nonetheless, I will speak what is just to you."[157] – He also engages in war with *the king of ce-*

---

[155] Proverbs 20:8 reads in full: "The king, who sits on the throne of judgment, scatters away all evil with his look." See Hugh of St. Cher, p. 222a, where he quotes Sirach 20:8 in its entirety.

[156] Bonaventure has changed third person plurals into first person plurals. Revelation 5:10 goes: "You have made them for our God a kingdom . . . and they will reign over the earth."

[157] On p. 379, n. 1 QuarEd cite the Glossa Interlinearis: "*Or what king setting out to engage in war*, etc. as if to say: To engage in war with God means that someone thinks that he is saved by himself through his just merits."

lestial providence when he steels himself for a test of patience, as it is said in Job 6:8–9: "Who will grant that my request may come and that God may give me what I look for? And that he who has begun may destroy me?" In this fashion there is a threefold war waged with the three aforementioned kings. – In the first *repentance* for sins. In the second *confidence* in one's merits. And in the third *patience* in affliction.

62. Second, concerning *the calculation of risk* the text adds: *Does not first sit down and consider* how to be provident in accordance with Deuteronomy 32:29: "O that they would be wise and would understand and would provide for their last end!" On account of this Ephesians 5:15–17 has: "See to it . . . that you walk with care, not as unwise, but as wise, making the most of your time, for the days are evil. Therefore, do not become foolish," etc. – *Whether he is able with ten thousand men to meet*, namely, to resist, *him who with twenty thousand is coming against him*, to attack him. Like the preceding parable this one, too, has three expositions. For if the interpretation deals with *the king of pride*, we meet him with the works of the virtues, which consist of adhering to a middle course,[158] and are specified as *ten thousand* on account of the observance of the ten commandments. And the adversary comes with a double number, for to each virtue there corresponds a double vice as its opposite according to superabundance and deficiency. Whence, since there are more ways to be turned aside than to be steered straight ahead, *more* are said to be in the army of the king who is proceeding against us. So Judith 1:4 reads: "He gloried as a mighty

---

[158] It seems that Bonaventure is alluding to the Aristotelian principle of *virtus in medio*, that is, virtue consists in adhering to a middle course between excess and deficiency. See Bonaventure's next sentence: "superabundance and deficiency."

one in the force of his army and in the glory of his chariots." But one must not flee nor be afraid, because, as it is said in 1 Maccabees 3:18–19: "It is an easy matter for many to be shut up in the hands of a few. And there is no difference in the sight of the God of heaven to deliver with a small company or with a great multitude.[159] For the success of war is not in the multitude of the army, but in strength from heaven."

63. Now if the interpretation concerns *the king of justice*, we sally forth with *ten thousand*, that is, with confidence in the merits from the observance of the ten commandments. And the king with *twenty thousand* refers to the severity of the judgments to be used in weighing deeds and thoughts. So Bede comments: "Although the person who presents the works of the ten commandments goes forth, God comes against him as it were with double the force, since God scrutinizes him not only for these works, but also for his deeds and thoughts."[160] – From this the meaning is clear that just as it is not safe to fight with *ten thousand* against *twenty thousand*, so too one is not secure in contending with this judge. For this reason Job 9:2–3 reads: "Indeed, I know that a human being cannot be justified in comparison with God. But if he will contend with him, he cannot answer him one for a thousand." So Malachi 3:1–2 says: "Behold, he comes, says the lord of hosts. And who will be able to ascertain the day of his coming? . . . For he is like a refining fire," etc. And the Psalmist says: "You inspire terror, and who will resist you?" (75:8). – Now if the inter-

---

[159] The Vulgate reads *in multis et in paucis* ("with a great multitude or with a small company").
[160] On p. 379, n. 7 QuarEd state that Bede's opinion, taken from Gregory, occurs in the words of the Glossa Ordinaria. For Gregory, see PL 76:1278CD. For Bede, see CCSL cxx, p. 283. See Hugh of St. Cher, p. 222b, for yet another version of "Bede's" commentary.

pretation focuses on *the king of celestial providence*, then the king who marches forth with *ten thousand* is the person who wants to endure great and many things for Christ. But the king, who is said to proceed with *twenty thousand*, is he who has endured incomparably more things for us, since he is "a giant of twin substance."[161] For which reason the Psalm asks: "What shall I render the Lord for all that he has rendered to me?" (115:12). And Micah 6:6 reads: "What will I offer the Lord that is worthy?"

64. (Verse 32). Third, with regard to a *provision for relief* the text continues: *Or else, while the other is yet at a distance, he sends a delegation and asks for the conditions of peace*, namely, if he acknowledges his own weakness in the face of this threefold battle, he labors to avoid this battle. Now the mission of this delegation is nothing other than the mission of prayer. The angels carry our prayer before the face of God as our legates. Tobit 12:12 reads: "When you prayed . . . and gave alms and buried the dead, I offered your prayer before the Lord."[162] This delegation is sent *to repulse the battles of temptation* that issue from *the king of pride*. In this way

---

[161] QuarEd on p. 379, n. 9 have led me to chapter 8 of Augustine's *Liber Unus Contra Sermonem Arianorum*. See PL 42:689 where Augustine is commenting on Philippians 2:5–11: "Nonetheless, Christ himself appears the same, a giant of twin substance, in a certain respect obedient, in a certain respect equal to God. In one sense Son of Man, in another sense Son of God. . . ." The editors also helpfully refer to Augustine's Commentary on Psalm 87, n. 10 where he brings in Psalm 18:6. See NPNF 1, Volume 8, p. 427: "But if we take the word giant in a good sense, as it is said of our Lord, 'he rejoices as a giant to run his course,' that is Giant of giants, chief among the greatest and strongest, who in His Church excels in spiritual strength."

[162] Bonaventure has both abbreviated and expanded this text. Tobit 12:12 reads: "When you prayed with tears and buried the dead and left your dinner and hid the dead by day in your house and buried them by night, I offered your prayer to the Lord."

Paul prayed as 2 Corinthians 12:7–8 states: "There was given me a thorn for my flesh, a messenger of Satan, to buffet me. Concerning this I thrice besought the Lord," etc. – Likewise, this delegation is sent *to repulse the battles of divine judgments*, which issue from *the king of justice*, as the Prophet prayed in the Psalm: "And enter not into judgment with your servant, O Lord, for in your sight no person alive will be justified" (142:2). – The delegation is also sent *to repulse the battles of afflictions*, which issue from *the king of providence*, as Jonah prayed in Jonah 2:2–3: "Jonah prayed to the Lord, his God, from the belly of the fish and said: I cried out to the Lord from my affliction, and he heard me." – From these reflections one garners that consideration of danger and risk prompt one to seek a remedy. So the Glossa observes: "Keeping in mind the deficiency we experience because of our fragility, we must petition peace from the severe judge by sending ahead a delegation of tears, good deeds, and pure affections."[163] Therefore, it is said in Sirach 18:20–21: "Before you take sick, have medicine at hand. And before judgment examine yourself, and you will find mercy in the sight of God. Humble yourself before you are sick, and in the time of sickness change your way of life," so that through the delegation of the priests you may find that God has been appeased.

65. (Verse 33). *So, therefore, everyone of you*, etc. After setting forth the parabolic example of the builder and of the king going forth to battle, here in a third place he provides *an application of both*. And since these examples were introduced to spur us to have foresight about a matter that is opportune and caution about a harmful

---

[163] On p. 380, n. 4 QuarEd state that this is the Glossa Ordinaria (from Gregory, whom Bede quotes) on Luke 14:31. For Gregory, see PL 76:1278D–1279A. For Bede, see CCSL cxx, p. 283.

matter and to provide spiritual counsel about both, it
follows that in this part an application is given of the
aforementioned examples with regard to: *foresight about
an opportune matter, caution about a harmful matter*,
and *spiritual counsel about both.*

First, then, relative to *foresight about an opportune matter* the text says: *So, therefore, every one of you who has
not renounced all that he possesses*, through contempt of
temporal matters, *cannot be my disciple*, through the
perfection of spiritual matters. As if he is saying: Just as
the builder cannot complete his project without money,
nor can the king safely engage in combat without soldiers, so no one can perfectly follow Christ unless that
person renounces everything.

66. And note that the following of Christ is twofold. The
first is that of *necessary obligation*, as it is said in Acts
9 and 6 that Jesus' followers were wont to be called *disciples* at that time, but they are now called *Christians*.[164]
About this following Isaiah 1:16–17 says: "Cease to do
perversely. Learn to do the good." The second is that of
supererogation, by which a person follows Christ
through the evangelical counsels. About this Matthew
5:1 has: "Seeing the crowds, Jesus went up the mountain. And when he was seated, his disciples came to
him." It is a necessary obligation *to renounce everything*
in the first type of discipleship with regard to contempt
for earthly things. But in the second type it is necessary
to leave everything behind, not only with regard to attachment to things, but indeed with regard to the things
themselves. Wherefore, the Glossa reads: "This is the

---

[164] This is a strange statement. Indeed in Acts 6:1 and 9:1, 10, 19, 25
the followers of Christ are called "disciples." Acts 11:26, however,
states: "And it was in Antioch that the disciples were first called
'Christians.'"

difference between *to renounce everything* and *to leave everything behind*, for *to renounce* is fitting for all those, who licitly use the mundane things they possess in such a way that they keep their mind focused on eternal things. But *to leave behind* pertains only to the perfect, who put aside all temporal matters and yearn only for eternal matters."[165] And this is necessary for the perfect disciples of Christ, that they may be conformed to the poverty of the Master. Thus, about this Matthew 19:27 states: "Behold, we have left everything behind and have followed you."[166] Bernard observes: "Behold, Peter, you have spoken well and are no fool. . . . For burdened down with things, you could not follow him who was running ahead. For *he rejoiced like a giant to run the course*."[167] For since "blessed are the poor in spirit" holds primary place among Christ's teachings, the person who ignores it suffers the consequence of not knowing "the rudiments of the words" of Christ.[168] And therefore, Antiochus, who is interpreted to mean *the silence of pov-*

---

[165] On p. 380, n. 11 QuarEd state that this is the Glossa Ordinaria (from Bede) apud Lyranum on Luke 14:33. See CCSL cxx, pp. 283–284. See Hugh of St. Cher, p. 222g, who quotes basically the same passage from "Bede." The interpretation of the Glossa/Bede is not far removed from the interpretation of Hans-Joachim Degenhardt, *Lukas, Evangelist der Armen: Besitz und Besitzverzicht in den lukanischen Schriften* (Stuttgart: Katholisches Bibelwerk, 1965).

[166] See Luke 18:28 for the same thought.

[167] On p. 380, n. 11 QuarEd point the reader to Chapter II "On Leaving All Things" of *Declamationes de Colloquio Simonis cum Jesu, ex S. Bernardi sermonibus collectae* of Geoffrey the Abbot. See PL 184:438B. The first part of Bonaventure's quotation, which is an abbreviation of "Bernard's" interpretation, is verbatim with his quotation from "Bernard" on Luke 9:23 (#38) above. The second part of the quotation is from Psalm 18:6. See Hugh of St. Cher, p. 222g: *Ubi Beatus Bernardus. Recte fecisti, Petre, quia sequi non poteras oneratus eum, qui exultavit ut gigas ad currendam viam* ("Where Blessed Bernard gives this interpretation. You have done rightly, Peter, for burdened down with things, you could not follow him, who rejoiced like a giant to run the course").

[168] In an uncharacteristic way of quoting scripture Bonaventure refers here to Matthew 5:3 and Hebrews 5:12.

erty, undermined the foundations of Jerusalem, for a person who contemns the counsel of poverty cannot be a disciple of the poor Crucified One.[169]

67. (Verse 34). Second, relative to *caution about a harmful matter* the text adds: *Salt is good, but if salt loses its strength*. By *salt* is understood any perfect disciple, who by example and word must season the hearts of others. Thus, Matthew 5:13 reads: "You are the salt of the earth." This is said that a disciple must have utmost *discretion* in *conversation*, according to what Colossians 4:6 states: "Let your speech, while always gracious, be seasoned with salt." For, just as food cannot be eaten unless it is seasoned with salt, so too the heart cannot stomach an indiscrete word.[170] Job 6:6 has: "Can an unsavory thing be eaten, that is not seasoned by salt?" The disciples must also possess *savory wisdom*[171] through *contemplation*. Whence it is commanded in Leviticus 2:13 that salt be offered with every sacrifice.[172] And persons who are prudent and wise are fitting condiments for the Church through their words and example. So the Glossa explains: "Salt seasons food, kills worms, preserves meat. So preaching preserves human nature unharmed for its creator from the worms and putrefaction of vices."[173] – But then *salt loses its strength*, when the dis-

---

[169] On p. 380, n. 14 QuarEd try to make sense of this interpretation. See CCSL lxxii, p. 155 for Jerome's interpretation of "Antioch" in Galatians as "the silence of poverty." 1 Maccabees 1:22–25 describes "Antiochus'" plunder of the silver and gold of Jerusalem's temple.

[170] Bonaventure is responsible for this strange image. Literally, he writes "the stomach of the heart."

[171] My translation attempts to capture Bonaventure's playfulness with the root meaning of *sapientia* ("wisdom"), namely, *sapio* ("to taste; to savor").

[172] Leviticus 2:13 reads: "Whatever sacrifice you offer, you shall season it with salt. Neither shall you take away the salt of the covenant of your God from your sacrifice. In all your oblations you shall offer salt."

[173] On p. 381, n. 2 QuarEd state that this is the Glossa Ordinaria on Luke 14:35.

ciple of Christ becomes irreligious in contemplation and
indifferent in deeds and in preaching, as it is said of
those in Romans 1:21: "Their reasonings were weak-
ened, and their senseless minds have been darkened,"
etc. And this is the greatest danger. – Thus the text
adds: *What will it be seasoned with?* As if to say: With
nothing. So Sirach 12:13 reads: "Who will take pity on
an enchanter bitten by a snake?" As if to say that such a
person is thoroughly despicable and useless both before
God and human beings, both in spiritual and in temporal deeds.

68. (Verse 35). So the text concludes: *It is fit neither for
the land nor for the manure heap,*[174] *but must be thrown
out.* The Glossa comments: "For the person who turns
back cannot bear fruit himself nor build up others."[175]
Moreover, what is worse is that he renders the earth
sterile, for the perfect man, who falls, renders others
useless for doing good through his evil example. And
therefore, the man who turns his back is compared to
Lot's wife, about whom it is said in Genesis 19:26 that
"looking back, she was turned into a statue of salt."[176]
And so Proverbs 6:12 reads: "A person who is an apostate, a useless man, walks with a perverse mouth," etc.
– Therefore, just as *a building begun, but not completed*
is useful for nothing and a man, who began and did not
finish the job, is derided by everyone, and similarly the
man who *is conquered in battle*, so too is *the disciple
who becomes an apostate* despised like *tasteless salt.* So

[174] On p. 381, n. 5 QuarEd rightly mention that the Vulgate reads
neque in terram neque in sterquilinium ("neither for the land nor for
the manure heap") whereas Bonaventure has *neque in terra neque in
sterquilinio* ("neither for the land nor for the manure heap").
[175] On p. 381, n. 5 QuarEd state that this is the Glossa Ordinaria
(from Bede) apud Lyrannum. See CCSL cxx, p. 284.
[176] In his commentary on Luke 9:62 (#110) above Bonaventure also
quotes Genesis 19:26.

Matthew 5:13 says: "It is no longer of any use but to be thrown out and trodden underfoot by people."

69. Third, concerning *the spiritual understanding of both* the text adds: *The person who has ears to hear, let him hear.* The text invites us to perfect understanding, so that the aforementioned words are not only heard with regard to their vocal sound, about which Matthew 13:15 says: "The heart of this people has been hardened, and with their ears they have been hard of hearing." These words must also be heard with regard to their *spiritual comprehension*, according to what Job 42:5 states: "With the hearing of the ear I have heard you, but now my eye beholds you."[177] The Psalm has: "I will hear what the Lord God will speak in me," etc. (84:9). And further with regard to *manual effectiveness*. James 1:22 reads: "Be doers of the word, not hearers only." Therefore, his desire is to say that the aforementioned words are *parabolic*. And therefore, they are to be heard and scrutinized spiritually and not carnally, according to what Proverbs 1:5–6 says: "A wise person will hear and will be wiser. And the person who has understanding will possess governments. He will understand a parable and its interpretation, the words of the wise, and their mysterious sayings." The persons who hear the word of God in this manner receive it most efficaciously, according to what Sirach 24:30–31 has: "The persons who listen to me will not be confounded,[178] and they that work in me will not sin. They who explain me will have life everlasting."

---

[177] See Hugh of St. Cher, p. 222h–p, who in his commentary on Luke 14:34–35 uses the same seven scripture passages that Bonaventure does and in the same sequence. Hugh's sequence is: Matthew 5:13; Job 6:6; Leviticus 2:13; Romans 1:21; Sirach 12:13; Lot's wife (Genesis 19:26); Job 42:5.

[178] In the Vulgate the verbs are third person singular. Bonaventure seems to have made all the verbs in this quotation third person plural.

LUKE 15

1. *Now the publicans and sinners were drawing near,* etc. After he has confuted the deceit of the Pharisees who were maligning Christ's power to perform miracles, in this part *he confutes the lack of mercy* of those murmuring against the manifestation of Christ's clemency through his works of compassion. Now this part is divided into three sections. In the first *an expression of the Jewish lack of mercy* is set forth. The second presents *a manifestation of divine compassion* where verse 3 reads: *And he spoke to them this parable,* etc. The third section deals with *the commendation of and teaching about human compassion* where Luke 16:1 below reads: *He also said to his disciples: There was a certain rich man.*

---

[1] The context prompts me to translate *impietas* by "lack of mercy" and *pietas* by "mercy, compassion" rather than by "ungodliness" and "godliness." In his commentary on Luke 15:1 (#2) below Bonaventure will ring a series of changes of the meaning of these words.

Luke 15:1-2
A threefold expression of Jewish lack of mercy

Now concerning *the expression of Jewish lack of mercy* three points are made, namely, *the occasion for the expression of the lack of mercy, the expression in murmuring of their lack of mercy,* and *the simulation of the righteousness of justice.*

2. (Verse 1). First, then, with regard to *the occasion for the expression of a lack of mercy* the text says: *Now the publicans and sinners were drawing near to him.* This manifests the supreme compassion of Christ to public sinners and provided the Pharisees with the occasion of judging him mercilessly. For it is customary to decrease one's visible works of mercy towards the wicked and to increase one's lack of respect for them. Thus the Psalmist says: "He has distributed; he has given to the poor," etc. and then immediately adds: "The sinner will see and will be angry" (111:9-10). Now Christ was showing great compassion, for he was receiving *the publicans,* who were public sinners. Therefore, the Glossa states: "*Publicans,* those who demand and collect public taxes, who deal with the lucre of the world through business transactions."[2] And such people were involved in many unjust money deals. Now sinners of this type, although they seem to need to be rejected for justice's sake, are open, nonetheless, to mercy. Confident of this mercy, *they were drawing near to him* as *the most merciful Lord,* according to

---

[2] On p. 382, n. 2 QuarEd state that this is the Glossa Interlinearis according to Bede. In his commentary on Luke 3:12 (#28) above Bonaventure quotes what Bede (and the Glossa Ordinaria) say about "the publicans." The two quotations agree in essential matters. See CCSL cxx, p. 79 on Luke 3:12. See Hugh of St. Cher, p. 222v, a, whose quotation of "the Glossa of Bede" is virtually identical with that of Bonaventure.

what James 4:8 says: "Draw near to God, and he will draw near to you."[3] *Draw near*, I say, through devout supplication. The Psalmist prays: "Let my supplication draw near in your sight, O Lord" (118:169). They were also drawing near to him as to *a most expert teacher*. Thus the text adds: *to listen to him*, according to the counsel provided by the wise man in Sirach 51:31: "Draw near to me, you unlearned, and gather together into the house of my teaching." For, as it is said in Deuteronomy 33:3: "Those who draw near to his feet will receive of his teaching."

3. Both the Pharisees and the publicans were drawing near to the supreme teacher Christ, but *the Pharisees deceitfully* according to what Jeremiah 12:2 has: "You are near and in their mouths, but far from their inmost being."[4] For such people seem to be *close* through feigned justice, but are *faraway* through hidden pride, according to what Isaiah 58:2–3 states: "For they seek me from day to day and desire to know my ways as a nation that has done justice and has not forsaken the judgment of their God. They ask of me just judgments, and they want to draw near to God. Why have we fasted, and you have not looked upon us? Have we humbled our souls, and you have not taken notice?" And the text continues: "Behold, in the day of your fast your own will is found," etc.[5] But *the publicans* were drawing near in a genuine way to hear, and having heard to turn from their evil deeds through repentance, according to the Lord's exhortation in Matthew 4:17: "Repent, for the kingdom

---

[3] Hugh of St. Cher, p. 222v, e also quotes James 4:8.
[4] Hugh of St. Cher, p. 222v, e also quotes Jeremiah 12:2.
[5] Bonaventure continues with Isaiah 58:3, which concludes with: ". . . and you exact from all your debtors."

of the heavens will be drawing near."[6] And when they have heard, they might be obedient to what they have heard, according to Qoheleth 4:17: "Guard your step when you enter the house of God, and draw near, so that you may hear. For obedience is much better than the victims of fools."

4. (Verse 2). Second, with regard to *the expression in murmuring of their lack of mercy* the text adds: *And the Pharisees and the scribes were murmuring. Murmuring* is oral communication which is not quite articulate speech, but not quite silence either. Wisdom 1:10–11 reads: "The ear of jealousy hears all things, and the tumult of murmuring will not be hidden. Therefore, keep yourselves from murmuring, which is of no profit. And refrain your tongue from detraction, for a derogatory utterance will not go for naught." And therefore, 1 Corinthians 10:10 says: "Neither murmur as some of them murmured and perished at the hands of the destroyer."[7] The Lord exceedingly hates this murmuring, for *it is of no profit* either for you or for your neighbor. Lamentations 3:39 says: "Why has a living person murmured, a man for his sins?" As if he were saying: In vain. The Lord also hates murmuring because it proceeds from *a wicked mouth*, which dares not argue openly, but, nevertheless, cannot conceal the wickedness of its heart. Wherefore, this word itself, *to murmur*, has such a

---

[6] On p. 382, n. 7 QuarEd correctly mention that the Vulgate reads *appropinquavit* ("has drawn near") while Bonaventure, along with many others, has *appropinquabit* ("will be drawing near").

[7] On p. 382, n. 8 QuarEd refer to Augustine's Commentary on Psalm 132, n. 12. See NPNF1, p. 623 (on Psalm 133, n. 8): "For murmurers are admirably described in a certain passage of the scriptures, 'The heart of a fool is as the wheel of a cart' (Sirach 33:5). What is the meaning of 'the heart of a fool is as the wheel of a cart?' It carries hay, and murmurs (creaks). The wheel of a cart cannot cease from murmuring (creaking)."

sound. About it Huguccio maintains that it stems from the root *I mutter, you mutter,* as if *a person wants to speak* and *does not venture to do so.*[8] But sometimes murmuring stems *from weakness,* as Numbers 11:1 reads: "There arose a murmuring of the people against the Lord, as if they were grieving on account of their labor." Sometimes it arises *from ignorance and error,* according to what John 7:12–13 has: "There was much murmuring . . . among the crowd. Some were saying: He is a good man. But others were saying: No, rather he seduces the crowds. Yet no one spoke openly about him. . . . " Sometimes it also issues *from wickedness,* as in Deuteronomy 1:26–27: "Being unfaithful to the word of the Lord your God,[9] you murmured in your tents and said: The Lord hates us, and therefore he has brought us out of the land of Egypt that he might deliver us into the hands of the Amorite. . . . " Similarly, these also were turning good into evil, both the repentance of the publicans as well as the mercy of Jesus. And they fell into this vice because they were proud and inhuman. Of them could be understood what Isaiah 65:5 says: "They say: Depart from me. Do not draw near to me, for you are unclean. These will be smoke in my anger, a fire burning all day long."

5. Third, concerning *the simulation of righteous justice* the text adds: *saying: This man welcomes sinners,* because of the affable nature of his conversation, *and eats with them,* because of the friendly nature of a banquet. By saying this, they wanted to accuse him of being a patron of evil persons and one who contemns the com-

---

[8] As far as I have been able to ascertain, Bonaventure is referring to Huguccio (Hugh of Pisa) who wrote a very influential *Liber derivatorum,* and died in 1210.
[9] The Vulgate reads *Dei nostri* ("our God").

mandments. So the Glossa says: "As if they were saying: He is against the Law, which prohibits this."[10] For in the Law contact with an unclean thing is forbidden. See Leviticus 11 and 13.[11] By this is understood avoidance of evil company. So Deuteronomy 7:2–3 reads: "You shall not enter into a covenant with them. . . . Neither shall you enter into marriage with them."[12] But, as the Glossa notes: "They are guilty of a double error, for they consider themselves righteous whereas they are proud, and the others sinners, whereas they are already repentant."[13] Therefore, the Pharisees, by feigning righteousness, sinned by their lack of mercy and by taking pride in themselves. This is what the Pharisees were wont to do. Luke 16:15 below states: "You are the ones who declare yourselves righteous in the sight of men and women." Likewise, by rendering an evil judgment, *they were sinning against their neighbors*, so that what Luke 6:42 has could be said of them: "You hypocrite, first cast out the beam from your own eye," etc. Furthermore, by impugning Christ's mercy, *they were sinning against Christ*, who *welcomed* sinners, according to what he had promised through Jeremiah in Jeremiah 3:1: "It is commonly said: If a man puts away his wife and she goes from him and marries another man, will he return to her any more?... But you have prostituted yourself to many lovers. Nevertheless, return to me, says the Lord,

---

[10] On p. 383, n. 2 QuarEd state that this is the Glossa Interlinearis.

[11] For example, Leviticus 11:47: "So that you may know the difference between the clean and the unclean, and know what you ought to eat and what to refuse"; Leviticus 13:46: "All the time that he is a leper and unclean he shall dwell alone outside the camp."

[12] It seems to me that Bonaventure has omitted a key clause from Deuteronomy 7:2, to wit, "nor show mercy to them." Hugh of St. Cher, p. 222v, h also quotes Deuteronomy 7:2–3, but in its entirety.

[13] On p. 383, n. 3 QuarEd state that this is the Glossa Interlinearis (from Homily 34, n. 2 of GGHG). See PL 76:1247A. Gregory's Homily 34 is on Luke 15:1–10.

and I will welcome you." For this is the action of most excellent mercy. So John 6:37 states: "Every-one[14] . . . who comes to me I will not cast him out." They were also reproving him for his merciful conduct because *he condescended to eat*, although this is an action of deepest mercy, according to Revelation 3:20: "I stand at the door and knock," etc. And Matthew 11:28 reads: "Come to me, all you who labor and are burdened." And John 7:37 has: "If anyone is thirsty, let him come to me and drink," etc.[15] For the Prophet, filled with the spirit, also invites everyone. Isaiah 55:1 says: "All you who are thirsty, come to the waters." And the reason for this is that, as it is said in Romans 10:12, "there is no distinction between Jew and Greek, for there is the same Lord of all, rich towards all who call upon him," etc.

Luke 15:3–32
The manifestation of God's mercy is described in three parables

6. *And he spoke to them this parable.* After he has disclosed the Jewish lack of compassion, he *displays divine compassion* in this second section in such a manner as to refute Jewish lack of mercy. And since God's mercy towards humankind is especially manifested in the human race's redemption, which humans needed as *a sacrifice of reconciliation, a liberating ransom*, and *a spirit of adoption*, it follows that in this section a triple par-

---

[14] Bonaventure has abbreviated John 6:37 and changed *omne* ("all that") to *omnis* ("everyone"). Bonaventure uses this same abbreviated text in his commentary on Luke 8:42 (#77) above.

[15] On p. 383, n. 6 QuarEd helpfully cite Homily 34, n. 2 of GGHG. See PL 76:1247B: "Rendering judgment against the Lord for welcoming sinners, they used their parched hearts to censure the very font of mercy."

able is introduced. Furthermore, God's mercy towards humankind is especially manifested by reason of the three things God has placed in humans, namely, by reason of an *instilled meekness, a stamped image,* and *a conferred likeness.* Now through the first, humans are assimilated to *the sheep*; through the second to *the imperial coin*; through the third to *the Son of the Eternal Father.* Therefore, in this section the Evangelist, illumined by the Spirit, sets forth a threefold parable, proffered by the mouth of the flesh of God, to accentuate God's mercy towards human nature. The first of these parables concerns *the shepherd and his sheep.* The second deals with *the woman and her drachmas* where verse 8 reads: *Or what woman, having ten drachmas.* The third deals with *a father and his sons* where verse 11 has: *A certain man had two sons.* In this he clearly manifests that every creature in a certain manner extends the mercy which God displays for humankind: *the brute creature* like the sheep, and *the creature which has only physical characteristics*[16] like the drachma, and *the rational creature* like human beings.

Luke 15:3–7
THE PARABLE OF THE LOST SHEEP

So the parable of *the lost sheep* develops in this fashion. For first the text expresses *the sorrowful anxiety* over the lost sheep, and then secondly *the great joy* for the sheep that has been found, where verse 5 has: *And when he has found it*, etc.

---

[16] I have given a paraphrase of Bonaventure's *corporalis*, which literally means "bodily."

Now in expressing *the sorrowful anxiety* for the lost sheep the Evangelist introduces four considerations, namely, *the possession of the multitude intact, the loss of the hundredth sheep, the abandonment of the rest of the multitude,* and *the search for the lost sheep.*

7. (Verse 3). So first, with regard to *the possession of the multitude intact,* which he wants to be understood not literally, but as a parable, he says: *And he spoke to them this parable.* So he is speaking in parables, because *this befits his wisdom.* The Psalm says: "I will open my mouth in parables," etc. (77:2). Also because *the infidelity of the Jews required it,* for whom the mysteries had to be veiled, according to what Matthew 13:13 notes: "This is why I speak to them in parables, because seeing they do not see, and hearing they do not hear." Another interpretation is: Because *it was suitable to the nature of Sacred Scripture,* in which not only words, but also things are signs to give instruction for the comprehension of the little ones and the simple folk so that they may conceive in themselves the multiform understanding of divine things. In accordance with Proverbs 1:1–4: "The parables of Solomon . . . to know wisdom and instruction, to understand the words of wisdom and to receive the instruction of doctrine . . . so that astuteness may be given to little ones and knowledge and understanding to youth."

8. (Verse 4). And since he is speaking to little ones, he sets forth clear examples when he says: *What man of you, who has a hundred sheep.* This man among men and women is the Son of God, of whom Baruch 3:38 says: "After these things he was seen on earth and conversed with men and women." And Philippians 2:7 reads: "being made in human likeness and found in human appearance." *The sheep* of this man are rational

creatures by reason of instilled meekness. Matthew
10:16 reads: "Behold, I am sending you forth like sheep
in the midst of wolves," etc. John 10:27–28 states: "My
sheep hear my voice...and I give them everlasting life."
Now these are numbered as *one hundred* on account of
perfection, which is intimated by a hundred on account
of the multiplication of ten by ten. So Bede comments:
"Since the number one hundred is perfect, God had one
hundred sheep, that is, the perfect number when he
created the substance of angels and humans."[17] For this
reason Matthew 13:8 uses this number to designate *perfect merit*: "Other seeds fell on good soil and yielded fruit
a hundredfold." And Genesis 26:12 states: "Isaac sowed
in that land, and he found that year a hundredfold."[18]
Similarly it refers to *the perfection of reward*. Matthew
19:29 has: "And everyone who has left house . . . will receive a hundredfold and will possess life everlasting."
Wherefore, *to have one hundred sheep* is to possess creatures in perfect number and in the state of their perfection.

9. Second, relative to *the loss of the hundredth sheep* the
text continues: *And if he loses one of them*. God lost *one*
sheep out of one hundred when man sinned. So Bede
comments: "One sheep is lost, when man abandons the
pastures of life by sinning."[19] Of this sheep it is said in
the Psalm: "I have gone astray like a sheep that is lost.
Seek after your servant, O Lord" (118:176).[20] So man is

---

[17] See CCSL cxx, p. 285. On p. 384, n. 6 QuarEd indicate that Bede is
following Homily 34, n. 3 of GGHG. See PL 76:1247BC.
[18] Bonaventure reads *sevit* ("sowed") whereas the Vulgate has *seruit*
("sowed"). Bonaventure reads *in anno illo* ("in that year") while the
Vulgate has *in ipso anno* ("in that very year").
[19] See CCSL cxx, p. 285, which is a quotation from Homily 34, n. 3 of
GGHG. See PL 76:1247C.
[20] Bonaventure has added *Domine* ("O Lord").

also said to be *one sheep*, for all have proceeded from one man, in whom they have also sinned, according to what Romans 5:12 says: "Through one man sin entered into the world, and through sin death . . . in whom all have sinned." But on account of the various sins added onto that of the one man they are said to be *many sheep*. Isaiah 53:6 states: "All we like sheep have gone astray. Everyone has turned aside into his own way." And 1 Peter 2:25 reads: "You were like sheep going astray," etc. And this happened as long as man lacked a shepherd. 1 Kings 22:17 has: "I saw all Israel scattered upon the hills like sheep without a shepherd." For this sheep had fallen prey to the wolf, the devil, about which John 10:12 says: "The wolf snatches and scatters the sheep."

10. Third, with regard *the abandonment of the rest of the multitude* the text adds: *Does he not leave the ninety-nine in the desert?* By *ninety-nine* are understood the Angels. There are two reasons for this. First, nine best fits the designation of the number of the angels on account of three times three in the orders of the Angels which designates the God who is three and one.[21] Second, after the angels had fallen and man was lost, their number remained imperfect and incomplete. So the Glossa says: "He left the ninety-nine, since the number of rational creatures was diminished with the loss of man."[22] Christ *left* these, not deserting them in a physi-

---

[21] Bonaventure's exegesis here becomes more comprehensible when one recalls that there were three orders of angels, each with three choirs. The seraphim, cherubim, and thrones comprise the first order. The dominations, virtues, and powers made up the second order. The principalities, archangels, and angels formed the third order.

[22] On p. 384, n. 13 QuarEd state that this is the Glossa Ordinaria (from Homily 34, n. 3 of GGHG). See PL 76:1247C. Readers might better grasp Bonaventure's thought here if they saw the powerful influence on it of Gregory the Great. I modify the translation of Gregory's Homily 34 made by Hurst, p. 282: "Because one hundred is

cal, local sense, since he is always everywhere, but because he is least concerned about their welfare. Hebrews 2:16 states: "At no time was he concerned about the angels, but was concerned about the seed of Abraham." Now it is said that *he left them in the desert*, that is, in heaven, which had been deserted by angels and humans, and no one could now enter therein. For which reason the heavenly homeland is compared to *a desert*. So the Glossa says: "*In the desert*, that is, in heaven, which man deserted when he sinned."[23] Heavenly Jerusalem is also called *deserted and desolate*, for according to Galatians 4:26–27: "That Jerusalem which is above is free, which is our mother. For it is written: Rejoice, you barren one, who does not bear. . . . For many are the children of the deserted and desolate one, more than of her who has a husband." And Isaiah 35:1 has: "The desert and impassable land will rejoice, and the wilderness will rejoice and will flourish like the lily."

11. Fourth, concerning *the search for the single lost sheep* the text says: *And go after that which is lost*. That is, God, the Son of God, came into this world to save this sheep, namely, man. Luke 19:10 below has: "The Son of Man has come to seek and to save what was lost." So 1

---

a perfect number, he himself possessed a hundred sheep when he created the substance of angels and men and women. But one sheep was lost when man abandoned the pasture of life by sinning. He left the ninety-nine in the desert, since he left the majestic choirs of angels in heaven. But why is heaven called a desert, unless it is because we call what we have left behind deserted? Man deserted heaven when he sinned. The ninety-nine sheep remained in the desert when the Lord was seeking the one on earth, because the number of rational beings, of angels and of men, which had been created in order to see God, was diminished when man was lost. Man who had been lost was sought on earth, in order that the perfect sum of the sheep might be restored in heaven."

[23] On p. 385, n. 1 QuarEd state that this is the Glossa Interlinearis (from Gregory).

Timothy 1:15 states: "The saying is true and worthy of all acceptance, that Christ Jesus came into this[24] world to save sinners." And Christ did this as *the good shepherd*. Thus, Ezekiel 34:11–12 reads: "Behold, I myself will seek my sheep and will visit them, as the shepherd visits his flock." – And since the good shepherd does not stop his quest until he saves, the text adds: *until he finds it?* Now Christ finds this sheep when he rescues it from perdition through his blood, according to what Deuteronomy 32 has: "The Lord alone was his leader, and there was no strange god with him" (verse 12). "The Lord found him in a desert land, in a place of horror, and of vast wilderness" (verse 10). Now despite great obstacles God found men and women who were lost, according to what Hosea 9:10 says: "Like grapes in the desert I found Israel . . . and like the first fruits of the fig tree." So this shepherd labored to the point of death to find the sheep, according to what John 10:11 has: "The good shepherd lays down his life for his sheep." For this reason the shepherd has also become *a lamb* among the sheep, so that he might redeem the sheep, according to what Isaiah 53:7 states: "He will be led like a sheep to the slaughter. And like a lamb before his shearer he will be dumb and not open his mouth." – So this search was prefigured by that search by which Abraham, willing to sacrifice his son, found a ram. Genesis 22:13 reads: "Abraham lifted up his eyes and saw a ram . . . amongst the briars sticking fast by the horns, which he . . . offered as a holocaust instead of his son." So all the rest of those sacrifices that had been offered whether of sheep or lambs and goats or rams and heifers signify that "Christ by virtue of his own blood entered once for all into the Holy of Holies, having ob-

---

[24] The Vulgate does not have *hunc* ("this").

tained eternal redemption."[25] And this is to say: "She searches carefully for it until she finds it."[26]

12. (Verse 5). *And when he has found it.* After detailing the sorrowful concern over the lost sheep, the text continues here with an expression of *the great joy over the sheep that was found.* About this three points are made: *the private exultation, the public rejoicing,* and *the principal point of the parable.*

So first, relative to *the private exultation* over the sheep that has been found the text reads: *And when he has found it, he lays it upon his shoulders rejoicing.* "These shoulders," as Ambrose says, "are the arms of the cross"; "to that place, he says, I have brought my sins. I have rested on that noble neck of the gibbet."[27] So he placed the sheep that had been lost on his shoulders, because he carried our sins there. Thus Isaiah 53:4 states: "Truly he himself has borne our illness, and he himself has carried our infirmities."[28] And 1 Peter 2:24 reads: "He himself bore our sins in his body upon the tree, so that we, having died to sin, might live to justice." And this is what Bede says: "He placed the sheep on his shoulders, because, taking on human nature, he himself

---

[25] Bonaventure is alluding to Hebrews 9:12–13 and has added *Christus* ("Christ") in his actual quotation of Hebrews 9:12.

[26] Luke 15:8.

[27] See CCSL xiv, p. 287. On p. 385, n. 11 QuarEd rightly indicate that Ambrose's original text has *in illa patibuli nobilis ceruice* ("on that neck of the noble gibbet").

[28] Bonaventure reads *infirmitates nostras* ("our infirmities") rather than the Vulgate's *dolores nostros* ("our sorrows"). It is the same reading of Isaiah 53:4 he has in his commentary on Luke 5:34 (#34) above. Hugh of St. Cher, p. 223c also quotes Isaiah 53:4, but simply writes "etc." after quoting its first three words.

carried our sins."²⁹ And he carried our sins on the cross and carried the cross on his shoulders, according to what Isaiah 9:6 has: "Dominion was placed upon his shoulders." And Isaiah 22:22 says: "I will lay the key of the house of David upon his shoulder." – *Rejoicing* he carried us upon his shoulder on account of the greatest love which he manifested for our liberation. Isaiah 40:11 reads: "He will feed his flock like a shepherd. He will gather together the lambs in his arm. . . . He himself will carry the young." And this with the greatest joy, according to Isaiah 66:12–14: "You will be carried at the breasts, and upon the knees they will caress you. As one whom the mother caresses, so will I comfort you. . . . You will see, and your heart will rejoice, and your bones will flourish like the grass."³⁰

13. (Verse 6). Second, with regard to *public rejoicing* the text adds: *And on coming home, he calls together his friends and neighbors.* This house is celestial Jerusalem, about which Isaiah 60:7 says: "I will glorify the house of my majesty." And John 14:2 states: "In my Father's house there are many mansions." Into this house Christ *came* on his ascension. Concerning this advent Isaiah 63:1 reads: "Who is this who comes from Edom, with dyed garments from Bozrah?" Into this house *he carries the sheep*, since, as it is said in Ephesians 4:8: "Ascending on high, he led captivity captive." And *he calls together* the Angels, who are said to be *friends* on account of their intimacy through knowing secrets. For this is a

---

²⁹ See CCSL cxx, p. 285. Bede quotes verbatim from Homily 34, n. 3 of GGHG. See PL 76:1247D. Hugh of St. Cher, p. 223c specifies *Christus* ("Christ") as the subject in his quotation from Bede.
³⁰ Bonaventure applies the imagery of Mother Jerusalem to the cross. Contrast Bonaventure's exegesis with that of Hugh of St. Cher, p. 223c–d, where in #c Hugh also quotes Bede, 1 Peter 2:24, Isaiah 53:4, and Ambrose (as well as 1 Corinthians 6:20).

sign of friendship. John 15:15 says: "But I have called you friends," etc.[31] And *neighbors*, because of their nearness to provide support. So Matthew 18:10 says: "Their angels in heaven always behold the face of my Father in heaven."[32] – The Lord calls these together for common rejoicing in the salvation of men and women. Therefore, he also adds: *Saying to them: Rejoice with me, because I have found my sheep that was lost.* He says this, as if giving them matter for rejoicing over the accomplishment of so great a boon and of the sheer love God showed to men and women. So Eternal Wisdom says in Proverbs 8:31: "My delights are with the human family." Therefore, Bede comments: "He does not say: Rejoice over the sheep that was found, but *with me*, because our life is his joy."[33] Wherefore, also to give expression to this magnificent rejoicing the joyous finding of the human race is called *nuptial joy*, in which the heavenly citizens exult. Revelation 19:6–7 says: "I heard as it were the voice of a multitude of angels saying: Alleluia. . . . Let us rejoice and exult and give glory to God. For the marriage of the Lamb has come, and the spouse of the Lamb has prepared herself."[34] For the Lamb has

---

[31] John 15:15 reads: "No longer do I call you servants, because the servant does not know what his master does. But I have called you friends, because all things that I have heard from my Father I have made known to you."

[32] On p. 386, n. 3 QuarEd cite the Glossa Ordinaria (from Homily 34, n. 3 of GGHG) on Luke 15:6: "Having redeemed humankind, the shepherd returns to heaven. There he finds the choirs of Angels, who are *friends*, because they continuously and steadfastly keep his will, who are also *neighbors*, because they enjoy the clarity of his vision." See Hugh of St. Cher, p. 223g, where it is clear that he is dependent on the Glossa Ordinaria. Hugh also quotes John 15:15, but in its complete form, and also Matthew 18:10.

[33] See CCSL, cxx, p. 286. Bede borrows from Homily 34, n. 3 of GGHG. See PL 76:1248A.

[34] Bonaventure's has adapted Revelation 19:6–7 to his purposes, especially at the beginning of 19:6. The Vulgate reads *Audivi quasi*

espoused for himself the holy church gathered together from sinners, and the Lamb possesses the little sheep that had been found.

14. (Verse 7). Third, about *the principal point of the parable* the text continues: *I say to you that thus there will be joy in heaven over one sinner who repents.* Isaiah 49:13 reads: "Give praise, O you heavens, and rejoice, O earth. You mountains, give praise with jubilation, because the Lord has comforted his people and will have mercy on his poor ones." – There is great joy, since it is greater to heal an infirm person than to preserve a healthy person. And therefore, the text adds: *more than over ninety-nine just who have no need of repentance.* Now this is said, not because the sinner who repents is better than the ninety-nine just, but because in the redemption of the human race God performed greater things than in the conservation of the entire heavenly multitude. For this manifests *greater power, wisdom,* and *mercy.* Greater *power* since it is greater to justify the ungodly than to create heaven and earth.[35] Greater *wisdom,* because as Job 26:12 states, "His wisdom has struck the proud person." Greater *clemency* or mercy. Thus Luke 1:78 above says: "Because of the loving kindness and mercy of our God, wherewith the Orient from

---

vocem turbae magnae ("I heard as it were a voice of a great crowd"). On p. 386, n. 6 QuarEd surmise that Bonaventure may have been influenced by Revelation 5:11: "I heard the voice of a multitude of angels."

[35] Bonaventure seems to be alluding to Romans 4:5: ". . . who justifies the ungodly." On p. 386, n. 9 QuarEd refer to Augustine. See Tractate 72, n. 3 in *St. Augustine: Tractates on the Gospel of John 55–111,* trans. John W. Rettig, (FC 90; Washington: Catholic University of America, 1994), p. 83: " Let him understand who can, let him judge who can, whether it is greater to create the just than to justify the ungodly. For assuredly if both are of equal power, the latter is of greater mercy."

on high has visited us." For greater was *the condescension in Christ.* Greater also was *the raising up of the human race*, according to the Psalm: "Because your magnificence has been elevated above the heavens" (8:2). So the latter is understood with regard to *the reason for our repentance*, namely, the redemption of the human race, in which the grounds for joy are greater than in all the other works of God.[36] – But if it is understood of *any sinner whatsoever by himself*, then the focus is on joy as *the new thing that is greater* or the meaning is that the sinner is frequently *more fervent* than the just person. So Gregory in his *Moralia* maintains: "Certain people in God's service are strengthened by the past weakness of someone, and both the desire of future things and the memory of past deeds draws them and impels them to keep the commandments."[37] So this statement does not refer to all sinners nor to all the just, but to the sinners who are fervent after their conversion and to the just who remain tepid. So as Gregory has taught and as Bede says in the Glossa: "There is greater joy over a sinner than over one who remains just. Just as the leader in a battle has more love for a soldier who returned after deserting and fought valiantly against the enemy than the one who never deserted, but never fought valiantly."[38] Another interpretation is that this is said be-

---

[36] Bonaventure now gets ready to address a new question: Is Christ's statement universally valid? How does it apply to someone like John the Baptist who was sanctified in his mother's womb?

[37] On p. 386, n. 11 QuarEd refer to Book XVIII, chapter 26, n. 43 of Gregory's *Moralia*. Bonaventure's quotation is very close to that of CCSL cxliiia, p. 913. Gregory goes on to talk about the love that draws one to the future and the shame that impels one to resist committing the sins of the past.

[38] On p. 386, n. 12 QuarEd refer to the Glossa Ordinaria apud Lyranum on Luke 15:7. The Glossa is based on Homily 34, n. 4 of GGHG, which Bede copied. For Gregory, see PL 76:1248C. For Bede,

cause the adversary has been conquered, in accordance with what Isaiah 9:3 says: "They will rejoice before you, as they that rejoice in the harvest, as conquerors rejoice after taking a prey, when they divide the spoils."

Luke 15:8–10
THE PARABLE OF THE LOST COIN

15. (Verse 8). *Or what woman*, etc. After the parable of the shepherd and his sheep, the parable of *the woman and the drachmas* is added here. In this parable under the metaphor of *the drachma, God's loving mercy to men and women* is revealed. There are four aspects of God's loving mercy: *the creation* of men and women, their *fall*, their *restoration*, their *justification*.

So first, concerning *God's loving mercy* with respect to *human creation* the text says: *Or what woman having ten drachmas.* This *woman* is divine wisdom,[39] which is said to be *a woman*, because she is to be loved as a most precious spouse.[40] The wise man says of wisdom in Wisdom 8:2: "I have loved her and have sought her out from my youth. And I have desired to take her as my spouse, and I have become a lover of her beauty." But she is said to be *a woman*, not because of the weakness of her sex, but because of the loving devotion of divine affection and mercy. For this reason God compares himself to a mother's affection. Isaiah 49:15 says: "Can a woman forget her infant, so as not to have mercy on the child of

---

see CCSL cxx, p. 286. Hugh of St. Cher, p. 223k paraphrases Gregory/Bede/Glossa, but indicates no source for his interpretation.

[39] On p. 387, n. 3 QuarEd cite Homily 34, n. 6 of GGHG. See PL 76:1249A: "While the shepherd is God, the woman is God's wisdom."

[40] In his commentary on Luke 13:21 (#44) above Bonaventure also interprets the woman of the parable of the leaven as divine wisdom.

her womb?, etc." And therefore, Wisdom says of herself in Sirach 24:24: "I am the mother of beautiful love," etc. So since God's wisdom is most powerful, most beautiful, most provident, and also most merciful, it may be taken to refer to *the valiant and strong woman*, spoken of by Proverbs 31:10: "Who will find a valiant woman?" That is, wisdom, which "reaches mightily," etc.[41] It refers also to *a valiant and good and beautiful woman*. Sirach 26:21 reads: "As the sun when it rises to the world," etc.[42] To *a provident woman*. Proverbs 14:1 states: "A wise woman builds her house," that is, wisdom. To *woman with loving devotion*, as in this parable. So the Glossa observes: "The woman, that is God's wisdom, had ten drachmas, since she created human beings and angels."[43] Now the drachma is the rational creature, sealed with the divine image. Thus, the Glossa says: "A drachma is a coin of a certain weight, which bears the image of the king."[44] *Man* is such a coin. About him it is said in Genesis 1:26: "Let us make man in our image and likeness." So Sirach 17:1 also says: "God created man from the earth and made him after his own image." *The angelic spirit* is such a coin. So Ezekiel 28:12–13 reads: "You are the seal of his[45] likeness, full of wisdom and perfect in beauty. You were in the pleasures of God's paradise." Therefore, the ten drachmas are the nine orders of angels with the tenth being human beings

---

[41] Bonaventure quotes part of Wisdom 8:1: "She (wisdom) reaches, therefore, from end to end mightily, and orders all things gently."

[42] Sirach 26:21 reads: "As the sun when it rises to the world in the high places of God, so is the beauty of a good wife for the ornament of her house."

[43] On p. 387, n. 6 QuarEd state that this is based on the Glossa Ordinaria (from Gregory) on Luke 15:8, which ends with "she created them in her image." See PL 76:1249C for Gregory's original text, which differs from that of the Glossa and of Bonaventure.

[44] On p. 387, n. 7 QuarEd state that this is the Glossa Interlinearis.

[45] Bonaventure has adapted the quotation by adding *eius* ("his").

to complete the entire universe. For the totality of numbers is encompassed in the number ten. Wherefore, the number ten also conveys a certain status. So Bede says: "The woman had ten drachmas, with nine orders of angels and human beings added as the tenth to complete the number of the elect."[46] Wherefore, in this God manifests his loving mercy towards rational creatures which he has created and sealed with his image.

16. Second, with respect to *God's loving mercy* towards *fallen man* the text says: *And*[47] *if she loses one drachma,* that is, through human transgression. For *the drachma that is lost* is human nature. Thus the Glossa says: "The woman, that is, God's wisdom, had ten drachmas, since she had created men and women and angels in her image. But she lost one, when man withdrew from the Creator's likeness."[48] Wherefore, since man is the tenth after the nine orders of Angels, he is rightly referred to by *the tenth drachma.* From this it follows that the liberation of men and women was prefigured when God commanded that *a tenth* be offered.[49] From this it also follows that *ten commandments* were given to men and women, by which they may ascend to God as through certain steps. Furthermore, it follows that in a prefiguration of the incarnation it is said that the sun turned

---

[46] See CCSL cxx, p. 287 for Bede's longer text, which is abbreviated in Bonaventure's quotation. Bede, for his part, is dependent on Homily 34, n. 6 of GGHG. See PL 76:1249CD. Hugh of St. Cher, p. 223i does not quote this passage.

[47] On p. 387, n. 10 QuarEd correctly mentioned that the Vulgates does not read *Et* ("And").

[48] On p. 387, n. 11 QuarEd state that this is the Glossa Ordinaria. See Homily 34, n. 6 of GGHG in PL 76:1249A, where Gregory concludes with: ". . . by sinning withdrew from the image of his Creator."

[49] See Exodus 22:29: "You shall not delay to pay your tithes (tenths) and your first fruits."

back *ten degrees,* as it is said in 2 Kings 20:11.[50] For the sun turned back by ten degrees, when God descended past the angels to man, who is the tenth.[51] Moreover, it follows that *the denarius* is the payment for everyone who labors in the vineyard of the householder. Matthew 20:2 says: "Having agreed," etc.[52] Therefore, it is fitting that *the tenth that was lost* designate fallen human nature.

17. For this lost drachma divine wisdom manifests *loving devotion stemming from mercy.* For which reason the text adds: *Does she not light a lamp* in the incarnation? *A lamp* is a light in a vessel of clay. That is, God in human flesh. So the Glossa states: "The wisdom of God lights a lamp to search, when she appeared in the flesh, because a lamp is light in a vessel of clay, that is the Word in the flesh."[53] Concerning this lamp it is said in the Psalm: "There I will bring forth a horn for David. I have prepared a lamp for my Christ" (131:17). So about the lighting of this lamp it is said in John 1: "The Word was God" (verse 1). He was the true light, which en-

---

[50] Isaiah the prophet is giving a sign to Hezekiah the king through the sun dial: "So Isaiah the prophet called upon the Lord, and he brought the shadow ten degrees backwards by the lines, by which it had already gone down in the dial of Ahaz."

[51] On p. 387, n. 13 QuarEd cite Isidore's *Quaestiones* sive *Commentarium* on IV Kings chapter 6, n. 4ff: "The first degree of God's descent was in an angel. . . . The second degree of descent was from angels to patriarchs. . . . The third in the giving of the Law. . . . The fourth degree in Joshua , son of Nun. . . . The fifth in the Judges. . . . The sixth in the Kings of the Jews. . . . The seventh in the Prophets. . . . The eighth in the priests. . . . The ninth in man. The tenth in the passion."

[52] Matthew 20:2 reads: "And having agreed with the laborers for a denarius a day, he sent them into his vineyard."

[53] On p. 388, n. 2 QuarEd state that this is the Glossa Ordinaria (from Homily 34, n. 6 of GGHG). See PL 76:1249A for Gregory's text which the Glossa modifies.

lightens every person" (verse 9). And afterwards: "The Word became flesh and dwelt among us" (verse 14).[54] – Not only this, but *she also shakes up*[55] *the house*, as happens in preaching. The Glossa interprets: "She shakes up the house, for she troubled the consciences of men and women about their sins."[56] And this refers to preachers. So it is said in Zephaniah 1:12: "I will search Jerusalem with lamps, and I will punish the men who are settled on their lees." – *And searches carefully, until she finds it?* with our redemption. So Wisdom 6:17 reads: "She goes about seeking such as are worthy of her, and she presents herself to them cheerfully along the ways and meets them with all solicitude." So what the Psalm says is also fittingly applied to her: "If I will give sleep to my eyes or slumber to my eyelids...until I search out a place for the Lord, a tabernacle for the God of Jacob" (131:4–5).

18. (Verse 9). Third, relative to loving mercy to *restored man* the text adds: *And when she has found it, she calls together her friends and neighbors.* By *the friends* and *neighbors* of divine wisdom are understood the good Angels and holy souls. So the Glossa explains: "The friends and neighbors are the heavenly powers, to the extent that they draw near to God to contemplate him more closely."[57] Therefore, these are said to be *the friends* of

---

[54] Contrast Hugh of St. Cher, p. 223v, d: "Just as the lamp is Christ, so too the candelabrum is the cross, upon which he had to be raised."

[55] On p. 388, n. 4 QuarEd accurately indicate that the Vulgate reads *everrit* ("sweeps clean") whereas Bonaventure (along with Gregory, Bede, Albert, Thomas, and Gorranus) has *evertit* ("shakes up").

[56] On p. 388, n. 4 QuarEd state that this is the Glossa Ordinaria (from Homily 34, n. 6 of GGHG). See PL 76:1249B for Gregory's text, which the Glossa modifies.

[57] The translation "more closely" renders *vicinius*, which comes from the same root as *vicinae* ("neighbors"). On p. 388, n. 7 QuarEd state that this is the Glossa Ordinaria (from Gregory). See Homily 34, n. 6

Wisdom because they love her and are loved by her, according to what Wisdom 7:27–28 reads: "Through nations she conveys herself into holy souls and makes them friends of God and prophets. For God loves only those who dwell with wisdom." Now *to call together* is nothing else but to join together in the unity and conformity of love. Job 25:2 states: "Power and terror are with him, who fashions harmony in his high places." And through this harmony of mutual love he granted them a common ground for joy. – And so the text continues: *Saying: Rejoice with me, for I have found the drachma that I had lost.* For Wisdom invites people *to rejoice together*, because that is the law of love. 1 Corinthians 13:6 says: "Love does not rejoice over wickedness, but rejoices with the truth." And the wise person says in Wisdom 8:17–18: "Thinking these things . . . , that there is immortality in thinking of wisdom, and that there is great delight in her friendship," for she wants the joys of all things to be *common* as especially is the case in that heavenly Jerusalem, not *private*. So Tobit 13:12 reads: "Jerusalem, give glory to the Lord for your good things and bless the eternal God, so that he . . . may call back to you all the captives and that you may rejoice forever and ever." For in this finding of the drachma is accomplished the restoration of the number of the elect in the heavenly Jerusalem. And that is a great cause for rejoicing. Isaiah 65:18 has: "Behold, I create rejoicing for Jerusalem, and for its people joy," for they rejoice with divine wisdom and in our salvation. And this in accordance with what Isaiah 66:10–11 states: "Rejoice with Jerusalem and exult with her, all you who love her. Re-

---

of GGHG. See PL 76:1249C for a text that is somewhat different from that of the Glossa. See Hurst, p. 285: "They (the heavenly powers) are close to supernal Wisdom in proportion as they draw near to him through the gift of uninterrupted vision."

joice for joy with her, all you who mourn over her, so that you may suck and be filled with the breasts of her consolation, so that you may also flow with delights from the abundance of her glory."

19. (Verse 10). Fourth, concerning *God's loving mercy* towards *men and women who had been justified* the text adds: *In the same way I tell you: there is joy for the angels of God*[58] *over one sinner who repents.* Now *the angels rejoice* over the repentance of a sinner. For *sin is destroyed; justice is recovered; the pride of the demons is confounded; protection by the angels is rendered efficacious; the Church is repaired; divine wrath is placated;* and *the heavenly Jerusalem* is restored. And the blessed angels rejoice especially over these seven effects. And so God's angels find joy in *a sinner's repentance*, in which they see these seven aforementioned effects take place.[59] – First, because *sin is destroyed.* Acts 3:19 reads: "Repent and be converted, so that your sins may be destroyed." Thus, it is said in Mark 1:4 that "John preached a baptism of repentance for the cancellation of sins," etc. – Second, because through repentance *justice is recovered.* So Revelation 2:5 reads: "Remember whence you have fallen, and repent and do the former works." And Sirach 17:20 says: "To the penitent God has given the way of justice and has strengthened those fainting."[60] – Third, because through repentance *the pride of the demons is confounded.* The Psalm says: "Depart from me, all you workers of iniquity, for the Lord has heard the voice of

---

[58] On p. 388, n. 13 QuarEd rightly mention that the Vulgate reads *Gaudium erit coram Angelis Dei* ("There will be joy among the angels of God").
[59] There is no parallel to these "seven effects" in Hugh of St. Cher.
[60] The Vulgate reads *conrogavit deficientes* ("has called together those fainting") whereas Bonaventure has *confirmavit deficientes* ("has strengthened those fainting").

my weeping" (6:9). And afterwards it continues: "Let all my enemies be ashamed and be very much troubled," etc. (6:11). For when a sinner is ashamed of his sin through repentance, then the demons are ashamed of their shamelessness. Jeremiah 31:19 states: "After you converted me, I did penance. . . . I was confounded and ashamed, because I have borne the reproach of my youth." – Fourth, because through repentance *protection by the angels is rendered efficacious*. Therefore, Revelation 3:19–20 has: "Those whom I love I rebuke and chastise. Be earnest, therefore, and repent. Behold, I stand at the door and knock." For our guardian angel does this diligently.[61] – Fifth, because through repentance *the Church is repaired*. For which reason it is said in Matthew 9:13: "I have not come to call the just, but sinners" to repentance.[62] For Christ calls to ecclesiastical unity, in which there is cancellation of sins and heavenly grace is given, according to what Ezekiel 18:21 says: "If the wicked did penance for all his sins . . . he will surely live and will not die." – Sixth, because *divine wrath is placated*. Sirach 12:3 reads: "The Most High hates sinners and has mercy on the penitent." And Jeremiah 18:8 reads: "If that nation . . . will repent of its evil, I also will repent of the evil that I have thought to do to it." – Seventh, because through repentance *the heavenly Jerusalem is restored*. So Matthew 4:17 says: "Repent, for the kingdom of the heavens will be drawing near."[63] And wherefore, the heavenly citizens exult, as it is said here: *There is joy for God's angels over one sinner who repents*. For they see the great power of repentance which not

---

[61] Apparently Bonaventure takes the guardian angel as the one knocking on the door and not Christ, "the Amen . . . the beginning of God's creation" (Revelation 3:14).

[62] In reality Bonaventure is quoting Luke 5:32. Matthew 9:13 reads: "For I have come to call sinners, not the just."

[63] See Bonaventure's commentary on Luke 15:1 (#3) note 6 above.

only recovers what was lost, but also obtains much more from God's loving mercy. Thus, Job 42:10 reads: "The Lord was turned at the repentance of Job. . . . The Lord doubled all[64] that Job had had before."

20. And for this reason all, who love God, who love good and who have the affection of loving mercy must exult with the angels over the conversion and repentance of sinners. So the Apostle in 2 Corinthians 7 says: "Even if I made you sorrowful for a while, I now rejoice, not because you were made sorrowful, but because your sorrow led you to repentance. For you were made sorrowful according to God, so that you might now suffer no loss at our hands. For the sorrow that is according to God produces repentance that surely tends towards salvation" (verses 8–10). And then he adds: "For it wrought in you earnestness, nay, defensive explanations, indignation, fear, yearning, zeal, readiness to avenge" (verse 11). And from these fitting honor is given to the divine majesty, the heavenly number is restored, and the unity of ecclesiastical peace is recovered. And therefore, in the conversion and repentance of one sinner the supercelestial, celestial, and subcelestial hierarchy fittingly exults.[65]

---

[64] The Vulgate reads *omnia quaecumque* ("all whatsoever") while Bonaventure has *omnia* ("all"). A smoother translation would be: "The Lord gave Job twice as much as he had before."

[65] See Bonaventure's commentary on Luke 13:33 (#72) above.

Luke 15:11–32
THE PARABLE OF THE FATHER AND HIS SONS[66]

21. *And he said to them: A certain man had two sons.*
After the parable of the shepherd and his sheep and of
the woman and the drachmas here in a third position is
added the parable of *the father and his sons*, so that
through the very great love the father has for his son
God's very great love may be shown here for the converted sinner, who is referred to by *the prodigal son.*
And since the mercy of the father is shown in that he
alleviated the misery of his son, who was first a sinner
and then a penitent, it follows that the Evangelist
makes four descriptive points in this parable. For first
he describes *the insolence* of the prodigal son. Second,
his *misery and indigence* where verse 14 reads: *And after he had spent all.* Third, his *repentance* where verse
17 has: *But when he[67] came to himself, he said,* etc.
Fourth, *the mercy of the father* where verse 20 says: *but
while he was yet a long way off.* And indeed the Evangelist describes the process in a most fitting order. For
insolence cast the prodigal son headlong into misery and
indigence. But *indigence* stirred him to repentance, and
repentance prepared him to obtain his father's mercy.

---

[66] See Dennis J. Billy, "Conversion and the Franciscan Preacher:
Bonaventure's Commentary on the Prodigal Son" *Collectanea Franciscana* 58 (1988): 259–275. See also *A Commentary on The Parable
of the Prodigal Son by Hugh of St. Cher (†1263)*, translated, with
introduction and notes by Hugh Bernard Feiss (Toronto: Peregrina,
1996).

[67] On p. 389, n. 11 QuarEd correctly mention that the Vulgate reads
ipse ("he [himself]") while Bonaventure does not.

Luke 15:11–13
THE INSOLENCE OF THE PRODIGAL SON

The Evangelist introduces three things to express *the prodigal son's insolence*, namely, *the condition of human freedom, the perpetration of voluntary sin*, and *the dissipation of the good of grace and nature*.

22. (Verse 11). So first, with regard to *the condition of human freedom* the text says: *And he said: A certain man had two sons.* By this *man*, as has often been said,[68] we understand the benign and loving Lord. For he himself, by reason of the supreme love, which renders him benign and human towards man, can rightly be called *man*. Thus Daniel 10:18 states: "The one that looked like a man touched me and strengthened me." Also as a designation of this, God frequently appeared to the holy Patriarchs and Prophets in the human form of a subject creature. But by *two sons* we understand the universality of the human race, not only with regard to Gentiles and Jews, as the Glossa explains it,[69] but also in a more general sense to encompass the innocent and the repentant, as must be understood from the application of the parable itself. Therefore, Bede comments: "This parable about Jew and Gentile can be understood generally of the repentant and the righteous, or the person who seems to himself to be righteous."[70] And these

---

[68] See Bonaventure's commentary on Luke 14:16 (#36) and 15:4 (#8) above, where "the man" is Christ and the Son of God respectively.

[69] On p. 390, n. 3 QuarEd state that this is the Glossa Ordinaria (from Bede who follows Augustine) apud Lyranum. For Augustine, see Book II, Question XXXIII, n. 1 in *Sancti Avrelii Avgvstini Quastiones Evangeliorvm cum appendice Qvaestionvm XVI in Matthaevm*, ed. Almut Mutzenbecher, CCSL xlivb (Turnhout: Brepols, 1980), p. 73. For Bede, see CCSL cxx, p. 287.

[70] On p. 390, n. 4 QuarEd state that this is what the Glossa Interlinearis on Luke 15:11 says. It stems from Bede. See CCSL cxx, p. 295.

are called *sons* because they have been created with free will and destined to possess the eternal inheritance. John 8:35 says: "But the slave does not abide in the house forever, but[71] the son abides there forever." Wherefore, the Psalmist says: "As a father has mercy on his sons, so does the Lord have mercy on those who fear him" (102:13).

23. (Verse 12). And since freedom of will in people who are vain and in sinners frequently presumes on its own powers and usurps to itself what belongs to God, the text adds: *And the younger of them said to his father: Father, give me the share of the property that falls to me.* This *younger son* is said to be the one who is more vain and who is highly oriented towards sensual goods, according to what Qoheleth 11:10 says: "For youth and pleasure are vain." And Qoheleth 11:9 reads: "Rejoice, O young man, in your youth. . . . And know that for all these God will bring you to judgment." This young man seeks *his own portion*, because he wants to be left to his own freedom, so that he may now conduct his life, not according to the rule of grace, but according to the whim of his own will. Therefore, Bede says: "*The property* is everything that we do, our life, our wisdom, our thought, and our speech. So the younger asks that a portion of this property be given to himself, since man, having taken delight in his own rational sense, sought to govern himself by his free will and to withdraw from the rule of his Creator."[72] This petition was not made for his own

---

[71] The Vulgate does not read *autem* ("but").

[72] On p. 390, n. 8 QuarEd state that Bede's interpretation comes from the Glossa Ordinaria apud Lyranum. For Bede himself, see CCSL cxx, pp. 287–288. See also CCSL xlivb, pp. 73–74. See Jerome's Letter 21, n. 5–6 in *The Letters of Jerome,* Volume I, Letters 1–22, translated by Charles C. Mierow, ACW 33 (Westminster: Newman Press, 1963), p. 114. "Everything is the substance (prop-

benefit, but rather to his detriment. For he sought to be placed in his own hands and to be left to his own judgment. It was like the petition of the sons of Israel when they petitioned for a king. 1 Samuel 8 states: "The sons of Israel[73] said to Samuel: Make us a king to judge us" (verse 5). "The Lord said to Samuel . . . : They have not rejected you, but me, that I should not reign over them" (verse 7). – And since the Lord in his just judgment leaves the person who is presumptuous about himself to his own devices, the text adds: *And he divided his property among them.* For it was fitting to do so, according to what Sirach 15:14 has: "God made man from the beginning and left him in the control of his own counsel." For to do so is the Lord's just judgment, according to what Matthew 25:15 says: "To one he gave five talents, and to another two, and to another one, to each according to his particular ability," etc.

24. (Verse 13). Second, with regard to *the perpetration of voluntary sin* the text continues: *And not many days after, having gathered up all his possessions,* through the rule of free will which he has over all his natural powers, *the younger son took a journey into a far country,* and this by committing sin. For *the country* is said to be *far* from God, not because of its spatial location, since God is everywhere, but because of the difference of will. So the Glossa observes: "*He went away into a far country,* not by changing his residence, but his soul. For the more a person sins by engaging in evil deeds, the farther

---

erty) of God: life, reason, thought, speech. This is the gift God has bestowed upon all alike, and in equal measure. . . . That is, he gave them free choice, he gave their hearts' desire, that each might live, not in accordance with God's command, but to please himself; that is, not out of necessity, but by free will. . . ."

[73] According to the Vulgate it was not "the sons of Israel" who petitioned Samuel, but "all the elders of Israel."

away he moves from God's grace."[74] Therefore, Proverbs
15:29 reads: "The Lord is faraway from the wicked and
will hear the prayers of the just."[75] But sin is *the country
that is faraway* from God, for, since it is *iniquity*, it distances one from the highest *goodness*, according to what
Isaiah 59:2 says: "Your iniquities have separated you
from your God, and your sins have hid his face from
you." Since sin is also *darkness*, it distances one from
the highest *light and truth*. 1 John 1:5–6 reads: "God is
light, and in him there is no darkness. If we say that we
have fellowship with him and walk in darkness, we lie
and are not practicing the truth." And a little later he
notes what he means by darkness: "The person who
hates his brother is in the darkness," etc.[76] Further,
since sin is *nothing*, it distances one from the highest *being*. For which reason Jeremiah 2:5 says: "What iniquity
have your fathers found in me, that they have distanced
themselves from me and have walked after nothing?"[77]
About these three matters together 2 Corinthians
6:14–16 states: "What has justice in common with iniquity? Or what fellowship has light with darkness? What
harmony is there between Christ and Belial? . . . And
what agreement has the temple of God with idols?" And

---

[74] On p. 390, n. 11 QuarEd state that this is the Glossa Ordinaria
(from Bede) apud Lyranum. See CCSL cxx, p. 288. The Glossa's quotation is almost verbatim. See Jerome, Letter 21, n. 7: "We must understand, therefore, that it is not by spatial distances but through
affection that we either are with God or depart from him." Augustine,
Book II, Question 33, n. 1 in CCSL xlivb, p. 74: "Therefore, *the faraway country* is forgetfulness of God."
[75] Hugh of St. Cher, p. 224h also quotes Proverbs 15:29.
[76] 1 John 2:11.
[77] On p. 390, n. 14 QuarEd refer to Augustine's Tractate 1, n. 13 on
John's Gospel. See *St. Augustine: Tractates on the Gospel of John
1–10,* translated by John W. Rettig, FC 78 (Washington: Catholic
University of America Press, 1988), p. 52: "Certainly sin was not
made through him (the Word), and it is clear that sin is nothing and
that men become nothing when they sin."

therefore, it is fitting that the sinner, who distances himself from God through sin, travels to a country far away from the heavenly realm, is cast into hell, which is the land of death and darkness, according to what Job 10:21 has: "Before I go ... to a land that is dark and covered with the mist of death, a land of misery and darkness, where the shadow of death and no order," etc.[78]

25. Third, concerning *the dissipation of the good of grace and nature* the text continues: *He squandered his property.*[79] I say that *he squandered* it through *spiritual* sins which especially dissipate the soul.[80] And this truly happens through *pride.* Nahum 2:2 reads: "As the Lord has responded to the pride of Jacob, so too with the pride of Israel, because the destroyers have dissipated them and have broken their vine branches into pieces." – Likewise, through *vainglory.* Isaiah 3:12 says: "O my people, they who call you blessed, the very same deceive you and dissipate the way of your steps." – Furthermore, through *envy,* according to what the Psalm says: "Our bones are dissipated by the side of hell" (140:7). Supply:

---

[78] Job 10:22 concludes with: "... where the shadow of death and no order, but everlasting horror dwells." On p. 391, n. 2 QuarEd quote the Glossa Ordinaria (from Ambrose) apud Lyranum on Luke 15:13: "What is farther away than to walk away from God? The person who walks away from God is an exile from the homeland, a citizen of the world. The country faraway is the shadow of death." See CCSL xiv, p. 288. The Glossa is a fine summation of Ambrose's interpretation.

[79] On p. 391, n. 3 QuarEd accurately mention that the Vulgate reads *ibi* ("there"). On p. 391, n. 7 QuarEd cite the Glossa Interlinearis (from Ambrose): *"There he squandered his property,* etc.: voluptuousness consumes all the goods of nature." See CCSL xiv, p. 289: "... by living voluptuously he consumed all the adornments of nature."

[80] In his treatment of "the spiritual" sins Bonaventure rings many a change on the verb *dissipare,* which I have consistently translated as "to dissipate," although some English translations, e.g., "to scatter," may produce more concinnity.

through envy, concerning which Proverbs 14:30 reads: "The rottenness of the bones is envy." – Moreover, through *anger*. The Psalm states: "They were dissipated and did not repent. . . . They gnashed their teeth against me" (34:16). Therefore, anger is like the demoniac in Luke 9:39 above: "He suddenly cries out and throws him down and dissipates him so that he foams." – Finally, he dissipated his soul through *sloth*, according to what Proverbs 18:9 has: "The person who is loose and slack in his work is the brother of the person who dissipates his own works." – And since *spiritual* sins often lead to *carnal* ones, the text adds: *by living voluptuously* relative to *gluttony* and *voluptuousness*, according to what Proverbs 20:1 says: "Wine is voluptuous, and drunkenness riotous. Whosoever delights in these things will not be wise." Therefore, the consummation of dissipation occurs in these things, according to what Job 31:12 states: "It is a fire that devours to the point of consummation and eradicates all things that spring up."[81] Wherefore, through these sins not only are the powers of the soul dissipated, but also the members of the body and temporal riches. And through this all man's property is dissipated, namely, material things, bodily members, and spiritual practices. For which reason Proverbs 29:3 reads: "A man who loves wisdom gives joy to his father. But the one who maintains harlots will squander away his property."[82] For in this way the Psalm is fulfilled: "Men and women, although they were in honor, did not understand," etc. (48:13).[83]

---

[81] Job is referring to adultery.

[82] Hugh of St. Cher, p. 224i also quotes Job 31:12 and Proverbs 29:3.

[83] Psalm 48:13 continues: ". . . they are compared to senseless beasts and have become like them." The Latin text of Luke 15:13 seems to read that verse in the light of 15:30 where "harlots" are specifically mentioned by the elder brother and thus clearly points to the

Luke 15:14–16
THE MISERY AND INDIGENCE OF THE PRODIGAL SON

26. (Verse 14). *And after he had consumed everything*, etc. After the description of the insolence of the prodigal son, the Evangelist depicts his *misery and indigence*. He makes three points: *the calamity of the famine, the opprobrium of servitude, the extreme form of want.*

So first, with regard to *the calamity of famine* the text says: *And after he had consumed everything*, namely, *by sin that devastates everything*, according to what Wisdom 3:19 reads: "Dreadful are the consummations of a wicked nation."[84] Of this consuming James 1:15 says: "When concupiscence has conceived, it brings forth sin. But when sin has been consummated, it begets death." – *There came a grievous famine over that country*, namely, through divine *avenging justice*. This *famine* is the lack of spiritual goods. Thus, the Glossa observes: "*A grievous famine in the faraway country* is the lack of the word of truth because the Creator has been forgotten."[85] And about this famine Amos 8:11 states: "I will send forth a famine into the land. Not a famine for bread, not a thirst for water, but for hearing the word of God."[86] And about this famine the Psalm says: "He called a famine

---

younger son's sins of lust and voluptuousness. The Greek text of 15:13 is not so clear. See Fitzmyer, p. 1088.

[84] Hugh of St. Cher, p. 224k also quotes Wisdom 3:19.

[85] On p. 391, n. 12 QuarEd state that this is the Glossa Interlinearis (from Bede who followed Augustine). See CCSL cxx, p. 288 where Bede introduces his quotation of Amos 8:11 with "has been written in the prophets." See Augustine, Book II, Question 33, n. 1 in CCSL xlivb, p. 74: "Therefore, *the faraway country* is forgetfulness of God. Now *the famine in that country* is the lack of the word of truth."

[86] Hugh of St. Cher, p. 224m also quotes Amos 8:11.

upon the land," etc. (104:16).[87] – *And he himself began to suffer want*, that is, *with no one offering him assistance.* So Ambrose comments: "He was suffering the lack of virtues, for their font had been abandoned. Therefore, it is just that the person who abandoned the treasures of wisdom and the height of heavenly riches is in want."[88] Wherefore, Proverbs 13:18 has: "Want and shame upon the person who refuses instruction," and this on account of sin. For as Proverbs 14:34 states: "Sin makes people experience misery." For this reason Bede says: "Every place, without the father, is penury."[89] For just as when wisdom arrived, all good things of wisdom came with her – Wisdom 7:11 says: "All good things came to me together with her and innumerable riches through her hands" – so too when wisdom is absent, all good things vanish and want takes over, according to what Proverbs 3:33 states: "Want from the Lord is in the house of the wicked, but the habitations of the just will be blessed."

27. (Verse 15). Secondly, concerning *the opprobrium of servitude* the text adds: *And he went and joined one of*

---

[87] The Psalm refers to the famine at the time of Joseph. See Genesis 41–42.

[88] The second part of this quotation is heavily dependent upon Ambrose. See CCSL xiv, p. 289. For the first part see Jerome, Letter 21, n. 10 in CSEL liv, p. 119: "He began to want in virtues, since the font of virtues had been abandoned." See Hugh of St. Cher, p. 224o: "And he himself began to suffer want] for virtues, for their font had been abandoned. Therefore, it is just that the person who abandoned the treasures of wisdom and the height of heavenly riches is in want." Hugh, however, gives no reference for this interpretation.

[89] On p. 391, n. 16 QuarEd state that this is the Glossa Interlinearis apud Lyranum on Luke 15:14 and that Hugh of St. Cher also attributes it to Bede. They cite Jerome, Letter 21, n. 10: "Every place in which we live without the father is a place of famine, penury, and want." It seems to me that Bede has nothing resembling the quotation attributed to him. See CCSL cxx, p. 288. See Hugh of St. Cher, p. 224o: "Bede. Every place, without the father, [is] penury."

the citizens of that country. Now *the citizen* in the country of dissimilitude and sin is the person who has set up a permanent home in sin. Among these citizens the first and primary citizen is the devil himself. So the Glossa says: "One of the citizens is that one who, having been set over the worldly concupiscences befitting his depravity, is called *the prince of the world,*"[90] according to what John 14:30 has: "For the prince of this world is coming," etc. To this citizen a person joins himself when he desires to do his will in all things. This is what sinners do, according to what is designated in 2 Maccabees 4:16 concerning those about whom it is said that "In all things they desired to be like those who were their enemies and destroyers." – And note that he is said *to have joined,* for the devil does not have *the power* over an individual except in so far as the sinner grants that power to him by his own will. So in the person of the devil Isaiah 51:23 says: "Bow down that we may go over." – And since, once the transfer of power has taken place, the devil always urges humans to sins, the text adds: *And he sent him to his farm to feed the pigs.* By *pigs* are understood the demons on account of their *wild crudity.*[91] Because of this Matthew 7:6 cautions: "Do not give to dogs what is holy nor cast your pearls before

---

[90] On p. 392, n. 1 QuarEd state that this is the Glossa Ordinaria (from Bede). See CCSL cxx, p. 288. The Glossa accurately quotes Bede.
[91] On p. 392, n. 5 QuarEd state that Ambrose, Jerome, Augustine, and Bede understand *the pigs* as demons. See Jerome, Letter 21, n. 12 in Mierow's translation, p. 116: "The pig is an unclean animal, because it delights in swill and filth. Such is the horde of demons. . . ." See Hugh of St. Cher, p. 224v, e: "To feed the pigs], that is, the demons, who like pigs delight in the sordid deeds of sinners." See Hugh of St. Cher, p. 224v, f: "Glossa Bedae: The food of demons is drunkenness, etc."

pigs, lest perhaps they trample them under their feet."[92]
Likewise, on account of their *carnal sensuality*. 2 Peter
2:22 reads: "What that true proverb says has happened
to them: . . . a sow, even after washing, wallows in the
mire." And this is what *carnal sensuality* does. So Proverbs 11:22 states: "A golden ring in a pig's snout, a
beautiful, but foolish woman," for the devil defiles many
through carnal sensuality. Now the demons have this
wild crudity in themselves, but suggest *carnal sensuality*
to others. So it is fitting that they are associated with
pigs, according to what Matthew 8:31 says: "If you cast
us out, send us into the pigs." For these pigs are fed off
the unclean deeds of sinners, since in these only do the
demons take delight. So Ambrose comments: "The food
of the demons is drunkenness, fornication, and things of
this sort which are soothing and entice one to engage in
them. The only care voluptuous people have is to fill
their own bellies. *Their god is the belly*."[93] About these
Philippians 3:19 reads: "Their god is the belly, and their
glory is in shame.[94] They mind the things of the earth."
So these pigs are fed by pig-like people, in whom reign
the wild crudeness of intelligence, *the carnal sensuality*
of concupiscence, *the cupidity* of avarice. And such people
in the manner of swine engage in nothing profitable for
life, but only for *hell*. A designation of this is provided in

---

[92] Matthew 7:6 concludes: ". . . under their feet and turn and tear you."
Bonaventure also quotes Matthew 7:6 in his commentary on Luke
8:4 (#8) above.

[93] On p. 392, n. 7 QuarEd state that only the last statement comes
from Ambrose. The entire interpretation stems from the Glossa Ordinaria on Luke 15:16. The scripture quotation at the end of the
Glossa is from Philippians 3:19. For Ambrose, see CCSL xiv, p. 289.
See also Jerome, Letter 21, n. 13 in Mierow's translation, p. 117:
"The food of demons is drunkenness, luxury, fornication, and all the
sins."

[94] On p. 392, n. 8 QuarEd rightly mention that the Vulgate reads *in
confusione ipsorum* ("in their shame").

Luke 8:33 above: "With a great[95] rush the herd of swine . . . went into the lake and was drowned," etc.

28. (Verse 16). Now third, with regard to *the extreme form of need* the text continues: *And he longed to fill his belly with the pods that the pigs were eating.* As the Glossa says, "*pods* are a kind of legume, hollow and creating the sound of bellows, that stuffs the belly, but offers little nourishment."[96] And therefore, it designates the pleasures of the vices, which at times attract the sinner in some exterior manner, but have no inner value. So pleasures of this kind are compared to dreams. Isaiah 29:8 reads: "As the person that is hungry dreams and eats. But when he has been awakened, his soul is empty. And as the person who is thirsty and dreams and drinks, and after he has been awakened, is yet faint with thirst, and his soul is empty. So will be the multitude of all the Gentiles who have fought against Mount Zion." The pigs are eating these *pods*, because, as Proverbs 2:14 says, "they are happy when they've done evil and exult in the most wicked things." And the sinner seeks and wants to be satiated with these pleasures as if they were genuine delights. Wherefore, of such people Job 30:3–7 says: "Barren with want and hunger, they gnawed in the wilderness, disfigured with calamity and misery. And they ate grass and the barks of trees. And the root of junipers was their food. . . . They found

---

[95] The Vulgate does not read *magno* ("great").

[96] On p. 392, n. 10 QuarEd refer to the Glossa Interlinearis, which gives the gist of Ambrose's commentary. See CCSL xiv, p. 289. Hugh of St. Cher, p. 224v, f quotes "Ambrose" and uses the same words as Bonaventure does in his quotation of "The Glossa." See Fitzmyer, p. 1088: ". . . the leguminous fruit of the carob tree. . . . Its long pods contain a sweet pulp and indigestible seeds and were used for food for animals, sometimes even for humans." Today the pulp of the pods is used as a chocolate substitute.

pleasure among these sorts of things and counted it a delight to be under the briers."[97] – And since no one can be satisfied with such things, the text adds: *And no one gave them to him.* For when the sinner seeks delights of this kind, he often loses them through God's just judgment. So the sinful soul says in Hosea 2: "I will go after my lovers that provide me with my bread and my water and my wool and my linen and my oil and my drink. Wherefore, behold I will hedge up your way with thorns, and I will stop it up with a wall. And she will not find her way" (verses 5–6). And further on: "I will cause all her joy to cease and her new moons, her Sabbaths and all her festivals" (verse 11). And God does this, so that he may call to himself through afflictions sinners who have departed from him for the sake of pleasures. Thus, Augustine in his Book of Confessions comments: "You sprinkled bitterness over all my pleasures, Lord God, so that I might seek to be gladdened without committing an offense and be found only in you."[98] So *no one gives him some of these pods*, when carnal satisfaction is withdrawn from the sinner, so that through this experience he might at all events be turned to knowledge of God and of himself. And just as the inebriated person is on the lookout for pleasure, so too are the sinner's

---

[97] On p. 392, n. 12 QuarEd cite Jerome, Letter 21, n. 13. See Mierow's translation, p. 117: "And this is why the young man, given to excess, could not be satisfied: because pleasure always creates a hunger for itself and when indulged does not satisfy."

[98] On p. 393, n. 2 QuarEd cite Book II, chapter 2, n. 4 of Augustine's *Confessions*. Bonaventure's text is an abbreviation. See *The Confessions of St. Augustine*, translated by F. J. Sheed (New York: Sheed & Ward, 1943), p. 28: "You were always by me, mercifully hard upon me, and besprinkling all my illicit pleasures with certain elements of bitterness, to draw me on to seek for pleasures in which no bitterness should be. And where was I to find such pleasures save in You O Lord, You who use sorrow to teach, and wound us to heal, and kill us lest we die to You."

senses heightened through tribulation, according to what Isaiah 28:19 has: "Vexation alone will make you understand what you hear." So Leviticus 26:25–26 reads: "I will send the pestilence into your midst, and you will be delivered into the hands of your enemies. . . . And you will eat and not be satisfied."[99]

Luke 15:17–20a
THE REPENTANCE OF THE PRODIGAL SON

29. (Verse 17). *But when he came to himself.* After describing the insolence and misery of the prodigal son, he depicts here in a third place *his repentance* and does so in great detail by treating the humility of *contrition, confession,* and *satisfaction.*[100]

So first, relative to *the humility of contrition* the text says: *But when he came to himself,* namely, through recognition of his own iniquity, for the sorrow of compunction makes one *consider one's internal conscience.* For this reason the text has: *Came to himself,* according to what Isaiah 46:8 says: "Return, you transgressors, to

---

[99] This a prediction of famine. I modify the NAB translation of Leviticus 26:26: "And as I cut off your supply of bread, ten women will need but one oven for baking all the bread they dole out to you in rations – not enough food to satisfy your hunger."

[100] For a brief treatment of Bonaventure's teaching about confession or the Sacrament of Penance, see Dennis J. Billy, "Conversion and the Franciscan Preacher: Bonaventure's Commentary on the Prodigal Son," *Collectanea Franciscana* 58 (1988): 259–275, esp. pp. 266–267. See also José L. Larrabe, "Teología de la penitencia y de la confesión segun S. Buenaventura," *Estudios Franciscanos* 77 (1976): 193–201. Further, Joseph A. Spitzig, *Sacramental Penance in the Twelfth and Thirteenth Centuries,* Catholic University of America Studies in Sacred Theology 2.6 (Washington: Catholic University of America Press, 1947), pp. 125–137. Finally, cf. *Opera Omnia* 4:317–587.

the heart."[101] – The sorrow of compunction also made him *consider the happiness that had been lost*. Therefore, the text continues: *He said: How many hired men in my father's house have bread in abundance*. That is, in God's house they are living happily and comfortably. – And note that some are *evil* hired men. About them John 10:13 states: "But the hired man flees, because he is a hireling."[102] Although these sometimes abound in material food in the house of the supreme Father, they, nevertheless, do not abound in spiritual food. On account of this Matthew 6:2 says: "Amen, I say to you: They have received their reward."[103] And to such people it is said in Isaiah 55:2: "Why do you spend money for that which is not bread?" Others are *good* hired men. About these Genesis 49:14–15 reads: "Issachar, a strong ass, . . . saw the rest that it was good, and the land that is was excellent, and he bowed his shoulders."[104] And these are the ones who serve for the sake of an eternal reward, and such abound frequently on the bread of faith, hope, and charity. About these Luke 11:5 above says: "Friend, lend me three loaves." And about these the Psalm speaks: "I will satisfy her poor with bread" (131:15).[105] – All this notwithstanding, compunction

---

[101] Hugh of St. Cher, p 224v, i also quotes Isaiah 46:8.

[102] Hugh of St. Cher, p. 224v, g also quotes John 10:13.

[103] Hugh of St. Cher, pp. 224v–225 k also quotes Matthew 6:2, Isaiah 55:2, and Genesis 49:14–15.

[104] On p. 393, n. 8 QuarEd correctly mention that the Vulgate reads *humerum suum* ("his shoulder"). Genesis 49:15 concludes: ". . . his shoulder(s) to carry, and became a servant under tribute." The "rest" of Genesis 49:15 may be "the rest" of non-nomadic life.

[105] On p. 393, n. 8 QuarEd quote the Glossa Ordinaria (from Bede): "*How many hired men*, who are diligently engaged in performing worthy deeds for the purpose of a future reward, are nourished by the daily food of heavenly grace. But *the person who is dying of hunger* is the one who is outside the house of the father, that is, living without faith, seeking in inane philosophy the life of the blessed."

makes a person *ponder his own calamity.* So the text adds: *While I am perishing here with hunger*, that is, on account of a lack of divine grace and instruction. And this is a grievous calamity. Lamentations 4:9 reads: "It was better for those who were slain by the sword than for those who were killed by hunger. For these latter wasted away entirely, having been consumed for want of earth's produce." And for their sake it is said in Lamentations 2:19: "Lift up your hands...for the lives[106] of your little children, who have fainted for hunger at the head of all the streets." Now the spirit is provoked and urged by the affliction of compunction. For this reason the Psalmist prays: "I am afflicted and humbled exceedingly. I roared with the groaning of my heart. . . . For I am ready for scourges" (37:9, 18).

30. (Verse 18). Second, concerning *humility of confession* the text adds: *I will get up and go to my father, and I will say to him: Father, I have sinned against heaven.* By this he is confessing that he has sinned against *ecclesiastical unity* which is what the word *heaven* means. For in it God dwells. Isaiah 66:1 reads: "Heaven is my throne." And the Psalm states: "The Lord is in his holy temple. The Lord's throne is in heaven" (10:5).[107] – He

---

See CCSL cxx, p. 289. The Glossa provides an accurate abbreviation of Bede's commentary.

[106] On p. 393, n. 10 QuarEd correctly mention that the Vulgate reads *anima* ("the life").

[107] On p. 393, n. 13 QuarEd refer to Question 3, n. 3 of Book II of Augustine's *Questions on the Gospels.* See CCSL xlivb, p. 76 where Augustine gives possible interpretations of *against heaven and before you*: "Does *I have sinned against heaven* refer to the heaven *before you*, so that he called heaven the very summit of the father, a meaning that is also contained in the Psalm: *His going forth is from the summit of heaven* (18:7) and so could be understood of the father himself? Or does *I have sinned against heaven* refer to the holy souls among whom is God's throne with *before you* referring to the interior depths of conscience?"

also confesses that he has sinned against *the divine majesty*. So he adds: *and before you*, since all things are manifest to him. Hebrews 4:13 reads: "All things are naked and exposed to the eyes of him to whom we have to render an account." For which reason it is said in Proverbs 16:2: "All the ways of men and women are open to his eyes, and the Lord weighs spirits."

31. (Verse 19). And since an offence against so great a majesty deprives us of the dignity of divine sonship, he confesses his unworthiness: *I am no longer worthy to be called your son*. And he makes a just and true confession, because the condition of being a son of God is the result of the greatest love, according to what 1 John 3:1 says: "See, brothers,[108] what manner of love the Father has bestowed on us that we should be called children of God. And such we are." The sinner is unworthy of that name, for he has treated his Father with contempt, according to what Isaiah 1:2 has: "I have brought up children and have exalted them, but they have despised me."[109] – And since it is a characteristic of a sincere confession, not only to confess the wickedness of sin and the unworthiness of the sinner, but also *to beg for mercy*, the text adds: *make me as one of your hired men*. – And note that this is the distinction between *a son, a servant*, and *a hired man*. For *the son* serves out of *love*. Galatians 4:6 reads: "Since you are sons, God has sent the Spirit of his Son," etc.[110] *A servant*, out of *fear*. Malachi 1:6 states: "A

---

[108] The Vulgate does not have *fratres* ("brothers").

[109] On p. 394, n. 2 QuarEd cite Jerome, Letter 21, n. 16. See Mierow's translation, p. 120: "He had sinned against heaven, since he had forsaken the heavenly Jerusalem, his mother. . . . He is not worthy to be called a son of God, since he had preferred to be the servant of idols. For everyone that commits sin is born of his father the devil."

[110] Galatians 4:6 concludes: ". . . the Spirit of his Son into our hearts, crying, 'Abba, Father.'"

son honors his father, but the servant will fear his master."[111] But *a hired man* is the person who serves out of *the hope of an eternal inheritance.* About this hired hand Job 7:1–3 reads: "The life of human beings upon earth is a warfare, and his days are like the days of hired man. And a servant longs for the shade, and as the hireling looks forward to the end of his work, so I also have had empty months and have tallied up my wearisome nights." – Therefore, from these considerations it follows that confession must be *sincere* and *humble,* so that with a desire born of humility *the gravity of the sin and the unworthiness of the sinner may be acknowledged* and *the mercy of a loving father be implored.* For it is said in Sirach 35:21: "The prayer of the person who humbles himself will pierce the clouds." An example of this is found in the case of the tax collector in Luke 18:9–14 below.

32. (Verse 20). Third, relative to the *humility of satisfaction* the text continues: *And he rose up and went to his father. This rising up* means abandoning sin and a certain withdrawal from it, which is *the beginning* of satisfaction. For "to make satisfaction is to excise the causes of sin and not to grant them access so that they bring about sin."[112] Thus there is a figure of this in what was

---

[111] The Vulgate does not read *timebit* ("will fear"), but the verb "to fear" occurs later in Malachi 1:6: "And if I be a master, where is my fear?"

[112] On p. 394, n. 6 QuarEd say that this definition is attributed to Augustine, but actually comes from Gennadius (of Marseilles, d. ca 500). See his *Liber De Ecclesiasticis Dogmatibus,* chapter 54 in PL 58:994C: *Satisfactio poenitentiae est, causas peccatorum excidere, nec earum suggestionibus aditum indulgere* ("The satisfaction of penance is to excise the causes of sins, and not to grant access to their suggestions"). Bonaventure's quotation is: *Satisfacere est causas peccatorum excidere et eis peccandi aditum non indulgere.* See *Catechism of the Catholic Church,* 2nd edition (Vatican City: Vatican Press, 2000),

said to the young man who was still *dead* in Luke 7:14 above: "Young man, I say to you, arise," so that in this way *sin* may be left behind. Christ said to a man similarly *restricted* in John 5:8: "Arise, take up your pallet and walk," so that in this fashion *the consequences of sins* may be left behind. Similarly it was said to Peter *bound in chains* in Acts 12:7: "Arise quickly," so that in this manner *occasion of sin* or bad company and habits may be left behind. On account of these considerations it is said to the sinner in Ephesians 5:14: "Wake up, sleeper, and arise from the dead," etc.[113] – And since "it is a small thing not to do evil, unless a person is also eager to labor at good deeds,"[114] the text immediately adds: *He went to his father*, on account of his example. John 14:6 reads: "No one comes to the Father except through me." *He went*, I say, so that the person who earlier had gone away through his arrogant transgression, now may return to his father with humble satisfaction, according to what Isaiah 60:14 states: "All who slandered you will come to you and will worship your footprints," etc.[115] Everyone, who comes like this, *is drawn* by God. John 6:44 states: "No one comes to me, unless my Father draws him."[116] And thus *drawn, he is aided*. Job 23:3 says: "Who will grant me that I may know and find him and proceed up to his throne?" And thus *aided, he is re-*

---

p. 366 (#1459): "Raised up from sin, the sinner must still recover his full spiritual health by doing something more to make amends for the sin: he must 'make satisfaction for' or 'expiate' his sins. This satisfaction is also called 'penance.'"

[113] Hugh of St. Cher, p. 225d and m also quotes Ephesians 5:14.

[114] On p. 394, n. 8 QuarEd point to Homily 13, n. 1 of GGHG. See PL 76:1123D–1124A where the text that "is immediately added" is not Luke 15:20, but Luke 12:35: "Let your lamps be burning."

[115] Bonaventure has adjusted and abbreviated Isaiah 60:14ab.

[116] The Vulgate reads differently: "No one can come to me unless the Father who sent me draw him."

ceived. John 6:37: "And the person who comes to me I will not cast out."

Luke 15:20b–32
THE MERCY OF A LOVING FATHER

33. *But while he was yet a long way off.* After describing the younger son's insolence, misery, and repentance, the Evangelist provides a fourth description: *the mercy of a loving father.* Now this section is divided into two parts. The first part depicts *the mercy of the loving father in accepting the conversion of the sinner.* In the second *he placates the indignation of the obedient son* where verse 25 says: *Now his elder son was in the field,* etc.

The Evangelist portrays *the mercy that accepts the conversion of the prodigal son* in three acts. First, in *receiving back the unworthy.* Second, in *clothing the naked* where verse 22 reads: *But the father said to his servants.* Third, in *feeding the hungry* where verse 23 has: *and bring out the fatted calf.* For this is the order by which the soul is restored through the gift of fatherly mercy. First, *it is welcomed back* through the kindness of grace. Second, *it is clothed* with the robe of justice. Third, *it is nourished* by the sweetness of joy and internal happiness. – So two things are said about *the mercy that welcomes the unworthy,* namely, *the clemency of the father who welcomes him back* and *the deep respect of the son who accuses himself.*

34. First, then, with respect to *the clemency of the father welcoming him back* the text says: *But while he was yet a long way off,* on account of sin which distances one from God. The Psalm says: "Far away from my salvation are the words of my sins" (21:2). And again: "Salvation

is far away from sinners, because they have not kept
your justifications" (Psalm 118:155).[117] – *His father saw
him and was moved with mercy*,[118] and poured upon him
antecedent grace. About the effects of divine regard see
Luke 22:61–62 below: "The Lord looked upon Peter. . . . And Peter went outside and wept bitterly."[119]
And about this Exodus 3:7–8 says: "I have seen the affliction of my people in Egypt. . . . And I have come down
to deliver them." The Prophet pleaded for this regard
when he said: "Regard my humiliation and my labor,
and forgive all my sins" (Psalm 24:18). And again he
says: "Look upon me and have mercy on me" (Psalm
85:16). – *And ran and fell upon his neck*, by means of
concomitant grace. As if to say: He embraced him according to what The Song of Songs 2:6 has: "His left
hand is under my head, and his right hand will embrace

---

[117] On p. 395, n. 2 QuarEd rightly indicate that the Vulgate reads
non exquisierunt ("have not sought"). Did Bonaventure read *non cus-
todierunt* ("have not kept") from Psalm 118:158? Hugh of St. Cher, p.
225q also quotes Psalm 118:155.

[118] See Hugh of St. Cher, p. 225r: "His father saw him] with the eyes
of mercy. Luke 22g[61–62] below: The Lord looked upon Peter...and
he wept bitterly."

[119] I make three points to help clarify Bonaventure's interpretation.
First, the father of the prodigal son is God. Second, Bonaventure is
stressing the fact that the father *saw* the prodigal son. Just as the
Lord's regard of Peter led to Peter's repentance, so too the father's
regard of his son leads to his son's articulated conversion. Third,
Bonaventure introduces a medieval understanding of grace. See Opera Omnia 2:669 where he writes: ". . . although grace is one, nonetheless it has multiple divisions according to diverse considerations."
So considered from its effect, grace is antecedent or subsequent. "For
it is said to be antecedent grace, in so far as it makes the will itself
good. And therefore, it is antecedent, because it does not stem from
free will, but rather it is poured upon the person by God himself. But
it is called cooperating or subsequent grace in so far as it aids free
will in eliciting a good work." Hugh of St. Cher, p. 225v, a uses the
terminology of "prevenient grace," "assisting or cooperating grace,"
and "finishing or perfecting grace."

me." And this takes place through *concomitant grace*, which aids a person in bearing the yoke of the divine law. Thus Ambrose comments: "He fell *upon the neck* of his son, when he imposed upon him love's light yoke."[120] For this *yoke* assists in carrying the burden. *The embrace* of the divine arm is the humanity of the incarnate Word. So the Glossa observes: "He humbled the arm, that is, the Son, in embracing the returning son."[121] About this arm the Psalm says: "The Lord's right hand has wrought salvation for him, and his arm is holy" (97:1).[122] And through this *embrace* the bonds of sinners are snapped according to what Isaiah 52:2 states: "Break the bonds off your neck, O captive daughter of Zion." – *And kissed him*, namely, by *subsequent grace*. For a kiss is a sign of love and of peace. So Bede states: "The son who has returned receives the kiss of love from his father and at the same time is assured of forgiveness

---

[120] On p. 395, n. 6 QuarEd state that Ambrose's interpretation is conveyed by the Glossa Ordinaria on Luke 15:20. See CCSL xiv, p. 293. Jerome, Letter 21, n. 20 provides background for this interpretation and the next one. See Mierow's translation, pp. 120–121: ". . . he fell upon his neck – that is, he assumed a human body – and just as John leaned on his bosom, he who was made the confidant of his secrets, so he placed on the younger son (by grace rather than because of merit), his light yoke, that is, the easy precepts of his commandments." Hugh of St. Cher, p. 225t gives basically the same interpretation as Bonaventure and calls it "The Glossa of Ambrose."
[121] On p. 395, n. 7 QuarEd state that this is the Glossa Ordinaria (from Bede, who quotes Augustine). For Augustine, see CCSL xlivb, p. 77: "Now what does it mean *to fall upon his neck*, except to incline and to humble his arm in embracing him? *And to whom has the arm of the Lord been revealed?* (Isaiah 53:1), who is truly our Lord Jesus Christ."
[122] In his commentary on Luke 1:38 (#69) Bonaventure writes: "For the word and the hand of the Father are identical." See *Bonaventure on Luke, Chapters 1–8*, p. 79, n. 100 and Augustine's Sermon 291.2: "Christ, you see the hand of the Lord, the Son of God is the hand of God, the Word of God is the hand of God."

through this grace,"[123] according to what Ephesians 1:13–14 has: "In him . . . believers were sealed with the Holy Spirit of the promise, who is the pledge of our inheritance." The spouse of The Song of Songs 1:1 is in search of this kiss of peace and of love: "Let him kiss me with the kiss of his mouth, for they are better," etc.[124] In this, God the Father's loving affection is exceedingly apparent, as he gives the greatest indication of his love towards the sinner who returns. And when we willingly kiss him out of mutual love, God the Father realizes that we are his sons. Genesis 27:26–27 reads: "Come near me, my son, and give me a kiss. He came near and kissed him." And the text continues: "He blessed him,"[125] for the fullness of a blessing issues from this kiss.[126] Therefore, the Psalmist says: "Lord, you have blessed your land" (84:2) and then adds: "Mercy and truth have met each other. Justice and peace have kissed" (84:11). The origin of this kiss is found in the Word Incarnate,[127] in whom there exists a union of the highest love and the connection of two natures, through which God kisses us,

---

[123] On p. 395, n. 8 QuarEd state that Bonaventure quotes Bede, who follows Augustine, from the Glossa Ordinaria. See CCSL cxx, p. 290. The Glossa abbreviates Bede (and Augustine). Hugh of St. Cher, p. 225v, a also quotes "Bede" and has the very same wording as Bonaventure.

[124] The last part of The Song of Songs 1:1 reads: ". . . for your breasts are better than wine." Hugh of St. Cher, p. 225v, a also quotes The Song of Songs 1:1a.

[125] The reference is to Isaac's blessing of Jacob.

[126] Hugh of St. Cher, p. 225v, a also quotes Genesis 27:26–27.

[127] Bonaventure's interpretation is christological. Contrast the moral interpretation of Hugh of St. Cher, p. 225v, a in Feiss' translation, pp. 59–60: "His left arm is the remission of guilt, his right hand the promise of glory. . . . The statement 'he kissed him' calls attention to finishing or perfecting grace because the kiss is a sign of perfect reconciliation and peace and love. . . . In a kiss, the lips of those kissing are joined. There are two lips of the soul of the penitent; namely, confession of sin and confession of praise."

and we kiss God, according to what The Song of Songs 8:1 says: "Who will give me you as my brother . . . that I may find you outside and kiss you, and now no person may despise me?"[128]

35. (Verse 21). Second, with regard to *the deep respect of the son who accuses himself* the text adds: *And the son said to him: Father, I have sinned against heaven*, namely, by contempt against the Majesty who governs all things. Job 11:8 reads: "He is higher than the heavens, and what will you do? He is deeper than hell, and how will you know?" And Job 22:12 has: "Do you not think that God is higher than heaven and elevated above the height of the stars?" Therefore, the person who holds in contempt the God of heaven sins *against heaven*. So it is said in Ezra 9:6: "My iniquities are multiplied over my head,[129] and our sins have sprouted up to heaven," etc. *And before you*, through *contempt of the Truth who watches over all things*. Sirach 23:28–29 states: "The eyes of the Lord are far brighter than the sun, beholding round about all the ways of men and

---

[128] On p. 395, n. 11 QuarEd refer to Bernard of Clairvaux, whose Sermon 2, n. 2 on The Song of Songs provides the christological background behind what Bonaventure says in #34. See *On the Song of Songs I,* translated by Kilian Walsh, Cistercian Fathers Series 4 (Kalamazoo: Cistercian Publications, 1976), pp. 9–10: "The mouth that kisses signifies the Word who assumes human nature; the nature assumed receives the kiss; the kiss however, that takes its being from both the giver and the receiver, is a person that is formed by both, none other than 'the one mediator between God and mankind, himself a man, Christ Jesus.' . . . In this way they (the saints) paid tribute to that prerogative of Christ, on whom uniquely and in one sole instance the mouth of the Word was pressed, that moment when the fullness of the divinity yielded itself to him as the life of his body." See SBOp 1.9–10. Is there some weak analogy here to the British use of "the kiss of life" for artificial respiration?

[129] The Vulgate has *iniquitates nostrae* ("our iniquities") and has no adjective before *caput* ("head").

women and the bottom of the depth, and looking into the hearts of all,[130] into their most hidden parts. For before they were created, all things were known to our Lord God. Also after they were perfected, he beholds all things." The Psalm says: "Against you only have I sinned and have done evil before you" (50:6). – *I am no longer worthy to be called your son*, on account of *contempt of the Goodness who provides for all things*. Wisdom 12:18–19 reads: "But you, Lord of power, judge with tranquility, and you make decrees for us with great favor. For your power is at hand for you, when you will. But you have taught your people . . . that they must be just and humane. And you have made your children to be of good hope, since in judging, you leave room for repentance for sins." Therefore, you say: *I am not worthy to be called your son*, because you have contemned this highest goodness, who in his largess has given us "the spirit of adoption as sons," according to Romans 8:15: "You have not received a spirit of bondage so as to be again in fear, but a spirit of adoption as sons." Whose largess it is also to regenerate us through water and the Holy Spirit[131] into the kingdom of the sons of God, according to Colossians 1:13: "He has rescued us from the power of darkness and transferred us into the kingdom of his beloved Son."

36. And note that although the father ran to meet him, hugged his neck with an embrace, and welcomed him with a kiss, nonetheless the genuine penitent never forgets his sin, according to what the Psalm says: "For I am ready for the scourge, and my sorrow is always be-

---

[130] On p. 395, n. 14 QuarEd correctly indicate that the Vulgate reads *hominum corda* ("hearts of men and women") for Bonaventure's *omnium corda* ("hearts of all").

[131] Bonaventure seems to allude to John 3:5. See also Titus 3:5.

fore me. For I will declare my iniquity, and I will take cognizance of my sin" (37:18–19). And although his father accepts him, he, nevertheless, is desirous of *perfect love*. And therefore, he does not seek here *the love extended to a hired man*, as he declared earlier, when he still lacked infused grace. But now, by being fully converted to his father, he gives evidence of being sincerely repentant and asks for divine grace. And this is what the Glossa says: "He wants, he says, to become through grace what he declared he was unworthy to be through merit,"[132] as that penitent petitioned in the last chapter of 2 Chronicles: "Now I bend my knees before you, imploring your kindness. I have sinned, O Lord, and I acknowledge my iniquity. I beg and petition: Lord, forgive me, lest you destroy me together with my iniquities and store up evil things for me for eternity. For you will save me, unworthy as I am, according to your great mercy. And I will praise you continually all the days of my life. For the power of the heavens praises you, and glory is yours forever and ever."[133]

37. (Verse 22). *But the father said to his servants*. After depicting the father's manifest mercy in welcoming back the unworthy person, the text continues with a description of his *mercy in clothing the naked* person. And since the sinner is stripped naked of *the garment of interior purity* and *the adornment of exterior respectability*, the text

---

[132] On p. 396, n. 5 QuarEd state that this is the Glossa Interlinearis (from Bede, who follows Augustine). For Bede, see CCSL cxx, p. 290. For Augustine, see CCSL xlivb, p. 77.

[133] On p. 396, n. 6 QuarEd indicate that this is the "Prayer of Manasseh." See "Oratio Manasse" verses 11–15 in Vulgate, 1909 for a text that is close to that quoted by Bonaventure. In his commentary on Luke 7:48 (#82) Bonaventure also quotes the "Prayer of Manasseh." See *Bonaventure on Luke, Chapters 1–8*, p. 647, n. 153.

shows how the father's mercy came to the aid of the prodigal in these two matters.

So first, relative to *the garment of interior purity* it states: *But the father said to his servants: Fetch quickly the best robe and put it on him.* The best robe is the garment of *interior purity*, with which our mind must be clothed and with which our mind was clothed from the beginning of its creation. Therefore, Bede comments: "The best robe is the garment of innocence, in which the first man was created. But after he sinned, he realized that he was naked and clothed with a garment of leaves, that is, he took on the garment of mortality."[134] Revelation 3:18 speaks of this garment of purity: ". . . you may be clothed in white garments and that the shame of your nakedness may not be manifest." The person who preserves himself in purity with the aid of divine grace is the person who is clothed with these garments according to Revelation 3:4: "You have a few persons in Sardis, who have not defiled their garments. And they will walk with me in white, for they are worthy." Now this garment of purity is given in the reception of the Sacraments, namely, *baptism*, which washes away all filth – the baptized wear a white garment as a designation of this – and also *penance*, which "is an attempt to restore the purity of baptism," as Augustine says.[135] And since this dispensation of the Sacraments takes place through the care of the ministers, the text says that *the*

---

[134] On p. 396, n. 8 QuarEd state that Bede's interpretation is conveyed in the words of the Glossa Ordinaria. See CCSL cxx, p. 291. The Glossa condenses Bede's thought which assumes Genesis 3:7.

[135] On p. 396, n. 10 QuarEd state that this quotation is from Ps-Augustine, *Liber de Vera et Falsa Poenitentia*, chapter 9, n. 24. See PL 1121: *Poenitentia enim vera ad Baptismi puritatem, poenitentem conatur adducere* ("For true penance is an attempt to bring the penitent to the purity of baptism").

father said to his servants, that is, to the ministers. For so it is said in John 20:22–23: "Receive the Holy Spirit. Whose sins you will forgive," etc.[136]

38. Secondly, with regard to *the adornment of exterior respectability* the text adds: *And give him a ring for his finger*,[137] through *the beauty of modesty*. For *a ring on the fingers* signifies betrothal through chaste love.[138] From this we understand that the person who preserves modesty in his deeds wears *a ring on his finger*. This modesty, even though it is manifest in the integrity of the flesh, consists especially in the integrity of *faith*, according to what 2 Corinthians 11:2 has: "I have betrothed you to one spouse, to present a chaste virgin to Christ." Therefore, *a ring* is a sign of faith and fidelity,[139] by which the soul is espoused so that its works may please Christ. For Hebrews 11:6 reads: "Without faith it is impossible to please God."[140] Wherefore, Blessed Agnes also said: "He has espoused me with the ring of his faith and fidelity."[141] Now the ring is *on the*

---

[136] John 20:23 concludes: ". . . they are forgiven them. And whose sins you will retain, they are retained." On p. 396, n. 11 QuarEd offer some background for Bonaventure's thought here. For Augustine, see CCSL xlivb, p. 77: "The best robe is the dignity which Adam lost. The servants who bring it are the preachers of reconciliation." The Glossa Interlinearis has: ". . . *servants*, the co-workers in the vineyard . . . *the best robe*, that is, the garment of the Holy Spirit."

[137] On p. 396, n. 12 QuarEd correctly mention that the Vulgate reads *in manum eius* ("for his finger") while Bonaventure has *in manu eius* ("for his finger").

[138] The commentary of Hugh of St. Cher, p. 225v, k also relates the ring to marriage.

[139] I have resorted to a double translation of *fides* as "faith and fidelity" to capture Bonaventure's play on this word.

[140] Hugh of St. Cher, p. 225v, k also quotes Hebrews 11:6 and James 2:26.

[141] Agnes' words are taken from the response to the third reading during the first nocturn of Matins for the feast of St. Agnes of Rome on January 21. It may not be happenstance that Bonaventure quotes

finger, when faith shines forth in action. For, as James
2:26 says: "Faith without works is dead." So the Glossa
of Ambrose observes: "*A ring*, that is, a sign of faith and
fidelity, by which are signified the promises in the
hearts of the faithful. *Put on his finger*, that is, into operation, so that through works faith may radiate forth,
and the works may be strengthened by faith."[142] A designation of this is given in Genesis 41:42: "Pharaoh took
his ring from his own finger and put it on Joseph's finger." – And since it is not sufficient that a person be
modest in his deeds, but also be *obedient and humble*,
the text continues: *and sandals for his feet*, namely, for
the *promptness of obedience*. For the person who is shod
is ready for travel. For which reason Ephesians 6:15
reads: "Having your feet shod with the readiness of the
gospel of peace." Now this obedience is especially
pleasing when it issues from filial affection. The Song of
Songs 7:1 has: "How beautiful are your feet in sandals,
O daughter of the prince." And since no one is suitable
to journey "from this world to the Father,"[143] unless he
possesses prompt obedience, this formula is given in
Exodus 12:11 for eating the paschal lamb: "You shall
gird your loins, and you shall have sandals on your feet,

---

these words, for this feast may have had special significance for
Franciscan men and women in the thirteenth century, as the liturgy
for Agnes of Rome's feast influenced the four letters that St. Clare of
Assisi wrote to Agnes of Prague. See Joan Mueller, *Clare's Letters to
Agnes: Texts and Sources* (St. Bonaventure, New York: Franciscan
Institute Publications, 2001), esp. pp. 107–148.
[142] On p. 397, n. 3 QuarEd state that this is the Glossa Ordinaria,
pieced together from Ambrose and Bede. See CCSL xiv, p. 294: "Can
the ring be anything else but the sign of sincere faith and an expression of truth?" See CCSL cxx, p. 291: "And it is good that a ring is
placed on the finger, so that faith may radiate forth through works
and works be strengthened by faith."
[143] See John 13:1.

holding staves in your hands, and you shall eat in haste. For it is the Passover, the passing over of the Lord."

39. And this obedience is especially required in *preachers* by the example of Christ and of the Saints. Isaiah 52:7 states: "How beautiful upon the mountains are the feet of the person who brings good tidings and preaches peace . . . who preaches salvation and says to Zion: The Lord will reign."[144] Thus, Bede comments: "*Sandals on the feet*, that is, protected by the example of those who were predecessors in the office of preaching, so that his work may be adorned by good living and prepare him for the journey to the eternal realm."[145] So since sandals are made from the skins of dead animals, and on account of this can designate *the examples of the fathers*, as Bede says here in the Glossa, it follows that it is said that

---

[144] The Vulgate concludes *Regnavit Deus tuus* ("Your God has reigned"). On p. 397, n. 8 QuarEd cite the Glossa Ordinaria apud Lyranum (dependent on Jerome) on Luke 15:22: "*And sandals*, lest a snake strike, so that he can tread upon scorpions, so that Isaiah 52:7 may fittingly be applied to him: *How beautiful are the feet of those who preach good tidings*, etc." See Jerome, Letter 21, n. 25 in Mierow's translation, p. 122: "*And shoes on his feet*, lest anywhere a lurking snake might attack the sole of his foot as he walked, and that he might tread upon serpents and scorpions, that he might be prepared for the gospel of peace, no longer walking according to the flesh but according to the spirit, and that the prophetic saying might be applicable to him: *How beautiful are the feet of those that preach peace and that bring good tidings*." See CSEL liv, pp. 128–129. Hugh of St. Cher, p. 225v, l also refers to Isaiah 52:7.

[145] On p. 397, n. 9 QuarEd state that Bede's exposition is conveyed in the words of the Glossa Ordinaria. In its simplification of Bede's complex thought the Glossa has obscured it somewhat. See CCSL cxx, p. 291. The editors also quote Book xxxiv, chapter 9, n. 19 of Gregory's *Moralia*: "Indeed, in Sacred Scripture sandals refer to the protection of preaching, as it is written (Ephesians 6:15): *the feet shod with the readiness of the gospel of peace*."

they may be given for the feet.[146] Since they can designate
the former way of sin, it is said, therefore, to Moses in
Exodus 3:5: "Remove the sandals from your feet."[147] And
Luke 10:4 above has: "Carry neither purse . . . nor sandals." Luke 10:4 refers to sandals *in the literal sense*, but
here *a parabolic similitude* is at work.

40. (Verse 23). *And bring out the fatted calf*. After the
description of mercy in welcoming back the unworthy
and clothing the naked, here the text depicts *mercy in
feeding the hungry*. And this occurs in the proper order,
for after the remission of sins and clothing with the virtues *the enjoyment of divine delights* follows. This arises
from a twin consideration, namely, of *our Savior* and of
the human being saved.

So first, relative to *the consideration of our Savior* the
text reads: *Bring out the fatted calf and kill it*. This *fatted calf* is Christ slain for our sakes, who is offered to us
in the Sacrament of the altar as most delectable food.
Now Christ is said to be *a calf*, for he was offered for
sins. Leviticus 1:5 states: "He shall immolate the calf
before the Lord, and the priests, the sons of Aaron, shall
offer its blood, pouring it round about the altar, which is

---

[146] On p. 397, n. 10 QuarEd state that this is the Glossa Ordinaria
and quote Homily 22, n. 9 of GGHG, which provides the background
for Bonaventure's highly condensed interpretation. See PL
76:1180D–1181A . I modify Hurst, p. 173: *"You shall have sandals on
your feet*. What are our feet, but our works, and what are sandals,
but the skins of dead animals? Sandals protect the feet. What are the
dead animals whose skins protect our feet except the fathers of old,
who have gone before us to our eternal homeland? When we regard
their example, we protect our feet, namely, our works. Therefore, to
have sandals on our feet means to regard the lives of those who are
dead, and to guard our footsteps against the wounds of sin."
[147] On p. 397, n. 11 QuarEd quote Homily 17, n. 5 of GGHG. See PL
76:1141A: "And what is the significance of sandals in this instance if
not the examples of dead works?"

before the door of the tabernacle." Further, it is said to be *fatted*, because it is filled with all good things and most delectable as spiritual food. Wherefore, the Glossa observes: "Christ is the fatted calf, so rich with every spiritual power that he is sufficient for the salvation of the whole world."[148] Genesis 18:7 speaks of this in the figure of Abraham preparing a banquet for the angels: "Abraham ran to the herd and took from it the best and most tender calf."[149] Christ's servants *bring out* this calf *and kill it*, when they immolate it on the altar for the salvation of sinners and distribute it to us as food. So the Glossa says: "Christ is always being sacrificed for believers."[150] Another interpretation is that *it is brought forth and killed*, when his death and the Sacrament of the altar are recalled to memory by the preacher as sustenance and food. Thus, Bede says: "Preach Christ born and teach his death, so that a person may believe in his heart by imitating the one killed and receive with his mouth the Sacrament of the passion for his betterment."[151] Wherefore, even though all Christians find nourishment in the passion of Christ, those are delighted above all, who experience themselves as being rescued and liberated through Christ's passion from grave evils and dangers and sins. – And so the text adds:

---

[148] On p. 398, n. 1 QuarEd state that this is the Glossa Interlinearis (from Bede). See CCSL cxx, p. 291. The editors also refer to Ps-Jerome's Letter 35 or Homily about the Two Sons, chapter 11. Hugh of St. Cher, p. 225v, m quotes the very same words as Bonaventure does, but attributes them to Bede.

[149] Hugh of St. Cher, p. 225v, m also quotes Genesis 18:7.

[150] On p. 398, n. 2 QuarEd state that this is the Glossa Interlinearis (from Jerome). I quote Jerome's Letter 21, n. 26 and modify Mierow's translation, pp. 122–123: "The fatted calf, which is sacrificed for the salvation of penitents, is the Savior himself, on whose flesh we daily feed, whose blood we drink." See CSEL liv, p. 129.

[151] On p. 398, n. 3 QuarEd state that Bede's words are couched in those of the Glossa Ordinaria. Bede, for his part, is following Augustine. See CCSL cxx, pp. 291–292. See also CCSL xlivb, p. 78.

And let us eat and make merry, not at a *carnal* banquet, about which the wicked say in Isaiah 22:13: "Let us eat and drink, for today we die." Rather at a *spiritual* banquet, of which 1 Corinthians 5:7–8 says: "Christ, our Passover, has been sacrificed. Therefore, let us keep festival, not with the old leaven, nor with the leaven of malice and wickedness, but with the unleavened bread of sincerity and truth." About this banquet The Song of Songs 5:1 states: "Eat, O friends, . . . and be inebriated, my dearly beloved."[152] – In this banquet Christ is *the food, the guest,* and *the steward,* for he himself is delighted with us, and we with him, and he himself brings this about. Revelation 3:20 says: "Behold, I stand at the door and knock. If anyone . . . opens the door to me, I will come in and will dine with him, and he with me."

41. (Verse 24). Second, with regard to *the consideration of the human being saved* the text adds: *Because this son of mine had been*[153] *dead*, through *sin*, which renders a person dead. The Psalm says: "The dead will not praise you, O Lord" (113:7). And again John 8:24 reads: "You will die in your sin." *And has come to life again*, through *repentance*. Ephesians 5:14 states: "Awake, sleeper, and arise from among the dead, and Christ will enlighten you." And the Psalmist prays: "You will take away their spirit, and they will fail. . . . Send forth your spirit," etc. (103:29–30).[154] *He had been lost*, through *the loss of justice*. Romans 2:12 reads: "Whoever has sinned without the Law, will perish without the Law." And 2 Peter 2:12–13 has: "They will perish in their own corruption,

---

[152] Bonaventure does not have *bibite* ("drink"), which the Vulgate reads.
[153] On p. 398, n. 6 QuarEd correctly mention that the Vulgate reads *erat* ("was"). Bonaventure reads *fuerat* ("had been").
[154] The Vulgate reads *Emittes* ("You will send forth").

receiving the recompense of their own injustice."[155] *And has been found*, through *the recovery of grace*, according to what Job 33:24 states: "I have found wherein I may be merciful to him." And the Lord does this, when he pours his grace into the soul. The Psalmist says: "I have found David my servant. With my holy oil I have anointed him" (88:21). – And since everyone must rejoice in this, the text adds: *And all began to eat and make merry.*[156] Bede observes: "Not only is the son, for whom the calf was killed, given refreshment, but also the father and his servants, for the refreshment of God and the Saints is the salvation of sinners."[157] As a figure of this reality it is said in Deuteronomy 16:14: "And you shall make merry at your festival time, you and your son and your daughter, your man servant, and your maid servant, the Levite also and the stranger, and the fatherless and the widow that are within your gates."

42. *Now his elder son*, etc. After the Evangelist has shown the mercy of the loving father in accepting the conversion of the penitent, here in a second point he shows *his mercy in placating the indignation of his obedient son*. Now this section has two components. The first gives voice to *the son's impatience* that leads to his indignation. The second expresses *the father's clemency* which strives to mollify his elder son's indignation where verse 28 reads: *His father, therefore, came out,*

---

[155] The Vulgate does not have the second "their own" (*suae*).

[156] The Vulgate reads *et coeperunt epulari* ("and they began to make merry").

[157] On p. 398, n. 10 QuarEd indicate that Bede's interpretation is given expression in the Glossa Ordinaria. See CCSL cxx, p. 292 for Bede's more detailed exposition. See also CCSL xiv, p. 294: ". . . in order to show that the father's food is our salvation and that the joy of the father is the redemption of our sins." Hugh of St. Cher, p. 225v, n quotes this interpretation as Bede's in the very same words that Bonaventure uses.

etc. – The Evangelist makes three points about the origin of *the impatience of the indignant son*, namely, *the difficulty of protracted labor, the solemnity of the rejoicing he has heard*, and *the gracious kindness evidenced by his father's largess*. As he pondered these matters, the elder son became indignant.

43. (Verse 25). So first, relative to *the difficulty of protracted labor* the text continues: *Now his elder son was out in the field*. This son is called *the elder son*, because he is more mature in good conduct, more obedient to and more in conformity with his father's directives. For, as Wisdom 4:8–9 says, "The understanding of a person is gray hair, and a spotless life is old age."[158] And since a good life is never unproductive,[159] the text says that he was in *the field*, namely, involved in necessary labor, so that he could say what Zechariah 13:5 has: "I am a farmer, for Adam is my example from my youth." Wherefore, he was laboring in the field according to the counsel of Proverbs 12:11: "The person who tills his land will be satisfied with bread." And Proverbs 24:27 reads: "Prepare your work outside, and diligently till your field."[160] For thus it was said to man in Genesis 3:19: "In the sweat of your brow will you eat bread."

44. Secondly, relative to *the solemnity of the rejoicing he has heard* the text adds: *And as he came and drew near*

---

[158] On p. 398, n. 14 QuarEd cite Jerome, Letter 21, n. 28. Mierow, p. 123, translates: "Now the story goes on to the older son, whom many interpret simply as the person of all the saints, but many – quite correctly – refer to the Jews."

[159] See Bonaventure's commentary on Luke 7:45 (#76) above: "For as Gregory says: 'God's love is never unproductive.'"

[160] Hugh of St. Cher, p. 226 b also quotes Proverbs 24:17.

to the house, he heard music and choral dancing.[161] This
house means the congregation of the just. The Psalm
states: "God is in his holy place, God, who makes people
of one way of life to dwell in a house" (67:6–7). And 1
Timothy 3:15 reads: "So that you may know how you
ought to conduct yourself in the house of God, which is
the Church of the living God." In this house *singing and
choral dancing* are heard because of the harmonious
happiness that comes from interior and exterior conformity of soul and speech. "For singing together as one is
the harmonious gathering together of whatever
sounds"[162] and designates the happiness that issues from
a harmony of souls. Therefore, Ambrose also comments:
"Singing is the undivided harmony of diverse age groups
and voice ranges or various chords, according to what is
said in Acts 4:32: *The multitude of the believers was of
one heart and one soul.*"[163] "*Choral dancing* indeed is a
gathering together of voices" and signifies the joy that
stems from *a harmony of voices and words* in the
preaching about and praising of God, according to the
words of the Prophet in the Psalm: "Praise him with
timbrel and choir" (150:4). And this harmony occurs in
the holy Church. 1 Corinthians 1:10 says: "I beseech . . . that you all say the same thing." And of these
two things it is said in Philippians 2:1–2: "If there is any
comfort in Christ, any encouragement from charity, any

---

[161] I have translated the Latin *symphonia et chorus* in such a way as
to express the singing and harmony of different voices involved in
both activities: *singing and choral dancing*. It seems that Bonaventure is not concerned with the harmony of dancing.

[162] On p. 399, n. 4 QuarEd state that this interpretation is that of the
Glossa Interlinearis (from Jerome). Jerome says less than the Glossa
Interlinearis. See CSEL liv, p. 131: *chorus in unum concinens* ("a
choir singing in unison").

[163] On p. 399, n. 4 QuarEd state that Ambrose's opinion is conveyed
by the Glossa Ordinaria apud Lyranum. See CCSL xiv, p. 296 for
Ambrose's more prolix interpretation.

fellowship in the Spirit, any feelings of mercy, fill up my joy by thinking alike, having the same charity, united in heart, thinking the same thing." – So the person who *draws near* to this house hears this joyful harmony. This *drawing near* comes about through a consideration of Sacred Scripture, which is, as it were, a certain leisure to recognize those things that are within the unity of the holy Church. Sirach 51:31 reads: "Draw near to me, you unlearned, and gather together in the house of learning."[164] And then, when someone attends to Scripture, in it he hears the concord and harmony of that Church within his members. For all of Scripture teaches nothing else but the concord and harmony of love, according to what Matthew 22:40 says: "On these two commandments," etc.[165] Romans 13:8 states: "The person who loves his neighbor has fulfilled the Law." For 1 Timothy 1:5 has: "The purpose of this mandate was love from a pure heart," etc.

45. (Verse 26). Third, with regard to *the gracious kindness evidenced by his father's largess* the text adds: *He called one of the servants and inquired what these things meant.* This *one servant* has been called the order of preachers and teachers. About this servant Luke 14:17 above said: "He sent his servant at supper time to tell those invited." At this verse the Glossa observes: "The servant is the order of preachers."[166] The ecclesiastical

---

[164] Hugh of St. Cher, p. 226b has a different approach to "leisure" or contemplation. Feiss, p. 67 translates: "For as a field is said to be an exercise of action, so also the study of contemplation is said to be a field."

[165] Matthew 22:40 reads: "On these two commandments depend the whole Law and the prophets." Matthew 22:37 gives the commandment to love God, and Matthew 22:39 the commandment to love one's neighbor.

[166] This is the Glossa Interlinearis. See Bonaventure's commentary on Luke 14:17 (#38) and the note there about the interpretations of

Sacraments and the mysteries of the Scriptures are required of this servant, for as Malachi 2:7 says: "The lips of the priest will guard knowledge, and they will seek the law from his mouth. For he is the angel of the Lord of hosts."

46. (Verse 27). And since the genuine preacher is the special herald of divine mercy, the text adds: *And he said to him: Your brother has come back,* through *the humility of repentance.* Isaiah 21:12 says: "If you seek, seek. Return and come back." And Isaiah 60:4 reads: "Your sons will come from afar, and your daughters will rise up at your side." – *And your father has killed the fatted calf,* through the repast of the Eucharist, according to what John 6:56–57 has: "My flesh is food indeed, and my blood is drink indeed. The person who eats my flesh and drinks my blood abides in me and I in him." – *Because he has got him back safe,* through *the restoration of justice,* which only Christ can restore, according to Acts 4:12: "There is no other name under heaven given to men and women by which we must be saved." Now all of *Sacred Scripture* preaches these three things, namely, repentance, grace, and salvation. Thus, *Christ's precursor* preached these things, namely, *Repent,*[167] and promised grace and salvation. Similarly, *Christ himself* said: *Repent.*[168] And likewise *the entire choir of Apostles,* especially Peter and Paul, who not only by word, but also by example cried out, according to what 1 Timothy

---

Gregory the Great and Bede about the servant as the order of preachers. Hugh of St. Cher, p. 226g in Feiss's translation, p. 68, comments: "The servant who is asked about this is the order of preachers or the assembly of teachers from whom the cause of wonder and doubt is sought."

[167] Matthew 3:2.

[168] Matthew 4:17.

1:15–16 states: "Christ Jesus came into this[169] world to save sinners, of whom I am the foremost. But for this reason I obtained mercy, so that in me above all Christ Jesus might show forth all patience, as an example[170] to those who will believe in him for the attainment of life everlasting." So he was also saying that *the fatted calf had been killed* on behalf of sinners, since he said in Romans 5: "But God commends his love towards us, because when we were still sinners, Christ died for us. Much more now that we are justified by his blood, will we be saved through him from the wrath" (verses 8–9). And a little later: "Where the offense has abounded, grace has abounded yet more, so that as sin has reigned unto death, so also grace may reign by justice..." (verses 20–21).

47. (Verse 28). And since the just person, presuming on his own merits, does not accept this justice, but rather is indignant over God's mercy, as if God is acting wickedly by rendering good things to evil people, the text adds: *But he was indignant and would not go in.* For the person who does not accept the affluence of God's mercy, but the sufficiency of his own justice, cannot enter into the love of ecclesiastical unity. And this is what Romans 10:3 says of such people: "Ignorant of God's justice and seeking to establish their own, they have not submitted to the justice of God." So for this reason also the Jewish people do not wish to enter into ecclesiastical unity, for, being proud of their own justice, they do not accept that the mercy of the highest Father has been extended to sinners.[171] And against such folk it is said in Romans

---

[169] The Vulgate lacks *hunc* ("this").

[170] The Vulgate reads *ad deformationem* ("as an example") while Bonaventure reads *ad informationem* ("as an example").

[171] On p. 400, n. 3 QuarEd cite Jerome, Letter 21, n. 31–32. See CSEL liv, p. 131. I modify Mierow's translation on pp. 124–125: "The

3:24–28: "They have been justified freely by his grace through the redemption which is in Christ Jesus, whom God has set forth as a propitiation by his blood through faith. . . . So that he himself is just and justifies the person who is of the faith of Jesus Christ.[172] Where, then, is your[173] boasting? It is excluded. . . . For we reckon that a person is justified by faith independently of the works of the Law." This elder son, therefore, presuming of his own justice and indignant over the mercy extended to his brother, is not walking according to justice, but according to injustice, for Proverbs 29:22 reads: "The person who is easily stirred up to indignation will be more prone to sin."

48. *His father, therefore, came out*, etc. After depicting the elder son's impatience that led to indignation, the Evangelist describes in a second point *the father's clemency in striving to placate his son's indignation*. There are three considerations: the father's *gracious overture* to his son; the son's *impudent response* to his father; the father's attempt to *appease and persuade* his son.

So first, relative to the father's most gracious overture the text reads: *His father, therefore, came out and began to entreat him.*[174] Now the father *comes out* to the external area by means of condescension, according to what Habakkuk 3:13 states: "You came out for the salvation

---

cause of rejoicing, which is sung in praise of God with equal fervor all over the world, is the salvation of Gentiles, the salvation of sinners. The angels rejoice, every creature unites in happiness, and of Israel alone is it said: *And he was angry and would not go in.* . . . And now Israel stands outside. . . ."

[172] The Vulgate does not have *Christi* ("Christ").

[173] The Vulgate does not read *tua* ("your").

[174] On p. 400, n. 7 QuarEd rightly mention that the Vulgate reads *illum* ("him") while Bonaventure reads *eum* ("him").

of your people, for salvation with your Christ." That is, this coming forth is nothing other than his external manifestation in the flesh. Isaiah 62:1 reads: "For Zion's sake I will not hold my peace, and for the sake of Jerusalem. I will not rest till her just one comes forth like brightness," etc.[175] – And since this coming forth took place because of great love to save humanity, the text continues: *He began to entreat him.*[176] Hebrews 12:7 says: "God deals with you as with sons." Therefore, he entreats, even though we are angry with him, according to what Isaiah 30:21 advises: "You will hear the word of a person admonishing you behind your back: This is the good path. Walk on it."[177] So God the Father himself is not indignant against his indignant son, but rather entreats and comforts him, so that what Isaiah 66:13 states may be fulfilled: "As one whom a mother caresses, so will I comfort you." And such action is fitting, for, as it is said in 2 Corinthians 1:3–4, "he is the Father of mercies and the God of all comfort, who comforts us in all our afflictions." So it is said in Jeremiah 3:4 about the father's appeal: "Therefore, at least from this time say to me: You are my father, the guide of my youth," etc.[178] And thus is fulfilled what Job 19:17 says: "I prayed for the children of my womb."

---

[175] Isaiah 62:1 concludes: ". . . and her savior be lighted as a lamp."

[176] See Jerome, Letter 21, n. 33 in Mierow's translation, p. 125: "How kind and merciful a father! He entreats His son to become a participant in the joy of the house; He asks him through the apostles, preachers of the gospel. Of these Paul says: *For Christ, we beseech you, be reconciled to God.*"

[177] I translate the Vulgate of Isaiah 30:21: "And your ears will hear the word of the person admonishing you behind your back: This is the way. Walk on it." Obviously, Bonaventure has adapted this quotation.

[178] It seems that Bonaventure's point is actually contained in his "etc." For Jeremiah 3:5 reads: "Will you be angry for ever?"

49. (Verse 29). Second, concerning *the impudent response* of the son the text adds: *But he answered and said to his father: Behold, these many years I have been serving you*. In saying this, he reveals his impudence. And he also *boasts of his righteousness*, saying that he has served his father for a long time, even though the Father himself has no need of our obedience, according to what the Psalmist says: "I have said to the Lord: You are my God, for you have no need of my good things" (15:2). And Job 35:7 reads: "Furthermore, if you act justly, what will you give him or what will he accept from your hand?" So he shows himself as an example by boasting that he has done great things for his father. He also shows himself as an example by saying that he has done nothing against his father, when he adds: *And I have never transgressed your commands*. And in this he justifies himself, even though the Apostle says in 1 Corinthians 4:4: "I have nothing on my conscience, yet I am not thereby justified." Against this type of arrogance it is said in 1 Kings 8:46: "There is not a person who does not sin." And 1 John 1:8 has: "If we say that we have no sin, we are liars."[179] For it is said in Romans 3:23: "All have sinned and have need of the glory of God."[180] – Therefore, *he sets his righteousness forth as an example and reproaches his father for his hardness* where the text reads: *And yet you have never given me a kid that I might make merry with my friends*. As if he

---

[179] The Vulgate has *quoniam* ("that") for Bonaventure's *quia* ("that") and *ipsi nos seducimus* ("we deceive ourselves") for Bona-venture's *mendaces sumus* ("we are liars"). See Bonaventure's commentary on Luke 11:13 (#34) above where he offers this same reading of 1 John 1:8. Hugh of St. Cher, p. 226v, p also quotes 1 John 1:8, but according to the Vulgate.

[180] See Jerome, Letter 21, n. 34 in Mierow's translation, p. 125: "As if this very thing were not transgression of a commandment: to begrudge another his salvation, to boast before God of his justice, when no one is clean in His sight." See CSEL liv, p. 132.

were saying: You have never acted kindly in my regard and have not given me any interior consolation, which would be indicative of your love.[181] And nonetheless, God does this by means of his just and hidden judgment, in accordance with Qoheleth 9:1–2: "There are just men and wise men, and their works are in the hands of God. And yet human beings do not know whether they be worthy of love or hatred, but all things are kept uncertain till the future." But the elder son, by not attending to God's hidden judgments, charges his father with hardness, as if he were saying what Job 30:21 states: "You have changed and become cruel to me, and in the hardness of your hand you are against me." So in this regard he rebukes his father for his hardness.

50. (Verse 30). In a similar way *he reproaches his father for his clemency* where the text has: *But after this son of yours.* As if to say: He is not my brother – as the Lord in indignation said in Exodus 32:7: "Descend from the mountain, for[182] your people has sinned."[183] *Your,* he says, not mine, for on account of his sin I refuse to acknowledge him as my brother. – Wherefore, the text continues: *Who has devoured his means with prostitutes, comes back,* and thus should be worthy of your wrath, because he is a prodigal, unclean and detestable, and therefore to be cast aside. The Psalmist says: "You destroy those who commit fornication by departing from you" (72:27).[184] And Lamentations 1:17–18 states: "Jeru-

---

[181] Hugh of St. Cher, p. 226v, q in Feiss's translation, p. 73 sheds some light on Bonaventure's interpretation: "And you never gave me a goat, that is, reproach of sins and compunction of heart."

[182] The Vulgate does not read *quia* ("for").

[183] Hugh of St. Cher, p. 227v, b also quotes Exodus 32:7

[184] Bonaventure has adapted the first words of the Vulgate, which I translate: "You have destroyed everyone who. . . ." The Latin *fornicantur* could well be translated by "are disloyal," but Bonaventure's

salem has become like an unclean menstruating woman among them. The Lord is just, for I have provoked his mouth to wrath." – *You have killed the fatted calf for him*,[185] by showing the most gracious benevolence, which he shows when he proffers love to anyone from the beneficence of the Lord's Passion,[186] according to what The Song of Songs 1:12–13 says: "A bundle of myrrh is my beloved to me. He will abide between my breasts. A cluster of cypress is my love to me, in the vineyards of Engedi." *He has killed for him*, that is, you have given it out of love, as if it were killed solely for him, as even Paul said in Galatians 2:20: "The life I now live in the flesh, I live in the faith of the Son of God, who loved me and gave himself up for me." Wherefore, Paul also said earlier in Galatians 2:19: "With Christ I have been nailed to the cross." – So by means of his impudent response this son rebukes his father for his clemency and reproaches him for his hardness and lack of kindness. He also trumpets his own righteousness, never taking into consideration that "God resists the proud, but gives grace to the humble," as it is said in James 4:6. Thus, God is *gentle* with sinners, so that he may stir them to hope, and *hard* with the righteous, so that he may bend them towards humility. For this reason Luke 17:10 below reads: "When you have done everything that was commanded you, say: We are unprofitable servants."

---

context calls for "commit fornication." Hugh of St. Cher, p. 227b also quotes Psalm 72:27, but reads *omnes* ("all") instead of Bonaventure's *eos* ("them").

[185] On p. 401, n. 7 QuarEd correctly mention that the Vulgate reads *illi* ("for him") while Bonaventure has *ei* ("for him").

[186] Hugh of St. Cher, p. 227e in Feiss's translation, p. 77 helps explain Bonaventure's exposition here: "'The fatted calf': that is, Christ, by giving him compunction and devotion at the recollection of the Lord's passion which is not given to all."

51. (Verse 31). Third, with regard to the father's *appeasing and satisfying his son*, the text says: *But he said to him: Son, you are always with me.* Note here the most gracious response of the father. For, although he could reproach his son for his presumption, indignation, impudence, and inhumanity, he, nonetheless, does not rebuke him, lest he disturb him further. Rather he lovingly coaxes him to be lenient. For Proverbs 15:1 reads: "A mild mannered answer crushes wrath." So he does not reproach the distraught, but gently and reasonably appeases the wrathful, namely, *by praising his son's obedience* with the words: *Son, you are always with me.*[187] That is, you always obey me, so that you may be numbered among those about whom Luke 22:28 below says: "You are the ones who have remained with me in my trials." So that you can say with the Psalmist: "I have become like a beast among you, and I am always with you" (72:23). *You are always with me*, remaining in the house as a son. John 8:35 has: "The son abides in the house forever."[188] – He also appeases him *by being benevolent to him* with the words: *And all that is mine is yours*, namely, through the benevolence of love, according to what 1 Corinthians 3:22–23 says: "All things are yours, whether Paul or Apollos...or things present or things to come. All are yours, and you are Christ's, and Christ is God's."[189] For as it is said in Romans 8:32: "who did not spare his own son, but handed him over for us all. How can he fail to grant us also all things with

---

[187] On p. 401, n. 11 QuarEd cite the Glossa Ordinaria (from Augustine): "*Son, you are*, etc., not as if he were contradicting his son's lie, but he is giving his stamp of approval to his perseverance with him and is inviting him to the enjoyment of greater exultation." See CCSL xlivb, pp. 80–81.

[188] Bonaventure adapts the second part of John 8:35 by adding *in domo* ("in the house").

[189] Hugh of St. Cher, p. 227k also quotes 1 Corinthians 3:22–23.

him?"[190] So he wants to say that although he does not manifest great things now, he, nevertheless, has great things reserved for him, according to what Isaiah 64:4 states: "Eye has not seen, O God, apart from you, what things you have prepared for them that wait for you." Therefore, all things belong to the righteous man, either in reality or in hope. For there are some things that are *higher*. Others that are *inferior*. Yet others that are *equal. The higher things* are for the just man *to enjoy.* The Psalm says: "You are the God of my heart, and the God who is my portion forever" (72:26). *The equal things* are the Angels *to assist* the just man. Hebrews 1:14 reads: "Are they not all ministering spirits, sent for service, for the sake of those who will inherit salvation?" *The inferior things* are for the just man *to use* and *to dominate.*[191] The Psalm says: "What is a human being, that you are mindful of him or the son of man that you visit him? . . . You have subjected all things under his feet" (8:5, 8).[192] And in this the wonderful benevolence of the father is manifest.

52. (Verse 32). He also appeases him *by underlining the goodness of the mercy extended to the younger son* by saying: *But we were bound to make merry*, namely, love urges us to do so, for love is the power that compels us to rejoice in the good. Wherefore, the Apostle says in 2

---

[190] Hugh of St. Cher, p. 227k also quotes Romans 8:32.

[191] On p. 402, n. 2 QuarEd cite the Glossa Ordinaria apud Lyranum: ". . . *The superior things* will be ours to see. *The equal things* will be ours to feast with. *The inferior things* will be ours to dominate." The Glossa's interpretation ultimately stems from Augustine. See CCSL xlivb, p. 83. Hugh of St. Cher, p. 227i has a different view. See Feiss's translation, p. 78: "The higher are the three persons which are ours to enjoy. The equal are the angels, who will be ours to live with. The inferior are the demons, who will be ours to dominate."

[192] Hugh of St. Cher, p. 227k also quotes Psalm 8:8.

Corinthians 5:13–14: "If we were ecstatic, it was for God. If we are in our right mind, it is for you. For the love of Christ impels us." And just as it is the nature of love *to be inflamed* over the person who causes another to stumble, according to what 2 Corinthians 11:29 says: "Who is made to stumble, and I am not inflamed?", so too it is in love's nature *to rejoice and be strengthened* over another person's restoration to health. – Therefore, he says: *For this brother of yours had been*[193] *dead and has come to life. He was lost and has been found. He had been dead because he deserted Christ*, who says of himself in John 14:6: "I am the way, the truth, and the life." And John 1:4 has: "The life was the light of men and women." *He was lost*, by *loving sin*, because Sirach 3:27 says: "The person who loves sin will perish in it." But *he has come to life, returning to the grace of Christ*. John 11:25 reads: "I am the resurrection and the life," etc. *And has been found, by returning to repentance*, just as in verse 5 above *the little sheep* was found and in verse 9 above the lost *drachma* was found. And so *we must make merry and rejoice*, for as it was said in verse 10 above: "There is joy among the angels of God over one sinner who repents." It is the joy of the shepherd over his lost sheep and likewise the joy of the woman over her lost drachma. So how much more joy must a brother experience over the return of his lost brother and a father over his son who has been found.

---

[193] On p. 402, n. 4 QuarEd accurately mention that the Vulgate reads *erat* ("was") while Bonaventure has *fuerat* ("had been").

LUKE 16

Luke 16:1–17:19
COMMENDATION OF AND TEACHING
ABOUT HUMAN COMPASSION

1. *And he also said to his disciples*, etc. After mentioning Jewish lack of mercy and detailing divine merciful love, the Evangelist now *commends and provides an exhortation about human compassion*. This part is divided into two. In the first section he exhorts the disciples themselves through Christ's teaching and parabolic *exempla* to engage in *corporal works of mercy*. In the second section he turns to *spiritual works* where Luke 17:1 reads: *And he said to his disciples*, etc.

Luke 16:1–31
HUMAN COMPASSION AND CORPORAL WORKS OF MERCY

The first section encompasses the present chapter, which has three parts. The first part gives a *parabolic exemplum of provident mercy*. The second part propounds *teaching of perfect mercy* where verse 9 reads: *And I say to you: Make friends*, etc. The final part adds *an exemplum of punishment for a lack of mercy* where verse 19 has: *There was a certain rich man*, etc.

Luke 16:1–8
THE PARABOLIC *EXEMPLUM* OF PROVIDENT MERCY

So concerning *the exemplum of provident mercy*, which features a steward who was free and easy with the goods of his master, it must be noted that it is partly *an explicit exemplum* and partly *a parabolic saying*.

For if this passage were not *an explicit exemplum*, the end of the parable would not read in verse 8: "The master commended the unjust steward because he had acted prudently," etc. But on the other hand, if this passage were not *parabolic in nature*, the Lord would never be proposing the detestable and fraudulent action of the steward in the exemplum. From these considerations it follows that the interpreter must realize that this exemplum must be understood partly in a literal sense and partly in a parabolic sense. For this parable and the one about the rich glutton that follows bear the nature both of *an example* and of *a parable*. Now this parable has more of the parable about it while the parable of the rich glutton has more of the example about it. So the latter parable is to be understood more from the literal sense while the parable under present consideration is to be understood partly as metaphor and partly in a literal sense.[1] – Now one must attend carefully to the

---

[1] Luke 16:1–8 has given interpretive fits to both ancient and contemporary interpreters. Bonaventure's explanation is quite adept. See Stephen L. Wailes, *Medieval Allegories of Jesus' Parables*, UCLA

manifest interpretation of this parabolic exemplum. It proposes something *to be acknowledged,* something *to be repulsed,* something *to be feared,* something *to be tolerated,* something *about which to be provident,* something *to be imitated,* and something *to be commended.*[2] – For *the origin of human power is to be acknowledged* where verse 1 reads: *There was a certain rich man.* – What *is to be spurned* is *the abuse of the power entrusted to a person.* See verse 1 which intimates this: *who was reported to him as squandering his possessions.* – *The judgment of heavenly justice is to be feared.* See verse 2: *And he called him and said to him.* – *To be tolerated* is *the imperfection of human weakness* which verse 3 suggests: *And the steward said within himself.* – *What is to be provided for* is *the finding of faithful friends* where verse 4 reads: *I know what I will do, when I am removed from my stewardship.* – *The display of generous mercy is to be imitated.* About this verse 5 says: *He summoned each of his master's debtors.* – *A wise and provident decision is to be praised* or commended as verse 8 states: *The master praised the unjust steward.*

2. (Verse 1). So first through this parable he teaches his disciples *to acknowledge the origin of earthly power,* for verse 1 reads: *And he said also to his disciples,* to whom he said in Luke 8:10 above: "To you it is given to know the mysteries of the kingdom of God." And John 15:15 has: "I have called you friends, because all things that I

Center for Medieval and Renaissance Studies 23 (Berkeley: University of California Press, 1987), p. 247: "The most careful justification of interpretive method comes from Bonaventure, who explains that the parable is obviously a mixture of literal and parabolic teaching. . . . "

[2] Need I remind my readers of Bonaventure's love of "seven"? See, for example, his commentary on Luke 15:10 (#19) above where he also makes seven points.

have heard from my Father I have made known to you."
Therefore, he now spoke to *the disciples*, for, the Jews
having been confuted, he had to persuade them of
mercy.[3] Since a consideration of *the origin of earthly
power* is a powerful incentive to the practice of mercy,
the text adds: *There was a certain rich man, who had a
steward*. *This man*, singular and singularly rich, is
rightly understood to be God, according to what Romans
10:12 states: "There is the same Lord of all, rich towards
all who call upon him." Only this one is *rich*, since he
possesses all things in abundance. The Psalms say: "For
the world is mine and its fullness" (49:12). And again:
"All the beasts of the forest are mine" (49:10). And yet
again: "The earth is the Lord's and its fullness, the
world," etc. (23:1). – *The steward* of this rich man is any
person who possesses some earthly *power* either by dignity or by wealth to dispense goods. So the Glossa
states: "*The steward* is the person to whom God has
committed some money for the aid of the poor."[4] And as
another Glossa comments: "*The steward* is properly
speaking the guardian of the villa, but it is used here for
the steward, that is, the person who dispenses."[5] Therefore, human power, since it is only temporary and
granted by another, is nothing else but a certain stew-

---

[3] On p. 403, n. 8 QuarEd cite the Glossa Ordinaria on Luke 16:1: "*To
the disciples*. Since the Pharisees are proud and avaricious, who first
denied forgiveness to those seeking it and now money to those in
need, the Savior first spoke to them, but now, with them listening
on, he addresses words about mercy to his disciples." The editors also
refer to Jerome, Letter 121, chapter 6 (see PL 22:1018) and Homily
121 of the Haimo of Auxerre's (d. ca. 855) Homilies on the Seasons
(see PL 118:647A).

[4] On p. 403, n. 10 QuarEd state that this is the Glossa Ordinaria
apud Lyranum.

[5] On p. 403, n. 10 QuarEd state that this, too, is from the Glossa Ordinaria, which ends with "who dispenses all the goods of the household."

ardship and management. So 1 Chronicles 29:14–15 states: "All things are yours. And we have given you what we have received from your hand. For we are sojourners before you and strangers, as were all our forbearers. Our days upon earth are as a shadow, and we have no permanent stay." Wherefore, the Apostle, too, did not want to be considered a master, but a manager and steward, when he said in 1 Corinthians 4:1: "Let a person account us as ministers of Christ and stewards of the mysteries of God." Job regarded himself as such a steward of present things when he said in Job 1:21: "The Lord has given. The Lord has taken away. As it has pleased the Lord, so it has been done."[6]

3. Secondly, that *all must spurn the abuse of power entrusted to them*, the text adds: *And this man was reported to him as squandering his*[7] *possessions*. For a person *squanders the possessions* of God, when he either evilly *retains* or evilly *receives* or evilly *dispenses* these temporal things. Thus, the Glossa observes: "Squandering occurs when things are evilly collected or poorly expended."[8] And the reason for this is that temporal goods exist so that through them eternal goods may be acquired. So when these temporal goods are disposed of in such a way that eternal goods are lost on their account, then undoubtedly *they are squandered*. Thus, those persons, who expend these temporal goods in such a way that they do not seek to gain salvation through them, but rather fleshly comfort, *are dispensing* them

---

[6] On p. 403, n. 11 QuarEd summarize the comments of Ambrose and Theophylactus, who teach that it follows from this passage that we are not masters, but only stewards or dispensers of things that do not belong to us, but have only been committed to our trust.

[7] On p. 403, n. 13 QuarEd rightly indicate that the Vulgate reads *ipsius* ("his") while Bonaventure has *illius* ("his").

[8] On p. 404, n. 1 QuarEd state that this is the Glossa Interlinearis.

not like a good steward, but *are squandering* them like the prodigal son. About the prodigal son it was said in Luke 15:13 above that "he squandered his fortune in loose living." Against these the Lord says through the mouth of the Prophet in Hosea 2:8–10: "I gave her corn and wine and oil, and I multiplied her silver and gold, which they used in the worship of Baal. Therefore, I will return and take away my corn . . . and wine in its season, and I will remove my wool and my flax that covered her disgrace. And I will reveal her folly to the eyes of her lovers." Wherefore, since there are many who wrongfully squander and few who rightfully dispense, it is said in 1 Corinthians 4:2: "Now here it is required in those who dispense that they be found trustworthy." – Now then these temporal goods are dispensed in a good way when they are distributed in works of mercy, according to what Luke 12:42 above says: "Who, do you think, is the person who faithfully and wisely dispenses and whom the master will set over his household," etc.? So *the origin* and the mother *of the squandering* of this steward is mercilessness. For which reason Proverbs 29:7–8 reads: "The just person notices the cause of the poor. The wicked lacks knowledge. Corrupt people squander the goods of the city." – Now then this steward *is reported* to his master, when the clamor of the poor rises up to the Lord. Thus, it is said in James 5:1, 4: "Come now, you rich, weep and howl over the miseries that will come over you. . . . Behold, the wages of the laborers who reaped your fields, which have been kept back by you unjustly, cry out. And their cry has entered into the ears of the Lord of hosts." And since the merciless person is heedless of his reputation, and every person is especially fearful of a bad reputation, it follows that such abuse of good things is to be shunned, lest through squandering goods a steward be plunged into opprobrium and public derision, according to what

Sirach 20:17–19 states: "A fool will have no friend, and there will be no thanks for his good deeds. . . . How often and how many will laugh him to scorn! For he does not distribute with right understanding that which was to be had, and in like manner also that which was not to be had."

4. (Verse 2). Third, relative to *the judgment of divine justice, which is meted out to each one and is to be feared,* the text continues: *And he called him and said to him: What is this I hear of you?* The Glossa comments: *"He calls,* when he instills the fear of eternal damnation."[9] Ezekiel 3:12 says this about this call: "And I heard behind me the voice of a great commotion, saying: Blessed be the Lord of glory from his place." Having been called by this voice, a person is spurred to consider future judgment, where he will be accused not only on the basis of his reputation, but also for what he has on his conscience. – For which reason the text adds: *Render an account of your stewardship.* For this voice must reverberate in the ear of everybody, for there is no doubt that divine justice demands an account of *good deeds that have been done.* Matthew 18:23 reads: "The kingdom of the heavens is like a king who desired to settle accounts with his servants." About *evil deeds that have been forgiven.* Matthew 18:24, 27 says: "And when he had begun the settlement, one was brought to him who owed him ten thousand talents. . . . Moved with compassion, the master of that servant released him." And afterwards it is added that he demanded from him an explanation of

---

[9] On p. 404, n. 7 QuarEd state that this is the Glossa Interlinearis. They also cite Haimo of Auxerre. See PL 118:647D: "God calls us in a twofold manner: in the present to repentance, and in the future to judgment."

why he failed to be forgiving in turn.[10] Also, about *good deeds that have been omitted*. Matthew 25:19 has: "After a long time the master of those servants came and settled accounts with his servants." And it adds about the lazy servant that he was cast out "into the darkness outside" (25:30). Moreover, about *evil deeds that have been perpetrated*. 1 Peter 4:3, 5 states: "For sufficient is the time past for those to have accomplished the desire of the Gentiles, walking, as they did, in voluptuousness, lust, drunkenness, revelings. . . . They will render an account to him who is ready to judge the living and the dead." Not only for *grave* evil deeds, but also for *small* ones, according to what Matthew 12:36 reads: "For every idle word people speak, they will give an account on judgment day." Therefore, an account of the stewardship of this steward is required from all the four previously mentioned considerations. For just as Bernard says: "Just as a hair from your head will not perish nor a second of time pass without an account of it being rendered."[11] – And after the submission of this account there will be no possibility of meriting. Thus, the text continues: *For you can be steward no longer*, because as Qoheleth 9:10 reads: "Neither deeds, nor reason, nor

---

[10] I have clarified Bonaventure's point here. Matthew 18:27 concludes: ". . . released him, and forgave him the debt." Matthew 18:32–35 deals with the master's condemnation of the servant he had forgiven, but who failed to show mercy and forgiveness to a fellow servant who owed him far less.

[11] On p. 404, n. 12 QuarEd point their readers to Chapter XLIV n. 54 "On the Excuse of Secular Matters" of *Declamationes de Colloquio Simonis cum Jesu, Ex S. Bernardi sermonibus collectae* of Geoffrey the Abbot. See PL 184:465D for a text and thought that differs from Bonaventure's: "Sit down, calculate what you want to acquire every single day. Indeed, you are certain that in no way will God fail to remunerate every good deed. And just as not a hair from the body, nor a second of time will perish." Bonaventure also quotes Ps-Bernard's *Declamationes* in his commentary on Luke 9:23 (#38) and 14:33 (#66) above.

wisdom, nor knowledge will be in hell, whither you are hastening." So, too, does Proverbs 27:24 say this to each and every steward: "You will not have perpetual power." And Sirach 10:11 states: "All power is short-lived." Wherefore, the Prophet says in the Psalm: "Put not your trust in princes nor in human beings, in whom there is no salvation. His spirit will go forth, and he will return to the earth. On that day all their thoughts will perish" (145:2–4).

5. (Verse 3). Fourth, concerning *the imperfection of the human weakness to be tolerated* in the steward, the text adds: *And the steward said within himself: What will I do, since my master is taking my stewardship away from me?* For since fear of judgment stirs up the mind to find a solution, the steward, realizing that he is to be judged, searches for a solution, according to what Sirach 18:19–20 states: "Before judgment prepare your case for justice . . . and before sickness take medicine. And before judgment examine yourself." – And since the perfection of repentance consists in affliction and corporal labor and humility and mental shame and since the spirit of the weak human being refuses these, the text continues: *To dig I am unable*, because of the difficulty of corporal labor. For, as it is said in Proverbs 29:21, "the person who rears his servant delicately from his childhood will afterwards find him insolent." *To beg I am ashamed*, for it is a contemptible and vile action. Sirach 29:30, 35 read: "Be content with little instead of much, and you will not hear the reproach of going abroad. . . . These two things are painful for a person of understanding: abuse from his household and reproaches from his creditor." So the person who flees from the Order of the Cistercians is similar to this steward, for they engage in labor. Or flees from the Order of the Minors, for they beg. And nonetheless, this is what sustains him, for he

shrinks from *labor* and *shame* because of his weakness, the first as being unendurable, the other as contemptible.[12]

6. But although these things are difficult for the weak human being, they are, nevertheless, easy for the Christian made perfect by Christ. For Christ became poor for our sake and was in many labors, in accordance with the Psalm: "I am poor and in labors from my youth" (87:16). He makes labor palatable and begging honorable, for "it is a great honor to follow the Lord," as it is said in Sirach 23:38. Now the Lord himself says this about himself: "But I am a beggar and poor, and the Lord is solicitous for my welfare" (Psalm 39:18). Now this is not said with regard to spiritual things, in which the Lord abounds, but relative to temporal things. In these he became needy and a beggar for our sakes, according to what 2 Corinthians 8:9 states: "You know the graciousness of our Lord Jesus Christ that, although he was rich, he became poor for our sakes," etc.[13] And therefore, blessed Francis says in his Rule that his brothers "must not be ashamed of begging, because the Lord made himself poor in this world for our sakes."[14] Nevertheless, the grace, which would have made the steward perfectly conformable to Christ, had not been given to him. So as

---

[12] I have tried to make sense of Bonaventure's somewhat obscure sentence. On p. 405, n. 6 QuarEd cite the variant reading of Vat.

[13] The Vulgate reads *propter vos* ("for your sakes") while Bonaventure reads *propter nos* ("for our sakes"). The Vulgate concludes with: ". . . that by his poverty you might become rich."

[14] Bonaventure has adapted Chapter VI, n. 4 of the Regula Bullata of 1223. See *Fontes Franciscani*, ed. Enrico Menestò and Stefano Brufani (Assisi: Porziuncola, 1995), 176: *Nec oportet eos verecundari, quia Dominus pro nobis se fecit pauperem in hoc mundo* ("Nor must they be ashamed (to beg), because the Lord made himself poor in this world for our sakes"). Both Bonaventure and Francis allude to 2 Corinthians 8:9.

an imperfect individual, he gives voice to his weakness: *I am ashamed to beg.*[15] He does not say: *I despise begging*, for that would not be weakness to be tolerated, but wickedness to be detested.

7. (Verse 4). Fifth, relative to *the need to be provident and find faithful friends*, the text adds: *I know what I will do*, so that I may make faithful friends. Thus the Glossa observes: "The steward is the person to whom God has committed some money to give to the poor. If this person realizes that his stewardship ends with this life, he will devote greater efforts in making friends than in accumulating wealth."[16] For the person who strives to make friends with his neighbor can rightly say: *I know what I will do.* A contrary example is given in 1 John 2:11: "The person who hates his brother is in darkness and walks in darkness, and does not know whither he is going, because the darkness has blinded his eyes." On the contrary, the person who loves knows what he is doing, for he is acting according to Christ's teaching, through which he seeks rescue from danger. – Wherefore, the text continues: *That, when I am removed from my stewardship*, through divine verdict, according to what Revelation 2:5 says: "I will come[17] to you and remove your lamp stand from its place," *they may receive me into their houses* through compassionate friendship. For the law of friendship is: Do not abandon

---

[15] Bonaventure's interpretation in this paragraph becomes clearer when the reader recalls its opening sentence: "But although these things are difficult for the weak human being, they are, nevertheless, easy for the Christian made perfect by Christ."

[16] On p. 405, n. 10 QuarEd state that this is the Glossa Ordinaria apud Lyranum and cite the Glossa Interlinearis: "*I know what I will do*, during the time of this stewardship."

[17] The Vulgate reads *venio* ("I am coming") while Bonaventure has *veniam* ("I will come").

a friend in time of need. So Proverbs 17:17 reads: "The person who is a friend loves at every moment, and a brother is proven in difficult circumstances." For Sirach 6:14–15 states: "A faithful friend is a strong defense. The person who has found him has found a treasure. Nothing can be compared to a faithful friend, and no weight of gold and silver is able to provide a counterbalance to the goodness of his fidelity."

8. (Verse 5). Sixth, relative to *the display of generous mercy to be imitated*, the text adds: *Therefore, he summoned each of his master's debtors.* Here *the literal sense* shows forth the steward's generous munificence and gracious mercy, for he shows largess to *many* in a *great* way and in a *proportionate* manner. *To many*, because he calls in each of his master's debtors, according to what the Lord promotes in Luke 6:30 above: "Give to everyone who asks of you." And Isaiah 32:20 reads: "Blessed are you who sow upon all waters, sending thither the foot of the ox and the ass."[18] And since mercy must be extended to the needy, he does not give to each and everyone, but to *the debtors*, in accordance with Isaiah 58:6–7: "Let those who are broken go free, and break asunder every yoke. Break your bread with the hungry, and bring the needy and the wayfarers into your home. When you see a person naked, cover him and despise not your own flesh." – *In a great way*, for he forgives a great sum of money. Thus the text says: *He said to the first: How much do you owe my master? He said*, I say, in a friendly tone of voice. Sirach 4:7–8 reads: "Make yourself affable to the assembly of the poor. . . . Give the poor person a courteous hearing, and pay what you owe, and respond

---

[18] The point of the Vulgate of Isaiah 32:20 seems to be the largess of the sower. The NAB translates the Hebrew: "Happy are you who sow beside every stream, and let the ox and the ass go freely."

to him peacefully," etc. And Sirach 18:16 says: "Will not
the dew moderate the heat? So also a good word is better than a gift."[19]

9. (Verse 6). *And he said to him*[20]: *A hundred caduses of
olive oil*, in honest acknowledgement of his debt. For
each person must honestly acknowledge his debt, lest
perhaps it be said of him what Revelation 3:17 has: "You
say that I am rich and have grown wealthy and have
need of nothing. And you do not know that you are
wretched and miserable and poor and blind and naked."
Now the *cadus* is a measure containing three urnas.
Thus, the Glossa comments: "A *cadus* is Greek; *amphora*
in Latin, containing three urnas."[21] Now this calculation
suggests the magnitude of the debt weighing down on
the debtor, for Proverbs 22:7 has: "The borrower is the
servant of the person who lends." – *And he said to him:
Take your bond and sit down at once and*[22] *write fifty*,
through a gracious pardoning of the debt. For the person
who removes half of another's burden gives great support
and relief to him.[23] And in this the law of love is fulfilled,

[19] The Vulgate reads *datus* for "gift" while Bonaventure has *datum*.
[20] On p. 406, n. 5 QuarEd correctly indicate that the Vulgate does not
read *ei* ("to him").
[21] On p. 406, n. 6 QuarEd state that this is the Glossa Ordinaria
(from Bede). See CCSL cxx, p. 297, where the editor indicates that
Bede is borrowing from Isidore of Seville's *Etymologia*. See Fitzmyer,
p. 1100 who states that the Greek text refers to 900 gallons of olive
oil. It is far more difficult to compute the amount of olive oil referred
to by the Latin text. On one account the debt is a mere 50 gallons; on
another it is 575 gallons. If the average contemporary price for olive
oil is $20 a gallon, one begins to glimpse the amount of money in-
volved in the debt.
[22] On p. 406, n. 7 QuarEd accurately indicate that the Vulgate lacks
et ("and").
[23] On p. 406, n. 7 QuarEd cite the Glossa Interlinearis: "*Write fifty.*
He pardons half of it."

according to what Galatians 6:2 states: "Bear one another's burdens, and so you will fulfill the law of Christ."

10. (Verse 7). He also is generous *in a proportionate manner*, for he acts in accordance with the urgency of the debt. For which reason the text adds: *Then he said to another: You, how much do you owe?* So he is seeking for a measuring stick, so that he may distribute things in a measured way, for Sirach 42:7 reads: "Where there are many hands, close yours. And whatever you deliver, give number and weight. Put all in writing that you give out and take in." – *Who said: One hundred kori of wheat.* Here he expresses a large measure, so that he may obtain a great pardon. As the Glossa says: "A *korus* is comprised of thirty modii," and so is a larger measure than a *cadus*.[24] And since in the matter of larger gifts the number must be smaller, so that the measure of indebtedness might be observed,[25] the text adds: *And he said*[26] *to him: Take your bond and write eighty.* The Glossa notes: "He forgives one-fifth."[27] Now although it seems he pardons less according to strict mathematical calculations, for he only pardons a fifth for the second person and a half for the first person, he actually pardons the second person more according to geometric cal-

---

[24] On p. 406, n. 9 QuarEd state that this is the Glossa Ordinaria (from Bede). See CCSL cxx, p. 297. A *modius* is a peck or eight quarts or a quarter bushel. So 100 *kori* would amount to 750 bushels of wheat. Fitzmyer, p. 1101 calculates the amount from the Greek text at about 150 bushels.

[25] On p. 406, QuarEd give no guidance as to the origin of this principle.

[26] On p. 406, n. 10 QuarEd rightly notice that the Vulgate reads *ait illi* ("he said to him") while Bonaventure has *Dixitque illi* ("And he said to him").

[27] On p. 406 n. 10, QuarEd state that this is the Glossa Interlinearis and then cite the Glossa Ordinaria (from Bede): "The text can be simply taken this way: Whoever alleviates the need of the poor either by one-half or by one-fifth is to be given a reward for his mercy." See CCSL cxx, p. 298 for Bede's far more elaborate interpretation.

culations. For there is more in the quantity of twenty kori of wheat than in fifty cadi of olive oil.[28] So it is shown in this that this steward generously pardons, for he pardons not only *many* and *in many ways*, but also *in a proportionate manner* according to what Tobit 4:8–9 says: "According to your ability, be merciful. If you have much, give abundantly. If you have little, take care also to distribute it willingly." Now in this forgiveness of *fifty* parts and of *twenty* parts the full remission of most generous mercy is rightly understood. For *fifty*, which stems from seven times seven and the addition of one, designates the remission of sevenfold mercy. As a designation of this there was a full remission during the jubilee, according to what Leviticus 25:10–11 says: "You shall sanctify the fiftieth year and shall proclaim remission to all the inhabitants of the earth. For it is the year of the jubilee. . . . Because it is the jubilee and the fiftieth year." Now this number, with twenty added to it, comes to *seventy*, which is understood as complete remission.[29] As a figure of this reality the people of the Lord, led off into captivity, were freed after seventy years, as it is said in Jeremiah 29:10: "When the seventy years will begin to be completed in Babylon, I will visit you and I will again speak my good word in your favor to bring you back to this place."

11. (Verse 8). Seventh, with regard to the consideration that *a wise and provident decision is to be praised*, the text has: *And the master praised the unjust steward, because he had acted prudently.*[30] The Glossa comments:

---

[28] I have to take Bonaventure's word for this geometric calculation.

[29] On p. 406, n. 12 QuarEd refer to Book II, Homily 5, n. 15 of Gregory the Great's *Homilies on Ezekiel*.

[30] On p. 407, n. 2 QuarEd rightly mention that the Vulgate reads *fecisset* ("had acted") whereas Bonaventure reads *egisset* ("had acted").

"He even praises a sinner, but not for his fraud, but for his prudence."[31] So, although the steward has done something reprehensible in itself, nevertheless, his manner of providing for his future can be taken as an example for good people. For just as the serpent, in injecting poison, is detestable, but is to be imitated by perfect men in its prudence in protecting its head – for which reason it is said in Matthew 10:16: "Be prudent as serpents as simple as doves" – so this steward is to be despised because he committed fraud, but praised because he prudently found a solution to the perilous situation in which he found himself. – And since people could wonder why the Lord provided such a steward as an example of prudence, the Evangelist gives an answer to them in what follows: *For the children of this age, in relation to their own generation, are more prudent than the children of light.* He does not say that they are more prudent *pure and simple*, but more prudent in those things that pertain to their *carnal generation*, just as the owl and the cat see more clearly at night than hu-

---

[31] On p. 407, n. 2 QuarEd state that this is the Glossa Interlinearis. See Haimo of Auxerre in PL 649:D–650A: "The master did not praise the unjust steward that he had committed fraud, but that he had prudently provided for his future, so that we may learn from his example, that we do not have a permanent city here, but should seek after our future city with all our desire." See also Jerome, Letter 121, chapter 6, in PL 22:1019, who interprets the parable as an elaborate similitude: "Therefore, if the steward of wicked mammon is praised by the words of the Lord that he took advance steps to win justice for himself from a wicked thing and if the Lord, having suffered a loss, praises the prudence of the steward who indeed had acted fraudulently against him, but had acted prudently for his own sake, how much more will Christ, who can sustain no loss and is prone to mercy, praise his disciples if they are merciful with the things that will be entrusted to them?"

mans do, not to read texts and gain knowledge, but to catch mice.[32]

12. Now *the prudence of the Spirit* that is in the children of light is more excellent than the prudence of the flesh that is in carnal men according to what Romans 8:6 says: "The prudence of the flesh is death, but the prudence of the Spirit is life and peace."[33] Nevertheless, worldly prudence has something about it that urges us to and teaches us about divine prudence, just as the solicitude of the person pursuing money is proposed as an example to the person in pursuit of wisdom. Proverbs 2:3–5 reads: "If you will call for wisdom and incline your heart to prudence, if you will seek her as money and will dig for her as for a treasure, then will you understand the fear of the Lord and will find the knowledge of God." Wherefore, since no sin destroys the last traces of human nature,[34] it follows that every sinful person has some

---

[32] On p. 407, n. 4 QuarEd cite Cardinal Hugh. See Hugh of St. Cher, p. 228v, g: "For clerics study secular prudence more diligently and with more enthusiasm than spiritual prudence. But how can the children of darkness see more clearly than the children of light, when nothing can be seen unless there is light? I answer: The owl and the cat see more clearly at night than do men and women, not to read texts and gain knowledge, but to catch mice." Hugh's answer is virtually identical to Bonaventure's statement about the owl and cat.

[33] On p. 407, n. 5 QuarEd call attention to a helpful parallel from Augustine. See his Book XI, chapter 2 n. 4 in *St. Augustine: The Literal Meaning of Genesis*, Volume II, Books 7–12, translated and annotated by John H. Taylor, ACW 42 (New York: Newman Press, 1982), 136: "And our Lord says that *the children of the world are wiser than the children of light* in providing for their own future – by means, however, that are fraudulent, not just."

[34] On p. 407, n. 7 QuarEd helpful refer their readers to Book XIX, chapter 12, n. 2 of Augustine's *De Civitate Dei*. See *Saint Augustine: The City of God* Books XVII–XXII, translated by Gerald G. Walsh and Daniel J. Honan, FC 24 (New York: Fathers of the Church, 1954), p. 215: "For, no man's sin is so unnatural as to wipe out all traces whatsoever of human nature."

quality that stirs the just person to good. For example, from a consideration of the *voluptuous* person one may be urged to *love*, from a consideration of the *avaricious* person to *care for others*, from a consideration of the *proud* person to *magnanimity*.[35] – So from this parable and exemplum we are not only given instruction on a particular point, but also on a general matter, that we can learn how to derive knowledge from everything that stirs us and forms us towards the good. For just as the Saints must give testimony by their excellent goodness and have a good reputation among those outside, so all sins display some form of virtue and piety.[36] Virtue is approved by all with a certain unanimity, but the wicked is condemned by all.

Luke 16:9-18
TEACHING OF PERFECT MERCY

13. *And I say to you*, etc. After the presentation of the exemplum of provident mercy the text adds *teaching about perfect mercy*, which indeed flows from the sense of the aforementioned parable. So first, teaching is given *to form the obedient disciples*, and secondly *to confute the rebellious Pharisees* where verse 14 reads: *Now the Pharisees heard all these things*, etc.

---

[35] On p. 407, n. 8 QuarEd refer their readers to Book II, chapter 7 of Aristotle's *Nicomachean Ethics*.

[36] On p. 407, n. 9 QuarEd point to the parallel of 1 Timothy 3:7: "Besides this he (the bishop) must have a good reputation with those who are outside. . . ." They also refer to Satire XIV of Juvenal. I quote lines 107–110 from LCL: "All vices but one the young imitate of their own free will. Avarice alone is enjoined on them against the grain. For that vice has a deceptive appearance and semblance of virtue, being gloomy of mien, severe in face and garb."

Luke 16:9–13
TEACHING GIVEN TO FORM PERFECT DISCIPLES

Concerning *the formation of disciples in mercy* the Evangelist proceeds in this fashion. For he first urges them to mercy, by reason of *the reward to be obtained.* Second, by reason of *fidelity to be preserved* where verse 10 says: *The person who is faithful in a very little.* Third, by reason of *duplicity to be avoided* where verse 13 states: *No one[37] can serve two masters.* – Now in making his first point he follows this order. After setting forth *an exhortatory instruction* he adds its *motivation.*

14. (Verse 9). First, then, relative to *exhortatory instruction* the text says: *And I say to you: Make friends for yourselves with the mammon of wickedness.* As the Glossa observes: "*Mammon* is the Syriac word for riches."[38] Now they are said to be the riches of *wickedness* since they are frequently linked with wickedness, according to what Sirach 11:10 states: "If you become rich, you will not be free from sin." Thus Augustine maintains: "Every rich person is either iniquitous or the heir of someone who was iniquitous."[39] Or as Bede explains in a homily: "*Mammon*, mammonis is the Punic for lucre."[40] One should not understand this text to mean that

---

[37] On p. 407, n. 12 QuarEd accurately mention that the Vulgate of Luke 16:13 reads *Nemo servus* ("no servant"). The dominant influence of Matthew's Gospel on churchmen in the Middle Ages seems evident here, for the parallel passage in Matthew 6:24 reads the simple *Nemo* ("No one").

[38] On p. 408, n. 1 QuarEd state that this is the Glossa Ordinaria (from Jerome). See PL 22:1019.

[39] Bonaventure quotes this same passage from "Augustine" in his commentary on Luke 11:13 (#34) above. See the note there.

[40] On p. 408, n. 3 QuarEd mention that they have been unable to find this homily, which is also quoted by Cardinal Hugh. They note that this opinion is found in Book II, chapter 14, n. 47 of Augustine's

a person must give alms from those things he has acquired through robbery or wickedness and has an unjust claim to. Against that interpretation Sirach 34:23 says: "The Most High does not approve the gifts of the wicked." And again in the same chapter: "The person who makes a sacrifice from the goods of the poor is like the person who sacrifices the son in the presence of his father" (34:24). Rather this text is to be understood to be talking about riches that a person has a just claim to. And nonetheless, they bring forth iniquity, unless they are distributed, according to what Sirach 10:10 states: "There is not a more wicked thing than to love money. For such a person even puts a price tag on his soul." From these riches, I say, they must make friends through the largess of alms, which display the affection of mercy.[41] For it is said in 1 John 3:17: "The person who has the goods of this world and sees his brother in need and closes his heart to him, how does the love of God abide in him?" And therefore, Sirach 29:13 reads: "Lose your money for the sake of . . . your friend, and do not

---

work *On the Sermon of the Mount.* Hugh of St. Cher, p. 228v, k quotes the same three sources that Bonaventure does and in virtually the same words "Augustine," the Glossa (of Bede), and "Bede's Homily."

[41] On p. 408, n. 5 QuarEd refer to Bonaventure's Opera Omnia 4:369–371where he discusses riches, almsgiving, and restitution. They also refer to Augustine's Sermon 113, chapter 2, n. 2 and state that other interpreters such as Paul the Deacon and Cardinal Hugh distinguish between two types of wickedness, namely, *a wickedness of injustice,* when riches are acquired through an unjust claim, and *a wickedness of inequality,* through which a rich person through the possession of wealth does not maintain equality with other men and women. The riches of the first wickedness must be returned in restitution. From the riches of the second type of wickedness alms must be given. See Hugh of St. Cher, p. 228v, k where the aforementioned twofold distinction is made. As far as I can determine, however, Hugh does not give an explanation of the wickedness of inequality.

hide it under a stone to be lost."[42] For Proverbs 11:26 has: "The person who hides his harvest will be cursed among the people," etc.

15. Second, with regard to *the motivation* the text adds: *So that when you fail, they may receive you into the everlasting dwellings.* From this it is understood why a gift should be given and what must motivate a person to give alms: For it is not *present comfort,* but *everlasting reward*; not on account of *a transient dwelling,* but *an everlasting,* according to what Matthew 6:2–3 says: "When you give alms, do not sound a trumpet before you, as the hypocrites do. Amen I say to you. . . . But when you give alms, do not let your left hand know what your right hand is doing." Now these everlasting dwellings are the mansions of glory, about which Isaiah 32:18 speaks: "My people will sit in the beauty of peace, and in secure dwellings and in opulent repose." Those who alone are perfect *receive* others *into the everlasting dwellings,* so that their merits may also assist others and that on account of their merits they may acquire everlasting dwellings for themselves and others. Wherefore, commenting on the present text, "Make friends for yourselves," the Glossa observes: "Not just any poor, but those who can receive them into the everlasting dwellings."[43]

16. For these are not the involuntary poor, but the poor in spirit. About them Matthew 5:3 says: "Blessed are the

---

[42] Bonaventure's text varies from the Vulgate in two regards: 1) the Vulgate reads *pro frate et amico* ("for your brother and friend"); 2) the Vulgate has *non* ("not") whereas Bonaventure has *ne* ("not").

[43] On p. 408, n. 9 QuarEd state that this is the Glossa Interlinearis (from Augustine).

poor in spirit, for theirs is the kingdom of the heavens."[44] Therefore, it is their responsibility as *kings and possessors* of this reign to lead people into the kingdom of the heavens. It is also their responsibility as *judges*, according to what Job 36:6 has: "He will not save[45] the wicked, but gives judgment over to the poor." I say, to the perfect and voluntary poor. About these Matthew 19 says: "You, who have left all things and followed me, will sit upon twelve thrones, judging the twelve tribes of Israel."[46] It is also their responsibility as *kin and friends*. Therefore, James 2:5 reads: "Has not God chosen the poor of this world to be rich in faith and heirs of the kingdom which God has promised to those who love him?"[47] Such poor people escort their friends and benefactors into heaven by means of that judicial law which the Lord will use in rendering future judgment and is found in Matthew 25:40: "What you have done to one of the least...you have done to me,"[48] and by means of that other law, which the Lord pronounced in Matthew 10:41:

---

[44] In this paragraph Bonaventure is dealing with those who have voluntarily taken a vow of poverty and for this reason are considered "perfect."

[45] On p. 408, n. 11 QuarEd correctly mention that the Vulgate reads *salvat* ("saves").

[46] Bonaventure seems to have conflated, adapted, and universalized Matthew 19:27–28, so that Peter and the first disciples are no longer the addressees. On p. 408, n. 11 QuarEd point to Opera Omnia 4:971 where Bonaventure argues for this *Conclusio*: "Christ alone pronounces the sentence at the judgment, but the Apostles and their perfect imitators are judges who assist the one pronouncing judgment and approve of the judgment."

[47] I have eliminated the *etc.* of the critical text and added the last words of James 2:5 ("to those who love him") which make Bonaventure's point.

[48] In the context of Bonaventure's discussion in this paragraph of the polyvalent word "poor" it seems significant that he has dropped *de his fratribus meis* ("of these my brothers").

"The person who receives a just person because he is just will receive a just person's reward."

17. (Verse 10). *The person who is faithful in a very little*, etc. After he has urged them to mercy from a consideration of the reward to be obtained, here in a second point he urges them by means of a consideration of *fidelity to be preserved*. For there is fidelity to be preserved in the disposition of temporal goods both from the angle of *merit and demerit* and from that of *danger and loss*.

So first, relative to a consideration of *the merit of fidelity* in earthly things of this kind the text says: *The person who is faithful in a very little thing is faithful also in much*. As if he were saying: Although these temporal things are to be contemned as of least value, nevertheless the faithful disposition of them must not be slighted. For it is the same faithfulness involved in large and small matters, and the faithful disposition of temporal things leads to a faithful disposition and preservation of spiritual and everlasting things. Thus, the Glossa comments: "*The person who is faithful in a very little thing*, that is, in sharing money with the poor, *is faithful also in much*, through clinging to his Creator."[49] And therefore, it is said to a servant of this kind in Revelation 2:10: "Be faithful unto death, and I will give you the crown of life." Similarly Matthew 25:23 states: "Well done, good and faithful servant. Since you have been faithful over a few things, I will set you over many. Enter into the joy of

---

[49] On p. 409, n. 1 QuarEd state that this is the Glossa Ordinaria (from Bede). See CCSL cxx, p. 299 where Bede's commentary makes more sense than the Glossa's abbreviation of it: ". . . *The person who is faithful in a very little thing*, that is, in sharing money with the poor, *is also faithful in much*, namely, by that act through which he specially clings to his Creator and desires to become one spirit with him."

your Lord." Wherefore, fidelity concerning small matters also gives evidence of fidelity with regard to large matters. And the opposite is also true: Infidelity concerning very little matters gives evidence of infidelity relative to major matters.

18. And therefore, the text adds: *And the person who is unjust in a little thing is unjust also in much. A little* is rightly said of everything that possesses the quality of time, both because of its smallness in *quantity*. Wisdom 11:23 reads: "For the whole world before you is as the least grain on the balance. And because of its shortness in *duration*. Wisdom 5:9 states: "All these things have passed away like a shadow." And the Psalm says: "They have slept their sleep, and all the rich men have found nothing in their hands" (75:6). Also because of its fleeting *happiness*. Thus Gregory observes: "The goods of the present life are few, although they seem many," since they come mixed with some vexation.[50] But many are the everlasting goods that exist without any corruption. So the person who is unjust in these cannot have the love of God, for he contemns the greatest things for the paltry few. For he sells his faith and justice to obtain something that has no value. Wherefore, Augustine says:

---

[50] On p. 409, n. 4 QuarEd cite Homily 9, n. 2 of GGHG. See PL 76:1107B: *Pauca quippe bona sunt omnia praesentis vitae, quamlibet multa esse videantur* ("Indeed, all the goods of the present life are few, albeit they seem to be many"). Bonaventure's quotation is fairly accurate. Hugh of St. Cher, p. 228v, p comments: *Ibi Glossa Gregorii. Pauca sunt bona praesentis vitae, quamvis multa videantur, quia non sine alicujus molestiae admixtione sunt, multa autem bona aeterna, quae sunt sine omni corruptionis molestia* ("This is what Gregory's Glossa says: The goods of the present life are few, although they seem many. Since they come mixed with some vexation. But many are the everlasting goods that exist without any vexation of corruption"). A good case can be made for Bonaventure's dependence on Hugh of St. Cher here.

"Lucre in one's safe, condemnation on one's conscience. He made off with a garment and lost trust. He acquired money and lost justice."[51] So by evilly disposing of money, he loses happiness and love and justice, which are God's greatest gifts. Thus, the Glossa states: "The person who does not dispose in a good manner of the temporal things he possesses annuls for himself the glory of the everlasting things of which he boasts. *For how can the person who does not love his brother, whom he sees, love God, whom he does not see? And if the person who has possessions sees his brother in need,* etc. *how does the love of the Father abide in him?*, as 1 John 3 says."[52]

19. (Verse 11). Second, with regard to a consideration of *danger and loss* the text adds: *Therefore, if in the case of the wicked mammon you have not proved faithful, who will entrust to you what is true?* As if to say: There is great danger in evilly disposing of these temporal goods, for through unfaithful disposition a person loses true riches. Thus, the Glossa has: "If you do not dispose in a good way of carnal riches, which are slipping away, who will give you true and everlasting riches?"[53] Now these riches are called *wicked mammon*, since, as the Glossa says, "wicked mammon is in charge of riches and uses

---

[51] In his commentary on Luke 9:25 (#40) above Bonaventure also quotes from Augustine's Sermon 220 on the Feast of the Holy Innocents. See PL 39:2152 where Augustine uses present tense verbs.

[52] On p. 409, n. 6 QuarEd state that this is the Glossa Ordinaria (from Bede). Bede is clearer than the Glossa. See CCSL cxx, p. 299: "But the person who dissimulates that he is rightly disposing of the temporal things he possesses annuls for himself the glory of the everlasting things of which he boasts." The scripture references are 1 John 4:20 and 3:17. The Vulgate of 1 John 3:17 reads *caritas Dei* ("the love of God") for the Glossa's *caritas Patris* ("the love of the Father").

[53] On p. 409, n. 7 QuarEd state that this is the Glossa Ordinaria (from Jerome). See PL 22:1019 where Jerome ends his interpretation with: ". . . who will entrust to you the true and everlasting teachings of God?"

them to tempt people."[54] As it tempted Ananias, of whom Acts 5:3 says: "Why has Satan tempted your heart," etc. That temptation was to theft. Something similar is said of Achor in Joshua 7.[55] Now that good which always remains is called *true*. For all these temporal things, which are transitory, are vain, according to what Qoheleth 1:2 says: "Vanity of vanities, and all is vanity." Now what is *true* is God's grace or God's glory or rather God himself, who is the reward of good persons. And therefore, the Psalm confesses: "The truth of the Lord remains forever" (116:2). And again: "Your[56] truth is from generation to generation" (Psalm 99:5). And in this truth beatitude consists, according to what Augustine says in the book of his Confessions: "Blessedness consists in the joy that comes from the truth."[57] For since "the true is that which exists,"[58] he alone is truth pure and simple who says: "I am who am," in Exodus 3:14. And the truthful and the faithful submit to and believe in that *truth*. Wherefore, John 3:20–21 states: "Everyone who does evil hates the light and does not come to the light, lest his deeds be exposed. But the person who does the truth comes to the light, so that his deeds may be manifested, for they have been performed in God." And John 8:31–32 reads: "If you abide in my word . . . you will know the truth, and the truth will

---

[54] On p. 409, n. 8 QuarEd state that this is the Glossa Interlinearis.

[55] On p. 409, n. 8 QuarEd correctly mention that the Vulgate reads *Achan* ("Achan") in Joshua 7:1. Joshua 7 tells the story of Achan's disobedience to God's ban, his confession of sin for his greed, and punishment of being stoned to death.

[56] The Vulgate reads *eius* ("his").

[57] On p. 409, n. 10 QuarEd refer to Book X, chapter 23, n. 33 of Augustine's *Confessions*, which Bonaventure also quotes in his commentary on Luke 11:28 (#62) above. See the note there.

[58] On p. 409, n. 10 QuarEd cite Book II, chapter 5 of Augustine's *Soliloquies* where he defines truth: "It seems to me that the true is that which exists."

make you free." Therefore, the danger of unfaithfulness is great in these small matters, for truth is lost for the sake of what is *vain*, the great is lost for the sake of *the small*.

20. (Verse 12). Nonetheless, since what is one's own is lost for the sake of *what belongs to another*, the text adds: *And if in the case of what belongs to another, you have not been faithful*, through the proper disposition of an earthly good. Wherefore, the Glossa observes: "Whatever pertains to the world does not belong to us, because it is outside our true nature."[59] Indeed, these are said to be *someone else's goods*, for we cannot bring them in or take them out with us. 1 Timothy 6:7 reads: "We brought nothing into this world, and certainly we can take nothing out." And Job 1:21 states: "Naked I came out of my mother's womb, and naked will I return thither." – *Who will give you what is yours?*, through the realization of a heavenly reward. For what is *ours* is that for which we were created and preordained and which, once possessed, cannot be lost. So Matthew 25:34 says: "Come, blessed of my Father, take possession of the kingdom prepared for you," etc. And Luke 6:20 above has: "Blessed are you poor, for yours is the kingdom of God." Now this kingdom is nothing else but God and the Lord Jesus Christ. Thus, the Glossa comments: "*What is your own*, that is, those things that have been properly destined for a human being. Christ is ours, because

---

[59] On p. 410, n. 1 QuarEd state that this is the Glossa Interlinearis (from Jerome and Ambrose). See PL 22:1019: ". . . everything that pertains to the world does not belong to us." See CCSL xiv, p. 297: "Riches do not belong to us, because they are outside of our true nature. They were neither born with us nor will they end with us in our death. But Christ is ours, because he is our life." Hugh of St. Cher, p. 229d attributes this interpretation to "Bede" and goes on to explain what "outside our true nature" (*praeter naturam*) means.

Christ is our life."[60] Colossians 3:4 says: "When Christ, your life, appears, then you too will appear with him in glory."

21. (Verse 13). *No one*[61] *can serve two masters*, etc. After urging them to mercy from a consideration of the reward to be gained and of faithfulness to be preserved, here in a third point the Evangelist spurs them on from a consideration of *the duplicity to be avoided*. For a person cannot at the same time show piety towards God and avarice towards the world. He makes this third point in this way. First, he *rejects duplicity* and then *gives voice to this rejection*.

So first, relative to *the rejection of duplicity* the text has: *No one can serve two masters*. This proposition is self-evident. For which reason it is said in Sirach 2:14: "Woe to those who have a duplicitous heart and wicked lips . . . and to the sinner who travels on the earth along two roads." And James 1:8 reads: "Being a double-minded man, unstable in all his ways." And so it is said in Sirach 1:36: "Do not come to the Lord with a double heart." That is, you do not want to serve two lords at the same time, because it cannot be done in a rightful way. – Now the two lords, who are divided from one another and who cannot be served at the same time, fall into four different categories. For there are the lords, *vice* and *virtue*. For which reason 1 Kings 18:21 reads: "How long will you hobble along in two directions? If the Lord is God, follow him. But if the Lord is Baal," etc.[62] And Isaiah 28:20 states: "The bed is severely narrow, so that

---

[60] On p. 410, n. 5 QuarEd state that this is the Glossa Interlinearis, which is dependent on Ambrose. See the previous note. Hugh of St. Cher, p. 229c attributes this exposition to "Bede."
[61] The Vulgate reads *Nemo servus* ("No servant").
[62] The speaker is Elijah.

one must tumble out, and a short cloak cannot cover both." – There are also the lords, *flesh* and *Spirit*. Galatians 5:17 says: "The flesh lusts against the Spirit, and the Spirit against the flesh. For these are opposed to one another, so that you do not do what you would." Therefore, Romans 8:13 has: "If you live according to the flesh, you will die. But if by the Spirit you put to death the deeds of the flesh, you will live." – Furthermore, these lords are *Christ* and *the devil*. 2 Corinthians 6:15 reads: "What harmony is there between Christ and Belial?" And 1 Corinthians 10:20–21 states: "You cannot drink the cup of the Lord and the cup of demons. You cannot be partakers of the table of the Lord and of the table of demons." – Moreover, there are the lords, *God* and *this world*. James 4:4 has: "Adulterers, do you not know that the friendship of this world is enmity with God? If a person wants to become a friend of this world, he is made an enemy of God."[63] And wherefore, 1 John 2:15 reads: "Do not love the world . . . for, if anyone loves the world, the love of the Father is not in him."[64] – By means of these two lords the text dissuades from worldly cupidity and urges towards divine mercy. Wherefore, the Glossa notes: "He castigates avarice and says that lovers of money cannot love God. So the person who

---

[63] Bonaventure's text of James 4:4b differs from the Vulgate which I translate: "Therefore, whoever wants to be a friend of this age is made an enemy of God."

[64] Hugh of St. Cher, p. 229k has much in common with Bonaventure. He observes: "Note that the two lords that cannot be served at the same time, are vices and virtues, heavenly things and earthly things, God and the devil, true glory and vain glory, flesh and Spirit." In explaining the meaning of these two lords, Hugh quotes eight scripture passages, five of which he has in common with Bonaventure: Sirach 2:14; 1 Kings 18:21; Isaiah 28:20; 1 Corinthians 10:20–21; 2 Corinthians 6:15. Bonaventure holds over two of Hugh's scripture quotations for later in his commentary. See #24 below where he quotes 2 Kings 17:41 and Leviticus 19:19. Bonaventure does not quote Zephaniah 1:5.

ST. BONAVENTURE'S COMMENTARY ON THE GOSPEL OF LUKE

loves money holds God in contempt."[65] From this it is evident that the person who wants to be a servant of Christ cannot be a servant of this world. Thus, Bede comments: "You must faithfully distribute these temporal things, so that you are lords over the temporal, not their servants."[66]

22. Secondly, with regard to *the articulation of the rejection* the text adds: *For either he will hate the one and love the other*, which is said about *the love* that makes one hate evil and love good, according to what Romans 12:9–10 has: "Hate what is evil. Hold to what is good. Love one another with fraternal charity." And the Psalmist says: "I have hated the unjust and loved your law" (118:113). – *Or he will stand by the one and despise the other*. This is said of *cupidity* that stands by the world and the devil in contempt of God, according to what Jeremiah 2:13 has: "My people have committed two evils. They have forsaken me, the fountain of living water, and have dug for themselves cisterns...which cannot hold water."[67]

23. And the reason why a person cannot serve the aforementioned masters at the same time is fourfold. The first reason is *the opposition of ministerial service*.

---

[65] On p. 410, n. 13 QuarEd state that this is the Glossa Ordinaria (from Bede, who is following Jerome and Ambrose). Hugh of St. Cher, p. 229k attributes this interpretation to "Bede."

[66] On p. 410, n. 14 QuarEd state that this quotation, found in the Glossa Ordinaria apud Lyranum on Luke 16:13, comes from Book I of Bede's Commentary on Matthew 6:24 and that Bede is following Jerome.

[67] Bonaventure has adapted and abbreviated the Vulgate of Jeremiah 2:13, which I translate: "For my people have committed two evils. They have forsaken me, the fountain of living water, so that they might dig cisterns for themselves, broken cisterns, that cannot hold water."

For service of God consists in the exercise of *the virtues*, according to what Luke 1:74–75 above said: "We may serve him in justice and holiness before him." And 1 Peter 1:15 reads: "As the one who called you is holy, be you also holy," etc. But service of the devil consists in the exercise of *the vices*. So Luke 15:15 above said of the prodigal son that "he sent him to his farm to feed the pigs." – The second reason is *the difference between the ministers*, for the Lord wants servants who are *sharp-eyed*. So it is said in Revelation 4:6 that "the living creatures were full of eyes before and behind."[68] And Proverbs 14:35 states: "A wise minister is acceptable to the king." But the devil wants *one-eyed* ministers. Thus, 1 Samuel 11:2 says: "On this condition I will make a covenant with you, that I may pluck out all your right eyes."[69] The Lord also wants ministers who are *presentable and well-ordered*. So 1 Kings 10:4–5 reads: "When the Queen of Sheba saw . . . the apartments of his servants and the order of his ministers," etc. But the devil wants ministers who are *shamed and in disarray*. So 2 Samuel 10:4 says: "Hanun, king of the Ammonites, cut away the garments of David's servants even to their buttocks and shaved off half of their beards."[70] The Lord also wants *humble* servants, according to what the Psalm says: "The person who acts arrogantly will not dwell in the midst of my house. The person who speaks unjust things," etc. (100:7).[71] But the devil wants *arro-*

---

[68] It seems that Bonaventure presupposes that his readers will recall that Revelation 4 describes those who "minister" at God's throne.

[69] The person setting down this condition is conqueror Nahash the Ammonite for the purpose of bringing "ignominy on all Israel."

[70] Bonaventure adapts this text. I translate the Vulgate of 2 Samuel 10:4: "Therefore, Hanun took David's servants and shaved off half of their beards and cut away half of their garments to their buttocks and sent them away."

[71] Psalm 100:7 ends with: ". . . did not prosper before my eyes."

gant servants. Job 41:25 reads: "He beholds every high thing, and he is king over all the children of pride." – The third reason is *the incompatibility of places*, for the Lord wishes to be in a *sublime and clean* place. The Psalmist prays: "To you have I lifted up my eyes, who dwells in the heavens" (122:1). And The Song of Songs 2:8 has: "Behold, my beloved comes leaping upon the mountains, skipping over the hills." But the devil, in *unclean* places. Job 40:16 says: "He sleeps . . . in the covert of the reed, in moist places."[72] – The fourth reason is *attention day and night*, for the devil wants *himself* to be served at every moment. Jeremiah 16:13 states: "You will serve strange gods who will not give you rest day and night," etc.[73] In a similar way the Lord wants *himself* to be served at every moment. The Psalm says: "On the law of the Lord he will meditate day and night," etc. (1:2). So since the Lord wants to possess all one's time and all one's heart, according to what Deuteronomy 6:5 has: "You will love the Lord your God with your whole heart and your whole soul and with your whole strength," and the devil and the world similarly want total service, it is impossible to serve both at the same time.[74]

---

[72] Bonaventure also quotes Job 40:16 in his commentary on Luke 8:33 (#57) and Luke 11:24 (#52) above. On Luke 11:24 (#52) Bonaventure writes: "*Arid and waterless places* are places where carnal propensities and concupiscence do not thrive." And the devil cannot rest there.

[73] Bonaventure has switched around what the Vulgate says. I translate: "And there you will serve strange gods day and night, who will not give you rest."

[74] On p. 411, n. 8 QuarEd observe: "Card. Hugh proposes the same four reasons." Hugh of St. Cher, p. 229k lists the four reasons as the opposition of offices, the diversity of places, the diversity of ministers, and singleness of time. He bolsters each reason with many of the same scripture quotations that Bonaventure employs.

24. And therefore, he concludes: *You cannot serve God and mammon.* That person *serves mammon* whose affections are so dominated by riches that he could be said to be *avaricious,* for he has thereby become a slave of idols. For, as it is said in Ephesians 5:5, "avarice is servitude of idols."[75] Wherefore, the Glossa observes: "He does not say: *to possess riches,* but *to serve.* The person who guards his riches like a servant is their servant, but the person who casts off the yoke of servitude distributes his riches like their master."[76] And so the Apostle said in 1 Corinthians 7:29–31: "It remains that . . . those who buy, as though they did not possess, and those who use this world, as though not using it," etc. But some want to possess God and the world at the same time and are like those nations, spoken of in 2 Kings 17:41: "The nations feared the Lord, but nevertheless served their idols." Against these it is said in Leviticus 19:19: "You shall not wear a garment that is woven of two kinds of thread."[77] Also against these is what the Lord says here, and what Jerome writes: "It is impossible that a person enjoy both present and future goods with the result that he fills his belly here and his mind there, that he progresses from pleasures to delights, that he may rejoice with the world here and reign with God there, that in both ages he may appear first, glorious in heaven and on earth."[78]

---

[75] This is not exactly what Ephesians 5:5 says: "For know this and understand that no fornicator or unclean person or avaricious person (which is servitude of idols) has any inheritance in the kingdom of Christ and God."

[76] On p. 411, n. 9 QuarEd state that this is the Glossa Ordinaria (from Bede, who is following Jerome's Commentary on Matthew). See CCSL cxx, p. 300.

[77] Hugh of St. Cher, p. 229k quotes 2 Kings 17:41 and Leviticus 19:19. See n. 64 above.

[78] On p. 411, n. 12 QuarEd cite Jerome's Letter 118 n. 6: "It is difficult, nay impossible . . . that he may progress from pleasures to de-

Luke 16:14–18
CHRIST'S TEACHING REFUTES THE REBELLIOUS PHARISEES

25. *But they heard all these things*, etc. After setting forth
teaching that provides formation for the humble, the
Evangelist introduces teaching that *is aimed at curbing
the rebellious*. And since the Pharisees were rebelling
against the teaching of Christ as man on account of the
pride they took in their merits and since this pride came
from a literal observance of the Law, this section has
two parts. The first deals with *curbing the arrogance of
the Pharisees*. The second focuses on *the voiding of the
observance of legal prescriptions* where verse 16 reads:
The Law and the Prophets were until John, so that the
vain glorification of the Pharisees may be eliminated by
showing that the Law is null and void.

So first, *the repression of the arrogance* of the Pharisees
is described in this fashion. First comes *the rebellion* of
the Pharisees. This, in turn, is followed by *the censure
of the rebellion*, which is followed by *the reason for the
censure*.

26. (Verse 14). Thus, the first point, *the Pharisees' revolt*
is shown by their mocking of Christ: *Now the Pharisees
who were avaricious were listening to all these things
and mocked him.*[79] As *the proud, they mocked* him for
his *words of simplicity*, according to what Job 12:4–5
says: "The simplicity of the just person is laughed to
scorn, a lamp derided in the thoughts of the rich."[80] And

---

lights, so that he may be first in both ages, so that he may appear
glorious both in heaven and on earth." As fas as I can tell, Hugh of
St. Cher does not quote Jerome here.
[79] On p. 412, n. 2 QuarEd rightly indicate that the Vulgate reads
illum ("him") while Bonaventure has *eum* ("him").
[80] Hugh of St. Cher, p. 229v, b also quotes Job 12:4–5.

like *the obtuse*, because of his *beneficial counsel*. Proverbs 15:5 reads: "A fool laughs at his father's instruction." Or like *the stupid*, because of his *admonitions to mercy*, according to what the Psalm says: "Their madness is according to the likeness of the serpent, like the deaf asp that stops her ears" (57:5). Therefore, the Glossa comments: "They deride him, the teacher of mercy and humility and frugality, as if he were commanding harmful things, things less than beneficial and never to be done."[81] And like *the avaricious*, they mock his *praises of largess*. So the Glossa observes: "*They mocked him*, understanding that he was addressing this parable to them, as they preferred present carnal goods to future and uncertain spiritual goods."[82] And this is what is said in Proverbs 18:2: "A fool does not accept the words of wisdom, unless what you say agrees with what he has in mind." Or like *the lawyers*, they mock his *commendations about poverty*. Thus, the Glossa notes: "They deride the one arguing against love of money as if his arguments are contrary to the Law and the Prophets, since in the Law many rich people please God, and since the Law promises the goods of the earth to those who keep the Law."[83] So Proverbs 9:7 reads: "And the person who rebukes a wicked person creates a blot for himself."[84] And all this used to issue from any rebellion that was arrogant and foolish.

---

[81] On p. 412, n. 3 QuarEd state that this is the Glossa Interlinearis (from Bede) on Luke 16:14.

[82] On p. 412, n. 4 QuarEd state that this is the Glossa Ordinaria (from Bede) on Luke 16:14. See CCSL cxx, p. 300, where Bede's interpretation also forms the basis for the view of the Glossa Interlinearis, cited in the previous note.

[83] On p. 412, n. 5 QuarEd state that this is the Glossa Ordinaria (from Bede) on Luke 16:16. See CCSL cxx, p. 301.

[84] It would seem that the first part of Proverbs 9:7 is more apropos for Bonaventure's argument: "The person who teaches a scorner does an injury to himself."

27. (Verse 15). Second, about *the censure of the rebellious Pharisees*, by which Christ deflates their inflated view of themselves, the text adds: *And he said to them: You are those who declare yourselves just in the sight of men and women*, through a display of your righteousness, *thinking* that thereby you yourselves are just. Romans 10:3 states: "Ignorant of God's justice and seeking to establish their own, they have not submitted to God's justice." By such a display you also *say* that you are just, contrary to what Job 9:20 has: "If I would justify myself, my mouth will condemn me. If innocent,[85] he will prove me wicked." By such a display *you externally pretend* to be just. Against this Matthew 6:1 says: "Take heed, lest you perform your justice before men and women in order to be seen by them." – And since such justification engenders sin, the text continues: *But God knows your hearts*, because God abhors pride. So God does not *know* them in order to test them, but to judge them. The Psalmist says: "The Lord is high, and has regard for the humble. And the high he knows from afar" (137:6). So it is said in Proverbs 16:2: "All the ways of a human being are open to the Lord's eyes. The Lord is the weigher of spirits." Jeremiah 17:9 reads: "The heart of men and women is perverse and inscrutable, and who will understand it?"[86] So it is of little value for you to be approved by human testimony, when you are disapproved by the judgment of God, who searches the heart. Thus, 1 Corinthians 4:5 reads: "Do not pass judgment before the time, until the Lord comes, who will both bring to light the

---

[85] Bonaventure's text is elliptical. The Vulgate reads *Si innocentem ostendere* ("If I would show myself innocent").

[86] On p. 412, n. 7 QuarEd rightly indicate that the Vulgate reads *cor omnium* ("the heart of all people") while Bonaventure has *cor hominum* ("the heart of men and women").

things hidden in darkness."[87] So it is that this justice did not issue from the truth, but from vanity. It was not truly real, but merely human. It did not come from inside, but from outside. It was rather a sin to be detested than a virtue to be commended. It was more deserving of punishment than everlasting recompense.[88] So Matthew 5:20 states: "Unless your justice exceeds that of the scribes and Pharisees, you will not enter the kingdom of the heavens."

28. Third, with regard to *the reason for the censure*, through which he expresses the divine judgment, the text adds: *For that which is exalted high before men and women is an abomination before God.* Note that he does not censure *the height of perfection*, about which 2 Corinthians 8:2 says: "Their highest poverty has abounded in their rich sincerity," etc. Nor *the height of contemplation*, about which Romans 11:33 speaks: "O, the heights of the riches of the wisdom and of the knowledge of God. How incomprehensible are his judgments," etc. And Sirach 24:7 states: "I have dwelt in the highest places, and my throne rests on a pillar of cloud." Nor *the height of desire and expectation*, about which the Psalmist prays: "You, O Lord, are my hope. You have made your refuge most high" (90:9). For these are *the heights before*

---

[87] 1 Corinthians 4:5 ends with statements that reinforce Bonaventure's exposition: "and make manifest the counsels of hearts. And then everyone will have their praise from God."

[88] On p. 412, n. 8 QuarEd cite the Glossa Ordinaria (from Bede) on Luke 16:15: ". . . While you contemn sinners as weaklings and desperate, you believe that you yourselves are perfect in everything and experts in every human weakness, having no need of the remedy of almsgiving. But that this height of pride is quite justly to be condemned is seen by him who *brings to light things hidden in darkness and makes manifest the counsel of hearts*." The text in italics is from 1 Corinthians 4:5, which Bonaventure has just quoted. See CCSL cxx, p. 300

God. – But there is *another height* that distances one
from the Most High, and this is *the height of presumption*, about which Jeremiah 48:29–30 says: "We have
heard of the pride of Moab that he is exceedingly proud.
His haughtiness and his arrogance, and his pride, and
the loftiness of his heart, I know, says the Lord." There
is also *the height of ambition.* Jeremiah 49:16 reads:
"Your arrogance has deceived you . . . who tries to lay
hold of the height of the hill." Further, there is *the height
of ostentation.* Ezekiel 31:10–11 has: "Because he was
tall in stature and his head reached up to the rich foli-
age, his heart was proud of his height.[89] Now[90] I have
delivered him into the hands of the strongest of the nations," etc. Such height in the sight of men and women
is *an abomination before God*, according to what Proverbs 16:5 states: "Every proud person is an abomination
to the Lord. Though hand be joined to hand, he is not
innocent." Now the Lord is said to consider height of this
kind as *an abomination* because it rejects him utterly,
according to what Isaiah 2:11 says: "The lofty eyes of a
person have been humbled, and the haughtiness of men
will be brought low, but the Lord alone will be exalted
on that day."

29. So this threefold high exaltation is spoken against as
abominable to the Lord. The first is *the height of presumption.* Sirach 3:22 reads: "Seek not the things that
are too high for you." And Romans 11:20 states: "Be not
high-minded," etc. The second is *the height of ambition.*

---

[89] This translation clarifies Bonaventure's point about the lofty, ver-
dant tree that glories in its height and the thickness of its crown.
The Douay reads: "Because he was exalted in the height and shot up
his top green and thick and his heart was lifted up in the height,
now. . . ."
[90] On p. 413, n. 2 QuarEd accurately mention that the Vulgate does
not read *nunc* ("now").

Romans 12:16 has: "Do not set your mind on high things, but be of the same mind as the humble," etc. Third, he speaks against *the height of ostentation*. The Psalm says: "Do not lift up your horn on high. Do not speak iniquity against God" (74:6). – But this high exaltation is an abomination to the Lord, because it is *haughty*. 1 Samuel 16:7 has: "Do not regard...the height of his stature, because I have rejected him."[91] Because it is *counterfeit*. Daniel 3:1 says: "King Nebuchadnezzar made a statue of gold, sixty cubits high," etc. Because it is *disastrous*. Therefore, Proverbs 17:16 reads: "The person who builds a high house is looking for disaster." And so it is said in 2 Corinthians 10:4–5: "The weapons of our warfare are not carnal, but powerful before God for the demolishing of strongholds, for the destruction of plans and of every lofty thing that exalts itself against the knowledge of God, bringing every mind into captivity to the obedience of Christ."[92]

30. (Verse 16). *Until John came, there were the Law and the Prophets*, etc. After the repression of the arrogance of the rebellious Pharisees the Evangelist presents in a second point a description of *the voiding of the legal pre-*

---

[91] The text deals with God's instructions to Samuel about selecting a king.

[92] In his exposition of Luke 16:15 (#27–29) Bonaventure has nine of his twenty-five scripture quotations in common with Hugh of St. Cher, p. 229v, d–h: Romans 10:3; Matthew 6:1; Psalm 137:6; Proverbs 16:2; Romans 11:33; Jeremiah 49:16; Proverbs 16:5; Isaiah 2:11; Psalm 74:6. Hugh has a much more elaborate view of "height," which he divides into "good height" and "evil height." Under "good height" are the two categories "of God and of human beings." "Evil height" has two categories: "of the devil and of human beings." Under "the evil height of human beings" Hugh places "ambition." Hugh also has the category of "indifferent height." It seems to me that Bonaventure has been very selective in what he has adapted from Hugh of St. Cher and very creative in his use of this "traditional" material. More detailed investigation is needed.

cepts. In their observance of these the Pharisees laid the foundation for their pride, scorned the teaching of Christ, and masked their own avarice. And since the Mosaic Law was voided by Christ, so that what remained pertained to *the spiritual understanding of the ceremonial law* and *the literal observance of the moral laws*, it follows that in this part he teaches not only *the voiding of the Law itself* relative to *literal observance*, but also its *fulfillment* relative to *its spiritual understanding* and its *duration* relative to *the moral law and conjugal union.*

So first concerning *the voiding of the Law* relative to its *literal observance*, the text reads: *Until John came, there were the Law and the Prophets.* As if he was saying to the Pharisees: You must not lay the foundation for your pride on the observance of the Law, since it is now ended with regard to letter and figure. And note that, although Christ could say: *Until I came*, for Romans 10:4 has: "Christ is the end of the Law unto justice," etc., he preferred, nevertheless, to nominate the Precursor as his voice. For John himself in his ministry pointed him out as the Lamb. John 1:29 reads: "Behold, the Lamb of God, who takes away," etc.[93] And he had already begun to point the clear way to the truth and through this to void the figure. For since the Law and all the Prophets promised that Christ would come and John pointed to him as present, the point is clear: *"Until John came, there were the Law and the Prophets*, for he could no longer be prophesied as *to come* when it was clear from John's testimony that *he had come."*[94]

---

[93] John the Baptist is speaking, and John 1:29 ends with "...takes away the sin of the world."

[94] On p. 413, n. 12 QuarEd state that this is the Glossa Ordinaria apud Lyranum on Luke 16:17 and derives from Bede. See CCSL cxx, p. 301 on Luke 16:17.

31. And since the Law ceases to exist with the beginning of the new testament, it follows that: *From his time the kingdom of God is being preached*, that is, with him the gospel of grace begins. Therefore, Mark 1:1–2 states: "The beginning of the Gospel of Jesus Christ . . . as it is written in Isaiah: Behold, I send my messenger," etc. Thus, too, blessed Luke began his Gospel with the conception of blessed John. Luke 1:5 above reads: "In the days of Herod there was." Thus, so that his preaching might be shown to be *new,* it is said in Mark 1:4 that John "was baptizing and preaching a baptism of repentance for the forgiveness of sins."[95] – And since John's preaching focused on repentance, by which men and women do violence to themselves, the text adds: *and everyone is forcing his way into it.* Matthew 11:12 is more expansive: "From the days of John the Baptist the kingdom of the heavens has been enduring violent assault, and the violent have been seizing it by force." Now this is a violence by which people *exceed their natural strength.* Therefore, Bede comments: "It is a great force, when people born of earth seek to possess heaven through a strength that they did not have by nature."[96] This is also the violence by which people *conquer nature's incurvation.*[97] So the Glossa observes: "Let us use violence against nature, so that it may not sink to

---

[95] On p. 413, n. 13 QuarEd cite the Glossa Interlinearis: *"The Law,* where temporal things were treated, *and the Prophets until John,* who by word and example taught repentance and austerity of life for the sake of heavenly things, who is the end of the Law and the beginning of grace; *from him*, from his time, *the kingdom of God,* etc."
[96] On p. 414, n. 3 QuarEd state that Bede's opinion comes from the Glossa Ordinaria. See CCSL cxx, p. 301 for Bede's more extensive and complex interpretation.
[97] See Bonaventure's commentary on the stooped woman in Luke 13:11-13 (#23–27) for more detail on the incurvation or stoop caused by sin.

earthly things, but lift itself up to heavenly things."[98] This is also the violence by which people *overcome the torpor of sloth*. Wherefore, Bede states: "Everyone, who is forcing his way, is hastening along with vigorous discipline, not lulling around in laggardly sloth. Therefore, the one displays the religious violence of faith, the other punishable sluggishness."[99] For there is great violence when through the rigorous exertion of repentance a person mitigates the severity of divine judgment and through humble prayer bends sublime judgment. What was said in Genesis 32:28 about Jacob in his strenuous wrestling match is a figure of this: "If you have been strong against God, how much more will you prevail against humans."

32. And note that blessed Bernard distinguishes between four types of people who possess the kingdom of heaven: "For some *seize* it violently. Others *buy* it. Still others *steal* it. Yet others *are compelled* to enter it."[100] "For the ones who leave everything and follow Christ

---

[98] On p. 414, n. 4 QuarEd state that this is the Glossa Ordinaria (from Ambrose). See CCSL xiv, p. 299.

[99] On p. 414, n. 5 QuarEd state that Bede's opinion comes from the Glossa Ordinaria, the first part of whose commentary stems from Bede, the second from Ambrose. As far as I can determine, the entire commentary that Bonaventure attributes to Bede comes from Ambrose. See CCSL xiv, p. 298. Hugh of St. Cher, p. 229v, l writes: "A third type of force is distinguished in the Glossa of Ambrose: Everyone, who is forcing his way, etc."

[100] This is Sermon 99 from Bernard of Clairvaux' *Sermones De Diversis*. See SBOp 6.365–366. Bernard's text has provided the general outline for the interpretation of Hugh of St. Cher, who, in his turn, provides a quotable text for Bonaventure's exposition. That is, Bonaventure does not quote Bernard independently, but indirectly via Hugh. For more details see Robert J. Karris, "Bonaventure's Commentary on Luke: Four Case Studies of his Creative Borrowing from Hugh of St Cher," *Franciscan Studies* 59 (2001): 133-236, esp. pp. 214-227, 235-236.

are those who *seize* it." What Genesis 49 states can be applied to them: "Judah is a lion's cub. To the prey, my son, you have gone up" (verse 9). And again later: "Benjamin, a ravenous wolf, will seize[101] the prey in the morning and will divide the spoil in the evening" (verse 27).[102] – "The people who *buy* it are those who give temporal things to receive eternal things." About these Luke 12:33 above states: "Make for yourselves purses that do not grow old." And Luke 16:9 above has: "Make friends for yourselves with the mammon of wickedness." Augustine's remarks fit such people: "I have something to sell. What is it? It's the kingdom of heaven. How is it bought? A kingdom is bought for poverty. Glory for low esteem. Joy for pain. Rest for labor. Life for death."[103] – "The ones who *steal* it are those who perform good deeds furtively, and avoiding human praise, are content with

---

[101] On p. 414, n. 8 QuarEd correctly indicate that the Vulgate reads *comedet* ("will eat") while Bonaventure has *rapiet* ("will seize"). Hugh of St. Cher, p. 2301 quotes Genesis 49:9 and reads *capiet* ("will catch").

[102] Hugh of St. Cher, p. 2301 also quotes Genesis 49:9, 27.

[103] On p. 414, n. 10 QuarEd refer to Augustine's Commentary on Psalm 93 n. 24. See *Sancti Avrelii Avgvstini Enarrationes in Psalmos LI–C*, ed. D. Eligius Dekkers and Joannes Fraipont, CCSL xxxix (Turnhout: Brepols, 1956), 1325 "Pay attention, brothers. There is something for sale. God says to you: I have something to sell. Buy it. What do you have for sale? I have rest for sale. Buy it with your labor. Make sure that we are strong Christians in the name of Christ: This is what the remainder of the Psalm tells us: Let us not grow weary. . . . Pay attention. God, as it were, decided to sell the kingdom of heaven. You say to him: How much does it cost? Its asking price is your labor. Now if he had said that its price was gold, that would not have been an adequate answer, for you would ask how much gold. . . .") Augustine expostulates the meaning of the psalm for over a page and nowhere expresses his point with the brevity of Bonaventure's quotation. But Hugh of St. Cher, p. 2301 comments: "Augustine. I have something to sell. And what is it? It's the kingdom of heaven. How is it bought? A kingdom is bought for poverty. Glory for low esteem. Joy for pain. Rest for labor. Life for death." I am drawn to the conclusion that Bonaventure quoted Augustine not directly, but indirectly from Hugh of St. Cher.

divine attestation alone." What Matthew 6:17 says fits
them: "But you, when you fast, anoint your head and
wash your face."[104] – "The poor *are compelled* to enter
whom the fire of poverty, in God's dispensation, proves
here, lest the fire of judgment engulf them as worthy of
damnation in the future." About these Luke 14:23 above
says: "Go out into the highways and hedges and compel
them to come in, so that my house may be filled."
Wherefore, although the time of the Law was a time for
buying, now after John is a time for *seizing*. For, just as
riches were promised then, so poverty is urged now.[105]

33. (Verse 17). Second, relative to *the fulfillment of the
Law according to its spiritual understanding* the text
continues: *Yet it is easier for heaven and earth to pass
away*, by a conflagration of the world. The Psalm says:
"And you in the beginning established the earth.
. . . They will perish," etc. (101:26–27).[106] – *than for one
tittle of the Law to fall*, through *the nullification of one
promise.* Rabanus comments: *"Heaven and earth will*

---

[104] Hugh of St. Cher, p. 230l also quotes Matthew 6:17.
[105] By "the riches promised then," it seems that Bonaventure is referring to the promise of a "land flowing with milk and honey." See, e.g.,
Ezekiel 20:6: "That day I swore to bring them out of the land of
Egypt to the land I had scouted for them, a land flowing with milk
and honey, a jewel among all lands." Hugh of St. Cher, pp. 229v–230l
also quotes blessed Bernard and goes so far as to have a very brief
section on the men and women who buy, seize, steal, and are compelled to enter hell before giving another interpretation of the first
three groups of people. Bonaventure quotes extensively from this
later interpretation of Hugh. If I interpret Bonaventure correctly, he is
saying that during the time of the Law people used their possessions
to help the poor. After John they should become the poor. The old
covenant promised the riches of a choice land which flowed with milk
and honey. During the new covenant poverty is the choice.
[106] Besides abbreviating Psalm 101:26–27, Bonaventure quotes the
first part of verse 26 the way it is quoted in Hebrews 1:10. That is,
he has *in principio* ("in the beginning") rather than *initio* ("in the
beginning").

pass away, the form having been put aside through the change of renewal while the prior substance remains. But the words of the Lord will in no way pass away without having been fulfilled."[107] Therefore, it is said in Matthew 24:35: "Heaven and earth will pass away, but my words will not pass away." For, as it is said in the Psalm: "Forever, O Lord, your word stands firm" (118:89). So although the old law seems to be transitory, it, nonetheless, remains and is greater than an earthly creature. It also remains through *the spiritual understanding of the divine word*. Thus, Matthew 5:17–18 states: "I have not come to destroy the Law . . . ,[108] but to fulfill. Amen I say to you . . . not one iota or one tittle will pass away from the Law, until all things have been accomplished." – And note that it says *one tittle*. For *a tittle* is properly called the top of a letter, which is used to decorate the letter itself and is, as it were, the least

---

[107] On p. 414, n. 14 QuarEd point to Rabanus Maurus' commentary on 1 Corinthians 7:31 as the source for this quotation. In searching through PL 112:72CD, I did not find this quotation. QuarEd rightly indicate that Rabanus Maurus' commentary on Matthew 24:35 is not extant. See PL 107:1077CD. The editors do, however, find a parallel in Book IV of Bede's commentary on Matthew 24:35: "Heaven and earth will pass away through the change of renewal, but the word of God will in no way pass away without having been fulfilled." See Hugh of St. Cher, 230c who seems to provide Bonaventure's quotation from Rabanus: *Rabanus. Coelum, et terra transibunt per commutationem innovationis, deposita priori forma, manente priori substantia. Sed verba Domini sine effectu completionis nullo modo transibunt. Matthew 24c[35]: Coelum, et terra transibunt, verba autem mea non transibunt* ("Rabanus: Heaven and earth will pass away through the change of renewal, the prior form having been set aside, while the prior substance remains. But the words of the Lord will in no way pass away without having been fulfilled. Matthew 24c[35] says: Heaven and earth will pass away, but my words will not pass away").

[108] In his adaptation of Matthew 5:17 Bonaventure has added *Legem* ("the Law") from the earlier part of this verse.

possible thing.[109] From this it follows that there is nothing at all, neither small nor large, in Scripture, nor anything, that does not have its fulfillment.[110] For all things are related to human salvation which will last perpetually, although earthly creatures are transient according to their external appearance. Isaiah 51:6 reads: "The heavens will vanish like smoke, and the earth will be worn away like a garment. . . . But my salvation will be forever, and my justice will not fail." So the book of Scripture is closer to the book of life than to the book of creation, and therefore it cannot remain unfulfilled.

34. (Verse 18). Third, with regard to *the permanence of the Law* according to *the law of nature* and *conjugal union* the text adds: *Everyone who puts away his wife and marries another commits adultery.* First, because he can put away his first wife solely for one reason, namely, immorality, according to Matthew 19:9: "Whoever puts away his wife, except for immorality, and marries another, commits adultery." Second, because for whatever reason he puts her away, it is not licit for him, while she is living, to marry another woman. And this is according to the law of nature divinely instituted when the human race was established. Genesis 2:24 reads: "A man will leave his father and his mother," etc. And what results is the decree that "marriage is the union of hus-

---

[109] See Hugh of St. Cher, 230c for almost the identical definition of a tittle.

[110] On p. 414, n. 16 QuarEd refer to Bede and Augustine for this interpretation. See *Saint Augustine, Commentary on the Lord's Sermon on the Mount with Seventeen Related Sermons*, trans. Denis J. Kavanagh, FC 13 (New York: Fathers of the Church, Inc., 1951). On p. 38 Kavanagh translates Book I, chapter 8 n. 20 of Augustine's Commentary thus: "Now, because the *'iota'* is formed by a single stroke, it is the smallest of those letters, and the *'tittle'* is merely a small part of it, placed on top. By these words, He indicates that every slightest detail in the Law is being fulfilled in practice."

band and wife who share together a common way of life."[111] It also decrees that it is an indissoluble bond. – And therefore the text continues: *And he who will have married*[112] *a woman who has been put away from her husband commits adultery.* The reason for this is that she was the wife of the first husband, no matter how she seems to be separated from him. So the Apostle says in Romans 7:2–3: "The married woman is bound by the Law while her husband is alive. . . . Therefore, while her husband is alive, she will be called an adulteress if she has been with another man." And wherefore, Jeremiah 3:1 states: "If a man puts away his wife, and she goes from him and marries another man, will he return to her any more? Will not that woman be polluted and defiled?" – Now it is to be noted that, although no mention is made of wives, the Lord, nevertheless, wanting to show the permanent nature of the Law relative to *moral issues* and its transitory nature with respect to *ceremonial and judicial matters*, makes an example of marriage because in its formulation there was *the writ* of dismissal. And the law of matrimony is confirmed in the Gospel as a *moral* right, and the writ of dismissal is rejected. Thus, Matthew 19:7–8 says: "Moses gave a command to give a writ of dismissal and to put her away.[113] He said to them: Because Moses, by reason of the hardness of your heart, permitted you to put away your wives." – From these considerations, therefore, one comes to un-

---

[111] On p. 415 n. 4 QuarEd state that this definition of matrimony comes from Book IV, distinction 27, article 1, question 1 and doubt 1 of his *Commentary on the Sentences*. See especially Opera Omnia 4:684.

[112] On p. 415, n. 5 QuarEd correctly indicate that the Vulgate reads *ducit* ("marries").

[113] Bonaventure has changed this first sentence from an interrogatory sentence to a declarative one and made it more difficult to understand. Matthew 19:7 reads: "They said to him: Why then did Moses command to give a writ of dismissal and to put her away?"

derstand how the Law *perdures*, how *it is made void*, how *it is fulfilled*, and at the same time the arrogance of the Pharisees, who glory in the letter of the Law, is put down.

Luke 16:19–31
AN EXEMPLUM OF PUNISHMENT FOR LACK OF MERCY

35. *There was a certain rich man*, etc. After the exemplum of provident mercy and the teaching about perfect mercy the Evangelist supplies here *an exemplum of punishment for a lack of mercy*. As was said above,[114] this passage has more the character of *an example* than of *a parable*, for on the literal level this rich man was enjoying pleasures, but now is suffering torments. So the Glossa of Bede states: "Against the avaricious who were deriding what he had proposed he gives an example, namely, that of the rich man tormented in hell because he did not make Lazarus his friend who could have received him into the everlasting dwellings. And it seems to be more a narrative than a parable."[115] So also the saintly teachers adduce the words of this parable as testimony about the state of the damned. And in order to show that their point is literally true, they refer to the fact that the poor person is named here. – Therefore, to explain the narration of this example, the Evangelist mentions three things: *the reason for, the sin of, and the*

---

[114] See Luke 16:1 (#1) above.

[115] On p. 415, n. 7 QuarEd state that this is the Glossa Ordinaria on Luke 16:19, whose last part is taken from Ambrose and whose first part from Bede. See CCSL xiv, p. 302 and CCSL cxx, p. 302. The Glossa has typically abbreviated Bede's thought. The editors go on to refer to commentators who have taken Luke 16:19–31 to be narrative/history or parable/image. See also Stephen L. Wailes, *Medieval Allegories of Jesus' Parables*, pp. 253–260.

punishment for the lack of mercy. The reason for the lack of mercy was *love* of oneself. *The sin* of lack of mercy was *merciless indifference* towards one's neighbor, where verse 20 says: *And there was a certain poor man. The punishment* for merciless conduct was *being cast into the calamity of hell*, about which verse 22 speaks: *But the rich man also died*, etc.

Relative to *the reason for the merciless conduct*, which is love of one's own good, the text says that the rich man was characterized by three things, namely, *the lust of the eyes, pride of life, and lust of the flesh.*[116]

Luke 16:19
THE REASON FOR LACK OF MERCY WAS LOVE OF SELF

36. (Verse 19). First, then, concerning *the lust of the eyes* the text says: *There was a certain rich man.* This *man* is said to be *rich*, not only on account of his possession of riches, but also because of his love of them. For which reason 1 Timothy 6:9 reads: "Those who seek to become rich fall into temptation and the snare of the devil," etc.[117] For through its love for earthly things the spirit grows fat and is weighed down, so that it cannot travel into the higher realms of heaven. For which reason Matthew 19:24 has: "It is easier for a camel to pass through the eye of a needle than for a rich person to enter into the kingdom of the heavens." Mark 10:24–25 says explicitly: "Children, with what difficulty will they who trust in riches enter the kingdom of God! It is easier for

---

[116] Bonaventure refers to 1 John 2:16: "Because all that is in the world is the lust of the flesh, and the lust of the eyes, and the pride of life, which is not from the Father, but from the world."

[117] The Vulgate does not read *diaboli* ("of the devil").

a camel," etc. About this sort of rich person Sirach
13:21–24 states: "As the wolf would have fellowship
with the lamb,[118] so a sinner with the just person. What
fellowship does a holy person have with a dog? Or what
good part does the rich have with the poor? The wild ass
is the lion's prey in the desert; so also the rich devour
the poor. And as humility is an abomination to the
proud, so also the rich man abhors the poor person."

37. Secondly, concerning *pride of life* the text adds: *and
used to clothe himself in purple and fine linen.* Bede
comments: "*Purple* is the color of royal garments and
issues from seashells cracked open by a knife. *Byssus* is
a type of white and very soft linen."[119] Now he is wearing
handsome and precious garments for the sake of vainglory. Therefore, Gregory observes: "No one shops for
precious garments except to seek glory, so that he may
be considered worthy of more honor than others."[120] And
this is indeed reprehensible and a sin, for as Sirach 11:4
says: "Glory not in apparel at any time and be not exalted
on the day of your honor."

38. Now there are four types of sins in the matter of
clothing.[121] The first deals with *costliness.* Thus, Bede

---

[118] On p. 416, n. 3 QuarEd correctly mention that the Vulgate has a
different reading. I translate: "If the wolf will at any time have fellowship with the lamb. . . ."

[119] On p. 416, n. 4 QuarEd indicate that Bede's words are actually
found in the Glossa Ordinaria on Luke 16:19. See CCSL cxx, p. 302
where Bede is actually quoting from Isidore.

[120] On p. 416, n. 5 QuarEd refer to Homily 40 n. 3 of GGHG. See PL
76:1305B. Bonaventure's quotation is not verbatim.

[121] Hugh of St. Cher, p. 230v, b has five: costliness, multiplicity,
anxiety, indecency, and ostentation. Hugh also employs most of the
same scripture quotations found in Bonaventure: Job 24:7; James
5:2–3; Matthew 6:28; Deuteronomy 22:5; Zephaniah 1:8. In my mind
there is little doubt that Bonaventure is adapting Hugh's commentary at this point.

comments: "If the practice of wearing costly garments were not a sin, the word of God would not have said so precisely that a rich man, clothed in purple and fine linen, was being irremediably tormented in hell."[122] For it is exceedingly absurd that a putrid corpse should be adorned with costly clothing when many poor people could be given sustenance from the money spent on it. But there are some excusing causes for such clothing: *the dignity of the person, a mark of office, protection.*[123] – Secondly, on account of *superfluity.* James 5:2–3 reads: "Your garments have become moth-eaten. . . . You have laid up for yourselves the treasure of wrath in the last days."[124] And this because of your injustice to the poor. Therefore, Job 24:7 says: "They send people away naked, taking away the clothes of those who have no covering in the cold." Jerome states: "The person who is proven to retain temporal goods beyond what is necessary is accused of seizing someone else's property."[125] – Thirdly,

---

[122] On p. 416, n. 6 QuarEd mention that Bede's opinion is given in the words of the Glossa Ordinaria, which are a close approximation to what Bede says. See CCSL cxx, p. 302. It should be noted that almost all of Bede's commentary on Luke 16:19–31 is taken verbatim from Homily 40 of GGHG.

[123] On p. 416, n. 7 QuarEd point to Cardinal Hugh. See Hugh of St. Cher, p. 230v, a: "There are excusing causes for various costly garments: Out of custom such as various bishops in Germany; because of the dignity of the person such as the gray and purple of the Pope; on account of necessity such as monks who have nothing else to wear; for protection, as when someone important wishes to hide for the sake of a good deed, like Sebastian." If Hugh was Bonaventure's source, he has surely generalized his source.

[124] The Vulgate does not read *vobis iram* ("for yourselves, wrath").

[125] On p. 416, n. 9 QuarEd refer to Ps-Jerome's *Regula Monachorum*, chapter 4. My research has indicated that this is a sense parallel only. See PL 30:396B: "The Gospel forbids you to have two garments, so that you might learn to possess only those things which nature requires and not those things that feed the worms. Indeed, if there are some extra garments, let them be put aside in one place, so that if any Sister whosoever has need, she may be clothed with it." See

on account of *anxiety*. Matthew 6:28–29 says: "As for clothing, why are you anxious? Consider the lilies of the field. They neither toil nor spin, yet I tell you that not even Solomon in all his glory was arrayed like one of these." – Fourthly, on account of *indecency*, for it is indecent for a cleric to be dressed like a woman or like an actor. Zephaniah 1:8 states: "I will visit upon . . . all the men who are clothed in strange apparel."[126] And Deuteronomy 22:5 reads: "A man shall not be clothed in woman's garments." – Now in all these ways people were wont to be excessive in their vesture, and in being excessive to glory, and in glorying to sin, and this glorying is vain and similar to the glorying of the crow.[127] For an egg that issues from wool or a worm that springs forth from silk should glory,[128] but "human beings are rottenness, and the son of man is a worm."[129]

39. Thirdly, with regard to *the lust of the flesh* the text continues: *And who feasted every day in splendid fashion*. The Glossa explains: "Behold, gluttony,"[130] which is

---

Hugh of St. Cher, p. 230v, b: *Hier. Aliena rapere convincitur, qui ultra necessitatem sibi retinere comprobatur* ("Jerome: The person who is proven to retain for himself beyond what is necessary is accused to seizing someone else's property"). It seems clear to me that Bonaventure has copied his quotation from Jerome directly from Hugh.

[126] The speaker is the Lord, and the visitation occurs "on the day of the victim of the Lord."

[127] On p. 416, n. 12 QuarEd refer to Aesop's Fables for Bonaventure's meaning here. The point of these fables is that a crow tries to be something that it is not (a pigeon, a raven, a peacock), is uncovered as a fraud, and is disgraced.

[128] Hugh of St. Cher, p. 230v, b has virtually the same statement: *Oportet enim ovem de lana gloriari non te, et vermem de ferico* ("For an egg that issues from wool should glory, but not you, and a worm that springs forth from silk").

[129] Job 25:6.

[130] On p. 416, n. 13 QuarEd state that this is the Glossa Interlinearis. Hugh of St. Cher, p. 321a quotes most of the same passages as

very often voluptuousness' companion. James 5:5 says: "You have feasted upon earth and have nourished your hearts on voluptuousness." – And note that there is a *splendid nature* to *spiritual feasting*, which produces *wisdom*. And here it is to be praised, as also that feast, about which Luke 15:23–24 above spoke: "Let us eat and feast, because my son," etc. This feast is *splendid*, because it has nothing sordid about it, but springs from the fountain of everlasting light. The Psalm says: "They will be inebriated with the abundance of your house . . . for with you is the fountain of life, and in your light we will see light" (35:9–10). Again the Psalm says: "Because I will go over into the place of the wonderful dwelling . . . with the voice of joy and praise, the sounds of one feasting" (41:5). – Likewise, there is *sumptuousness* in *the bodily feast*, which *compassion* spreads on the table, and this, too, is to be praised. About this 2 Corinthians 9:7 states: "Not grudgingly or from compulsion, for God loves a cheerful giver."[131] And this splendor consists in a cheerful countenance and generous almsgiving. About it Sirach 31:28 has: "The lips of many will bless the person who is generous with his food, and the testimony of his truth is faithful."[132] – There is also *sumptuousness* in *the fleshly feast* that *voluptuousness* hosts. Zechariah 7:6 reads: "Did you not eat for yourselves and drink for yourselves?" And this splendor ex-

---

Bonaventure, to wit, Luke 15:23–24; James 5:5; Sirach 31:28; 2 Corinthians 9:7; Zechariah 7:6; Lucan; Bernard. This seems to be another instance of Bonaventure's heavy dependence on Hugh of St. Cher.

[131] 2 Corinthians 9:7 begins: "Let each one give (to the collection for the poor in Jerusalem) according as he has determined in his heart, not grudgingly. . . . "

[132] The last clause doesn't make too much sense. Translating from a better text and numbering verses differently, NAB translates Sirach 32:23: "On a man generous with food, blessings are invoked, and this testimony to his goodness is lasting."

tends not only to the appealingly prepared courses, but also to silver vases, dazzling furniture, and a multiplicity of lights. About this Lucan writes: "O greed that searches over land and sea, To furnish forth the banquet! Pride that joyst In sumptuous tables!"[133] About this Bernard writes: "Of all the others the pleasure of the throat, which is so highly regarded today, takes up scarcely two fingers' space. The small enjoyment of that little fragment is prepared with such trouble and gives rise to such anxiety!"[134] Now this superfluity of banqueting brings about a paucity of wisdom and virtues and frequently even of temporal goods. Thus, Proverbs 21:17 says: "The person who relishes feasting will be in want. The person who delights in wine and fatty things will not grow rich."[135]

---

[133] On p. 417, n. 3 QuarEd refer to Book IV, lines 375–376 of Lucan's *De Bello Civili*. My translation is that of Sir Edward Ridley, available from The Online Medieval and Classical Library. In Ridley's translation these verses are 420–422. Bonaventure's Latin text is the same as the critical text found in: *M. Annaei Lvcani Belli Civilis Libri Decem,* ed. A. E. Hovsman (Cambridge: Harvard University Press, 1926), 102. Hugh of St. Cher, p. 231a cites this same text from Lucan.

[134] On p. 417, n. 4 QuarEd refer to Bernard of Clairvaux' *Sermo ad Clericos de Conversione* chapter 8, n. 13. I have modified the translation of G. R. Evans, *Bernard of Clairvaux: Selected Works* (New York: Paulist, 1987), 77. Bonaventure's text is very close to that of Bernard. See SBOp 4:87, but it is also close to the text of Bernard cited by Cardinal Hugh. See Hugh of St. Cher, p. 231a. On the basis of Bonaventure's considerable borrowing from Hugh in this section I judge that he also borrowed his citation of Bernard from Hugh. A future detailed study, however, is necessary for any permanently firm judgment.

[135] On p. 417, n. 5 QuarEd, at the end of Bonaventure's commentary on Luke 16:19 where he has borrowed extensively from Hugh of St. Cher, have the simple advisement: "Cf. Card. Hugh on Luke 16:19."

Luke 16:20–21
THE SIN OF LACK OF MERCY WAS MERCILESS INDIFFERENCE

40. (Verse 20). *And there was a certain poor beggar*, etc. After mentioning the reason for the lack of mercy, the Evangelist introduces here *the sin of lack of mercy* which he shows to be reprehensible from the three conditions of the poor man. These circumstances show that the poor man was worthy of mercy and consequently that the rich man was merciless and impious. For the rich man is shown to lack mercy relative to *a sick poor man, an abandoned poor man, a poor man dear to God and just.*

First, then, with respect to *the neediness of the sick poor man* the text continues: *And there was a certain poor man, named Lazarus.* And note here that while the rich man is designated by a general term, the poor man is presented with his own name, so that what the Psalm says may be demonstrated: "He will spare the poor and the needy. . . . And their names will be honorable in his sight" (71:13–14). Wherefore, the Glossa comments: "The humble poor man is approved and known by name."[136] Thus, the Lord said to Moses in Exodus 33:12: "You have found favor before me, and I know you yourself by name."[137] And that indeed is a weighty matter. So although the Psalm may say this about the rich "They have given their names to their lands" (48:12), this is said to the poor in Luke 10:20 above: "Rejoice that your names are written in heaven."

41. And note that the rich man's lack of mercy is aggravated in that this poor person was *alone*. Therefore, a

---

[136] On p. 417, n. 8 QuarEd state that this is the Glossa Interlinearis.
[137] Bonaventure has inverted the order of the Vulgate and has added *ipsum* ("yourself").

certain Psalm states: "Look upon me and have mercy on me, for I am alone and poor" (24:16). – For he was *a beggar*. The text adds *a beggar*, as if he were knocking at the door seeking alms. Sirach 4:4 has: "Reject not the petition of the afflicted and do not turn your face away from the needy. – For he was *right out in the open*. As the text says, *who lay at his door*, so that he could not now use ignorance as an excuse. Therefore, 1 John 3:17 states: "The person who sees his brother in need and closes his heart to him," etc.[138] Oh, how unlike he was to Job, of whom Job 31:32 says: "The stranger did not stay outside; my door was open to the traveler." How unlike he was also to Abraham, who sat "at the door of his tent," so that he might immediately receive strangers, as Genesis 18:1–8 recounts. – His lack of mercy is further aggravated because the poor beggar was *sick*, as the text says: *covered with sores*. Sirach 7:39 reads: "Be not slow to visit the sick, for by these things you will be confirmed in love." So he could say in this instance: "I am poor and sorrowful," etc.[139]

42. (Verse 21). The situation is also made worse because *he was famished*. Thus, the text adds: *longing to be filled*. Isaiah 58:7 states: "Break your bread with the hungry and bring the needy and the wanderers into your house," etc. And Sirach 4:2 says: "Despise not the hungry soul, and do not provoke the poor in their need." – The situation is likewise made miserable because *he would be content with crumbs*, as the text reads: *with the crumbs that fell from the rich man's table*. Job 22:7 has: "You have not given water to the weary, and you have withdrawn bread from the hungry." And Ambrose observes:

---

[138] 1 John 3:17 concludes: ". . . , how does the love of God abide in him?"

[139] Psalm 68:30.

"The rich, situated, as it were, above nature, seize upon the sufferings of the poor as reasons to relish their own pleasures."[140] – Now from these six considerations it is manifestly clear that this poor man is in need, a need that made him worthy of compassionate mercy and demonstrated how reprehensible the rich man was because of his hardness of heart.

43. Second, concerning *the abandonment of the poor man* the text adds: *And no one gave any to him.*[141] So Lazarus could say what Isaiah 63:5 has: "I looked about, and there was no one to help. I sought, and there was none to give aid." And Qoheleth 9:15 reads: "No one afterward remembered that poor man."[142] For as it is said in Proverbs 19:7: "The brethren of a poor man hate him. Moreover, his friends have also abandoned him." Thus, this poor person was truly abandoned, according to what the Psalm says: "To your care is the poor man abandoned" (9:35), for no one has remedied his neediness. Nor has anyone cared for his sickness. – Wherefore, the text continues: *But even the dogs used to come and lick his sores.* The Glossa comments: "Neither could he chase them away from him nor did he have a protector to do so."[143] From this it is obvious that the rich man was inexcusable, when he saw the poor man so abandoned. In this instance the astonishing cruelty of this rich man can be noticed, because he was more generous to the dogs than to the poor man, and the dogs were more tender towards that poor man than the rich man was. Wherefore, Peter of Ravenna states: "At nature's

---

[140] See CCLS xiv, p. 303. Bonaventure's quotation is almost verbatim.
[141] This sentence is not in the Vulgate, but is a variant.
[142] All of Qoheleth 9:15 reads: "Now there was found in the city a man poor and wise, and he delivered the city by his wisdom. And no one afterward remembered that poor man."
[143] On p. 418, n. 4 QuarEd state that this is the Glossa Interlinearis.

teaching the dogs care for the poor man's sores whereas the rich man neglects him with nature accusing him."[144] And this is against what is said in Job 5:24: "In protecting your own kind, you will not sin." So the same Peter of Ravenna says: "Miserable rich man, even if you did not give a crumb of bread to the poor man, why didn't you at least drive off the dogs? But your dogs are gentler than you are, even though you are harsher to them. And you were more kind to your dogs than to the poor man. From time to time your dogs got a succulent treat, but the poor man never once received a crumb from your table."[145] Therefore, the rich man's lack of mercy is spotlighted by a comparison with the poor man's great misery, and the patience of the poor beggar is stockpiled in comparison with the rich man's abundance. So Gregory comments: "In one incident two judgments of God are fulfilled. A massive damnation comes upon the rich man who does not have mercy at *the sight of the poor man.* Further, the poor man, who

---

[144] On p. 418, n. 5 QuarEd refer to Sermon 121, n. 18 of Peter of Ravenna or Peter Chrysologus. See PL 52:533A: *Canes currant pauperem magisterio naturae, et homo hominem negligit, ipsa graviter accusante natura* ("At nature's teaching the dogs care for the poor man whereas man neglects a fellow human being, with nature herself gravely accusing him"). Bonaventure's quotation is not verbatim. It does, however, agree word for word with Hugh of St. Cher's quotation of Peter of Ravenna. See Hugh of St. Cher, p. 231v, d. Peter's Sermons 121–124 bear the title, "On the Rich Man and Lazarus," and are found in PL 52:529C–543A.

[145] On p. 418, n. 6 QuarEd refer to Peter Chrysologus' Sermon 121 and state that the last part of the quotation, which Cardinal Hugh also cites, is not found in Peter Chrysologus. See PL 52:533A: *Miser dives, si panem non dedisti, quare vel canes abigere noluisti? Sed mitiores te canes tui, immo tu saevior canibus tuis* ("Miserable rich man, even if you didn't give bread, why did you not even want to drive away the dogs? But your dogs are more gentle than you are, even though you are more cruel to your dogs?"). See Hugh of St. Cher, p. 231v, d for a quotation from Peter of Ravenna that is virtually the same as that found in Bonaventure.

is daily tempted at *the sight of the rich man*, is approved."[146] Proverbs 22:2 reads: "The poor and the rich have met one another. God is the maker of both."

Luke 16:22
THE POOR MAN IN THE BOSOM OF ABRAHAM

44. (Verse 22). Third, with regard to *the holiness of the poor man* the text continues: *And it came to pass that the poor man died and was borne away by the angels into Abraham's bosom*. From this it is clear that this beggar was holy and good, for when he died, he was received by the angels and carried to a place of peace. Wisdom 3:2–3 reads: "In the sight of the unwise they seemed to die. . . . But they are in peace." Such people are borne there by the ministry of angels. So Peter of Ravenna says: "The angels do not disdain to carry the person to whom they used to minister here. Hebrews 1:14 states: *All are ministering spirits*, etc." And Peter continues later: "Angelic services are fittingly assigned to the poor man, to whom the ministrations of human decency were cruelly denied."[147] Now the angels transport this beggar into the bosom of Abraham, that is, into

---

[146] On p. 418, n. 7 QuarEd state that Gregory's words are quoted from the Glossa Ordinaria on Luke 16:21. See PL 76:1306A. Cf. Hurst, p. 376: "But when in one incident . . . he (the Lord) indicated at once the massive condemnation that awaited the pitiless rich man as a result of his seeing the poor one, and his approval of the poor man who was tempted daily by seeing the rich one."

[147] On p. 418, nn. 9–10 QuarEd cite the pertinent passages from Peter Chrysologus' Sermon 121 n. 2 and say: "In such a way Cardinal Hugh also quotes this opinion of Peter of Ravenna." See PL 52:530AB and Hugh of St. Cher, p. 231v, g. While Peter Chrysologus does not refer to Hebrews 1:14 and Hugh of St. Cher and Bonaventure do, Hugh of St. Cher also quotes Baruch 5:6. Bonaventure does not cite Baruch 5:6. In brief, Bonaventure is quoting Peter Chrysologus from Hugh of St. Cher.

a place of rest. Indeed, before the opening of the door to heaven this place was in limbo and is called *the bosom of Abraham*. For Abraham himself was received there as into a bosom by reason of his faith, by which he was said to be *the father of many nations*.[148] And those who are received there are said *to be received into his bosom*. So he also was the first to receive the promise of Christ's incarnation.[149] Now it is called *a bosom*, because, just as in a bosom things are hidden, cherished, and protected in an intimate place, so too the holy fathers were protected in that place. Isaiah 4:5–6 states: "Over all the glory will be a protection. And there will be a tabernacle for shade against the daytime heat and . . . for a covert against the whirlwind and rain."[150] And the Psalmist says: "For he has hidden me in his tabernacle. In the day of evil he has protected me in the hidden place within his tabernacle" (26:5). In this bosom Lazarus was placed, having been delivered by death from all evils, according to what Job 5:19–24 says: "In six tribulations he will deliver you, and in the seventh evil will not touch you. In famine he will deliver you from death, and in war from the hand of the sword. You will be hidden from the scourge of the tongue, and you will not fear calamity when it comes. . . . And you will know that your tabernacle possesses peace."

---

[148] Genesis 17:5. On p. 418, n. 11 QuarEd cite Book IV, chapter 16, n. 24 of Augustine's *De Anima et ejus Origine*. See NPNF1, Volume 5, p. 364: ". . . you must understand by 'Abraham's bosom' that remote and separate abode of rest and peace in which Abraham is; and that what was said to Abraham did not merely refer to him personally, but had reference to his appointment as the father of many nations, to whom he was presented for imitation as the first and principal example of faith."

[149] See Bonaventure's commentary on Luke 13:28 (#60) above.

[150] Hugh of St. Cher, p. 231v, b quotes Isaiah 4:5–6 in its entirety.

45. And note that there is a *sinful* bosom, a *praiseworthy* bosom, and a *desirable* bosom. – The *sinful* bosom is threefold. The first is *the bosom of carnality*. Proverbs 5:20 reads: "Why are you seduced, my son, by a strange woman and are cherished in the bosom of another?" And Proverbs 6:27–29 has: "Can a man hide fire in his bosom and not set his clothes on fire? . . . So he that goes into his neighbor's wife will not be clean when he will touch her." Further, there is *the bosom of cupidity*. Proverbs 17:23 says: "The wicked person takes gifts out of the bosom, so that he may pervert the paths of judgment." Then there is *the bosom of cruelty*. 1 Kings 3:20 reads: "She took my child from my side, while I your handmaid was asleep, and laid it in her bosom. Then she laid her dead child in my bosom." And Job 31:33 states: "If, as a human being, I have hidden my sin and have concealed my iniquity in my bosom."[151]

There is also *a praiseworthy bosom*, namely, one that is *humble in hiding*. Exodus 4:7 says: "Put your hand back into your bosom. He put it back and brought it out,[152] and it was like his other skin." There is further *the bosom of benignity in cherishing*. Proverbs 21:14 has: "A secret gift quenches anger, and a benefaction in the bosom the greatest wrath." Moreover, there is *the bosom of long-suffering perseverance*. Job 19:27 reads: "This my hope is laid up in my bosom." And Ezekiel 43:13 states: "In the bosom thereof was a cubit . . . and the

---

[151] I have completed this quotation, for Bonaventure does not cite the second clause, which contains the key word "bosom." On p. 419, n. 2 QuarEd state the Hugh of St. Cher distinguishes six bosoms of evil: voluptuousness, cupidity, vanity, powerlessness, negligence, and evil conscience. See Hugh of St. Cher, p. 232g.

[152] On p. 419, n. 3 QuarEd correctly indicate that the Vulgate reads *rursus* ("again") and does not have *eam* ("it").

border thereof until its edge," namely, the cubit of perfect reward.[153]

And third is *the desirable bosom*, and this is mentioned here: "It came to pass that the beggar died and was borne away by the angels into Abraham's bosom." The rest of blessed souls is understood by this bosom. Matthew 8:11 says: "Many will come from the east and the west and will recline with Abraham, Isaac, and Jacob in the kingdom of the heavens."

Luke 16:22–31
THE PUNISHMENT OF MERCILESS CONDUCT

46. *But the rich man also died*, etc. After descriptions of the reason for and the sin of lack of mercy the text introduces here *the punishment for mercilessness* and makes two points. The first deals with *the misery inflicted*. The second considers *the mercy denied* where verse 25 has: *And Abraham said to him*, etc.

Luke 16:22–24
THE PUNISHMENT FOR MERCILESSNESS

Now the delineation of *the misery inflicted* on account of the sin of merciless non-action is threefold: *being cast*

---

[153] On p. 419, n. 5 QuarEd try to make sense of this application of Ezekiel 43:13 by referring to Cardinal Hugh's use of it for "the bosom of vanity." See Hugh of St. Cher, p. 232g: "The cubit is the perfect measure. So the cubit is in the bosom of the person who in his own opinion seems to himself to be perfect. And the border thereof till the edge, when he proffers boastful words about his own perfection. Exodus 4b[7]: When Moses put his hand into his bosom, he brought it out leprous."

down into the place of misery; separation from the place of the just; the multitude of manifold calamities.

47. First, concerning *being cast into the place of misery*, the text reads: *But the rich man also was dead* through *the cessation of temporal joys*. And note that the text uses the past tense to suggest that that pitiable rich man had experienced not just a single death, but a threefold death. First is the death of *sin*, by which the soul is separated from God. He had been already dead from this while he was alive. 1 Timothy 5:6 states: "The widow, who gives herself over to pleasure, is dead while she is still alive." *Widow* indicates the soul separated from God. – Second is the death of *nature*, by which *the soul is separated from the body*. Sirach 41:1 says: "O death, how bitter is the remembrance of you to the unjust[154] person, who enjoys peace in his possessions." – Third is the death of *hell*, by which the soul is separated from beatific life. About this Revelation 20:14 has: "And hell and death were cast into the pool of fire." Relative to this designation of a threefold death it is said in Revelation 8:13: "Woe, woe, woe to the inhabitants of earth," etc. – *And he was buried in hell*, by *being cast into the place of misery*. And this on account of *the sin of pride*. Isaiah 14:11 reads: "Your pride is brought down into hell. Your carcass is fallen down." On account of *the sin of voluptuousness*. Job 21:13 says: "They spend their days enjoying good things, and in an instant they go down to hell." On account of *the sin of being unmerciful*. The Psalm says: "They have been placed in hell like sheep. Death will feed upon them" (48:15). And again the Psalm states: "Let death come upon them, and let them go down into hell alive. For there is wickedness in

---

[154] On p. 419, n. 9 QuarEd correctly mention that the Vulgate does not read *iniusto* ("unjust").

their dwellings," etc. (54:16).[155] – From this it is clear how great a difference exists between the adherents of Christ and of the devil, for the former *are elevated* in heaven while the latter *are buried* in hell where there is an exceedingly deep pit. Job 17:16 reads: "All that I have will go down into the deepest part of hell," etc.[156] And the Psalmist says: "They will go into the depths of the earth, will be handed over to the sword, will be the prey of foxes" (62:10–11).[157]

48. (Verse 23). Second, with regard to *the separation from the place of the just* the text adds: *And lifting up his eyes, being in torment*, namely, in the place of continual affliction. Revelation 14:11 states: "The smoke of their torments arises forever and forever." Isaiah 30:33 reads: "Topheth has been prepared from yesterday. . . . It is fed by fire and much wood: the breath of the Lord like a torrent of brimstone kindling it."[158] – *He saw Abraham afar off and Lazarus in his bosom.* Truly, he is *faraway* both in terms of *place* and *status*, because the rich man is in *the lowest* place while the beggar is in *the highest.* Proverbs 29:23 states: "Humiliation follows the proud, and glory will uphold the humble of spirit." And Proverbs 14:19 reads: "The evil will fall down be-

---

[155] On p. 419, n. 12 QuarEd cite Book II, q. 38 n. 1 of Augustine's *Qvaestiones Evangeliorvm.* See CCSL xlivb, p. 89: *"The sepulcher of hell,* the depths of the punishments which devour the proud and the unmerciful after this life."

[156] On p. 419, n. 13 QuarEd accurately indicate that the Vulgate reads *profundissimum infernum* ("the deepest hell").

[157] In this commentary Bonaventure has liberally adapted the interpretation of Cardinal Hugh. See Hugh of St. Cher, p. 232a. With Hugh Bonaventure shares the idea of a threefold death and many of the same scripture quotations, e.g., Revelation 8:13; Revelation 20:14; Isaiah 14:11.

[158] On p. 420 n. 1 QuarEd quote Jerome: *"...Thopheth,* that is, *broad and spacious hell,* which burns them with everlasting flames, etc." Isaiah 30:33 is referring to the funeral pyre of an enemy king.

fore the good, and the wicked before the gates of the just." Furthermore, the rich man was *in affliction* while the poor man was *in peace*. Isaiah 65:13 has: "My servants will eat, and you will be hungry." Moreover, because the rich man is *in need* while the poor man is *in abundance*. Luke 1:53 above says: "He has filled the hungry with good things, and the rich he has sent away empty." The Psalm states: "The poor will eat and be filled" (21:27). And in another Psalm: "The rich have been in need and were hungry, but those who seek the Lord," etc. (33:11).[159] Now it is said that *he saw Abraham*, but this was no comfort to him but rather added to his torments. Thus Gregory comments: "We must believe that before they receive their recompense at the final judgment, the unrighteous behold some[160] at rest. This is so that when they see them in their joy, they may be tormented not only by their own suffering, but also by the good the others have received."[161] The Psalm says: "The sinner will see and be angry. He will gnash his teeth and waste away. The desire of sinners will perish" (111:10). And Wisdom 5:2 reads: "Those seeing it will be troubled with a terrible fear," etc.

49. (Verse 24). Third, with respect to *the accumulation of multiple calamities* the text continues: *And he exclaimed*[162] *and said: Father Abraham, have mercy on me,*

---

[159] The end of verse 11 contains Bonaventure's punch line: ". . . but those that seek the Lord will not be deprived of any good."

[160] On p. 420, n. 5 QuarEd correctly indicate that Gregory reads *quosdam justos* ("some just"). See PL 76:1309A. They also note that Cardinal Hugh does not read *justos* ("just"). See Hugh of St. Cher, p. 232v, c for Hugh's quotation of Gregory which is similar to Bonaventure's.

[161] See Homily 40, n. 8 of GGHG. I have modified the translation of Hurst, p. 381. See PL 76:1308D–1309A.

[162] On p. 420, n. 7 QuarEd accurately mention that the Vulgate reads *clamans* ("cried out") while Bonaventure has *exclamans* ("exclaimed").

so that from his cry the greatness of his suffering may be clear, according to what Isaiah 65:14 says: "Behold . . . my servants will give praise out of the joyfulness of their hearts, and you will cry out of the sorrow of your hearts and will howl from grieving spirits." And this was indeed fitting for the rich man. Proverbs 21:13 reads: "The person who stops his ears against the cry of the poor will himself cry and will not be heard." – *And send Lazarus to dip the tip of his finger in water*, so that from the plea for a drop of water *the magnitude of his want* may thus be obvious. Job 27:19–20 has: "The rich man, when he will fall asleep, will take nothing with him. He will open his eyes and find nothing. Neediness will cover him like water."[163] The Psalm states: "They have slept their sleep, and all the men of riches have discovered that there is nothing in their hands" (75:6). Thus, Chrysostom observes: "The person who sinned through excess in extravagant things, now in his suffering pleads for the most common of things." And again, speaking to the rich man, Chrysostom says: "You did not deign to look at Lazarus at that time, and now you desire the tip of his finger?"[164] And Bede notes: "That rich man, who refused to give the smallest of foodstuffs from his table, is now situated in hell and pleads for the smallest amount of relief. For the person who refused Lazarus a crumb of bread now is petitioning for a drop

---

[163] Bonaventure's text varies in two significant ways from the Vulgate, for Bonaventure reads *aperiet* ("will open") for the Vulgate's *aperit* ("opens") and *operiet* ("will cover") for the Vulgate's *apprehendit* ("seizes").

[164] On p. 420, n. 10 QuarEd refer to Chrysostom's Homily on Psalm 25,11 and to his Homily 1 on Luke 16, but also say: "Cardinal Hugh also says this." Hugh of St. Cher, p. 232v, f has both these quotations from Chrysostom, but in reverse order. The quotations from Chrysostom found in Bonaventure and Hugh are substantially the same.

of water."[165] Proverbs 28:27 reads: "The person who gives to the poor will not want. The person who despises his entreaty will suffer indigence." – *To cool my tongue*. From the affliction of the tongue *the rectitude of divine justice* is thus clear. So Peter of Ravenna comments: "If the fire of hell has already taken hold of you entirely, why are you desirous of relief solely for the heat of your tongue? May it be that your tongue suffers such great heat because it ridiculed the poor man and denied him mercy? That which is the first thing to be judged was the first thing to sin. That which tasted costly foods and savored drinks with pleasant aromas is the first to taste torments,"[166] according to what Wisdom 11:17 says: "By what things a person sins, by the same also is he tormented." Therefore, Bede in the Glossa says: "Note that as is the custom, he was given to loquacity during banquets."[167] For which reason Proverbs 10:19 cautions: "In the multitude of words sin will not be absent." – *For I am tormented in this flame*, so that *the sternness of divine punishment* may be clear. The Psalmist states: "You will make them like a fiery oven when you manifest your face" (20:10). And Deuteronomy 32:22 reads: "A fire is kindled in my wrath, and will burn even to the depths of hell." Wherefore, Sirach 7:19 says: "Humble

---

[165] Hugh of St. Cher, p. 232v, g attributes this interpretation to Gregory. See CCSL cxx, p. 304, where Bede is quoting from Gregory the Great. See PL 76:1306D–1307A for Gregory's exposition.

[166] On p. 420, n. 12 QuarEd refer to Peter Chrysologus' Sermon 122, n. 11 and state that many things have been changed in the quotation. See PL 52:535A. Hugh of St. Cher, p. 232v, g has virtually the same text as Bonaventure and follows it immediately with a quotation from Wisdom 11:17. Cardinal Bonaventure again has quoted an authority through the good graces of Cardinal Hugh.

[167] On p. 420, n. 14 QuarEd state that this is the Glossa Interlinearis (from Bede who is quoting Gregory). See CCSL cxx, p. 304. For Gregory, see PL 76:1707A, whose interpretation of the sin of loquacity is more nuanced. But see Hugh of St. Cher, p. 232v, f for a quotation of Bede which is almost identical to that of Bonaventure.

your spirit very much, for the punishment on the flesh of the wicked is fire and worms."

50. And note that this flame was real, but the tongue was imagined, because real fire afflicts spirits, according to what Matthew 25:41 says: "Depart from me, accursed ones, into the everlasting fire," etc. And *the soul* is also afflicted in the images that it has generated through the body, according to what Wisdom 17:6 states: "There appeared to them a sudden fire, very dreadful. And being struck with the fear of that face, which was not seen, they thought the things which they saw to be worse." And later Wisdom 17:20 states: "Therefore, they were more violent to themselves than the darkness." So from this one garners that in the affliction of the reprobates there is simultaneously a real and an imagined punishment, at the same time a natural and supernatural action, simultaneously intrinsic and extrinsic affliction, at the same time suffering that is one's own and suffering that comes from outside, so that in this way what Wisdom 5:21 says may be fulfilled: "The whole world will fight on his behalf against the unwise."[168] Real flames indeed burned, and the imagined and imaginary tongue showed the fuel it supplied for the burning of the soul of the rich man. Now the tongue provides a more apt expression than any other member, which is tormented and afflicted in the fire of hell, because in the realm of sinning it is like kindling for all iniquity. James 3:5–8 reads: "The tongue also is a small member, but it boasts mightily. Behold, how small a fire sets so great a forest ablaze! And the tongue is a fire, the very world of iniquity. The tongue is placed among our members, defiling the whole body and setting on fire the course of our life,

---

[168] On p. 421, n. 3 QuarEd accurately state that the Vulgate reads *cum eo* ("with him") while Bonaventure has *pro illo* ("on his behalf").

being itself set on fire by hell. For every kind of beast . . . has been tamed, but no one can tame the tongue." For it is "a restless evil, full of deadly poison."

51. Now this is said, because the tongue itself assails divine *majesty, truth* and *goodness, mutual charity*, and all norms of *decent behavior*.[169] – It attacks God's *majesty* through *arrogant* speech. The Psalm says: "Who have said: We will highly praise our tongue," etc. (11:5). And because of this the preceding verse stated: "May the Lord destroy all deceitful lips and the tongue that speaks proud things" (11:4).[170] Likewise through *blasphemous* words. Revelation 16:10–11 reads: "They gnawed their tongues for pain and blasphemed God." And 2 Maccabees 15:33 says: "He commanded that the tongue of the wicked Nicanor should be cut out and given piecemeal to the birds," for he had blasphemed.[171] – *Truth,* through *lying* words. Proverbs 26:28 states: "A deceitful tongue does not love truth, and a slippery mouth wreaks ruin." Jeremiah 9:3, 5 read: "They have bent their tongue, like a bow, for lies and not for the truth. . . . They have taught their tongues to speak lies," etc. The Psalmist says: "They loved him with their mouth," etc. (77:36).[172] – Through *duplicitous* words. The Psalm has: "All the day long your tongue has devised injustice. As a sharp razor you have wrought deceit" (51:4). And again the Psalm states: "Your tongue has

---

[169] Although Bonaventure was in the habit of adapting lists from Hugh of St. Cher, this is his own list of five.

[170] It would seem to me that the unquoted part of Psalm 11:5 is key to Bonaventure's point about an attack on God's majesty: ". . . our lips are our own. Who is Lord over us?"

[171] The reference is to the actions of Judas against Nicanor, governor of Judea.

[172] Bonaventure's "etc" hides the key last part of the verse: ". . . and with their tongues they lied to him."

framed deceits" (49:19). And Sirach 5:11 reads: "Winnow not in every wind, and do not go into every lane. For thus is every sinner proven by a double tongue." – *Goodness*, by *flattering* words. Proverbs 6:24 has: "That they may keep you from a wicked woman and from the flattering tongue of a stranger." And Sirach 20:17–18 states: "A fool will have no friend, and there will be no thanks given for his good deeds. For those who eat his food use their tongue for falsehood." Proverbs 28:23 says: "The person who corrects a man," etc.[173] Likewise, by *calumniating* words. Wisdom 1:11 reads: "Keep yourselves from murmuring, which profits nothing, and refrain your tongue from calumny." And Sirach 28:28 cautions: "Hedge in your ears with thorns, and don't listen to a wicked tongue." And Proverbs 25:23 advises: "The north wind drives away rain, and a stern countenance a calumniating tongue." Job 20:12 states: "When evil will be sweet in his mouth, he will hide it under his tongue."

52. *Mutual charity* through *wrangling* words. The Psalmist prays: "You will protect them in your tabernacle from the disagreement of tongues" (30:21). Sirach 8:4 says: "Do not litigate with a person who is eloquent, lest you strew fire upon his wood."[174] And Sirach 4:34 reads: "Do not be hasty with your tongue." In addition, through *provocative* words. The Psalm warns: "The sons of men, whose teeth are weapons and arrows," etc. (56:5).[175] And Jeremiah 9:8 prophesies: "Their tongue is a piercing arrow. It has spoken deceit." The Psalmist states: "They

---

[173] The full text is: "The person who corrects a man, will afterward find favor with him, more than the person, who by a flattering tongue deceives him."

[174] On p. 421, n. 11 QuarEd correctly indicate that the Vulgate reads *et non strues in ignem illius ligna* ("and you will not strew wood upon his fire").

[175] Psalm 56:5 concludes with: ". . . and their tongue a sharp sword."

have sharpened their tongues like serpents" (56:5). – *All norms of decent behavior*. Through *impure* words Sirach 51:4–7 reads: "You have delivered me...from an unclean tongue and from lying words." James 3:6 says: "The tongue is placed among our members, defiling the whole body and setting on fire," etc. Moreover, through *useless* words. James 1:26 has: "If anyone thinks himself to be religious, not restraining his tongue," etc.[176] And Sirach 19:17 states: "For who is there who has not offended with his tongue?" Therefore, James 3:2 pronounces: "If anyone does not offend in word, he is a perfect man." Thus, it is said in Proverbs 16:1: "It is the responsibility of a human being to prepare the soul, and of God to govern the tongue." Proverbs 18:21 adds: "Death and life are in the power of the tongue." And so the preacher prayed in Sirach 22:33: "Who will set a guard before my mouth and a sure seal upon my lips, so that I do not fall because of them and my tongue destroy me not?" – So for these reasons the rich man, situated in hell, says here: *so that he may cool my tongue, for I am tormented in this flame*.

53. *But Abraham said to him*, etc. Having described the punishment from the angle of the suffering inflicted, the Evangelist next depicts the punishment relative to *the mercy denied*. There are two parts. The first is *the denial of mercy to the person himself*. The second is *the denial of mercy to relatives* where verse 27 has: *And he said: Then, father, I beseech you*, etc.

Concerning *the denial of mercy to the rich man himself* there are three points: *the dissimilarity between rewards*,

---

[176] James 1:26 concludes: "... but deceiving his own heart, that man's religion is vain."

the contrast between recompenses, and *the unalterable nature of divine judgments.*

Luke 16:25–31
MERCY DENIED

54. (Verse 25). First, then, with respect to *the dissimilarity between rewards* the text says: *But Abraham said to him: Son, remember that you in your lifetime have received good things.* He calls him *son* not because he imitates him, but because of natural generation. The Psalm states: "The sons who are strangers have lied to me. Strange sons have faded away" (17:46). Thus Peter of Ravenna comments: "You call me *father*, and I (call) you *son*, so that you may grievously mourn over what you have lost, what you were born to, what grace and nature had given you."[177] He says to this son that *he should remember the good things*, not for his consolation, but rather for his torment. Therefore, Boethius states: "The most unhappy type of fortune is to have known happiness."[178] And he received this in payment for his good

---

[177] On p. 422, n. 7 QuarEd refer to Peter Chyrsologus' Sermon 123 n. 3. See PL 52:536C: *Tu vocas patrem, ego voco filium ut te graviter doleas perdidisse quod natus es. Adhuc voco filium, ut amarius doleas perdidisse te quod tibi gratia dederat et natura* ("You call me father. I call you son, so that you may grievously mourn over what you have lost, what you were born to. I still call you son, so that you bitterly mourn that you have lost what grace and nature had given you"). Compare Hugh of St. Cher, p. 233a: *Petrus Raven. Tu vocas me patrem, et ego voco te filium, ut tu graviter doleas perdidisse, ad quod natus es, quod tibi gratia dederat et natura* ("Peter of Ravenna comments: You call me father, and I call you son, so that you may grievously mourn over what you have lost, to what you were born, what grace and nature had given you"). Bonaventure's quotation of Peter Chrysologus is closer to Hugh of St. Cher's than to the original.

[178] On p. 422, n. 8 QuarEd refer to Book II.4 of Boethius' *Consolation of Philosophy*. I use the Latin text of LCL and the translation thereof

things. So Bede observes: "Note that this rich man had some good thing, from which he received a transitory good in this life."[179] So he was among those of whom it is said in Matthew 6:2: "Amen I say to you: they have received their reward." Therefore, this reward was transitory and preliminary to punishment. – But in contrast was Lazarus' reward. So the text adds: *And Lazarus in like manner evil things*, because there is *similarity in contrast*. For Lazarus received evil things for a time to purge the evil of sin and to acquire the good things of everlasting happiness. Therefore, Bede says: "Lazarus had some bad things, but the fire of want purified him."[180] And Gregory maintains: "If we see the poor doing something reprehensible, we must not disdain them, for perhaps the medicine of poverty heals those whom the weakness of morals wounds."[181] And this is the way of entering the kingdom. Acts 14:21 says: "Through many tribulations we must enter the kingdom of God." Thus in this is verified what Qoheleth 8:14 states: "There are just people, whom evils befall, as if they had

---

by S. J. Tester, pp. 190–191: *Nam in omni adversitate fortunae infelicissimum est genus infortunii fuisse felicem* ("For in all the adversities of fortune, the most unhappy kind of misfortune is to have known happiness"). See Hugh of St. Cher, p. 233b: *Unde Boetius: Infelicissimum genus infortunii est fuisse felicem* ("So Boethius comments: The most unhappy type of misfortune is to have known happiness"). Bonaventure's Latin text is: *Unde Boetius: Infelicissimum genus fortunae est, fuisse felicem*. Did Bonaventure copy directly from Boethius?

[179] On p. 422, n. 9 QuarEd state that Bede's exposition comes via the Gloss Ordinaria, which attributes it to Augustine. See CCSL cxx, p. 304 for Bede's text, which he borrows from Homily 40 n. 6 of GGHG. See PL 76:1307C. See Hurst, p. 379 for Gregory's context: Some external good in this world "may have been given you in return for your good actions; the judge who is paying you in this life with external goods may deprive you of your recompense in interior ones."

[180] See CCSL cxx, p. 304. Bede borrows from Gregory.

[181] See Homily 40 n. 10 of GGHG. See PL 76:1310A.

done the works of the wicked," for as Tobit 12:13 fittingly says: "Since you were acceptable to God, it was necessary that temptation should prove you."

55. Second, relative to *the difference between recompenses* the text continues: *But now here he is comforted whereas you are tormented. Here*, in this life, I say, he was comforted in tribulation. John 16:20 reads: "The world will rejoice, but you will be sorrowful. But your sorrow will be turned into joy." So Matthew 5:5 states: "Blessed are they who mourn, for they will be comforted." For just as it is said in 2 Corinthians 4:17: "Our tribulation in the present is light and momentary...beyond measure."[182] And therefore, James 1 says: "Esteem it all joy, brothers, when you fall into various trials" (verse 2), and afterwards: "Blessed is the man who endures temptation" (verse 12). And therefore, Chrysostom observes: "If we become sick, if we are poor, let us rejoice. Let us accept evil in our lives, so that afterwards we may receive good things."[183] For the Prophet speaks thus: "We have passed through fire and water, and you have brought us into a place of refreshment" (Psalm 65:12). And as a figure of this the water of the chief steward at the wedding feast was changed into wine in John 2:1–11. Therefore, the poor man is thus comforted, and the rich man, on the contrary, is tormented. Luke 6:24 above states: "Woe

---

[182] 2 Corinthians 4:17 concludes: ". . . prepares for us an eternal weight of glory that is beyond measure."

[183] On p. 422, n. 14 QuarEd refer to Chrysostom's Homily 1 on Luke 16. See Hugh of St. Cher, p. 233f where Hugh quotes 2 Corinthians 4:17, John 2:1–11, John 16:20, and Chrysostom. Bonaventure's quotation of Chrysostom is identical to that of Hugh with one exception: Bonaventure has *post* ("afterwards") whereas Hugh reads *postea* ("afterwards"). To me it is clear that Bonaventure quoted Chrysostom through the mediation of Hugh.

to you. You rich,[184] who are now having your comfort."
And Proverbs 14:13 reads: "Laughter will be mingled
with sorrow, and mourning follows upon the heels of
joy." For this temporal pleasure casts a person into everlasting torment. So Gregory comments: "Momentary is
that which gives pleasure, but everlasting is that which
torments."[185] So there is a harmony in God's just judgment, so that there is a transition from one extreme to
the other, namely, from tribulation to consolation and
from comfort to everlasting affliction in the form of a
type of cross. A figure of this is mentioned relative to
Jacob in Genesis 48:13–14: in blessing Joseph's sons he
didn't stretch his hands straight out, but crossed them
over.

56. (Verse 26). Third, with regard to *the unalterable nature of divine judgments* the text continues: *And besides
all that, between us and you a great gulf is fixed*, which
suggests the impossibility of moving between the reprobates and the elect. Qoheleth 11:3 says: "If the tree falls
to the south or to the north, in whatever place it will
have fallen, there will it be." This non-transgressing
zone is called *a gulf*, because neither can the good descend into the darkness of the sinners nor can the
wicked into the light of the good. For which reason it is
said in John 12:35: "Walk while you have the light, so
that darkness may not overtake you." Ambrose in the
Glossa comments about this intransgressibility: "Between the poor man and the rich man there is a gulf,

---

[184] On p. 422, n. 15 QuarEd correctly indicate that the Vulgate has
Vae vobis divitibus ("Woe to you rich").
[185] On p. 423, n. 1 QuarEd indicate three references: Book XIV chapter 8 n. 10 and Book XV, chapter 13 n. 15 of Gregory's *Moralia* and
Homily 40, n. 12 of GGHG. Gregory gives the same opinion in those
places, but in different words. Hugh of St. Cher, p. 233g has the
identical quotation from Gregory that Bonaventure has.

because after death rewards cannot be changed."[186] And further, because of this there can be no mutual comforting. – And so the text continues: *so that they who wish to pass over from this side to you cannot,* to offer merciful assistance, *and they cannot cross from your side to us,* to attain an everlasting reward. Thus, Gregory comments: "Although the souls of the just possess mercy in the goodness of their natures, they are bound by their Creator's great rectitude, united with their own justness, so that they cannot be moved by compassion for the condemned."[187] In addition, *the wicked* cannot escape from the prison of infernal Tartarus. The Psalm says: "They will leave their riches to strangers, and their sepulchers will be their homes forever" (48:11–12). From this they cannot escape, for Qoheleth 9:10 states: "Neither work, nor reason, nor knowledge, nor wisdom will be in hell, whither you are hastening." For neither can they exit from hell nor can they enter into the rest of the elect. Isaiah 52:1 reads: "It will no more be permitted that the uncircumcised and unclean pass through you." Wherefore, Revelation 22:15 has: "Outside are the dogs and sorcerers, the impure . . . and the idolaters," etc. *The good,* for their part, cannot pass over to help the wicked. They can, however, see them. Therefore, Isaiah 66:24 says: "They will go out and see the carcasses of the men who have transgressed against me. Their worm will not die, and their fire will not be quenched. And they will be loathsome in everyone's sight."

---

[186] On p. 423, n. 4 QuarEd state that this is the Glossa Interlinearis. See CCSL xiv, p. 304. The Glossa is quite faithful to Ambrose's interpretation.

[187] On p. 423, n. 5 QuarEd refer to Homily 40, n. 7 of GGHG. See PL 76:1308B. Bonaventure follows Gregory's text almost verbatim. I have modified the translation of Hurst, p. 380.

57. (Verse 27). *And he said: Then, father, I beseech you,* etc. After the denial of mercy for his own person the text adds here *a denial for his relatives.* There are four considerations: *the petition for mercy* for his relatives; *the denial of the mercy requested*; *the reason for the proffered petition*; *the approbation of the response already given.*
So, first, relative to *the petition for mercy towards his relatives* the text reads: *And he said: Then, father, I beseech you to send him to my father's house.* Now this petition was *carnal*, for its extent was to his brothers only.

58. (Verse 28). Wherefore, the text adds: *For I have five brothers.* Sirach 18:12 states: "The compassion of human beings is towards their neighbors," etc. Therefore, it was *carnal*, for it was for his brothers in the flesh who were living according to the flesh. And the number five also suggests this. By the number five is understood that they had been given over to the five senses of the body, according to what is said to the Samaritan woman in John 4:18: "You have had five husbands, and the one you now have," etc. And Luke 14:19 reads: "I have bought five yoke of oxen."[188] He is also carnal, because he did not make this request to prevent someone else's punishment, but rather lest his own be increased by their arrival. – Therefore, the text adds: *that he may testify to them, lest they, too, come into this place of torment.* Truly, he said this, lest by their presence his own misfortune may multiply through seeing his relatives being tormented so greatly. So Bede observes: "The recognition of the poor man, whom he had disdained, and the memory of his brothers, whom he had left behind,

---

[188] Hugh of St. Cher, p. 233v, c thinks that, perhaps, the five brothers refer to the pleasures of the five senses and also quotes John 4:18 and Luke 14:19. For Hugh, though, this is point three of seven messages of the literal sense.

added to the punishment of the rich man, so that he might be further tormented by seeing the glory of the one he despised and the punishment of those he had loved to no avail."[189] And this is especially true, when the imitators of crimes against strangers share in the punishments. So Gregory says: "So that sinners may be more grievously tormented, they will see both the glory of those whom they have contemned and the punishment of those whom they have loved to no avail."[190] – Now this petition was not only carnal in his own regard, but it was also *cruel* with regard to his neighbor, for on account of his love for his own kin he wanted Lazarus to abandon the bosom of rest and travel to a place of dangers. In this what Proverbs 12:10 says will be verified: "The just have regard for the lives of their animals, but the hearts of the wicked are cruel." Therefore, even Christ, who called Lazarus, Mary's brother, back to life, is said in John 11:35 to have wept: "And Jesus wept." – This petition was also *in vain*, because he believed that the word of a dead man was of more value than that of the immortal God. So Qoheleth 10:3 is fulfilled: "But the fool, walking along life's way, thinks that all people are fools, whereas it is he himself who is the fool." Thus, the Glossa comments: "This rich man is beginning to be a zealous preacher, although now he has time neither to

---

[189] On p. 423, n. 12 QuarEd state that Bede's interpretation is couched in the words of the Glossa Ordinaria. See CCSL cxx, p. 305. The Glossa has simplified Bede's exposition, which in reality is Gregory the Great's. Hugh of St. Cher, p. 233v, c quotes "Bede" in almost the identical words as Bonaventure.

[190] On p. 424, n. 1 QuarEd refer to Homily 40, n. 8 of GGHG. See PL 76:1308D and Hugh of St. Cher, p. 233v, c. Hugh and Gregory have almost the same wording. Bonaventure is the lone wolf. The reason that this quotation is so similar to the quotation from Bede which Bonaventure just quoted is that Bede was quoting Gregory.

learn nor to teach."[191] – Likewise, his petition was *shameless*, because he had refused to do small things and now was requesting the greatest benefits, contrary to what is said in Sirach 4:36: "Let not your hand be stretched out to receive and shut when you should be giving."

59. (Verse 29). Second, concerning *the refusal of the mercy petitioned* the text adds: *And Abraham said to him: They have Moses and the Prophets. Let them hearken to them. Moses*, that is the teaching of the Law, which should be listened to because of its great authority. For as Proverbs 28:9 states: "The prayer of the person, who turns away his ear lest he hear the Law, will be an abomination."[192] And therefore, the Legislator said in Deuteronomy 32:1–4: "Hear, O heavens, the things I say, let the earth give ear to the words of my mouth. . . . Give magnificent praise to our God. The works of God are perfect." And they also have the Prophets, that is, the teaching of the Prophets is to be listened to because of their certain truth, according to what 2 Peter 1:19 says: "We have the more secure word of prophecy, to which you do well to attend, as to a lamp shining in a dark place, until the day dawns and the morning star rises in your hearts." The person who refuses to hear the words of this twofold teaching, which is both authentic and certain, is totally without an excuse. For which reason the Lord says through Jeremiah the Prophet in Jeremiah 26:4–6: "If you will not hearken to me to walk in my Law, which I have given to you, and if you do not hearken to the words of my servants the

---

[191] On p. 424, n. 3 QuarEd state that this is the Glossa Ordinaria (from Ambrose). See CCSL xiv, pp. 304–305. Ambrose, however, reads *magister* ("teacher") rather than *praedicator* ("preacher").

[192] Hugh of St. Cher, p. 233v, e also quotes Proverbs 28:9.

Prophets, whom I sent to you from early in the morning, I will make this house like Shiloh and will make this city a curse. . . . " Wherefore, if those who do not heed the Law and the Prophets are inexcusable, those who do not listen to the Apostles and Evangelists are entirely without excuse. Even more inexcusable are those who do not hearken to Wisdom Incarnate himself. So wisdom complains in Proverbs 1:24–26: "Since I called and you refused, I stretched out my hand, and there was no one who paid attention. . . . I will also laugh at your destruction and will mock when what you feared shall come upon you." The person who does not want to listen to this Wisdom, who "preaches abroad in the streets," is wholly inexcusable, because the Law and the Prophets bear witness to him.[193] Thus, Matthew 17:3–5 reads: "There appeared to them Moses and Elijah speaking with him. . . . And a voice out of the cloud said: This is my beloved Son. Listen to him." And therefore, it is said in Hebrews 2:1–3: "We ought the more earnestly to observe the things that we have heard, lest perhaps we drift away. For if the word spoken by angels proved to be valid . . . how will we escape if we neglect so great a salvation?" And Hebrews 12:24–25 reads: "You have drawn near to Jesus, mediator of a new covenant, and to a sprinkling of blood which speaks more eloquently than that of Abel. See that you do not refuse him who speaks."

60. (Verse 30). Third, concerning *the reason for the petition proffered* the text adds: *But he answered: No, father Abraham, but if someone from the dead would go to*

---

[193] Bonaventure quotes Proverbs 1:20 and, as QuarEd on p. 424, n. 9 suggest, alludes to John 5:39: "You search the Scriptures. . . . And it is they that bear witness to me."

them,[194] *they will repent.* In this he demonstrated *the carnality* of his brothers, who would be more greatly moved by a bodily resuscitation than by spiritual revelation. So they belong to the number of those, about whom Wisdom 2:1 says: "The wicked have said, reasoning among themselves, but not rightly . . . : There is no rest when human life is ended, and no one has been known to have returned from hell." In this he also showed *the perversity* of his brothers, that they would prefer the witness of a dead man to the witnesses of the living God, contrary to what Isaiah 8:19–20 states: "Will the people not seek from their God a vision of those who are alive from the dead?[195] Rather they should seek in the Law and in the testimony. If they speak not according to this word, they will not have the morning light."[196] In this he also manifested *the unbelief* of the brothers in that they would not believe unless they saw signs and wonders like that official in John 4:48: "Unless you see signs and wonders, you do not believe." In this he likewise showed *the folly* of the brothers, for they should be moved to repentance more from seeing that human beings die than from the possibility that they may see them resuscitated. Sirach 38:23 reads: "Remember my judgment. For yours will be the same. Yesterday for me, today for you."[197] And Sirach 17:26 states: "Give praise before death. Praise perishes from the dead as nothing."

---

[194] On p. 424, n. 12 QuarEd rightly indicate that the Vulgate reads *eos* ("to them"). Bonaventure has *illos* ("to them").

[195] On p. 425, n. 1 QuarEd point to Bonaventure's divergent reading here. The Vulgate does not have *visionem* ("a vision") and has *requirit* ("seeks") for Bonaventure's *requiret* ("will seek"). Hugh of St. Cher, p. 233v, f also quotes Isaiah 8:19–20 and reads *requiret*.

[196] The first part of Isaiah 8:19 sets the context: It is the contrast between God's word and diviners, soothsayers, and enchanters.

[197] Hugh of St. Cher, p. 233v, g also quotes Sirach 38:23.

The Psalm says: "The dead will not praise you, O Lord, nor any of those who go down to hell" (113:17).

61. (Verse 31). Fourth comes *the approval of the response already given*, as the text continues: *But he said to him: If they do not hearken to Moses and the Prophets*, that is, by obeying them. For it is in this way that they should be heard, according to what Revelation 1:3 has: "Blessed is the person who reads and hearkens to the words of this prophecy and keeps them," etc.[198] The persons who do not hearken to so many witnesses contemn God's truth, according to what Ezekiel 3:7 states: "The house of Israel does not want to hearken to you, because they will not hearken to me. For the entire house of Israel is stubborn and has an obstinate heart."[199] – So since those who are obdurate and incapable of believing resist such a great truth, the text adds: *Even if someone rises from the dead, they will not believe him.*[200] And the reason for this consequence is that the person who does not believe in testimony that is very credible also does not believe in testimony that is less credible. We have an example of this in the case of *Lazarus*, a person who was resuscitated. The unbelieving Jews not only did not believe that he had been raised from the dead, but also, as it is said in John 12:10–11, "the Jews planned to put Lazarus to death, for many of the Jews began to leave them and to believe in Jesus." But the obstinate Pharisees not only did not believe, but also wanted to extinguish the

---

[198] Bonaventure has adapted Revelation 1:3, which reads: "Blessed is the person who reads and those who hear the words of this prophecy and keep. . . ."

[199] On p. 425, n. 5 QuarEd rightly mention that the Vulgate reads *duro corde* ("hard heart") while Bonaventure has *indomabili corde* ("obstinate heart").

[200] On p. 425, n. 6 QuarEd accurately indicate that the Vulgate does not have *ei* ("him").

faith of believers. We also have an example of this in *Christ*, whom the Jews also refused to believe in after he had been raised from the dead. Therefore, Chrysostom says: "Christ has risen from the dead, and he announced what evil things there were in hell. He also descended from heaven, and preached about the good things that were there. Nevertheless, he was not believed."[201] And this is because such people had refused the testimony of the Law and the Prophets. John 5:46–47 reads: "If you believed Moses, you will perhaps believe me also, for he wrote about me. But if you do not believe his writings, how will you believe my words?" – So from the preceding it is clear that most merciful father Abraham had totally refused mercy to the merciless rich man, so that what Isaiah 63:16 says may be fulfilled: "You, Lord, are our father, and Abraham has not known us." And also is verified what James 2:13 states: "Judgment is without mercy to the person who has not shown mercy." And Wisdom 19:1 reads: "To the wicked, even to the end there came upon them wrath without mercy." For what Matthew 25:41 says is spoken to such people in the judgment: "Depart from me, accursed ones, into the everlasting fire, which was prepared for the devil and his angels."

---

[201] On p. 425, n. 8 QuarEd state that Hugh of St. Cher also has this quotation and that they have been unable to find it in Chrysostom. See Hugh of St. Cher, p. 233v, g for a quotation from Chrysostom that is virtually identical to the one Bonaventure has.

INDEX OF SCRIPTURE PASSAGES

This index reveals how well versed Bonaventure was in Sacred Writ. Attentive readers will discover that Bonaventure quotes all seventy-two books of the Vulgate Bible with the exception of two tiny letters: Philemon and 2 John. They will also find that he quotes extensively from Wisdom Literature, e.g., Proverbs, and from christologically rich passages in the New Testament such as John 1:1-14 and Philippians 2:6-11.

6:42	1400	9:5	807,
6:45	1183		944 n 59
7	999 n 179	9:6	799, 808
7:14	872 n 141,	9:7	809
	1091 n 198,	9:7-8	809,
	1440		810 n 23
7:16	830,	9:7-9	808 n 20
	847 n 92,	9:9	811,
	1276 n 96,		1300 n 157
	1304	9:10	798, 812
7:22	1369	9:11	814, 815
7:27	902 n 204	9:12	812, 816
7:36-50	996 n 173	9:13	817,
7:38	948 n 70,		818 n 35
	996, 1223	9:14	816, 819,
7:39	999		819 n 39
7:45	1456 n 159	9:14-15	819
7:48	1447 n 133	9:16	821,
8:1	994		824 n 46
8:4	1432 n 92	9:17	822,
8:8	847 n 93,		823 n 45
	1278 n 105	9:18	798, 827,
8:10	831, 1471		827 n 53,
8:13	1383		829 n 56
8:15	872 n 141,	9:19	829,
	1091 n 198		829 n 57
8:16	1097 n 209	9:20	831
8:21	1084 n 179	9:21-22	833
8:33	1433,	9:23	826, 836,
	1500 n 72		942 n 55,
8:35	888 n 177		1153 n 55,
8:38	898		1391 n 167,
8:39	1321		1476 n 11
8:42	1401 n 14	9:23-27	837 n 72
8:51	846	9:24	839,
9	994		839 n 78
9:1	799, 941,	9:25	840,
	941 n 47		1493 n 51
9:2	800,	9:26	841, 896,
	941 n 49		1146
9:3	799, 802,	9:27	842,
	803 n 10,		843 n 84,
	805 nn 13-		896
	14	9:28	826, 844,
9:4	806,		845,
	936 n 38		845 n 89,

14:23	1370, 1370 n 121, 1512	15:9	1417, 1468
		15:10	1419, 1468, 1471 n 2
14:24	1371	15:11	1402, 1423, 1423 n 70
14:25	1315, 1372		
14:25-26	1374	15:11-32	1035
14:25-33	1375 n 132	15:12	1424
14:26	1216, 1375 n 132	15:13	1425, 1427 n 78, 1428 n 83, 1429 n 83, 1474
14:27	1376		
14:28	1372, 1379		
14:29	1382, 1384 n 154	15:14	1422, 1429, 1430 n 89
14:29-30	1383	15:15	1430, 1499
14:31	1379, 1384, 1389 n 163	15:16	1432 n 93, 1433
14:32	1388	15:17	1035 n 44, 1036, 1235, 1422, 1435
14:33	838 n 75, 911, 1379, 1389, 1391 n 165, 1476 n 11		
		15:18	1437
		15:19	1438
14:34	1392	15:20	1263, 1422, 1439, 1440 n 114, 1443 n 120
14:34-35	1394 n 177		
14:35	1392 n 173, 1393		
15:1	1052, 1133, 1395 n 1, 1396, 1420 n 63	15:21	1445
		15:22	1441, 1447, 1451 n 144
		15:23	1441, 1452
15:1-10	1371 n 126, 1400 n 13	15:23-24	1521, 1521 n 130
15:2	1398	15:24	1454
15:3	1403	15:25	1441, 1456
15:4	1403, 1423 n 68	15:26	1458
		15:27	1459
15:5	1402, 1408, 1468	15:28	1455, 1460
		15:29	1463
15:6	1409, 1410 n 32	15:30	1428 n 83, 1464
15:7	1411, 1412 n 38	15:31	1466
		15:32	1467
15:8	1402, 1408 n 26, 1413, 1414 n 43	16	1534 n 164, 1542 n 183
		16:1	1395, 1471, 1472 n 3,

5:8-9	1460		1507 n 92
5:12	1405	12:3	1269
5:20-21	1460	12:9-10	1498
6:12	1063	12:16	878 n 157,
6:13	1070		1507
6:21	841	12:19	907,
7:2-3	1515		907 n 217
7:7	1376 n 137	13:3	1151
7:23	1364	13:8	988, 1458
7:24-25	1365	13:8-9	1114
8:3	991	13:9	977,
8:6	1485		977 n 139,
8:13	840, 1497		980 n 147,
8:14	1177		1114 n 256
8:15	1017, 1446	13:12	1101
8:24	1047	13:12-14	861
8:26	1014, 1050	13:13	1344,
8:26a	1014 n 3		1345 n 60
8:26b	1014 n 3	14:17	801,
8:30	1258		962-963,
8:32	860, 889,		1067, 1176,
	1466,		1215, 1273
	1467 n 190	15:1	899
9:5	1085	15:7	815
9:15	965 n 109,	15:18	1189 n 147
	1179 n 124	16:16	933
9:18	965		
9:22-23	1070 n 137	**1 Corinthians**	
9:27	1314	1:3	1215 n 222
10:2	906	1:5-7	1164
10:2-3	1259	1:10	831, 1457
10:3	1460, 1504,	1:17	800
	1507 n 92	1:18	1239,
10:4	1508		1240 n 17
10:10	831, 963,	1:19	964
	1145,	1:20	964, 1163
	1145 n 32	1:22	1059
10:12	1176, 1401,	1:23-24	1069
	1472	1:24	1009 n 201,
10:15	800		1092,
10:17	1350		1122 n 270
11:20	1269, 1506	1:25	1069 n 133,
11:20-21	956, 1372		1369
11:25-26	1298, 1313,	1:26	1177
	1313 n 193	1:26-29	1367
11:33	1314, 1505,	1:28-29	912

3:17-18	920, 1213
3:18-19	1213 n 216
4:2	998
4:4	977
4:8	1070, 1409
4:14	830
4:22	1376
4:25	977
4:30	923
5:5	1501, 1501 n 75
5:8	1101
5:8-9	1100
5:14	1440, 1440 n 113, 1454
5:15	1158
5:15-17	1386
5:16	1049
5:32	1330
6:12	957, 1024, 1385
6:15	1450, 1451 n 145

Philippians

1:10-11	1250
1:18	898, 898 n 196
1:21-24	1006
1:23	866
2:1-2	1457
2:3-7	894
2:5-11	1388 n 161
2:7	991, 1270, 1403
2:7-8	859
2:8	1376
2:8-9	1339
2:10	897
2:13	1365, 1382
2:15	861, 861 n 120, 1098
2:15-16	1102
2:21	1200,

	1200 n 180
2:21-22	899
3:13-14	919
3:19	1326, 1432
3:20	855, 1186
4:6	1001, 1040, 1152, 1166
4:7	1215
4:18	1165

Colossians

1:5-6	1271
1:10	1271
1:13	942, 1273, 1446
1:20	934
2:3	1092
2:5	828
2:18	1325 n 21
3:4	1496
4:2	825, 1039
4:6	1392

1 Thessalonians

2:5	804
2:7	894
2:13	950
2:19	1202, 1202 n 188
4:16	1138 n 16
5:2	1195 n 167
5:2, 4	1195
5:3	1163, 1214
5:4	1195 n 167
5:17	1014-1015, 1039
5:19-20	951
5:23	1277

2 Thessalonians

2:10	1236

1 Timothy

1:5	1113, 1458
1:12	1198 n 176
1:12-13	1198

	1021, 1449, 1449 n 140
11:33	1046
12:1	843
12:7	1462
12:11	1250, 1251 n 42
12:15	839, 1382
12:17	1290
12:24-25	1548
13:12	1305, 1377
13:12-13	1307 n 177
13:13-14	843
13:14	867
13:15	963
13:17	1208

James

1:2	1542
1:5	1041, 1152
1:6	810
1:8	1496
1:11	1173
1:12	1029, 1542
1:13-14	1028
1:15	1429
1:17	1050
1:19-20	908
1:21	939
1:22	1084, 1394
1:23	978
1:23b-24	978 n 142
1:26	1539, 1539 n 176
2:5	1490, 1490 n 47
2:13	1027, 1350, 1551
2:26	836 n 67, 1449 n 140, 1450
3:2	1539
3:5-8	1536
3:6	1539
3:14	906
3:18	1250

4:3	1042
4:4	1497
4:4b	1497 n 63
4:6	963, 1465
4:7	1074
4:8	1397, 1397 n 3
4:9	1181 n 128
4:14	1164
4:17	946, 1206, 1206 n 200
5:1	840
5:1, 4	1474
5:2-3	1518 n 121, 1519
5:5	1162, 1162 n 81, 1344, 1345 n 60, 1521, 1521 n 130
5:7	1250
5:9	1187 n 143
5:10-11	1284
5:16	963

1 Peter

1:3-4	1165
1:13	1188, 1188 n 145
1:15	1499
2:3	865
2:13	1334
2:21	1284
2:24	991, 1408, 1409 n 30
2:25	1405
3:7	1262
4:3, 5	1476
4:10	941, 1201, 1342
4:11	815
4:18	1298
5:1-2	817
5:1-3	930
5:2, 4	1202

5:5	1369
5:6	948 n 71,
	1339
5:7	803, 1001,
	1143, 1166
5:8	863, 1194,
	1274
5:10	1356

2 Peter
1:10	997,
	997 n 175
1:16-18	873
1:19	1098, 1296,
	1547
2:4	955, 1372
2:9	1372
2:12-13	1454
2:14-15	804
2:21	1078, 1206,
	1206 n 201
2:21-22	919,
	919 n 242
2:22	1432
3:3-4	1203
3:9	844, 1235

1 John
1:5-6	1426
1:8	1050, 1463,
	1463 n 179
2:11	1426 n 76,
	1479
2:15	1497
2:16	1295 n 147,
	1359 n 91,
	1517 n 116
2:18	1358,
	1358 n 85
2:20	1153 n 54
2:27	1153,
	1153 n 54
3	1493
3:1	1438
3:2	1022
3:15	1374

3:16	1213,
	1213 n 218
3:17	815, 1488,
	1493 n 52,
	1524,
	1524 n 138
3:18	815, 1033,
	1145
4:1	906
4:4	1151
4:20	1493 n 52
5:4	1046

3 John
8-9	943
5-6	1343

Jude
12-13	1246

Revelation
1:3	1550,
	1550 n 198
1:5	1213
1:7	1313,
	1313 n 192
1:10	1154
2:5	1419, 1479
2:7	1350
2:10	1198, 1491
3:4	1448
3:5	857
3:14	1420 n 61
3:17	1162,
	1162 n 79,
	1481
3:18	1448
3:19-20	1420
3:20	994,
	1043 n 66,
	1187,
	1187 n 143,
	1316,
	1401, 1454
4	1499 n 68
4:1	1043

CHURCH FATHERS, ECCLESIASTICAL AUTHORS, AND GLOSSAE

With few exceptions, this index is global and indicates the rich heritage upon which Bonaventure drew. The studious reader will need to explore each "source" of Bonaventure's exposition on its own terms. Was he really quoting Bede or Bede as represented by the Glossa Ordinaria? Further, was Bonaventure quoting John Chrysostom directly or borrowing his quotation from the one he found in the commentary of his contemporary, Hugh of St. Cher? Did Chrysostom actually write the work attributed to him, e.g, *Opus Imperfectum*?

PHILOSOPHERS, JURISTS, AND HISTORIANS

This index points to non-ecclesiastical influences upon Bonaventure's thought. It is my educated guess that Bonaventure may have been acquainted with the thought of these authors through excerpts from their writings. For an excerpt of Seneca's writings on the value of a frugal life, see *L. Annaei Senecae Philosophi Opera Quae Exstant Omnia a Ivsto Lipsio Emendata et Scholiis Illustrata*. Third edition; (Antwerp: Balthasar Moreti, 1632) 837-840 ("Excerpta Quaedam e Libris Senecae").

Aesop
Fables 1520 n 127

Aristotle 909 n 220,
932 n 30
Categoriae 856 n 109
De Anima 1170 n 104
De Caelo 1033 n 32
De Generatione et
Corruptione 1294 n 145
De Sophisticis Elenchis,
1051 n 88
Nicomachean Ethics
1133 n 2,
1249 n 38,
1486 n 35
Periherm. 1215 n 223

Josephus
Antiquities 1083 n 174,
1232 n 1,
1233 n 1

Juvenal
Satires 1486 n 36

Lucan 1521 n 130
De Bello Civili 1522,
1522 n 133

Pliny 909 n 220

Seneca 909 n 219
De Clementia 908,
908 n 219,
909 n 220
De Remediis fortuitorum
1139,
1139 n 19
Epistles 932,
932 n 30,
940,
940 n 45,
957 n 92,
1196,
1196 n 172

Stobaeus 1324 n 19

Strabo 1320 n 8,
1362 n 98

Virgil
Georgics 1033 n 35,
1034 n 36